A Centenary History of the Indian National Congress
(1964-1984)

Academic Foundation

A Centenary History of the Indian National Congress

A Centenary History of the Indian National Congress

(1964-1984)

Volume — V

INDIAN NATIONAL CONGRESS

ACADEMIC FOUNDATION

NEW DELHI

First published in 2011
by

ACADEMIC FOUNDATION
4772-73 / 23 Bharat Ram Road, (23 Ansari Road),
Darya Ganj, New Delhi - 110 002 (India).
Phones : +91-11-23245001 / 02 / 03 / 04.
Fax : +91-11-23245005.
E-mail : books@academicfoundation.com
www. academicfoundation.com

DISCLAIMER
The views expressed in this book are of individual contributors and do not necessarily reflect the views of the Congress Party. The book does not claim to be comprehensive in the coverage of historical facts.

Cataloguing in Publication Data--DK
Courtesy: D.K. Agencies (P) Ltd. <docinfo@dkagencies.com>

A Centenary history of the Indian National Congress.
v. cm.
Contents: v. 5. 1964-1984
ISBN 10: 817188864X
ISBN 13: 9788171888641

1. Indian National Congress--History. 2. India--Politics and government--20th century. I. Indian National Congress.

DDC 324.25408309 22

Typeset by Italics India, New Delhi.
Printed and bound in India.

10 9 8 7 6 5 4 3 2 1

Congress Centenary History—Volume V

Contents

Foreword

125 years is a long period in the journey of any institution or movement. For the Indian National Congress, it has been an equally momentous and inspirational journey which saw the emergence of a free nation from the shackles of colonial bondage. Congress has the rare privilege of belonging to a select group of political movements across the world to have traversed such a long distance. It is a movement which became synonymous with the saga of struggle and sacrifice against a repressive regime, which saw the birth of a free nation and has been witnessing its prosperity and growth, its dramatic transformation, which has captured the imagination of the world.

Twenty-five years ago, at the occasion of Centenary session of Indian National Congress, Rajiv Gandhi had stirred our collective conscience to reconnect with the masses, recalling the vision of our founding fathers and the ideals espoused by Mahatma Gandhi to collectively generate a mass movement to revitalise the Party. The task of rejuvenating and rebuilding the Congress has been a difficult one in a changed political ethos, which saw the emergence of political formations, with a divisive ideology, seeking to polarise our polity on narrow basis of religion, region, caste or language. Together, we have preserved the secular fabric of our country and nurtured our democratic traditions, which were an article of faith for our charismatic leaders.

The resurgence of Congress across the country personifies the faith reposed by the people of India in our ideology, which is rooted in a spirit of nationalism, secularism and democracy. Throughout its history, Congress has retained its mass character which has been its greatest strength, subsuming in its welcoming embrace divergent views and harmonising divergent ideologies.

During the last six and a half years, we have endeavoured to provide a Government which is transparent, responsive and accountable. We have remained true to our promise to the *'Aam Admi'*.

We have strived to reach out to the underprivileged and marginalised, to the rural masses and millions of farmers who tirelessly toil for our sustenance. In true Gandhian traditions, we have endeavoured to empower the unempowered, to give voice to the voiceless and remain sensitive to the aspirations of Dalits, tribals, other backward classes (OBCs), women and minorities.

Our philosophy of 'inclusive growth' is anchored in our abiding commitment to the welfare of the common man. We have guaranteed employment by law. This has seen a steady transformation in rural India, providing the biggest social security net ever conceived anywhere in the world. Our dream of building a new India has seen the creation of massive infrastructure in the rural hinterland. Our commitment to transparency in governance, has empowered the people through the Right to Information Act. We have kept our promises to provide free education to every child from 6-14 with the passage of the Right to Education Act.

Rajiv Gandhi dreamt of a modern India, prepared to face the challenge of the 21st century, and, today, we see the realisation of his dreams, foundations of which were laid by Jawaharlal Nehru by building institutions of higher learning. India's growing profile is today acknowledged by the world and we have achieved many a milestones on the global stage.

Last year, the people reposed their trust in Congress yet again in a greater measure and we have accepted the mandate with a sense of humility and gratitude. But we believe that the task of building India remains an unfulfilled mission. The dreams of our founding fathers will only be fulfilled when the fruits of development reach the poorest of the poor, when the darkness of ignorance is dispelled from the country, when harmonious co-existence becomes a way of life, when all citizens are equal partners in progress.

Several daunting challenges confront our great nation today. Violence, extremism and communal hatred threaten to rupture the composite culture of our society, which we have zealously guarded over decades. The idea of India personifies a spirit of conciliation and dialogue of peace and harmony and must always do so. Equally, all citizens of the country must share in the fruits of development and a special effort would be needed to reach out to those who have suffered on account of continuing violence leading to underdevelopment and unemployment.

As we peer into the future through the prism of the past, we hope to see a vibrant secular India, responding to the dreams and aspirations of a billion people, an India which will have the leadership of the 21st century world.

India is a young nation, though an ancient civilisation and the youth represent our collective hopes and aspirations for a brighter future and are, therefore, our greatest strength. Recording history of this epoch journey was the idea of Indira Gandhi carried forward by Shri Rajiv Gandhi and four volumes of Congress History were released on the occasion of Centenary celebration. On the special occasion of having completed 125 years of our journey, the 5th Volume of History is dedicated to the people of our country, especially the youth which will enable them to connect them with the struggle and sacrifice of our leaders, the challenges that they courageously faced and many a giant strides taken in this period towards Congress commitment to India's development.

This Volume captures an important period in the history of our country, following the demise of Pt. Nehru in whose passing, an age came to an end. His succession by Lal Bahadur Shastri, whose sudden death in 1966 created a void. Congress entrusted the responsibility of providing leadership to Indira Gandhi in a truly challenging period. This Volume traces the journey of the Party and captures the remarkable leadership of Indira who remained resolute even in the face of adversity. It was not an easy time nor was it an easy task to step into Nehru's shoes. She reaffirmed the resolve of the Party for the poor and underprivileged and steered the economic destiny of the country. Her historic decisions including nationalisation of banks and abolition of privy purses were significant development of the period. Many decisions taken during that period were enveloped in partisan political debate and it is now time to ponder and reflect and to recall the same and preserve it for posterity. This Volume is our collective tribute to Indira Gandhi.

I place on record my deep appreciation for the thorough research by the editorial team led by Shri Pranab Mukherjee and the Group of eminent Historians and all contributors who have made this publication possible.

— Sonia Gandhi

Preface

On December 28, 2009 the Indian National Congress began a year of celebrations to mark its 125th anniversary. The party began commemorating the occasion on that date, to reawaken the memory of all the struggles and successes of the Congress in the last 125 years. As a part of the celebrations, it was decided to publish and bring up to date, the volumes *'A Centenary History of the Indian National Congress'*. Telling the story of the Congress party is important for it straddles both the era of struggle for freedom and the making of modern India.

For the first time, in April 1976, the Congress Working Committee had appointed the Congress History Project Committee. It was under the aegis of this Committee that the first four volumes covering the period 1885-1964 were published. To cover the period of last 46 years, the Congress President Mrs. Sonia Gandhi thought it appropriate to bring the Congress narrative up to date with the publication of two more volumes covering the period 1964 to 1984 (Volume 5) and from then on to 2010 (Volume 6).

The present volume narrates and analyses a wide variety of issues which affected the Congress Party and which in turn impinged on national issues. It covers the trials and tribulations of the party over this crucial period. The narrative not only takes into account political issues such as performance of the party in six national elections, but also analyses in detail the split in the party in 1969.

The present volume has within its fold scholarly articles written by academics, journalists and other experts who have attempted to weave together a history of the Congress party during one of its historically most interesting periods. The volume focusses attention on a range of major issues affecting nation's interests, including foreign policy and defence and nuclear security. There is also an analysis of developments in the societal and economic sphere which provides the context in which party policies evolved and were adopted in one form or the other by the government.

Lest we forget, this was also a period marked by economic turbulence. The efforts made by Prime Minister Indira Gandhi to help India tide over this crisis have been chronicled in detail. There are comprehensive analyses of the foreign policy challenges and the triumphant liberation of Bangladesh. Clearly, this was the Indira Gandhi era and it was marked, as the contributions amply show, by her interventions in diverse areas such as foreign policy and environment, most of which still hold good. Apart from this, themes and areas of import such as Kashmir and the Northeast are narrated in detail and provide insight into the impact of the past on the present. The volume also has well-grounded analyses of the party's role and impact on issues such as gender, science and technology and education. There are several other areas which find mention and I am happy to note the diversity of issues that have been dealt with in this volume.

In attempting to summarise the essence of this volume, I could do no better than emphasise the basic approach of the Congress. This should be seen in the background of the fact that the Indian National Congress has been an integral part of India's journey for the past 125 years. When created, the Congress was democratic and secular. Under the influence of mass politics, it also became socialist, pledged to supporting the interests of the vast millions of landless and propertyless. It has always endeavoured to be an inclusive party.

The Congress had to find the ways and means of forging a consensus on issues affecting India's national interest even when they became extremely contentious. By creatively evolving a middle path, the party has so far steered itself and the nation along a steady course of growth and development and it continues to be India's political mainstream.

Historically, the strength of the Congress Party has been its ability to tide over a crisis, either of an evolutionary or revolutionary nature. In the past century and more the Congress Party has evolved as a party with a clear agenda, first as the leading light of the national movement for Independence and second as the party in power after independence in 1947. For anyone trying to understand the growth and development of the party, it is important to know the underlying strength of this approach.

On January 26, 1950 when India became a republic, India's first Prime Minister Jawaharlal Nehru said and I quote: 'Twenty years ago we took the first pledge of independence. During these twenty years we have known struggle and conflict and failure and achievement. The man who led us through apparent failure to achievement is no more with us, but the fruits of his labours is ours. What we do with this fruit depends upon many factors, the basic factors being those on which Gandhiji laid stress throughout his career—high character, integrity of mind and purpose, a spirit of tolerance and cooperation and hard work. I can only suggest to our people that we should find our republican freedom on these basic characteristics and shed fear and hatred from our minds and think always of the betterment of our people.' There can be no better message one can provide to the people of India on the occasion of the publication of the fifth volume of the history of the Indian National Congress.

It must be noted that the Congress Party desired that the volume is edited and contributed to by experts in order to generate an objective and scholarly perspective for the period under review and not necessarily have a party perspective. The views expressed by the authors in this volume, therefore, do not necessarily reflect the views of the Congress Party. It is not an 'official' history of the Congress between 1964 and 1984. It is rather an attempt to weave together the major developments, challenges, successes and failures of the period so that one can better understand the role of the Indian National Congress in the life of Indian nation in the last 125 years.

I do hope that this volume will serve both as an introduction and the means by which the party worker, the leaders of the Congress party, as well as all those interested in the history of this critical period in India's journey, will get a better perspective of how things evolved. It is my privilege to place this book in the hands of the readers and hope it will serve as a benchmark.

Pranab Mukherjee

About the Contributors

Aparna Basu, Ph.D, Cambridge, was formerly Professor of Modern History, University of Delhi. She has published several books and articles on history of education and women's history, including *Growth of Education and Political Development in India, 1898-1920*; *Essays in the History of Indian Education*; *History of Delhi University*; *Mridula Sarabhai: Rebel With a Cause* (with Bharati Ray); *Women's Struggle: A History of All India Women's Conference* (with Bharati Ray); *From Independence Towards Freedom: Indian Women since 1947*; and *Abbas Tyabji: A Biography*. She is on the Editorial Board of Indian Economic & Social History Review and Indian Journal of Gender Studies. She has been a Visiting Fellow of University of Malaya, Kuala Lumpur; St. Antony's College and Queen Elizabeth House, Oxford; Wolfson College, Cambridge; and Sophia College, Tokyo. Dr. Basu has been President of the All India Women's Conference (AIWC). Currently, she is Patron of AIWC. She is a member of the Governing Body of the Gandhi National Museum and Library and a Trustee of the Sarabhai Foundation.

Rakesh Batabyal studied history at St. Xavier's College, Ranchi, and earned his Masters and Doctoral degree in Modern History from Jawaharlal Nehru University, New Delhi. He has been a Fellow at the Indian Institute of Advanced Study (1996-1999), Shimla, and at the National Institute of Punjab Studies, New Delhi (2004). He has taught in Gujarat, Maharashtra, Karnataka, and at Kelaniya University, Sri Lanka (2004) and was appointed to the newly established India Chair for Contemporary Indian History at Tokyo University (2010). His books *Communalism in Bengal: From Famine to Noakhali* (2005), and *Penguin Book of Modern Indian Speeches* (2007) have been widely received. Presently an Associate Professor and Deputy Director of Academic Staff College of JNU, he is finalising his book on the History of JNU. With a background in philosophy and training in Romanian language at Bucharest University, he is currently working on contemporary history of Eastern Europe, particularly Romania and Poland, on the basis of the historical insights gained from the Indian National Movement.

Bipan Chandra is National Professor, Emeritus Professor of History, Jawaharlal Nehru University and Chairman, National Book Trust, India. Educated at Lahore, Stanford and Delhi, Bipan Chandra is one of the India's foremost and most respected historians. He has over the years lectured in many parts of the world. Among his numerous publications are: *Communalism: A Primer* (New Delhi, 2004); *In the Name of Democracy: The JP Movement and the Emergency* (New Delhi: Penguin, 2003); Essa*ys on Colonialism* (New Delhi, 1999); *India Since Independence* (jointly with Mridula Mukherjee and Aditya Mukherjee) (New Delhi, 2008); *Ideology and Politics in Modern India* (New Delhi, 1994); *Essays on Indian Nationalism* (New Delhi, 1993); *Essays on Contemporary India* (New Delhi, 1993); *The Epic Struggle* (New Delhi, 1992); *India's Struggle for Independence, 1857-1947* (New Delhi: Penguin, 1989); *Indian National Movement: The Long Term Dynamics* (New Delhi, 1988); *Communalism in Modern India* (New Delhi, 1984); *Nationalism and Colonialism in Modern India* (New Delhi, 1979); *Freedom Struggle* (jointly with Amalesh Tripathi and Barun De) (New Delhi, 1972); and *The Rise and Growth of Economic Nationalism in India: Economic Policies of Indian National Leadership, 1880-1905* (New Delhi, 1966). He is currently writing a biography on Bhagat Singh.

Sanjukta Das Gupta is an Associate Professor at the Department of History, Calcutta University. She studied Modern History at Presidency College, Calcutta, and Calcutta University. Her research interests include the agrarian economy and the social history of India and the history of *adivasis*. She has been a Visiting Fellow at Uppsala University (Sweden) and at the University of Rome, La Sapienza (Italy). A recipient of the Charles Wallace research grant in 2009, she has contributed extensively in academic journals and edited volumes. Her monograph entitled *Adivasis and the Raj: Socio-Economic Transition of the Hos, 1820-1932* is forthcoming in 2011 (Hyderabad: Orient Blackswan). She has also co-edited *Narratives of the Excluded: Caste Issues in Colonial India* (Calcutta: K.P. Bagchi, 2008) and *Narratives from the Margins: Aspects of Adivasi History in India* (Delhi: Primus Press, forthcoming in 2011).

David Devadas is a journalist, author, teacher and filmmaker, who is the author of *In Search of a Future: The Story of Kashmir* (Penguin, 2007). He is currently a senior fellow at Nehru Memorial Museum and Library, New Delhi, researching the processes through which identities are becoming rigid and antithetical, and are engendering conflict in various parts of Jammu & Kashmir state. He lives in Srinagar, from where he travels to different parts of the state, interacting with wide cross-sections of various communities. He has earlier served as Political Editor of *Business Standard*, Visiting Professor at the Centre for Jawaharlal Nehru Studies at Jamia Millia Islamia, and has edited Kashmir's leading English daily, and a website. He has written columns that were published in *Business Standard*, Gulf News, *The Tribune* and other newspapers.

V.P. Dutt is former Pro-Vice-Chancellor and acting Vice-Chancellor of Delhi University and a former Member of Parliament. He is currently Distinguished Fellow at Institute for Defence Studies and Analyses (IDSA), New Delhi. He has written widely on India's foreign policy, world affairs, East Asia and modern China. His books include *India's Foreign Policy since Independence* (National Book Trust); *China After Mao; China's Foreign Policy; India and the World; China's Cultural Revolution;* and numerous articles that include 'Problems of Modernization of Asia'; 'The World: Yesterday, Today and Tomorrow'; 'The International System and Japan's role'; 'Big Powers and the Indian Ocean; Pacific Region'; 'The Iraq War: An Overview'; 'The New World Order: An Indian Perspective'; 'Asian Security Problems'; 'World in the Eighties and Jawaharlal's Vision'; and 'Bangladesh: Shadow of the Big Powers'. He has lectured at the Sorbonne, Warsaw, Hong Kong, Japan and many US universities.

Bhashyam Kasturi is a Ph.D from Delhi University and is currently Head, Research and Publications Division at the Nehru Memorial Museum and Library, New Delhi. Starting out his career as a lecturer at Delhi University, he subsequently became a journalist and was associated with the *Selected Works of Jawaharlal Nehru*. He is a regular guest on the Lok Sabha TV channel and has also been interviewed by BBC Radio on issues of current relevance. He is the author of two books, one on India's Intelligence Services and another on Mahatma Gandhi and India's partition. He has written extensively on issues of military, intelligence, military history and terrorism. His writings have found a place in India's leading newspapers and journals. He has been commissioned to write papers on

Pakistan Occupied Kashmir (PoK) and other aspects of developments in Pakistan, including the role of the military.

Deepak Kumar teaches History of Science and Education at Zakir Husain Centre for Educational Research. He is known for his work *Science and the Raj* (2nd Ed., Delhi: OUP, 2006). In addition, he has edited four more books and has published more than 35 papers in the realm of history of science, technology, environment and medicine.

Inder Malhotra is one of India's most respected journalists. He has been a Syndicated Columnist since taking premature retirement as Editor of *The Times of India*, New Delhi (1978-1986). Before that he worked for *The Statesman* for 15 years, first as the Political Correspondent and Chief of the Bureau and then as Deputy Editor. He cut his journalistic teeth at the United Press of India which he joined immediately after graduating from the Punjab University. He also wrote for *The Guardian* (1965-1995). He is both a Nehru Fellow (1986-87) and a Woodrow Wilson Fellow (1992-93). He has lectured widely, in India and abroad, including at all major universities in the United States and England and at the International Institute for Strategic Studies, London, the Institute of Oriental Studies in Moscow, and the Foreign Policy Association in Tokyo. His publications include *Indira Gandhi: A Personal & Political Biography* (1989); *Dynasties of India and Beyond* (2003), and a fresh biography of Indira Gandhi (2006). He is now working on a book on *Indian Security: Past, Present and Future*.

Girish Mishra was educated at Motihari Zilla School, Patna College and Delhi School of Economics. He taught at Kashi Vidyapith, Kirori Mal College, and Delhi School of Economics; and was a Fellow at the Nehru Memorial Museum and Library, New Delhi. Some of his published works: include *Agrarian Problems of Permanent Settlement: A Case Study of Champaran; Balzac: Mirror of Emerging Modern Capitalism; Malthus and His Ghost; Sociology and Economics of Casteism in India: A Study of Bihar; Rammanohar Lohia: Man and His Ism; Nehru and Congress Economic Policies; An Economic History of Modern India; Economic Systems; and Comparative Economic Development*, etc.

Aditya Mukherjee is Professor of Contemporary Indian History, former Chairperson, Centre for Historical Studies, Jawaharlal Nehru University (JNU), New Delhi; and Director, Jawaharlal Nehru Institute of Advanced Study, JNU. He was elected President of the Indian History Congress (Modern India), 2007-08. He is editor of the Sage Series in Modern Indian History;

Selected Works of Jawaharlal Nehru, 2009 (Volume 43 in progress). He has been Visiting Professor at Duke University, USA, JSPS and Japan Foundation Fellow, at University of Tokyo, Visiting fellow at the Institute of Advanced Study, Lancaster, UK and Fellow, Nantes Institute for Advanced Study, France. His publications, apart from numerous articles, include *India's Struggle for Independence* (Penguin, 1989) (co-author); 50th reprint in 2010, translated into several languages; *India Since Independence* (Penguin, 2008) (co-author), also translated into many languages; *RSS, School Texts and The Murder of Mahatma Gandhi: The Hindu Communal Project* (Sage, 2008); *History in the New NCERT Text Books: A Report and an Index of Errors* (co-author), *Indian History Congress, 2003; and Imperialism, Nationalism and the Making of the Indian Capitalist Class 1927-1947*, (Sage, 2002).

Sudha Pai is Professor at the Centre for Political Studies, Jawaharlal Nehru University. Her areas of interests include state politics in India, Dalit politics, politics of Third World societies, globalisation and governance, and has published extensively in these areas. She was Senior Fellow, Nehru Memorial Museum and Library, New Delhi for a period of three years (January 2006-2009). She has been member of a number of projects including an International project on 'Democracy and Social Capital in Segmented Societies' funded by the SIDA (Sweden). Her recent books include *Dalit Assertion and the Unfinished Democratic Revolution: The BSP in Uttar Pradesh* (2002); *Political Process in Uttar Pradesh: Identity, Economic Reforms and Governance* (2007); and *Developmental State and the Dalit Question in Madhya Pradesh: Congress Response* (2010).

Mohinder Singh taught History at the University of Delhi and the Punjabi University, Patiala; Professor-Director, Guru Nanak Foundation, New Delhi (1982-90); Professor-Director, National Institute of Punjab Studies (1990-2010); awarded fellowship by the ICHR for research in UK; lectured at various Indian and foreign universities including University of California, Santa Barbara; author of several standard works on Sikh history and religion, including *The Akali Movement* (Macmillan, 1978); *Baba Kharak Singh* (NBT 2005); *Guru Granth Sahib: The Guru Eternal* (Himalayan Books, 2008). He has also edited Punjabi Classics: *Heer Warishah; Sohni Mahiwal; Bulle Shah;* and *Baba Farid; and* published eight pictorial books under the *Panjab Heritage Series;* contributed a chapter to *A Centenary History of the Indian National Congress*, 1985. He was Member of National

Commission for Religious & Linguistic Minorities (2005-2007); and is currently Member, National Commission for Minority Educational Institutions.

Shekhar Singh has taught Philosophy at St. Stephen's College Delhi, and at the North-Eastern Hill University, Shillong; and Environmental Management (IIPA), and Ethics and Administration, at the Indian Institute of Public Administration, New Delhi. As an environmentalist, he has been Advisor (Environment & Forests) to the Planning Commission, Government of India; Member, Indian Board for Wildlife, Government of India, New Delhi; Member, Central Board for Forestry, Government of India, New Delhi; Consultant, United Nations Food and Agricultural Organization (FAO), East Africa; Secretary, Island Development Authority, Government of India; Chairman, MoEF Appraisal Committee for Power Projects; Chairman, Task Force on Ecologically Vulnerable Areas, Planning Commission; Supreme Court of India appointed Commissioner on forests and other allied matters for the Andaman and Nicobar Islands; Chairman, Task Force on Governance, Participation, Transparency and Environmental Impact Assessment, Planning Commission; Senior Independent Advisor, Global Environment Facility, Washington DC.

Yogendra Singh is Professor Emeritus at the Centre for the Study of Social Systems, Jawaharlal Nehru University. He has served as Visiting Professor at universities in many parts of the world. Among his several books are: *For a Sociology of India* (Ed. and Contributed with Prof. Unnithan *et al.*) (New Delhi: Prentice Hall, 1965); *Towards a Sociology of Culture in India* (Ed. with Unnithan and Deva) (New Delhi: Prentice Hall, 1965); *Towards a Sociology of Non-violence & Peace* (with Unnithan) (New Delhi: Indian Council of Social Science Research, 1968); *Modernization of Indian Tradition* (New Delhi: Thompson Press, 1973); *Traditions of Non-Violence in the East and West* (with Unnithan) (New Delhi: Arnold Heinemann of India, 1973); *Social Stratification and Social Change* (New Delhi: Manohar Publishers, 1977); *Social Aspects of Scientific and Technological Revolution* (with R.K. Mukherjee *et al.*) (London: Sage Publications, 1977); Essays *on Modernization* (New Delhi: Manohar Publishers, 1978); *Image of Man: Ideology and Theory in Indian Sociology* (New Delhi: Chanakya Publishers, 1983); *Indian Sociology: Social Conditions and Emerging Concerns* (New Delhi: Sage Publications, 1986); *Sociology of Culture* (with Boris Erasov) (Moscow: Progress Publishers, 1991); *Social Change in India: Crisis and Resilience* (New Delhi: Har Anand, 1991);

Culture Change in India: Identity and Globalization (Jaipur: Rawat Publications, 2000); *Sociology of Culture* (with Boris Erasov) (Jaipur: Rawat Publications 2010); *Social Sciences: Communication, Anthropology and Sociology: History of Science, Philosophy and Culture in Indian Civilization* (Ed.) (Delhi: Pearson, 2010); *ICSSR Research Survey and Exploration in Sociology and Social Anthropology: 2003-2009* (Ed.) (New Delhi: ICSSR (forthcoming)). Since the past few years Prof. Singh has been working on a book *Sociological Theories and the Indian Sociology.*

Shantha Sinha, Chairperson, National Commission for Protection of Child Rights (NCPCR) India, is a Professor of Political Science, University of Hyderabad, and a pioneer in the field of child rights in India. She was awarded the Padma Shri in 1998 and the Ramon Magsaysay Award for Community Leadership in 2003. She is the Founder Secretary and Trustee of MV Foundation based in Andhra Pradesh, which has withdrawn over 6,00,000 children from work and mainstreamed them into schools. Hundreds and thousands of children were mobilised to join schools in areas of civil unrest in the states of Andhra Pradesh, Bihar and Chhattisgarh. She has published a book entitled *Maoists in Andhra Pradesh* (1985) and several articles on issues relating to child rights. She did her Masters in Political Science from Osmania University in 1972 and her Ph.D from Jawaharlal Nehru University in 1976.

B.G. Verghese was the editor of the *Hindustan Times* (1969-1975) and *Indian Express* (1982-1986). Verghese completed his schooling from the Doon School in Dehradun. He graduated from the St. Stephen's College in Delhi. He also attended the Trinity College in Cambridge. He started his career in journalism with *Times of India,* a leading English-language daily newspaper in India. He served as an information adviser to the Prime Minister of India (1966-1969). He also served as an information consultant to the Defense Minister in 2001. Veghese was honoured with the Magsaysay Award in 1975. He has served on a number of official and unofficial boards and committees and is associated with several NGOs in the fields of media, education, etc. He was a member of Kargil Review Committee and co-author of the *Kargil Review Committee Report*. He was also a member of the Editors Guild of India Fact Finding Mission to Gujarat in April 2002. He has authored several books such as *Design For Tomorrow; Waters of Hope; Harnessing the Eastern Himalayan Rivers; Winning the Future; India's Northeast Resurgent;* and *Reorienting India* and others.

Chapter I

Introduction

Aditya Mukherjee

The history of the Indian National Congress is inseparable from the history of the Indian people and the process of the making of the modern Indian nation since the last quarter of the 19th century. The early Indian nationalists who conceptualised and gave basic direction to this process of the Indian 'nation in the making'[1] created the Indian National Congress seeing it as a crucial vehicle for taking forward this process.

The first four volumes in the series take the story from the birth of the Indian National Congress in 1885 to the attainment of Independence in 1947 and the Nehruvian effort at nation building till 1964. These four volumes were released on the occasion of the Congress Centenary in 1985. I am privileged to present the current volume covering the period 1964 to 1984 in the 125th Year of the Indian National Congress.

I

The period 1964-1984 is a period when the gains of the first flush of political, economic and social developments after independence during 1947-1964, which were crafted with great care and brilliance under Jawaharlal Nehru's leadership, had to be consolidated and the country prepared for the next stage of development, amidst the rapidly rising expectations of the people freed from nearly 200 years of colonial bondage. This was a stupendous task which had to be undertaken at a time when the glow of the Indian National Movement, one of the greatest mass movements in world history, was beginning to fade and Jawaharlal Nehru its iconic leader who carried with him the prestige of this great movement was no longer at the helm of affairs. Also, this task had to be undertaken in a period when because of a set of national and international developments India faced some of its severest hurdles in the economic and political sphere. The challenge was how to accomplish this task in such difficult circumstances and that too within the paradigm of secular democracy, sovereignty and equity with which independent India started its journey.

The path was not easy and at times looked impossible. Critics at home and abroad began to predict that the Indian state was at the verge of collapse, its democracy beginning to disintegrate and the experiment of independent economic development based on self-reliance and equity proving a complete failure.[2] It is from this situation that Indira Gandhi rose like a phoenix and took up the challenge and guided India through numerous crises. However, the challenges were colossal and inevitably, even as they were being met, they succeeded in leaving deep scars, which the nation had to deal with for long, and some of them still refuse to go away.

The 19 essays in this volume evaluate the wide variety of challenges that emerged in this period and the efforts to meet them with varying degrees of success, whether the challenges be economic, political, social or environmental. The attempt in these essays is not to give accolades or apportion blame but to assess objectively the developments of this period. In fact this period which was dominated by Indira Gandhi has by and large not received a balanced treatment partially because of the intense heat generated by cataclysmic events like the 'emergency', 'operation blue star' and the anti-Sikh riots following Indira Gandhi's assassination. The volume does not gloss over these 'controversial' events but in fact looks back at them with greater complexity and objectivity, which is now possible with the passage of time and the necessary distancing from the immediate event. Also, the volume puts these events in perspective by fore-fronting a range of other issues that emerged in this period in areas of the economy, polity, external relations, gender equity, caste dynamics, science and technology, environment and the growth of the extreme left as well as the extreme right represented by fascist communal forces. It also details the developments in certain specific regions of the country like Punjab, Jammu and Kashmir and the Northeast as they had major repercussions at the national level. Many of the essays have taken a wider time span to make their arguments either because the theme could not be discussed without doing so or because the earlier volumes had not touched on those themes at all.

The volume begins with an overview of Indira Gandhi, as after Jawaharlal Nehru passed away in 1964, except for a brief initial phase under Lal Bahadur Shastri, she towered over the Indian landscape, till she fell martyr to assassins' bullets in 1984.

II

I will highlight below some aspects of this extremely important and difficult period in India's history and the role played by Indira Gandhi.

At independence India inherited an economy ravaged by colonialism. Its per capita income and per capita agricultural output had been falling for decades and industry contributed a mere 6 percent of the GDP.[3] Average life expectancy was less than 30 years and the poor died of famine in their millions at the end of 200 years of so called 'colonial benevolence'.[4] Add to this what centuries of subjugation did to the colonised people socially, culturally, morally and psychologically and one understands what the great Indian poet Rabindranath Tagore meant when he wrote shortly before his death in 1941:[5]

> When the stream of their (British) centuries' administration runs dry at last, what a waste of mud and filth will they leave behind them.

It is from this 'mud and filth' that resurgent India had to be rebuilt again. It fell upon Jawaharlal Nehru to lead the country in undertaking this arduous task but it had to be done within a paradigm which was the legacy of the Indian national movement which created the independent Indian state. Essentially it meant that the India would have to choose a path which was democratic, secular, pro-poor or equitous and uncompromising of her sovereignty. Nehru was deeply aware that this path of making the transition to industrial modernisation with democracy and civil liberties was a difficult one and was as yet 'uncharted' in history.[6] Nor was India to trade her independence and sovereignty to grow rapidly, by compromising her principles and accepting the hegemony of the then dominant global power. How difficult this was, is evident from the fact that almost all the post colonial countries that tried to develop quickly as well as countries like Japan which made a quantum jump in her growth trajectory since the 1950s, were forced to compromise on one or the other or both of these two principles of democracy and sovereignty.

India under the Nehruvian consensus, which was a product of the legacy of the national movement, was able to strike out a new path. The democratic structure was assiduously built, the newly won sovereignty zealously guarded, economic and political dependence on the advanced countries gradually diminished, steps taken, including land reforms, to meet the rights and needs of the poor and all this while relentlessly fighting the fissiparous tendencies based on language, region and religion faced by the newly born Union which had been so painfully torn into two at birth as a result of religious communalism. We have charted out elsewhere how this path was painstakingly crafted with considerable degree of success.[7]

III

After Nehru passed away in 1964 the big question was how to take this process forward. Lal Bahadur Shastri took on this heavy burden sturdily on his frail shoulders and he creditably saw India through the 1965 war with Pakistan. However, his tenure at the helm was short-lived as he passed away about 18 months after he took charge. It was Indira Gandhi who now had to rise to this challenge. But as I mentioned above the task had now become much more complex and difficult because of a variety of reasons.

Indira Gandhi took charge in the mid-1960s when India was economically at its most vulnerable moment. The wars of 1962 and 1965, two successive monsoon failures of 1965 and 1966, a fall in agricultural output by 20 percent, high inflation, food stocks so low as to threaten famine conditions in some areas and a deteriorating balance of payment situation with very low foreign exchange reserves had pushed India to a 'begging bowl' situation. Following soon after the economic crisis of the mid-1960s there was the genocide in East Pakistan resulting in the huge burden of over 10 million (more than the total population of a large number of countries) refugees from that region taking shelter in India and contributing to the 1971 (Bangladesh) war with Pakistan followed by, two droughts of 1972 and 1974, the major oil shock of 1973 involving a quadrupling of international oil prices and hence of cost of oil imports, the oil shock of 1979 when oil prices again doubled and the disastrous harvest of 1979-80 caused by the worst drought since independence. Taken together the period appeared to present an almost impossible economic situation, especially for a poor and backward country.

Moreover these crises had their political implications with regards to India's external relations, as well as internally. For example, the United States chose the vulnerable moment of the mid-1960s, when India was critically dependent on her for aid, especially the food loans under the PL 480 agreement, to flex its muscles. She tried to pressurise India into toeing the preferred US line globally, as well as with regard to India's domestic policy. Again during the Bangladesh war the US now with China's support tried to put major impediments in the way of India's sovereign right to follow an independent path suited to her interests.

The deteriorating economic situation in the mid-1960s contributed to some fundamental changes in the internal political situation as well. The Congress Party was beginning to lose its total hegemony over Indian politics reminiscent of the Nehruvian days, especially in some of the North Indian states. The opposition parties sensing a chance tried to make a combined front with strange bedfellows from the extreme right to the extreme left entering into 'promiscuous' relationships with each other with the sole objective of overthrowing the Congress. Non-ideological 'anti-Congressism', which was to become a major bane of Indian politics over time, made its first appearance in this period. The Congress Party itself was divided, with the party organisation representing the conservative sections actually trying to clip Prime Minister Indira Gandhi's wings, forcing a split in the party.

The economic crisis of the early 1970s combined with misgovernance in certain states contributed to the rise of protest movements which later merged into the powerful JP movement. This movement soon came considerably under the grip of extreme right wing fascist forces represented by the RSS and was reduced to just an anti-Congress, in fact anti-Indira, agenda where it sought to remove her (a democratically elected Prime Minister) from power at any cost, not democratically or constitutionally but by any means whatsoever.

With the setting in over time of the process of the decline of the societal cohesion that the national movement had generated, the fissiparous tendencies based on language, region, class, caste and religion reared their head once again. Many of these tendencies were actively encouraged from across borders, as for example in Kashmir, Punjab, the Northeast (and even Naxalbari) . This created at times situations where the very unity and integrity of the country was threatened.

In sum this period saw the basic fundamentals of the path charted out by India after independence getting seriously threatened. The unity of the country, its sovereignty, its democratic structure and its capacity to protect its poor were all under severe stress and it appeared that India might be overwhelmed by it as were so many other newly independent countries.

IV

This is when Indira Gandhi took on these challenges with courage and conviction setting aside forever the misplaced description of her as a *goongi gudiya.* The fearless protector from evil, Durga, or 'the only man in her cabinet' was how she soon began to be popularly viewed.

From the experience of the mid-1960s economic crisis and American efforts at domination, Indira Gandhi was quick to realise that India would not be able to maintain a sovereign independent stance *vis-à-vis* the advanced countries if her economy remained weak and dependent on those countries, especially for food. She therefore set about addressing this issue on a war footing.

She pushed the 'Green Revolution' vigorously and it began to pay immediate dividends. Between 1967-68 and 1970-71 food grain production rose by 35 percent. Net food imports fell from 10.3 million tonnes in 1966 to 3.6 million in 1970, while food availability increased from 73.5 million tonnes to 89.5 million tonnes over the same period. Food availability continued to increase sharply to 110.25 million tonnes in 1978 and 128.8 million tonnes in 1984 and food stocks had crossed the 30 million tonnes mark by the mid 1980s, putting an end to India's 'begging bowl' image and creating considerable food security even in extreme crisis situations.

Apart from food self-sufficiency, a series of other steps were taken to ensure that the fiscal deficit came down sharply, foreign aid as proportion of net national product declined and remained low and the debt service ratio fell to an easily manageable level. Further, the Nehruvian effort at reducing India's dependence on the external world for maintaining her rate of investment and thus growth by creating the capacity (mainly through the public sector) to produce capital goods indigeneously was taken forward sharply in this period. The share of equipment that needed to be imported in the total fixed capital investment in India which was nearly 100 percent at independence and had fallen to 43 percent by 1960 was brought down to a mere 9 percent by 1974, whereas the value of the fixed investment in India increased by about two and a half times over this period (1960-1974).[8] In other words, by 1974 India could sustain nearly 91 percent of her fixed investments on the basis of indigeneously produced capital goods, without depending on imports from advanced countries.

Indira Gandhi was to also expand enormously Nehru's effort at creating indigeneous scientific and technical capacities including in frontier areas like nuclear science. India's expenditure on science and technology had increased from $1 million in 1947-48 to $ 1450 million in 1984. India's stock of scientific and technical manpower had increased more than 12 times from 190 thousand to 2.32 million between 1949 and 1977. The Pokhran nuclear test in 1974 and the launch of the Aryabhatta in 1975 were testimony to the advances made in nuclear and space research.

It is the autonomy from the advanced countries in feeding her own population and most importantly in determining her own rate of capital accumulation or growth, including in areas involving high levels of technology, which went a long way in giving India the flexibility to have an independent foreign policy and pursue it with vigour as Indira Gandhi did, to the great annoyance of superpowers like the United States and their acolytes. She could adopt 'an attitude of dismissive disdain' making even the American president 'nervous'.[9] Indira Gandhi was to play a leading role in the Non-Aligned Movement, and mobilise international support in a manner that she was able to resist the severest international pressure. Her courage in withstanding the combined Chinese and American pressure during the Bangladesh war with the US Seventh Fleet threateningly moving into the Indian Ocean is now a legend.

Having, to a considerable degree, promoted self-reliance in the economy and asserted India's sovereignty by maintaining an independent economic and political trajectory, Indira Gandhi was to simultaneously turn towards the third basic element in the national movement and the Nehruvian paradigm—addressing the concerns of the poor.

While the land reforms under Jawaharlal Nehru had made considerable headway with feudal *zamindaris* essentially becoming a thing of the past, the main beneficiaries were the upper tenants or occupancy tenants and not the poor tenants, tenants at will and landless labourers. Indira Gandhi was acutely aware of this and as she said at a land reform conference of the State Chief Ministers called by her in September 1970:[10]

> The land reform measures implemented have failed to match the legitimate expectations which were first fostered among millions of cultivators during the national movement...we have yet to create institutional conditions which would enable small farmers, tenants, and landless labourers to share in the agricultural New Deal.

She therefore launched the second wave of land reforms to address the issue. The land ceilings issue was taken up in right earnest, reducing the ceiling and attempting better redistribution of surplus lands. Where no progress could be made on this front she went about distributing homestead lands or even just home sites to the landless. Equally important she launched a series of massive schemes of loans, subsidies, etc., for small and marginal farmers so that they could access key inputs and thus the benefits of the Green Revolution. The nationalised banks, service cooperatives were all persuaded to extend their net to these poorer sections. This ensured that the Green

Revolution did not lead to depeasantisation (selling out by the small farmers) but in fact became the key to their survival. The Green Revolution in fact did not, as predicted by many sceptics in the Left, turn into a Red Revolution but became one of the most important anti-poverty measures.[11]

Indira Gandhi's campaign of 'Garibi Hatao' (in place of the prevalent 'Indira Hatao' campaign) was not mere rhetoric as many have argued it to be. Certainly the poor did not think so. I was touring some of the most backward districts of Andhra Pradesh when she was assassinated. We saw, as the newspapers widely reported, poor villagers weeping inconsolably and refusing to light their cooking fires for days on end. Significantly, while many poor villagers told us that her death meant the disappearance for them of the protection of a mother, the rural elite scoffed at the poor, threateningly saying 'now that your mother is dead you better watch out.'

V

As I discussed in the last section Indira Gandhi met to a considerable measure the national movement and Nehruvian objectives of economic growth with self-reliance and equity as well as the maintenance of India's independence and sovereignty in her external relations. What was the record on the other two pillars on which the Indian state was envisioned, secularism and democracy? Her successes on both these fronts have often been overshadowed by basically three scars left by the political turmoil of this period, the centralisation of the power structure within the Congress Party, the Emergency and Operation Blue Star. If one may take the simile further the survival of scars does not mean a bona fide operation to cure the disease was not made or that the operation was unsuccessful.

Moreover, looking back at these events with a historian's hindsight one finds that it is too simplistic to hold Indira Gandhi alone responsible for these three scars as is often done. In many ways they reflected the collective failure of the Indian political system. As we saw above in Section III the Congress hegemony was in decline in the mid-1960s and the opposition rallied together on the basis of an unscrupulous anti-Congressism putting a major challenge to the Congress. Indira Gandhi, however found herself in an unfavourable situation to meet the challenge, as the Congress organisation and a group of regional party bosses around whom the right wing elements in the Congress had consolidated, now began to openly plot against her even when she was the duly elected Prime Minister.

Driven to the wall she had no option but to jump the party organisation and appeal directly to the people to return to power and keep the party geared on its social democratic agenda. Also, because of the opportunistic positions taken by the provincial party bosses and the general degeneration in public ethic which was destructive of collegial trust, she increasingly began to centralise power around her in the party. This over time led to the party organisation increasingly becoming a top-down one and there remaining hardly any mechanism for large number of leaders emerging in the party who were democratically elected from below and who commanded a substantial mass base. In recent years the Congress has been making repeated efforts to reverse this trend for example by trying to hold elections for the party organisation from the lowest levels. These efforts have not had easy success because of problems common to the entire political system in India. Parties other than the Congress too share the same denouement as that faced by the Congress on this issue.

The emergency again was the product of the political impasse that had got created by the JP movement which as I mentioned above had, to a great extent, come under the grip of the fascist right wing represented by the RSS and which sought to remove Indira Gandhi by exercising coercion outside the democratic path sanctioned by our constitution. Once democracy was held at abeyance, whatever the provocation, its inevitable misuse was to follow, what we now remember as the 'excesses'. If the emergency was a blot on Indian democracy, it must be remembered that Indira Gandhi revoking the emergency on her own, allowing free and fair elections and handing over power graciously, once defeated, marked the 'triumph' of Indian democracy. Dictators are not known to behave in this manner. Perhaps, in the long run, as the chapter in this volume on the JP movement and the emergency argues,

> Paradoxically, even the Emergency experience strengthened democracy. It inoculated Indian people not only against another bout of authoritarianism but also against an irresponsible movement like the JP Movement. Democracy, freedom and parliamentary form of government were further entrenched. Since 1977, there has been little talk of the need to scrap or change the existing political system and replace it by military rule or dictatorship or some sort of non-party democracy in order to have faster economic development or to end corruption, even though corruption has vastly increased since 1974-75.

The Indian people, who under the influence of the national movement had imbibed democracy as a non-negotiable value in itself, had no hesitation in voting out Indira Gandhi, one of their most popular Prime Ministers till barely a few years earlier, once she was seen as having abrogated their democratic rights, however briefly. However, they had no hesitation in bringing her back with a resounding victory not only because of the appalling record of the Janata regime even on the count of maintaining democratic norms, but because they were confident that she was committed to the democratic path.

One of the senior most ministers in her Cabinet, and for many years thereafter, told me a very telling anecdote recently. His illiterate house maid of many years who was an Indira loyalist had voted against her after the emergency. But when asked why she proposed to vote for her in 1979-80 she said that she voted against her in 1977 to teach her a lesson, now that the lesson was learnt she was happy to welcome her back. She explained further that when an angry mother exasperated with the behaviour of her son wishes him dead she only does that to chide him, not to actually see him dead. The minister told me that this conversation gave him the clue that Indira Gandhi going to come back with a big bang as she had not lost the people's trust.

On the secular front Indira Gandhi had remained steadfast throughout her life. The popular slogan during her election campaign '*Na jaat per na paat per mohur lagegei hath per*' was symptomatic of her strong desire to contain caste and communal politics in India. In fact given the amazing resurgence of casteism and communalism in the years following her death, the Congress Party and the country as a whole needs to learn from the experience of how Jawaharlal Nehru and Indira Gandhi were to keep the casteist and communal forces at bay. Indira Gandhi was perhaps the last to launch an active ideological struggle against these forces through, for example, the education system, media, etc. The tendency since then has been to pander to these forces, in a populist and opportunist manner, in order to obtain short-term electoral gains but causing immense damage to the long-term vision with which the Indian nation was imagined.

The tendency to paint the Congress with a communal brush because of the Operation Blue Star is to miss the wood for the trees. The chapter on Punjab in this volume shows the long history behind the Punjab crisis. It shows how communalist forces grew and spread in Punjab over a long period of time. It also shows that while some Congressmen, like Zail Singh, may have played ball with the Sikh communalists with disastrous consequences, the Congress was not a Sikh communal organisation. Nor was there anything in Congress politics or ideology which was anti-Sikh (unlike say the BJP whose *raison-d-etre* is being anti-Muslim and anti-Christian). Yet, after the anti-Sikh riots following Indira Gandhi's assassination the effort has been to generalise that event and repeatedly brand the Congress as a communal (presumably now Hindu communal) anti-Sikh Party. How Congress could be both Sikh communal and be anti-Sikh is difficult to explain. This could be argued only in the sense that all communal parties are objectively destructive of the communities they claim to represent but this is not the sense in which the Congress is accused of being anti-Sikh, i.e., it is anti-Sikh because it is Sikh communal.

The Congress Party and certainly Indira Gandhi was never anti-Sikh. She had to launch Operation Blue Star as events in Punjab had led to a situation where the Sikh sacred shrine in Amritsar was being desecrated by some of the worst criminals against humanity who had congregated there, fortified themselves, unleashing mayhem and terror from its premises. She paid with her life by taking on this challenge frontally at a time when even the brave people of Punjab, barring a handful, had by and large (from Judges to law makers to teachers and common citizens) been 'silenced' under terrorist fear.

To the last she insisted on keeping Sikh guards in her personal security even when warned against it. It is to be noted that she did not do it as a public act to make a point but a private decision which threatened her own life. As a deeply secular person she would not allow herself distrust against anybody simply on the basis of his religious origin. While it is the same guards who were to mercilessly shred her frail body with bullets, it is this trust and faith in secularism which is the legacy she leaves behind.

Endnotes

1. Early nationalists like Surendranath Banerjea used this phrase 'nation in the making' being deeply conscious that it was a continuing process and a task which had to be consciously and creatively taken forward.
2. See Bipan Chandra, Mridula Mukherjee and Aditya Mukherjee, *India Since Independence.* Penguin, New Delhi, 2008, pp.4-7 and Selig Harrison and Neville Maxwell, etc., quoted therein.
3. See Angus Maddison, *The World Economy*: *Vol. I A Millennial Perspective, Vol.II Historical Statistics,* OECD, 2006, Indian Edition, New Delhi, 2007, table 8b, p. 641; George Blyn, *Agricultural Trends in India, 1891-1947: Output, Availability, and Productivity,* Philadelphia, 1966, p.123 and p.102 and ch.5 below.
4. Yet many like Tirthankar Roy, Meghnad Desai, etc., till today talk of the positive impact of colonial rule. See for a detailed critique of this neo-colonial position, Aditya Mukherjee, "Return of the Colonial In Indian Economic History: The Last Phase of Colonialism in India", Presidential Address, Modern India, *Proceedings of the Indian History Congress,* New

Delhi, 2007, reprinted in *Social Scientist,* Vol. 36, No. 3-4 and 5-6, Mar.-Apr., and May-June, 2008.

5. Quoted in Bipan Chandra, Mridula Mukherjee, Aditya Mukherjee, *India Since Independence, op.cit.*p.19.
6. See *Selected Works of Jawaharlal Nehru,* Volume 28, p. 371.
7. See Bipan Chandra, Mridula Mukherjee, Aditya Mukherjee, *India Since Independence,* and Iqbal Narain, ed., *Centenary History of the Indian National Congress,* Volume IV: 1947-1964.
8. These figures are from an extremely persuasive piece by Vijay Kelkar, "India and the World Economy: A Search for Self Reliance", Paper read at Seminar on Jawaharlal Nehru and Planned Development, New Delhi, 1980.
9. Henry Kissinger quoted by V.P. Dutt below, chapter 6.
10. Louis J. Walinsky, ed., *Agrarian Reform as Unfinished Business, The selected papers of Wolf Ladejinsky*, OUP, 1977, (hereafter Ladejinsky papers), p.483.
11. See my chapter on the Green Revolution in Bipan Chandra, Mridula Mukherjee, Aditya Mukherjee, *India Since Independence, op.cit.*

Chapter II

Indira Gandhi: An Overview

Inder Malhotra

For full two decades, from the mid-1960s to the mid-1980s of the last century, Indira Gandhi dominated the Indian scene like a colossus, irrespective of whether she was in power or out of it. As in life, so over 25 years after her death, she looms large in modern Indian history. To be sure, like all human beings, she had her share of flaws and failings. As Prime Minister for more than 15 years in two innings, she did make mistakes, some of them serious, and a few with lasting effects. But the yeoman services she rendered her country because of her clear-eyed, hardheaded leadership outweigh overwhelmingly the wrongs she did or allowed to be done. She is unquestionably the second greatest Prime Minister India has had, the first being, of course, her illustrious father, Jawaharlal Nehru.

Even during the early 1960s when India and much of the world fretted about 'After Nehru, Who?' Indira Gandhi's name had figured on the shortlist of his possible successors. However, Welles Hangen, a Delhi-based American journalist and author of a thoughtful book on precisely this question, had argued that she could surely reach the room at the top but only with the help of the 'parental key'. Interestingly, the impression was widespread that Nehru wanted to pass on his mantle to his daughter and had 'groomed' her for this purpose assiduously. But however brisk the speculation and whatever Nehru's ambitions for his daughter, he did absolutely nothing to catapult her to the highest office. In fact, the succession issue was settled in favour of Lal Bahadur Shastri in Nehru's lifetime and with his consent. A group of Congress Party bosses in states headed by K. Kamaraj, then chief minister of Madras (now called Tamil Nadu) and later Congress president, had masterminded this. For its exertions it was promptly nicknamed 'the Syndicate'.

Who could have thought that Shastri would die in just 19 months? His death—at the Central Asian city of Tashkent where he had gone to negotiate, under Soviet auspices, with President Ayub Khan of Pakistan to bring the subcontinent back to peace after the 1965 war—was sudden. Nobody had given any thought to this possibility. The Syndicate had seen Shastri's selection through consensus, but it was in no position to repeat that performance. For, Morarji Desai, stating that he had been 'cheated out' of his due once and would not let that happen again, had made it clear that he would contest whoever the Syndicate's candidate was. Moreover, though Kamaraj instinctively felt that Indira Gandhi would be the best bet of the Congress and the country, some of his cohorts did not agree with him immediately. S.K. Patil, the Bombay boss, indeed suggested that Kamaraj should accept the onerous responsibility himself. To this the silent strong man replied: 'No Hindi, No English. How?'

It would be idle to pretend that Indira Gandhi's parentage had nothing to do with her choice as the future prime minister. But there was another more powerful reason to opt for her. In less than 13 months the fourth General Elections, the first without Nehru, was due. Who among the Congress leaders could be a better garner of votes than her? True to his word, Desai insisted on a vote by the Congress Parliamentary Party and lost to Indira Gandhi, polling 169 votes against 355 for her. The popular goodwill surrounding her election was enormous. Huge crowds cheered what they called the 'return of the red rose', the reference being to Nehru's lifelong habit of sporting a red rose in his buttonhole.

Indira Gandhi's rise to power was both popular and spectacular. But this honour had come to her at a very difficult time. Two wars during three years and two leadership successions within half of that period were accompanied by two successive years of savage drought that decimated crops, particularly in Bihar where the spectre of famine haunted the land. The country did not have the foreign exchange to buy food in the world market. The already substantial dependence on the import of American wheat under the US Public Law 480 on rupee payment and at relatively low prices now became critical. At the same time, she had to cope with some other grave problems. The long-standing demand for Punjabi Suba—a Punjabi-speaking state—was one. In the strategic and sensitive Northeast, the tribal insurgency until then confined to the Nagas had suddenly spread to the Mizos, too.

Rising food prices led to mass discontent that found expression at the All India Congress Committee session at Jaipur barely a month after she had become Prime Minister. No wonder then that she decided to go on an official visit to the US where she had been a dozen times before, with her father or on her own. Her agenda was clear but totally unstated: to get food and financial aid without appearing to do so. On the way to Washington DC she departed from the standard practice of Indian leaders to halt in London before flying across the Atlantic.

Instead, she made a stopover in Paris. Her two sons then studying in Britain crossed the English Channel to be with her. Her decision to break journey in the French capital had a dual purpose: to snub the British Prime Minister, Harold Wilson, who had had the temerity to blame India for starting the 1965 war and then explaining that he had been 'misled' by an adviser; and, by establishing rapport with President Charles de Gaulle, she wanted the world to know that her ambitions for her country were like his for France. All through her meeting and lunch with her host she spoke in fluent French. *Le Grand* Charles was charmed. Many years later it became known that he had told some of his colleagues: 'Women don't usually succeed in politics, but this one would'. (See author's *Indira Gandhi*—NBT 2006, p. 188.)

America's welcome to Indira Gandhi could not have been more effusive. There was media hype even before her arrival. President Lyndon Johnson's praise for 'this proud, able and gracious lady' was gushing. He even broke protocol at a reception for her and decided to stay at the house of the Indian Ambassador, B.K. Nehru, to dine with her. And he took every opportunity to declare 'all-out support' to her. Only after an interval it became clear that the outcome of the US visit was mixed. There was a feeling that she had conceded more than she should have. The first disturbing sign was a storm of protest by Indian educationists, academics and scholars against her acceptance of the US proposal for establishing an Indo-US Educational Foundation, modelled on the Ford Foundation that was to be financed by the huge funds America had accumulated in this country because of massive supplies of PL 480 wheat. Eventually, she rescinded this agreement. Secondly, and more importantly, there was criticism of what was perceived to be the 'softening' of her criticism of America's war in Vietnam. Remarkably, she first encountered it in Moscow where she had stopped over before having to face a lot more of it at home. Critics did not know, however, that before going to see Johnson she had summarily rejected the advice of her senior aides to tell him that she 'shared' America's 'agony' over Vietnam. The farthest she went was that she 'understood' the agony. Even after this became known the critics, including Krishna Menon and other members of the Congress Party, were unrelenting. On the grim food situation confronting India and its new Prime Minister, Johnson's response was both prompt and generous. He promised to send 10 million tonnes of PL 480 wheat. But even this promising transaction turned sour before long, as we will see presently.

On June 6, 1966, barely six months after her ascent to power, Indira Gandhi's government devalued the rupee by 35 percent. Both the US and the World Bank were insistent on this, and the matter was secretly discussed between her and Johnson. This decision hit the country with the force of a mini-nuke. Indira was taken aback by the ferocity of the reaction. Never before, except during the Chinese invasion in 1962, had public opinion been so aroused as over devaluation. To cap it all, Kamaraj took over the leadership of all those calling devaluation 'a surrender to American dictates'. The irony is that the decision to devalue the rupee had been all but taken during the time of Lal Bahadur Shastri and would probably have been announced by him but for his untimely death. Indira Gandhi was in no position to reverse her predecessor's resolve. Also at that stage of her career her understanding of the intricacies of high finance was limited. Stoically, she carried the can. Meanwhile, her difficulties had grown partly because of her generally shy nature and inexperience in running the affairs of State. In Parliament she tended to be tongue-tied which gave one of her inveterate political adversaries, Socialist leader Ram Manohar Lohia, an opportunity to nickname her *goongi gudiya* (the dumb doll) that caught on. In this atmosphere she never received the full credit for having resolved the issue of Punjabi Suba that had bedeviled the country's northwest region, both its breadbasket and sword arm, for long years.

On the other hand, this must be reckoned to be the moment when she decided to show the steel that was in her though, as was her wont throughout her political career, she never acted impetuously. Her first decision was to replace L.K. Jha, her Secretary and chief bureaucratic adviser, who was an ardent advocate of devaluation, by P.N. Haksar, a Foreign Service Officer and a Nehru family acolyte known for his left-leaning views imbibed during a long stay in England in the 'Pink Thirties'. But she carried out the change only after the 1967 General Elections. On the issue of Vietnam, however, she acted quickly.

Three weeks after devaluation she embarked on a three-nation journey to Egypt, Yugoslavia and the Soviet Union carrying with her a statement on the war in Vietnam's paddy fields. The first two countries, together with India, provided leadership to the Non-Aligned Movement. By the time she had reached Moscow, the carefully crafted statement had morphed into an 'Indian initiative' to bring peace to Vietnam. A complete and immediate cessation of American bombings was obviously the first step in the process to which the other side was required to reciprocate. Back home the move was welcomed. But no sooner was the statement issued Lyndon Johnson in Washington hit the ceiling. He was enraged. He did not withdraw the offer of food, but did something much worse. He put food shipments on such a tight leash that India literally lived from 'ship to mouth'. With every morsel we Indians had to swallow a bit of humiliation. No wonder many started demanding that India should say no to American wheat. Indira

Gandhi characteristically remained silent. Privately, she commented that if food shipments stopped, the 'agitating ladies and gentlemen won't suffer. Only the poor would starve'. She vowed that India must never be in the same situation, and ensured this through the Green Revolution, one of her earliest achievements.

As the elections drew nearer, bickering within the Congress Party grew. At every party forum there was carping criticism of the Prime Minister. Desai made no bones about his determination to challenge her leadership after the poll. In this atmosphere the Hindu extremists, anxious to exploit the cow-slaughter issue for electoral purposes, brought a procession of *sadhus* to the doorstep of Parliament where it degenerated into vicious violence. Seven persons were killed and there was widespread arson. Indira used the ghastly event to ease out her ineffectual and troublesome home minister, Gulzari Lal Nanda. He appealed to the Syndicate to 'save him' but his lament fell on deaf ears. However, the Syndicate arrogantly overruled her when she wanted to replace also her finance and foreign ministers also. She was miffed but again kept quiet. Worse followed. In distributing party tickets and disbursing party funds to the candidates, the Syndicate gave short shrift to the Prime Minister's followers. It even brushed aside her simple plea that so senior a leader as Krishna Menon should not be denied his traditional constituency.

On Christmas Day, exactly 11 months after being sworn in, she spoke out. Without raising her voice, she told the Press: 'Here is a question. Who the party wants and whom the people want? My position among the people is uncontested.' This was the essence of her political strategy all through her life, in good times and bad: Appeal to the people over the heads of the party bosses, and carry the masses with you. Having announced this she left for the countrywide election campaign. Everywhere—except at Bhubaneswar where she was injured as a result of stones hurled at her—she was greeted with tremendous enthusiasm and applause.

However, the election results when they came in did not reflect affectionate outpourings of the crowds along the campaign trail. In fact, the outcome was a major setback to the Congress and the Prime Minister. The party's vote was down from 45 percent in 1962 to 42 percent. It lost not only the southern state of Madras (now Tamil Nadu) but also seven states in North India, giving rise to the jibe that one could travel all the way from Calcutta (now Kolkata) to Amritsar 'without having to traverse a single inch of Congress-governed territory'. In the Lok Sabha, with a total membership of 520, the Congress Party's two-third majority plummeted to 283 seats. But, paradoxically, this worked to Indira Gandhi's advantage, rather than disadvantage. For, several Syndicate stalwarts had bitten the dust. In a class by itself was the fall of Kamaraj. He had lost not only his state, of which he was an 'uncrowned king' until then, but also his seat. Unconcerned with all this, Desai wanted a contest between Indira and him. But the Congress's instinct for self-preservation took over. The party did not want a divisive contest for leadership. Though itself deflated the Syndicate rode again and forced a compromise under which Desai became deputy prime minister in Indira Gandhi's cabinet. He was assigned the Finance portfolio he had held twice under Nehru.

So tenuous and phony was the Congress compromise that, far from being mitigated, the struggle between Desai's supporters and Indira's followers, was aggravated. True to his style, Desai would encourage his close associates to undermine the Prime Minister's authority but would not say anything against her because as a 'man of principles' he did not wish to invite the charge of 'disloyalty'. (Tarakeswari Sinha, a staunch supporter of Desai to a group of journalists, including the author in October 1968 when power struggle was escalating.) It is often said by Indira's critics that having decided to lurch Leftwards after the 'devaluation bombshell' and especially in the wake of the 1967 election she used 'populism' to strengthen her position in the country and thus in the party. This is a half truth. The reality is a lot more complex. Whatever her own convictions and predilections, she had to be responsive to the strong feelings of the party ranks. And yet she did this in a way that in formulating policies she could carry the Conservative section of the party with her. Let the sequence of facts speak for itself.

In May 1967, the All India Congress Committee (AICC) met for the first time after the electoral shock. The rank and file, especially the radicals among them, promptly nicknamed 'Young Turks', denounced the 'old and reactionary leaders' for having alienated the traditional voters of the Congress, especially the Harijans (now called Dalits), religious minorities and the poor in general. The party, they thundered, would never be able to recover the lost ground until it returned to earlier socialistic policies diluted by 'pragmatism' in recent years. Desai protested against the attempts to 'malign elderly leaders' and some stalwarts of the Syndicate endorsed him. This was the first indication that the Syndicate and Desai, bitter enemies of each other previously, were now drawing close. The reason for the Syndicate's change of heart was that Indira's declaration of independence of it. This had dashed the party bosses' hope that she would only reign while they would rule. She had earlier brushed aside the joint suggestion of Desai and the Syndicate that the outgoing president, S. Radhakrishnan, be given a second term, and insisted that Vice-President Zakir Hussain should be elevated. She prevailed and Hussain's victory was welcomed as a triumph of Indian secularism and of hers.

However, the attention at the AICC was focussed on giving the government's economic policies a leftwards push. But despite the din and noise, neither side, least of all Indira Gandhi, wanted to force the issue. Consequently, the leadership drafted a 10-point programme on which the radicals and the Conservatives could agree. The only point of contention in it was the key issue of nationalisation of private banks for which there was considerable sentiment within the political class. The Young Turks wanted immediate nationalisation. Desai, as Finance Minister, was vehemently opposed to it. He was agreeable to 'social control' of banks, which really meant appointment of watchdog committees to monitor the banks' workings. When the Young Turks opposed this idea, to their surprise, Indira gave Desai full support. Social control, she said, must be a given a fair trial for two years after which the matter could be reviewed. The radicals were frustrated and angry but they could not dare oppose her. Her priority was to shift her policies leftwards so as to be able to carry all sections of the party with her.

The bank nationalisation issue was thus settled. Everybody relaxed and debate on other less controversial items droned on and on until late at night. By then Indira, Desai and some other senior leaders had gone home. The Young Turks suddenly perceived the opportunity to assert themselves. The 10-point programme included in the Congress agenda the abolition of the 'privileges' enjoyed by the rulers of former princely states, ranging from gun salutes to immunity from certain laws and regulations. The resolution said nothing, however, about the privy purses of the princes obviously because these were guaranteed in perpetuity by the constitution. Regardless, the Young Turks moved an amendment demanding that the privy purses also be abolished forthwith. It was carried out by only 17 votes to six but became the Congress policy, amidst vigorous protests by a hurriedly organised trade union of princes.

Thereafter differences and bickering within the ruling party escalated fast and virtually paralysed the government. In these circumstances, the chances of implementing the 10-point programme with alacrity were slim. The radicals were impatient and on the warpath. Chandra Shekhar, who was to become Prime Minister in 1990, made serious allegations of corruption against Desai's son, Kanti, on the floor of the House. His demand for a prime ministerial reprimand to the 'offending member' remained unfulfilled.

By early 1968 Desai and the Syndicate had decided that Indira Gandhi had to be removed from the office of Prime Minister but did not know how. In the Indira camp her staunch supporters were beseeching her to carry her struggle against the Desai-Syndicate combination to its logical conclusion. She refused because she knew better. External challenges had to be met before taking on challenges within the party. Almost precisely at that time providence provided the Desai and the Syndicate with the opportunity they were hankering for. It was the sudden death of President Zakir Hussain barely a year after taking over. The task of Indira's adversaries was simple: to choose one of themselves as the future President and once in Rashtrapati Bhavan he would do the rest. Indira knew she had to checkmate this plan, and she was determined to do so. But she had other goals to achieve first.

The regional party, Dravida Munnetra Kazhagam (DMK) that had replaced the Congress in Tamil Nadu was strong and stable. But in the seven North Indian states the Congress had lost to cacophonic and comprehensive coalitions that included every opposition party from the extreme right to extreme left. No wonder, they started falling one after the other under the weight of their contradictions. By February 1969, the Congress, even though itself torn by factional warfare, had regained control of all these states, except West Bengal that was a much tougher nut to crack.

Here, in 1967, the Left Front had come to power. Its nominal leader and chief minister was Ajoy Mukherjee, a highly respected Congressman hounded out of the fold by the party boss, Atulya Ghosh. But it was the Communist Party of India, CPI (Marxist), led by Jyoti Basu, who wielded the real power. In a highly tense atmosphere, power went to the heads of Marxist cadres. Social, economic and political conflict led to such violence that many alarmed industrialists and business executive starting leaving the state. Some screamed foolishly that West Bengal was becoming 'another Vietnam'. Indira dismissed the state government within a few months, and the CPI (M) carried the battle to the streets. In 1969, the Marxist-dominated Left Front returned to power with an even larger majority. This was worrisome for Indira but her attention was focussed on the critically important struggle over the choice of the party's presidential nominee. Matters came to a head in July 1969. At a meeting of the Congress Parliamentary Party at Bangalore, her opponents succeeded in overruling her and selected Sanjiva Reddy, a Syndicate stalwart. Though technically bound by the Bangalore decision she was furious.

On returning to Delhi, her first move was to divest Desai of the Finance portfolio but asked him to stay on as deputy prime minister—an offer he understandably refused. She took over Finance herself. She had prepared the ground for this move rather shrewdly. A day before the climatic Parliamentary Board meeting she had sent to the Congress

Working Committee a note on economic policy, under the title "Some Stray Thoughts, Hurriedly Dictated", in which she hinted, rather than say explicitly, that the issue of bank nationalisation could be reconsidered even though the two-year trial period was not yet over. To Desai she wrote that she did not want to burden him with the responsibility of carrying out policies he 'did not believe in'. A few days later, she called Economic Affairs Secretary, I.G. Patel, and said to him: 'For political reasons it has been decided to nationalise the banks. You have to prepare within 24 hours the bill, a note for the cabinet and a speech for me to make to the nation. Can you do it and make sure there is no leak?' (I.G. Patel, *Glimpses of Indian Economic Policy* (OUP, p. 135.) The next morning all the documents were on the Prime Minister's desk, and by that afternoon 14 major banks had been nationalised by ordinance. The effect across the country was electric. In Delhi rickshaw drivers and other poor people danced in the streets. None of them had ever been inside a bank or was likely to. But they said something was at last being done for the poor and the rich were being put in their place.

Meanwhile, the epic battle for the presidency was in full swing and had taken several dramatic twists and turns. The Syndicate, Desai and hopeful Sanjiva Reddy were dismayed when they learnt that Indira Gandhi's followers in Parliament and all state assemblies (the President is elected by all members of Parliament and of state assemblies, with varying value of their votes) were clamouring for 'conscience vote' and were planning to vote for V.V. Giri, the Vice-President who had resigned and was contesting as an independent candidate. When the votes were counted Giri won though with a narrow majority. However, in Indian elections, as in love and war, the winner takes all, the loser can only lick his wound.

In the circumstances, a split in the Congress was inevitable. But such is the mystique of 'Congress unity' that the unavoidable took two and a half months to materialise in slow motion. For, neither side wanted to attract the odium of having broken up the party of the Mahatma and Nehru. Eventually, the bizarre charade ended. On November 7, 1969, the great Congress split took place. Indira Gandhi's dominance of the party was impressively manifested.

Of the 282 Congress members of the Lok Sabha—the House that sustains or brings down governments—220 went with Indira and 68 with the Syndicate-Desai combination. However, her government was clearly in a minority in the House. Yet, she had no difficulty in running it because the CPI, DMK and several Independents fully supported the Congress (I) government. When she summoned a meeting of the AICC, of its 705 members 446 attended.

At this stage she devoted a lot of her time and energy to see the bank nationalisation overcome judicial objections. The measure to abolish the privy purses, needing a two-thirds majority, failed in the Rajya Sabha by a fraction of a single vote. Unperturbed, she got the princes 'de-recognised' by Presidential order. She was anxious to make good of her other promises to the people not only because of their intrinsic merit but also because she wanted to disprove her noisy critics who were screaming that her radical rhetoric was only a 'smokescreen for her quest for personal power'. She abolished the managing agency system that had been a part of the Indian mercantile scene since Robert Clive. She halted the trend towards decontrolled economy and set up a Monopolies and Restrictive Trade Practices (MRTP) Commission in 1970. On the other hand, she turned down her radical followers' demand for nationalisation of foreign trade and for the withdrawal of concessions already given to foreign investors. Significantly, this important nuance went unnoticed.

Indira Gandhi's government was stable enough but she continued to brood that dependence on other parties and groups could lead to political blackmail. While she was still planning her next step, an interesting opportunity presented itself in distant Kerala. A Left Front ministry, headed by the CPI(M) since 1967, collapsed because of internal differences, especially between the Marxists and the CPI. In 1959, as Congress president, she was the main driving force behind the dismissal of the Kerala government of the undivided CPI(M) led by EMS Namboodiripad. Now, she entered into an alliance with the right CPI, to keep the Marxists, still led by EMS, at bay. In the fresh elections to the state assembly in September 1970, the Congress-led alliance won easily. Thereafter, Kerala apparently became what a trailer is to the feature film! For, on December 27, she went on air to announce that since she needed a fresh mandate, the Lok Sabha had been dissolved and fresh elections would be held in mid-February of the new year—full 12 months ahead of schedule. Probably anticipating this, almost all her opponents—the rival Congress that called itself the Congress (Organisation), the Hindu right-wing party Jana Sangh (the forerunner of the BJP), the big business party Swatantra, now defunct, and a farmers' outfit of North India named Bharatiya Kranti Dal (BKD)—formed a 'Grand Alliance' with a single-point manifesto: 'Indira Hatao' (remove Indira). Her masterly counterstroke was: 'Garibi Hatao' (remove poverty) that mesmerised the country. The poor, a majority of the population, felt that they had at last found their redeemer. In next to no time, the 1971 parliamentary poll turned into a referendum on Indira's leadership.

During the election campaign no holds were barred. But the election results when they came in stunned friends and foes alike.

Indira's party, without any political machine worth the name, won 352 Lok Sabha seats or 70 more than the undivided Congress had managed to muster four years earlier. The Congress (O)'s share had plummeted from 68 to 16. Some other Opposition parties were virtually wiped out. No one was in any doubt that Indira Gandhi's sweeping victory was primarily personal. Newspapers that until the previous day had ranted against her suddenly wrote appreciatively about the 'Indira Wave'. Until then nobody had perceived it.

Buoyed by the stupendous renewal of mandate, she started working on a politically attractive and economically sound plan of action to place before the new Parliament. But that was not to be. For, exactly eight days after being sworn in for the third time she was confronted by a wholly unexpected and tremendously terrible problem, with profound implications for India, that had started unfolding itself at the country's doorstep in what was then East Pakistan and is now the Islamic Republic of Bangladesh. The Bangladesh Crisis erupted on March 25 with the fury of the cyclones that frequently devastate that unfortunate land. It immediately invited Pakistani repression and atrocities worse than the Nazi war crimes, driving 10 million hapless refugees to flee to adjacent Indian states. It also led, inevitably, to the war for the liberation of Bangladesh in December. All this was to preoccupy the Prime Minister and the people at large all through 1971.

It is fair to add, however, that Indira Gandhi did manage to bring about two important amendments in the Constitution. The first that had repercussions for so many years afterwards was to restore to Parliament the right to amend all sections of the basic law. In 1967 when K. Subba Rao was the Chief Justice of India, the Supreme Court had, by a majority of four to three, debarred Parliament from amending the fundamental rights. Parliament's reversal of this verdict was not the end of the matter. On the contrary, it became the starting point of her conflict with the judiciary that was technically resolved by the Supreme Court in 1973 by letting Parliament change any part of the Constitution but without altering its 'basic structure'. However, her tug-of-war with the higher judiciary, with several senior judges being superseded in the process in the midst of public hue and cry, persisted. The second amendment made Parliament, rather than the judiciary, the final arbiter of the amount of compensation to be paid for private property acquired for public purpose in pursuance of the directive principles of state policy.

Interestingly, these crucial changes in the Constitution attracted little attention because all minds were focussed on Bangladesh. Since this climatic development with far-reaching consequences is the subject of a separate chapter in this volume, I will avoid well-known details and concentrate on critically important landmarks, including those underscoring the brilliant and inspiring leadership Indira Gandhi provided the country in extremely testing times.

Her first exasperating problem was to control and calm down not just the public at large but prominent political leaders across the spectrum, including a few of her colleagues, who had begun clamouring for immediate Indian military intervention. Curiously, the respected Gandhian leader, Jayaprakash Narayan, better known as JP, also joined this howling crowd. P.N. Dhar, the Prime Minister's Secretary from 1970 to 1977, was 'astonished' at the 'unbalanced judgment and emotionalism of this otherwise lovable man' until he (JP) was persuaded to divert his energies to 'mobilising world public opinion against Pakistan'. (*Indira Gandhi, the "Emergency", and Indian Democracy*, OUP, 2000. p.157)

Understandably, the Prime Minister gave priority to harmonising the political, diplomatic and military strands in Indian response to Pakistan's challenge. Also, from the very start, she and her Chief of the Army Staff, General (later Field-Marshal) Sam Manekshaw, were in complete agreement on the strategy to be followed. She took good care not to make any warlike statements in her future speeches but kept the focus on the ten million refugees. 'Pakistan's internal problem has become our problem', she told a succession of visiting foreign dignitaries.

By the end of August she had come to the conclusion that her top priority should be to influence and mould the international opinion. She started with a visit to Moscow where she refused to hold negotiations with lesser Soviet leaders until Leonid Brezhnev returned home. This he did immediately, interrupting his holiday. He and other Soviet leaders listened to her with attention and respect. Three weeks later she embarked on a hot-paced tour that took her to Austria, Belgium, France, West Germany, Britain and the United States. It was an essay in masterpiece diplomacy. Her message found acceptance everywhere, except in the US where the Nixon-Kissinger duo, for its own dubious reasons, was hell-bent to be on the side that was morally in the wrong and militarily doomed to defeat.

Meanwhile, the world order and the international configuration of forces underwent a tectonic change as a result of Henry Kissinger's secret visit to China. The inveterate foes of two decades suddenly became not just friends but virtual allies. Indira Gandhi showed no sign of panic or worry even though China's reaction to, and role in, any India-Pakistan conflict was always a matter of concern. A few days after the sea change in the US-China relationship, Kissinger told the Indian ambassador to Washington, L.K. Jha, that in case China intervened in an India-Pakistan war over Bangladesh, New Delhi must not expect any help from Washington. Indira was unflappable. Her response was to send her trusted aide D.P. Dhar to Moscow to clinch the Indo-Soviet Treaty of Peace, Friendship and Cooperation. Remarkably, this treaty had been in the works for two years because Indira was not particularly keen to conclude it. But a radically changed situation called for a radically different approach. At the same time, she saw to it that the treaty had no clause on defence or military cooperation. It only provided for immediate mutual consultations whenever the security of either side was threatened. Also, the treaty specifically recognised India's non-aligned status.

When the war was on, the US, evidently still bewitched by Yahya Khan and other butchers of Bangladesh, took the extraordinary and provocative step of sending a nuclear naval task force to the Bay of Bengal. Indira was furious with this attempt at intimidation but remained cool. A few days later, she quietly called in Raja Ramanna, then director of the Bhabha Atomic Research Centre and country's principal nuclear physicist, and told him to go ahead and start working on India's first nuclear detonation that took place on May 18, 1974.

In view of the foregoing it is my contention that India, being a country completely lacking in strategic thinking, has never given Indira Gandhi full credit for her strategic virtuosity and the skill and diligence with which she defended the nation's security and supreme interests, whatever the odds. This is as good a place as any to make another pertinent point. Indira Gandhi did not have her father's grand vision or his phenomenal grasp of world history and dynamics of international forces. But in her comprehension of uses of power and willing to use power, internally or externally, when necessary, she excelled her 'Papu'.

On the afternoon of December 16, 1971, she was in her office in Parliament House waiting for a call from her Army Chief. Rather delayed, the call came in the midst of an interview she was giving to a Swedish TV team. Taking leave of it, she rushed to the House to announce, amidst thunderous applause: 'Dacca is now the free capital of a free country...'. During the short walk back to her office she told her Information Adviser, H.Y. Sharada Prasad: 'I must now declare a ceasefire on the western front, because if I don't do it tonight, I won't be able to do so tomorrow'. Clearly, she, unlike some of her starry-eyed colleagues, was aware of the perils of euphoria.

This was her finest hour. The country's admiration for her turned into adoration. Almost overnight the *goongi gudiya* morphed into invincible goddess Durga. Women, especially in villages, saw her as an incarnation of *shakti*, female energy. On behalf of a grateful nation,

President Giri awarded her Bharat Ratna, the highest civilian honour. She was now at the pinnacle of her power and glory. *The Economist's* description of her as the Empress of India seemed apt. Her popularity among the people was intact. But the trouble with scaling Olympian heights is that thereafter there is nowhere to go except down. Nobody at that time could have foreseen that her downward slide would begin so soon.

On way to her apotheosis Indira Gandhi had done the country a lot of good, as she was to do afterwards. But it is only fair to recognise that there were at least three deleterious consequences of the concentration of practically all power in her hands and of her constant glorification by her overzealous supporters. First, almost immediately after her rise to supremacy a cult of personality had developed. In this essentially feudal country a courtier culture grew fast and spawned rampant sycophancy that eventually blossomed into Dev Kanta Barooah's infamous rubbish: 'Indira is India, India is Indira'. It was a surprise that someone of her sophistication and refinement could tolerate the crudest flattery as each of the competing courtiers tried to outdo every other to catch the benign attention of the sole disperser of patronage. Backbiting, backstabbing and intrigue became the order of the day. On the other hand and rather paradoxically, despite her absolute power, Indira Gandhi did not shed her paranoia or quest for absolute security that may have been understandable during the years of struggle with the Syndicate and Desai but made little sense in the changed milieu. Consequently, she could not stand anyone in her party who could even remotely be a rival power centre.

Secondly, total concentration of power meant an erosion of the democratic institutions, so carefully nurtured by Nehru, which underpin the necessary checks and balances in any democratic system. However, to put all the blame for this on Indira would be wrong. What did the worthies heading the institutions concerned do to preserve their autonomy? More importantly, since her time there have been no fewer than 12 governments at the Centre. All political parties, big, small or minuscule, have shared power in one form or the other. But at no stage has anyone tried to end or even reduce the manipulation of institutions. All these have to bow to the rulers of the day. Mercifully, the Supreme Court and the Election Commission are two honourable exceptions!

The third deleterious development at the peak of Indira Gandhi's power was a strange new twist to the curse of corruption and abuse of authority that has been an enduring part of India's life all through history though today it has obviously taken a quantum leap, compared with what prevailed in her time. The sophistry that entered the situation during her primacy was this: intoxicated by the vast majority of their party in both Houses of Parliament and almost all state assemblies, the large number of Congressmen blessed with the 'gift of grab' took it for granted that they were immune from accountability. However, the Opposition in Parliament and vigilant sections of the media tried to expose major scams and scandals. Their perpetrators told the Prime Minister that the attack on them was in reality an attack on her. She somehow accepted this absurd proposition and thus became a shield for the corrupt. Consequences, in terms of disruption of Parliament and loss of the people's respect and confidence were disastrous.

It was in this ambience that, in the summer of 1972, Indira Gandhi, having won the war, addressed the more arduous task of making peace with Pakistan in the hope of using India's strong position to find a permanent solution on the Kashmir issue. Negotiations between her and Zulfiqar Ali Bhutto held at Shimla were tough and tortuous. One evening it seemed that the talks were on the brink of breaking down. Yet, by midnight the agreement was signed. Its essence was a private and verbal assurance by Bhutto that the Line of Control (LoC) in Jammu and Kashmir would, over time and gradually, be converted into a permanent border. The key word was 'gradually'. For the first time since the 1971 General Elections, Indira Gandhi came under criticism on account of the Shimla Accord. Her critics said it was a 'sell-out', not settlement. As it became clear that Bhutto had no intention of living up to his commitment, the criticism of Indira became sharper. The only mystery still is as to why and how did Indira Gandhi trust Bhutto's word? For, she knew better than anyone else that he was so slippery that, compared with him, an eel would be a leech!

By the start of 1973, the afterglow of the Bangladesh had faded. On the contrary the heavy bills of that glorious event had started coming in. The government's overflowing granaries had been emptied out to feed the ten million Bangladesh refugees who had by now gone home. At this very moment the weather gods turned cruel and the rains failed again. Indira's hitherto ascendant career had run into a bad patch. The Budget deficit shot up and foreign exchange reserves plummeted. Prices soared by 24 percent, the largest surge in one go since Independence. This inevitably led to economic discontent on a mass scale and political turbulence. Destructive polarisation that had become dormant during and after the Bangladesh War also resurfaced.

This was disastrous enough. What made it catastrophic was the first Oil Shock in the wake of the Arab-Israeli war later in the year 1968. Petroleum prices quadrupled over a very short time, shattering the Indian economy already under heavy strain. India needed a huge loan from the International Monetary Fund (IMF). The IMF's conditions went against the entire gamut of Indira Gandhi's policies in pursuance of 'Garibi Hatao'. Stoically, she accepted the conditions and enforced a wage freeze, compulsory deposits by all salaried employees and drastic cuts in government expenditure that meant more unemployment. She balanced this with a ceiling on dividends but this did not dent the outcry against her new economic policies. Slimmer dividends did not affect the lavish lifestyle of the rich, said the critics, but the poor were being crushed.

Both the drought and the Oil Shock were beyond her control. But surely she could have done something to control her wayward party men who were no different from, and perhaps more venal than, their opposite numbers in the despised Congress (O). One of these worthies was Chimanbhai Patel in Gujarat, popularly called 'Chiman Chor' (Chiman, the thief). Much to Indira's annoyance he had toppled the chief minister of Gujarat nominated by her and taken his place. He then permitted the 'oil kings' of his state to raise their prices in return for 'donations', ostensibly for the party. The dam of pent-up fury against corruption burst with such intensity that curfew had to be imposed in 106 cities and towns of the state. Before the dust could settle 103 persons had been killed, 300 injured and more than 8,000 arrested. The protesters called their movement 'Nav Nirman' or Resurgence. The Prime Minister bought peace with them by accepting their strange demand for the dissolution of the state assembly in which her party had a stable two-third majority.

Against this bleak backdrop, moved to centre-stage JP, the respected Gandhian leader who has already found mention in this narrative in the context of the Bangladesh crisis and war. His objective was to canalise stray and often directionless agitations against Indira into a powerful and united countrywide movement to oust her and her government. To an extent he succeeded in this effort though not fully. He even appealed to the Army and the police to disobey her. In the midst of it all, a railway strike began with the declared goal of 'starving the country'. Indira crushed it with an iron hand. As for the JP Movement, it is my view that she might have contained it, just as she had done it in the case of Nav Nirman, were it not for the June 12 judgment of the Allahabad high court judgment 'convicting her of corrupt election practices', setting aside her 1971 election to the Lok Sabha and disqualifying her from holding public office for six years. The Supreme Court's 'conditional', not unconditional stay left her with only two options: to step down at least temporarily or resort to extreme measures. Since all of her confidants, especially her increasingly powerful son Sanjay had ruled out her withdrawal from office 'even for a day', the hammer-blow of Emergency and Indira's monumental mistake became unavoidable.

Thus it was that at the midnight hour of June 25, when JP, Desai and others were woken up and marched to prison they did not know what had hit them. Sanjay and his cohorts had made elaborate preparations for the Emergency in total secrecy. Because of its critical importance, the Emergency is the understandably the subject of a separate chapter. So I will avoid gory details and concentrate only on broad and significant points.

There is no question that the Emergency was a sordid chapter in independent India's history and a 19-month nightmare for all those who lived through it. Nearly, 100,000 citizens were imprisoned without trial. Many times more than that number were harassed. It took an excruciatingly long time to flush out of the body politic the poison the Emergency had pumped into the system.

Yet ugly though the Emergency undoubtedly was, in all fairness, India under it was never anything like Germany under Hitler, the Soviet Union under Stalin, China under Mao or Pakistan under Zia. It was also noteworthy that Indira Gandhi's dynasty building and the Emergency went hand in hand. Sanjay's power was more than considerable even earlier. Behind the ramparts of the Emergency it became uncontestable. People saw him as an 'extra-Constitutional authority' and resented this. But the question is whether the dynastic pattern of politics, in not just the Congress but also almost all political parties, has ended or expanded during the 35 years since then.

Most importantly, Indira Gandhi decided to end the state of Emergency as abruptly and unexpectedly as she had hit the country with its proclamation, and having predictably lost the Elections she had called surrendered power without hesitation. No less significantly, in the 35-year perspective there has a major change in the country's perception. More and more people now accept that the Emergency was 'scripted jointly by her and JP'.

The Janata Party—a hurriedly merged combination of all the parties that were arrayed against her—came into power, with Desai as prime minister. Euphorically, it concluded the mood that Indira Gandhi had been 'consigned to the dustbin of history' for good. How wrong it was!

Once again let us not get bogged down in the shabby details of what happened during the Janata period, such as Indira Gandhi's victory in a by-election but prompt expulsion from Parliament and brief imprisonment thereafter. This was symptomatic of the Janata's manic persecution of her and Sanjay. The Shah Commission appointed against her turned into a cross between a US Congressional inquiry and a Chinese people's court. Even those who wanted her to be called to account were appalled. There was also the daily display of the epic clash of ambitions of the three top Janata leaders with a collective age of 235 years and egos of cosmic proportions. Suffice it to say that in 30 months flat, the Janata was history and Indira had returned to power spectacularly.

In this moment of triumph, she rejoiced doubly, for herself and for her son. The election had conferred some legitimacy on him and there was greater acceptance of him as the Crown Prince than earlier. Within the party his word was law. About 150 of the more than 350 Congress candidates that had won were his nominees. He also chose the chief ministers of the states that the Congress had won in a series of assembly elections.

Everything was going very well, but then the tremendous triumph was followed by heart-breaking tragedy. On June 23 in an air crash that could have been averted easily, had he paid attention to air safety regulations, Sanjay killed himself. Indira was shattered beyond words. She did regain enough composure to function as the head of the government but she never recovered from the traumatic shock fully.

If during her previous tenure she was confronted by the Bangladesh challenge, this time around she had to cope with the nettlesome problem of the Soviet invasion of Afghanistan against which the US and Pakistan, in close collaboration with China, had organised the 'Afghan jihad'. In fact, the Soviet tanks and troops had rolled into Kabul on December 26, 1980 when India was in the throes of elections. In early January, the UN was to discuss an American resolution on the Afghan War. Indira Gandhi had been elected by then but yet not sworn in. Even so, the Foreign Office sought her directive, not of Charan Singh, still the caretaker prime minister. Surrounded by surging crowds of admirers amidst deafening noise of celebrations, she delegated the task to two of her trusted foreign policy advisers, G. Parathasarthy and T.N. Kaul. What they conveyed to South Block was ambiguous and somewhat one-sided. At the UN it evoked sharp and wide criticism. Indira did the course correction, first in a joint statement with the visiting French President Giscard d' Estaing, stating that there should be no foreign troops anywhere and the Afghan problem should be solved 'politically, not militarily', and then after the veteran Soviet foreign minister, Andrei Gromyko, arrived to explain the Soviet stand and seek her support. She listened to him patiently, but told him: 'On this I cannot support you.' (I.K. Gujral, then ambassador to Moscow, who sat through the meeting to the author.)

Indira Gandhi had always been deft in handling international problems, but shortly after Sanjay's death, a series of grim internal difficulties started overtaking her foreign policy worries and eventually overwhelmed her. Religious, regional, linguistic, caste and other parochial conflicts were nothing new in India. Tribal insurgencies in the country's northeast were also endemic. But these started taking a new turn.

Assam the largest and most important northeastern state virtually exploded over the issue of 'foreigners' who were changing the state's demography. The students who led the anti-foreigners agitation wanted the aliens detected and deported at once. The unwanted foreigners were mostly illegal immigrants from what was East Pakistan first and then became Bangladesh. The new state refused to accept any responsibility for migrants before its birth in 1971. Moreover, though the movement was ostensibly directed only against Bangladeshis, the Indian Bengalis settled in Assam were also a target. Furthermore, the Assamese society itself was full of intricate divisions. It is a measure of the resultant insanity that in March 1983, during a highly successful Non-Aligned Summit in New Delhi, warring groups massacred 3,000 children in an Assamese village named Nellie.

Traditional atrocities on the Dalits had stopped during the Emergency. When these were resumed during the Janata rule, Indira had fought against them. On one famous occasion she went to the marooned venue of a particularly savage slaughter of the innocents on an elephant. Now these atrocities were becoming fairly frequent during her reign. Mass conversion of Dalits to Islam in a Tamil Nadu village worsened the situation. On the other hand, in Gujarat, the birth state of Mahatma Gandhi, virulent anti-Dalit riots started, on the curious pretext that they were getting away with too many places in institutions of higher learning. In Andhra, the long-standing demand for a separate state of Telangana touched off trouble.

Myriad and multiplying problems may be crowding in on her, but the issue uppermost in Indira's mind was how to fill the vacuum left behind by Sanjay. She did not take long to make up her mind that the void left by her younger son should be filled by his elder brother Rajiv. Basically apolitical he was reluctant to plunge into politics. He was happy to be a pilot of the Indian Airlines and to live quietly with his Italian-born wife Sonia and their two children. It is remarkable that neither anyone in her cabinet nor any of the leaders in the higher councils of her party tried to influence her judgment. Everyone knew that reluctant Rajiv would be persuaded to be on his mother's side sooner or later. A 'draft Rajiv' campaign had already begun.

The only opposition to this move came from Sanjay's young, highly ambitious and fiery widow, Maneka. She thought and said so aggressively that she, not her 'slothful' brother-in-law, was the rightful heir to her husband's legacy. Indira would not countenance this effrontery. While Rajiv was still making up his mind and Maneka was fuming and fretting, the Prime Minister acted fast to strip Sanjay's key associates of whatever, power, privilege and influence they were enjoying. Then the rather bizarre posthumous Sanjay cult was first halted and then reversed. Maneka retaliated by forming a Sanjay Vichar Manch (the Sanjay Thought Forum). Living in the Prime Minister's House with her infant son, Varun, she also staged the *saas-bahu* drama that is a staple of Indian cinema and television soap operas that mint millions by depicting the tyranny of the mother-in-law on the hapless wife of her son. Just when Indira was about to leave for London to inaugurate the Festival of India, Maneka announced that she would hold a rally of Sanjay's followers in Lucknow. Indira forbade her to do so. But the young woman went ahead with her resolve. On return home Indira told Maneka to leave her house; the latter went but only after prolonged bickering and in the midst of a blaze of publicity. Her subsequent efforts to confront Rajiv politically came to naught. Today Maneka and her son Varun are both MPs owing allegiance to the BJP, the party totally hostile to the Congress that is currently led by Sonia Gandhi, Indira's elder and favourite daughter-in-law and Rajiv's widow.

A large section of the Indian intelligentsia—that remained critical of Indira Gandhi from the late 1960s to long after her assassination, irrespective of the masses' virtual veneration of her—lamented that Rajiv's anointment was a proof that for Indira Gandhi dynasty was 'above all', and this would make India a 'dynastic dictatorship'. But the large majority of Indians, happy with the familial pattern in all walks of life, did not bother. They liked Rajiv because of his image as 'Mr. Clean', and since his advisers and associates had studied, along with him, in the elite Doon School, there was much talk of 'Rajiv's Doons *versus* Sanjay's goons'.

While her energies were focussed on settling the issue of 'After Sanjay, Who?' the unrest and resentment among the Sikhs of Punjab—a minority of no more than two percent of the population but enjoying a much larger share in the economy and professions and vastly disproportionate representation in the Army—started becoming sinister and was eventually to become searing. To try to explain the bewilderingly complex and highly emotional roots of the Sikh discontent in a short essay would be futile. A brief outline of the problem as it was in 1980-81 when Indira Gandhi returned to power should suffice.

Even after the formation of the Punjabi-speaking political party in 1966 when Indira had just become Prime Minister, the Akali Dal that claimed to represent the entire Sikh community was still frustrated because it could not come to power despite the achievement of Punjabi Suba it had dreamed of for so long. The reason was simple. All Sikhs did not vote for the Akali Party although it permanently controlled all the Sikh shrines with their huge landed properties and enormous income. A minority of Sikh votes plus the bulk of Hindu votes enabled the Congress to be in power in Punjab. In 1977, when the tidal wave of anti-Emergency sentiment made clean sweep of the Congress, the Akalis, for the first time, rose to power in Punjab entirely by themselves though they shrewdly shared power with the Janata both in the state and the Centre.

Immediately after the 1977 parliamentary poll, the Janata government arbitrarily dismissed Congress governments in nine states while their term was not yet over. In all nine, the Janata or its allies won. The Akalis, already well entrenched in Chandigarh were not interested in this manoeuvre. However, when the Janata government fell and fresh Parliamentary elections were held, the Akali Party found to its horror that it had lost the bulk of the parliamentary seats. Yet it remained confident that it would rule Punjab for two more years and then win the fresh elections to the state assembly. It did not foresee that Indira would repay the Janata in the same coin. She dissolved state governments in the same nine states, and won back all of them, including Punjab. Political parties in other eight states took their defeat in their stride. But the Akalis were incensed and alleged that the whole exercise was a 'conspiracy' to eliminate the only Sikh government in the country. This was the start of a no-holds-barred, all-out Akali campaign to get even with Indira and her party in which many Sikhs outside the Akali ranks also joined. The subsequent developments turned into a calamity of gigantic proportions for the country that also took Indira's life.

The main motive force behind it was, of course, the Akali-led Sikhs backed by the Sikh Diaspora but Indira's Party's contribution to the colossal tragedy cannot be overlooked. Her main fault was not to send the Army into the Golden Temple, the holiest of the Sikh shrines, when she did it in June 1984 because at that time the sacred shrine had been converted into a heavily fortified, extremely well-armed citadel of secession and terror. Her egregious error was to allow the situation to degenerate to this unspeakably dangerous level.

Giani Zail Singh who was Congress chief minister of Punjab in the 1970s—and first became home minister in Indira's 1980 cabinet and later still President of the republic—had unwisely but ostentatiously tried to steal the Akalis' clothes by pandering heavily to the religious sentiments of the Sikhs. He did not realise that in this game he could not beat the extremists. The Akalis retaliated by passing an ambiguous resolution at Sri Anandpur Sahib making many demands on behalf of the Sikhs, principally the one for the 'utmost autonomy' to them, limiting the 'interference into their affairs by the Delhi *durbar* to the barest minimum'. While in power in Punjab (1977-1980), the Akalis had said nothing about this resolution but after losing power they revived it with vengeance.

Meanwhile, during their years in the wilderness, Zail Singh, in complete collaboration with Sanjay, picked up a relatively obscure, young and fundamentalist lay preacher named Jarnail Singh Bhindranwale with a view to building him up as a rival to the Akali leadership. It is inconceivable that they could have done so without Indira Gandhi's consent. Sanjay and Zail Singh believed that by advocating extremist causes the young preacher would embarrass the Akali Dal. Precisely, the reverse happened. Bhindranwale soon turned into a classic Frankenstein's Monster and embarked upon devouring his creators. The Akali Dal then started a *dharma yudh* (holy war) against the Indira government over the Anandpur Sahib resolution and sundry Sikh demands including one for a separate Sikh personal law. Bhindranwale took it over and stretched the resolution into demanding an independent and sovereign state of Khalistan. His young followers started a reign of murder and terror. This was a godsend to Pakistan that immediately extended all help to the 'Sikh insurgency'. The Akali leaders surrendered to Bhindranwale who had become something of a messianic figure. There is no point reciting all the painful succession of events that led to Operation Blue Star in which Bhindranwale and all his associates were killed, with very heavy damage to the shrine. The Sikhs across the world were enraged.

No wonder that Indira Gandhi knew that when she had sanctioned military action at the Golden Temple, she had also signed her own death warrant. Those fateful shots by her Sikh security guards were less than four months away. However, of the far too many important episodes in the last year and a half of her life, at least four need to be discussed. Two of these preceded Blue Star and two came later.

In February 1983, Indira got a rude political jolt when her party was defeated in the state assembly elections in Andhra Pradesh and Karnataka, the two states that were her bastions and had remained loyal to her even after the Emergency. The defeat in Karnataka was a reflection of nothing more than declining support to her. But the far more shattering defeat in Andhra was for a totally different reason that had a bearing on her style of nominating any non-entity as chief minister of a Congress-ruled state and changing him or her at will. In Andhra at one time she chose as chief minister T. Anjaiah, a well-meaning but totally ineffectual man. While welcoming Rajiv Gandhi at Hyderabad airport one day the bumbling Anjaiah made a *faux pas* that so infuriated the usually well-mannered young man that he gave the chief minister a tongue-lashing on the tarmac.

Opponents of the Congress in the state seized this opportunity to denounce the episode as 'insult to the whole of Andhra'. N.T. Rama Rao, an icon of the Andhra film industry, vowed to avenge this affront. He founded a party called Telugu Desam that trounced the Congress at the 1983 polls.

Later that year, in Sri Lanka, an island republic separated from the Indian peninsula by a 21-mile stretch of seawater, there were stirrings of a revolt by the Tamil minority against the Sinhala majority dominating the government. This was to develop later into an ethnic war that continued for nearly a quarter of a century. At that point of time, however, vicious anti-India riots broke out in Colombo. Indian business establishments, including banks, as well as many Indian nationals were attacked brutally. Without a word to Colombo, she told her foreign minister, P.V. Narasimha Rao, to fly to Sri Lanka and read out the Riot Act to its president, J.R. Jayawardene. When told that this was a violation of Sri Lanka's sovereignty, she replied: 'In relation to Sri Lanka, India cannot be treated as any other third country.'

The two things that Indira did or permitted her henchmen to do in the wake of the cataclysmic events in Punjab were worse. The first had to do with Jammu and Kashmir, a state even more sensitive than Punjab. On June 30, she spoke to half a dozen of us who were either editors or senior commentators on a background basis. We had thought that she would discuss Punjab. But it was Kashmir that was on her mind. She told us bluntly that the Kashmir chief minister, Farooq Abdullah, had to go or be sacked. This was not exactly a surprise because in informed circles it was well known that she wanted Farooq out. Some of us argued with her that whatever her reasons to take the proposed precipitate action would create an upheaval in Kashmir at a time when Punjab was still aflame. However, her mind was made up.

There is some irony in the complex backdrop to this. Very briefly, Farooq's father Sheikh Mohammed Abdullah was Kashmir's towering leader and first chief minister. Indeed, it was under his leadership that the state acceded to the Indian Union in 1947. But during the next six years his politics changed so drastically that Nehru was constrained to dismiss and detain him in 1953. Of the next 22 years, the Sheikh spent 14 in jail. But, wisely assessing that without the Lion of Kashmir, as Abdullah senior was called, Kashmir could not be stabilised. She patiently negotiated an agreement with him under which he returned to power in Jammu and Kashmir with the Congress Party's support. In September 1982 the Sheikh died. By then he had made it clear that he wanted his son Farooq to succeed him. Indira smoothened the succession. Yet relations between Farooq and her deteriorated fast. During the 1983 elections, some of his acolytes treated her with not just churlishness but indecently.

B.K. Nehru, an uncle of Indira and an outstanding civil servant and diplomat, was then Governor of Kashmir. He refused to sack Farooq by executive order and insisted that Farooq's majority must be tested in the legislature. Her response was to transfer him to Gujarat. His successor, Jagmohan, sent Farooq packing. Consequences were grave and lasted for many years after her death.

This should normally have been a deterrent to any further rash action. But so chaotic the system became which she was supposed to be controlling strictly, that on August 16, the governor of Andhra, a particularly inept Congressman from Himachal Pradesh named Ram Lal, dismissed the redoubtable N.T. Rama Rao and appointed one of his renegade colleagues as chief minister. Indira swore that she had no advance information of this and most people believed her. The governor claimed that someone in her 'inner circle' had directed him to act against NTR. The country's reaction was one of anger. Many said that Indira was back to her authoritarian ways. Unable to erode NTR's solid majority for a whole month, the Prime Minister and the Congress Party had to eat the humble pie and restore him to his office. The tragic date of October 31 was just six weeks away.

This is only a brief sketch of the many-splendoured life of an outstanding leader that was also full of high drama and searing tragedy as well as of her times that she both shaped and was herself shaped by. So a short summing up of her voyage is called for in both personal and political terms.

Indira Gandhi was complex, controversial and, above all, compelling. She could also be contradictory. For instance, charm and graciousness came naturally to her. But these could instantly change to irritation and disdain. She could be generously forgiving as well as vindictive. A year after her death, James Callaghan, the British Prime Minister then, wrote that while she had a 'taste for the sharp retort', Indira Gandhi could also be the 'mistress of eloquent silence'. He could have added that she had the additional gift of the 'glacial glance'. I once watched her look through a former aide who was in high enough favour earlier but had since fallen from grace. Her wit and humour could be devastating. To give only one example, Pakistan's military ruler, Zia-ul-Haq, met her for the first time in April 1980 during Zimbabwe's independence celebrations. Unfortunately, for him morning newspapers had repeated some of his uncomplimentary remarks about her. The first thing he said on arrival was: '"Madam, please, do not believe everything you read in newspapers". "Of course, not", she replied, "Aren't they calling you a democrat and me a dictator?"'

Cooks, warriors and rulers, as someone said ages ago, must be judged not by what they say but what they actually do and achieve. By this yardstick Indira Gandhi's record is exceptionally creditable. The performance of none of the dozen prime ministers since her time comes even remotely close to it. About her contemporaries, friends or foes, the less said the better.

In her time, despite her grievous mistakes for which she paid grievously, India became the third largest reservoir of highly skilled scientific and technical manpower in the world, the fifth military power, the sixth member of the most exclusive Nuclear Club, the seventh in the race for space and the tenth industrial power, which clearly became the foundation for today's 'Rising India'.

Transcending all this, however, were her two enviable attributes unlikely to be equalled for as long as we can foresee. The first was her empathy with the people, especially the poor and dispossessed that had to be seen to be believed. At work, it was not just her charisma and magnetism but something much more. To be sure she could do little to make good of her promise to banish poverty, but through some alchemy the poor believed her and they believe today that she 'cared'. Worthy of even greater honour and respect was her second attribute: deep and unswerving devotion to India and cause of its sovereignty, independence, unity and autonomy in every sphere of life. It is no exaggeration to say that she would have readily killed or swallowed poison herself rather than compromise with India's honour.

Almost immediately after her assassination by her Sikh security guards disgraceful anti-Sikh riots had begun. But she could in no way be held responsible for them. On the contrary, one of her last acts was to reject a suggestion by her advisers to exclude all Sikhs from the Prime Minister's security cordon simply by asking: 'Aren't we secular?' In the parliamentary elections in December 1984, Rajiv Gandhi won a majority so huge as to be mind-boggling. It was really a grieving nation's tribute to the slain leader.

'Strong' and 'decisive' are the two words the younger generation of India uses the most in relation with Indira Gandhi. And because its search for such a leader today in vain, it yearns for her all the more.

Chapter III

The Congress Party and Six National Elections: 1964-1984

Sudha Pai

The Indian National Congress—India's Grand old Party—has been in existence since 1885. Unlike parties in western democracies that historically emerged out of a struggle for representation; the Indian National Congress as in many countries of the developing world, is the product of an anti-colonial movement. Led by tall nationalist leaders, it has functioned both as an anti-colonial movement and a single dominant party after independence. An examination of the post-independence journey of the Congress Party reveals that there has not been a single, but many Congress parties: the Nehru Congress, the Indira Gandhi Congress, the Rajiv Gandhi Congress, and more recently the Sonia Gandhi Congress. In each of these periods the party has exhibited specific characteristics: outlook, leadership, style of functioning and impact on democratic politics, which can be examined apart. In this context the period from 1964 to 1984 can be described as the Indira Gandhi period and due to her towering personality has in fact been described as 'Indira Gandhi's India.'(Kochanek, 1976).

This chapter examines the performance of the Congress Party in the six national elections held between 1964 and 1984. It employs the lens of electoral politics to understand the interrelationship between the significant political events of the period, changes within the party and the manner in which the Congress leadership dealt with these developments and their impact on the electoral performance of the party. It argues that the assumption of the leadership of the Congress Party by Mrs. Indira Gandhi in 1965 marked the beginning of a new epoch during a formative period in the development of the party and the process of nation building. It was a volatile period when the single dominant party model of the Nehru era was challenged and redefined over the next two decades. Developments within the polity and society contributed to the questioning of Congress dominance and the beginnings of a gradual move towards a more broad-based multiparty system particularly in the states. This period witnessed the rise of new opposition parties such as the Jana Sangh and Swantantra Party which brought together the Socialist, Communist and other parties on the platform of anti-Congressism. The Green Revolution led to the emergence of a rich peasant class while increasing democratisation led to backward caste and lower caste mobilisation, both of which led to the rise of new parties such as the Bharatiya Kranti Dal (BKD) and later the JD/SP and the BSP which challenged the dominance of the Congress in the Hindi heartland. Regional forces in the southern states also began to assert themselves.

Indira Gandhi's impact on the Congress Party and the country was definitive and long lasting. Under her leadership the party could successfully deal with poor electoral performance in 1967; manage a major split in 1969; introduce a radical economic programme to meet the challenge of the party bosses and rising anti-Congressism; resist external pressures for change in economic policy; restore its position as a dominant party in 1980 after the short-lived Emergency; and cope with her assassination in 1984. Despite these problems, the party was able to obtain 40 percent of the votes in all the elections in this period with the exception of the 1977 elections when it could obtain only 34.52 percent of the votes cast.

However, there were many developments that have affected the long-term growth and the electoral fortunes of the party. Following the vacuum created by the sudden demise of Lal Bahadur Shastri, Mrs. Gandhi was selected as the Prime Minister by the Syndicate who felt they could control 'her' and through her the 'party'. After a period of considerable struggle she was able to meet the challenge posed by the party bosses and emerge as the undisputed, sole leader of the party by the early 1970s. This was mainly because of her new radical socialist agenda which won her the support of progressive elements in the party and an electorate increasingly disillusioned with the Congress in the late Nehru era. But rather than adopting a consensual style of leadership needed in a federal and loosely organised mass party, with many factions and state leaders, which would have enabled her to implement her agenda, Mrs. Gandhi adopted personality based politics and through a systematic process of centralisation and personalisation of power. She dismantled the party, removed the intermediate leadership and the process of consultative decision-making and re-built it without a democratic structure and with office-bearers personally responsible to her—a process that extended to personnel within the government as well.

Mrs. Gandhi had inherited a fairly well-organised party machine with several capable leaders in the states across the country. But her bypassing of the party machinery inaugurated the decline of single party dominance, and a process of long-term decay of the party organisation, particularly in north India. As a consequence, despite her strong leadership and efforts to re-orient the party, Mrs. Gandhi could not introduce faster economic growth or fulfill many of the promises contained in her radical agenda of the early 1970s. The Congress Party faced failures in the planning process, food shortages and droughts, low growth rate of the economy, high poverty levels, autonomy movements in the northeast, and later demand for separation of Telengana, etc. Equally important, the entry into politics of Sanjay and Rajiv Gandhi created the space for the allegation that the Congress was becoming a 'family' controlled party and that it was establishing the 'dynastic' principle.

These developments cumulatively impacted on the social and regional base of the party and its electoral fortunes. In the six national elections held during this period the party's position constantly fluctuated: from 361 seats in the 1962 elections to a sharp drop to 283 in 1967; a recovery in 1971 with 352 seats; a defeat due to the emergency leading to only 154 seats in 1977; and recovery with 353 and 404 seats in 1980 and 1984 respectively. While the impact of these developments was not immediately felt, they contributed to the virtual collapse of the party in the 1990s.

The period from 1964 to 1984 is divided into four phases in order to examine the relationship between developments within the party under the leadership of Indira Gandhi, changes in the larger polity and electoral politics: 1964 to 1971; 1971 to 1977; 1977 to 1980; and 1980 to 1984. The concluding Section reflects on the relationship between electoral politics, the trajectory of the Congress Party during this period and its implications for Indian democracy.

I

1964–1971: Challenge of Generational Change and Anti-Congressism

In the period 1964 to 1971 the Congress Party moved from a position of strength as reflected in the results of the 1962 national elections when it obtained 361 seats and 44.7 percent votes, to a position of weakness in 1967 when its seat and vote percentage dropped to 283 and 40.7 percent. However, in 1971 the party was able to meet a number of challenges and recover obtaining 352 seats and 43.8 percent though it did not return to the 1962 position. During this period the Congress Party faced two internal and one external crisis, which cumulatively impacted on its electoral performance in the elections of 1967 and 1971. The former were the succession crises following the death of Nehru and Shastri and the Congress Split in 1969 both of which were managed efficiently by the party leadership; and the latter the anti-Congressism of the opposition parties prior to the 1967 elections hoping to defeat a party which was no longer led by tall leaders such as Nehru.

Even before the death of Nehru in May 1964 a number of developments had led to rising discontent in the country with the Congress Party, which eventually translated into the poor performance of the party in the 1967 national elections. An immediate event was the Chinese invasion of October 1962 which led to outrage and unhappiness with the ruling party including Nehru, leading to the exit of his trusted advisors—Krishna Menon and K.D. Malaviya—from the cabinet (Kochanek, 1966: 288). Rising prices, increased taxes, drastic financial measures calling for gold control and compulsory deposits and continuation of the emergency declaration all aroused opposition. The unexpected defeat of the Congress candidates in three important by-elections in May 1963 created unhappiness within the party and senior leaders felt it was necessary to devote time to rebuild the organisation from the lowest levels upwards. Soon afterwards the opposition parties introduced, for the first time during the Nehru government, a no-confidence motion in parliament, which though easily defeated, caused much consternation. These feelings crystallised into the 'Kamaraj Plan' adopted by the Working Committee on August 10 under which a number of leading Congressmen were to voluntarily relinquish their ministerial posts and work full-time to rebuild the party organisation.[1] Nehru's introduction of a list of 12 names in the Committee meeting, which included leaders such as Jagjivan Ram, Morarji Desai and Shastri, who were to resign and work for the party, led to the feeling that he was removing potential successors thereby using the Plan for his own ends.

Consequently, the Kamaraj Plan gave birth to the Syndicate, a faction[2] whose aim was to retain control of the Congress presidency and ensure that their supporters were in the AICC, which enabled them to play an important role when Nehru fell ill in January 1964 leading to his death in May. The Syndicate particularly Kamaraj, ensured that Lal Bahadur Shastri—a leader acceptable to all sections—was made Minister without Portfolio which kept out Morarji Desai and ensured the former's elevation to Prime Minister later. Although both the right and left wing of the party tried to keep out Shastri and some tried to bring in Mrs. Indira Gandhi, Kamaraj's skill as a leader, extensive consultations with all groups and an appeal to the need for unity ensured within 48 hours, the 'unanimous' selection of Shastri as the successor to Nehru (Kochanek, 1966: 294).

The sudden death of Lal Bahadur Shastri on January 11, 1966 created a vacuum and crisis of much greater magnitude as it caught the party leadership unprepared. There was neither a candidate who commanded the widespread support Shastri did, nor were the pressures for unanimity as strong and despite best efforts, an open contest could not be avoided between Morarji Desai and Mrs. Gandhi. The Congress parliamentary party by an overwhelming majority of 355 to 169 out of 526, elected Mrs. Gandhi as the Prime Minister. Two factors were responsible for her selection: her relative inexperience and perception that she would be least threatening to the party bosses; and the support of the left wing of the party. However, the decision was viewed as transitional; the 'final' decision would be taken after the Fourth General Elections due in 1967 which was expected to introduce a generational shift in the party (Kothari, 1967).

The 1967 Elections: Loss of Monopoly

On assuming office, Mrs. Gandhi faced the urgent task of evolving a new, broad-based, all-India leadership that could assume the task of managing the national elections in 1967, the first without Nehru, heading of the party. The approaching elections forced a process of 'mutual understanding' and the open rift between the government and the party wings was forgotten. The party settled down to election of a Central Election Committee (CEC), Pradesh Election Committees (PECs) and selection of candidates, a process that required accommodating personal/group differences for mobilising the party organisation for a common purpose (Kothari, 1967: 89). In this process the Prime Minister appeared to be no longer dependent on Kamaraj and seemed to be on an equal footing until at least the elections were over. But intense factionalism around selection of candidates due to rising aspirations led to deadlocks and unaccommodated dissidents leaving; rival lists presented to the Chief Election Commission; a Disciplinary Action Committee to settle personal and group rivalries though this had little effect in the states. In some states rival Congress parties were set up by dissident Congressmen, good examples being in Orissa under Hare Krishna Mahtab and in West Bengal under Ajoy Mukherjee (Kothari, 1967: 91).

Discontent among the people which had begun during the Nehruvian period with the failure of the Congress to fulfill promises such as land reform and faster economic growth, now erupted against the new government. A wave of agitations and violence commenced a few days after Mrs. Gandhi was sworn in as Prime Minister on January

24, 1965 and continued until the elections. They took many forms: food riots, student riots and *bandhs* that upset the governmental machinery in many states. The severe drought especially in Bihar and East UP and the war with Pakistan had shattered the process of economic planning. There was considerable indiscipline in parliament from the opposition parties and Congress members who called for a debate on economic policy and indulged in 'government-baiting'. The new Prime Minister faced trouble from the Naga tribes, the Mizo National Front, demands for Punjabi Suba and tough decisions on agricultural policy of economic aid (Kothari, 1967: 86). The decision to devalue the Rupee in June 1966 following a severe foreign exchange crisis and the new fertiliser policy with US aid aroused much resentment not only from the opposition parties particularly the Left, but from within the Congress including the Congress President Kamaraj who felt that the party was being kept in the dark and not consulted or even informed.

Opposition parties long frustrated at their powerlessness, decided to take advantage of the new situation. They joined hands on the platform of anti-Congressism as they realised that given the weaknesses within the Congress Party they had a chance to defeat it at the polls. They were also keen to harness the rising disillusionment among the electorate with Congress rule. The Socialists, Communists and a section of the Jana Sangh launched joint rallies against government policies; leading to electoral adjustments between opposition parties in the states: in Kerala all left parties except the Praja Socialist Party (PSP) formed an alliance; in Rajasthan a Swatantra-Jana Sangh alliance emerged while in Madras the DMK, Swatantara, Muslim League and the Communists joined hands.

However, the situation was handled fairly well by the Prime Minister. She took a number of policy decisions with great firmness: to form the Punjabi Suba, negotiated with the Nagas and put down the Mizo rebellion. She also made attempts to improve her relationship with the Congress President and other senior leaders to which they reciprocated; replaced older ministers bringing in new leaders such as Y.B. Chavan who as Home Minister was able to efficiently handle a number of difficult situations: the law and order situation; the anti-cow slaughter agitation; and procurement and distribution of food grains in drought hit areas. Although Mrs. Gandhi decided to devalue the rupee in the face of much opposition at home, once the crisis passed, she took the bold step of not continuing with liberalisation of the economy despite considerable external pressures from the IMF and the US (Kothari, 1967). Mukherji points to the 'executive orientation' or leadership qualities, which enabled Mrs. Gandhi to take this bold decision regardless of advice from internal and external advisors (Mukherji, 2000: 379).

Despite these efforts as Table 1 shows, the Congress Party performed badly. The 1967 national elections[3] was the first one faced by the Congress without Nehru at the helm. Mrs. Gandhi's link with Nehru proved too weak to reverse the downward trend in popular support for the Congress Party. At the national level and as Table 1 shows, the party obtained only 283 seats and 40.78 percent of the votes cast. As Appendix Table A-1 in the Appendix shows, the rest of the seats and votes were divided among an array of opposition parties: Jana Sangh 25, CPI 23, Swantantra 44, the two socialist parties (PSP+SSP) 36 and independents 35 seats; no party obtained more than 10 percent of the seats, the exception being independents who together obtained 13.78 percent. Analysis of the results for the Lok Sabha seats alone shows that, except in Rajasthan and Kerala, the Congress vote was reduced in many other states: in Maharashtra, by 6.69 percent, in West Bengal by 8.6 percent, in Gujarat by 3.18 percent, in Punjab by 4.18 percent, in Mysore by 2.47 percent and in Orissa by 34.12 percent (Gupta, 1967: 1229-30). Only in Andhra, Assam, Gujarat, Kashmir, MP, Maharashtra and Mysore was the Congress able to form a majority government. Due to opposition alliances, a small decline in vote for the Congress in certain areas resulted in massive defeats. The index of Opposition unity rose in many states particularly if one considers opposition coalitions as a single party for the purposes of analysis: in Madras the Congress vote declined from 46.1 percent to 41.8 percent which placed it ahead of the 40.8 percent won by the DMK, but the latter won 138 seats and the Congress only 49.

Table 1

Performance of the Congress Party in Six Lok Sabha Elections: 1962-1984

Elections	*Seats Won*	*Vote Percentage*
1967	283	40.78
1971	352	40.78
1977	154	34.52
1980*	353	42.69
1984	404	49.10

Source: Election Commission of India *(www.eci.nic.in).*

The immediate reasons as outlined earlier were serious food shortages, growing unemployment in the industrial sector, steep rise in prices and the slowdown of the government's developmental programmes, which created disillusionment and unhappiness among the electorate in the post-Nehruvian phase. However, certain longer term changes within the polity help explain the poor performance of the Congress particularly its defeat in the states, where it created space for an incipient multiparty system. Many of the states where the Congress lost its monopoly were in north India where the party had its traditional stronghold. The decline in these states was not sudden: from 1952 to 1957, the Congress share of votes had declined from 41.47 percent to 33.1 percent in Bihar, from 47.9 percent to 32.2 percent in UP and from 47.5 percent to 36.6 percent in the Punjab (Brass, 1968b: 1174).

The Congress here was a party supported by the top and the bottom of the caste/class hierarchy, i.e., largely the Brahmins and the scheduled castes. This near monopoly was challenged by backward caste mobilisation in the states of the Hindi heartland in the 1960s particularly Uttar Pradesh where Charan Singh left with his followers to form the Bharatiya Kranti Dal (BKD). This category was able to make use of the Green Revolution and prosper; mobilisation of a rich peasant class was strengthened by their simultaneous mobilisation as a status order (Pai, 1993: 51). The 1969 mid-term assembly elections in UP show that the BKD won in the better-off districts where bigger farmers were able to make use of the new technology while the Congress was pushed into the poorer districts in the east with poor, small landholders. The BKD also gave a blow to the Jana Sangh in 1969 which was developing as the second largest party in the state, signalling that new forms of horizontal alignments based on agrarian issues were replacing customary unequal ties between landlords and landless labour (Ibid). In the south, the victory of the DMK points to the challenge posed by emerging regional movements/parties. The overall decline in the Congress vote from eight to three percent in almost all the states suggests that important changes were taking place, which were reflected in the elections.

Changes in the internal working of the Congress Party also had implications for its structure of dominance and electoral fortunes. Rajni Kothari writing prior to the elections pointed to seminal changes within the Congress Party that help explained its poor performance in 1967. Nehru, he argued, had contributed immensely to the consolidation of single party dominance, but his towering personality had created 'vast crystallisation of internal competition within the Congress Party and the consequent strain on its internal thermostat' (Kothari, 1967: 95). It was only towards the end of his life that independent forces could emerge in the party. Consequently, the Congress system by 1967 exhibited major inadequacies that pointed to lack of sufficient institutionalisation: a neglect of the communications and consultation continuum with regard to the outside world;

organisational weaknesses visible in the struggle for leadership in the mid-1960s, the rivalries in the selection of candidates during 1966-67 and the enormous shifting of political loyalties at the state level. The situation was more institutional than in 1962: 'organised' sabotage had created rival Congress parties that it seemed would not rejoin the party after the election and the leadership situation was in 'great turmoil'. In the post-Nehru period, the leadership had to deal with three institutional forums that began to play a critical role: the national parliament, the small but effective opposition parties at regional and national levels, and above all, the growing body of opposition within the ruling party. The 'Congress system' Kothari warned, needed to take correctives towards its own institutionalisation without which it would find it difficult to win elections, most immediately the approaching 1967 elections (Ibid).

As the elections had introduced considerable change in India's Party system, there was a need felt to develop new theoretical frameworks. So far the model widely used by commentators was that of one-party dominance, but in actual reality, it consisted of a national party joined to a number of state multiparty systems, in each of which the Congress structure of dominance was different. After 1967 certain features of this structure began to work against the Congress: factions unlike in the past were willing to consider defections even if it meant defeating the parent party; opposition parties were no longer acting as a 'margin of pressure' but were willing to join hands with Congress factions; and independents/defectors had emerged who were prepared to move from party to party in search of power and position. In fact, Brass argued, 'the decline of the Congress is only partly reversible and the return of Congress dominance throughout the Indian Union is the remotest of the possibilities to be considered for the future development of politics in India' (Brass, 1968b: 1175).

II

1971-1977: The New 'Indira' Congress, Emergency and Defeat

A development within the Congress which held important portents for the 1971 elections was the split in the party in December 1969 following four months of intense inner-party conflict. The reason lay in the conflicts within the party since the mid-1960s, which the poor performance in the 1967 elections worsened. The Syndicate representing the party bosses hoped to control Mrs. Gandhi and thereby both the party and the government; the widespread defeat inflicted on the party in the 1967 elections had led to loss of power in a number of the states which they controlled. Humiliating defeats were suffered by S.K. Patil, Atulya Ghosh and even Kamaraj that weakened the organisation wing of the party (Hardgrave, 1970: 256). Consequently this time Mrs. Gandhi was unanimously elected as the leader of the Congress parliamentary party on March 12, 1967. But for the Syndicate members the issue of leadership of the parliamentary party had not been fully resolved and after the elections Morarji Desai once more made clear his desire to become the Prime Minister (Guha, 2007: 435). Under a compromise he was made both the finance minister and deputy Prime Minister—a post no one had held since the death of Vallabhbhai Patel.

The immediate occasion for the split was the election of the President of India in 1969 for which both sides had different candidates and for whom they sought support within the party. However, the real reason was an intense power struggle between the two antagonistic groups for control over the party, the outcome of which would determine its future trajectory. Keen to re-establish the dominance of the Prime Minister over the party and secure her choice of candidates in the approaching 1972 national elections, Mrs. Gandhi at the AICC meeting at Bangalore on July 12, 1969 proposed a left-oriented agenda:[4] nationalisation of 14 major commercial banks, effective implementation of land reforms, ceilings on urban income and property and curbs on industrial monopolies, among others. By doing so she tried to portray the Syndicate as conservative and the approaching election as 'the beginning of a bitter struggle between the common people and the vested interests in the country' (Frankel, 1978: 419). She also removed ministers—including Morarji Desai, the deputy Prime Minister—who according to her did not subscribe to her Socialist agenda. In the presidential elections on August 20, she allowed a 'free vote' of conscience to the Congress parliamentary party, which led to the victory of her candidate. Accordingly, the Congress Working Committee (CWC) full of Syndicate members on November 12, 1969 led by S. Nijalingappa expelled Mrs. Gandhi for indiscipline from the Congress Party and instructed the parliamentary party to elect a new leader. But by this time due to her socialist agenda she had the support of the 'Young Turks' who had formed Socialists groups within the party.[5] Mrs. Gandhi in a landmark decision announced the de-linking of national and state elections, which has impacted on all subsequent elections. The split created two Congress parties that fought for recognition: one led by the Syndicate bosses in the organisation or Congress (O) and the other by Mrs. Gandhi the Congress (I) or the new Indira Congress, representing mainly the parliamentary wing. It is against this background that the performance of these two disputatious parts of the Congress Party in the 1971 elections must be analysed.

The 1971 Elections

The 1971 elections were advanced by 14 months because Mrs. Gandhi held that she wanted a popular mandate to implement her progressive agenda held up by reactionary forces in parliament. As Table 1 shows, in the 1971 Lok Sabha elections the Congress (I) won 352 seats gaining an absolute majority; while the Congress (O) won barely 16 seats. This made the Congress (I) the recognised party and Mrs. Gandhi its undisputed leader throwing out the Syndicate. As Appendix Table A-1 in the Appendix shows the four major opposition parties who formed an alliance obtained a total of just 49 seats: the Congress (O) got 16, Swatantra 8, Jana Sangh 22 and SSP 3. No party could gain more than 10 percent of the votes apart from the Congress (O) which obtained 10.43 percent. In many states in the assembly elections held a little later, the Congress returned to power ending the period of coalition governments, but the verdict did not 'indicate a trend towards return to the one-party dominant system' (Narain, 1971: 2023).

The reasons for the victory of the Congress (I) lay in the promise in the party manifesto of a 'genuine radical programme of economic and social development' upholding the interests of the small farmer and landless labourer, and small entrepreneur against the big capitalist. It offered a 'strong and stable government' and asked for support against the 'dark and evil forces of Right reaction' intent on destroying democratic and socialist objectives (Ibid). The slogan 'Garibi Hatao' (remove poverty) caught the imagination of an electorate unhappy with slow economic growth, shortages and unstable coalition governments in the states which had created dependence on regional parties leading to a 'virtual coalition' at the Centre. The electorate preferred the programmatic policies of the Congress which avoided both the extreme left and right represented by the Communists and the Swatantra. The verdict was suggestive of a differentiated, secular and national, rather than de-regionalised politics.

Narain argued that the breakdown of one-party dominance in 1967 and the victory of the Congress in 1971 represented two ends of a continuum. In 1967, the voter registered a negative vote in protest against the immobilism of the political elite and their failure to achieve social justice; while in 1971 the voter gave a positive vote for the promise of an egalitarian social order and commitment to its realisation. Following a period of instability and economic uncertainty, the elections provided a 'democratic interlude for nation building' and were a vote for the new Congress (Ibid: 2024). At the same time the election was characterised as a Prime Ministerial election, as Mrs. Gandhi played a critical role in the victory of her party and was described as a charismatic leader elected directly by the people. Narain held that it was not 'hereditary charisma'. Rather it was a 'cultivated and a functional charisma which is built around and projects her image to the people as an agent of change-oriented and action-based politics...' (Ibid: 2025).

Analysis of both the national and state assembly elections made it difficult to predict whether there would be a return to a one-party system. The voters displayed a 'split psyche' in the case of some states where elections were held simultaneously with the national elections by voting for state level parties in the case of the former and national parties in the case of the latter. However, most scholars agreed that India continued to move towards a more competitive democratic polity with prospects of alternation of power between different parties at the state level. The elections also pointed to a more viable party system through a process of merger and fusion of parties. Parties such as the Congress (O), Swatantra, SSP, PSP it was felt had little future and the party system could move towards three or four major national parties leading to relatively stable and like minded coalitions in some states, a two-party situation in others and majority rule in some others (Ibid: 2027).

The Emergency and Erosion of Support

The elections of 1971-72 marked the return of Congress dominance and political stability at the Central and state level. But the new Congress under Mrs. Gandhi could not fulfill the radical promises it had made to the people, evident from the imposition of Emergency just four years later. By the mid-1970s there were intractable problems faced by Mrs. Gandhi's government: slow economic growth of 3-4 percent, high poverty levels of 40-50 percent in both rural and urban areas, the Bangladesh crisis, famine, the oil crisis of 1973 and significant regional variations due to slow spread of the Green Revolution. Also she had little help from the Congress Party which by 1975 had few strong state level leaders due to the absence of democratic functioning within the party: elections were not held and chief ministers were constantly changed in the name of 'revitalisation' weakening the party (Frankel, 1978: 474). Following the 1972 assembly elections, conditions were favourable for the realisation of Mrs. Gandhi's vision of social transformation through democratic and constitutional methods. Rising political consciousness was visible among large numbers of the urban and rural poor ready to participate in Mrs. Gandhi's programme. However, this required two steps: involvement of the new Congress leaders in the states; and considerable organisational efforts to involve the poorer castes and classes in the implementation of social and economic reform. But this did not happen, on the contrary the party from the early 1970s was immobilised by both factional divisions and increasing personalised control from above.

From the early 1970s these developments contributed to the formation of oppositional organisations/movements such as the Nava Nirman Yuvak Samiti in Gujarat and Chhatra Sangharsh Samiti in Bihar, student bodies that spread rapidly to other states, which voiced the unhappiness of the youth against the failures of the government. A succession of strikes, demonstrations, looting, rioting and arson of public property were an outlet for feelings of frustration, but soon acquired political focus. Equally important was Jayaprakash Narayan's call for 'Total Revolution' in 1974 together with leaders such as J.B. Kriplani (Ibid: 526). The economic situation translated these movements into a national anti-Congress alliance. There was rising opposition to Mrs. Gandhi's regime particularly the failure to fulfill radical promises made earlier, high levels of dissidence within the Congress due to increasing centralisation of power and the erosion of Congress Party support. Eventually the Emergency was imposed in response to breakdown of the shared political consensus on legitimate methods of resolution of differences between the government and the opposition. But the immediate reason was the Allahabad High Court judgment setting aside Mrs. Gandhi's election to parliament in 1971. Although the actual charge on which this was done was minor, it led to pressures on her to resign and pushed her to declare the Emergency on June 25, 1975 (Ibid).

The decision to impose the Emergency and its impact on the Congress Party and the country has remained, a highly controversial subject. Writing in 1976, V.P. Dutt argued that it was an 'interim measure' without which India might have faced disaster and disintegration. He pointed out that some opposition parties and groups put forward the most irresponsible demands, created a situation of chaos, attempted to paralyse the government and began a campaign of calumny against Mrs. Gandhi; the slightest resistance by the government led to agitations and demonstrations which often ended in violence (Dutt, 1976). But other scholars argued that signs of centralisation of power in her hands and even 'creeping dictatorship' had begun in the early 1970s itself before these oppositional movements started, that quickened and became more open in 1975 (Guha, 2007: 492). Some pointed to not merely attempts to dismantle India's opposition parties, but also the establishment of 'new political institutions' which gave immense power to the Central government such as the Central intelligence organisations, Central government police forces, the Prime Ministers secretariat and the Youth Congress (Weiner, 1976).

On her part Mrs. Gandhi claimed that the Emergency was imposed to 'save the country from disruption and collapse' and to 'put through the new economic programme'. She felt that there was a 'deep-seated conspiracy of the opposition parties against the interests of the country' and 'dangers from within and without' (Frankel, 1978: 484). She pointed to a number of improvements in the performance of the government: corruption went down, bureaucrats came to office on time, trains kept to schedule, the administration enforced laws better, unions did not strike and both hoarding of essential commodities and 'black money' went down. However, these changes did not unleash forces in the country that could lead to faster economic development, removal of poverty or opportunities for the poor. The attempt to achieve economic development and reduction of disparities in the absence of basic institutional changes led to neither growth nor redistribution, creating discontent. The Emergency left India's political economy fundamentally unchanged, but the Congress shifted from being a party based on decision-making by consensus and multiple centres of power, to a more centralised organisation.

More important for our purposes, the Emergency introduced long-term seminal changes in the Congress Party; and more immediately led to its defeat in the 1977 elections. Mrs. Gandhi tried to create a new party and restore strong Central rule (as under Nehru) free from the evils of bossism. It had three features: unprecedented centralisation and personalisation of power in the Prime Minister's hands over all party and governmental organisations such as the Parliamentary board, CWC and Central cabinet; strengthening of the unitary tendencies of the Constitution aimed at weakening federal institutions; and an attempt to change the support base of the party 'from above' by recruiting under-represented sectors of society such as women, youth, intellectuals, SC, ST, etc., into the party organisation.

By the mid-1970s, Mrs. Gandhi's consolidation of power had resulted in the creation of a 'pyramidal decision-making structure' in the party and government in which all key posts were manned by loyal men (Kochanek, 1976). With the emergence of the High Command as a powerful Central organisation there were important changes in the relationship between the party and the government. The Prime Minister's secretariat emerged as a large, independent, executive force comparable to what exists in presidential systems with control over senior bureaucracy. The government's 20-point programme did not emanate from the cabinet or the Congress party but from staff directly under the Prime Minister. The party could no longer control policy decisions or ministerial appointments. The Youth Congress under the leadership of her 29-year old son Sanjay Gandhi emerged as a militant cadre based organisation taking over many of the functions of the regular Congress organisation with a strong base in the major cities. Mrs. Gandhi actively sought to prevent the rise of powerful state political leaders and chief ministers who might threaten the position or programme of the Prime Minister (Kochanek, 1976).

However, while Indira Gandhi succeeded in centralising power within her hands, she could not alter the nature of the Congress Party. The pyramid system created at best a 'brittle Centre' unable to manage the tensions and cleavages of a heterogeneous party operating within a federally governed polity (Kochanek, 1976). The Congress, especially at the local level, remained a broad aggregative electoral coalition rather than a cohesive ideologically coherent party. Her attempt to create a closed party led to revolt as factions found ways to evade her control, which she tried to quell with more centralisation. There was also need to reconcile the tensions between the need for organisational mobilisation and reconciliation. Without this the new 20-point programme could not be implemented through bureaucratisation and centralisation; compromise and negotiations were needed. Mrs. Gandhi was not heading a revolutionary mass party capable of pushing the country in a radical direction and her attempt to control and restructure the party organisation proved unworkable leading to weak, ineffective and inept leadership in the states which led to the economic crisis.

An important result of centralisation was the decay and disintegration of the Congress Party machinery in states where it had been strong. As James Manor observed: 'Both in ideas and action, the old Congress machine had crumbled during the 1970s... By the early 1970s, the Congress machine suffered from mounting complacency and corruption as old men grew weary, retired or died... (Mrs. Gandhi's) efforts to centralise power in her own hands led her to abandon the principle of representation for the selection of personnel at every level of the party. After 1972, Congress committees and party offices, both great and small, were filled by appointment rather than by election.' (Manor, 1981: 28)

In Uttar Pradesh a key state for the Congress, after 1977 there were no elections to the party's 8,000 cooperative societies which formed an essential link to local constituencies. The local party organisation (*zila parishads*) largely went out of existence when the Congress lost the 1977 elections and did not reappear (Stone, 1988: 1024). By the mid-1970s in contrast to the 1950s and 60s the party hardly had any important national or state level leaders with independent bases of political power. While earlier factions attempted to be inclusive of various religious, caste and regional groups, from the 1970s they became largely caste or religious lobbies due to the growing intervention of the Central government into UP politics and the related decay of the Congress machinery. Intervention and decay were part of the same broad trend. The High Command felt that a robust party machine in UP would be more difficult to manipulate and consequently made no effort to resurrect the apparatus after it was repeatedly damaged in the late 1960s due to the split and then the Emergency in 1975-1977. Mrs. Gandhi seemed to believe that her control over the party units in the states was more important than a healthy state party that could reach down, absorb, and be responsive to the people (Ibid: 1024).

The 1977 Elections: Defeat and Further Decline

The term of the Lok Sabha elected in 1971 had been extended by the Congress government after the imposition of the Emergency. Among the reasons proffered were that economic development and elections were antithetical as the latter would wipe out the gains of the Emergency, and that the forces of subversion and disruption that had forced its imposition were still active. Hence, the announcement of the national elections on January 18, 1977 just one year after the declaration of the Emergency was sudden and took the political class by surprise. A reason given was that the Emergency was becoming 'routinised' with its gains showing a tendency towards dissipation, rising prices and the grip on the economic front loosening. Hence, elections needed to be held early if the Congress Party had to capitalise on the gains of the Emergency (Narain, 1977: 106). Second, was the growing tension between the Youth Congress of Sanjay Gandhi and the parent party with factionalism reaching high levels necessitating perhaps, a 'new Kamaraj Plan' (Ibid: 106). Mrs. Gandhi also found it necessary to heed the considerable criticism, from both the international media as well as political leaders of many countries, of the Emergency as destructive of the only democratic regime in Asia and legitimise her regime by holding elections. Within the Congress Party however, the feeling was that, 'the Congress Party is at present in an especially strong and advantageous position to face the elections as most opposition parties were in a state of enforced hibernation for over 18 months; many of their leaders and large numbers of their active cadres were in detention.' (*Economic and Political Weekly*,1977: 69)

Despite the announcement of the elections, the Emergency was not withdrawn. Fundamental rights remained under suspension, though press censorship was relaxed and election meetings could be held without special permission. But the caretaker government remained armed with extraordinary discretionary powers that could be used as it wished. Despite its optimism the Congress Party faced a number of internal problems which contributed to its defeat. The most important was the second split in the party and exit of Jagjivan Ram with his supporters on January 2, 1978 to form the Congress for Democracy (CFD). The CFD immediately put forward an eight-point demand to create conditions for a fair and free election including lifting the Emergency, which strengthened such a demand by all other parties. While the 1969 Congress split was a long-drawn affair over a number of months preceding the 1971 elections, the revolt in 1977 took place less than six weeks before the polling. It shocked the Congress leadership which initiated attempts to make adjustments with the CPI in some states which was not liked by the Congress cadres. The Youth Congress which had demanded 50 percent of the 542 seats in the elections was now ignored and old timers, Chief Ministers and other senior leaders in the states were consulted. The Congress leadership had little time to select candidates and only two considerations were followed: avoiding further defections and selecting those with a record of winning (Ram, 1977: 175).

There were important differences in the position of the Congress Party in 1971 and 1977. In the 1969 split and the subsequent 1971 elections, the initiative had been with the Prime Minister due to adoption of the socialist programme; in 1977 the Congress leadership felt vulnerable and the rank and file confused. The party was also bereft of a Harijan leader of stature. In 1971, Mrs. Gandhi went to the polls early not because of opposition demand but because she saw great advantage in the timing. In 1977, the Prime Minister had given—even her own party—the impression that elections would not be held before March 1978 because the life of the Lok Sabha had been extended. Thus, Congressmen were caught unawares. The Janata Party launched its campaign in New Delhi with a rally on January 30 and held a second one with the rebel CFD group led by Jagjivan Ram and other leaders a few days later to the discomfiture of the Congress leadership. The Congress rally in contrast held in February was not well managed, it gained a poor political response and key leaders such as Sanjay Gandhi and D.K. Barooah did not attend.

The sudden announcement gave the opposition parties a 'psychological edge' compared to the 1971 elections (Ibid). Moreover, in 1971 the Congress had relied on Mrs. Gandhi's personal popularity as a leader while the opposition made her its principal target; in 1977 the 'personality factor' worked in favour of the opposition. The halo of being in prison and campaigning for democracy put opposition leaders on an elevated platform in the public eye. There had also been strong resistance movements against the Emergency by political activists, writers and artists and the media. The Bharatiya Lok Dal (BLD), Jana Sangh, CFD and Swatantra had jointly opposed the Constitution Amendment Bill and demanded a special mandate for it through a free and fair elections. But the extension of the life of the Lok Sabha on November 5, 1976 had lessened their urgency for joint action. The announcement of elections united them and led to a race to obtain an election symbol which made the quick merger of these parties in time for the election, possible. The opposition emerged in the role of 'emancipators' committed to ending the Emergency including its excesses and the Congress found itself on the defensive because it appeared in the role of an instrument of coercion committed to prolonging it. The opposition parties attacked 'extra-constitutional authorities'—a euphemism for Sanjay Gandhi's position in the government and the Congress—and the Congress leadership found it difficult any longer to defend him as in the past. They put forward a twofold platform to fight the elections: 'bread' and 'liberty' which they contrasted with the Congress Party's platform of 'stability' interpreted as continuation of the Emergency. Finally the election campaign narrowed down to the single issue of restoring democracy and based on the slogan of 'power to the people' the Janata Party won. Although Indira Gandhi in her January 18 broadcast held that she was going to the polls with the resolve to 'reaffirm the power of the people', this did not happen (Ibid: 177).

The 1977 Lok Sabha elections produced a stunning electoral verdict. As Appendix Table A-1 in the Appendix shows, the Congress Party obtained only 154 seats and 34.52 percent of the votes, while the newly formed Janata Party with 295 seats and 41.32 percent obtained a majority in parliament. The two major parties obtained the bulk of the votes leaving very little for smaller groups and independents. Most important was the defeat of both Mrs. Gandhi and her son Sanjay Gandhi. The national elections was a 'people's poll, retributive in the North and affirmatory in the South' because the resentment against the excesses of the emergency regime was much stronger in the former; Congress leaders in this region who chose to disassociate themselves organisationally were largely spared this resentment (Gupta, 1979: 390). In UP and Bihar the Congress lost all the 85 and 54 seats respectively, in Rajasthan the Congress won only one seat out of 25, in MP one out of 40. The strong resentment in the north, enabled the constituents of the Janata Party—most of whom were identified with the Hindi heartland—to offer a united alternative to the Congress, which despite having strong feelings of anti-Congressism had not been able to do in the past. The south in contrast remained relatively beyond the reach of Sanjay Gandhi, the excesses of the family planning programme and the absence of sycophantic chief Ministers (Rao, 1977). Here the pro-Indira wave persisted: in Andhra Pradesh the Congress obtained 41 out of 42 seats; in Karnataka 26 out of 28; in Maharashtra 20 out of 48; in Tamil Nadu 14 out of 39 and in Kerala 11 out of 20 Lok Sabha seats. In no other state did the figure rise above 10 (Narain, 1977). The assembly elections held in June 1977 in 10 states and three union territories also pointed to continuity with the parliamentary poll. Elections analyses[6] also point to a pronounced congruence in the perception of the urban and rural electorate on the one hand and the elite and the masses on the other. The suffering of the former in the wake of demolitions, unwarranted arrests and firings; and the experience of the latter with the inhuman and unimaginative administrative of the family planning sterilisation programme led both to realise the importance of the democratic rights they had lost.

The 1977 elections was hence primarily a political battle in which the issues of democracy *versus* dictatorship and stability *versus* chaos, occupied centre stage. These issues relegated economic issues to the background, as the single most important goal that emerged was to drive Indira's Congress out of power particularly in the north. Considerations such as personality, caste, creed of the candidate and all forms of vote-banks seem to have been subordinated except at micro-levels. The question of whether it heralded a shift from a single dominant party system to a competitive alternative system occasioned much controversy. Some scholars argued that the election struck the final blow to the dominant Congress system which was already disintegrating under the weight of its internal contradictions. In January 1978, the Congress Party split again into two parts as some Congressmen unhappy with Mrs. Gandhi's regime testified before the Shah Commission. The section of the party supporting Mrs. Gandhi easily won the state elections in AP and Karnataka, but it remained weak in the north. These 'develoPrime Ministerents' led Narain to wonder 'if the Congress could survive out of office, let alone a political recovery.' (Ibid: 112). Others held that it was not a two party system but a two party situation that had briefly appeared for a time (Desai and Joshi, 1978).

III

The Janata Interlude: 1977-1980

While it is true that the Emergency was responsible for the victory of the Janata Party, an important issue worthy of consideration is whether it represented a new social force thrown up by changes in the polity and economy that attempted to challenge Congress dominance both at the Centre and in the states. Two features of the Janata Party make this question pertinent. First, it consisted of a number of groups the most important of which was the BLD headed by Charan Singh who represented the rising rich peasant class thrown up by the Green Revolution. Having achieved a modicum of economic power, this group was now keen to attain political power so that it could ensure that state policy was oriented towards agriculture and farmers' needs and not towards industrialisation as they alleged it had been so far. This is seen in the agrarian policies introduced by Charan Singh as the Prime Minister (Byres, 1981). The election manifesto of the Janata Party had promised that a non-Congress coalition would implement developmental policies and programmes more responsive to popular needs. This was to be accomplished through a Gandhian alternative path of decentralised development, small scale industry rather than heavy industry, with an emphasis on immediate employment generation for the poor. The new draft Fifth Five-year Plan (1978-1983) differed significantly from its predecessors with almost 43 percent earmarked for rural development. Its objectives were: employment, poverty reduction and direct provision by the state to meet selected basic needs of the poorest.[7] Based on these programmes the Janata Party had hoped to create a social base different from that of the Congress Party in order to emerge as a strong alternative national party.

However, while the Janata Party was able to fulfill its restorationist mandate that reversed the authoritarian perceived usurpation of democratic power, it could not provide an alternative set of policies and programmes. Consequently, the function of restoration yielded a 'thin base of political capital that evaporated very fast' (Gupta, 1979: 390). While the JP's rural strategy of development was fairly well planned, the time period proved too short and difficulties arose in its execution. Another reason was the dramatic increase in atrocities against Dalits and scheduled castes, particularly in north India where the Janata Party had its base among the backward castes a fallout of the increasing confrontation between the two groups in the countryside (Pai, 1993). Equally important were the endemic conflicts between the various components of the JP particularly between the former members of the BLD and the Jana Sangh manifested both at the Centre and in the states that did not allow them to function effectively; the best example being Charan Singh's exit from the cabinet in 1978 and his re-entry in early 1979. In short, the different groups did not become any better integrated than they were following the 1977 victory.

Thus, the Janata phase proved to be merely an interlude, mainly one of restoration. While Mrs. Gandhi's government repealed the Emergency immediately following announcement of its defeat, it was the Janata government that restored the democratic system when it assumed office. The suspension of fundamental rights was withdrawn; the freedom of the press restored and the 42nd Amendment was partially withdrawn. A composite bill to repeal the Maintenance of Internal Security Act (MISA) and simultaneously provide for preventive detention by including a new chapter in the criminal procedure code 1973 was introduced in the Lok Sabha. However, the leaders of the Janata Party were determined to punish Mrs. Gandhi for imposing the Emergency. As many as eight enquiry commissions were set up, each headed by a retired judge; the most important being the Shah Commission to punish those guilty of the excesses of the Emergency. This factor also contributed to the return of Mrs. Gandhi in the 1980 elections.

IV

The 1980s: Congress Restored?

Given the record of the Janata government, in the 1980 national elections it was widely expected that the Congress would emerge as the largest party in the Lok Sabha, but without a majority. This was because there was no supportive wave, nor a solid organisation behind Indira Gandhi, seen in the fact that she chose to contest from a second safer seat—Medak in Andhra Pradesh. But the Congress won 351 seats with almost 43 percent of the popular votes compared to 352 seats and nearly 44 percent of the votes in 1971. As Appendix Table A-1 shows the Janata Party split into two parts which together obtained only 72 seats and less than 10 percent of the votes. A feature of the 1980 elections was the increased 'nationalisation' of electoral politics seen in the extent to which the vote for the Congress swung in each state in accordance with the national results (Weiner, 1982). This trend began in 1967 and increased over every elections. In the 1971, 1977 and 1980 elections, 12 states consistently conformed to the national trend or, created the national trend.[8] The reasons lay in exposure to a common communications network and shared national economic experiences as a result of the growth of a national market. A third reason was the de-linking of the parliamentary and state elections in 1971 as a result of which many states followed the national voting pattern. But the variations from state to state in the strength of Congress Party were greater under Mrs. Gandhi than under Nehru. This Weiner held pointed to the fact that India had 'many different party systems', reflecting the varied social cleavages, class structures, and historical circumstances of each of the states. All they shared by 1980 was a national Congress Party (Ibid).

The election restored the Congress Party to the position of preeminence it had held since Independence. It now had an overwhelming majority in parliament, controlled all but a few state governments, and a national leader who commanded both domestic support and international respect. The reasons for the Congress victory lay in the failures of the Janata Party outlined earlier. But an immediate factor was the attempt by the Janata Party leaders to malign and humiliate Mrs. Gandhi during their regime, seen in the abortive attempt to arrest her for corruption in October 1977. Also her election to parliament in late 1978 from a safe constituency from the south—Chikmaglur in Karnataka—was set aside due to a 'privilege motion' against her as soon as she re-entered parliament which landed her in jail for a week. However, she contested by-elections from the same constituency again and won. Mrs. Gandhi was able to overcome these attempts to harass her by reaching out to the people, a good example being her visit to Belchi in Bihar on an elephant to visit Dalit families burned to death by an upper caste mob in May 1977; a visit which made her popular and contributed to her comeback.

Pointing to the similarities between the massive victories of the Congress Party in the 1971 and 1980s national elections under Mrs. Gandhi, an important issue raised was whether the 1977 elections in which the Congress performed badly was an 'exception'. In both the 1971 and 1980 elections the Congress won the support of a wide cross-section of the people in terms of caste, class and religion and did least well among caste Hindus. In both elections it was the only national party winning seats across states. The Janata Party was the most national of the opposition parties, but in votes polled it was the second largest party in only nine states, with its strength mainly in the north. The Congress Party won a majority in all but two of the 10 states that held state assembly elections in the early 1980s. In 1972 also it had won 70 percent of all assembly seats, following its parliamentary victory a year earlier. In 1977 with the formation of the Janata Party India was close to a two-party system: the two together won 78 percent of the vote and 83 percent of the seats in parliament. Hence, Weiner argued that the breakup of the Janata coalition and the victory of the Congress in 1980s restored India to its 'normal political state: one national and many opposition parties confined to a single region or single state, with almost all of the parties further divided into factions' (Weiner, 1982: 342). In sum, the electoral results for the Congress Party from

1952 to 1980 show how stable the vote for the Congress has been with the exception of the elections of 1977. In the six parliamentary elections, its vote-share never fell below 40.7 percent or rose above 47.8 percent (Ibid).

However, analysis of major shifts in the social and regional base of the Congress shows that the victory of 1980 did not mark a 'restoration' of the earlier model of single party dominance (Rudolph and Rudolph, 1982). In the Nehru era, the traditional stronghold of the party had been the six states of the Hindi heartland, the Congress getting 49 percent of the seats and 42 percent of the votes in the area in 1957. In the 1967 and 1977 elections Congress support fell below the national average in this region, which the two elections of 1971 and 1980 only 'partially restored' (Ibid: 39). In 1980 while registering a considerable recovery as against 1977, the party extended the downward trend line by getting seats and votes not only below its good performance in 1971 but even below those of its poor performance in 1967 in this region. Rather, the results indicate that the regional base of the Congress moved towards the upper south (AP and Karnataka) and the west (Maharasthra and Gujarat), a trend that had began in 1967 itself. Second, the support gained by the party from the SCs, STs and the minorities—which in the Nehruvian era was an essential condition for its disproportionate support in the Hindi heartland—and had broken down in 1977 due to the excesses of the Emergency and was not restored in 1980. In 1980, the Congress won 60 percent of the reserved seats as against 65 percent in 1971. In the five Hindi heartland states where almost half (49 percent) of the reserved seats are located, Congress's recovery fell 23 percent short of its 1971 level. The Congress did not have a single backward or lower caste leader in the northern states at a time when ascriptive identities were becoming salient. The leadership remained mainly from the upper castes. Nor did the minorities support the Congress either in 1977 or 1980 in any part of the country. Only the ST voters returned to the Congress fold; in 1980 the Congress managed to win 82 percent of the seats reserved for the tribals. In the long run the loss of support of the SCs and minorities contributed to the collapse of the Congress in the states of the Hindi heartland and the emergence of parties such as the SP, RJD and the BSP (Ibid).

The massive victory of the Congress Party in 1980 was also somewhat deceptive (Roy, 1980). The Congress secured 67 percent of the seats in the Lok Sabha by polling less than 43 percent of the total valid votes cast. In absolute figures, out of a total electorate of 351 million, about 201 million took part in the polling. Out of this, only about 86 million voted for the Congress. Thus, less than one in every four of the eligible voters in India positively voted for the return of the Congress. Roy further estimated that over 100 seats were won by the Congress because of the split prior to the 1980 elections between the rump Janata and the revived Lok Dal, in the combined votes that had been cast for the Janata Party in the 1977 elections. Additionally in the 1980 elections, the proportion of the electorate actually exercising their franchise declined by 5 percentage points compared with 1977—from 61 percent to 56 percent (Ibid). Roy further argued that the Congress performed well, but the people were not swayed by Mrs. Gandhi's charisma. Wherever there was the option of a radical alternative as in Kerala, West Bengal and Tripura and even in some constituencies in Bihar, people voted for the left parties. In the southern states also of AP and Karnataka the Congress performed well as in 1977. In the Hindi belt states of UP, Bihar, MP, Haryana, Rajasthan and Delhi which had rejected her so decisively in 1977, there was a shift towards the Congress. Here the Congress increased its votes by over 10 million from 19.6 million in 1977 to 29.8 million in 1980 and from 25.94 percent to 39.12 percent. In the rest of the Hindi heartland the Muslims and the Harijans in particular, and a large mass of the people in general, decided to vote for the Congress on mature consideration, but without exuberance or overt enthusiasm (Ibid).

Another pertinent issue was whether the Emergency and the Janata Party rule was merely an 'interlude' in what was otherwise a remarkable pattern of continuity and stability in democratic institutions and processes; or, could the tremendous stresses and strains of the 1980s lead to authoritarianism again even if it did not mean imposition of an Emergency. There were continuities from the past with implications for the future of the Congress Party: centralisation within the party and corresponding weakness of the state/local organisation (Weiner, 1982: 339). In 1980 Mrs. Gandhi returned to power tempered by the experiment of the Emergency, but her 'sense of personal insecurity and vulnerability' persisted despite her own position in the party being stronger and the party even more dependent upon her to sustain its electoral support. The reinstating elections of 1980 produced an even more fragile system of authority than was produced by the elections of 1971 and 1972. Congress remained organisationally weak. Consequently, her style of autocratic control over the party organisation continued, with the help of a trusted 'caucus' including Sanjay Gandhi. Following his death, she came to depend upon her elder son Rajiv Gandhi. The Youth Congress had 42 MPs apart from other MPs close to Sanjay Gandhi capable of fomenting trouble within the party. Mrs. Gandhi's cabinet consisted of political unknowns with no social base. As state party organisations/

governments became increasingly subservient to the Centre, intra-party democracy within the Congress declined. Meetings of the AICC and CWC became less frequent and as local elections were very infrequent, the party 'atrophied' (Ibid).

Further, by 1980 intervention by the High Command in the states in all matters—selection of candidates for election, for the Pradesh Congress Comittee (PCC) and particularly CMs—became the norm. It was able to control state units to a large extent because of the high level of corrosion of the local Congress Party machine. For example, in 1982 Sripat Misra a 'nobody' was selected as CM in UP and selection of members of his cabinet was 'micromanaged' by High Command members sent to Lucknow for the purpose (Stone, 1988: 1023). This was true of all CMs in the 1980s in UP: V.P. Singh in 1981, Sripat Misra in 1982, N.D. Tiwari in 1984, Bir Bahudar Singh in 1985 and Tiwari (again) in 1988. In fact, by the 1980s the party system was characterised by a national party—the Congress which had lost much of its support in key regions enabling it to compete effectively only in the Hindi belt states—and a complex array of regional, ideological and communal parties that competed for power among themselves and with the Congress (Ibid).

Moreover, despite her victory Mrs. Gandhi faced serious challenges: price rise fuelled by inflation and shortages, a significant fall in food grains production due to the severe drought the previous year, rising cost of petroleum, oil & lubricants [POL] imports leading to heavy deficits in the balance of trade, rising disparity between the prices of agricultural commodities and the soaring costs of agricultural production which made peasants concerned about the price and availability of agricultural inputs. There was also a growing class of educated unemployed linked to the slow industrial growth of the 1970s and early 1980s and the increasing demand for reservations from the backward castes in north India particularly in UP and Bihar. The early 1980s also witnessed the rise of autonomy movements espousing conflict and violence in Assam, Nagaland and Punjab and regional parties and ethnicity movements that began to gradually occupy the space earlier held by the Congress such as AP and Jharkhand (Weiner, 1982: 349 and Roy, 1980: 228). These problems could also push the opposition to revive anti-Congressism leading to further confrontation. In sum, a combination of difficult economic problems, a weak party structure unable to manage factional conflict and a leadership inclined to centralise power led to a perception that a shift to authoritarianism was once again possible.

The 1984 Elections: Assassination and 'Sympathy' Wave

Despite the massive victory of the Congress in 1980, the diminution of its national stature increased Mrs. Gandhi's sense of precariousness of her party's position. This increased her inclination to constantly intervene in state politics. This style of functioning was responsible to a great extent for 'Operation Blue Star' in the Punjab involving the army, which culminated in her assassination on October 31, 1984 by two of her own Sikh security guards. There had been tension between the Central government and the Akalis in the Punjab ever since the Anandpur Sahib Resolution was adopted by the Akali Dal in 1973. The politics of agitation and assassination co-existed uneasily during the early 1980s leading to the rise of the Sikh religious leader Bhindranwale and finally the use of the army on June 5-6, 1984 to flush out militants hiding in the Golden Temple in Amritsar code-named Operation Blue Star. As a result, the 1984 national elections were overshadowed by the assassination and the riots and killing of Sikhs which followed it in retaliation in many towns in north India including Delhi where over a thousand died in the violence. Rajiv Gandhi was sworn in as Prime Minister within hours of Mrs. Gandhi's assassination and national elections were held in late December 1984.

Although it was expected that the Congress Party would obtain some 'sympathy' votes, the Congress obtained 404 seats and 49.10 percent of the votes surpassing any election held under Mrs. Gandhi and reaching the levels obtained under Nehru in 1957. As Appendix Table A-1 shows apart from the Prime Minister who got 22 seats, no party could obtain more than 10 seats and no opposition party got more than about 8 percent of the votes cast. The party also improved its position in the Hindi heartland states gaining 210 seats against 143 in 1980. The 1984 elections has been described as an 'authentic wave election' built upon 'sympathy' for Mrs. Gandhi or rather, in respect for her martyrdom and for the bereaved son. A 'wave' elections according to Brass is one in which a clear tendency begins to develop in one direction or another, towards a national party or its leader(s). It is based upon an issue or set of issues that transcend local calculations and coalitions and draws the bulk of the uncommitted and wavering voters in the same direction with increasing momentum in the last days of the campaign as the word spreads across the country (Brass, 1984). After the de-linking of parliamentary and state legislative elections in 1971, which led to the freeing of the former from their dependence on the latter, all parliamentary elections were 'wave' elections affecting the electoral fortunes of the Congress Party, though there were important differences among them. In 1971, it was because of the slogan of 'garibi hatao'; in 1977 it was based on the resentment among the people against the 'Emergency' regime excesses and on the promise of a new era held forth by the JP. The 1980 'Indira wave' was less formidable but was possible due to the discontent of the people with the disintegration of the Janata coalition, a sense of identification once again with Mrs. Gandhi and widespread scarcities of essential commodities and high prices.

The 1984 elections was similar to the Janata wave of 1977 in the north in terms of seats won, and increase in the Congress vote share. This is evident from the absence of major economic issues that had played a role in earlier election campaigns such as scarcity, high prices, poverty, low food grain and sugarcane prices for producers. Nor did issues such as caste calculations affect the results. In fact, just prior to the election a devastating accident took place on December 3 which did not figure in the campaign: the Bhopal Gas tragedy in which the leak of the deadly gas methyl isocyanate from the Union Carbide chemical plant, killed over 2,000 people and seriously affected 50,000 leading to thousands trying to flee the city. Brass describes it as a 'lamppost election' in which voters voted for the local Congress candidate irrespective of his character and abilities (Brass, 1984). But describing Rajiv Gandhi as a 'colorless national leader' and the 'dullest public speaker' who could not hold the attention of crowds very effectively, Brass argued that it was not an election swayed by a charismatic personality. Rather, Gandhi was a known personality with a 'clean image'; people voted for him without enthusiasm, but with hope (Ibid).

At the same time it is questionable to what extent it was the 'sympathy' factor that provided the Congress a massive electoral victory. While sections of the middle class admired Mrs. Gandhi, they were dismayed by the Khalistan movement in the Punjab and other secessionist movements in the country. Writing about the elections in UP, Brass points out that after the election, few observers credited the sympathy factor as causing a vote shift towards the Congress, of more than 5 percent to 7 percent (Ibid). Most Congressmen thought it was likely that the sympathy factor did affect uncommitted voters and women who voted disproportionately in favour of the Congress. Rather, another significant reason that contributed to the massive Congress victory was the focus by the party almost exclusively, on the theme of 'save India' from internal and external enemies by using the theme: 'Desh Akhand'—a rewording of the old Jana Sangh slogan, 'Akhand Bharat' (one country or the country indivisible). The Congress campaign presented Rajiv Gandhi as the logical heir to his mother's legacy and the party itself as the bulwark against the forces of secession. A poster pointed out that the electorate had a choice of 'unity or separation'. The Congress campaign wrote a commentator 'capitalised on the growing mass insecurities and Mrs. Gandhi's assassination was equated in the public mind with an assault on the Indian State and that perception was constantly reinforced.' (Khare, 1985)

These slogans to a large extent could not be separated from the feelings aroused by Mrs. Gandhi's assassination which was depicted as martyrdom caused by enemies of the country, a murder of the nation's leader and defender. The feeling was widespread among Hindu middle and upper class people in the cities and towns where a large number of Sikhs were killed. The Congress succeeded in capturing a large number of votes of the Brahmins and Rajputs and to a lesser extent some of the backward castes that used to go to the Jana Sangh. It was widely reported that prominent Jana Sangh/BJP leaders had openly or secretly urged voters to support the Congress this time as the best hope for preserving the unity of the country. Some RSS workers in UP usually thought of as only strong supporters of the BJP were also reported to be working for Congress candidates. The Congress therefore was able to create a winning coalition consisting of the middle class, the upper castes, a section of the BCs, SCs and lower backwards (Brass, 1984).

The electoral campaign in which Rajiv Gandhi was presented as his mother's heir and his elevation as Prime Minister, indelibly shaped the future of the Congress Party. It is questionable whether Nehru had groomed his daughter, and it is well accepted that Mrs. Gandhi from an initial position of weakness was able to carve out a position of strength for herself emerging as a strong and accepted leader of the Congress Party. The encouragement given to Sanjay Gandhi by his mother, and the succession of Rajiv Gandhi where the Congress Party opened itself to the allegation of following the dynastic principle. Mrs. Gandhi by centralising all power in her hands throughout the 1970s and early 1980s created a situation within the party where few leaders could have been considered after her death. Consequently, Rajiv Gandhi despite being a political novice emerged as the undisputed leader of the Congress Party. However, the massive victory overshadowed this feature as well as did the rapid decline, decay and collapse of the party organisation, which became evident by the end of the decade.

V

Conclusion

From our narrative of the trajectory of electoral politics in the country during the period 1964 to 1984, some conclusions can be drawn of the impact on the electoral fortunes of the party. This was a decisive period in the history of the Congress as it witnessed the beginnings of the gradual transition from a single dominant party system that had emerged out of the national movement, towards multi-partyism in the states, more in keeping with a diverse federal polity. Equally important, this phase falls in between the Nehruvian era when the party enjoyed considerable electoral support and the second half of the 1980s when it began to experience rapid decline both electoral and organisational.

Our analysis suggests that rapid socio-economic and political changes in the larger context and developments within the organisation of the Congress Party played a determining role in its electoral fortunes. A number of significant developments took place during this period: rise of new opposition parties particularly on the right and the regrouping of social forces on the left, which despite their differences joined hands on the platform of anti-Congressism in the hope of wresting power from the Congress following the death of Nehru. Social movements among the backward castes and the lower castes leading to rising political awareness and discontent with the failure of Congress policies to bring in improvements in their position and fulfill their demands. Agrarian change and class formation and conflicts in the countryside led to the formation of the BKD that played a central role in electoral politics in north India. The de-linking of national and state politics also led to the emergence of two separate political arenas that encouraged the rise of state/regional parties. Changes in the states were beginning to drive national politics, as a parliamentary majority for the Congress at the Centre depended on winning in the states.

The Congress Party under Mrs. Gandhi's leadership faced a number of challenges when she assumed office. It was a troubled period in India's economy and polity due to food shortages, rising prices, unemployment, failures in the planning process, internal demands for autonomy, pressures from outside to liberalise the economy and devalue the rupee leading to disenchantment with the Congress Party. She faced opposition from within the party and from opposition parties who hoped to defeat the Congress in the post-Nehru period. However, Mrs. Gandhi was able to hold together the party, meet the challenge of the party bosses and win the 1967 national elections, albeit with a reduced majority. Her victory in the 1971 elections showed that the Nehru Congress had been reorganised by her into a more cohesive party with lower levels of factionalism, a radical ideology and programme. She was perceived by the people based on her leadership qualities, her socialist programme, and as an agent of rapid economic development. Thus, India seemed poised on the brink of change. This is evident in the 1972 assembly elections when the electorate in large parts of the country preferred the Congress—under the leadership of Mrs. Gandhi—to the unstable coalitions formed by opposition parties. Rising levels of politicisation and improvement in agriculture led to considerable support and enthusiasm for the Congress Party.

However, paradoxically just when the conditions in the country and the party were ripe for achieving Mrs. Gandhi's vision of radical change, she got pushed into personality-oriented politics that resulted in centralisation and personalisation of power in her hands. The effort that was needed to involve the participation of the poorer sections for implementation of the Congress programme of social and economic transformation in the states was not attempted. Rather, Mrs. Gandhi sought to transform the Congress Party in order to maintain her hold over it, win elections, control state power, and through it introduce change in the polity. Beginning in the early 1970s centralisation of power resulted in a severe political and economic crisis that threatened the legitimacy of the system and ended in the imposition of the Emergency, curtailment of fundamental rights, postponement of elections and revision of the Constitution. The Congress High Command—meant under Nehru to be a central organisation for conflict management and arbitration within the party—developed into a powerful centre through which she tried to control all institutions: the parliament, CWC, Congress Parliamentary board, CEC and the Cabinet through regulation, patronage, ideology, ticket distribution, etc. She attempted to reach down to the bottom level and restructure the party from the top into an 'oligarchy' controlled with the help of her close aides. This led to the breakdown of the 'machine' character of the Congress which had been the strength of the party in some states.

But Mrs. Gandhi did not succeed in her efforts to transform an open mass party with a loose organisation, federal structure, factions, broad umbrella support structure and centrist ideology, into a revolutionary vanguard that would under her leadership rapidly implement the desired radical socioeconomic change. There was revolt within the organisation and some cardinal features of the party since its inception—federal structure, diffused power, presence of factional leaders in the states whom the leadership could not ignore, and a process of consensual decision-making—defeated her purpose. There emerged a contradiction between the federal organisation of the party and her attempt to centralise all power at the Centre. By the mid-1980s, considerable damage had occurred to the organisation and electoral base of the Congress Party from which it has not yet fully recovered. The two were closely related and fed on each other. Organisational decline began in the mid-1960s and continued during the 1970s and 1980s until it was no longer possible to talk about a dominant party. Her attempt to control the party led to absence of internal democracy leading to collapse of branches of the party in key states such as UP. Another contributory factor was that Mrs. Gandhi's dependence on her sons contributed to a liberal democratic party under Nehru, becoming dependent on just one family. Consequently, since the early 1980s the Congress has remained bereft of any leader outside the 'family' with the exception of P.V. Narasimha Rao. The massive 'wave' victories in the 1980 and 1984 elections hid the electoral decline in the social and regional base of the Congress Party most particularly among the scheduled castes and minorities—who had been its mainstay—in its traditional stronghold of the Hindi heartland states, from which it has not recovered. While it is true that democratisation of politics in the northern states was responsible for the rise of identity-based lower caste parties such as the SP, BSP and RJD. It was the collapse of the Congress—earlier the party of the lower castes—in the 1990s that provided the political space for these parties.

In sum, Mrs. Indira Gandhi presided over a very difficult formative period in India's post-independence history and faced enormous economic difficulties and political uncertainties which she handled fairly effectively. However, under her leadership the party experienced organisational decline and decay that weakened it providing room for other parties in the 1990s.

Endnotes

1. *Congress Bulletin*, No. 7-8, July-August, 1963: 12-13 quoted in Kochanek, 1966.
2. The members of the Syndicate were K. Kamaraj, Sanjiva Reddy, S.Nijalingappa, Atulya Ghosh and S.K. Patil.
3. The first four Lok Sabha elections (1952, 1957, 1962 and 1967) were held simultaneously with state assembly elections.
4. It was based on the 10-Point Programme worked out earlier by Mrs. Gandhi. For this programme see Frankel, 1978: 397-98.
5. During this period two groups within the Congress Party—the Socialist Forum and the Congress Forum for Socialist Action (CFSA) were active. For details see Frankel 1978.
6. See, Special issue, *Seminar,* 1977.

7. For a detailed study of the party's economic plans, see Franda: 1979.
8. These included Karnataka, Maharashtra, Punjab, Himachal Pradesh, Orissa, Delhi, Madhya Pradesh, Rajasthan, Bihar, Uttar Pradesh, Haryana, Jammu and Kashmir and Assam, and they contain two-third of the Indian population.

References

Brass, Paul R. (1968a). "Uttar Pradesh", in Myron Weiner (ed.), *State Politics in India.* New Jersey: Princeton University Press.

———. (1968b). "Coalition Politics in North India", *The American Political Science Review* 62(4): 1174-1191. December.

———. (1986). "The 1984 Parliamentary Elections in Uttar Pradesh", *Asian Survey* 26(6): 653-669. June.

Byres, T.J. (1981). "The New Technology, Class Formation and Class Action in the Indian Countryside", *Journal of Peasant Studies* 8(4): 405-454, July.

Das Gupta, Jyotirindra (1979). "The Janata Phase: Reorganisation and Redirection in Indian Politics", *Asian Survey* 19(4): 390-403.

Desai, Ashok V. (1967). "Small Thoughts on the Elections", *Economic and Political Weekly* 4: 1230. March.

Desai, Kirti and Ram Joshi (1978). "Towards a More Competitive Party in India", *Asian Survey* 18(11): 1091-1116. November.

Economic and Political Weekly (1977). Editorial XII(4) 22: 69. January.

Franda, Marcus (1979). *Small is Politics Organisational Alternatives in India's Development.* New Delhi: Wiley Eastern Limited.

Frankel, Francine (1978). *India's Political Economy 1947-77.* Delhi: Oxford University Press.

Guha, Ramachandra (2007). *India After Gandhi The History of the World's Largest Democracy.* New York, USA: Harper Collins.

Gupta, Sulekh C. (1967). "Small Thoughts on the Elections", *Economic and Political Weekly* 1229-1230. July 8.

Hardgrave, Robert L. (1970). "The Congress in India - Crisis and Split", *Asian Survey* 10(3): 256-262. March.

Khare, Harish (1985). "The State Goes Macho", *Seminar* 497.

Kochanek, Stanley (1966). "Post Nehru India: The Emergence of the New Leadership", *Asian Survey* 6(5): 288-299. May.

———. (1976). "Mrs. Gandhi's Pyramid: the New Congress", in Henry C Hart (ed.), *Indira Gandhi's India: A Political System Reappraised.* Colorado: Westview Press.

Kothari, Rajni (1967). "India: the Congress System on Trial", *Asian Survey* 7(2): 83-96. February.

Manor James (1981). "Party Decay and Political Crisis in India", *Washington Quarterly* 28. Summer.

Mukherji, Rahul (2000). "India's Aborted Liberalisation - 1966", *Pacific Affairs* 73(3): 375-392. Autumn.

Narain, Iqbal (1971). "Democratic Interlude for Nation Building Fifth Lok Sabha Elections", *Economic and Political Weekly* 2023-2028. September 18.

———. (1977). "From Promise to Disenchantment?", *Asian Survey* 14(2): 103-116. February.

Pai, Sudha (1993). *Uttar Pradesh: Agrarian Change Electoral Politics.* New Delhi: Shipra Publications.

Ram, Mohan (1977). "The Key Issue", *Economic and Political Weekly* Annual Number: 175-177. February.

Rao, G.V. Prasad (1977). "Why no Tremor in the South? The Janata Earth", *The Times of India,* New Delhi, March 29.

Roy, Ajit (1980). "Seventh Lok Sabha Elections", *Economic and Political Weekly* Annual Number: 227-228. February.

Rudolph, Lloyd I. and Susanne Hoeber Rudolph (1981). " Transformation of the Congress Party: Why 1980s was not a Restoration", *Economic and Political Weekly*: 811-18. May 2.

Seminar (1977). "The Elections and the System" No. 212. Special issue.

Stone, Brewer (1988). "Institutional Decay and Traditionalisation of Politics: The UP Congress Party", *Asian Survey* XXVII (10): 1018-1030. October.

Thapar, Romesh (1977). "The Election and After", *Economic and Political Weekly* 12: 91. January.

———. (1977). "Week to Week", *Economic and Political Weekly* Annual Number: 168-172. February.

Weiner, Myron (1976). "India's New Political Institutions", *Asian Survey* 16(9): 898-901. September.

———. (1982). "Congress Restored: Continuities and Discontinuities in Indian Politics", *Asian Survey* 22(4): 339-355. April.

Appendix

Table A-1

Party	1967		1971		1977		1980		1984	
	Seats	*Votes (in %)*	*Seats*	*Votes (in %)*	*Seats*	*Votes (in %)*	*Seats*	*Votes (in %)*	*Seats*	*Votes (in %)*
INC	283	40.73	352	43.68	154		353	42.69	404	49.10
BJS	35	9.31	22	7.35	-		-	-	2#	7.74
CPI	23	5.11	23	4.73	7	34.52	17	2.49	6	2.71
CPRIME MINISTER	19	4.28	25	5.12	22		9	6.24	22	5.87
PSP	13	3.06	2	1.04	-	2.82	-	-	-	-
SSP	23	4.92	3	2.43	-	4.29	-	-	-	-
SWA	44	8.67	8	3.07	-		-	-	-	-
NCO	-	-	16	10.43	3		-	-	-	-
BLD	-	-			295		-	-	-	-
LKD	-	-			-	1.72	-	-	3	5.97
INC(I)	-	-			-	41.32	-	-	-	-
INC(U)	-	-			-		13	5.28	-	-
JNP	-	-			-		31	18.97	10	6.89
JNP(S)	-	-			-		41	9.39	-	-
INDS	35	13.78	14	8.38	9	5.50	9	6.43	9*	9.44^
ICS										

Note: * This includes 4 seats won by the ICS; ^ This includes 1.52 percent won by the ICS; and
BJP formed after breakup of Janata party.

Source: Election Commission of India (*www.eci.nic.in*)

Chapter IV

Economic Challenges 1964-1984

From Increased Dirigisme to Beginnings of Liberalisation

Aditya Mukherjee

The years 1964-1984 were in many ways extremely turbulent and eventful years in both political and economic terms at home and internationally. This led to the Indian economy facing some of its gravest challenges since independence. Largely under Indira Gandhi's leadership, these challenges were faced squarely with critical shifts made in economic strategy in response to the changing political and economic scenario. Broadly speaking the period witnessed the taking forward of the Nehruvian paradigm emerging out of what can be called the Nehruvian consensus to its logical conclusion and in later years, in response to changing circumstances, one sees a creative shift away from some aspects of this paradigm without giving up the basic objectives of the Nehruvian consensus.

I

The Nehruvian Consensus

Any attempt to evaluate India's economic journey after independence from a protectionist planned economy to economic reform and participation in the globalisation process must place the Indian experience both in a historical and comparative context. We have to evaluate the early Nehruvian effort taking into account the level and stage from which the beginning was made, the uniqueness of the effort to undertake an industrial transformation within a democratic framework and the global constraints prevailing at that time. Similarly, the reassertion of the Nehruvian path after a brief interlude in the 1960s and the shift in economic strategy made since the 1980s under Indira Gandhi and Rajiv Gandhi leading to the dramatic turn in 1991 under Narasimha Rao, has to be placed in the context of the Indian situation and the changes in the global context that had occurred during those periods.

The strategy adopted by Nehru in the 1950s reflected the need of the times and a consensus evolved around it, what may be called the Nehruvian consensus. Similarly by the last decades of the 20th century the needs and opportunities had changed and a consensus evolved around economic reform. In other words, Manmohan Singh, the architect of India's economic reform since the 1990s, would have been part of the Nehruvian consensus in the 1950s just as Nehru would have been part of the reform consensus in the 1980s and 1990s. Implied in the above argument is the inference that the shift from the first to the second did not involve the abandoning of the basic paradigm within which independent India set out to meet, in Nehru's words, its 'tryst with destiny'.

This paradigm was historically given to the makers of independent India as a legacy of the movement which led to the creation of the new state. The Indian national movement was a prolonged, nearly hundred years long, movement. It was also a mass movement, involving millions upon millions of people, perhaps the biggest mass movement in world history. The movement therefore, unlike coups or guerilla or 'professional revolutionary' led movements, carried the ideas of the movement to deep layers of Indian society, making the overlooking of these ideas and their reversal an extremely difficult process. The key ideas of the Indian national movement which are important in the current context are: a) the notion of sovereignty or independence, b) the notion of democracy, and c) a pro-poor (not necessarily socialist) orientation. [The kind of strong resistance governments in India have faced to any move to distance themselves from these principles (witness the response to the temporary restriction on democratic rights during the emergency, 1975-1977) makes an interesting comparison with the ease with which the Soviet Union and China were able to do a virtual about-turn from the legacy of their socialist revolutions.] The wide range of political actors on the Indian stage at independence, from the far left to the far right, had to and did debate strategies within this paradigm. Nobody could or did argue, for example, for a semi-sovereign or semi-democratic, leave alone a neocolonial or authoritarian, path for India's economic development at independence. The shifts in India's economic policy including towards the economic reforms also occurred broadly within the same paradigm.

II

Initial Conditions

In order to understand the Nehruvian paradigm at independence and its evolution over time it is necessary to highlight the initial conditions at independence from which India had to attempt an economic take off. This becomes necessary because of the resurgence of the colonial viewpoint, for example, in the Cambridge Economic History, Volume 2, in the early 1980s and more recently a caricature version of the same argument in Tirthankar Roy's *Economic History of India,*[1] where it is argued that colonialism led to 'positive economic growth', 'rapid growth of real income in industry and services', setting up of 'modern infrastructure', etc., thus creating conditions for an economic take off after independence.[2]

Actually, what India inherited after 200 years of colonial 'benevolence', was a very sorry state of affairs indeed. As Angus Maddison's monumental work shows, India was the largest economy of the world for the entire thousand years of the first millennium accounting for close to 30 percent of the world's GDP. Till as late as the beginning of the 18th century India's was still the largest economy contributing about 25 percent of the world's GDP, more than eight times that of the United Kingdom. The decline started soon after and at the end of nearly 200 years of colonial rule—India's share of the world GDP was reduced to a mere 4.2 percent in 1950. It was a few decades before India could sufficiently shrug off the colonial legacy and begin to gradually claw her way back into improving her share of the global pie.[3]

The impact of colonialism in human terms was traumatic and all too visible. At independence the average life expectancy was barely 30 years. The poor obviously died much younger. India was faced with acute food shortages creating near famine conditions repeatedly in different areas. The Bengal famine of 1943, just four years before the British left, claimed more than 3 million lives.[4] Between 1946-1953 about 14 million tonnes of food grains worth Rs.10,000 million had to be imported, seriously affecting India's planned development after independence. In 1951, 84 percent of the people (92 percent women) were illiterate. The legacy of colonialism which neocolonialists like Tirthankar Roy misjudged so completely was anticipated by the poet Rabindranath Tagore, shortly before his death in 1941, in his inimitable way:[5]

> The wheels of fate will someday compel the English to give up their Indian Empire. What kind of India will they leave behind, what stark misery? When the stream of their centuries' administration runs dry at last, what a waste of mud and filth will they leave behind them.

III

The Nehruvian Breakthrough and After

The growth that India witnessed after independence was thus not all about carrying on the 'good' work started during colonialism. It was a product of a structural break from colonialism, painstakingly crafted through a multi pronged planned effort—an unique effort of trying to industrialise and build capitalism with democracy and civil liberties. Jawaharlal Nehru and other leaders were deeply aware that India was experimenting with a hitherto uncharted path as none of the industrialised countries of the world had democracy and civil liberties during the initial period of transition to capitalism and industrialisation, the period of primitive accumulation.

A consensus had emerged on critical aspects of the development path to be followed, what I refer to as the Nehruvian consensus. For example, the Gandhians, the Socialists, the capitalists as well as the Communists (barring brief sectarian phases), were all more or less agreed on the following agenda: rapid industrialisation based on import substitution including of capital goods industries; promotion of self-reliance and prevention of imperialist or foreign capital domination; land reforms involving abolition of *zamindari*, tenancy reforms, introduction of cooperatives, especially service cooperatives for marketing, credit, etc.; growth to be attempted along with equity, i.e., the growth model must be reformist with a welfare, pro-poor orientation; the state to play a central role in promoting economic development including through direct state participation in the production process, i.e., through the public sector, and so on.

I have detailed elsewhere the breakthroughs made since independence by moving along this path.[6] I will only outline here a brief comparison of some of the features of the colonial period, especially the period of so called 'decolonisation' and 'positive' growth since World War I with those of the period after independence. This may help underline the enormity of the break required, and to a considerable extent achieved.

Table 1

Rate of Growth of per capita GDP
(Annual average compound growth rates)

	(1) 1820-1870	(2) 1870-1913	(3) 1913-1950	(4) 1950-1973	(5) 1973-2001	(6) 2001-2007
France	1.01	1.45	1.12	4.04	1.71	
UK	1.26	1.01	0.93	2.42	1.86	
USA	1.34	1.82	1.61	2.45	1.86	
Japan	0.19	1.48	0.88	8.06	2.14	
India	0.00	0.54	**-0.22**	1.40	**3.01**	5.65*

Note: * per capita net national product.

Source: Column 1 to 5 from Angus Maddison, *op. cit.*, Table 8b, p. 643. Column 6 is based on *Economic Survey, 2006-07*, Government of India, New Delhi 2007, and Aditya Mukherjee, "Indian Economy in the New Millennium," in Bipan Chandra, Mridula Mukherjee and Aditya Mukherjee (2008). *India Since Independence*. Delhi: Penguin.

The growth of per capita income in India in the colonial period was either zero or very low, remaining way below that of the independent countries of Europe, USA and Japan between 1820 and 1913. (See Table 1). In the last decades of colonial rule, after colonialism had had its full impact, the per capita income in India actually declined at an annual rate of -0.22 percent between 1913- 1950. [7] After independence, on the other hand, India's national income or gross national product (GNP) grew at an average rate of about 4 percent per annum over the first three plans, between 1951and 1964-65 (omitting the last year of the third plan, i.e., 1965-66, which saw an unprecedented drought and a war). This was roughly four times the rate of growth achieved during the last half century of colonial rule. It was higher than what Japan could achieve in a comparable period of its development between 1893 to 1912.[8] India's per capita income grew at 1.4 percent in the first couple of decades (about three times faster than the best phase, 1870-1913, under colonialism) and much faster at 3.01 percent in the next 30 years, 1973-2001 (a rate considerably higher than that achieved by West Europe,[9] USA or Japan) and in the last four years (2003-04 to 2006-07) at an astounding 7 percent (it was over 8 percent in 2006-07) comparable to the explosive rates achieved by Japan (though in very special circumstances) between 1950-1973.[10]

Similarly, the colonial period saw a process of deindustrialisation where traditional industry was largely destroyed and modern industry grew very slowly. Despite the growth of modern industry since World

War I, at about 3.8 percent per annum, it contributed a mere 6 to 8 percent of the national product in 1950, having started from an extremely low level of 4 percent of national product in 1913.[11] Moreover, modern industry was yet dominated by consumer goods industry with a near total and debilitating dependence on the advanced countries for capital goods and technology. Contrast this with the period after independence. Industry during the first three plans (1951-1965) grew at 7.1 percent per annum. More important 'the three-fold increase in aggregate index of industrial production between 1951 and 1969 was the result of a 70 percent increase in consumer good industries, a quadrupling of the intermediate goods production and a ten-fold increase in the output of capital goods.'[12]

This pattern of industrial development led to a structural transformation of the colonial legacy. From a situation where to make any capital investment, virtually the entire capital equipment had to be imported (in 1950, India met nearly 90 percent of its needs of even machine tools through imports) the share of imported equipment in the total fixed investment in the form of equipment in India had come down to 43 percent in 1960 and a mere 9 percent in 1974, whereas the value of the fixed investment in India increased by about two and a half times over this period (1960-1974).[13] This broadening of the industrial base was a major achievement of the Nehru-Mahalanobis strategy as it considerably increased India's autonomy from the advanced countries in determining her own rate of capital accumulation or growth.

Agriculture, the largest sector of the Indian economy, was in a state of ruin under colonialism. Per capita agricultural output actually fell at the rate of 0.72 percent per year during 1911-1941. Per capita food grains output fell even more sharply by 1.14 percent per year, a 29 percent fall over the period.[14] No wonder the food shortages and famine conditions mentioned above. After independence, a combination of institutional changes (land reforms) and massive state sponsored technological change transformed this situation.[15] During the first three plans (leaving out 1965-66, a drought year), Indian agriculture grew at an annual rate of over 3 percent, a growth rate more than eight times faster than the annual growth rate of 0.37 percent achieved during the half a century (1891-1946) of the last phase of colonialism in India.[16]

The Green Revolution in the late 1960s maintained a rate of growth ranging from about 2.5 to 3.5 percent (primarily through increases in yield) till the mid 1990s.[17] The Green Revolution areas like Punjab and Haryana did not have any continuities with trends in the colonial period as Tirthankar Roy, for example, argues.[18] Haryana was largely an extremely backward area in colonial times and even Punjab showed meagre growth rates in terms of all-crop yields per acre of 0.36 percent per annum between 1901-1941 by one estimate and of only 0.06 percent between 1906-07 and 1941-42 by another. The highest increases in yield seen in Punjab were in non-food crops of an average of 1 percent per annum between 1891-1951. In contrast the value productivity of eleven major crops in Punjab increased between 1950-51 and 1969-70 by 255 percent, i.e., an average annual increase of more than 12.5 percent.[19] The huge productivity difference certainly signifies a structural break.

The rate of capital formation, the key to economic development, occurred at a very slow pace during the colonial period. India was in fact losing to Britain as drain or tribute an equal proportion, if not more, of what was invested in India. The drain has been variously calculated to be between 5 to 10 percent of her national income.[20] The average annual rate of capital formation between 1901 to 1913 was 6.92 percent of GDP, falling to 6.75 percent between 1914-1946. Public expenditure, an important engine of capital formation in backward countries, declined sharply from Rs. 75.4 crore annually during 1925-1930 to Rs. 41.7 crore during the Depression years 1930-1938, when the opposite needed to be done.[21] The massive cut in government expenditure along with other deflationary fiscal and monetary policies greatly exacerbated the negative effects of the Depression on the Indian economy.

The contrast between the colonial and the post-independence scenario is evident. While public expenditure was low and declining during the last decades of colonial rule the initial 40 years of independence (1950-1990) saw it rise by more than three times Similarly, while the last 50 years or so of colonial rule (1901-1946) saw the gross capital formation in the economy hover around 6 to 7 percent of GDP annually, the first 50 years after independence saw the rate of capital formation rise consistently and sharply, ending up at a rate of 33.8 percent in 2005-06 about five times the colonial rate.[22]

Also, Jawaharlal Nehru and the early Indian planners were acutely aware of India's backwardness in science and technology (an area left consciously barren in the colonial period) and therefore made massive efforts to overcome this shortcoming. An unprecedented increase occurred in the educational opportunities in science and technology in the universities and institutes. Admission capacity in technical education (engineering and technology) at the degree and diploma levels was higher by 6 and 8.5 times, respectively between 1950 and 1965.[23] National expenditure on scientific research and development kept growing rapidly with each plan. For example, it increased from Rs. 10 million in 1949 to Rs. 4.5 billion in 1977. Over roughly the same period the stock of India's scientific and technical manpower increased more than 12 times from 190 thousand to 2.32 million. A spectacular growth by any standards, a growth whose benefits India reaps today as the world moves towards a 'knowledge' society.

IV

1964-1984: The Challenges

By the mid-1960s, when Indira Gandhi took the baton after Jawaharlal Nehru, with a very brief interlude under Lal Bahadur Shastri, the Indian economy was in the grips of a massive crisis, which rapidly changed India's image from a model developing country to a 'basket case'. Two successive monsoon failures of 1965 and 1966, superimposed on an agriculture which was beginning to show signs of stagnation, led to a fall in agricultural output by 17 percent and food grain output by 20 percent. The rate of inflation which was hitherto kept very low (till 1963 it did not exceed 2 percent per annum) rose sharply to 12 percent per annum between 1965 and 1968 and food prices rose nearly at the rate of 20 percent per annum. The inflation was partly due to the droughts and partly due to the two wars of 1962 (with China) and 1965 (with Pakistan) which had led to a massive increase in defence expenditure. The government consolidated (state and Centre) fiscal deficit peaked in 1966-67 at 7.3 percent of GDP.

The balance of payments situation, fragile since 1956-57, deteriorated further, with the foreign exchange reserves (excluding gold) averaging about $340 million between 1964-65 and 1966-67, enough to cover less than two months of imports. The dependence on foreign aid, which had been rising over the first three Plans, now increased sharply due to food shortages as well as the weakness of balance of payments. Utilisation of external assistance, which was 0.86 percent of net national product (NNP) at factor cost in 1951-52, increased to 1.05 percent in 1956-57, 2.37 percent in 1957-58, 2.86 in 1960-61 and 3.8 percent in 1965-66. Amortisation and interest payments as percent of exports (debt service ratio) rose sharply from 0.8 upto the end of the first plan to 3.9 during the Second Plan, 14.3 during the Third plan to 20.6 in 1966-67 and a whopping 27.8 in 1966-67. Given the overall situation, long-term planning had to be temporarily abandoned and there were three Annual Plans from 1966 to 1969 before the Fourth Five-year Plan could commence in April 1969.

It is at this most vulnerable time for the Indian economy—with high inflation, very low foreign exchange balance, food stocks so low as to threaten famine conditions in some areas, calling for large imports, and nearly half the imports having to be met through foreign aid—that the United States of America, the most important donor at that time, decided to suspend its aid in response to the Indo-Pak war (1965) and refused to renew the PL 480 (wheat loan) agreement on a long-term basis. Also, the United States, in President Johnson's words, wanted to keep India 'on a short leash' so that she (like the wayward puppy) did not stray too much from the economic policies preferred by the US, which they now sought to pressurise India to accept apart from pressurising her to support the US stand on Vietnam.

The US, the World Bank and the IMF wanted India to: (a) liberalise its trade and industrial controls, (b) devalue the Rupee, and (c) adopt a new agricultural strategy. While there was considerable indigeneous support for a new initiative in agriculture (which was successfully implemented), there was plenty of suspicion over trade and industrial liberalisation and particularly over devaluation. As it happened, the devaluation of the Rupee (nominally by 36.5 percent though effectively much less) and the trade liberalisation that was initiated by Prime Minister Indira Gandhi in the mid-1960s got associated with the continuing recession in industry, inflation, and the failure of exports to pick up, all of which was at least partly caused by 'exogeneous' circumstances like the second major drought of 1966-67 and partly by the inadequate manner in which these policies were initiated. In any case, these policies were condemned before their long-term effect could be realised.

The perceived failure of the devaluation and liberalisation of controls on trade and industry combined with the resentment at the 'arm twisting' resorted to by external agencies in favour of these policies, using India's economic vulnerability, led to an 'economic nationalist' response based on a reversal to (and in fact, considerable accentuation of) the earlier policies of controls and state intervention. The immediate imperative was seen to be the restoring of the health of India's balance of payments situation, creation of sufficient foreign exchange reserves and the removal of dependence on food imports by improving agricultural production and creating food reserves.

The method chosen for meeting the balance of payment crisis and reducing the fiscal deficit (the two being linked) was a severe tightening of the belt, involving drastic cuts in government expenditure rather than increases in tax levels. The cut fell mainly on government capital expenditure, which in real terms decreased by about 50 percent between 1966-67 and 1970-71. This was an important factor in the continued industrial recession in this period. The industrial slowing down continued till the mid-1970s, the industrial growth rate coming down from an average of 7.8 percent per year between 1951 and 1966 to 4.99 percent per year between 1966 and 1974.

Further, the political developments in this period had important implications for economic policy. In the 1967 elections, the Congress Party received a major setback in the Centre and particularly in the States. The Prime Minister, Indira Gandhi, responded by adopting a radical stance which led to differences within the Congress and eventually a split in November 1969. After the split Mrs. Gandhi could retain the Government only with the support of the Communist parties and some regional parties, and this accentuated the radical Left turn in her policies. In December 1970, she called for General Elections and, campaigning on the slogan of 'garibi hatao' (remove poverty) and promising radical socialist policies, she romped home with a landslide victory in March 1971.

The post-1967 period therefore saw the launching of a series of radical economic policies which on the one hand helped meet the immediate economic crisis and take forward many of the Nehruvian pro-poor objectives but on the other hand they also had certain long-term implications on India's developmental effort. Some of these policies accentuated the shortcomings that had begun to emerge during the first phase of planning itself, i.e., in the 1950s and early 1960s, others created new distortions. The major private commercial banks in India were nationalised in 1969. The same year the Monopoly and Restrictive Trade Practices (MRTP) Act, severely restricting the activities of large business houses, was passed. After the 1971 elections victory a series of further such measures increasing government control and intervention were introduced with the active support of Left radicals, intellectuals like P.N. Haksar, D.P. Dhar and Mohan Kumaramangalam. Thus, insurance was nationalised in 1972 and the coal industry was nationalised in 1973. A disastrous effort was made to nationalise wholesale wheat trade the same year, which was abandoned after a few months. The Foreign Exchange Regulation Act (FERA) was passed in 1973, putting numerous restrictions on foreign investment and the functioning of foreign companies in India, making India one of the most difficult destinations for foreign capital in the world. The government also decided to take over and run 'sick' companies, such as a number of textile mills, rather than allow such loss-making companies to close down.

The debilitating long-term effects of many of these measures on the overall economy have been discussed in Section IX below.

It must be remembered, though, that the new policies, which were partially a result of the historically-specific economic and political situation, met many of the critical problems faced by the country at that time. They pulled India out of the economic crisis most creditably and restored her independence and dignity *vis-à-vis* the advanced countries. Equally important, this was not achieved by tightening the belt at the cost of the poor but keeping the needs of the poor in focus. We shall briefly review these achievements in the next section.

V

1964-1984: The Achievements

In the considerable economic achievements between the mid-1960s and the mid-1980s, Indira Gandhi, (often too easily dismissed as populist) as Prime Minister for most of the period, i.e., from 1966 to 1984, barring a brief interregnum between 1977-1979, played a major role. These achievements have to be evaluated keeping in view the series of formidable internal and external shocks witnessed during this period. For example, following the economic crisis of the mid-1960s discussed above, there was the genocide in East Pakistan (Bangladesh) resulting in the huge burden of over 10 million refugees from that region (nearly half the population of a country like Australia!) taking shelter in India, the 1971 war with Pakistan, two droughts of 1972 and 1974, the major oil shock of 1973 involving a quadrupling of international oil prices and hence of cost of oil imports, the oil shock of 1979 when oil prices doubled and the disastrous harvest of 1979-80 caused by the worst drought since independence.

Concerted efforts were made after the mid-1960s to, *inter alia*, improve the balance of payments situation, create food security, introduce anti-poverty measures and reduce dependence on imports for critical inputs like oil. These enabled India to weather the impact of the droughts, war and the oil shocks without getting into a debt crisis and a recessionary spin as happened in the case of a number of developing countries, especially in Latin America in the 1980s, and without serious famine conditions, leave alone famine deaths, that occurred in Communist China by the millions in the late 1950s.

On the food front the situation improved rapidly. The adoption of the 'Green Revolution' strategy of introducing a package of high yield variety (HYV) seeds, fertilisers and other inputs in a concentrated manner to some suitable select areas paid immediate dividends in creating food security and poverty reduction (discussed in detail below in Section VIII). Between 1967-68 and 1970-71 food grain production rose by 35 percent. Net food imports fell from 10.3 million tonnes in 1966 to 3.6 million in 1970, while food availability increased from 73.5 million tonnes to 89.5 million tonnes over the same period. Food availability continued to increase sharply to 110.25 million tonnes in 1978 and 128.8 million tonnes in 1984 and food stocks had crossed the 30 million tonnes mark by the mid-1980s, putting an end to India's 'begging bowl' image and creating considerable food security even in extreme crisis situations. For example, the economy was able to absorb the massive successive droughts of 1987-88 without undue pressure on prices of food or imports. In fact the rural poverty index continued to show a decline in these crisis years as rural employment and incomes were maintained through Government programmes using the surplus food stocks. This was the first time since independence that rural poverty was not exacerbated during a drought or a poor harvest.

The success of the Green Revolution Strategy of technological reforms in Indian agricultutre, and particularly making the strategy inclusive and pro-poor required taking forward radically the process of institutional land reforms started in the Nehruvian period. In the following section we will look at how these two phenomenon evolved complimentary to each other from the mid-1960s to the mid-1980s.

VI

Second Wave of Land Reforms

At independence, under Nehru's leadership India witnessed the unique phenomenon of wide ranging land reforms being implemented within a modern democratic structure without any violence or use of authoritarian force. There was no forced collectivisation as in the Soviet Union or forcible expropriation of land and pushing of peasants into communes as in China, processes that had cost millions of lives. Nor was there any external army of occupation undertaking the task of land reforms among a defeated people as in Japan. India had to attempt this task with adult franchise, full civil liberties to the opposition and an independent judiciary. Yet, basing itself on the heritage of long, powerful national and peasant movements independent India successfully transformed the colonial agricultural structure (with all its semi-feudal characteristics) which it had inherited. Zamindari was abolished, tenancy reforms were started and even land ceiling legislations were introduced. However as I have discussed at length elsewhere[24] the reforms were successful in essentially abolishing the feudal elements but the main beneficiaries were the upper tenants or occupancy tenants and not the poor tenants, tenants at will and landless labourers. The Congress leadership and the Planning Commission were aware of this and now looked towards redressing this situation.

Land Ceilings

Creating effective land ceilings was a major challenge. Despite the ceiling legislations which were passed by most states by 1961, till the end of 1970 not a single acre was declared surplus in large states like Bihar, Mysore, Kerala, Orissa and Rajasthan. In Andhra Pradesh, a mere 1400 acres were declared surplus but no land was distributed. Only in Jammu and Kashmir were ceiling laws fully implemented and by the middle of 1955 about 230,000 acres of surplus land were handed over to tenants and landless labourers, that too without having to pay any compensation. However, taking India as whole, only 2.4 million acres were declared surplus by the end of 1970, and the area distributed constituted only about half the surplus land, constituting a mere 0.3 percent of the total cultivated land of India.

The dismal record in using ceiling legislation for a more equitable distribution of land combined with a sharply increasing polarisation in the countryside since the mid-1960s called for a new initiative in land reform. The Indian countryside on the one hand saw the growing consolidation of the owner cultivator/rich peasant interests (similar to what the Rudolphs call 'Bullock capitalists')[25] and their finding a distinct political voice in formations such as the Bharatiya Kranti Dal (BKD) (formed by Charan Singh after he brought down the C.B. Gupta-led Congress government in UP in 1967). The BKD later merged with Swatantra and other parties to become Bharatiya Lok Dal (BLD) in 1974 and the BLD was the principal component of the Janata Party which came to power in 1977, after the emergency, bringing the strong influence of the owner cultivator/rich peasant interests, which was hitherto felt mainly at the state level, to the Central or national level.

On the other hand, in the wake of the political and economic crisis of the mid-1960s there emerged a strong strand of agrarian radicalism in large parts of the country. The Naxalite Movement led by the CPI (ML) peaked in West Bengal and parts of Andhra Pradesh, Orissa and Bihar towards the end of the 1960s. The year 1970, and in some cases like in West Bengal the preceding few years, saw a widespread 'land grab' movement by the landless in many parts of the country under the leadership of the Communist and Socialist parties. Disturbances were reported from Assam, Andhra Pradesh, Bihar, Gujarat, Punjab, Rajasthan, Tamil Nadu, UP and West Bengal in 1969-70. The total amount of land seized was not very significant and most of the land seized was Government wasteland, land taken over by the Government but not distributed and to some extent homestead land. Also, the movement was effectively suppressed. About 20,000 political activists were arrested. However, despite the very limited success in land seizure and the quick suppression of the movement, on the whole the movement had a significant symbolic effect. The nation's attention was drawn dramatically to the agrarian question.

This was the context in which the second spurt of land reform efforts was to occur in the 1960s and early 1970s. The Land Reform Implementation Committee of the National Development Council met in June 1964 and made sustained efforts to put pressure on the Chief Ministers of the States to plug the loopholes in the land reform legislations and implement them effectively. With the political shift of Mrs. Indira Gandhi to the left in the late 60s, particularly after 1969, these efforts received a further momentum. At a land reform conference of the State Chief Ministers called by Prime Minister, Indira Gandhi, in September 1970, she forcefully argued that social discontent and violence in the countryside had erupted because:[26]

> The land reform measures implemented have failed to match the legitimate expectations which were first fostered among millions of cultivators during the national movement...In short, we have yet to create institutional conditions which would enable small farmers, tenants, and landless labourers to share in the agricultural New Deal.

Reduction of ceiling limits was one of the main issues discussed in the Conference with most of the Chief Ministers rejecting such a proposal outright. The matter was referred to the Central Land Reforms Committee, which was to look into this and other contentious issues that emerged in the Conference. In August 1971, the Committee made a series of recommendations including a substantial reduction in the ceiling limits, withdrawal of exemptions such as those in favour of 'efficient' or mechanised farms and making ceilings applicable to the family as a unit and not to individuals as was the case in most states.

The Congress, now further strengthened after the electoral victories of 1971 and 1972, was able to get the Chief Ministers' Conference held in July 1972 to approve new national guidelines following months of bitter opposition. The new guidelines were based essentially on the August 1971 recommendations of the Central Land Reforms Committee. Some of the important features of the July 1972 guidelines, which marked a break in the history of ceiling legislation in India, were:

1. The ceiling for double-cropped perennially irrigated land was to be within the range of 10 to 18 acres, it was 27 acres for single cropped land and 54 acres for inferior drylands.
2. Ceiling was to be applicable to a family as a unit of five members, (husband, wife and three minor children). Additional land per additional member could be permitted for families

which exceeded this number but upto a maximum limit of double the ceiling for the five member unit.

3. In the distribution of surplus land, priority was to be given to landless agricultural workers, particularly those belonging to the scheduled castes and scheduled tribes.
4. Compensation payable for surplus land was to be fixed well below market price so as to be within the capacity of the new allottees.

Following the 1972 guidelines most states (barring some north-eastern states and Goa which had no ceiling laws) passed revised ceiling legislation lowering the ceiling limits within the range prescribed in the guidelines. Resistance to the ceiling laws and efforts to evade the ceiling continued in a variety of ways. A common method was to seek judicial intervention on a number of grounds. Hundreds of thousands of ceiling cases were filed in the courts all over the country. One estimate mentions 5,00,000 pending cases in Andhra Pradesh alone!

In an attempt to stem this menace the Government got the 34th Amendment to the Constitution passed in Parliament in August 1974, getting most of the revised ceiling laws included in the Ninth Schedule of the Constitution so that they could not be challenged on constitutional grounds.

While the renewed effort of the 1970s did lead to some progress in surplus land being redistributed, the overall results were still far from satisfactory. As a result of the ceiling laws of the 1970s, an additional area of about 2.27 million acres of land was distributed by the early 1980s, but, quite symptomatic of the resistance to the entire effort at ceiling reform, an estimated 32.25 million acres of land was willfully dispersed to avoid ceilings.

Nevertheless, by March 1985, 7.2 million acres were declared surplus out of which 4.3 million acres were distributed to about 3.3 million beneficiaries. Moreover, more than half, 54.6 percent of the beneficiaries were members of the scheduled castes and scheduled tribes who received about 43.6 percent of the area distributed.

However, an important impact of the ceiling laws, and perhaps in the long run the most critical one, was that it killed the land market and prevented an increasing concentration in landholdings through depeasantisation. As the eminent scholar of Indian agriculture and policymaker, C.H. Hanumantha Rao, puts it, 'The law discouraged concentration of landownership beyond the ceiling level and thus prevented the possible dispossession of numerous small and marginal holders which would probably have occurred through a competitive process in the land market in the absence of a ceiling on landholdings.'[27]

Also, though the opportunity to acquire large areas of surplus lands for redistribution was missed because of the stiff resistance to the ceiling laws, in the long run the high population growth and the rapid subdivision of large holdings over several generations (in the absence of the practice of primogeniture for inheritance in India) led automatically to little land remaining over the ceiling limits. In fact the number of holdings and the area operated under the category of large holdings, 25 acres or above (even 15 acres and above) kept falling in the decades since independence right upto the 1990s. Except in certain small pockets in the country, very large landholdings of the semi-feudal type are now things of the past. Inequality among landowners was no longer a key issue, as it was not very skewed any more. By one estimate, by 1976-77 nearly 97 percent of the operated holdings were below 25 acres and 87 percent of the holdings were below 10 acres.[28] The problem of the landless or the near landless, who it is estimated constituted nearly half the agricultural population still required urgent attention.

However, any further attempt at land redistribution through lowering of ceilings was not politically feasible or even economically viable. Given the adverse land man ratio in India and particularly given (unlike many other countries with similar ratios) the fact that a very high proportion of the population continued to be dependent on agriculture (nearly 67 percent of the total workforce was engaged in agriculture in 1991) and that consequently the number of potential competitors for land was very large, any attempt to further reduce ceilings to provide land for the landless labourers would vastly increase the number of uneconomic and unviable holdings. Also, it would range the entire, now very powerful and politically important, landowning classes against any regime which tried to do so. Perhaps the only viable programme left for the landless was the one, which was to some extent taken up, of distributing homestead lands or even just home sites, ensuring the payment of minimum wages, as well as providing security of tenure and fair rents to share croppers and tenants.[29] Other answers were to be found in increasing off-farm employment in rural areas, in increasing animal husbandry and other activities associated with cultivation but not requiring land.

Cooperatives

A wide spectrum of the Indian national movement including Mahatma Gandhi, Jawaharlal Nehru, the Socialists and Communists was agreed that cooperativisation would lead to major improvement in Indian agriculture and would particularly benefit the poor. Cooperativisation was therefore seen as an important element in the agenda for institutional changes sought to be achieved through land reform. However, as in the case of the land ceiling issue, there was no general consensus in the nation, particularly among the peasantry, on the question of cooperatives and hence the movement had little success in terms of cooperative farming.

The service cooperatives, which fared much better than the farming cooperatives, also suffered from some major shortcomings requiring constant efforts to ensure that they met the objectives set out by the planners. To begin with, the service cooperatives not only reflected the iniquitous structure of the Indian countryside but also tended to reinforce it. Typically the leadership of the cooperatives, i.e., its president, secretary and treasurer, consisted of the leading family or families of the village which not only owned a great deal of land but also controlled trade and moneylending. These well to do families, the 'big people' or the 'all in alls' of the village, were thus able to corner for themselves scarce agricultural inputs including credit. In fact, quite often, low interest agricultural credit made available through cooperative rural banks was used by such families for non-agricultural businesses, consumption and even moneylending! It was a case of public subsidy being used by a non target group for private investment. To the extent that the Congress and other political formations with similar objectives, *viz.*, the Socialists and the Communists, failed to use the political space provided at the grassroots level by the *panchayats*, the Community Development Programme and the cooperatives in favour of the underprivileged in the countryside by mobilising them into action, these institutions were taken over by the dominant sections in the village, who used them to further buttress their economic and political influence.

The village poor, the landless, got little out of these institutions in the early years. An example at hand is the constant refusal to implement the elaborate recommendation made by the Reserve Bank of India in 1954 that rural credit cooperatives were to give credit to the cultivator as the producer of a crop and not as the owner of land. This refusal of the cooperatives to issue 'crop loans' or loans in anticipation of the crop being produced, and their insisting on credit being given against land as security, meant that the landless were essentially excluded from this scheme. In 1969 the Reserve Bank observed that tenant cultivators, agricultural labourers and 'others' secured only 4 to 6 percent of the total credit disbursed. The Report of the All-India Credit Review Committee, 1969 and the Interim Report on Credit Services for Small and Marginal Farmers produced by the National Commission on Agriculture, 1971, confirmed the virtual exclusion of the landless and added that the small and marginal farmers were also at a considerable disadvantage *vis-à-vis* the bigger cultivators in accessing credit from the cooperatives and even from the nationalised banks. As we shall see presently, it required a special targeting of these groups through programmes like the Marginal Farmers and Landless Labourers Scheme (MFAL) and the Small Farmers Development Agency (SFDA) under the broad rubric of the 'garibi hatao' (remove poverty) campaign launched by Indira Gandhi, for this bias to be considerably mitigated.

A common shortcoming of the cooperative movement in India was that what was to be a popular movement involving people's participation soon became like a huge overstaffed Government department with officials, clerks, inspectors, etc., replicated at the block, district, division and state levels. A large bureaucracy generally not in sympathy with the principles of the cooperative movement and quite given to being influenced by local vested interests, instead of becoming the instrument for promoting cooperatives, typically became a hindrance.

Yet, over time the service cooperatives, particularly the credit cooperatives, performed a critical role for Indian agriculture. After all, while in 1951-52 the Primary Agricultural Credit Societies (PACS), which were village level cooperative societies, advanced loans worth only about Rs. 23 crores (230 million), in 1960-61 about 212 thousand such societies disbursed nearly Rs. 200 crore (2 billion). By 1992-93 these societies were lending as much as Rs. 4,900 crore (49 billion).

As Table 5.2 shows, in 1951-52 cooperatives supplied only 3.3 percent of the credit requirements of the cultivator, whereas by 1981 they supplied nearly 30 percent. Seen in another way, we find that in 1951 the cultivator was dependent on non-institutional and generally rapacious sources of credit such as the moneylender, trader or landlord for 92.7 percent of his credit requirements. By 1981, however, low cost institutional credit looked after over 63 percent of the cultivator's requirements. Nearly 30 percent was met by the cooperatives and another nearly 30 percent was met by the commercial banks which, after their nationalisation in July 1969 by Indira Gandhi, were prevailed upon to provide credit to agriculture on a priority basis.

The cooperative credit societies, however, suffered from a major drawback, that of failure to repay loans and consequently a very large percentage of overdues. Between 1960 and 1970 overdues of the primary societies rose from 20 to 38 percent of the credit disbursed. The situation continued to deteriorate with the all India average of overdues rising to 45 percent in the mid-1970s and many provinces reaching totally unviable figures, like 77 percent in Bihar. Quite significantly, it has been observed that the defaulters were not necessarily the poor and small farmers but more often the well to do ones. With the growing political and economic clout of the well to do peasants, the problem of overdues had reached dangerous proportions, affecting the viability and growth rate of rural credit institutions. (Populist measures like the decision of V.P. Singh's National Front Government in 1990 to write off all rural debts upto Rs. 10,000 not only put a heavy burden on the national exchequer but further eroded the viability of rural credit institutions.)

Table 2

Different Sources of Credit for the Cultivator 1951-1981

(figures in percentages)

	1951-52	*1971*	*1981*
Moneylender, trader, landlord, etc.	92.7	68.3	36.8
Cooperative	3.3	22.0	29.9
Commercial Banks	0.9	2.6	29.4
Government	3.1	7.1	3.9

Source: All India Debt and Investment Survey, 1961-62, 1981. (Cited in Ruddar Datt *et al., Indian Economy*. p. 469.)

As mentioned above, one positive result of the concerted effort in the early 1970s to reach institutional benefits to the rural poor was that a much larger proportion of cooperative and bank credit started becoming available, particularly to the small and marginal farmers. In 1979-80 about 34 percent of the short-term loans given by scheduled commercial banks went to households holding less than 2.5 acres, when such households constituted only 33 percent of the total households. Similarly, 57 percent of such loans went to households owning up to five acres, while the proportion of households in that category was only 49 percent. No longer was institutional rural credit the preserve of the rural elite. Policy initiatives were to follow which led to the rural banks giving a much higher proportion of the credit to the weaker sections. As for the cooperatives (PACS), those with holdings up to 5 acres received 34 percent of the credit and those holding above 5 acres received 62 percent. The situation of the landless however remained the same, only 4 percent of the credit went to them.[30]

It is thus evident that service cooperatives had started to play a very important role in rural India. Their role in making available a much increased amount of cheap credit to a wider section of the peasantry was critical. They not only helped in bringing improved seeds, modern implements, cheap fertilisers, etc., to the peasants, they also provided them with the wherewithal to access them. And, in many areas they also helped market their produce. In fact in many ways they provided a necessary condition for the success of the 'Green Revolution' strategy launched in the late 1960s, which was based on intensive use of modern inputs in agriculture. It is not surprising then that Wolf Ladejinsky, who was fully aware of all the shortcomings of the cooperative movement in India, was to record in his annual note to the World Bank in May 1972: 'millions of farmers have benefited from them (cooperatives) and rural India without this landmark is hard to visualise'.[31]

VII

The Green Revolution

The two wars with China (1962) and Pakistan (1965) and two successive drought years in 1965-66 led to fall in agricultural output by 17 percent and food output by 20 percent. Consequently food prices shot up, rising at the rate of nearly 20 percent per annum between 1965 and 1968. India was forced to import more than 10 million tonnes of food grain in 1966. It is in this moment of crisis with famine conditions emerging in various parts of the country especially Bihar and UP, that the USA threatened to renege on commitments of food exports to India. The Indo-Pak War, India's stand on Vietnam and the desire to arm twist India into accepting an economic policy package favoured by the USA had convinced President Johnson that India should be put 'on a short leash' and what better way to do it than to cynically use India's desperate dependence on USA for food!

Given this scenario of the mid-1960s, economic self-reliance and particularly food self-sufficiency became the top priority objective of Indian economic policy and for that matter of foreign policy. The New Agricultural Strategy began to be implemented in right earnest. The then Prime Minister, Lal Bahadur Shastri, Food Minister, C. Subramaniam, and Indira Gandhi, who followed Shastri in 1966 after his brief tenure, all gave full support to and crafted this basic transition in the strategy for developing Indian agriculture. The World bank appointed Bell Mission recommended such a transition and the USA pressed in its favour but they appear to have been 'leaning on open doors' as a considerable consensus in favour of such a change had emerged within India. Critical inputs like High Yield Variety (HYV) seeds (the suitability to Indian conditions of the high yielding Mexican dwarf wheat proved to be an extremely timely scientific breakthrough), chemical fertilisers and pesticides, agricultural machinery including tractors, pump sets, etc., soil testing facilities, agricultural education programmes and institutional credit were concentrated on areas which had assured irrigation and other natural and institutional advantages. Some 32 million acres of land, about 10 percent of the total cultivated area, was thus initially chosen for receiving the package programme benefits on top priority.

Government investment in agriculture rose significantly. Institutional finance made available to agriculture doubled between 1968 to 1973. The Agricultural Prices Commission was set up in 1965 and efforts were made to see that the farmer was assured a market at sustained remunerative prices. Public investment, institutional credit, remunerative prices and the availability of the new technology at low prices raised the profitability of private investment by farmers and as a result the total gross capital formation in agriculture began to grow faster. This was reflected in, for example, the rate of increase in the gross irrigated area rising from about one million hectares per annum in the pre-Green Revolution period to about 2.5 million hectares per annum during the 1970s. Also, between 1960-61 and 1970-71 the number of electric and diesel pump sets increased from 421,000 to 2.4 million, tube wells increased from 90,000 to 460,000 and tractors from 31,000 to 140,000. Also, consumption of chemical fertilisers, nitrogen, phosphorus and potassium, increased from 306,000 metric tonnes in 1960-61 to 2,350,000 in 1970-71. Most of this increase occurred in the second half of the period.

The results of this new strategy began to be witnessed within a short period. Between 1967-68 and 1970-71 food grain production rose by 35 percent. Again, between 1964-65 and 1971-72 aggregate food production increased from 89 to 112 million tonnes, calculated to be a 10 percent per capita increase. Net food imports fell from 10.3 million tonnes 1966 to 3.6 million in 1970, while food availability increased from 73.5 million tonnes to 89.5 million tonnes over the same period. It has been estimated that' 'But for the new agricultural strategy India would have to import a minimum of about 8 to 10 million tons of wheat yearly at a cost of $600 to 800 million.'[32] Food availability continued to increase sharply to 110.25 million tonnes in 1978 and 128.8 million tonnes in 1984 putting an end to India's 'begging bowl' image. By the 1980s not only was India self-sufficient in food with buffer food stocks of over 30 million tonnes but was even exporting food to pay back earlier loans or as loans to food deficit countries. It was this comfortable food situation which enabled India to successfully deal with the severe and widespread droughts of 1987 and 1988 without large scale foreign help as was needed in the mid-1960s. By the end of 1990s food grain production in India was nearly 200 million tonnes, up from 51 million tonnes in 1950-51, a growth rate of about 3 percent, ahead of the high population growth rate of 2.1 percent.

A major impact of the Green Revolution strategy was that through increases in agricultural yields it enabled India to maintain, once again, the high rate of agricultural growth achieved since independence. The average rate of growth achieved between 1949-50 to 1989-90 was about 2.7 percent per annum. In the pre-Green Revolution period, 1949-50 to 1964-65 about 51 percent of the growth in agricultural output was accounted for by increase in area (which grew at 1.61 percent per year) and 49 percent by increase in yield (which grew at 1.5 percent per year), i.e., both area and yield increases were equally important in maintaining growth levels. Once the possibilities of area increases reached a saturation point rapid yield increases became necessary if a similar growth rate was to be maintained. This is what the Green Revolution strategy succeeded in doing. Between 1967-68 and 1989-90 about 80 percent of the growth of agricultural output was explained by increases in yields per acre (which grew at 2.5 percent per year) while increase in acreage (which grew only at 0.26 percent per year) explained only 20 percent. In fact in recent years virtually the entire output growth has been attributed to increases in yield, as agricultural acreage has remained stagnant and even shrunk.

It must be recognised that, apart from the maintaining of the agricultural growth rates, the critical impact of the Green Revolution was that it generated a rapid increase in the marketable surplus of food grains. This aspect has perhaps not been sufficiently highlighted. A number of factors explain why the new agricultural strategy generated large marketable surpluses, such as the fact that the initial breakthrough in food production occurred in the relatively developed regions in northwestern India and parts of southern India where food consumption levels being already high a large proportion of the additional output was marketed; the use of labour per unit of output tended to decline creating a marketable surplus from the rural areas to the extent that the proportion of the output which had to set aside for consumption by labour declined, and the fact that output increases occurred mainly as a result of yield increases and not increases in acreage led to a fall in the need for food grain as seed per unit of output.

It was the marketed surpluses as a result of the Green Revolution (and not any unprecedented rise in aggregate all India growth rates) which enabled internal procurement of food by the government and the building up of large food stocks. The food requirements generated by a strategy of rapid industrial development, the rapidly growing urban and general population and the periodically food deficit areas could now be met internally. The liberation from dependence on PL 480 or other imports for the above was a major step in the direction of self-reliant independent development for India. The other alternative to external dependence, that of forced procurement from the countryside, was never a real option for democratic India.

However, doubts about the new agricultural strategy began to be expressed from the very early stages of its implementation. One persistent argument had been that by concentrating resources on the regions that already had certain advantages the Green Revolution strategy was further accentuating regional inequality. Clearly the solution to such fears lay in spreading the Green Revolution further and not opposing it *per se*. Recent works of scholars such as G.S. Bhalla[33] show that instead of promoting further inequality, the Green Revolution over time actually spread to large parts of the country bringing prosperity to these regions. In the first phase of the Green Revolution, 1962-1965 to 1970-1973, an all India compound growth rate of 2.08 percent per year was achieved but it was mainly the result of sharp increases in yield in wheat in the northwestern region of Punjab, Haryana and western UP, which grew at a much faster rate than the average, Punjab registering a stupendous rate of 6.63 percent.

In the second phase, 1970-1973 to 1980-1983, with the extension of HYV seed technology from wheat to rice, the Green Revolution spread to other parts of the country, notably east UP, Andhra Pradesh, particularly the coastal areas, parts of Karnataka and Tamil Nadu and so on. Regions like Maharashtra, Gujarat, Andhra Pradesh now grew much faster than the all India growth rate of 2.38 percent per year.

The third phase of the Green Revolution, 1980-1983 to 1992-1995, showed very significant and encouraging results. The Green Revolution now spread to the erstwhile low growth areas of the Eastern region of West Bengal, Bihar, Assam and Orissa, with West Bengal achieving an unprecedented growth rate of 5.39 percent per annum. Other regions, particularly the southern region and Madhya Pradesh and Rajasthan of the central region grew rapidly as well. In fact for the first time the southern region registered a higher rate of growth than the northwestern region. By the end of the third phase, the coefficient of variation of the output growth levels and yield (per hectare) levels between the various states had fallen substantially compared to earlier decades. This period therefore saw not only a marked overall (all India) acceleration of the growth of agricultural output touching an unprecedented growth rate of 3.4 percent per year, but also witnessed a much more diversified growth pattern considerably reducing regional inequality by increasing the spread of rural prosperity.

In the early stages of the Green Revolution, particularly the early 1970s, a considerable opinion emerged that the Green Revolution was leading to class polarisation in the countryside. It was argued that the class of rich peasants and capitalist farmers were getting strengthened partly at the expense of the small peasants, tenants, etc., who, unable to access the modern inputs, were being pushed into the rank of the landless, i.e., a process of depeasantisation was in progress. Further, the mechanisation of agriculture was displacing labour leading to increasing unemployment and a fall in wages of agricultural labour. In other words, on the whole a process of relative immiserisation of the rural poor and for some sections even absolute immiserisation was taking place, creating conditions for agrarian unrest and revolt. 'The Green Revolution will lead to the Red Revolution' was the catchy slogan doing the rounds in some circles in the late 1960s and early 1970s.

Later events and recent scholarship has shown most of these misgivings to be unfounded, as were the misgivings about regional inequality. From the very beginning of the initiation of the new agricultural strategy there was the awareness that steps will have to be taken to ensure that the poor farmers could access the benefits of the new technology and the agricultural labourers' interests were protected. (It may be noted that the immediate, though somewhat alarmist, warning signals put out by sections of the Indian intelligentsia regarding the negative effects of the new strategy on the poor perhaps contributed to the early consciousness and efforts to prevent such a denouement.) Shortly after the strategy was fully on course a concerted effort was made once again, as part of the 'garibi hatao' campaign launched by Indira Gandhi in the late 1960s and 1970s, to reach the rural poor, small farmers and the landless. A series of programmes such as the Rural Works Programme (RWP), Small Farmers Development Agency (SFDA), Marginal Farmers and Agricultural Labourers Scheme (MFAL), Crash Scheme for Rural Employment (CSRE), The Employment Guarantee Scheme (EGS) in Maharashtra, were launched. The SFDA and the MFAL, for example, identified more than a million small farmers and over half a million marginal farmers who were given short, medium and long-term loans. Small and marginal farmers were also assisted by Government subsidies of 25 percent and 33.3 percent of the investments for which they borrowed, respectively. Millions of poor farmers also benefited from the massive increase in institutional credit made available to agriculture, through cooperative societies, Land Development Banks, nationalised commercial banks, Agricultural Refinance Corporation, etc., with a special effort, which was considerably successful, to see that the credit reached the poorer sections as well. (See section on cooperatives above.)

With all their weaknesses and loopholes these programmes had a considerable cumulative effect. So much so that eminent economist Raj Krishna reported in 1979 that, 'small farmers, as a class, command more productive assets and inputs per unit of land than large farmers.'[34] Though the small farmers with operational holdings of five acres or less cultivated only 21 percent of the total cultivated area, their share of net irrigated area was 31.4 percent, of total fertiliser use was 32 percent and of total agricultural credit 33 percent. The new Green Revolution technology proved to be not only scale neutral but appears to have evolved an inverse relationship between scale and productivity. Small farmers applying more inputs per unit of land compared to large farmers were able to produce 26 percent of the value of agricultural output with 21 percent of the land.

Thus the Green Revolution far from pushing the small farmer into the ranks of the landless actually enabled him to survive. Studies have shown that with the adoption of the new technology, improved seeds and other agricultural inputs the small farmer became relatively more viable and did not have to sell out to the large farmer in distress.[35]

Similarly, the fears of the Green Revolution leading to increasing rural unemployment because of labour displacing mechanisation proved to be baseless from a very early stage. On the basis of a field trip made as early as February 1969 in Punjab, Wolf Ladejinsky (who advised General Mac Arthur in planning land reforms in Japan during the period of allied occupation after the War and after that was closely associated with land reforms in Taiwan, South Vietnam, Nepal, Indonesia, the Philippines and India) reported that with the spread of the new technology 'the demand for casual labour has increased and so have wages and the landless laborer is somewhat better off than in the past.'[36] The 'victims' of tractorisation were bullocks not labour. The net impact of tractorisation taking into account increase in cropping intensity etc., was an increased demand for labour. The fear that that indiscriminate mechanisation in the next, post-tractorisation phase, such as large scale introduction of combine harvesters and threshers would lead to displacement of labour also does not appear to have materialised on a significant scale in any part of the country till today. In Punjab, for example, the number of agricultural labourers is said to have trebled between 1961 and 1981, while the number of landless agricultural households declined. The additional demand for labour was met through large-scale migration of labour from the poorer districts of Eastern UP and Bihar.

Moreover, the general experience of the Green Revolution in region after region—Punjab, Haryana, Coastal Andhra, Maharashtra, Tamil Nadu, etc.,—has been that apart from the growth in agricultural employment, it has generated non-agricultural rural and semi-urban employment, through the development of agro industries, rapid increase in trade and warehousing of agricultural produce and agricultural inputs like fertilisers and pesticides, massive growth of the transport industry, manufacturing of a large range of farm implements and other inputs, heavy demand for repairs and servicing of trucks, tractors, electric and diesel pumps and other modern agricultural equipment and machinery and so on. Since over time almost all the agricultural machinery and equipment was produced indigeneously, mechanisation in agriculture created urban factory employment. Also, the increase in rural incomes following the Green Revolution led to increased demand for masons, carpenters, tailors, weavers, etc., in the rural areas and for factory produced consumer durables from transistor radios, watches, cycles, fans, televisions, washing machines, motorcycles, sewing machines to cars and air conditioners. Since the rural demand for some of these commodities began to exceed the urban demand, forcing their manufacturers to turn their face towards the countryside, its impact on generating urban employment is not inconsequential. It is significant that Punjab saw a striking increase of about 50 percent in urban employment between 1971 and 1981, partly reflecting the impact of development in agriculture in the non-agricultural sector.

However, all the employment generated by the Green Revolution was still not sufficient to meet the employment requirements of the rapidly growing population, a large proportion of which lived in the countryside. Urgent short-term and long-term steps were therefore necessary to deal with this situation. Here, too, the Green Revolution proved critical. The surplus stocks of food grain that became available as a result of the agricultural breakthrough made it possible to launch employment-generating poverty alleviation programmes on a considerable scale, particularly in the agriculturally backward areas. As the agriculture expert and policymaker C.H. Hanumantha Rao put it:[37]

> From about 20 million person-days of employment generated in the mid-Sixties, the employment generated under such programmes in the country as a whole amounted to 850 million person-days in 1988-

> 89. These employment programmes, together with the income generated under the Integrated Rural Development Programme (IRDP), seem to make up for about half the deficiency in employment generation in agriculture in the post-green revolution period...These programmes were made possible because of the increased availability of foodgrains from internal procurement.

The Green Revolution did however contribute to an increase in inequality in the countryside. But the poor too benefited in absolute terms though their well to do neighbours did relatively far better. Yet pursuing a strategy which was more 'equitable' and 'politically correct' but left the rural poor, already living at the edges of survival, worse off would be cruel. Some of the earliest reports of the impact of the new agricultural strategy, such as those of Daniel Thorner based on field visits to Coastal Andhra, Thanjavur in Tamil Nadu, parts of Haryana, West UP, etc., in 1966 and 1967[38] and those of Ladejinsky from Punjab in 1969 confirm that, while inequity increased, the poor including the small peasant and the landless agricultural labourer benefited. Real wages of agricultural labour have consistently risen in areas where the Green Revolution spread. Increase in wages in the high growth areas, such as Punjab, would have been much sharper but for the migration of labour from low wage areas of Bihar and UP. But then not only were the migrant labour beneficiaries of considerably higher wages the wage levels in the areas they came from also tended to rise. Inter-state disparities in agricultural wages, began to decline since the mid-1970s partly because of the migration of labour from the backward regions to the Green Revolution areas.

In sum the Green Revolution had a major impact on rural poverty levels through its impact on food availability, decline in relative prices of food (the most important item of expenditure for the poor), generating of agricultural and non-agricultural employment, rise in wages and so on. The link between the spread of agricultural growth or the Green Revolution to an area and the fall in the numbers of the rural population living below the poverty line in that area is now widely accepted and can be seen to be operating in a large and growing part of the country. With the overwhelming proportion of the Indian population still dependent on agriculture (over two-thirds even today) the critical importance of spreading the Green Revolution type of development as an anti-poverty measure has been widely recognised. (The slowing down in recent years of public investment in irrigation and other infrastructure, which is critical for the spread of rapid agricultural growth, has been widely criticised from this perspective.)

The Green Revolution, therefore, has not spawned any 'Red Revolution' in the countryside.

VIII

Other Indicators of Growing Autonomy

Apart from food self-sufficiency, certain other features emerged in the Indian economy after the crisis of the mid-1960s that pointed towards a greater autonomy of the Indian economy and increased self-reliance. The fiscal deficit was brought down sharply from 7.3 percent of GDP in 1966-67 to 3.8 percent in 1969-70. The balance of payments situation improved considerably with reduced food and other imports, a certain improvement in exports and particularly with the surge in remittances made by Indian workers from the oil boom rich Middle East. By 1978-79, the foreign exchange reserves had risen to a peak of about $ 7.3 billion (including gold and SDRs), more than nine months of imports cover compared to less than two months cover in 1965-66.

Given the arm twisting done by the donors, self-reliance was seen as the need to reduce dependence on foreign aid not only in a crisis situations such as those created by droughts or other natural disasters but also on aid as a short-term means to develop key capabilities as was envisaged in the earlier Nehru-Mahalanobis strategy. Partly as a result of this shift in perspective, foreign aid began to decline rapidly. Net aid as a proportion of net national product (NNP), which had peaked to an average of 4.22 percent during the Third plan (the last few crisis years of the plan partly accounting for this high rate), came down to 0.35 in 1972-73 and rose only slightly after the 1973 oil crisis, but yet averaged not more than 1 percent of NNP till 1977-78. The debt-service ratio, i.e., the annual outflow of interest and repatriation of principal due to existing debt as a proportion of exports of goods and services, fell to a low and easily manageable 10.2 percent in 1980-81 from an estimated 23 percent in 1970-71 and 16.5 percent in 1974-75.

We have already seen that the rapid expansion in the indigeneous capital goods industry, which started in the Nehru years, had greatly reduced India's dependence on the external world for maintaining her rate of investment (and growth) as the share of equipment that needed to be imported in the total fixed capital investment in India had fallen from 43 percent to 9 percent between 1960 and 1974, whereas the value of the fixed investment in India increased by about two and a half times over this period (1960-1974).[39] This autonomy from the advanced countries in determining her own rate of capital accumulation or growth is what gave India the flexibility to have an independent foreign policy and pursue it with vigour as Indira Gandhi did, to the great annoyance of superpowers like the United States and their acolytes.

Private foreign investment, which had always been very low in proportion to total investment, continued to be so. Unlike many Latin American and some East Asian countries, foreign capital or multinational corporations played a very minor role in India. In 1981-1982, only about 10 percent of value added in the factory sector of mining and manufacturing was accounted for by foreign firms which included FERA companies with diluted foreign shareholding. Till the 1980s, most foreign collaborations were technological collaborations without involving any foreign share or equity capital. For example, in 1977-1980, 86.5 percent of technology import agreements did not involve any foreign equity. Foreign capital was marginal in the financial sphere as well. It was negligible in the insurance sector and foreign banks accounted for only 8.9 percent of total deposits in the organised banking sector in 1970. Between 1969 (the year bank nationalisation occurred) and 1981, while the number of branches of all commercial banks in India rose from 8,262 to 35,707, the number of branches of foreign banks rose from 130 to 132. By 1992, the corresponding figures were 60,601 and 140. It must be noted that more than 60 percent of the massive branch expansion of the Indian banks was in the rural areas, not only creating a much wider base for mopping up savings but also for extending credit, including priority credit to agriculture, and that too increasingly to the poorer households as part of the second wave of land reform as discussed above.

Table 3

Gross Domestic Savings and Gross Domestic Capital Formation (As percent of GDP at current market prices)

Annual Average	*Gross Domestic Savings*	*Gross Domestic Capital Formation (Adjusted)*
1950-51 to 1959-60	10.58	11.84
1960-61 to 1969-70	13.53	15.63
1970-71 to 1979-80	18.92	19.06
1975-76 to 1979-80	21.22	20.68
1980-81 to 1989-90	20.03	21.99

Source: Calculated from *Economic Survey*, 1996, GoI.

Thus, while the volume of foreign private investment remained marginal and foreign aid declined and the ratio of foreign savings to total investment remained low and fell throughout the 1970s, the rates of domestic savings and investment increased rapidly. As Table 3 shows, from an average savings rate of 10.58 percent and a rate of gross domestic capital formation or investment of 11.84 percent in the 1950s, the savings and investment rates nearly doubled to 21.22 percent and 20.68 percent respectively between 1975-76 and 1979-80. The 1980s saw further increases in the rates of domestic savings and capital formation, making them comparable to several high growth economies.

The early 1980s also saw a highly successful breakthrough in the import substitution programme for oil under the supervision of the Oil and Natural Gas Commission (ONGC), a public sector organisation. The large loan received from the IMF in this period helped this effort considerably. (Strong critics of this loan, including major intellectuals of a section of the Left, were predicting yet another sell out to 'imperialism' were once again proved wrong. Rather than a sell out the loan which was not even fully taken contributed to increased autonomy rather than external dependence). In 1980-81, domestic production of oil was 10.5 million tonnes and imports 20.6 million tonnes, the oil import bill taking up 75 percent of India's export earnings! With new discoveries at the Bombay High oil fields, by the end of the Sixth Plan (1980-1985), the target of indigeneous production of 29 million tonnes was achieved. As a result, in 1984-85, the net import of oil and oil products was less than a third of the domestic consumption and the oil import bill was also down to a third of export earnings.

By the mid-1970s, the industrial growth rate also started picking up from a low of about 3.4 percent between 1965-1975 to about 5.1 percent between 1975-1985. If the crisis year of 1979-80 was omitted, then the industrial growth rate during 1974-75 to 1978-79 and 1980-81 to 1984-85 was about 7.7 percent per annum. In the 1980s as a whole the industrial growth rate maintained a healthy average of about 8 percent per year. Again it was in the 1980s that the barrier of the low, so-called 'Hindu rate of growth' of 3 to 3.5 percent that India had maintained over the previous two decades was broken and the economy grew at over 5.5 percent. By one estimate the average real GDP growth rate between 1980 to 1989 was an impressive 6 percent.[40]

A new feature of the 1980s was the phenomenal increase in new stock market issues, the stock market thus emerging as an important source of funds for industry. It has been estimated that in 1981 the capital market accounted for only 1 percent of domestic savings, whereas by the end of the 1980s this proportion had increased by about seven times. The new stock issue in 1989 was Rs. 6,500 crore, which was about 7.25 percent of gross domestic savings of 1989-90. Another estimate shows that in 1990 Indian companies raised an unprecedented Rs. 12,300 crore from the primary stock market.

Last, though certainly not the least, Indira Gandhi gave a great push to the Nehruvian goal of making India more self-reliant and less dependent on the advanced countries in the area of science and technology. As pointed out above (Section III), India's stock of scientific and technical manpower increased more than 12 times from 190 thousand to 2.32 million between 1949 and 1977. A spectacular growth by any standards, making India the third largest country in the world in terms of her scientific and technical manpower.

One may add here that she was equally determined that India should create an independent body of knowledge in the area of the social sciences as well, particularly in economics and history. It is with this perspective that the Jawaharlal Nehru University (JNU) was set up in 1969 squashing proposals to set up a university in India with a social science focus but with American sponsorship and an English Vice Chancellor! It is her deep seated anti-imperialism and fierce defence of India's national dignity and sovereignty which made her one of the most widely revered leaders of the third world.

IX

Need for Reform

What was it then which, despite the positive developments since independence discussed above which 'pushed' and 'pulled' India toward economic reform.

Broadly, there were three sets of problems which had emerged internally in the Indian economy over time and which were pushing in the direction of urgent reform. On the other hand certain fundamental changes that had occurred in the international situation and the nature of world capitalism after World War II, particularly since the 1960s and 70s, which 'pulled' in the direction of a change in the protectionist economic strategy successfully adopted by India in the early stages.

First, the excessive state intervention in the so called 'licence-quota *raj*' was leading to the creation of tremendous inefficiency. Prolonged protection to Indian industry from imports by following the import substituting industrialisation (ISI) strategy led to the killing of external competition. Similarly, industrial licensing effectively prevented free internal competition. In the absence of internal and external competition Indian industry grew very inefficient. Other regulations such as the MRTP Act further inhibited industrial development. The Act went against the basic principle of economies of scale, which is at the heart of capitalist development (or for that matter of socialist production). It also punished efficiency, as any company, which expanded due to efficient production, good management and research and development (R&D) would face severe restrictions, including refusal of permission to increase capacity once it crossed a prescribed limit. Again, reserving certain areas for small-scale industries meant excluding these areas from the advantages of scale and larger resources for R&D activities.

Second, the large public sector in India, which controlled 'the commanding heights' of the economy, also began to emerge as a major source of inefficiency. The early emphasis on the public sector was critical to India's industrial development. It is the public sector which entered the core areas, diversified India's industrial structure, particularly with regard to capital goods and heavy industry, and reduced India's dependence on foreign capital, foreign equipment and technology. However, over time, the political and bureaucratic pressure on the public sector undertakings gradually led to many of them running at a loss. They were overstaffed, often headed by politicians who had to be given sinecures, became victims of irresponsible trade unionism and were unable to exercise virtually any efficiency accountability on their employees.

All these factors led to the investment efficiency in India beginning to fall or the incremental capital output ratio (ICOR) rising. Low efficiency or low productivity levels are of critical consequence as economic superiority is established and transfer of surplus from one country to another occurs today not through direct political or economic domination but through processes such as unequal exchange occurring between countries with different productivity levels. Economic thinkers of the Left and the Right are agreed on placing the question of productivity at the centre of any national development. In today's context of rapid globalisation, pursuing excessively autarchic policies in search of autonomy (something a section of the Indian Left and the newly discovered *Swadeshi* path of the Right, such as the RSS, still argues for) may, through fall or stagnation of productivity levels, destroy precisely that autonomy and push the country towards peripheralisation.

The third set of problems, which overcame the Indian economy was the gradual abandoning of fiscal prudence since the late 1970s. In a major economic analysis of the period eminent economists, Vijay Joshi and I.M.D. Little described the 1979 budget during the Janata regime, 'as a watershed marking the change from previous fiscal conservatism.'[41] This led to a situation where the macroeconomic balance, (such as balance between government revenue and expenditure or balance between exports of goods and services and the liabilities caused by imports of goods and services as well as foreign borrowings) which was maintained in India (unlike many other developing countries) with great caution for the first 25 years or so after independence, was being slowly eroded. The gradual erosion of fiscal prudence was reflected in government expenditure rising consistently, mainly because of the proliferation of subsidies and grants, salary increases with no relationship to efficiency or output, overstaffing, and other 'populist' measures such as massive loan waivers or making huge budgetary allocations which were aimed at winning over support of electorally important sections of society rather than at achieving best overall development.

The long-term constraints building up over a few decades that were debilitating the Indian economy combined with certain more recent and immediate factors, emerging out of the crisis in the middle east following Iraq's invasion of Kuwait, to lead to a massive fiscal and balance of payments deficit, climaxing in 1991. The crisis pushed India into taking a big step forward in the process of economic reform which had already begun nearly decade earlier.

There were at the same time changes occurring in the international situation and in the world capitalism system, particularly since the 1960s and 1970s, which was pulling India towards a change in strategy. For example, the export pessimism inherent in the first three plans, a pessimism which, one must recognise, was shared widely by development economists the world over in the 1950s, was no longer necessary.

Some of the important changes that needed to be taken cognisance of were, very briefly, the following: First, the nature of foreign capital and multinational corporations was changing. A process of 'internationalisation of production' had started. Multi-national corporations, instead of just looking for markets or sources of raw material, now looked for cheaper production areas. Instead of creating enclaves in the backward countries, which had backward and forward linkages with the home country (this was the typical colonial pattern), they were now bringing in investments which had major multiplier effects on the local economy, including of technology transfer. Second, along with, and partially as a result of, the above process, there were massive capital transfers between countries, reminiscent of the capital transfers of the 19th century at the height of colonial expansion, but very different in character. The above two processes contributed to the third major international development, that of an unprecedented explosion of world trade. Between the 1950s and 1970s, world output of manufactures increased four times but world trade in manufactures increased 10 times. The percentage of world produce that went for export doubled between 1965 and 1990. What is most significant is that while there was a massive increase in global industrial exports, the Third World was able to rapidly increase its share of total industrial exports, especially since the 1970s, from about 5 percent in 1970 to double the figure in 1983.[42]

The East Asian Miracle, i.e., the rapid industrialisation of the East Asian countries, beginning in the 1960s, which gradually shifted the industrial base of the world from the West to the East, took advantage precisely of these kinds of opportunities of capital and market availability. Japan's example of explosive post-World War II growth was being repeated by South Korea, Taiwan, Singapore, Hong Kong and, more recently, Thailand, Malaysia, China and Indonesia. The four Asian Tigers, South Korea, Hong Kong, Singapore and Taiwan increased their share in world export of manufactures more than five times from 1.5 percent in 1965 to 7.9 percent in 1990. Even the newly industrialising economies (NICs), Indonesia, Malaysia and Thailand increased their share from 0.1 percent to 1.5 percent over the same period.[43]

India did reasonably well till the mid-1960s, basing herself on an inward oriented, import- substitution based strategy. However, she failed to respond adequately to the new opportunities thrown up by the changing world situation despite the availability of the East Asian experience. In fact India's share in world exports actually shrunk from about 2.4 percent in 1948 to 0.42 percent in 1980, rising to a still paltry 0.6 percent by 1994. In contrast, South Korea's manufactured exports, which were negligible in 1962, amounted to four times those of India by 1980.

India thus needed to use the opportunities provided by the changed world situation to reform its economy, participate in the new phase of globalisation, rapidly industrialise and transform its economy, increase income levels and drastically reduce poverty levels, as did many of the East Asian countries.

X

Shift towards Economic Reforms

We have seen above that during the period 1964-1984 Indira Gandhi under her leadership not only successfully dealt with the enormous economic challenges faced by India due to internal and international events but that she did so keeping two critical aspects of the Nehruvian consensus in the forefront. First, she maintained and indeed increased India's economic self-reliance which was the key to keeping her sovereignty intact. Second, she extended the pro-poor orientation of the Nehruvian paradigm to a considerable extent. As for the third critical element, maintaining India's democracy, she was able to achieve all the economic breakthroughs of her period within the democratic framework, though she did get politically pushed into a situation where for a brief period during the emergency days India saw the abrogation of democratic rights. It was an aberration unacceptable to the Indian people and she, respecting the people's verdict, on her own restored full democratic procedure including free elections, a course, dictators are not known to follow.

In pursuing the Nehruvian economic objectives Indira Gandhi initially used nationalisation and the public sector to much greater lengths than Nehru did in his lifetime. However, with internal and external imperatives calling for change (as discussed in the previous section) Indira Gandhi began to take the first steps towards economic reform. The 1970s itself witnessed some, what has been described as, 'reform by stealth', with the rupee, for example, being allowed to depreciate in response to market conditions not by an outright devaluation, which was then politically unviable, but by pegging it to a depreciating sterling. Particularly after her return to power in 1980, Indira Gandhi tried to bring in liberalisation measures, mainly in the area of deregulation of industrial licensing and reduction of restrictions on large 'monopoly' enterprises. Though by the standards of the post-1991 reforms these efforts would appear puny, a glance at the newspapers of the 1980s would suggest that they were seen as quite path-breaking (particularly by the critics) at that time.

The need for reform had been recognised early enough in India. Among economists, Manmohan Singh, Jagdish Bhagwati and others had been arguing for it since the 1960s and 1970s.[44] Other economists, who were closely associated with her as advisers, like Sukhamoy Chakravarti and Arjun Sengupta, had also begun to see the need for change.

Yet, it was many years before the reforms could be launched. This was partly because the internal political situation in India was not suitable for such a shift given the fact that in the late 1960s and 1970s Indira Gandhi was able to stave off the political challenge to her from within the party and outside with the support of a broad spectrum of the Left including many Communists. The Left, particularly at that time, was in no way prepared to accept internal or external liberalisation of the Indian economy. The Left position got further strengthened by the bullying tactics adopted by the United States at that time trying to take advantage of India's economic vulnerability (see Section IV above). Instead of reform one therefore witnessed a further recoiling into a more protectionist and dirigiste economic policy in the late 60s and early 70s. Also, apart form the ideological opposition from the orthodox Left there was a persistent opposition to economic reform from vested interests such as the bureaucracy and sections of business who benefited from the existing system of license and controls, using them to earn a kind of 'rent'.

Another reason why the shift to economic reform took so long in India and, even when it took place, it was not as sharp a turnaround as it was in China in 1978 or the Soviet Union after the mid-1980s was that in a democracy the change from one kind of societal consensus (such as the Nehruvian consensus) to the building up of an alternate consensus (around economic reforms) is a process and not an event, and consequently it has its own dynamic, very different from that operating in a non-democratic or totalitarian society, and inevitably takes longer.

The fiscal and balance of payment crisis of the late 1980s culminating in a crisis situation with the country at the edge of default in 1991, enabled even the minority Government of Narasimha Rao to break through the traditional mindset and attempt an unprecedented comprehensive change in economic strategy at a time when both the ideological opposition and the resistance of the vested interests was at a weak point. But the spade work in the sense of gradually building an alternative consensus had started long ago. Firm beginnings in the direction of reforms were made by Indira Gandhi, an initiative, which was carried forward by Rajiv Gandhi. The election manifesto with which Rajiv Gandhi campaigned had clearly chalked out the strategy of economic reform. After his cruel assassination Narasimha Rao and Manmohan Singh implemented that programme very ably. But this is a story which shall be taken up in the next volume.

Endnotes

1. Dharma Kumar (ed.) (2000). *Cambridge Economic History of India, Vol. II,* Cambridge, 1982 and Tirthankar Roy, *The Economic History of India: 1857-1947*, Oxford University Press, New Delhi, second edition 2006. All references in this paper are to the first edition.
2. For a detailed critique of the resurgent colonial positions see Aditya Mukherjee, "Return of the Colonial In Indian Economic History: The Last Phase of Colonialism in India", Presidential Address, Modern India,

Proceedings of the Indian History Congress, New Delhi, 2007, reprinted in *Social Scientist*, Vol. 36, No. 3-4 and 5-6, Mar.-Apr., and May-June, 2008. The arguments in this chapter draw liberally from this Address and my chapters in Bipan Chandra, Mridula Mukherjee and Aditya Mukherjee, *India Since Independence*, Penguin, New Delhi, 2008

3. Angus Maddison (2007). *The World Economy: Vol. I A Millennial Perspective, Vol.II Historical Statistics*, OECD, 2006, Indian Edition, New Delhi, Table 8b, p. 641.
4. Amartya Sen (1982). *Poverty and Famines: An Essay on Entitlements and Deprivation. Delhi: OUP.* Appendix D, pp. 195-216.
5. Quoted in Bipan Chandra, Mridula Mukherjee, Aditya Mukherjee, *India Since Independence*, *op.cit.*p.19.
6. Aditya Mukherjee and Mridula Mukherjee (1988). "Imperialism and the Growth of Indian Capitalism in the Twentieth Century", *Economic and Political Weekly*, XXIII (II), 12 March. Also reprinted in Ghanshyam Shah (ed.), *Capitalist Development: Critical Essays*, Bombay, 1990 and Aditya Mukherjee in Bipan Chandra, Mridula Mukherjee and Aditya Mukherjee, *India Since Independence, op.cit.*, Chs. 25-33.
7. The figures are all from Table 2 which is based on Angus Maddison, *op.cit.*, p.643 except where indicated. Sivasubramonian and Heston's estimates show an annual growth rate of per capita income between 1914 to 1946 which is somewhat higher at 0.26 and 0.13 respectively but nevertheless prove our point reflecting the sharp contrast between before and after independence. M. Mukherjee's estimates of income growth are much lower than even Maddison's. See R.W. Goldsmith (1983). *The Financial Development of India: 1860-1977.* New Haven: Yale University Press. Table 1.2, p. 4.
8. See K.N. Raj (1965). *Indian Economic Growth: Performance and Prospects.* New Delhi: Allied Publishers. p. 2.
9. West Europe as a whole grew at 1.88 percent between 1973-2001. Maddison, *op.cit.*, p. 643.
10. Figures for 2001-2007 are based on *Economic Survey, 2006-07*, Government of India, New Delhi 2007, Table 1.2, S-4, and Aditya Mukherjee, "Indian Economy in the New Millennium," in Bipan Chandra, Mridula Mukherjee and Aditya Mukherjee (2008). *India Since Independence*, Delhi: Penguin.
11. Goldsmith, *op.cit.*, p. 68.
12. A. Vaidyanathan (1983). "The Indian Economy Since Independence (1947-70)", in Dharma Kumar (ed.), *The Cambridge Economic History of India*, Vol. II, Delhi. p. 961, (emphasis mine).
13. See Aditya Mukherjee (2000). "Planned Development in India 1947-65: The Nehruvian Legacy", in Shigeru Akita (ed.), *South Asia in the 20th Century International Relations.* Tokyo. These figures are from an extremely persuasive piece by Vijay Kelkar (1980). "India and the World

Economy: A Search for Self Reliance", Paper read at Seminar on Jawaharlal Nehru and Planned Development, New Delhi.

14. George Blyn (1966). *Agricultural Trends in India, 1891-1947: Output, Availability, and Productivity.* Philadelphia, p.123 and p.102. See also Goldsmith, *op.cit.,* p.68.
15. See my chapters on Land Reforms and the Green Revolution in Bipan Chandra, Mridula Mukherjee, Aditya Mukherjee, *India Since Independence, op.cit.*
16. See Blyn, *op.cit.,* Table 5.8, p. 119, K. N. Raj, *op.cit.* for the pre and post independence figures respectively.
17. See my chapter "Agricultural Growth and the Green Revolution" in Bipan Chandra, Mridula Mukherjee, Aditya Mukherjee, *India Since Independence, op.cit.*
18. Tirthankar Roy, *op.cit.,* ch.3, e.g. p. 51.
19. See Mridula Mukherjee (2006). *Colonialising Agriculture: The Myth of Punjab Exceptionalism,* New Delhi: Sage, pp.157-62.
20. See for example Irfan Habib (1995). "Colonisation of the Indian Economy 1757-1900", in *Essays in Indian History,* New Delhi, pp. 304-5 and Bipan Chandra, chapter on "The Colonial Legacy" in Bipan Chandra, Mridula Mukherjee, Aditya Mukherjee, *India After Independence,* p. 10.
21. See Aditya Mukherjee (2002). *Imperialism, Nationalism and the Making of the Indian capitalist Class,* New Delhi: Sage. Ch. 4, and Aditya Mukherjee, *Presidential Address...., op.cit.,* p. 36.
22. *Ibid.* and *Economic Survey 2006-07. op.cit.,* Table 1.5, S-9.
23. Calculated from Jagdish Bhagwati and Padma Desai (1970). *India Planning for Industrialisation.* London, p. 74.
24. Bipan Chandra, Mridula Mukherjee, Aditya Mukherjee, *India Since Independence, op.cit.,* Chs. 29-32.
25. L. Rudolph and S.H. Rudolph (1987). *In Pursuit of Lakshmi: The Political Economy of the Indian State.* Chicago.
26. Louis J. Walinsky (ed.) (1977). *Agrarian Reform as Unfinished Business, The selected papers of Wolf Ladejinsky*. OUP, (hereafter Ladejinsky papers), p.483.
27. C.H. Hanumantha Rao, " Agriculture: Policy and Performance", in Bimal Jalan (ed.), *The Indian Economy: Problems and Prospects.* New Delhi: Viking. p.118.
28. D. Bandyopadhyay (1986). "Land Reforms in India: An Analysis", *EPW, Review of Agriculture,* June.
29. Wolf Ladejinsky, otherwise an avid supporter of ceilings and land distribution, came to a similar conclusion in may 1972. *Ladejinsky Papers,* p. 513.
30. The figures in this paragraph are from Rudolph and Rudolph, *In Pursuit of Lakshmi,* Table 42, p. 373.

31. *Ladejinsky Papers,* pp. 505-6.
32. *Ladejinsky Papers,* p. 494
33. See for example, G.S. Bhalla and Gurmail Singh (1997). "Recent Developments in Indian Agriculture: A State Level Analysis", *EPW,* 29 March. The statistics in the rest of the paragraph are taken from this source.
34. Raj Krishna (1979). "Small Farmers Development", *EPW,* 26 May, p. 913.
35. G.S. Bhalla and G.K. Chadha (1982). "Green Revolution and the Small Peasant—A Study of Income Distribution in Punjab Agriculture", *EPW* 15 and 22 May.
36. *Ladejinsky Papers,* pp. 436-440
37. See C.H. Hanumantha Rao (1992). "Agriculture: Policy and Performance", in Bimal Jalan (ed.), *The Indian Economy: Problems and Prospects.* New Delhi: Viking. pp. 128-29.
38. See Daniel Thorner, *The Shaping of Modern India,* pp. 202 ff. and 224 ff.
39. See f.n. 13 above.
40. C. Rangarajan (1998). "Development, Inflation and Monetary Policy", in Isher J. Ahluwalia and I.M.D. Little, (eds.), *India's Economic Reforms and Development: Essays for Manmohan Singh.* Delhi: OUP. p. 59.
41. Vijay Joshi and I.M. D. Little (1994). *India: Macroeconomics and Political Economy. 1964-1991.* Delhi: OUP. p. 58.
42. See E.J. Hobsbawm (1994). *Age of Extremes: The Short Twentieth Century.* Harmondsworth: Penguin, for a brilliant analysis of the changes in world capitalism since World War II.
43. See World Bank (1993). *The East Asian Miracle: Economic Growth and Public Policy.* New York: Oxford University Press. p. 38.
44. See Jagdish Bhagwati and Padma Desai, *op.cit.,* and Jagdish Bhagwati (1994). *India in Transition: Freeing the Indian Economy.* Delhi.

Chapter V

Foreign Policy Challenges 1964-1984

V.P. Dutt

India faced enormous challenges in foreign policy virtually all through 1964-1984. There were serious issued posed and contentions marked relations with virtually every important region and country India was reacting with. There were direct challenges to India's security and territorial integrity as well as indirect challenges to its basic interests. It required resilience and willingness to make sacrifices to adequately respond to the threats that came directly and the challenges that loomed prominently but somewhat tangentially and that required diplomatic finesse rather than a military response.

Independent India's first Prime Minister Jawaharlal Nehru, died on 27 May 1964 and was succeeded by Lal Bahadur Shastri. The country was facing a serious economic situation. But hardly had a year passed when it was confronted with a severe military threat from Pakistan. General Ayub Khan, President of Pakistan, stirred the hornet's nest, first in the Rann of Kutch in April 1965 and then launched a serious infiltration offensive in Kashmir on 5 August 1965 and, frustrated by failure, started a major war with India in September, but met with serious setbacks. There were heavy casualties on both sides, although more on the Pakistan side; but more particularly the losses in Pakistan's much-vaunted heavy armour was a severe blow to its army's pride.[1]

Pakistan also believed that Lal Bahadur Shastri was a weak Prime Minister, but Shastriji proved otherwise. With his slogan of 'Jai Jawan Jai Kisan', he galvanised the country and frustrated Pakistan's plans. The United Nations Security Council (UNSC) stepped in and on 22 September unanimously passed a resolution that called for an unconditional ceasefire. Thus the war ended, but peace had yet to be ensured. Unlike in previous times, it was the Soviet Union that decided to take the initiative between India and Pakistan.

Prime Minister Alexei Kosygin invited the leaders of India and Pakistan, Shastri, Prime Minister of India, and Ayub Khan, President of Pakistan, to Tashkent, then part of Soviet Uzbekistan and now capital of the Uzbek republic, the independent state, to reach a peace agreement. With considerable nudging from the Soviet Prime Minister the two leaders signed an agreement on 10 January 1966 that came to be known as the Tashkent Declaration, providing that the forces of the two countries would pull back to the pre-war positions, economic and diplomatic relations would be restored and the two leaders would work towards building good relations between the two countries, emphasising the principle of non-interference in each other's affairs.[2]

The Soviet intervention between India and Pakistan carried both positive and negative implications for India. The Soviet Union was a friendly country. It did not nurture preconceived biases against India, unlike some of the Western countries. It was not therefore intentionally going to harm Indian interests. If it could prevail upon Pakistan to adopt a reasonable and non-aggressive attitude towards India, it would be a gain for all. But there was apprehension in India whether the Soviet Union understood fully the Pakistani situation and motivations.

The Pakistani establishment was a great one in conveying different things at different places. To USA, the plea was that Pakistan had taken great risks in aligning with the West and should therefore be supported against India which had become non-aligned. To the Chinese the approach was very simple. They had no enmity against China but were merely reacting to the fear of Indian dominance and India's attempt to undo Pakistan. If they abused communism, it was really their way of getting even with Nehru. They could offer similar arguments to Russia. The Indian apprehension was whether Russia fully comprehended the complete picture.

Tragically, Shastri died of a massive heart attack the day after he signed the Tashkent Declaration. In his place Indira Gandhi was elected as the Prime Minister of India. She had a three-pronged fight in her hands, no sooner had she taken office. On one front was the internal political struggle, on second front the domestic situation and on the third and linked with the second was its impact on foreign policy and the challenges that were posed to the independent foreign policy of India. We are here concerned only with the last two, as the internal political struggles within the Congress Party are outside the ambit of this study.

Challenges in Relations with USA

A daunting domestic economic situation awaited Mrs. Gandhi as she assumed office. Conflict (China) and war (1965 Indo-Pakistan) had wreaked havoc on the economic situation. In addition, the country's woes were made worse by floods and drought during 1965-1967. A famine-like situation stared the people in the face. India became heavily, almost terminally, dependent on food imports from the West, chiefly from the United States. As it was said, the country lived from ship to mouth. This also put severe restraints on India's independent foreign policy.

It was under these forbidding circumstances that Mrs. Indira Gandhi undertook her first trip abroad—to the United States to ensure more regular supply of food grains and to establish a more durable relationship with the United States. The experience of the conflict with China had left behind a huge mass of bitterness that made a closer relationship with the United States a more desirable and feasible objective. She appeared to share these perceptions and was proceeding on her visit to USA (28 March to 1 April 1966) with high expectations, but this also turned out to be a painful lesson for her in international politics, or real politic.

She had gone there with the themes of joint commitment to democracy, India's developmental efforts within a free political system and the danger of the Chinese drive towards hegemony in Asia.[3] But the public reception given to her by the US administration was different from the private pressure exercised by it. In public President Lyndon B. Johnson was stated to have said in so many words: 'Give this girl whatever she needs.' Mrs. Gandhi told this writer in a special interview, Johnson tried to pressurise India and sat on its requests for speedy food shipments for sometime in order to bring about a modification of her relationship with the Soviet Union.[4]

Another issue that irritated Johnson greatly was Vietnam and the approach of India and other non-aligned countries towards it. Because of urgent domestic requirements. India's stance was somewhat moderated and there was a slurring over the American escalation of the war and its extension into North Vietnam. Mrs. Gandhi expressed the need for a political settlement and the contribution that a cessation of the bombing of North Vietnam would make towards a political settlement, but told the National Press Club that she was impressed in her talks with President Johnson by the sincerity of the President for a peaceful settlement.

But the lesson was both loud and clear and salutary as well. Self-reliance became an important element in the perception of Mrs. Gandhi. A new strategy of achieving self-sufficiency in food grains through massive inputs was launched at first dimly and then more clearly the impossibility of adhering to an independent foreign policy while suing for food grains was realised.

However, during 1966-1969 India needed to import a fairly large quantity of food grains, fertilisers, edible oil and many other essential items, many of them imported from the US, and Public law 480 (PL 480) became the symbol of India's dependence. In 1966 alone India had imported 1 million tonnes of grains from USA. It had also imported some 650,000 lakh tonnes of fertiliser in 1967, 45,000 lakh in 1968 and 200,000 in 1969 from the United States. Food imports began tapering off by 1969. When Mrs. Gandhi became Prime Minister, USA was the largest economic donor to India, contributing about Rs. 1602.5 crore, of this 648.8 crore in grants, Rs. 829.4 crore as loans repayable in dollars, and Rs.1124 crore on local currency repayment basis. Only 32 percent of the American aid involved repayment in foreign exchange and the bulk of this carried low rates of interest and repayable over a period of 40 years. As a result Washington came to hold enormous amounts of Indian currency that took many years of difficult negotiations to sort out.

We may also note that already by this time the Soviet Union was providing aid to the tune of Rs. 484 crore, the second highest of the aid givers, followed by West Germany (Rs. 445 crore), Britain (Rs. 345 crore), Japan (Rs. 273 crore), Italy (Rs. 81 crore), Czechoslovakia (Rs. 63 crore), France (Rs. 57 crore), Canada (Rs. 48 crore) and Poland (Rs. 40 crore). We may also note that US aid at this time, very useful as it was, generally went into areas like power, transport and surplus foodstuffs and agricultural products and the supply of fertilisers and other essential materials.[5] But this assistance though very important was not available for heavy industry. For that India had to turn to the Soviet Union. Of that later.

So the foreign policy challenges and the domestic challenges became intertwined. Resolving the latter helped the former. The domestic challenge of food self-sufficiency became the first priority of Mrs. Gandhi's government. The green revolution that was ushered in ending the era of large-scale food imports could be credited as perhaps her biggest achievement as it not only relieved the suffering of the people, but gave substance and muscle to India's independent foreign policy.

We may now take stock of the various strands in Mrs. Gandhi's foreign policy as they took shape and developed between 1966 and 1971. The strategy that she gradually worked out revolved around a number of elements and factors. So far as the question of foreign technology was concerned, it was needed to modernise the country. The government had to find a balance between the requirements for foreign aid, technology and investments and the objective of self-sufficiency. This became both a foreign policy and a domestic policy exercise, with the balance sometimes shifting towards one or the other side depending on the economic situation and the domestic balance of forces.

Another element in the new foreign policy strategy was to develop, strengthen and advance relations with the non-aligned and developing countries. India believed at the time that this was its area of operation. India's history, geography and past experience influenced its tilt towards the newly emerging and poorer countries of the world. India was one of the founders of the non-aligned movement. In their unity the non-aligned found greater strength and leverage. Even if they were not so united, they helped moderate the European conflicts and even if this was a marginal role, it was worthwhile in the maintenance of their newly won independence. But it needs some emphasis that non-alignment was an instrument of foreign policy, the product of a particular period in history. It was not coterminous with foreign policy, but a tool to fashion an independent course and maximise the advantages for the country.

Mrs. Gandhi continued India's policy of forging closer relations with Asian (including Arab) and African countries. Among the non-aligned, Jawaharlal Nehru had developed a special relationship with President Tito of Yugoslavia and Nasser of Egypt. Even when India faced severe economic difficulties during 1966-1968 and was seeking US aid for tiding over the crisis, among the first countries visited by Mrs. Gandhi were Yugoslavia (now reduced to Serbia) and the then UAR (now again limited to Egypt) in July 1966.[6]

The Third Tripartite conference of Yugoslavia, UAR and India was held in New Delhi in October 1966. The deliberations reflected the concerns of the three countries on the pressures applied on the newly independent and emerging countries, the visible and the invisible forms of imperialism and neo-colonialism, the threat to world peace by gross interference in the internal affairs of impendent countries and the use of economic and financial assistance for dominance. The three leaders expressed their 'deep concern' at the 'dangerous situation in South-east Asia' and the 'sufferings' of the Vietnamese people. They demanded a cessation of the bombing of North Vietnam, withdrawal of all foreign forces, the implementation of the Geneva accords and the participation of the South Vietnamese Liberation front for a peaceful revolution of the conflict in Vietnam.[7]

These statements were bound to anger Lyndon Johnson's administration. Even though for some of the period in the early 1960s India learned somewhat towards the United States, but despite the trauma of the Sino-Indian conflict and the early efforts of Mrs. Gandhi to achieve a new relationship, and despite the dire need to import foodstuffs from USA and the various economic difficulties during 1965-

1968, India and the United States could not overcome their differences or to keep them from souring their relations. These continued to be caught up in a declining curve in the subsequent developments: US arms supply to Pakistan, the Middle Eastern conflicts and the war in Vietnam. In the wars in West Asia, India was on the side of the Arabs, while Washington became the mainstay of Israel. In the case of Vietnam, India regarded the struggle there as basically a nationalist struggle and Vietnam as an emerging counterfoil to China. The US officialdom at the time, and even more so in view of American reverses, was hypersensitive about any expression of sympathy with Vietnam.

The relations between the two countries clearly headed towards another troubled phase. With appreciable increase in agricultural production, and the overcoming of the effects of the severe droughts in the years 1964 and 1965, and as a result of the crash measures taken to boost agriculture, the country's confidence returned that found its reflection in foreign policy and saw its rapid return to its old moorings. The seeds of discord with the US were already present, for over a long period of time, the world outlook of the two countries, their perception of their interests in this part of the world and their conceptual framework had been at divergence. Their conceptual frameworks rarely coincided except for a brief period after the Chinese attack. Whether it was non-alignment, the peace area approach, the cold war, the Indian Ocean, questions about colonialism, the international political and economic order, their outlooks had been wide apart. What should be done in South Asia, Southeast and West Asia or in Africa, etc., the two countries did not generally see eye to eye. But above all, the United States' stance in this subcontinent with its immediate and wider ramifications for the political and security interests of India, chiefly the persistent attempt to enforce an artificial parity between India and Pakistan, combined with the divergence in policies towards other important areas and issues clouded their relations and kept them at loggerheads.

The United States' approach towards this subcontinent was determined largely by the overall strategy of the Western bloc and, atleast initially by British experience and advise. Americans frequently bowed to the 'superior wisdom' and experience of the British in regard to their erstwhile colonies in the subcontinent. The concept of divide and rule and a balance of power approach towards the two major countries of the subcontinent was borrowed from the British and carried forward even more single-mindedly by successive US administration. The cold war reinforced this approach.

Pakistan's entrance into the Western military alliance and the provision of military facilities confirmed American assumption for support to Pakistan. No matter how much India protested that Pakistan had no intention of using the arms aid against China or Russia and that, arms would really be fired only against India, it cut no ice with Washington because America's strategic interests demanded alignment with a willing Pakistan. This gave the US a valuable foothold in South Asia, bases for extending the network of its military alliance system from Europe to Middle East to Southeast Asia and launching pads for overflights over China and the USSR to serve their security needs. It also provided a useful lever of pressure against a recalcitrant India that flaunted its independence. Although US alignment with Pakistan got a bit frayed during the 1960s and USA actually stopped the supply of military hardware to Pakistan in the wake of the Indo-Pakistan war of 1965, it was only a question of time before USA would resort once again to its old logic of drawing Pakistan into its strategic embrace and resume military aid. Richard Nixon became President in 1969 and if the US had stuck to its proclaimed new policy in Asia, including India, USA and India would have formed a much greater area of convergence of perceptions. Nixon was believed to have held the view that any failure of the Indian democracy would be 'a disaster of world-wide proportion'.[8] He had also moved away from his earlier brand of anti-communism and in an article in *Foreign Affairs* (October-December 1967) he had outlined a policy of not wishing to thrust American concepts on Asian countries who should solve their own problems. American aid would still be provided but Nixon now believed—in theory at least—that the US should not involve itself in any country's internal problems. Yet Nixon soon embarked upon a policy of creating a new equation, partly with the good offices of Pakistan, with China and was therefore pursuing a course that soon enough came into conflict with India's basic interests.

But the causes of the troubled relationship ran deeper. Among others, they encompassed US and Indian approaches and assessments towards Vietnam, West Asia and Pakistan and then to some extent China as well. In West Asia, India came out strongly in support of the struggle of the people of Palestine for a homeland, while the US gave unstinted support to Israel. About Vietnam, we have already noted the divergence in approach. It became aggravated because of the sensitivity of the Johnson administration in a losing war. In what was obviously an attempt at arm-twisting and applying more pressure on India, the US authorities let it be known that Washington proposed to lift the arms embargo on Pakistan imposed soon after the September 1965 Indo-Pak war. The then Secretary of State William P. Rogers declared at a press conference in Washington that the US Government had made a study to ascertain how many times they had been able to influence the policy of another government by withholding military aid and 'we find that it has not been successful in any instance.' A Government of India spokesperson criticised such a move as contrary to India's interests and to the interests of peace and stability in this area. The spokesperson added that what the Americans should go into was not in how many cases the stoppage of military aid was able to change the course of policy of the other country but that in how many cases the aid was used for the ostensible purpose for which it was given.[9]

The persistent US policy of maintaining an artificial parity of military power between India and Pakistan and its obvious tilt towards the latter remained a basic element of discord between USA and India. Despite the considerable effort Mrs. Gandhi made initially during this period to bring about a fundamental improvement of Indo-US relations and despite the softening of India's standpoint on various issues on which the US administration was sensitive, as for instance for a while on Vietnam, and the US quick response to advance credits to India in the highly troubled economic situation in the country, the more fundamental discord in outlook could not be hidden for very long. The crunch came in 1970 with Washington's official announcement on 7 October 1970 to resume the supply of lethal weapons to Pakistan and with the estrangement of India-US relations in the Bangladesh crisis soon thereafter.

But before that, we need to consider the rapid development of Indo-USSR relations in meeting foreign challenges.

Promise and Challenges of Indo-Soviet Relations

Jawaharlal Nehru had initiated the policy of friendship with all countries and while in the initial period of independence, the economic and political relations with the West had far out-weighed those with Soviet Russia, Nehru had extended the hand of friendship to Moscow. He had debunked the bogey of Russia's motivations that the British had assidiously fostered from the 19th century onwards. Stalin's misperceptions had hindered the development of relations, but with the passing away of Stalin, the Khrushchev era saw a spurt in Indo-Soviet relations. Even since Khrushchev (then Secretary General of the Soviet Communist Party) and Bulganin (then Soviet Premier) declared that Soviet Union regarded Kashmir as an integral part of India during their first visit in 1955, there came a quantum jump in India-USSR relations.

Another seminal development was the Soviet refusal to accept the Chinese arguments and their position on the conflict with India and even its open criticism for their armed attack against India. Soon thereafter came the first time Soviet offer and the agreement signed on

11 September 1964 for the supply of defence materials and for the setting up of a MIG aircraft factory in India.[10]

The Soviet Union came to play an increasingly significant, and from the point of view of India, helpful and valuable role on many issues central to India's security and economic development as well as a kind of counterfoil to the Western pressures on India. The Soviet economic assistance specially centred on the development of heavy industry in India.

Yet, ironically in the initial years of Mrs. Gandhi's Prime Ministership, some irritants and challenges also cast their shadow on Indo-Soviet relations, as we have noted earlier. The Soviet Union had begun to involve itself in the affairs of the subcontinent after the Indo-Pak war of 1965. The Tashkent Agreement had been arrived at through Soviet mediation with Alexei Kosygin, Prime Minister of the USSR, playing a crucial role. This tempted the Soviets to believe that they would develop a close relationship with both India and Pakistan and bring about a new situation in which they could carry both India and Pakistan with them in order to stem the American crusade for alignment against the Soviet Union and the ideological onslaughts unleashed by Beijing in Asia.

Pakistan encouraged the Soviet hopes in this regard by conveying the impression in Moscow that Pakistan's sole concern in joining the American military bloc was to enhance its security against India. If Moscow could help ensure its security, Pakistan would be willing to reduce its commitments to the West. As the Soviets saw new possibilities in this situation, they increased their presence, granting more economic assistance to Pakistan. Islamabad rapidly increased the pressure on Moscow for the supply of military hardware. To save their new policy, Moscow felt obliged to meet the mounting Pakistani campaign to come someway in meeting Islamabad's bid for weapons and to begin, however modest, a programme for the supply of weapons to Pakistan.

Thus, India was confronted with a situation in which USA and China had already bolstered Pakistan's military and now the Soviet Union too was starting a pipeline even though the objectives were different and the Soviet promised military aid was quite limited at the time. Nevertheless, it was a matter of deep concern for India. Mrs. Gandhi sent a strong letter of protest to the Soviet leaders and there was a hue and cry in India.[11]

Very soon, however, Indo-Soviet lines began to converge again and Moscow dropped the Pakistani connection. The dominant factor was that Soviet and Indian interests ran on similar lines not only in the subcontinent, but in Asia as well. The Sino-Soviet split had firstly severely restricted any Soviet initiative in Asia, and secondly, created a new stake for Moscow to work against either US or Chinese or their joint dominance in Asia. This led them to support a policy which ran close to the Indian approach in the subcontinent and generally in Asia: that of opposing foreign pressures on Asian countries. Specifically, in South Asia the complementarity of interests was even more pronounced as Pakistan moved into a double alliance with Washington and Beijing in its search for power compatibility with India. Soviet support to India on crucial national issues involving their countries, which was to be even more graphically illustrated during the Bangladesh crisis, cemented and underscored this complementarity. Consequently India developed extensive political, economic and defence relationship with the Soviet Union.

Bangladesh Crisis and Relations with the Two Big Powers

The events leading to the emergence of Bangladesh are now well-known and etched in the consciousness of the people in India and impacted on India's relations with the big powers for a number of years to come. The Bangladesh crisis came at a time when the American administration was set on a course of establishing a new balance of relationships in Asia, a relationship with China at the centre with very considerable help from Pakistan, a kind of US-China-Pakistan axis. Pakistan tried to brutally suppress the struggle in Bangladesh, indulging in unspeakable atrocities that led to the exodus of nearly 10 million people from the then East Bengal into India, but Washington winked at these developments and instead put pressure on India to desist from taking any forceful action. The strong official American disapproval and the various moves the Nixon-Kissinger duo took to prevent the emergence of Bangladesh, pitting Washington directly against Indian interests, was partly to please Beijing and partly to reward Islamabad for its go-between good offices. That is why when Mrs. Gandhi went to Washington as part of her visits to a number of countries to mobilise opinion against Pakistani rulers' murderous campaign in Dacca, President Richard Nixon and his Secretary of State, Henry Kissinger were so unresponsive. We have it on the authority of Kissinger himself that Nixon was rather nervous in meeting her because she appeared to adopt an attitude of dismissive disdain.[12] Perhaps the real reason might have been that Nixon was on such a weak wicket!

Faced with this hostile grouping, India needed a viable counter-force to protect its integrity and interests. This was the background in which India signed with the Soviet Union a Treaty of Peace, Friendship and Cooperation in August 1971,[13] the second of its kind that India had signed (although officially it was claimed that it was long in the making). It was the Soviet backing that became crucial in warding off the most serious threat to India's integrity and socio-economic polity. Perhaps for the first time Soviet friendship's bearing on the fundamental national interests of India seeped down in mass consciousness in India. No ideological justifications were needed. The Soviet Union came to be fully supportive of India on this issue.

On the other hand, a certain suspicion and resentment crept into the Indian thinking about US policies and intentions in regard to this region. Mrs. Gandhi told this writer in a special interview (already referred to) on 17 March 1979 in response to a question about Indo-US relations that Washington did not look kindly upon strong, independent countries in Asia. US administration did not apparently wish to see the emergence of a strong India and strove for a relationship of dependence to suit the changing perceptions and requirements of American foreign policy.

The events surrounding the emergence of Bangladesh are well-known and need no repetition here. During this period threatening noises were made by USA and China. Washington sent the Seventh Fleet demonstratively towards Chittagong in a show of force and Beijing bitterly denounced India but any serious intervention had been averted by the Indo-Soviet Treaty. It may also be noted that the Simla Agreement signed subsequently between Pakistan President Zulfiqar Ali Bhutto and the Indian Prime Minister Indira Gandhi in June 1972 was remarkable for the stress it laid on bilateral resolution of all problems between the two countries.[14]

Emergency and the Challenge to India-US Relations

Relations with the US were none too comfortable when under domestic pressures Mrs. Gandhi declared a state of emergency and most of the oppositions leaders were rounded up and put behind the bars. These developments were bound to adversely impact on relations with the United States. The US strongly disapproved the declaration of emergency. The US President Gerald Ford commented that, 'it was very sad that 600 million people have lost what they had since mid 1940s as I recall and think it is a very sad development.'[15] The US media was equally critical. Mrs. Gandhi reacted sharply to these criticisms. Speaking at the Indian National Congress session in Chandigarh on 31 December 1975 she accused the West of rank hypocrisy in its concern for the future of democracy in India after having played ball with every dictatorship in Asia. She had the impression that the West never displayed much friendliness towards India and that it was not particularly pleased with India's independent stand in world affairs and her growing strength.[16]

Yet unnecessarily and avoidably Indo-US relations dipped to almost a freezing point. India had always maintained a certain balance in its relations with major powers. This balance had now been disturbed somewhat out of pique, although it must be noted that, despite all the political tensions the economic ties remained fairly strong.

Apparently Mrs. Gandhi was herself conscious of the problem and during her second term as Prime Minister took steps to restore the balance. It is generally believed that the thaw came when she met US President Ronald Reagan at Cancun in October 1981. It was there that the US President acquired a new insight into the Indian thinking and a close re-examination of the US premises that India's close relations with the USSR meant hostility towards the West and that India was a surrogate power for Soviet causes. Followed a 9-day Prime Ministerial visit to the US on 28 July 1982 where Reagan recognised that India and USA were both strong, independent and proud nations and that their relations were based on enlightened national interests.

Mrs. Gandhi used the opportunity to provide the rationale for Indian policies. Symbolically, to a pointed question at the National Press Club in Washington, 'Does India Tilt? Which way?' She replied sharply, 'I think we stand upright.' Friendly relations with one country did not stand in the way of friendly relations with others.[17]

A certain political balance was restored with USA, but relations remained somewhat uneasy politically for a number of years to come.

The Challenge of Relationship with China

Relations with China were in deep freeze when Lal Bahadur Shastri became Prime Minister. However, Shastri's stint as Prime Minister was short-lived as he passed away almost in a year and a half after he became Prime Minister on 9 June 1964. The burden of the challenge of the relationship with China was borne by Indira Gandhi. During the early period the Chinese leadership was still looking for 'revolutionary masses' of India ready to overthrow the 'comprador-landlord dominated' Indian government dependent on imperialism for its existence.[18]

That this was a propaganda meant for the 'revolutionaries' in Asia, and perhaps also for their own people was evident later when Mao Zedong, taking the usual salute on 1 May 1970 called the Indian charge of affairs in Beijing at the time, Brajesh Mishra, up on the rostrum and chatted with him for a few moments. Mao said to Mishra that, 'India and China had been friends in the past and should be friends again.' This was an extraordinary gesture on the part of the helmsman and the great teacher, as the Chinese referred to him at the time. This was no off-the-cuff gesture, the Chinese leadership did not function that way. The matter must have deliberated at the highest levels of Chinese leadership. Mao must have concluded that continued hostility with India did not serve Chinese interests, particularly in its functioning in the Afro-Asian world. The Chinese leadership might also have been thinking of reducing the various fronts on which they were fighting or quarrelling. But the Indian leadership was caught off guard. Not sure how to respond, the external Ministry official asked for a written proposal which appeared as a strange response to the Chinese as the supreme leader had himself indicated he wanted an improvement in India-China relations. Perhaps once bitten–twice shy, the government was wary of finding itself trapped.[19]

In any case, the tentative feelers were deluged by the Bangladesh crisis. Like Washington, Beijing was furious at the developments for similar reasons. They too had just made an opening towards the US through the good offices of Pakistan and now they had to watch almost helplessly (and therefore more maddeningly) the diminution of Pakistan both in size and prestige. But they resisted the temptation of the bait offered by Kissinger to strike India militarily. Both Mao and Chou limited themselves to making fun of and denouncing India in their talks with Nixon and Kissinger and in their propaganda otherwise. China's representative at the UN, Huang Hua, described India's arguments on Bangladesh as 'gangster logic'[20] and he brought in the issue of Tibet also, accusing India of grooming the Dalai Lama as the 'chieftain of the counter revolutionary rebellion'.

The emergence of Bangladesh could not be prevented, but Beijing concerted its moves with Islamabad in regard to its recognition. The main concern of the Chinese regime at the time was to ensure the stability of Pakistan and its capacity to survive the secession of East Bengal (now emerging as Bangladesh).

China's reaction to India's first nuclear explosion in 1975 was again in line with its general denunciation of India. Beijing alleged that India's chief objective in exploiting the atom was to intimidate and blackmail its neighbours, ironically the same charge that others had made in regard to the Chinese nuclear explosion in 1964. A powerful member of the Politbureau Li Xiannian, subsequently the Chairman of the People's Republic of China, himself journeyed to Pakistan to assure it against any threat of nuclear blackmail by India and reiterated support to Pakistan on the Kashmir issue.[21]

The same acerbity in Chinese propaganda was noticeable when a popular revolt in Sikkim leading to a referendum resulted in Sikkim's merger with India. The Chinese verbal reaction was liberal in its stern language. 'India was "gobbling up" Sikkim, it had divided Pakistan and was encouraging "anti-national" elements in Nepal, and was giving protection and succour to Tibetan rebels. It had a 'black record' against neighbours.'[22] China absolutely did not recognise India's annexation of Sikkim. India has been trying to create 'a great Indian Empire with the backing of Moscow.'[23]

All these harsh words notwithstanding, both countries were certainly probing the possibility of a return to normalcy in relationship. A table-tennis team (shades of the ping-pong diplomacy with the United States), accompanied by a Vice-Minister, came to India in February 1975 and was given very considerable publicity in the Chinese media, a presentiment of things to come. Mrs. Gandhi was equally keen on an opening towards China to impart more flexibility to Indian foreign policy. She told this writer in the interview referred to earlier, 'I have always believed that we should have a foot in there.' Finally, India announced its decision on 15 April 1975 to send an ambassador to China and chose a seasoned diplomat, K.R. Narayanan to go there (Narayanan was subsequently elected President of India). Soon followed a Chinese ambassador to India. With the return of ambassadors began the slow trek to full normalisation.

The new Janata Government that came to power in 1977 took couple of significant moves in regard to relations with China. Indian External Affairs Minister Atal Bihari Vajpayee visited China in February 1979. Although his visit had to be cut short because Beijing chose the same time to attack Vietnam, Vajpayee claimed two gains from the visit. One, the border issue that had been frozen earlier was now on the agenda. Two, he took the occasion to explain India's position about Sikkim. The Chinese made no comment.[24]

Mrs. Gandhi came back to power in 1980 and the thread was picked up when she met the Chinese Prime Minister, Hua Guofeng, in May 1980 at Belgrade where they had both gone for the funeral of President Tito. Both agreed to persist with the process of resolving issues and improving relations.[25] Both sides were responding to each other. We need to recall that after the death of Mao and the disposal of the Gang of Four, China had embarked upon an ambitious programme of economic development and did not wish to get embroiled in conflicts around its periphery, India too, for the same reasons and some more wished to avoid any renewal of conflict with China. China sent its Vice-Premier and Foreign Minister Huang Hua in yet another move to push ahead in their relations. Mrs. Gandhi was also keen to end the era of frosty relationship that apparently constricted India's options. On the eve of Huang Hua's visit, in a discussion at the request of this writer, Mrs. Gandhi observed, 'we cannot take the view that here we stand and here we shall stand for all time to come'. In other words, she was looking for more flexibility for Indian foreign policy and bringing India-China relations back on the normal track. She also met the then Chinese Premier, Zhao Zeyang at Cancun in Mexico on 28 October 1981, where both were attending the North-South Conference,[26] reaffirming their resolve to mend relations.

The path was, of course, strewn with many obstacles. Central to the problems between India and China was the border dispute, difficult, contentious and almost intractable. Another roadblock was the issue of Arunachal Pradesh. China questioned India's sovereignty over it and kept reiterating its claim on it, linking it with the Tibetan issue. The merger of Sikkim with India was another acrimonious issue, but less intractable than the other two issues.

Nevertheless, the process of normalisation had begun and would continue on its course. Mrs. Gandhi showed considerable deftness in handling the challenge of India-China relationship.

Pakistan: The Enduring Challenge

Since its inception Pakistan's paramount problem has been that of identity and integration. Religion provided the impulse for separation and formation of a separate state. But religion by itself could not resolve the problem of identity, as was evident from the secession of East Bengal and its emergence as the new state of Bangladesh. The problem of identity remained. Was Pakistan's priority to remain an Islamic state with an Islamic agenda or was it to transform itself into a nation-state with an agenda of development and national integration? Its oscillation between these two concepts remained a critical obstacle to its evolution into a modern, rising state.

Added to this dilemma was the compulsive urge for parity with India, strengthened by the irrational belief sedulously fostered by the establishment that Pakistan was a martial race, superior in its prowess to the 'Hindu' state of India.

India was the chief antagonist from the act of birth of the two states. The belief that Pakistan's security was principally threatened by India became an act of faith constantly intoned by those who ruled Pakistan. The anxieties, real or imagined, about Pakistan's security were consequently heightened, and one fanned the other so that it became a self-perpetuating process. It was constantly dinned into the consciousness of the people that India had not reconciled itself to the creation of Pakistan and would take every step to undo it.

Pakistan had only brief stints with a democratically elected government, for, much of the time that Pakistan came into being, it has been ruled by a military-bureaucratic complex which suppressed the democratic movement and the political parties or briefly tolerated a democratically elected government with the unstated understanding that foreign policy was the domain of the army.

Making the situation more volatile was the decision of the Americans in 1955 to establish their military presence in the region, to induct Pakistan into the Western military alliance system and to provide military assistance to Pakistan. This gradually created a militarised state in Pakistan, posing a serious threat both to India and the democratic aspirations of the people of Pakistan by creating a siege mentality in the country.

The consequences have been well-known. We have already noted the Rann of Kutch conflict and the Indo-Pak war of 1965. America's intrusion into this region has generally contributed to conflicts and wars, rather than let Pakistan develop as a 'normal' state. At the time China also helped stoke the fires, although much later it modified its policy. China helped Pakistan recover its heavy losses in the 1965 war and 1971, the large-scale military assistance given almost gratis.[27]

The rationale of Pakistan's establishment was made amply clear by General Ayub Khan in his book, *Friends Not Masters*. He left no doubt that Pakistan's sole objective in joining the Western bloc was to acquire military strength against India. Ayub used the same logic for developing closer relations with China. In fact Ayub revealed how he tried to woo the Soviet Union as well so as to neutralise Soviet veto on Kashmir.[28] We have already considered this effort earlier.

Bangladesh Crisis and the Simla Conference

The break-up of Pakistan and the emergence of Bangladesh was not only a traumatic event for Pakistan and for Indo-Pak relations, it was also one of the biggest foreign policy challenges faced by India during 1964-1984. While the events connected with emergence of Bangladesh are well-known, we might take a brief look at the consequences of the emergence of Bangladesh. These were handled with tremendous sophistication by Indira Gandhi and her Government, more particularly in the face of open US-China combined hostility. Zulfiqar Ali Bhutto played his own game and released Sheikh Mujibur Rahman from captivity in the hope of wooing and weaning him away from India, although it did not cut much ice at the time. But the leftover problems from the Bangladesh conflict had still to be resolved. There were some 90,000 soldiers under the joint command of Bangladesh and India.

Their fate had yet to be decided. The new situation in regard to Indo-Pak relations had also to be resolved. There were areas in West Pakistan under Indian control and some Indian territory with Pakistan. There were Indian and Pakistani civilians on the wrong side. The lines of actual control on the various borders with Pakistan had to be accepted *de jure*—in other words full normalisation and final settlement between India and Pakistan. To address these complex problems, Zulfiqar Ali Bhutto met the Indian Prime Minister, Indira Gandhi, along with their aides at Simla (now Shimla) in June 1972.

Simla Conference and After

Bhutto's urgent requirements and the long-term strategy that he evolved comprised two-three essential elements. He desperately needed to get the huge contingent of Pak prisoners of war back in Pakistan in order to consolidate his position. At the same time he began taking vigorous step for recouping the military losses during this war and to restore the morale of the army. The main source of arms aid was once again China.[29] Indeed, the Pakistan army's losses both in 1965 and 1972 were made up by China, virtually free of charge. He also took many steps in regard to the recognition of Bangladesh so that it would appear to be done in an Islamic context.

India hoped for a full settlement, the fixation of the international line of control and the elements of a Kashmir settlement. Apparently the two sides held complex, intensive and extensive, and to all accounts frank discussions and negotiations.[30]

It is not possible to know all that transpired in Simla at this point of time. One thing was clear: Bhutto accepted at the time an essential bilateral approach to the outstanding problem between India and Pakistan. India asked for a final settlement in writing centred around the existing realities with some adjustments if necessary. Bhutto was not willing to ink that piece of paper. He pleaded that at that time his position could become untenable within the country were he to formally sign some kind of an agreement. Bhutto would not budge from that position.

It is well-known that the Simla Conference was on the verge of failure. It was saved at the last minute by Indira Gandhi by not insisting on a formal agreement. Undoubtedly, Bhutto promised to gradually work towards that kind of agreement after he had prepared public opinion for it.[31]

After protracted negotiations and after Bhutto felt he had sufficiently stabilised his position within Pakistan, he recognised Bangladesh, ostensibly at the request of the Islamic nations in February 1974, and thereby he got his captured soldiers back. In a long preamble to a tripartite agreement signed on 9 April 1974, Pakistan condemned any crimes that might have been committed by its personnel in Bangladesh and expressed its deep regret for such misdeeds. In a separate bilateral agreement, India and Pakistan expressed their resolve to build a cooperative and friendly relationship.[32]

Pokhran-I and Pakistan

India exploded (or imploded) a nuclear device on 18 May 1974 which India claimed was in the pursuit of peaceful uses of the atom (PNE) and that India was not manufacturing nuclear weapons. From hindsight this assertion appeared to have been a mistake. If India had declared itself then as a nuclear weapon state, many of the subsequent problems could have been avoided. Neither the American laws penalising any nuclear explosion by a country outside the P5 were in place nor had the Nuclear Suppliers Group (NSG) been organised by then.

Even so, the explosion riled the Western world, particularly its media a great deal. Yet the US official reaction as stated by Dr. Henry Kissinger was rather mild. He did not believe it changed the balance of power in the region, though he would have advised against it.[33] The reaction in Pakistan was, however, explosive. The media carried alarming forebodings and sinister implications Bhutto described it as a 'fateful development',[34] declared that he would never submit to Indian dominance over the subcontinent and sent emissaries around important countries to mobilise opinion against the Indian explosion. Even then Indira Gandhi tried to mollify Pakistani opinion and herself conveyed the assurance to Bhutto (on 22 May) that the nuclear explosion was 'entirely for peaceful purposes' and reiterated that India had no desire to acquire atomic weapons or threaten any neighbour.[35] Notwithstanding the hyper reaction from him, it soon became known that, even before the Indian explosion, Bhutto was energetically pursuing a nuclear programme of his own and had enlisted the services of A.Q. Khan[36] subsequently hailed as the father of the Pakistani nuclear bomb.

Afghanistan, Zia-ul Haq and India

Bhutto had no intention of living up to the understanding reached at Simla, but he himself became a victim of the army, civilian politics of Pakistan and his own handpicked army chief, General Zia-ul Haq hanged him and became the head of the government and the state. This was also the time when gradually the Afghan developments took centre stage in world politics with the entry of Soviet troops into Afghanistan. This allowed Zia to play his own game, strengthen his own position, secure huge arms aid with no questions asked from the United States and began a low-level terrorist insurgency in Kashmir. Despite the Soviet entreaty, India declined to support the Soviet troops' entry into Afghanistan and advised the Soviet leaders to withdraw their troops as early as possible. After some unfortunate initial hiccups, India's policy towards the developing situation in Afghanistan was firmed up and was now composed of three components. There should be a political solution, not a military imposition from either side. The Soviet troops should withdraw, but thirdly all foreign intervention should cease so as to allow the emergence of an independent, non-aligned Afghanistan.

This policy was also conveyed to General Zia by Swaran Singh, but also that India did not share the view that a grave and immediate threat had risen to Pakistan's security. Infact any involvement of Pakistan in the new cold war would make precisely that threat a reality.[37] Subsequently Narasimha Rao, as Foreign Minister, gave the assurance to Zia in Islamabad in June 1981 that India had a stake in the integrity and stability of Pakistan and to dispel the apprehension that India had any desire to see the undoing of Pakistan.[38]

But General Zia had his own calculations and his own game to play. Utilising the American decision to see the Soviets undone in Afghanistan at any cost, he secured an initial agreement with the United States in September 1981 for a military and economic aid programme of $3.5 billion over the next five years.[39] These programmes, particularly the supply of weapons tended to become open-ended. There was no accounting and it was very difficult to assess the amount of US-supplied weapons that went into Pakistan, many of them ostensibly for transfer to the rebel elements in Afghanistan supported by Pakistan.

This militarisation of Pakistan and the gradually escalating terrorism exported into India posed formidable challenges for India and for Indian foreign policy in the years to come.

Bangladesh's Woes and Challenges for India

The establishment of the new state of Bangladesh was a moment of triumph for both Mujibur Rahman and Indira Gandhi, but it very soon turned into a tragedy for both the countries. Mujib came to Calcutta to a rousing reception on 16 February 1972 and in a joint *communiqué*

Bangladesh and India stressed that their relations were based on the principles of 'democracy, socialism, secularism, non-alignment and oppositions to imperialism and colonialism in all its form and manifestations',[40] Indira Gandhi went to Dacca in mid-March to an equally ecstatic reception. India and Bangladesh signed a Treaty of Friendship and Peace on 19 March (1972), the third of its kind that India had signed with any other country, the first one being with Nepal and the second with the Soviet Union.[41]

Sheikh Mujibur was a grand leader, but not necessarily a grand administrator. The country confronted a horrendous situation. The government machinery had collapsed, the bureaucracy emasculated, administration in total disarray, transport and communication badly disrupted and trade and commerce fairly stagnated. It needed herculean efforts to put the country back on the rails. India tried to help as best as it could to revive Bangladesh's infrastructure and economy with the total aid from India by the end of March 1975 amounting to some Rs. 308 crore.[42]

But a storm was brewing in Bangladesh. All the anti-Mujibur elements, all the anti-India forces, the various Islamic organisations sympathetic to Pakistan were conspiring to bring about a change of regime in Dacca. A *coup d'tat* took place on 15 August 1975 under the leadership of rightwing elements led by Khondkar Mushtaq Ahmed, then Minister of Commerce and Trade, and an army officer killed Mujib and his family. A power struggle ensued in which finally the army chief, General Ziaur Rahman took over power in Bangladesh.

There was nothing that India could do about these grisly developments. The anti-India elements were having a hay day fomenting anti-India propaganda, arousing public emotions and blaming India for all the ills of the country. Gradually two or three issues came to the fore that troubled and were exploited to continue to poison Indo-Bangladesh relations.

Foremost, was the issue of the use of the Ganga waters and the Farakka barrage that India was building for their better use. Bangladesh insisted that the barrage denied Dacca its due share of the Ganga waters and that its construction should be stopped. India's pleas that India was the major ripararian country with its catchment area amounting to 98 percent, and that of the total population around Ganga, about 94 percent was in India and that India would take care of the needs of Bangladesh had no effect on the authorities in Dacca. Bangladesh even took the case to the UN.

It was only after the death of General Ziaur Rahman and when General Ershad came to power through another coup that some stabilisation took place in the India-Bangladesh relations. Obviously for his own reasons, General Ershad wanted to lower the hostility decible with India. Responding to Indira Gandhi's overture, which was preceded by India' official declaration that the events in Bangladesh were an internal matter, General Ershad came to India on 6 October 1982 for a three-day visit and described his talks with Mrs. Gandhi as 'historic' because 'we are making progress towards resolving the problems'. They finally settled the land border between the two. Subsequently, the two countries set up a Joint Water Commission for dealing with the various problems in regard to Farakka, with the assurance by India that Bangladesh would continued to receive the same quantity of water as in the previous agreement of 1977.[43]

We may take note of the other issues that arose that were exploited to create bad blood between the two countries. A serious irritant was the increasingly large influx of Bangla citizens into India. The problem became particularly acute in Assam, creating a dangerous social and linguistic problem. As a consequence, the Government decided to fence the border with Bangladesh resulting in vigorous protests from Dacca against the Indian action and a huge hue and cry was whipped up by the Bangla media. The issue continued to rile Bangladesh and at the same time the infiltration worried India equally greatly. It also resulted in an occasional exchange of fire at the border between the two countries.

The growing imbalance in their trade was a matter of concern to both the countries. Under Ershad, India took initiative to minimise irritants and achieve a better balance. The Indo-Bangla trade pact was renewed for another three years in July 1984 envisaging an annual 100 crore trade volume, but pledging earnest endeavour to address an escalating trade balance that had crossed Rs. 500 crore mark.[44]

Nepal: Compulsions of a Small Neighbour

The challenge of relations with Nepal was of a very different kind. Nepal was no ordinary neighbour. Nepal and India were bound together by the pull of history, geography, kinship, religion, faith, cultural legacy and linguistic affinity—a relationship that India did not have with any other country. The Himalayas were more than mountains to both the countries—they were a part of them.

Their relationship after India's independence came to be essentially based on the Treaty of Peace and Friendship signed on 31 July 1950 that joined the security of India with that of Nepal and provided that Nepal would consult India before importing military equipment from any country other than India but gave the right to Nepal after such consultation to import arms through Indian territory. Simultaneously, a Treaty of Trade and Commerce was signed by which India undertook to make available to Nepal to the maximum extent possible commodities essential for its economy through routes and methods of transport most convenient, while at the same time ensuring that the Indian market was not flooded by cheap goods coming from Nepal.

India built roads, highways, powers projects and airports. This is not the occasion to give details of these activities but we may keep one point in view that many rivers originated in Nepal (or even in Tibet) and that both Nepal and India had a joint interest in taming them and utilising their hydel potential for electricity and other purposes. We may also note that some of the Nepalese demands about trade issues were taken account of in the trade agreement of September 1961. It envisaged the creation of a common market but more immediately generally exempted from any duties or charges goods originating in one country for sale in the other and also transit facilities for goods produced in Nepal for export to third countries. The only exception was Pakistan as it was not willing to reciprocate in regard to India's trade with Afghanistan.[45]

But the Peace Treaty became the subject of acrimony and inflamed passions in Nepal with many regarding it as an unequal treaty. The sum and substance of it was that Nepal was a landlocked state and this state of dependency rankled and it was easy to arouse the emotions of the people. Indira Gandhi had to cope with the bouts of nationalism made worse by a King wanting to arrogate to himself all power through an attempt to exploit Nepalese nationalism.

The passing away of King Tribhuvan and the accession of King Mahendra to the throne changed the equation between Kathmandu and Delhi. King Mahendra played the China card against India and deliberately gave construction facilities to the Chinese close to the Indian border. For the Nepalese authorities under King Mahendra, the erosion of the special relationship with India became one of their principal preoccupation. China too had become a factor in India-Nepal relations, as it began to construct highways and some hydel projects. Indira Gandhi, however, tried to handle the problems with a soft approach. She visited Kathmandu in October 1966 and announced aid worth of Rs. 40 crore for Nepal's third five-year plan, almost twice the amount contributed for its second five year plan. In addition there were agreements about a paper factory and some hydro-electric projects.[46]

Despite Indira Gandhi's initiatives King Mahendra was determined to play the China card and arouse Nepalese nationalism, partly also to justify his own seizure of power and dismissal of the elected B.P.

Koirala government that he had done earlier on 15 December 1960. An orchestrated anti-India movement was launched. The press was up in arms and public demonstrations were organised. India lodged at least two protests against the anti-India campaign unleashed in Kathmandu. King Mahendra demanded free and unrestricted flow of trade with and through India. The visits of the then Deputy Prime Minister Morarji Desai (23-24 October 1967) and the subsequent visit of Dr. Zakir Hussain in October 1968 failed to mollify him. Indeed he repeated his call for Nepal's right to full access within and through India for Nepal's trade even during the visit of the Indian President.[47] The political problem continued to dog India-Nepal relations. Later in an interview to the officially-sponsored newspaper, *Rising Nepal,* the King saw no need for the continuation of the 1950 Treaty of Peace and Friendship and Arms Assistance Treaty of 1964.[48]

Kathmandu demanded on 25 July 1969 the withdrawal of the Indian Military Mission and the Military Liaison Group. India acceded to both the demands. The Nepalese replaced the Indian personnel on the northern check posts on 1 January 1970 and the Indian Military Liaison Group was withdrawn on 18 August.[49]

The real problem was not just one issue or the other. The King was trying to bring about a fundamental change in India-Nepal relations and he was using one issue or another for achieving that, including using the China card, declaring neutrality between India and China.

It is possible that the King was greatly riled over the asylum given to B.P. Koirala and his supporters in India. They moved around expounding their views. The King was both resentful and nervous, despite the repeated assurances given by India that it did not wish to destabilise the King. But Mahendra was not convinced and was fearful of being overthrown by a popular movement.

Indira Gandhi's government lost its patience. There was cold anger in Delhi that King Mahendra was deliberately whipping up sentiments against India and becoming the spokesperson of Nepalese nationalism in order to divert attention from the failure of the *panchayat* system and from popular discontent. The King's strategy was to separate the political from the economic issues, so as to burn the candle from both ends. This became unacceptable to New Delhi. The Government banned the import from Nepal of synthetic fibres and stainless steel and fixed a ceiling of 120 tonnes of jute per month for import from Nepal and their reexport to that country. Transit facilities from Radhikapur to Pakistan were also cancelled. Nevertheless, India extended the trade agreement that had expired on 30 October 1970 by two months even though there was no formal new agreement in place.

For a while the anti-India campaign was continued with even greater intensity. The student protests were intensified against Indian 'imperialism'. Nepal tried to lobby international opinion against India.[50] But finally the King had to backtrack in face of the economic realities. Indira Gandhi was also willing to soften her stance in reciprocation and a new Treaty of Trade and Transit valid for five years was signed on 13 August 1971. Foreign Minister Swaran Singh, with his flair for soothing tensions went to Kathmandu and secured the alignment of Nepal's policy with that of India in regard to the developments in East Bengal. Nor did Nepal try to stop Gurkha troops in the Indian army from fighting against the Pakistani army[51] and Nepal expeditiously recognised Bangladesh (16 January 1972).

The question, however, still arises whether it was necessary to 'teach a lesson' to a small landlocked state largely dependent on India, no matter how capricious its king was. We could have been more concerned with the sentiments of the people, rather than with those of their King.

In any case, the passing away of King Mahendra and accession to the Nepalese throne of King Birendra on 31 January 1972 led to a distinct improvement of relations. Indira Gandhi took the initiative to visit Nepal—a second time during her tenure as Prime Minister—in February 1973 and invited King Birendra to India for an extended stay in India. During her visit to a huge welcome, she underlined India's interests in the development and prosperity of Nepal and gave the assurance that India was not extending any assistance to rebel activity against the Nepalese government.[52]

Sri Lanka: Yet Another Foreign Policy Challenge

There were many more challenges that Indira Gandhi faced during the period under discussion. But for considerations of space, we discuss only one more—that of Sri Lanka.

Mrs. Gandhi's management of the crises she faced in dealing with the world in various areas, chiefly in regions around her own country, was fairly impressive. But there were situations which defied any statesman's talents and wits; like the crisis in Sri Lanka.

The genesis lay in the presence of two million Tamilians in Sri Lanka, a million of them dating their ancestors' entry there as anciently as the Sinhalese presence itself, and another million, many of them stateless, the consequence of the British policy of taking indentured labour to its various colonies. The former, the Ceylon Tamils as they were called, were mainly concentrated in Jaffna on the northern and eastern coast, where as the Indian Tamils lived mostly in the districts of Colombo, Candy and Trincomalee in the traditional tea gardens and estate areas.

The current problem began with large-scale rioting and violence (and not for the first time) in Colombo and elsewhere in the island against the Tamils in July 1983 escalating into a carnage against the Tamils involving the Sri Lankan army and police and finally blowing up into a virtual civil war with the Tamil militants including the LTTE and the EPRLF (which was then in control in Jaffna) as well as with the JVP militants. The details need not detain us here; we are concerned more with the broad contours of Mrs. Gandhi's response.

Mrs. Gandhi's response was based on three premises. One, that the unity and integrity of Sri Lanka should not be disrupted. Two, that the life, property and honour of the Tamils in Sri Lanka should be ensured. Three, that foreign interference and intervention must be excluded from the island republic. This last dimension was not a minor matter. India's security could not be compromised. India was determined to the best of its capacity to prevent any foreign intrusion. As Mrs. Gandhi told the Parliament what she had conveyed to the Sri Lankan President Junius Jayawardene that foreign intrusion in the area was harmful for both the countries. She had cautioned him about the forces of destabilisation at work '...and so we must minimise the possibility of foreign involvement.' The problem of Tamils in Sri Lanka was a matter in which India could not be treated as 'just another country.'[53]

These heightened concerns came in the wake of Sri Lanka's desperate bid to involve foreign powers, the West, Israel and Pakistan to face up to India and meet the mounting internal conflicts. Tamilian refugees had started coming into India. New Delhi also had to take into consideration the emotions and susceptibilities swaying the people in Tamil Nadu. It was an extraordinarily novel situation. India was dealing with another sovereign country; yet whatever was happening there had a direct bearing on peace and normalcy in parts of India and on the security of the country.

When an agreement was virtually reached at an all-party round-table conference in January 1984 and what was known as Annexure 'C' was signed detailing the devolution of power to the Tamil majority areas within the ambit of a unified country, Colombo gradually managed to get off the hook and to sneak out of the commitment.

There were also allegations by Colombo that the LTTE was being given material assistance by M.G. Ramachandran's AIADMK government in Tamil Nadu. The continued carnage against the Tamilians in Sri Lanka left little choice to them but to defend themselves by all possible means including force and in this exercise they turned for help to all those quarters whose help could be tapped. That is how many armed groups emerged in the Tamil-dominated areas.

No matter what slips might have been made, Mrs. Gandhi's broad framework for dealing with the crisis in Sri Lanka was a sound and sensible framework and still remains the only feasible framework for handling the tragic events there.

One could conclude by remarking that Indira Gandhi generally handled the challenges in foreign policy with a lot of maturity and with the minimum losses for India. Foreign policy remained anchored to the country's national interests and simultaneously Indira Gandhi retained the status that India had achieved earlier in the world community. It is not that no mistakes were made, but they did not outweigh the deft manner in which India's interests were preserved and the foreign challenges met with very considerable aplomb.

Endnotes

1. See B.C. Chakraborty (1992). *The Indo-Pak War, 1965.* History Division, Ministry of Defence, Government of India.
2. *http://www.kashmir-information.com/LegalDocs/Tashkent.html*
3. For the texts of Indira Gandhi's speeches in USA see *Foreign Affairs Record,* March and April 1966.
4. The interview was held at Indira Gandhi's residence at 12 Wellington Crescent on 19 March 1979 when she was out of government.
5. For all these figures, see *Asian Recorder,* 28 May-3 June 1966, page 103; and 9-13 September 1966, pp. 6028-29.
6. For Mrs. Gandhi's visits to Yugoslavia and the UAR, see *Foreign Affairs Record,* July 1966.
7. Text of the Joint Communique in Ibid: October.
8. *Asian Recorder,* 9-15 December 1968, p.86660.
9. *Indian Express,* 17 January 1970.
10. *Asian Recorder,* 21-27 October 1964, pp.6099 and 6101.
11. For reports of Mrs. Gandhi's letter to protest of 10 July 1968 and related development see, *Times of India and Hindustan Times* of July-August 1968.
12. See Henry Kissinger, *The While House Years.*
13. For text of the Treaty see *Foreign Affairs Record,* August 1971, p.161.
14. For the Text of the Simla Agreement see *Foreign Affairs Record,* June 1972.
15. *Indian Express,* 18 September 1975.
16. *Hindustan Times,* 1 January 1978.
17. *Time of India* and *Hindustan Times,* 28, 29 and 30 July 1982.

18. English Text of a commentary in *People Daily* released by *New China News Agency* (Beijing), 10 August 1968. Also see *People's Daily* , 1 October 1968.
19. Based on personal discussion with a number of high officials of the MEA at the time.
20. Text of Huang Hua's speech at the Security Council on 4 December 1971 circulated by *New China News Agency*, UN, 4 December 1971.
21. News from *Xinhua* News Agencies, 15 April 1975.
22. *Xinhua* news agency (Beijing), 24 March 1975.
23. *People's Daily*, 13 April 1975.
24. See Gargi Dutt, "China and India, an Uncertain Relationship", in V.P. Dutt (ed.), *China: The Post Mao View*.
25. *SWB* 10 May 1980 FE/6416/1
26. *Statesman* 29 October 1981
27. Defence Ministger's, Chavan's statement in Parliament on 8 August 1966. *Foreign Affairs Record*, August 1966, pp.214-15.
28. Mohammad Ayub Khan (1967). *Friends Not Masters*. London and New York: Oxford University Press.
29. See *New York Times*, 2 June 1972.
30. See *Foreign Affairs Record*, June 1972.
31. Based on discussions with high-ranking aides who were present there.
32. *Asian Recorder*, 7-13 May 1974, p.11985.
33. *Bulletin*, Department of State, 24 June 1974.
34. *Asian Recorder*, 4-10 June 1974, p.12035.
35. Ibid.
36. See Bhutto's *If I am Assassinated*.
37. See Inder Malhotra's "Dialogue with Pakistan", *Times of India*, 17 April 1986.
38. *Indian Express*, 12 June 1981.
39. *Times of India*, 17 September 1981.
40. *Foreign Affairs Record*, February 1972, p. 36.
41. Ibid, March 1972, p. 63
42. Deputy Foreign Minister, Bipan Pal Dass' statement in the Lok Sabha. *Asian Recorders*, 30 April-4 May, p. 12568.
43. *Hindustan Times*, 8 October 1982.
44. *Times of India*, 28 July 1984.
45. See Murlidhar Dharmadesni (1976). *Indian Diplomacy in Nepal*. Jaipur: Alekh Publishers. p.154.
46. *Asian Recorder*, 19-26 November 1966, p. 7403.
47. See *Hindustan Times*, 10 June 1969.

48. *Asian Recorder*, 30 July-5 August 1969, pp. 9057-58.
49. *Times of India*, 17-18 August 1970.
50. See *Statesman* 3 January, *Times of India*, 5 January and *Indian Express*, 7 January 1971.
51. *Times of India*, 27 November 1971.
52. *Asian Recorder*, 2-8 April 1973, p. 11319.
53. *Times of India*, August 6, 1983.

Chapter VI

Liberation of Bangladesh

Inder Malhotra

What came to pass in what was then East Pakistan and is now the Islamic Republic of Bangladesh on December 16, 1971—in Indira Gandhi's famous words, that day Dacca (now Dhaka) became 'the independent capital of an independent country'—was bound to happen sooner or later. For it was built into the situation. Indeed, some perceptive observers had foreseen this denouement. For instance, four years earlier in 1967, the British diplomat Robert Wade-Gerry, later his country's High Commissioner to India had told a closed-door meeting of the International Institute for Strategic Studies (IISS) in London that Pakistan could not survive in one piece for much longer. (K. Subrahmanyam, this country's leading strategist who was present at the meeting told this to author. Nehru's official biographer, S. Gopal, was the only other Indian at that gathering.) Lord Mountbatten's Papers show that even earlier he had recorded confidentially that the post-1947 structure of Pakistan would last, at most, for 25 years.

There were strong, indeed compelling, reasons for the gloomy forecasts. From the word go, Pakistan had been a geographical monstrosity. More than a thousand miles of Indian landmass separated its eastern and more populous wing from the western one where political power really resided. In Salman Rushdie's memorable phrase, Pakistan was 'a bird with two wings and no body'. To make matters a lot worse, the largely Punjabi military-bureaucratic elite that dominated the all-Pakistan government made no bones about its disdain for distant Bengalis. So much so that even in Dacca, the capital of East Pakistan, the Punjabis and others from the western wing held most of the top positions. In the Army, the share of East Pakistan, also called East Bengal, was negligible. An East Bengal Regiment was raised only a few years before the two wings parted company. There was only one Bengali officer of the two-star rank in an army half-a-million strong.

Almost immediately after the birth of Pakistan it started becoming clear that the two wings had no bonds other than religion. The rulers based in Karachi chose dangerously to aggravate the underlying divide by their language policy. They made Urdu the country's sole official language. When the Bengalis, deeply devoted to their mellifluous and highly developed language, protested, they were fired upon. Fierce anti-Urdu riots erupted and went on until the unwise decision was amended. The students killed during these became the eastern wing's first martyrs. Bangladesh reveres them every year on Martyrs' Day. Glaring and growing economic disparities widened the breach.

The wrongs done to the eastern wing could perhaps have been mitigated, thought not righted, had democracy taken roots in Pakistan. East Bengal's numerical superiority and its traditional, if volatile, commitment to political process and electoral politics might have provided some corrective to power imbalance and economic exploitation. It is noteworthy that no all-Pakistan elections were held before December 1970. But as early as 1954, the people of the eastern wing had forced Karachi to hold elections in their part of the country. The Pakistan Muslim League, then controlling the federal as well as all provincial governments, was roundly defeated in this poll. But the federal government annulled the election and sacked the newly elected East Pakistan government. In 1958, the Army, led by General (later Field Marshal) Ayub Khan took over and Pakistan went under military rule. The Army's contempt for the Bengalis far exceeded that of feudal-minded West Pakistani civilians.

To deprive East Bengal of the advantage of numbers, the military dictator merged all four provinces in the west, ethnically and linguistically diverse, into 'One Unit' and then ordained that the two wings would have 'parity' in the parody of a national assembly to be 'elected' on a very limited franchise under Ayub's brand of 'basic democracy'.

In these circumstances, it was inevitable that a movement for autonomy to East Pakistan should develop, and it did. Its leader was a charismatic, if also somewhat demagogic, Sheikh Mujibur Rahman, better known as Sheikh Mujibur, later to be the Father of Bangladesh and later still to be assassinated by some of his disgruntled followers. He argued that the long neglected and much exploited people of East Bengal should be able to 'use the fruits of their labour for their welfare' rather than 'helplessly watch them being carried away to the west'. This was music to the ears of long-suffering Bengalis. The 1965 war between India and Pakistan—started by Pakistan at the insistence of Zulfiqar Ali Bhutto, then Ayub's most favoured protégé and foreign minister, in the naïve hope of 'wresting Kashmir from India'—gave a big boost to Mujibur's movement. For, East Bengalis discovered to their dismay that they were virtually undefended and totally vulnerable.

India had no interest in occupying defenseless East Pakistan, if only because it did not want China to get an excuse to intervene in the war on behalf of its Pakistani allies.

Vague at first, Mujibur's campaign for autonomy eventually crystallised into a six-point charter of demands, which, in the unlikely event of being conceded, would have made East Bengal all but independent except for a loose confederation with the western wing. Originally, he had conceded only foreign affairs and communications to the federal government that the Army had shifted from Karachi to Rawalpindi. Later, he agreed to add defence to this list but strictly on condition that the east and the west would have equal representation in the Army. Infuriated military rulers arrested him immediately and charged him with treason 'in collusion with India.'

Ironically, his trial, known as the Agartala Conspiracy Case to underscore the India connection, was abruptly terminated because Ayub, to save himself from a powerful movement to overthrow him, sought the help of all political leaders, including Mujibur. This was of no avail. The movement for the restoration of democracy did sweep the Field Marshal out of power, but instead of democracy returning to Pakistan, martial law came back with a vengeance.

The bluff, blustering and often incredibly crude General Yahya Khan, who took over from Ayub lacked his predecessor's impressive personality as well as political skill. Over-indulgence in drink and dissolute living had further dulled his senses. However, he eventually redeemed himself by living up to his promise to hold free and fair elections, the first ever in Pakistan. After a few postponements, once because of a catastrophic cyclone that took a toll of nearly half a million lives, these elections were held in December 1970. The election results were stunning and no one was stunned more than Yahya! He was confident that no party would get a clear majority in the National Assembly, and he would continue to rule the roost. But the electorate willed otherwise.

Sheikh Mujibur's Party, the Awami League won all but two of the 162 seats in the National Assembly allotted to the eastern wing—on the basis of population, of course—apart from capturing almost every state in the provincial assembly of East Pakistan. He thus had a clear majority in the 300-member National Assembly even though his party had not contested a single seat in the western wing. Nevertheless, Mujibur's claim to be Prime Minister of Pakistan was obvious and uncontestable.

This, however, was not at all acceptable to Yahya and the Army though unfortunately not only the outside world but also even Mujibur became aware of this when it was too late. Worse, in the Army's ignoble resolve Yahya had a seemingly unlikely but actually enthusiastic collaborator, Zulfiqar Ali Bhutto, the man who had led the movement for the restoration of democracy against his mentor, Ayub. His Pakistan's People's Party had won in the National Assembly 82 seats of the 138 allocated to the four provinces constituting the western wing, but Mujib had twice that many seats. Bhutto's obsessive objective in life was to have absolute power. Suddenly, he discovered that the main obstacle to his cherished goal was Mujibur, no longer the military.

He and Yahya were therefore agreed that under no circumstances should power be transferred to Mujibur. But they took care to cover their evil design behind a façade of elaborate negations with the Awami League leader in which hints of conciliation alternated with acrimony and threats. However, the talks were kept going. Bhutto's last-ditch offer to Mujibur was that he should rule the eastern wing and leave the west alone. '*Iddhar hum, uddhar tum* (here we; there you)' were the four Urdu words he used. Mujibur's understandable reply was that all matters should be decided by the National Assembly due to meet in Dacca soon. Bhutto immediately announced a boycott of the assembly session and threatened to 'break the legs' of any West Pakistani legislator 'foolhardy' enough to go to Dacca. Yahya obliged him by cancelling his own summons to the inaugural session of the National Assembly that was fated never to meet. (See author's *Dynasties of India and Beyond*—HarperCollins India, 2004, p. 256. Let me add here that many of the details cited above and to follow are based on my primary research, including valuable conversations with K. Subrahmanyam. His book *Bangladesh and India's Security*—Palit and Palit, 1972, as well as Anthony Mascarenhas's *Rape of Bangladesh* published the same year have also helped.)

Some seven weeks before the Bangladesh crisis came to a head, two Kashmiri extremists had hijacked a Fokker Friendship aircraft of Indian Airlines to Lahore where it was brazenly blown up in the presence of Bhutto. India retaliated by banning all Pakistani flights over its territory. This naturally impeded the Pakistan Army's frantic efforts to augment its deployments in East Pakistan to prepare for the massive repression it had already decided to launch. It therefore started sending reinforcements in civilian aircraft that had to fly to Dacca via Colombo and be refuelled in the Sri Lankan capital. The troops, including those belonging to Special Forces, travelled under the garb of a mufti but their identity could not be hidden. Meanwhile, Yahya's negotiations with Mujibur continued to be a convenient camouflage for the Army's secret build-up.

In any case, no one in New Delhi's power structure was paying much attention to these developments because everyone who mattered was absorbed in the ongoing and undoubtedly historic election that coincided with the gathering storm in Pakistan. Even so, it is astounding that when the balloon went up in Dacca late in the evening of March 25, New Delhi was taken completely by surprise. Indeed, the prevailing view within the Indian establishment was that Yahya would be able to bring about some kind of a compromise between Mujibur and Bhutto, and that this would be to India's advantage, especially in East Bengal where Mujibur and his followers, unlike their West Pakistani compatriots, harboured no hostility to India. P.N. Dhar, Indira Gandhi's Secretary from 1970 to 1977, admits this candidly. (Dhar, *Indira Gandhi, the Emergency and Indian Democracy*—OUP, 2000, pp. 147-151.)

Incredible though it may seem the Army headquarters did not have even a contingency plan to cope with the grim situation. The government's only directive to the Eastern Command of the Army was that in the event of a war with Pakistan, it should 'protect' Calcutta (now Kolkata) and the narrow 'Siliguri corridor', the heartland's only land link with the strategic Northeast. Period!

No less astonishing was that policymakers in New Delhi completely misunderstood Yahya's arrival in Dacca on the morning of March 25 with a team of advisers ostensibly for negotiations with Mujib and other Awami League leaders. P.N. Dhar records that the Core Group of advisers to Indira Gandhi did not believe that Pakistani rulers 'would go over the brink and start a full-scale civil war. For at stake were the territorial and ideological foundations of the state.' This belief was buttressed by reports from Dacca that the talks between Yahya and Mujibur, 'though difficult, were going well'. Even after the first reports of the horrendous crackdown came in, New Delhi continued to believe that after a brief show of the military strength, negotiations between the two sides would be resumed.

'We were', adds Dhar, 'proved wrong'. Yahya Khan is believed to have told his officers: '"there can be no settlement with the "Bingos" till they are sorted out well and proper."' (Ibid: 151-52.) It took Dhar and his colleagues a relatively long time to realise that the show of negotiations with Mujibur was a 'diversion' to keep the Awami League leaders engaged while the military gave finishing touches to its well-thought-out plan to decapitate the Awami League leadership, terrorise or massacre Bengali intellectuals and cow down the eastern wing's population through a genocide so brutal as to put even the Nazi war crimes at shame. To ensure that there was no resistance from any Bengali quarter, the Pakistan Army attacked the police headquarters,

East Bengal Regiment and the East Bengal Rifles in a bid to disarm them. This operation succeeded only partially.

Before Sheikh Mujibur was arrested and whisked away to a dingy jail in West Pakistan to be placed in solitary confinement and later to be tried for treason, he declared unilateral Independence of Bangladesh. In another part of the city a serving army Major named Ziaur Rahman repeated the proclamation on an improvised radio station. The Bengali Muslims had thus been driven to reject the two-nation theory, the *raison d'etre* of their state. The entire Bangladeshi population was in revolt. The process of bifurcation of Pakistan had begun.

As the Pakistan Army's unspeakable atrocities escalated, streams of refugees from Bangladesh started flowing into adjacent Indian states—West Bengal, Assam, Meghalaya and Tripura. Constant illegal immigration into these states since 1947 had already caused acute economic, political and social problems. The burden of more refugees would be too much for them. But there was no way to stop the terror-stricken and miserable Bengali refugees coming in. If they did not flee they would almost certainly be killed. But here again the government's calculations were vague and unrealistic.

The Ministry of Rehabilitation, for instance, thought that no more than a couple of million refugees would come in. Actually, from April 14 to May 21 more than three and a half million had arrived. In the last week of May Indira Gandhi went to the northeastern states to meet the victims of Pakistani atrocities face to face. On seeing their physical plight and mental state and hearing their tales of woe, she was so shaken that on return to Raj Bhavan in Calcutta she declared grimly and firmly: 'The world must know what is happening here and do something about it. In any case, we cannot let Pakistan continue this holocaust'. By now the flow of refugees had turned into a flood. Soon their number rose to a staggering 10 million.

Yet there still was no clarity about India's strategy or policy. Discussions and debate, whether in the inner recesses of the government or out in the open at such institutions as the Indian Council of World Affairs (ICWA), the School of International Studies (SIS) and so on, were confused, confusing and cacophonic. For example, in the very first public discussion in Delhi at which political leaders, academics and other opinion-makers took part, Balraj Madhok, then president of the Jana Sangh, the forerunner of the Bharatiya Janta Party (BJP), emphatically declared that India must not support Bangladesh's separation from Pakistan because that would lead to a break-up of India, too. Nor was there any dearth of armchair strategists who argued that a united Pakistan rather then a bifurcated one was in

India's interest. Moreover, there were frightening forecasts that a war with Pakistan, if started, could continue for a very long time (some mentioned Vietnam while Bhutto talked of a thousand-year war), and that would lead to heavy bombing of Indian cities and industrial centres and displacement of population. K. Subrahmanyam, an officer of the prestigious Indian Administrative Service and director of the Institute for Defence Studies and Analyses (IDSA), was practically alone in refuting these assumptions and pleading that the Bangladesh crisis should be viewed as a threat to Indian security. Others tried to dismiss him as a 'maverick' opposed to official policy of restraint and the majority view.

On the other hand, a large number of people, including some members of Indira Gandhi's council of ministers, were clamouring for immediate military action against Pakistan to stem the tide of refugees. Critics said that her government's 'so-called restraint' was nothing but 'spinelessness masquerading as caution.' However, she managed to calm down the 'hotheads' within her ranks by quietly telling them that she and her Army Chief, General Manekshaw, were agreed that the monsoon was not the time for the military to move, especially when requisite logistics had yet to be put in place. She also made it clear that she had absolutely no intention to absorb the 10 million refugees in India. Pakistan's 'internal problem' had become India's problem, and this was 'unacceptable'. From the foregoing it is obvious that by then she knew that the war was inevitable and was thinking through things accordingly. But she did not want to give any public hint of this, and was taking care not to make any warlike statements.

On the other hand, the Prime Minister had no hesitation to help the Mukti Bahini, the liberation army that Bangladeshis had formed to fight the Pakistani army from occupation. She also allowed the freedom fighters to set up a Bangladesh government-in-exile at Mujibnagar near Calcutta though she discouraged all demands for its immediate recognition.

In this atmosphere, a closed-door seminar on Bangladesh at the ICWA on July 3 acquired extraordinary importance. For, at it K. Subrahmanyam presented a paper arguing that Pakistan's military junta would 'prefer defeat at India's hand to a political settlement.' Therefore, the crisis presented India 'an opportunity of a lifetime' to cut Pakistan to size and to liberate the people of Bangladesh. The paper was confidential and not meant for publication. But somehow it found its way to *The Times*, London, which published it as a full-page article on July 13. Instantly, it became a sensation and was quoted widely in India and abroad. Pakistan's foreign secretary of that day, Sultan Mohammed Khan, has recorded in his memoirs that he gave copies this paper to Zhou Enlai in Beijing and Andrei Gromyko in Moscow as proof of 'India's real intentions'. Since K. Subrahmanyam was an IAS officer though seconded to a government-financed think tank, it was generally assumed that he was reflecting the government policy. The reality, however, was that both the Ministry of Defence and the Army Headquarters were displeased with him.

In this context, some strange notions sprouted among gullible Indians. One was that the Mukti Bahini, directed by the government-in-exile, would take care of the beleaguered Pakistan Army, and India had to do nothing. Few of them knew that the government-in-exile was divided into several squabbling factions.

The United States that had been 'tilting' towards Pakistan all the time saw its opportunity and established contact with one of the ministers, Khondkar Mushtaq Ahmed of which the prime minister, Tajuddin, had no knowledge. The chain of command of the Mukti Bahini that the government-in-exile had formed had not been able to establish its authority fully. This was by no means all.

Neither Tajuddin nor Khondkar Mushtaq enjoyed the confidence of Sheikh Mujib whose five nominated confidants, called *Khalifas*, were headed by his nephew, Sheikh Moni. The *Khalifas*, fearing that the leadership of the resistance might pass from the Awami League to the Mukti Bahini formed a rival army called Mujib Bahini. Ironically, one Lieutenant General of the Indian Army trained the Mukti Bahini and another did the same for the Mujib Bahini. Pro-Moscow and pro-Beijing groups, ploughing their own furrows, further complicated the depressing situation.

In the midst of this all some unexpected tectonic changes took place in the international configuration of forces that profoundly changed the parameters within which to face the grave challenge confronting India. On June 28, presumably encouraged by the lack of pressure either from the people of West Pakistan or the international community, Yahya Khan announced a plan for the transfer of power to civilians that was not only fraudulent but also diabolic. He appointed a handpicked Bengali civilian, A.M. Khan, as governor of East Pakistan with a mandate to hold elections to National Assembly seats 'vacated' by members of the banned Awami League who 'disappeared'. Arriving in Delhi a week later Henry Kissinger, President Nixon's special assistant for national security, dismayed his interlocutors by calling Yahya's move as a 'conciliatory gesture'. However, his talks with Indian leaders were desultory. No one knew, of course, that he was really on a totally different and supremely important mission.

On July 16, Nixon announced that Kissinger had been on a secret visit to China and that he himself would go to Beijing in February 1972. A sea change in relations between the US and China, sworn enemies of each other for 20 years, startled the whole world. For India, it was a matter of the gravest concern, given China's unstinted support to Pakistan. Two days after the 'Nixon Shock', Kissinger told the Indian ambassador to the US, that if China intervened in a 'warlike situation' between India and Pakistan, New Delhi should not look to Washington 'for assistance'.

The US-China rapprochement bordering on an alliance had pronouncedly accentuated the threat to Indian security in the midst of the steadily worsening Bangladesh Crisis. Indira Gandhi's response to it was cool, quick, firm and superb. Displaying strategic virtuosity rare among this country's political leaders, she realised that the situation demanded a countervailing international linkage. Within 48 hours of the Kissinger-Jha conversation, therefore, she sent to Moscow D.P. Dhar, who had been ambassador to the Soviet Union and had just returned to Delhi to be one of her principal advisers on Bangladesh though his official designation was Chairman of the Policy Planning Committee in the Ministry of External Affairs. In the familiar environs of the Soviet capital he had no difficulty in negotiating the Indo-Soviet Treaty of Peace, Friendship and Cooperation, which was signed in New Delhi on August 9.

Of great help to him in his task was that two years earlier the then Soviet defence minister, Marshal Andrei Grechko, had offered India such a treaty during his visit to Delhi. He had indeed brought a Soviet draft of it with him. But it had remained in the works all the while because Indira was in no hurry to clinch it. However, a radical change in the power equations warranted a radically different approach. Even so, two important changes had to be made in Moscow's draft before India could agree to it. In the first place, the Soviet Union had similar treaties with a number of friendly countries each of which contained a clause on defence cooperation. Indira did not want it. Consequently, the Indo-Soviet treaty only provided that in the event of the security of either party being threatened, the two sides would immediately 'engage in consultations'. Secondly, making the solitary exception in the format of similar treaties, the Soviet Union recorded its endorsement of India's non-aligned status.

This made nonsense of the vociferous criticism in the West, especially the US, that India had abandoned non-alignment in which Indira Gandhi's inveterate critics at home had joined gleefully. They were silenced, however, when the crunch came and the Soviet Union delivered on the treaty to the resounding applause of the Indian people. Let these essential details together with one minor caveat by Moscow be outlined at an appropriate stage in this narrative.

Other developments in the month of August were disconcerting. In Pakistan, Yahya was going ahead with his plans for a sham transfer of power to civilians, and in this he was getting overt support of the US, especially after Kissinger had threatened us with American neutrality in case of Chinese intervention in the ongoing India-Pakistan crisis over Bangladesh. The under-secretary in the state department had the temerity to suggest to foreign secretary T.N. Kaul that India should 'control guerilla activity on its side of the border' and accept UN personnel to 'handle refugee aid'. America's clandestine contacts with Khondkar Mushtaq in Mujib Nagar were also continuing. To cap it all, Yahya had brusquely rejected the UN secretary-general, U. Thant's concern about Sheikh Mujibur Rahman's trial, declaring that Pakistan could not accept the proposition that any 'judicial verdict on the individual case will have repercussions outside the borders of Pakistan. No such repercussions are inevitable unless Pakistan's hostile neighbour, India, is encouraged to make them so'. (*Dawn*, August 16, 1971.)

Indira Gandhi realised that it was time to educate and build up international opinion on Pakistan's savage genocide in East Bengal. She, therefore, decided to go on an extended foreign tour. She began with Moscow where she apprised Leonid Brezhnev and other Soviet leaders of the growing danger of war in the subcontinent. Then she undertook a 21-day travel that took her to Brussels, Vienna, Paris, Bonn, London and Washington. As I have said in another chapter in this volume, it was a fascinating essay in masterly diplomacy. Everywhere she went hers was a virtuous performance. Typical of her style in private negotiations was an exchange with the British Foreign Secretary, Sir Alec-Douglas-Home. '"Our fear," said he, "is that there would be war". "We wouldn't start it"', was her laconic reply.

In every country she went to, including the US, public and media opinion over the unspeakable Pakistani atrocities on the Bangladeshi people was far ahead of their governments'. Yet appeals for reticence were ubiquitous. She used her public appearances to deal with them. When a BBC interviewer spoke of restraint, she burst out that such appeals to her were 'meaningless'. No government had shown such restraint as hers had 'despite such tremendous provocation and threat to our security and stability'. The interviewer persisted in his argument that restraint was indeed the need of the hour. She shot back: '"When Hitler was on the rampage, why didn't you say, '"Let's keep quiet, have peace with Germany and let the Jews die"'?

There is no point going into the murky and dreary details of the way the notorious Nixon-Kissinger duo treated her in Washington. In 2005, the US State Department published *South Asia Crisis, 1971*, Volume XI in the series Foreign Relations of the United States 1969-1976. A perusal of this tome would show that Indira Gandhi gave her interlocutors as good as she got but with dignity and courtesy. The volume also records that while waiting for her to arrive at the White House, the US president and his national security adviser called her a 'witch' and then added a rhyming epithet that no civilised individual would use for any lady, leave alone a foreign head of government. However, even American public opinion was on her side and against the perverse policies of Nixon and Kissinger.

At the National Press Club when a questioner inquired about the possibility of a meeting between her and Yahya she replied that she could not possibly 'shake hands with a clenched fist'. She also pointed out that while she had 'never used a rude word' about anybody, Yahya had been making offensive statements against her and about things in general, which precluded a 'friendly conversation'. The applause that followed was loud and prolonged.

All this was by no means without effect. When the Bangladesh War became the subject of heated discussion and hectic diplomatic activity at the UN Security Council, France and Britain abstained on resolutions unacceptable to India. Later, in early 1972 they were quick to recognise Bangladesh as a sovereign state.

During her stay in London, Indira Gandhi had told a meeting of the India League: 'I am sitting on top of a volcano and I honestly do not know when it is going to erupt'. Shortly after returning home in November she knew that the flashpoint was near. On the one hand, Yahya and his cohorts, in cooperation with leaders of religious parties and even Bhutto, were building up war psychosis in West Pakistan. On the other, the brutality of the Pakistani army in East Bengal had reached its crescendo. The 100,000-strong, India-backed Mukti Bahini was fighting the army of occupation with equal ferocity. However, the 'hot pursuit' of the East Bengali guerillas by the Pakistani troops was often leading to clashes between them and Indian armed forces along the border. Obviously, to allow such a situation to last indefinitely would be an invitation to disaster.

On the night of November 21/22 a Pakistani infantry brigade, supported by tanks, artillery and air force launched a large-scale attack on a Mukti Bahini base at Belonia in an area broadly called Boyra very close to Jessore on the border. During their operations, the Pakistani soldiers crossed the frontier and attacked several Indian villages. The Indian armed forces brought down three Pakistan Air Force (PAF) aircraft in Indian air space and arrested the three pilots who had baled out. I was in London at that time and on the next morning *The Times* declared under a huge headline that the India-Pakistan war over Bangladesh had begun. The American newspapers, I later learned, had done the same thing. They were embarrassed, however, because the Indian authorities had flown the world media to the Boyra area to see for themselves what the situation on the ground was.

A day before this episode, Yahya had suddenly extended his 'hand of friendship' and asked India to 'grasp it' so that the two countries could 'begin a new era of good neighbourly relations.' On November 23, however, he declared a 'national emergency', asserting that Pakistan was 'threatened by external aggression'. Indira Gandhi immediately repudiated his protestations, telling Yahya that his emergency was a 'climax of his efforts to put the blame on us for a situation he himself had created'. Almost simultaneously the Pakistani military dictator was telling *Newsweek*: 'I have no reason to tell you that the war is not imminent because it is. In ten days time, I might not be in Rawalpindi. I shall be fighting a war.' Sure enough, he kept his word.

Almost exactly ten days after his interview with the American magazine, on September 3 just before sunset Yahya launched what later came to be known as his 'Unlucky Strike' as bombers of the PAF attacked a number of Indian advanced air bases. It was a clumsy and unproductive effort that achieved little besides starting the War for the liberation of Bangladesh. Had he waited another 24 hours, the responsibility for starting the war would have been India's. For after the Boyra incident, this country had abandoned all hopes of avoiding a war and planned to march into Bangladesh on September 4. Evidently, by then there were a number of Indian military personnel in *mufti* within Bangladesh to help the Mukti Bahini. On the morning of September 4, they donned their uniforms.

Indira Gandhi was in Calcutta when the war began. She returned to Delhi rather late at night. After consulting her cabinet colleagues and leaders of opposition parties who all concurred with her war plans, she addressed the nation at the midnight hour, appealing to all Indians vigorously and valiantly to pursue the 'war forced on us'. She also told the world that both the Indian Army and the Mukti Bahini were fighting under the joint Indo-Bngladeshi command.

Since March 25, she had been resisting strident demands for immediate recognition of the provisional government of Bangladesh in Mujib Nagar. On December 6, she announced the recognition of Bangladesh to wild cheers by Parliament. Pakistan immediately broke diplomatic relations with India.

A detailed account of the progress of the war would be pointless for reams and reams of pages have been written on it. Suffice it to say that it was a lightning campaign leading to brilliant success. According to *The Sunday Times* (December 22, 1971), it was 'an achievement reminiscent of the German blitzkrieg across France in 1940'. Yet it would be only fair to take note of a few flaws in military plans and their execution. The most important of these was that occupation of Dacca was not part of the original war plan. The directive was to 'occupy as much of the Bangladesh territory as possible'. Lieutenant General J.R. Jacob, then Chief of Staff to Lieutenant-General J.S. Aurora, the overall field commander, claims that he added this objective to the plan later. It seems more accurate to say that local commanders, realising the importance of taking Dhaka, collectively proceeded to do so.

It is also worth mentioning that getting to Dhaka in a land crisscrossed by north-south rivers had its problems. Dropping of paratroopers did help. However, it was easier and faster to get to Dhaka from the north because there were no east-west rivers in the way. In fact, Major-General Gandharv Nagra, GOC of one of the two Divisions deployed in the north, did reach Dhaka earlier than anyone else. From Mirpur he even sent a note to Pakistan's General A. A. K. Niazi. Having been military attaché in Pakistan earlier. Nagra obviously knew Niazi well because he addressed the overall commander of the defeated Pakistan army in the east as 'My deal Abdulla'.

From this no one drew the wrong conclusion that the higher command of the Indian Army should have ordered both the Divisions in the north to move southwards to the Bangladeshi capital. The Indo-Soviet treaty by itself was a deterrent to China, no doubt. But not content with this, the Soviet Union deployed mechanised troops along its border with China, especially in Kazakhstan. It also conveyed to Beijing a stern warning about the consequences of its intervention in the war. With all that, however, this country could not possibly lower its guard against China. Who can say when a country might choose to act irrationally? General Manekshaw had ordered therefore that one of the two divisions deployed in north of Bangladesh must stay close to the China border.

This was a wise move because there were frequent reports of the movement of Chinese troops on their side of the frontier. I remember an occasion during the first week of the war when, in the course of the daily briefing on the war situation, an American correspondent asked what exactly was happening along the India-China border. The then defence secretary, K.B. Lall replied: 'Both sides are praying for snow'.

Later disclosures by the Americans themselves reveal that as late as on December 10, 1971, at a secret meeting with the Chinese Ambassador to the UN, Huang Hua, at a CIA safe house in New York, Kissinger was cajoling China to do something against India. The official 'top-secret/sensitive/eyes only' record quotes Kissinger as telling his Chinese interlocutor: 'The President wants you to know that it's, of course, for the People's Republic to decide its course of action...but if the People's Republic were to consider the situation on the Indian subcontinent a threat to its security, and if it took measures to protect its security, the US would oppose efforts of others (read the Soviet Union) to interfere with the People's Republic'. Kissinger went on to say: 'We are afraid that if nothing is done to stop it (Indian advance in Bangladesh), East Pakistan will become a Bhutan and West Pakistan will become a Nepal. And India with Soviet help would be free to turn its energies elsewhere'. (*The Kissinger Transcripts* (New York, 1998, p. 51.)

The commentary of the book's editor William Burr on the Kissinger-Huang meeting is also noteworthy: 'Huang's rhetoric in the conversation was militant; Kissinger concluded incorrectly that the Chinese were about to join the fighting. Beijing had as little interest in intervening as India had in escalating the fighting". (Ibid: 48.) All this undoubtedly vindicates Manekshaw's cautious approach.

Making allowance for the time differential between New York and New Delhi, within 24 hours of the secret parleys between Kissinger and Huang Hua, something spectacular happened in the Indian capital right in the open. By then it had also become known that the US had dispatched a naval Task Force of its Sixth Fleet, led by the nuclear aircraft carrier USS Enterprise from across the Malacca Strait to the Bay of Bengal. Indira Gandhi was furious but knew that this show of force was nothing more than symbolic and took it in her stride. However, to shore up the people's confidence and morale she decided to address a public meeting in the heart of the capital in broad daylight. At least a million men, women and children attended. Patriotic songs sung by legendary Lata Mangeshkar had stirred the vast audience before the Prime Minister spoke. She, however, was calm and composed. She indulged in no oratorical flourishes but did convey clearly her resolute defiance of the US attempts at intimidation. She knew that the Soviet submarines, some of them perhaps nuclear, were closely following the American naval vessels. At the same time she also knew very well that while the Soviet Union was standing by India fully, it was urging her government to finish the war as soon as possible. Evidently, Brezhnev was getting a message a day from Nixon. The Soviet deputy foreign minister, V.V. Kuznetsov, was camping in New Delhi to monitor the progress of the war.

While Indira Gandhi was addressing the cheering crowds, General Manekshaw was broadcasting over All India Radio a message to General Niazi asking him to lay down his arms. The beleaguered Pakistani general could draw no comfort from the American fleet's movement because his troops had already started throwing in the towel. In fact, his deputy, Major General Rao Farman Ali was appealing to the UN to intercede and bring the war to an end.

To cut a long story short a week after the Kissinger-Huang conversation, General Niazi, together with 93,000 Pakistani troops surrendered to General Aurora. No surrender on such a large scale had taken place anywhere since World War II.

Remarkably, the much-bruited US naval Task Force reached the Bay of Bengal when the game was already over. Apart from earning widespread opprobrium, its only significant achievement was to hasten Indira Gandhi's decision to start preparations for an underground nuclear detonation. Ordered immediately after the war's end, it was conducted at Pokhran on May 18, 1974.

So far we have discussed only the war in Bangladesh. What about the clash of arms on the Western front? The question is very important in view of the claim of the Nixon-Kissinger duo that they had declared a global alert and dispatched the nuclear naval Task Force to save West Pakistan, which is all that was left of Pakistan, from Indira Gandhi's 'design' to 'dismember it'. In his memoirs, *The White House Years*, that many have called 'The Whitewash Years', Kissinger has been strikingly inventive in trying to perpetuate a downright falsehood. For, the truth about Indian strategy in relation to West Pakistan was totally opposite of what Nixon and Kissinger alleged it to be.

If the directive in the east was to 'occupy as much East Bengal territory as possible' that in the west was to 'see to it that fighting takes place in Pakistan's territory'. Surely this could not have been a shortcut to dismemberment. In any case, as I have recorded several times during the lifetime of several actors in the drama, while walking back to her Parliament House office after announcing the glorious victory in Bangladesh, Indira Gandhi told her Information Adviser H.Y. Sharada Prasad, that she must declare a ceasefire on the western front that evening because 'if I don't do it tonight I wont be able to do so tomorrow.'

P.N. Haksar, her principal secretary, told me later that he had drafted the statement the Prime Minister made about the liberation of

Bangladesh. Its last sentence was the announcement of a simultaneous ceasefire in the west. He was surprised when Indira Gandhi left it out but appreciated the point she made subsequently that before declaring a ceasefire in the West it would be better to hold consultations with those who might hold a different point of view. She first had a private meeting with the Chief of the Army Staff and found him in complete agreement with her though he added that, as always, the Army would obey the government's orders 'whatever they be'. She then summoned a meeting of the Cabinet's Political Affairs Committee. All three Service Chiefs, General Manekshaw, Admiral S.M. Nanda, and Air Chief Marshal P.C. Lal, were in attendance.

When she asked what should be done on the western front, Defence Minister Jagjivan Ram, who apparently was unhappy that he was not always in the loop when decisions on the conduct of the war were taken, said the views of the Army ought to be ascertained. '"Well", remarked a smiling Indira, "let's ask your Chief of the Army Staff"'. Manekshaw repeated to the Cabinet Committee on Political Affairs (CCPA) exactly what he had said earlier to the Prime Minister. The meeting dispersed and Indira promptly declared the ceasefire.

Another pertinent point to be made in this connection is that at a fairly early stage of the war Indira Gandhi was advised that to capture 'a very large chunk' of Sindh in West Pakistan would give the country a useful bargaining chip in the post-war negotiations with Pakistan. But her answer was that the forces in the western region did not have the resources to do so. As it happened, an Indian army battalion almost literally walked uncontested into the Sindh desert and occupied an area of 5,000 square miles that was of no strategic or economic value. It was returned to Pakistan, along with 368 square miles in the Sialkot area of Pakistani Punjab, in accordance with the Shimla Agreement signed by Indira Gandhi and Zulfiqar Ali Bhutto on July 3, 1972. In the terms of the same agreement India retained 364 square miles of territory in northern Kashmir, and the old ceasefire line was accordingly converted into a Line of Control (LoC). Bhutto privately promised 'gradually' to convert this line into an international border but unsurprisingly went back on his word. That, however, is a different story.

The incontrovertible evidence gives the lie to the Nixon-Kissinger claim that Indira Gandhi indeed wanted to dismember West Pakistan but was deterred by US warnings conveyed through the USSR. For years Kissinger went on claiming that his conclusion on Indira's intention was based on the reports of the CIA that had a 'mole' in her cabinet. After long years, it was revealed that the 'mole' was Morarji Desai, a gentleman who had ceased to be a cabinet minister since July 1969.

The crowning irony, however, was that in 1974, when Kissinger, as secretary of state, revisited Delhi, this time around with the avowed purpose of 'improving relations with India', he told P.N. Dhar that were he, 'Mrs. Gandhi's adviser in 1971, he would have told her to do exactly what she did do'. (Dhar, *op.cit.* p. 172.)

After the humiliating defeat and surrender in Bangladesh a tidal wave of trauma, mortification and anger swept Pakistan or whatever was left of it. Brought up on the myth that a single Pakistani soldier was worth his 10 Indian counterparts, the people felt befuddled and betrayed. The army's prestige and awe, most of all Yahya's, plummeted. Air Marshal A. Rahim, Chief of the Air Staff, publicly stated: 'We have been let down by drunken pigs'. The reference to Yahya's fondness for the bottle could not have been clearer. Contemporary eyewitness accounts of the goings-on at the General Headquarters are revealing. Yahya did not dare come out of the President's House. His cronies also went into hiding. Among the senior generals present, Lieutenant-General Gul Hasan—then Chief of the General Staff—was giving the orders and 'he was being obeyed'.

At that time Bhutto was flying back from New York after having indulged in all kinds of theatrics at the UN Security Council. But instead of heading for home, he stayed put in Rome. Despite the tears he shed at Turtle Bay he was jubilant that his time had come because in view of the election results, the Army, with which he had collaborated fully, had no option but to transfer power to him. But he was cautious. Yahya and the Army may have been discredited thoroughly but he was still the Supreme Commander of the armed forces and the Army had got used to ruling the country since 1958. What if Yahya refused to transfer power? He took a plane to Rawalpindi only after Gul Hasan and others generals sent a colonel to Italian capital to assure Bhutto that he need have no worry or suspicion at all.

On December 20, 42-years old Zulfiqar Ali Bhutto was sworn in as the world's first and only civilian Chief Martial Law Administrator because there was no other constitutional or legal basis for transference of power to him!

Ironically, at that precise moment, Sheikh Mujibur Rahman, the hero of the historic turning point in the Indian subcontinent, was languishing in a Pakistani jail in solitary confinement and with absolutely no access to radio or newspapers. Therefore, he did not even know that his mission had been a glorious success, and that his people, delirious despite the horrors they had gone through, were eagerly waiting for him. Released by Bhutto—whose main concern was to convince Mujib that he alone was responsible for saving the life of the

Bangladesh leader—he was also offered a Pakistani aircraft to go wherever he wanted. Mujibur decided to fly to London where he was treated as a head of state and lionised by the Bangladeshi and Indian Diaspora. Having found his bearings he then headed home via Delhi. Indian welcome to him was expectedly exuberant. But it paled compared with the apparently unending outpouring of adoration and affection with which the Bangladeshis overwhelmed him. He was undoubtedly the Father of the new nation though his people chose to call him Bangabandhu (Elder Brother of Bangladesh).

A few months later, in the first General Elections in independent Bangladesh, Mujibur's Party, the Awami League, won with 73 percent of the votes polled. This was an achievement unheard of anywhere in the entire region before or since. The highest proportion of votes that Jawaharlal Nehru had got at the height of his power and glory was 47 percent. Only in the 1984 General Elections, held immediately after Indira Gandhi's assassination, her and her father's party got 49 percent that remains the highest ever in India. In Pakistan, Bhutto rode to supreme power with no more than 38 percent vote.

Mujibur was blessed with charisma. He also had the enviable gift of moving the masses by his powerful oratory. But he lacked the stature and vision of, say, Nehru or Jinnah. Yet, it seemed that that this relatively young man was destined to lead his country, consolidate its newly won freedom as well as its democratic system, and firmly put it on the path to progress. Alas, this expectation was not to be fulfilled, partly because of Mujibur's own shortcomings and largely because his party, the Awami League, was torn apart by factional divisions and implacable rivalries that had begun even during the freedom struggle and had now assumed alarming proportions within South Asia's most excitable and volatile society. The more radical groups that had fought bravely against he Pakistan army were disaffected as much by their exclusion from power as because of their ideological objections to Mujibur's 'moderate policies'. They accused him of 'betraying his promise to redistribute the country's wealth'. Even among moderate sections there was great resentment against the 'arrogance and greed' of Mujibur's family and favoured cohorts. Corruption and bad governance are common to the entire subcontinent but these afflicted Bangladesh, even at that early stage, to an uncommon degree.

No wonder the economic situation deteriorated fast. People groaned under the weight of rising prices and growing shortages. More disastrously, Bangabandhu failed to establish a grip on the faction-ridden and fractious army. As stated earlier, there were not many Bengalis in the undivided Pakistan army in any case. Those that were could come back home only in early 1974 when Pakistan at last recognised Bangladesh. Unfortunately, many of them were pro-Pakistan at heart and were, therefore, at loggerheads with the officers and men who had fought valiantly for freedom from Pakistan. To make matters worse, radical parties and groups had their adherents at almost all levels in the armed forces. They undermined discipline and aggravated confusion.

Mujibur's response to the mounting crisis was shockingly inept and counterproductive. He resorted to repression and emergency laws. When this did not work, he shook the system he himself had built up to its roots. First, he changed the parliamentary system into a presidential one, arrogating all powers to himself as founder-president of the country. And then, in February 1975, he suddenly converted Bangladesh, a passionate devotee to competitive politics even while under the jackboot of the Pakistani military, into a one-party state. India, itself drifting towards Indira Gandhi's Emergency at that time took no great notice of what was happening in its neighbourhood. But the rest of the democratic world was appalled, and some of the enraged Bangladeshis started plotting against the man they used to revere.

Indira Gandhi was gravely concerned when her intelligence agencies informed her of what was afoot in Bangladesh. She sent her most trusted spy chief, R.N. Kao, then head of Research & Analysis Wing, India's foreign intelligence agency better known by its acronym RAW, with instructions to give Mujibur full details of the threat to his life. Kao did the best he could but to no avail. As he told me many years later, the moment he started explaining how alarmed Indira Gandhi was because the threat to Mujibur's life was real, Bangabandhu started laughing. '"Kao Sahib", he said, "why are you worried? All these people are my sons; none of them would raise his hand against me"'.

On the morning of August 15, 1975—28th anniversary of Indian independence, incidentally—a group of relatively junior military officers assassinated Sheikh Mujibur Rahman, the founding father of Bangladesh. It was not just a case of the foul murder of an eminent leader; it was a savage massacre of all members of his family that were with him at his residence and Dhanmondi in the Bangladeshi capital. If his eldest daughter, Sheikh Hasina, survived the slaughter and is today Bangladesh's Prime Minister for the second time, it was only because she was travelling abroad on that darkest of dark days.

It is both relevant and necessary to mention here that Indira Gandhi was affected very seriously by the murder of the Chile's elected President, Salvador Allende two years earlier. How profound was the effect became public a year after her own assassination when Fidel

Castro wrote about it. On November 11, 1973 Castro was in New Delhi on way to Vietnam. An 'extremely pleasant' banquet Indira gave in his honour was 'rudely interrupted' by the 'stunning news' from 'far-off Chile where it was still morning': Allende had been killed in a *coup d'etat*. '"At that dramatic moment", recorded the Cuban leader, "Indira Gandhi, in a proof of intimacy and confidence, said to me: "what they have done to Allende they want to do to me also. There are people here, connected with the same foreign forces that acted in Chile, who would like to eliminate me."' If Mujibur's assassination saddened her even more it was understandable. For, here was a case of almost an entire family being wiped out.

Finally, the last word on Bangladesh and its liberation should belong to the distinguished Pakistani commentator Ayaz Amir who has said repeatedly over the years that the Father of Bangladesh was 'not Mujibur Rahman but Yahya Khan'. He could have added: 'with unstinted support by Zulfiqar Bhutto'.

Chapter VII

Defence and Nuclear Policy of the Congress

Bhashyam Kasturi

This paper attempts to review India's defence and nuclear policy in the period 1964 to 1984. It is an interesting period for analysis as it straddles two great Prime Ministers of Independent India. Nehru was at the helm of affairs, continuously for 17 years, while his daughter Indira was at the helm for a similar period, but with breaks. One cannot forget that Lal Bahadur Shastri was also Prime Minister in the crucial years after Nehru's death and led the nation in the war against Pakistan.

While studies of India's defence policy in this period have been undertaken with a focus on the nature of policy enunciated and its actual implementation, the impact of party politics and more particularly that of the Indian National Congress remains to be seen. It is argued that the party's focus right from 1947 had been on external relations, foreign affairs, of which defence was a subset. This was an outcome of the policy of non-alignment. Towards the end of Nehru's tenure as Prime Minister, the Sino-Indian war brought into sharp focus the need for party and government to pay attention to defence as a separate entity.

At the time of independence, the Congress Party was driven by an anti-colonial and anti-imperial attitude towards defence. Independent India began with the notion that armed forces while important for the country had to be kept in check and under civilian supremacy.

The basic objectives of India's path were defined by Nehru in a speech at Columbia University in 1949. He stated: 'India is a very old country with a great past. But it is a new country also with urges and desires...Inevitably she had to consider her foreign policy in terms of her enlightened self-interest, but at the same time brought to it a touch of her idealism. Thus she has tried to combine idealism with national interest. The main objectives of that policy are: the pursuit of peace, not through alignment with any major power or group of powers, but through an independent approach to each controversial or disputed issue; the liberation of subject peoples; the maintenance of freedom both national and individual...'[1]

The Nehruvian consensus on foreign policy was premised on three aspects. First, self-reliance, second, independence and, finally, autonomy of action independent of others. This was also the case in terms of defence, where Nehru took India out of the offensive-defence of the colonial authorities and made it into a defensive-defence in the context of Independent India. A defensive posture was premised on the policy of non-alignment and on the notion that it was important to focus national attention on development, of which defence was a part, but not essential part. At the same time, the Nehruvian model did not rule out the use of the armed forces in an offensive posture as was witnessed during the first Kashmir war in 1948.

The interface between the government's defence and nuclear policy and the Congress Party can be also understood or explained in terms of the decision-making process within the party. According to Nehru, 'It is basically the government policy and the implementation of that policy that affects the people. The Congress comes in only in broadly effecting that policy or pushing it in that direction or that, but much more so in carrying the message of that policy to the people...'[2]

What this meant is that the Congress Party was meant to act both as a sort of advisor to the Government and a mechanism to carry the message of government policy to the people. The party organisation could not of course determine government policy, as in the case of India's nuclear policy, but could debate and discuss a certain line of thought that was being articulated both within and outside the party.

At the top is the President of the party, followed by the AICC and then the PCC. The CWC is the chief executive organ of the party and is in fact the decision-making body of the party. There have been times, like when Mrs Gandhi was Prime Minister the individual's stamp on decisions of the party was felt more despite the fact that the individual was not a party president. This was true even in Nehru's time and was even apparent in the years when Indira Gandhi was in power.

Rajni Kothari refers to the strength of the 'Congress system' in the mid-1960s.[3] This is best explained as the capacity of the Congress Party organisation to network the dominant social groups through, for example, factions, and linking them with the party structure. The 'Congress system' was considered to be, in a sense, an effective channel for mobilising popular support in the election, and also putting popular demand on a higher political level, like the State Legislative

Assembly or Lok Sabha. This was another way of speaking of one party rule and with the electoral performance of the Congress Party being steady from one election to another and the centrality of the 'Congress system' to Indian political system could be justified. This one party dominance was shaken in the 1967 general election, when the Congress Party for the first time suffered a major setback both in the Centre and in many states.

The decade beginning in the early 1960s and extending a few years into the 1970s witnessed India's involvement in three wars on the subcontinent; one with China and two with Pakistan. These three wars significantly altered India's global views and challenged the efficacy of the Non-Aligned Movement. One of the underpinnings of the period under review in terms of party policy responses and government decision-making was India's commitment to the Parliamentary system of government. Except for two years during the emergency this has remained the driving force of defence policy. The only area in which a certain strategic independence/autonomy was witnessed was in the realm of nuclear matters. The 1964 Lop Nor nuclear test by China forced India to consider its options and led, in the next decade, to the Indian Peaceful Nuclear Explosion (PNE) in 1974. From 1964 to 1984 the Congress Party journeyed with the nation, in two wars with Pakistan, the creation of Bangladesh and witnessed the assassination of a Prime Minister.

It would be recalled that soon after the border war with China in 1962, India fought a war with Pakistan on the Western Front. Stalemated though it was, it was fought by the very same soldiers, with much the same equipment that the Army had in 1962. In August 1971, came the Indo-Soviet Treaty, followed by yet another war with Pakistan, leading to the creation of Bangladesh. What the 1971 conflict with Pakistan brought to the fore was the position of importance the armed forces had in the national decision-making process just prior to and during the war. This was a gradual process and did not happen overnight. It also involved individuals like General Sam Manekshaw, Chief of Army Staff and Chairman, Joint Chiefs of Staff, who attempted to synchronise military decision-making with the foreign policy decisions on Bangladesh. In 1974, India carried out our first nuclear explosion and 10 years later, the Indian Army carried out Operation Blue Star to rid the Golden Temple of Sikh terrorists followed by the assassination of Indira Gandhi.

The period under review witnessed increased allocation to defence and by 1984 India was spending roughly 3 per cent of its GDP on defence. The accent on self-reliance that Nehru propagated, one that persisted despite the necessity of imports in the aftermath of the 1962 war, is an aspect of India's defence policy that has stood the test of time. It was really Nehru's leadership of the Congress Party and the evolution of a second generation of leadership of leaders in the party who provided the political platform for defence and nuclear security.[4]

The narrative of the party and its relation to government on matters relating to defence and nuclear policy requires analysis of the various resolutions and discussions on these matters during Congress sessions. The first session of importance to the period under review was the one held at Bhubaneswar session in January 1964.

The border war with China in 1962 was a watershed for the Indian military. For Nehru, the war marked a decline in the importance of non-alignment and led to a escalation in India's defence budget. It was also an end of the road for Krishna Menon as Defence Minister and brought in Y.B. Chavan, the seasoned Congressman from Maharashtra. The details of India's defence expansion can be found in other texts, but the more important factor is the higher priority given to defence in the national matrix.

Immediately after the war, President Radhakrishnan concluded that, 'military weakness has been a temptation, and a little military strength may be a deterrent.'[5] In the aftermath, a ambitious five-year plan for expansion was put into place for the period April 1964-March 1969. This plan had a six-fold objective which *inter alia* included the expansion of the three armed forces, establishment of defence production industries to reduce import dependence and improvement of communications along the border.[6] The first budget after the war in 1963 doubled the defence expenditure from Rs. 473 crore allocated in 1962/63 and which included an emergency allocation of Rs. 100 crore for the war effort to Rs. 867 crore.[7] The following year, India increased spending on defence to 4 per cent of GDP. Soon thereafter came the first time Soviet offer and the agreement signed on September 11, 1964 for the supply of defence materials and for the setting up of a MIG aircraft factory in India. New ordnance factories (OFs) were planned and established during the next three decades. The number of OFs thus grew to 35 by the mid-1980s.

During the consideration of the draft resolution on international affairs in the Subjects Committee in January 1964 at Bhubaneswar, Morarji Desai defended the policy of non-alignment of India and expressed the hope that the Nuclear Test Ban Treaty (NTBT) would be followed up and would eventually lead to total disarmament and international concord. Reflecting the then prevailing Nehruvian worldview, Desai added that if it was not achieved, the winner and loser, both would perish in a world conflict.

Interestingly, he also raised the question of how India could reconcile her present efforts to raise her armed strength with the professions of peace. And answering the own question he said, 'To my mind, there is no contradiction between the two. We have to safeguard our freedom, which cannot be separated from freedom elsewhere.' The reason for building up the armed forces was obvious to anyone, the aftermath of the border war with China. Desai went a step further and added to say that if the Chinese refused to vacate Indian territory then 'we should keep ourselves prepared to turn them out by force.' In addition, he pointed to the 'intrasigence' of China with regard to the Colombo proposals and therefore, the nation was obliged to strengthen her defences.[8]

The resolution passed by the Congress on International Affairs in January 1964 stated that it had become imperative to put an end to war 'if the world is to avoid grave catastrophe or even to survive.' It was concluded that this could 'only be realised by full and complete disarmament and the outlawing of war which our Government has held as its firm position and advocated in the United Nations and the world generally.'

The Congress was also clear at this stage, that India 'adopted and consistently pursued a policy of freedom from entanglements with the world blocs, each poised against, suspicious and fearful of the other, and perpetuating the climate of cold war as between them and in the world' in the interests of world peace. In their understanding, the adoption of the policy of non-alignment, peaceful co-existence and support of human rights and freedoms 'have won increasing appreciation even amongst many aligned countries. Non-alignment is also increasingly regarded as a helpful and constructive force in the lowering of world tensions and in the containment of the area of the cold war itself.'[9]

Faced with increasing government attention to modernising the armed forces and keeping in mind the threat from Pakistan, the party had to take a strong supportive position *vis-à-vis* the nation's spending on defence. Therefore, the Congress in its statements at the AICC session at Bhubaneswar proclaimed, 'its full support of the firm resolve of the nation to resist Chinese aggression with all its strength, military, political, diplomatic of our people. The Congress supports the Government in its adherence to the position that they will continue to seek and entertain peaceful approaches and methods but are equally resolved not to yield to aggression or to acquiesce in the surrender of national sovereignty. The Congress firmly believes that the Government's acceptance and support of the Colombo proposals is based on this approach and, therefore, endorses it warmly.'

In October 1963, the Partial Test Ban Treaty came into force. It was a treaty signed in Moscow which banned all nuclear weapons testing, except for underground tests. The US, UK and USSR signed this treaty which had its focus in the then rising concern about radioactive fallout as a result of nuclear weapons testing underwater, in the atmosphere, and on the ground's surface, on the part of the nuclear powers. In its resolution passed in January 1964, the Congress welcomed and expressed the hope that the Nuclear Test Ban Agreement would help lower world tensions and would lead progressively to wider and more significant relaxations resulting ultimately in the ending of the cold war. The Congress also welcomed the continuance of the better world climate that this Agreement induced amongst the Bloc countries themselves and in the world in general.[10]

Coming just two years after the border war with China, the Congress Party had to make statements regarding the need to revitalise defence preparedness. It therefore stated that it supported the nation's, 'accentuated defence preparations forced on us by the continuing aggression by China is in no way inconsistent with or contrary to dedication to the cause of world peace and cooperation, our allegiance to the Charter of the United Nations or to our determination to strive for a warless world. In a totally disarmed world there can be no aggression.' The party was however, clear that given the experience with China in 1962 and the aggressive attitude of Pakistan, 'it became and remains the duty of our Government and people, and to the cause of world peace itself, to be prepared to contain, prevent and foil aggression and not to allow it to become gainful to the aggressor.'[11]

Just at the moment, India's troubles with Pakistan also began. Incidents of armed clashes occurred on the border with East Pakistan. Speaking at the Subjects Committee meeting at the 69th session at Durgapur in January 1965, Morarji Desai pointed out that it was necessary for Pakistan to learn to live in peace with India. It is interesting to note that while moving the resolution in the Plenary on January 10, P. Chengalvarayan from Tamil Nadu sounded a note of warning to both China and Pakistan by saying that while India sought peaceful resolutions to bilateral problems, it would do everything possible to 'counteract, prevent and fight aggression' and 'take back every inch of territory lost to the aggressors, whatever the sacrifice.'[12]

Congress President K. Kamaraj while delivering the Presidential address noted that, 'while we must continue to mobilise our resources to build our defence, we shall at the same time keep the door of negotiations open for finding a just and honourable solution. Pakistan's border agreement with China a year ago also came in for criticism from the Congress President who said that it was 'fishing in troubled waters' by concluding the border agreement in respect of territory to which she has no title whatsoever. It was observed that this and any future action showed that 'opportunism' guided Pakistan's actions.[13]

A few months later, intervening in the party debate, Nehru spoke on the international situation at Bombay in May 1964. The Prime Minister said that, 'the Chinese posed a great threat to India.' He stated that India was willing to talk to China provided the Colombo proposals were accepted. Nehru was alive to the constant criticism in Parliament and outside that India's defence preparedness had suffered under the stewardship of Krishna Menon and therefore made it a point to refer to it and said that defence preparations were for meeting any eventuality.

The Annual Report of the Congress Party for the year 1964 makes an interesting reference to the defence situation. It speaks of the unabated threat from China to India's northern frontiers and adds that the country's defence preparedness showed 'new signs of courage and consciousness.' The whole complexion of the armed forces underwent a great change. The party was clearly pushing for a defence buildup to meet any aggression. As mentioned earlier, the push for defence came from the modernisation plan put in place after the Chinese aggression. This gave the armed forces a level of importance both in terms of equipment and in terms of their role in the decision-making process in the governmental system. This process was further strengthened during the 1971 war with Pakistan.

There is also mention of the Chinese nuclear test at Lop Nor on October 16, 1964. This came close on the heels of the Test Ban appeal at the Cairo conference. The admission that there was no 'minimising the psychological and political impact' of the test on the minds of smaller nations and the statement that it posed a threat to the security and peace of the Asian region indicated that India, while adhering to its traditional on not making nuclear weapons was willing to state it would 'use nuclear weapons for peaceful purposes only.'[14]

On October 27, 1964 the CWC met to discuss the draft resolution on international affairs for the AICC meeting slated to meet on November 7 at Guntur. This draft prepared by then foreign minister Swaran Singh, approved the government's policy of not manufacturing nuclear weapons. At the AICC meeting, members received a petition signed by 100 members urging a debate on the nuclear issue. The aim was to get a large number of members to demand that India acquire nuclear weapons 'as an independent deterrent to protect herself against any possible threat from China.'

According to press reports, a majority of speakers at the meeting came out strongly in favour of India manufacturing atom bombs. And that Shastri and the other top leaders managed to stem the tide and got a resolution passed stating that India would continue to use nuclear energy for peaceful purposes was seen by one newspaper as 'nothing short of a miracle.' Shastri declared that, 'We cannot at present think of making atomic bombs in India. We must try to eliminate atomic bombs in the world rather than enter into a nuclear arms competition.' The final resolution proclaimed that, 'efforts should be redoubled for the development of peaceful uses of atomic energy for the prosperity and well-being of the Indian people.'[15]

Shastri was strongly opposed to pursuing the Indian nuclear option. But around this time Homi Bhabha, Secretary of the Atomic Energy Commission, made public statements in favour of the bomb intended to increase public support and put pressure on the political establishment. On October 4, 1964 Bhabha made his estimate public that India could build a bomb within 18 months of the decision to do so. This statement fuelled debate within the Congress Party about whether India should go in for the manufacture of nuclear weapons or not. Not only did this and subsequent statements of Bhabha fuel debate about the desirability of India initiating a weapons programme in the public domain, it also undermined support for Shastri and his 'no weapon' policy within his own Congress Party. That Bhabha was able to make such statement and get away with it can be attributed to his enormous public stature and the tight control over nuclear information which left no effective scientific voice to act as a counterweight.

At the end of 1964, the Congress Party appeared to be split on the nuclear issue. A large number of partymen, favoured the building by India of an independent nuclear deterrent, though it was not very clear in what form and in what time frame. On the other side, was a minority led by Prime Minister Shastri and others who were not in favour of an open shift towards production of nuclear weapons and emphasised India's policy of seeking global nuclear disarmament as the way forward to counter the Chinese threat. There was also a third group within the Congress Party which took a middle path and one which articulated the view that India should neither undertake to produce nor should it exclude the option, but instead look seriously at all options and enhance technological capacities in the light of the Chinese test. This, at the end of the day was what emerged as the stated policy of the government in subsequent years.

At the 69th Session of the Congress held at Durgapur held on January 7, 1965, Morarji Desai clarified India's stand when he said, while moving the resolution on International Affairs (at the Subjects Committee meeting) that, 'the entire world should confine the use of nuclear energy to peaceful uses'. Reiterating the government's stand that manufacture of the bomb would not fit in with the loyalty to the ideal of Mahatma Gandhi and Nehru, Desai added that, 'he did not consider it a fit answer to the Chinese challenge.'

Referring to the demand for a referendum on atom bomb issue, Desai said he was not prepared to leave such a serious issue to be settled by general referendum, but considered it a case for a firm decision by leaders. The discussion on the atomic issue must have been heated for it led T. Chengelvarayan to defend Nehru on the issue of global disarmament. He called disarmament as being in furtherance of defensive strategy for every part of the world. Similarly, the Test Ban Treaty was again in furtherance of the defensive strategy of the world. The Congress resolution pin-pointed some fundamental issues relating to foreign policy: non-alignment remained the sheet-anchor, disarmament was the main slogan and in the context of the Chinese nuclear explosion 'a sense of national danger' was being articulated which furthered the debate on whether India should go nuclear or not.

The Congressmen from Tamil Nadu then went on to say that, '"the question of atomic retaliation is not only politically, militarily or psychologically so easy" and urged all partymen "not to get lost in this dilemma as to whether they (India) should have the bomb or not and think of its far reaching consequences."' Another member Laxmiraman Acharya from UP echoing the same thoughts said that because of the Chinese nuclear fear, 'they need not give up their basic principles, and be frightened by the atomic bomb.'[16]

The next day, when the debate on the resolution on international affairs continued it emerged that there were several amendments that had been tabled seeking a change in India's present policy towards the atomic bomb. And that in view of the new situation arising from the explosion made by China, they should also enter into the race for the manufacture of the atom bomb 'in order to strengthen ourselves and to defend ourselves properly against the Chinese aggression.' There was a reference to the cost of manufacturing the atom bomb, to which Desai said that from an economic point of view also 'it was not desirable.' The logic used against the manufacture of the bomb was that if India were to undertake to make one at a heavy cost, 'she would have no ground to ask for international help for her economic development.'[17]

Despite the intense debate within the party, all amendments were withdrawn and the main resolution was passed unanimously. Lal Bahadur Shastri who was Prime Minister by this time, expressed his happiness at the fact that the resolution had been passed 'unanimously.' According to him, if the expression of such sentiments (as in the amendments) found validity in the policy of different countries, it would lead to the proliferation of atomic weapons.

Shastri then went on to give his reasoning as to why China had exploded a nuclear device at Lop Nor. He said that despite its economic difficulties, Beijing had produced a bomb because it considered the US as its biggest enemy and did not want to stay behind either the US or USSR in the arms race. The Prime Minister stated that India was wedded to the policy of disarmament and added that, 'this was the correct policy under the existing situation.' Shastri, however, added that 'if necessary' this policy might undergo changes in the distant future. He wanted India's relations with China to be seen in the context of New Delhi wanting friendly relations with its neighbours.[18]

The resolution passed on international affairs at Durgapur in January 1965 therefore deplored 'the nuclear explosion conducted by the People's Republic of China in defiance of world opinion and the sustained efforts being made by the vast majority of the nations of the world towards cessation of nuclear tests. This further proliferation of the atom bomb has increased the menace to the peoples of the world. The peace-loving nations should now unite together in raising their voice against this increasing threat to human existence. It is essential for the United Nations and the major unclear powers to give urgent and serious attention to this problem so that the danger of vast devastation to mankind by any use of nuclear weapons is obviated. The Congress recognised that the Moscow Partial Test Ban Treaty helped to achieve a measure of success and hopes that the countries who have not already done so should subscribe to the Moscow Test Ban Treaty which should also be extended to cover underground tests.'

The full text of the resolution is as follows: 'The Indian National Congress reaffirms its determination to continue to pursue the policy of non-alignment and peaceful co-existence which, in the context of the recent changes in the international situation, has an ever widening and constructive role to play in the maintenance and consolidation of international peace and security. The use of force in certain parts of the world and the danger to world peace arising therefrom has convinced the Congress more than ever of the need to pursue the objectives of general and complete disarmament including prohibition of use of nuclear energy for non-peaceful purposes. The vast advances in science which can do so much for the prosperity and well-being of humanity should be exploited only for the purpose of peaceful development and progress of mankind. The Congress declares that efforts be redoubled for the development or the peaceful use of atomic energy for the prosperity and well-being of the Indian people.'[19]

At the meeting of the CWC held on November 7, 1965 at New Delhi a letter from Trikamlal J. Patel, a AICC member from Gujarat, was considered. He requested the Congress President to call a meeting of the AICC to have the policy on the stand of the party or the government in this regard. But Shastri reiterated that it had been made very clear that India did not want to manufacture nuclear weapons, and nor was it trying to get any nuclear guarantee or umbrella from foreign countries. Since the matter did come up, the party decided to take up the matter at the next Plenary. So clearly the Chinese test and Bhabha's statements created problems for the government and the party in sticking to its no weapon policy.[20]

In September 1965, the war with Pakistan led the Congress Working Committee to pass a resolution recording its appreciation of the lead given by the government to the country in the great hour of trial and paid tributes to the armed forces 'on their glorious role in resisting the recent Pakistani aggression.' According to the resolution passed at New Delhi on September 25, 1965, India's strategy was better than that of Pakistan and inflicted heavy blows on the Pakistani armed forces on land and in the air and defeated their aggressive designs.[21]

One must refer here to two aspects of this resolution. One that it was Shastri's leadership that the decision was taken to send the armed forces on the road to Lahore. This was the counter to the Pakistani armed thrust at Chammb. It was also fortunate that the citizens of the Valley and the Indian armed forces foiled Operation Gibraltar, the Pakistani plan to infiltrate the state of Jammu and Kashmir and create trouble there.

As a whole the Congress Party showed its gratitude to the people of the nation for supporting the military campaign against Pakistan. That is why the resolution passed at New Delhi also notes with 'great satisfaction the unity and solidarity displayed by people of all sections...' For instance, it takes note of the farmers of Punjab who came forward to cut down their standing crops and showed great courage in successfully tracking down the paratroopers. This was part of the plan launched by Pakistan to para-drop troops onto three Indian airfields, i.e., Halwara, Pathankot and Adampur. This plan failed because of improper planning and preparation.[22]

When the CWC met again on November 7, at New Delhi it had before it the task of taking an overview of the situation arising from the war with Pakistan. Several interesting points were made which are worth summarising here. First, the CWC pointed to India seeking friendship with all the nations of the world. Second, referring to the Pakistani aggression, the resolution stated that the world must recognise 'the fact of the repeated and continuing aggression.' Keeping in mind the possibility of China coming to the help of Pakistan, the resolution drew attention 'to the threat posed by the aggressive expansions of China' and added that both Pakistan and China have acted in concert against India.[23]

In the wake of the 1965 war, Indira Gandhi sought to consolidate India's regional position after two decades of flux in defence and foreign policy coupled with an uncertain political environment at home. The first thing to do was to tackle the internal front. The Congress Party was split and in so doing unexpectedly consolidated her political position and guaranteed her political future by alienating the right with the backing of the left and centre of the party. This gave the Prime Minister an increasingly firm grip upon the political process and on the national security front. Between 1965 and 1971, activity on the defence front was slow. Post 1965 the main activity was political consolidation followed by tackling of the economic crisis faced by India.

The 70th Session of the INC was held at Jaipur in February 1966. The focus of attention was the Tashkent declaration which Shastri had signed before his unfortunate death. While the party was at pains to defend the declaration, it made no bones about why India chose to make a military thrust in the Lahore-Sialkot sectors. Morarji Desai said that this frustrated Pakistan's hopes of seizing Kashmir. Additionally, international calls for a ceasefire came up only after India's drive towards Lahore. Desai, observed that once the UNSC had given a call for a ceasefire and Pakistan had accepted it, it was difficult for India to ignore it because 'India always believed in a policy of peace.'

There were of course voices of dissent on the declaration itself or to specific parts of it. For instance, the decision to return Haji Pir pass captured by the Indian Army, which was and still is a major route of infiltration remained a bone of contention. But Congressmen were asked to look at the larger context of the Tashkent Declaration and in the context of India wanting peace with Pakistan. Y.B. Chavan, the then Defence Minister went a step ahead and said that the declaration should be seen as a solemn pledge by one nation to another.[24]

In the overall situation, however, Chavan thought it prudent to declare that every country had the basic responsibility of defending its sovereignty and territorial integrity. He added that the Chinese threat remained 'even today.' One must refer here also to the statement made by Mahavir Tyagi, a Congressman from UP and a former minister for defence production. He said the Tashkent declaration raised many doubts. He observed that Shastri received a shock when within three hours of the signing of the agreement, a Pakistani spokesman said that the declaration did not cover the question of withdrawal of infiltrators from Kashmir and that it opened a way for Pakistan to raise the question of political talks in the Security Council for settlement of the Kashmir dispute.[25]

Indira Gandhi, by now the Prime Minister, in her speech said the passing of the resolution unanimously on Tashkent demonstrated the AICC's tribute and homage to Shastri. She pointed out that Pakistan had committed aggression on Kashmir twice though under the UN Charter there could be no aggression on one another by member nations. The tenor of her arguments was that resolution of the conflict by peaceful means was and would remain the focus of India's policy.[26]

At the second sitting of the Plenary on February 12, 1966 Indira Gandhi said, 'no government could afford to neglect its defence. The Government, armed forces, and the people would have to remain vigilant and strong for that was the price of freedom.' The AICC passed a resolution in June 1967 that blamed Pakistan for continuing to take a bellicose and aggressive posture against India. It also drew the attention of the party and the government to the collusion between China and Pakistan in instigating and encouraging lawless and hostile elements in India including the Naga and Mizo hostiles.[27]

The June 17, 1967 hydrogen bomb explosion by China drew a sharp reaction from the AICC, when it stated that this act posed a grave problem for the international community and more especially for India. Towards this end, the party endorsed the stand of the Government in pursuing steadfastly the development of atomic energy for peaceful purposes. The CWC Resolution passed at New Delhi on June 23, 1967 states: 'The AICC fully endorses the policy pursued by the Government of India to adhere steadfastedly to the development of atomic energy for peaceful purposes. It calls upon the government to ensure that the proposed treaty for non-proliferation is designed to take tangible steps towards nuclear disarmament and lay down a balance of mutual obligations between the nuclear weapon powers and non-nuclear weapon powers.'[28]

At Hyderabad in January 1968 it was the turn of S. Nijalingappa as Party President to speak of the heritage of Nehru and Shastri in foreign policy. But the observation by him of China's 'virulent cold war against us in particular and against several other nations' was a reminder of the need for constant vigil. And the blame for the ills in bilateral relations were laid down, not on the peoples of both nations, but on the 'autocratic, dictatorial and expansionist leadership of the Communist Party.'[29]

In the same year, Indira Gandhi decided against signing the nuclear non-proliferation treaty. This was her way of seeking to demonstrate India's independent posture and also keep the nuclear option open. According to Ashok Kapur, the decision was not a carefully thought out one, but a decision crafted on the basis of a 'high-powered bureaucratic coalition headed by T.N. Kaul, who was then foreign secretary.'[30] The general perception was that the NPT legalised China's nuclear status. Therefore, it was logical that India refused to sign the NPT in 1968. A 1972 survey showed that 68.9 per cent of Indians were not in favour of the NPT.

The year 1969 was, as one authority aptly states, one of 'tectonic grinding' for the Congress Party as it split. The AICC met on November 22 and 23 at New Delhi to vote on direction and leadership. A majority of the party sided with Indira Gandhi. The party then split and two groups emerged, with Indira Gandhi's Congress becoming known as the Congress(R), for Requisition while the Old Guard became known as Congress(O), for Organisation.[31]

At the AICC meeting held in New Delhi in 1970 June, Swaran Singh speaking on the resolution on International affairs noted that after the 1965 conflict, Pakistan had been trying to increase its military strength from various sources. This had only placed a heavy responsibility on India for the defence of the sovereignty and integrity of the country. Swaran Singh also referred to suggestions made by some members that India should manufacture the Atom Bomb, he said that the Government had decided against this after mature thought. He concluded by saying that the threat to India for a long time to come would only arise from conventional weapons.[32]

The resolution adopted by the CWC at this point refers to the hope that was kindled by the Tashkent Declaration that Pakistan would also move towards the peaceful settlement of differences. It also advocated peaceful resolution of differences with China 'which would bring back the Indian territory illegally occupied by China.'[33]

Speaking at the AICC session at Patna in October 1970, Congress President Jagjivan Ram pointed out that the USA had '"taken the unfriendly step" of supplying bombers, tanks and other arms to Pakistan.'[34] He noted that this would only add to Pakistan's intransigence. This issue of arms supply to Pakistan by Washington had been in question since the 1965 war and it came up periodically in Congress sessions.

India went to war again with Pakistan in 1971 as a consequence of its support of the Bangladesh independence struggle in East Pakistan. India did not immediately become directly involved due to the fact that the Indian Army's Eastern Command was scattered throughout West Bengal supporting the recently concluded elections, and the summer monsoons had set in, making it difficult for India to employ its armour in East Pakistan. Instead, India provided support and training to the guerrilla forces of the independence movement until conditions improved in its favour. In the prelude to this impending conflict, India's concerns about the balance of power in the region compelled it to sign its first bilateral treaty of 'Peace, Friendship, and Cooperation' with the Soviet Union, which stated that each country would come to the aid of the other if attacked.[35]

Two events in particular pushed the Soviet Union and India into concluding a treaty in August 1971. The first was US Secretary of State Henry Kissinger's secret mission to Peking and second was the developing crisis in East Pakistan. The Soviets saw the Treaty as a diplomatic riposte to the American move to improve relations with China. Because the implicit US pledge of support against China was no longer valid, the Indians could look only to the Soviet Union to restrain China in the event of a clash with Pakistan. The Soviet Union was already a significant supplier of defence equipment to India, but with the signing of this first treaty, the Soviets quickly became India's primary supplier of defence equipment. By this time, India understood its ability to procure equipment was an important security objective, and its defence relations were singularly focussed on maintaining 'reliable suppliers.'

The day after Pakistan Air Force attacked Indian Air Force bases in December 1971, the CWC held an emergency session in Delhi. It is of note that the meeting was of the view that the party organisation should be active at all levels in mobilising defence efforts. The resolution adopted by the CWC on the Indo-Pak war spoke to the declaration of emergency and the need of all people to stand solidly behind the Government to face the crisis. Faced with an economic downturn, in the late 60s, the CWC also had to state that the nation was bearing the 'heaviest of burdens' and called on the international community to bring about a peaceful solution and prevent the annihilation of the entire people of Bangladesh.[36]

It is contended here that on defence the party was mainly driven by the Party president and compulsions of the day. In 1971, it was Mrs Gandhi who took the decisions on Bangladesh and delivered a political masterstroke. On the unfinished business of prisoners of war (PoWs), there was some discussion in the CWC in June 1972 in New Delhi. Replying to the debate on the international situation on June 1, 1972, Jagjivan Ram observed that there had been suggestions from party members that there should not be any talk of release of prisoners of war unless they had been prosecuted for the inhuman atrocities they had indulged in Bangladesh. Jagjivan Ram admitted that what had happened in East Pakistan had no parallel in world history. The unprecedented genocide and the behaviour of the Pakistan army with the women in Bangladesh had no parallel concluded Jagjivan Ram. But he opined that it was up to Bangladesh to take necessary action in the matter.[37]

Even more significant was the admission by Pakistan that this time the war had been decisive. Jagjivan Ram observed that this meant that Pakistan had admitted defeat and in such a situation India had offered bilateral talks. Acknowledging the role of the Indian Army, Ram spoke of the army winning the war, but also having to 'win the peace.'

India emerged stronger in political terms after the 1971 war but without the foreign exchange reserves to convert the strategic opportunity of Bangladesh for the acquisition of defence technology that would make the armed forces truly effective. It is interesting to note that at the 74th Calcutta session in December 1972, Shankar Dayal Sharma Congress President after his speech requested Indira Gandhi 'to address the meeting and guide the members.' In response to this Prime Minister Indira Gandhi stated: 'It is not very fair for the Congress President to announce that I am going to guide the deliberations, the deliberations have been going on for more than almost 24 hours already!' In many ways the reality of the situation was well reflected in terms of the Prime Minister's sway over the party at this stage of its existence.[38]

The resolution adopted by the Congress at the 74th Session held at Calcutta in December 1972, noted that India was forced to go to war with Pakistan in her own defence and in defence of the people of Bangladesh. It also observed that Indira Gandhi declared a unilateral ceasefire as soon as the limited purpose of armed conflict had been achieved. The reasoning for this was that India pursued a policy of peace. The resolution also stated that the country (read Congress) 'do not glory in military prowess; we seek friendship, lasting friendship. [with Pakistan]. This is the reason for the Simla agreement.'[39]

In September 1973, the AICC placed on record its appreciation of the policies of the Government of India with regard to relations with Pakistan. First, was the unilateral ceasefire of December 18, 1971; next, the Simla Agreement of July 1972; the delineation of the Line of Control in Jammu and Kashmir; the return of prisoners in the western sector; and the return of territories occupied during the 1971 conflict. Therefore, the credit for the entire campaign is given to Indira Gandhi, both in political and military terms.[40]

Shankar Dayal Sharma, Congress President spoke at the AICC in July 1974. There he took the line, one that the government of the day also made, that Bhutto, Prime Minister of Pakistan was raising the bogey of India to divert people's attention from internal problems. He said: 'In behaving the way he was doing, the Pakistan Prime Minister was following in the footsteps of his predecessors.' He also reminded his audience of the steps that Prime Minister Indira Gandhi had taken to ease the diplomatic pressure on Pakistan. And what did Bhutto do in return? He was rearming Pakistan with great speed, raising new divisions out of the PoWs that India had freed and was concentrating troops on India's border. Dr Sharma warned the people to be 'wary and alert' adding that the Prime Minister in her recent speeches had many times warned the people of external threats to the country's security and sovereignty.[41]

In the midst of political turmoil and increasing food shortages in 1974 India undertook to explode the first Peaceful Nuclear Explosion at Pokhran on May 18. Following the 1971 war, Prime Minister Indira Gandhi and others in India's political elite were concerned about the way New Delhi had become a pawn in the power-game between Washington, Moscow and Beijing, and were unhappy at not being treated as a major power. Consequently, the government began more actively pursuing development of a nuclear explosive device around 1972 and then tested it in 1974. However, it is important to note that this period was also one of great turmoil in internal politics, and therefore it is often argued that this achievement was a demonstration of India's technical know-how and an opportunity to inspire pride, nationalism, and a sense of achievement for the country. India opted not to weaponise its new capability and remained satisfied with the knowledge that it had clearly indicated it had the know-how.

The AICC meeting in New Delhi resolved to hail the achievement of Indian Scientists in carrying out successfully the underground nuclear experiment for peaceful purposes which took place on May 18, 1974. 'It marks an important milestone in the development of our nuclear technology, and reflects the determination of the Indian people to develop their resources through their own efforts for the progress of the country... For two decades the Indian scientists and experts have been active in this field, and the All India Congress Committee congratulates them and the Prime Minister for this latest achievement in which the whole country has rejoiced.'

The resolution further stated that the AICC 'welcomes the clear statement of the Government of India reaffirming their intention of not using nuclear weapons. The All India Congress Committee expresses its joy in the fact that this important scientific experiment by India has been based on indigenous efforts, and without violation of any of India's bilateral or international obligations. It is a matter of deep satisfaction that India's achievement of scientific excellence and her steadfast commitment to peace have been welcomed by the non-aligned and developing world and have been well received in a large number of industrialised countries and scientific circles.'[42]

It is of interest that the CWC resolution on Nuclear Explosions passed on May 24-25, 1974 while applauding the the Indian scientists for the underground nuclear explosion for peaceful purposes carried out on May 18, 1974 noted that it was an important milestone in the development of India's nuclear technology and added that it represented 'the resolve of the people of India to develop their resources through their own efforts for economic, scientific and technological progress of the country.' The resolution harked back to the 'vision and guidance of Jawaharlal Nehru' in establishing the Atomic Energy Commission (AEC) and gave kudos to the outstanding contribution made by Dr Homi Bhabha in organising the AEC with the objective of achieving self-reliance in technology and equipment.

Interestingly, the resolution did not give political credit for the nuclear explosion to the Prime Minister, Indira Gandhi, but instead chose to speak of the evolutionary nature of India's nuclear programme and highlighted the fact that for two decades Indian scientists and technologists had been active in the field of nuclear energy. The CWC opined that the Peaceful Nuclear Explosion would help in 'building up a better future for the people of this country.' The CWC also supported the Government in its position that the PNE was in effect a peaceful one and was not undertaken 'for manufacturing nuclear weapons.'[43] Also interestingly nowhere in the resolutions does one find mention of any debate on whether India should have gone in for more tests or seek to answer the question as to why Indira Gandhi chose to take the decision not to have more tests.

At the 75th Plenary session of the Congress held at Komagata Maru nagar in Punjab in January 1976, the resolution on International Situation moved by Dr Rafiq Zakaria was done in the context of further arms supplies to Pakistan. Dr Zakaria said that the Indian 'armed forces are quite capable of giving once more a crushing reply to any aggressor.'[44] When the AICC met again in November 1976, Indira Gandhi had an interesting take on foreign policy formulation for India. Speaking at Guwahati, she said: 'That is, to strengthen friendship where it exists, to create friendship where it does not exist and to try to minimise hostility where there is hostility.'[45]

In August 1977, the Congress met in New Delhi where interestingly, a resolution on India's nuclear policy was passed. Paying tribute to all the Indian scientists who had done Pokhran three years ago, the CWC noted with concern the statement made by Prime Minister Morarji Desai who is reported to have said: 'I have come to the conclusion that no explosion is necessary for a peaceful use.' He further declared that, 'there is no question of any other explosions now for peaceful purposes.'[46] This statement was made by the then Prime Minister in the Lok Sabha on July 13, 1977 in response to a query as to whether India had pleged to the US not to undertake further peaceful nuclear explosions. The Congress Party opined that this was an unfortunate departure from the policy so far pursued by India in our best national interest, as well as that of developing countries and world peace.

The Congress was reflecting the then prevailing view that external (read US) pressure was being brought to bear on the Janata Party government to get India to deviate from the chosen path of self-reliance in the field of nuclear technology. Given the explosion of a neutron bomb by the Americans, the CWC urged the government to play a more effective role in reaching at international agreements banning every weapon system of mass destruction, and general and complete disarmament.[47]

During the Janata government interlude, the Congress approach on such matters was to criticise their policy and to recall their own heritage created by Jawaharlal Nehru. For instance, the resolution on international affairs passed in April 1977 at New Delhi spoke of the distortion in foreign policy being pursued by Morarji Desai. The Congress claimed that while the label of the policy has been maintained 'but its content has been replaced with just the opposite policy.'[48]

In January 1980, Indira Gandhi was back at the helm of affairs. At this time it became clear that the armed forces needed a dose of money to modernise and expand. And it was immediately apparent that India was back on the nuclear table, for the AICC resolution of December 1980 made it clear that in safeguarding India's sovereign right to develop and use nuclear technology for peaceful purposes, India would continue to oppose discriminatory arrangements such as the Nuclear Non-proliferation Treaty while urging the conclusion of a general convention on the total prohibition of the use or threat of use of nuclear weapons.

What did the Soviet invasion of Afghanistan at the end of 1979 mean for the Congress Party? Following on Government policy, the party took the line 'of inadmissibility of interference in the internal affairs of sovereign states.' At Calcutta in 1983, the worry was still Afghanistan, which was termed as a 'complex issue'. The resolution stated that, 'the problem could be solved only on the basis of the fundamental principles of non-interference, withdrawal of foreign troops, non-use of force and respect for sovereignty, territorial integrity and non-aligned status of Afghanistan.'[49] The government's stand on Afghanistan was well articulated by Indira Gandhi in 1982, in an interview to Time Magazine. She said *inter alia*, 'We are opposed to a foreign presence, whether in the shape of troops or any other type of interference, anywhere. Everybody rushed in at once to condemn the Soviet Union. We said we disapproved, but we did not join in the condemnation because we felt that it would not improve the situation.'[50]

India's security was also being threatened by the large-scale induction into Pakistan of a vast arsenal of sophisticated weaponry of tremendous destructive power. The militarisation of Pakistan was the next worrying aspect for India. Soon after her re-election, Mrs. Gandhi signed a major arms supply agreement with the USSR. The significant part of the deal was the easy terms on which the Soviets were willing to give India their latest arms and their willingness to discuss technology transfer. At the same time, the Government negotiated both with the USA and UK for possible supply of much needed equipment for the armed forces. That nothing emerged immediately at this moment in time was a result of India's economic woes and a perception of the Soviet tilt in terms of arms supplies.

Throughout the early 1980s, Congress politicians were constantly alluding to the 'gathering war clouds', the imminent threat of war and of course the famous 'foreign hand' came in handy as a tool for both political consolidation as well as military modernisation. At the beginning of her second tenure as Prime Minister, Indira Gandhi declared that she would not foreswear further peaceful nuclear explosions (PNE). She noted that the 1974 PNE had been carried out for peaceful purposes and said that India had no intention of producing nuclear weapons.

And yet faced with an emerging nuclear threat from Pakistan, India was forced to upgrade its nuclear weapons potential in the early 1980s. And by 1982, India was preparing for another nuclear test. This test slated for 1983 was subsequently put off.[51]

In its resolution on atomic energy in the same session, the Congress stated that India had mastered the entire nuclear cycle. 1983 is a memorable year in this respect. The Madras Atomic power station of 220 MW was wholly designed, fabricated and put into operation by Indian scientists and technologists. While the self-reliance factor was ever present on their minds, when they say that India is committed to using the atom for peace and prosperity of its people and not for destructive purposes, perhaps for the first time, the party pays attention to the issue of nuclear power. At that moment, nuclear power accounted for barely three per cent of the total installed power generation capacity in India. The AICC urged the Government to increase the share of nuclear power generation which had clear advantage for areas situated far away from the coal fields. 'We must also intensify our work on the experimental fast breeder reactor with a view to utilizing our considerable resources of thorium.'[52]

Though the credit for the order to assemble the weapon goes to Rajiv Gandhi and the credit for restarting the development programme of the weapon after Morarji Desai halted it belongs to Indira Gandhi, it was Narasimha Rao who operationalised it. In other words, there has been a consistent continuity in the Indian nuclear policy under Congress governments. Even while working hard for nuclear disarmament, Congress prime ministers were hardheaded people who did not put all their eggs only in the basket of nuclear disarmament. During the time when Rao was Prime Minister, when India was under considerable pressure from the US to roll back its nuclear programme, he appears to have kept Vajpayee informed of the progress in the nuclear programme.

The evidence of this is that there was no pressure from the BJP in Parliament on the nuclear issue though there was a widespread impression in the country that the programmes had been slowed down under US pressure. Unfortunately, Rao's statesmanship in treating the nuclear issue as a non-partisan national issue did not appear to have been reciprocated by the National Democratic Alliance (NDA) leadership on the day of the Shakti tests.[53]

On her return to power, Indira Gandhi took command of the defence portfolio and did give an impetus to armed forces modernisation signing numerous agreements with the Soviet Union. But the real challenges faced by Indira Gandhi were internal. Punjab, Jammu and Kashmir, Tamil Nadu and Assam were just a few states from where the Indian state had to face security problems. The greatest challenge undoubtedly was Punjab where Sant Jarnail Singh Bhindranwale leading a radical faction of the Akali Dal began a campaign of violence. This led eventually to his fortifying the Golden Temple in Amritsar and the launching of Army operations in 1984 to flush out the Sikh terrorists hiding there.

Conclusion

As one looks back and attempts to get an overview of the situation as it unfolded, several themes come out. As stated in the beginning, the adherence to the Parliamentary system of government had its advantages and disadvantages in the realm of defence and nuclear security. The record demonstrates that defence was and remains rarely discussed in detail in Parliament.[54] The only substantive moment was in the post-1962 period when Nehru was forced to speak out with regards to policy on China and when the then Defence Minister Y.B. Chavan chose to highlight some of the recommendations of the Henderson-Brookes Committee Report in the Lok Sabha. At the same time, the debates in Parliament over the nuclear issue demonstrate that government policy could be and was in fact influenced by the public debate both within and outside the Legislature.

One must also see that the Congress Party resolutions were basically on international affairs/international situation and while as we have seen, serious amendments on national security issues were debated and discussed, these inevitably revolved around the issue of 'foreign policy' or defence in terms of 'Chinese aggression' or 'Pakistani intransigence.' What further complicated the matter was that all the Prime Ministers had a close link in the making of foreign policy, either by being their foreign ministers or putting their stamp on the same in the Government or in the party.

It would be appropriate to borrow the idea of the Congress system to state that single party rule also meant that there was little actual political opposition to policies relating to defence. This meant that while the Congress Party could while it was in power adhere to defence policies of a particular nature, it did not mean that inner party debate on defence and related subjects was completely absent. Since members of the Government were also members of the Congress Party it was possible to discuss matters of defence within the close confines of the party, without revealing secret issues. In terms of India's nuclear policy, this was not the case.

The closely guarded nuclear bureaucracy in India made it difficult to discern nuclear policy and debate it within the party. What was possible was a discussion on a possible Indian stance on the basis of international developments, as happened in the case of China. It was not until the Janata government came to power in 1977 that persons other than those from amongst the Congress Party came to have an idea of the nuclear programme.

It is contended that in the case of the PNE in 1974 , it was more a decision of the Prime Minister Indira Gandhi for political or other reasons and reinforced by the scientific establishment's need to operationalise their experiments. The historical record demonstrated the evolutionary nature of the nuclear programme and while defending the traditional stand of evoking the moral need for global nuclear disarmament, India went down the nuclear path in the aftermath of the

Chinese test in 1964 knowing fully well it would acquire the capacity to manufacture nuclear weapons one day.

The process of decision-making within the Congress Party while being a consensual one, was also at times determined by individual personalities. This was more so in politico-military terms when it came to issues such as defence and nuclear matters. In the period under review, the focus of attention was the persona of Indira Gandhi as the Prime Minister. Her remarks at various Congress sessions make it clear that her focus was on the internal dimension of state polity. The attention paid to foreign affairs is based on the idea that non-alignment was the best tool to stride forth on the international arena, but with certain caveats. On Afghanistan for example, India remained relatively quiet. The main thing that emerges is the 'foreign hand' the ubiquitous phrase that sounded loud and clear during the 1980s.

As is evident from the resolutions and the historical record, post-1962 defence became a more debated issue, both in Parliament and within the Congress Party. For the latter, international affairs became more oriented to security and gradually national security. Recall that India fought a war with Pakistan followed by another one in 1971. Clearly the latter was a major politico-military victory for India and therefore pride in the defence of India became a matter of routine. Tied in with the foreign policy objective of obtaining the status of a regional power, India moved swiftly to acquire the means to demonstrate that capability. Defence expenditure in the period 1980/81 to 1983/84 went up from 2.84 per cent of GDP to 3.05 per cent of GDP. Clearly, the demands of the services were growing, but it required political backing. The other visible trend was further indigenisation of the defence industrial base.

That this process was evolutionary rather than revolutionary was demonstrated only in 1988 when Indian paratroopers were airlifted into the Maldives during Operation Cactus, to rescue President M.A. Gayoom.

In this sense, the period under review throws up interesting points of examination *vis-à-vis* the Congress Party in relation to India's defence and nuclear security. First, the party debates on the nuclear issue bring about the sense of dilemma within the government on what direction to follow. This is true in the case of Shastri as Prime Minister. Later the pattern of decision-making in government changes when Indira Gandhi takes over. This is predicated on personal world views and perceptions of threats to national security. Seen in one way, the shift in focus from global nuclear disarmament to India's nuclear security actually occurs with Indira Gandhi.

Second, the defence as a issue was actively debated within the party in foreign policy terms. Most of the time, the debates are post crisis, but reflect the prevailing mood of the government and the public at that point in time.

Third, the nature of decision-making within the party in relation to these matters appears to shift from a consensual one, to one determined by the top party leadership. Sometimes, it was driven by factors extraneous to the party's views on the matter. This is apparent in the late 1960s and early 1970s when the party's attention was on the internal political and economic situation. And yet the nation is at war with Pakistan in 1971 and three years later explodes the first PNE.

The perspective of the Congress system provides the present analysis with an opportunity to view the debates and discussions within the party on defence and nuclear security in the historical context. It is assumed that given the specialised nature of national security issues, there is a limit.

Endnotes

1. Jawaharlal Nehru's Speeches Volume Two: 1949-1953 p. 394.
2. Wood, Glynn L. and Daniel Vaagenes (1984). "Indian Defense Policy: A New Phase"? *Asian Survey* 24(7): 721-35. July.
3. Kothari, Rajni (1964). "The Congress 'System' in India", *Asian Survey* 4(12): 1161-73.
4. Glynn L. Wood and Daniel Vaagenes (1984). *op.cit.*, p. 725.
5. President S. Radhakrishnan's statement in a Washington Television Interview, June 9, 1963. *Dawn*, June 10, 1963.
6. Kavic, Lorne J. (1967). *India's Quest for Security: Defence Policies, 1947-1965*. Berkeley and Los Angeles, California, University of California Press, pp. 192-93.
7. Smith, Chris (1994). *India's Ad hoc Arsenal: Direction or Drift in Defence Policy?* Stockholm International Peace Research Institute. pp. 79-80.
8. Zaidi, A.M. (1983). *The Encyclopedia of the Indian National Congress*, Volume Eighteen 1962-1964 Democratic Socialism. S. Chand & Company, pp. 426-27.
9. For full text of Resolution see Ibid: 488-91.
10. A.M. Zaidi, *op.cit.,*: 488-89.
11. Ibid: 490.
12. Ibid: 444-45.
13. Ibid: 451.
14. Ibid: 646-47.

15. Perkovich, George (1999). *India's Nuclear Bomb: Impact on Global Proliferation*, University of California Press. p. 81.
16. Zaidi, *op.cit.*, Volume Nineteen: 1965-1967, *The Ten-Point Programme*, pp. 31-34.
17. Ibid: 35-36.
18. Ibid: 38.
19. Ibid: 91-92.
20. Ibid: 157.
21. Ibid: 153-154.
22. Ibid: 154.
23. Ibid: 363.
24. Ibid: 174-177.
25. Ibid.
26. Ibid: 180.
27. Ibid: 205.
28. Ibid: 358.
29. Zaidi, *op.cit.*, Volume Twenty: 1968-1969. *Facing the City Bosses*. p. 62.
30. Indian Security and Defense Policies under Indira Gandhi, Y.K. Malik and D.K. Vajpeyi. E.J. Brill. Leiden (1988). *India: The Years of Indira Gandhi*. pp. 48-49.
31. Perkovich., *op.cit.*: 147.
32. Zaidi, *op.cit.*, Volume Twenty-One: 1970-1971. *The Split and the Aftermath*. p. 50.
33. Ibid: 64-65.
34. Ibid: 79.
35. This treaty was signed in August 1971.
36. Ibid: 391-392.
37. Zaidi., *op.cit.*, Volume Twenty Two: 1972-1973. *At War with Poverty*. (1984). pp. 172-173.
38. Ibid: 63.
39. Ibid: 139.
40. Ibid: 499-500.
41. Zaidi, *op.cit.*, Volume Twenty Three: 1974-1975. *The Lengthening Shadows*. p. 27.
42. Ibid: 67.
43. Ibid: 184-185.
44. Ibid: 402.
45. Om Prakash Ralhan (1998). *Encyclopaedia of Political Parties*, Volumes 33-50, Anmol Publications. p. 3446.

46. Zaidi, *op.cit.*, Volume Twenty Four: 1976-1977. *AICC Circular*. August 20, 1977. pp. 375-376.
47. Ibid: 317.
48. Zaidi, *op.cit.*, Volume Twenty Five: 1978-1983, *The Return of Priyadarshini*. (1985). p. 218.
49. Ibid: 471.
50. An Interview with Indira Gandhi, Interview with Time, August 2, 1982. At: *http://www.time.com/time/magazine/article/0,9171,925596,00.html#ixzz11I5gYxKo*
51. Perkovich, *op.cit.*: 242-243.
52. Zaidi, *op.cit.*: 431.
53. Subrahmanyam, K., Narasimha Rao and the Bomb (2004). *Strategic Analysis*, Volume: 28 (4) Commentaries, October, accessed at: *http://www.idsa.in/strategicanalysis/NarasimhaRaoandthe Bomb_ksubramanyam_1004*
54. Smith, Chris. *op.cit.*:103.

Chapter VIII

Indian National Congress

Science and Technology

Deepak Kumar

For almost nine decades since its inception in 1885, the Indian National Congress (INC) was more than a political party; it was a movement which debated and deliberated upon not only political but social and economic issues. It acted as 'the unofficial Parliament of an India which was politically subject but spiritually and nationally awake'.[1] It has been, as Mahatma Gandhi pointed out, 'not an organisation to enunciate theories but to anticipate national needs and wishes and forge practical sanctions for their fulfillment.'[2]

Early Years

Technical education was one of the important issues that attracted the attention of the early congressmen. The very third session of the INC in 1887 took up the question of technical education. K.T. Telang and B.N. Seal showed how in the name of technical education the government was imparting merely lower forms of practical training.[3] For D.E. Wacha, technical education signified higher education, especially of the sciences. Delivering the presidential address in 1901, he said:

> It is idle to talk of mere small industries in carpentry and brick waking and so forth. If there is to be an industrial revival of a practical character which shall change the entire surface of this country, you will have first to lay the foundation of teaching in the Applied Sciences. You cannot have the cart before the horse. Higher Education must precede industrial development.[4]

The inadequacies of the medical service also attracted the congress attention. In 1893 K.N. Bahadurji moved a resolution beseeching the government 'to raise scientific medical profession in India by throwing open fields for medical and scientific work to the best talent available and indigenous talent in particular'.[5] Congress was fast emerging as the most zealous vanguard of Indian interests. Whether it be education, agriculture or mining, Congress touched several problems in its wide sweep.[6]

At the Calcutta session in 1901, an industrial exhibition was organised. It drew the attention of ordinary delegates coming from distant parts of the country to the advantages of technological applications and new industries. It was so popular that it soon became a regular feature at Congress sessions. The fervour was such that the Congress later sponsored an Industrial Conference on an annual basis. It also supported the 'national education' efforts which had begun as an integral part of the Swadeshi movement in 1905. Even in the midst of the First World War, the INC continued the pressure. Its first example can be seen in the *Note of Dissent* submitted by Madan Mohan Malaviya as a member of the Indian Industrial Commission (1916-1918).[7] His critique and suggestions remain valid even now. A decade before Jawaharlal Nehru, Malaviya had asked for 'an integrated economic development' based on new knowledge and technologies.[8] Both, in their own way, realised the significance of modern technology as a new and strong linking of knowledge and power. State was to play the most important role in this equation which, in turn, would make the state all-powerful.

Gandhi—Nehru Dilemma

This was exactly the time Gandhi appears on the scene and takes a virtual control of both the INC and the national movement. In the middle of growing demands for self-rule, democracy, industrialisation and development, Gandhi emerged as an extraordinary dissenter and with an extraordinary vision. He seldom used the terms science and technology. He was opposed to the machine-based civilisation, though not machinery *per se*. He wrote:

> How can I be when I know that even this body is a most delicate piece of machinery? The spinning wheel itself is a machine. What I object to is the craze for machinery. Today machinery helps a few to ride on the backs of millions. The impetus behind it all is not philanthropy to save labours but greed. It is against this constitution of things that I am fighting with all my might.[9]

One of the very few occasions on which Gandhi touched the issue of science and people directly was while he was talking to some students at Trivandrum in 1925 and when he visited the Indian Institute of Science (IISc) at Bangalore in 1927. He said that he was not an opponent or foe of science. He recalled how he once wanted to become a doctor but could not stand the idea of vivisection and retreated. He wanted to put certain limitations 'upon scientific research and upon the uses of science' in terms of humanity and morality. Moreover, he wanted science to be pursued for the sake of knowledge, accurate thought and action. He cited how J.C. Bose and P.C. Ray pursued science for the sake of science and not for money or fame. Thereafter, Gandhi would pose the most important question:

> How will you infect the people of the villages with your scientific knowledge? Are you learning science in terms of the villages?[10]

There were no easy answers. The system prepared the students (and still does so) for an urban or industrial India or for a slot abroad. Many differed. Meghnad Saha, a pioneer astrophysicist and well-known for his deep social commitment, wanted India to choose 'the cold logic of technologies' and not 'the vague utopia of Gandhian economy.'[11] Gandhi's own political heir and independent India's first Prime Minister, Jawaharlal Nehru himself begged to differ with his mentor. For Gandhi, the individual, the society and technology formed one whole in a similar manner as did religion, politics and constructive work. Keeping them separate or autonomous was to him inconceivable. In a letter to Nehru is September 1945 Gandhi talked about the necessity to escape the 'moth-like circling'. 'When the moth approaches its doom it whirls round faster and faster till it is burnt up.'[12] To this Nehru replied:

> I do not think it is possible for India to be really independent unless she is technically advanced country. I am not thinking for the moment in terms of just armies but rather of scientific growth. In the present context of the world we cannot even advance culturally without a strong background of scientific research in every department.[13]

The INC had thus come a long way from 1885. As the party's policies evolved one finds dualism or parallel demands for alternatives in terms of traditional-modern, small-big industries, etc.[14] But what is most striking is the level and quality of the debate (something which we miss now). Their arguments and articulations reverberated in the provincial legislative councils, the Central Legislature and even at the District Board and municipality level.

The enthusiasm was not only for national independence but also for national reconstruction. A clear direction came from the Lahore Congress where Nehru talked not only about *Purna Swarajya* but also socialism and planned reconstruction. The dualism seemed to end here and the Nehruvian era virtually began. Taking advantage of the change, M.N. Saha persuaded the next Congress President, Subhas Chandra Bose to appoint a National Planning Committee (NPC). Under Nehru's Chairmanship it began work in 1938 with 29 expert sub-committees dealing with different areas of national reconstruction. The onset of the Second World War and the subsequent Quit India Movement, etc. disrupted the work of the NPC. But soon it regrouped and by 1949 the NPC had published 27 volumes of reports, outlining a Ten-Year Plan to be implemented by a government of free India.[15] This Committee was the creation of the INC and its significance seems to have been lost in the heat of Quit India, etc., and also our obsession with transfer of power and partition.

Nehruvian Era

Nehru was deeply committed to science and put a premium on scientific temper. Socialism fascinated him and the Russian Revolution fired his optimism. Nehru was a 'humanist' who resented being neatly categorised within the four corners of a single 'ism'.[16] His preferences were all for science and for the scientific method. But he also understood and appreciated the limitations of science in elaborating questions like the purpose of life or providing clues to absolute truth. His curiosity and fascination for science was child-like but he explained some of the recent advances in science in his letters to his daughter (February to July 1933 from Dehradun Jail) like an accomplished and devoted science populariser.[17] He looked into the history of sciences, cited examples of how dogmas were fought; reasoned about the relations between science and religion; discussed Darwin, Einstein and Pavlov; pondered over the good and bad applications of science; and what is unique, exulted over seeing women as doctors, teachers and engineers.[18] In September 1933 Nehru wrote to Aldous Huxley refuting his characterisation of Congress views as anti-science. He clarified that the Mahatma had never asked the Congress to accept or adopt all his ideas nor were his views anti-science.[19]

Despite certain differences, Nehru defended Gandhi and on science he goes almost lyrical in his message to the *Science and Culture* (Journal founded by M.N. Saha in 1935):

> Science is the very basis and texture of life today and without it we perish, or what is even worse, slide back to barbarism. Science does not mean the thousand and one applications of it that we see today, but even more so the scientific and rational approach to all problems of life. Science has made great progress in the West and raised the standard of living in some countries to unprecedented height. And yet that very science has failed to solve the major problems of the

> age and we see war with all its horrors ravaging the world. Thus science destroys itself if it is not extended to the political, economic and others fields of human life and endeavour. It would appear that science today is in a position to solve all these problems, or most of them, and to create conditions of well-being and progress for all humanity. Yet though we swear by science and accept it advantageously for many purposes, still the habit of unscientific approach remains. Vested interests, superstitions and out-of-date customs prevent the full application of the scientific and the rational method.[20]

Nehru understood the flip side of science. It turned humans into 'almost a geological force, changing the face of the planet earth chemically, physically and in many other ways.' But control over nature does not mean control over one's self. Still, an optimist that he was, Nehru felt that 'perhaps new developments in biology, psychology, and the interpretation of biology and physics, may help man to understand and control himself more than he has done in the past.'[21] This hope remains a valid hope for many of his succeeding generations!

On numerous occasions opening dozens and dozens of institutions, addressing scientific gatherings, conferences, etc., during his prime ministership (1947-1962), Nehru repeatedly hammered one point, i.e., scientific temper as a way of life, as 'an approach to life and all life's problems.'[22] The importance and urgency he attached to it can be gauged from the fact that in the very next week after independence, he placed scientific research under his own 'personal charge'. A decade later came the nation's declaration of faith in science in the shape of the Scientific Policy Resolution adopted by the Parliament on March 4, 1958. It promised *inter alia* 'to foster, promote and sustain, by all appropriate means, the cultivation of science, and scientific research in all its aspects—pure, applied and educational.' The party and the parliament stood behind the new helmsman. In fact, the manifesto of the Congress Party for the first national government in 1945 itself had declared scientific research as 'a basic and essential activity of the state' to be 'organised and encouraged on the widest scale.'[23] Nehru's stamp on this was unmistakable.

Nehru kept his doors always open to those scientists who wanted to build institutions like S.S. Bhatnagar, Director General, Council of Scientific and Industrial Research (CSIR) and Homi J. Bhabha, Director, Tata Institute of Fundamental Research (TIFR). The chain of laboratories established under CSIR during 1947-1954 was known as the result of 'Nehru-Bhatnagar Effect'. Nehru fondly called Bhatnagar 'a live-wire'. This close alliance between Nehru and scientists in industrial research and atomic energy probably had a negative influence on other sectors.[24] It is argued, for example, that agriculture and agricultural scientists were not given prominence. Our agriculture may have advanced a great deal had Nehru evinced the same interest in the Indian Council of Agricultural Research (ICAR) as he did with the CSIR and the Department of Atomic Energy (DAE).[25] Similarly, the university sector also suffered relative neglect. Many good scientific workers moved out of the universities to the mission-oriented government laboratories and institutes. Universities worldwide are the basic source of scientific talent. Thanks to the 'Nehru-Bhatnagar Effect', they suffered silently a bleak prospect. Well, national reconstruction was a daunting task and it seems Nehru did not have a free hand; he had to make choices with caution. In the midst of the Nehruvian heyday, he is reported to have said:

> Most of my Ministers are reactionary...but as long as they are my Ministers I can keep some check on them. If I were to resign they would be the government and they would unloose the forces that I have tried ever since I came to power to hold in check...I have to work with the people who are actually influential in the country. They may not be the kind of people I like but it is the best I can do.[26]

Not withstanding minor and friendly criticisms, Nehru faced little or no opposition. The Congress represented national aspirations and every section of the society stood to benefit from the proposed policies. It was an era of hope—problems appeared in the last years of Nehru's life but the system came to crisis only after his death.[27]

The Nehru period was also significant for it not only ended the dualism and vacillation of earlier periods but also laid down specific policies and established new institutions (like IITs, CSIR and DAE) as instruments of implementation. Nehru's personal popularity among scientists is simply legendary. In 1938, he had sent a message to the silver jubilee session of the Indian Science Congress Association (ISCA). In 1947, he even presided over the 34th session of the ISCA, an honour yet to be bestowed on any other politician.

Henceforth, he was invited to inaugurate the Science Congress every year. The scientists themselves wanted to hear the voice of the nation and feel reassured while for Nehru it was personal satisfaction. Sometimes he softly demurred; at the 44th ISCA session in Calcutta he said, 'I consider this a great privilege and honour for a variety of reasons although I sometimes fear that repetition of a practice makes it rather stale'. But this practice evoked a sharp response from C.V. Raman, India's only 'Nobel' scientist:

> Can you give me the example of any other country in which Science Congress is inaugurated by politician? Every year, for 17 years

continuously, the organisers of the Indian Science Congress could think of only Prime Minister Nehru to inaugurate it...How self-respecting scientists could go on listening to piffle spouted by politicians in a 'Science Congress' is something which I have never been able to understand.[28]

Notwithstanding criticisms, national patronage for science and technology continued. The Indian National Congress never wavered in its commitment to rural upliftment and sustained industrialisation in certain key sectors. Successive presidents of the INC reaffirmed it. The early 60s were difficult years. Growing food crisis and the Chinese aggression had left the nation and Pt. Nehru distraught. He fell ill at the Bhubaneswar session of the INC in 1964 and his subsequent death did cast a gloom. But it did not mean a break with his policies and priorities. As the then Congress President, K. Kamaraj, said at the Durgapur session in 1965:

It has been agreed that production of food should have top priority...Without waiting for chemical fertilisers, imported or indigenous, or both, and without looking forward to the completion of big power and irrigation projects, we should urgently set about the task of producing more food, by utilising, to the maximum extent possible, locally available resources, compost, green manure and other traditional soil feeds. Minor irrigation works should be undertaken on a planned and widespread basis. This, of course, does not rule out the building of big irrigation and power projects.[29]

The Indira Years

The year 1967 marks a watershed in the history of independent India. For the first time non-Congress coalition governments appeared in several states. The party itself was undergoing tremendous strain. Pt. Nehru's daughter Indira Gandhi was elected Prime Minister in 1966 but the growing rift between the organisational part of the Party and the legislative wing led to a split at the Faridabad session in 1969. Indira Gandhi soon took full command of both the party and the government. A new era had begun.

Jagjivan Ram was made the President of the rejuvenated Congress (which the media called Congress I) at a special session in Bombay. At this juncture the country was passing through a phase in which practically all parties were confronted with internal dissensions and divisions. These internal dissensions were probably 'expressions of conflicting attitudes to democracy and the challenges of a developing nation'.[30] One way to meet these challenges was to develop, nay enforce, commitment. To quote from Jagjivan Ram's presidential address, 'We need, clearly and inevitably, an apparatus with a purpose, a mind. We need a service committed to the ideal of democracy, socialism, secularism'.[31] A new term had now entered India's political lexicon, i.e., 'committed'.

The role of science and technology as the most important means for poverty alleviation returned to the Congress when in 1972 (fresh from the victory in Bangladesh war) its President implored the 'way and means of bringing the benefits of science and technology to our people':

> In this context, we must provide in due course for mass production of items of mass, daily consumption and make them available through cooperatives and other fair price stores at prices within the means of the common people. I am often appalled by the way the advantages of modern science and technology are today largely limited to the upper strata of society. While special units might be set up in the public sector, those in the private sector should be directed to reserve a major portion of their production for specified items of mass consumption.[32]

In the meantime agitations had taken over the political arena. Gujarat and Bihar became volatile over price-rise, maladministration and corruption issues. To stem the tide, the INC President, D.K. Barooah, at the Chandigarh session in 1975, referred to Nehru:

> In the context of economic development we must take note of the importance that our leader and mentor Jawaharlal Nehru attached to the development of science and technology. "It was science alone", he pointed out, "that could solve these problems of hunger and poverty, of insanitation and illiteracy, of superstition and deadening custom and tradition, of vast resources running to waste, of a rich country inhabited by starving people". Stressing the importance of science and technology, he said that, "a country can only survive today if it has enough of scientific and technical personnel". And true to his word, he went about in right earnestness to develop this personnel. Our scientific laboratories and institutes of technology which have contributed so much to our self-reliance in technical know-how stand as an eternal tribute to his memory. Their contribution to consolidation of our freedom is of no mean order; it is with their help that we are able to harness our resources scientifically to build-up a self-reliant economy for development as well as for defence of our frontiers. We are proud today to have a rich reservoir of technical intelligentsia capable not only for taking our country into the foremost rank of industrial advancement but

> also of assisting other developing countries in their endeavour for modernisation.[33]

Truly speaking, Mrs. Gandhi never wavered in her commitment to planned development. She always had one senior scientist as a member of the Planning Commission. In 1970, she had established a Committee on Science and Technology (COST) under the dynamic leadership of B.D. Nag Chaudhury. This Committee organised four Working Groups each dealing with: 1) science policy at the national level, 2) management of S&T institutions, 3) R&D for industrial development, and 4) higher education and manpower.[34]

Despite emphasis on industries and higher education, it must be noted to the eternal credit of Mrs. Gandhi that henceforth both party and government thinking took a definite turn towards rural India. For the first time, in 1971 (despite Indo-Pak War over Bangladesh and the economic strain caused by refugee influx) India's national expenditure on R&D in agriculture was on par with that on atomic energy. Under the Fifth Five-Year Plan (1974-1979) it rose higher than expenditure on defence and atomic energy. Experiments were made for introducing fertiliser, irrigation techniques, hybrid seeds, and plant and soil development. Under the remarkable and selfless leadership of C. Subramanian, India was soon to reap the benefits of Green Revolution. But the rural India needed (and still needs) more than agricultural experiments. Institutions like the Khadi Village Industries Commission (KVIC) *inter alia* promoted gobar gas plants. Even scientific bodies, like the Indian Science Congress (62nd session, Delhi, 1975) for the first time, decided that in their future sessions they should have a theme to focus on for cross-disciplinary discussion. It was decided that for the 63rd session the theme would be 'Science and Integrated Rural Development'. In January 1976 the Waltair session of the ISCA focussed on: (a) rural assets and liabilities, (b) science and technology as related to rural development, and (c) blueprint for action. Here Mrs. Gandhi proclaimed the nation's official commitment in no uncertain terms:

> Our science should give itself a rural bias. Rural life should be so enriched as to prevent the migration of people and resources from villages to towns...The village and the home should become laboratories for inter-disciplinary scientific and technological investigation...Our centre of science and higher technology should attach as much importance to the man who takes science to the field as to him who publishes a thesis.[35]

This was definitely a new emphasis and was backed by financial support. In 1947-48, India's expenditure on S&T was a meagre USD one million; by the end of Mrs. Gandhi's period (1984) it rose to USD 1,450 million.[36] The changes that took place during her regime can be put in following categories:

1. Creation of new agencies for research and administration in S&T.
2. Expansion in overall funding for existing agencies.
3. A restrictive and selective policy towards foreign investments and collaborations.
4. The expansion and revamping of the decision-making and consultative machinery for S&T and technology imports.
5. Efforts to link the S&T system with other production sectors of the economy through the science and technology plan, and
6. Formulation of a technology policy.[37]

In an article published in the influential American journal *Foreign Affairs* in October 1972, Mrs. Gandhi, fresh from the huge success at the Lok Sabha and later assembly elections, confidently argued, 'So marked has been the development of our industry and agriculture, our science and technology, our education and health, that some argue that India should not now be counted among the underdeveloped nations'. Yet she was acutely aware that, 'the process of development had widened the disparities between different social classes and has created new imbalances between states and, between districts within the same state.'[38]

Ten years later, on a visit to the US, she addressed the American Association for Advancement of Science (AAAS). There she outlined how apart from agriculture and rural crafts, Indian science covers a wide spectrum, 'encompassing work in some frontier areas of atomic energy, and fundamental research in mathematics, particle physics, molecular biology and so on'.[39] To the question why India, still struggling with basic needs, should step into frontier areas of S&T, she argued, 'new knowledge is often the best way of dealing with old problems. We see our space effort as relevant for national integration, education, communication, and the fuller understanding of the vagaries of the monsoon which rules our economic life. Mapping from the sky also gives information about natural resources. Oceanography augments food and mineral supplies. Modern genetics open out vast possibilities. Knowledge cannot be fragmented. How can one say which kind of knowledge is immediately applicable. Also, can we compel our scientists to be content with repeating the work of others?' This was indeed a succinct portrayal of a developing nation's perspective. But she did not stop here; she enquired why and how '95 percent of the world's R&D is still confined to the industrialised nations'. 'Almost 60 percent of this is military-oriented and of the rest, a good part of even basic scientific and engineering research is directed to problems specific to advanced economies', she argued.[40]

Such a candid observation, that too from a Third World leader, must have unnerved the American scientific establishment. The West was not favourably disposed to India's nuclear energy and space programmes. But pioneers like Homi Bhabha and Vikram Sarabhai remained steady and resolute and the nation stood behind them. The cultivation of nuclear science or space research was not for the sake of glamour or exclusive knowledge. As Bhabha quipped, 'there is no power so costly as no power'. Probably this meant both industrial and military power.[41] The objective was independence from foreign sources of nuclear power technologies and also satellite launch. Nuclear and space programmes, whether intended or not, provided the country with nuclear weapons and strategic nuclear delivery vehicles. The rationale was provided by the future combination of energy, telecommunications, and other development requirements in the civilian sector, and strategic necessities in the defence sector.[42] After Bhabha's sad demise in an air-crash, Sarabhai virtually ran both the departments of atomic energy and space research. In 1970 he presented 'a 10-year profile' of both departments. Its objectives were far too ambitious. In the space area, for example, the profile involved going from Rohini rockets to the Geosynchronous Satellite Launch Vehicles (GSLV) in 10 years![43] This nevertheless reflected the optimism and confidence of the Indira years. The result was the Pokharan atomic experiment in 1974 and the launch of Aryabhatta in 1975. GSLV, of course, had to wait for almost three more decades.

Another distinctive feature of the Mrs. Gandhi's period is the total integration of S&T into the Fifth Five Year Development Plan. At the discussions on the approach to the fifth plan, Mrs. Gandhi made it very clear that, 'science and technology should not be looked upon as a separate subject or sector, but as powerful tools which permeate all aspects of our thinking and action.'[44] It was this approach which finally culminated in the Technology Policy Statement in 1983 which aimed at 'the development of indigenous technology and efficient absorption and adaptation of imported technology appropriate to national priorities and resources'.[45] The nation sought 'technological advancement not for prestige or aggrandizement but to solve our multifarious problems and to be able to safeguard our independence and our unity'. New technology missions were launched with multiagency participation to provide S&T inputs for meeting immediate needs in critical areas such as drinking water, literacy, pulses and edible oils, immunisation, and rural communication.[46]

Perhaps the most distinctive and ironically less known feature of Indira Gandhi's leadership was her concern for environmental degradation and her efforts at conservation. Her critics may have denounced her so-called authoritarian style of functioning, Emergency, etc., but her concern for poverty alleviation and sustainable development were honest and genuine. In a recent article Mahesh Rangarajan, a noted environmental historian, has shown how she strove for a balance between nature, power and science.[47] He cites interesting and relatively unknown examples from Mrs. Gandhi's life and career to show her care and concern even under most trying circumstances. For example, she addressed the first meeting of the National Committee on Environmental Planning and Coordination (NCEPC) on the day (December 6, 1971) Indo-Pak War began. Later in the midst of the Simla Agreement discussions in May 1972, she dashed a letter to the Chief Minister of Bihar asking him to stop the diversion of forest land for a development project. Incredible indeed! At the first UN Conference on the Human Environment at Stockholm in June 1972, she asked:

> Are not poverty and need the greatest polluters? The environment cannot be improved in conditions of poverty. Nor can poverty be eradicated without the use of science and technology. For instance, unless we are in a position to provide for the daily necessities of tribal people and those who live in and around our jungles, we cannot keep them from combing the forests for their livelihood, from poaching and despoiling the vegetation. When they themselves feel deprived, how can we urge the preservation of animals?[48]

Project Tiger, launched in the same year, was a testimony to the new resolve. Nine tiger reserves were created with strict no to tree-felling, grazing or human habitation. In 1980, the Forest Conservation Act was passed. Through legislation and administrative fiats, the government, both at Centre and states, were acquiring more power over forest, common land, water resources, etc. An aggressive statism created popular protests, even unrest. Chipko movement is a classic example of ordinary people's reaction and power. Awareness about the tribals' plight and rights came to the fore. Civil society began to debate the right of livelihood; a host of issues emerged and attracted attention, for example, development for what and for whom?

During the early 1980s one may see a gradual but sure shift towards neoliberal policies. Focus was to be more on wealth creation than on distribution. The critics pointed to the increasing disparities between the urban rich and rural poor as result of the S&T based developments. Even the Green Revolution which had definitely lifted the country from droughts and virtual begging for food also came under scanner. The 'top-down' approach or 'trickle-down' theories which the country had witnessed since Macaulay's time, again showed its limitations, if not total failure. In the midst of protecting the forests, the tiger and the Silent Valley, the government failed to protect the neighbourhood and its environment from the polluting industries. Bhopal gas tragedy was just waiting to happen.[49] No worse were the happenings in Punjab which finally consumed one of the finest daughters India had produced.

The Indian National Congress was in crisis again. The baton passed to the young and techno-savvy Rajiv Gandhi. He was probably the first to talk about the 21st century and India's place in it. He fired the imagination of the nation and won a landslide victory in 1985. In his first broadcast to the country on November 12, 1984, he said:

> As we build today so will be the tomorrow. Together we build for an India of the 21st century...How are we going to prepare the nation to meet the challenges of the next century, to meet the challenges of the latest technology, as it comes? Development has to mean absorption of the most modern techniques at the most basic levels in our society.[50]

In 1986 the young Rajiv Gandhi introduced a National Education Policy. He ushered in a computer revolution and a paradigm shift in telecommunications. Technology missions were given top priority and they boosted the economy as nothing else had done in the previous eras. Success of companies like Reliance, Infosys, etc., was scripted in the 80s. Nehru talked of scientific temper, now the discourse was on knowledge economy and knowledge society. The stage was set for the forthcoming debates and initiatives on liberalisation, privatisation, and so forth. Sectors like oil, infrastructure, etc., were to witness quantum leaps while moral values nosedived. The consequences are too close for us to judge. However the whiff of change in 1985 seemed reassuring.

To conclude, a quote from Rajiv Gandhi's Presidential Address at the 1985 Bombay session of INC seems relevant:

> A century of achievement ends. A century of endeavour beckons to us. Our resplendent civilisation, with unbroken continuity from the third millennium BC looks ahead to peaks of excellence in the third millennium A.D.[51]

Endnotes

1. Gandhi, Indira (1983). "Presidential Address, INC", Calcutta session, in A.M. Zaidi (ed.) (1989). *Congress Presidential Addresses.* Vol. V (1940-1985), New Delhi. p. 566.
2. Quoted by Barooah, D.K. (1975). *Presidential Address, INC.* Chandigarh. Ibid: 551.
3. INC sessions of 1888 and 1892, Zaidi, A.M. (ed.) (1978). *The Encyclopaedia of the Indian National Congress.* Vol. II, New Delhi. p. 163.
4. Ibid: Vol. IV, p. 251.
5. Ninth session at Lahore in December 1893. Ibid: Vol. II, p. 406. This resolution was repeated at the 12th, 13th and 14th session in 1896, 1897 and 1898 respectively.
6. Kumar, Deepak (2007). *Science and the Raj.* 2nd Ed., Delhi. pp. 208-10.
7. For details see, Visvanathan, Shiv (1985). *Organising for Science.* Delhi. pp. 36-96.
8. Sinha, J.N. (1991). "Science and the Indian National Congress", in Deepak Kumar (ed.), *Science and Empire.* Delhi. pp. 161-81.
9. *Young India,* November 13, 1924. pp. 377-78.
10. *The Hindu,* 19 March 1925; *Young India,* 21 July 1927.
11. *Science and Culture* (1935). I: 3-4, June.
12. Young India (1925). "To industrialise India in the same sense as Europe is to attempt the impossible", 6 August.
13. Jawaharlal Nehru, *Selected Works,* Vol. 14. pp. 554-57.
14. Sinha, J.N., *op. cit.*
15. Sinha, J.N. (1995). "Technology for National Reconstruction: The National Planning Committee, 1938-49", in Deepak Kumar and Roy MacLeod (eds.), *Technology and the Raj.* New Delhi. pp. 250-61.
16. Gokhale, B.G. (19768). "Nehru and History", *History and Theory* 17(3): 311-22. October.
17. Singh, Baldev (ed.) (1988). *Jawaharlal Nehru on Science and Society.* New Delhi: NMML. pp. 3-14.
18. Unlike majority of his countrymen, Nehru happily lived with a single girl child! This personal example was conveniently ignored by his people.
19. For an interesting discussion see, Prasad, Shambhu (2001). "Towards an Understanding of Gandhi's Views on Science", *Economic & Political Weekly* 36(39): 3721-32. September 29-October 5.
20. *Science and Culture* VIII(I), July 1942, reprinted in Baldev Singh (ed.), *op. cit.*, pp. 28-29.
21. Ibid: 35.
22. Ibid: 52.

23. Cited in Krishna, V.V. (2001). "Changing Policy Cultures, phases and trends in science and technology in India", *Policy Cultures* 28(3): 179-194. June.
24. Ibid.
25. Pal, B.P. (1977). "Science and Agriculture", in B.R. Nanda (ed.), *Science and Technology in Modern India*. New Delhi. pp. 43-54.
26. Jawaharlal Nehru to J. D. Bernal at a meeting in Beijing in 1954. See, *Bernal Papers*, MSS. Add. 8287, Box 48, B. 3.349, Cambridge University Library.
27. Vyasulu, Vinod (1989). "Nehru and the Visvesvaraya Legacy", *Economic & Political Weekly* 24(30): 1700-84. July 29.
28. Cited in Singh, Rajendra (2003). "Indian Sciences Congress Association and the VIPs", *Current Science* 84(12): 1498-99. 25 June.
29. A.M. Zaidi, *op.cit*, pp. 412-22.
30. Presidential Address by Jagjivan Ram, Ibid: 477.
31. Ibid: 493.
32. Presidential Address by S.D. Sharma, Ibid: 513.
33. Presidential Address by D.K. Barooah, Ibid: 546.
34. Sharma, Dhirendra (1976). "Growth and Failures of India's Science Policy", *Economic and Political Weekly* 11(51): 1969-71. December 18.
35. Cited in Ibid.
36. Rao, J.S. (1985). "Science and Technology in India", *Science* (New Series) 229 (4709): 130-34. July.
37. Natarajan (1988). "Science and Technology under India Gandhi", in Yogendra K. Malik and Dhirendra K. Vajpeyi (eds.), *India :The Years of Indira Gandhi*. Leiden. pp. 98-115.
38. Gandhi, Indira (1972). "India and the World", *Foreign Affairs* 51(1): 65-77. October. The gulf which she had so astutely perceived was to widen even more under her successors in the years to some.
39. Gandhi, Indira (1982). "Scientific Endeavour in India", *Science (*New Series) 217(4564): 1008-09. September 10.
40. Ibid.
41. Anderson, Robert S. (1983). "Cultivating Science as Cultural Policy: A Contrast of Agricultural and Nuclear Science in India", *Pacific Affairs* 56(1): 38-50. Spring.
42. Thomas, R.C. (1986). "India's Nuclear and Space Programme: Defence or Development?", *World Politics* 38(2): 315-42. January.
43. Parthasarathi, Ashok (2001). "Leadership in Science and Technology: Some Aspects of the Indian Experience", *Economic and Political Weekly* 36(40): 3843-51. October 6-12.

44. Parthasarathi, Ashok (2007). *Technology as the Core: Science and Technology with Indira Gandhi*. New Delhi. p. 52. This interesting volume is full of anecdotes and liberal pats by the author on his own back!
45. Technology Policy Statement, DST (1983). New Delhi; Sikka, Pawan (2001). "Technology Policy in India—Key Issues and Future Perspectives", *International Journal of Services Technology and Management* 2 (3-4): 388-01.
46. Mohan, S. and Ashok Jain (1999). *India: 50 years of Independence 1947-97: Science and Technology*. New Delhi. p. 84.
47. Rangarajan, Mahesh (2009). "Striving for a Balance: Nature, Power, Science and India's Indira Gandhi, 1967-1984", *Conservation and Society* 7(4): 79-92.
48. Cited in Ibid.
49. It is interesting to note that to deal with pollution and industries in private sector, the NCEPC had constituted a sub-committee under the chairmanship of Keshub Mahindra (of the Bhopal Gas fame!)Ref. Ashok Parthasarathy, Technology at the Core, op.cit, p. 203.
50. Sikka, Pawan (2007). *Rajiv Gandhi's Modern India, Development with Science and Technology*. New Delhi, p. XVIII. See also, David Dickson (1985). "Gandhi shakes up Indian Science", *Science* (New Series) 230(4729): 1016-17. November 29.
51. A.M. Zaidi, *op. cit*, p. 607.

Research help received from Awadesh Kumar and Kaushalya Bajpai is gratefully acknowledged.

Chapter IX

Dynamics of Caste and Congress Policies of Social and Economic Development

Yogendra Singh

The contribution of the Congress towards incorporating caste as an institution into its policies and political discourses should be evaluated in the context of two important analytical dimensions: first, the historicity of the discourse on caste and its interface with the colonial legacy including vast theoretical and empirical data generated by social sciences in India. Secondly, the place that caste occupied in the ideology of Congress to achieve social transformation and development in the Indian society. This analytical framework for evaluation remains valid in general for any period of time. It may provide an objective perspective for the task of studying the relationships between the Congress policies of social and economic development and its interface with the dynamics of caste. The period of 1964-1984 which constitutes the boundary for analysis in this essay bears historical continuities with policies and programmes for development envisaged earlier as well as is embedded into challenges contemporaneous to the period under evaluation.

Traditionally, caste as an institution had a pivotal place in the social structure of India. Its role in social stratification and its institutionalisation in society, with all its implication to social and cultural exclusion and exploitation has been widely recognised. Caste, at the local level also performed a quasi-political role from time to time through caste *panchayats*. Most of these functions, however, remained local or at best regional, varying from one part of India to another. The systematic entry of caste into the political discourse of the state enters with the beginning and consolidation of colonial regime. It was motivated by multiple reasons, a few to promote reforms and inclusiveness, but many others with an eye on governance and consolidation of the British colonial regime across India. 'Divide and rule' indeed seems aptly to express it in large measure. Steps such as, divisions and organisation of army on caste based notion of 'martial' and 'non-martial' races, support to caste anchored governance in the village communities representing the traditional caste hierarchies which reinforced the economic and cultural domination of *zamindars* belonging mostly to the upper castes began to kindle caste consciousness among people. The Census operations particularly that of 1931, on caste lines led to widespread politicisation of caste. It led to numerous claims from castes lower in traditional reckoning with claims for upper caste status. It had many other associated cultural and social implications which Srinivas has characterised as the process of 'Sanskritisation' (see, Srinivas, 1966; Singh, 1973). It inaugurated the entry of state in the institutionalisation of possibilities of change in the traditional caste structure, and consequently it led to litigations and judicial interventions to settle the issues particularly in the southern regions of India.

The British regime under the Act of 1935 also introduced the policies specially to ensure protection and welfare of the 'depressed castes' and tribes (See, Davis, 1958). It accompanied several other measures to remove caste discrimination in state sponsored institutions. Several institutions were established to survey the social and cultural profiles of India, some on a long standing basis. In addition to the Census Commission, organisations such the Linguistic Survey of India (LSI), Anthropological Survey of India (ASI), etc., were entrusted with the task of enumeration and study of social and cultural attributes, such as languages, dialects, tribes and caste. No doubt, the social facts generated through these surveys, etc., proved helpful in promoting social science researches, but more importantly these helped the state in policy formulation as well as in legitimising the colonial policies of portraying India as a configuration of fragments rather than an organically integrated society capable of, by implication, to undertake the task of nation building and self-rule (Singh, 1986). These facts were often used to legitimise colonial ideology. This is reflected not only through out in formulation of state policies and political stances but also finds cross-mirroring in the writings of many Western social scientists.

The national movement for Independence led by the Congress not only undertook the cause of national mobilisation but also contested the colonial ideology which was being promoted through several fact-finding British reports and surveys. Many Indian social scientists joined this movement by laying bare many biases contained in such reports, and provided counterfactual evidence of facts which established that linkages existed among the regions, religions, ethnicities, tribes, caste and communities in India. This was in addition to the centuries-old strong cultural and civilisational ties of interdependence that existed across many of India's cultural regions. N.K. Bose, who served as the head of the ASI and was close to nationalist leaders contributed extensively through his writings to disabuse the biases which colonial administration and social scientist widely manifested in their policies and publications (Bose, 1977). Congress policies on caste, tribe and minority evolved throughout the entire period of the national movement for independence in consonance with the recognition of these realities. Its entire policy framework was embedded in the vision of an independent, republican future India. It was committed to the abolition of all institutions, structural and cultural which were founded upon legitimisation of inequalities, exploitation and marginalisation of the weaker sections of the society be they economic, social or cultural. Politics and political mobilisation were viewed as the instruments for the realisation of these goals.

Emergence of the National Discourse on Caste

The social and political discourse specifically on caste began to emerge and manifest its dynamics in course of the Congress-led national movement as it began to reach its point of culmination. The movement had to reckon with multiple dimensions, pulls and compulsions manifested by social and political interest groups embedded in local and primordial identities of which caste formed a vital structural foundation. These needed to be reconciled with its overall nationalist cosmopolitan approach to nation building whose agenda included radical social and economic reforms. Throughout the period of struggle for freedom the central theme of Congress ideology hinged on strengthening the unity of India as a nation state where the plurality of traditions and social and economic wellbeing of all communities, classes, castes, tribes and ethnicities were protected; where state constitutionally guaranteed commitment to secularism, universal human rights and freedom and welfare to all its citizens. Yet, the Congress realised and affirmed its commitment to pursue special policy goals to offer protection and, where relevant, positive discrimination in favour of members of depressed castes, tribes and others who have suffered and continued to suffer from social and economic deprivation and marginalisation in society. It also consistently fought the attempts of the colonial regime to divide caste, tribes and religious communities in India to promote its political interest as also such political parties and movements which endorsed divisive policies on sectarian lines (Chandra, 1979).

The social and political consequences of these complex dimensions of nation building which devolved upon the Congress at the beginning of Independence is reflected in the debates in the Constituent Assembly constituted in order to frame the Constitution of India (Batbayal, 2007). The composition of the drafting committee of the Constituent Assembly was highly representative, it also had membership representing the interests of depressed castes, classes, tribes, ethnicities and minorities, etc., and the debates amply reflect the political and social discourses on castes, its place in future policies of the state for overall social, economic and cultural development of these communities. Particularly noteworthy is the contribution made by the leaders who represented the tribes, depressed castes and minorities. They articulated the urgent need to offer constitutional protection of the interests of castes and tribes who have suffered centuries of oppression, exploitation and marginalisation in the traditional Indian society. As is known widely, B.R. Ambedkar, who personified the representation on behalf of the depressed classes and caste played an architectural role in the making of the Constitution and made it possible to integrate the policies of positive discrimination in favour of the depressed communities within the framework of a Constitution fundamentally anchored on the principles of universal citizenship rights and civil liberties for all. The 'Objectives Resolution' of the Constitution moved by Jawaharlal Nehru reflects this concern. Out of its eight clauses which enunciate the fundamental spirit and objectives of the Constitution, clauses five and six refer particularly to such measures. These read as follows:

> (The Constituent Assembly declares its firm and solemn resolve to draw up for the future governance a Constitution: (5) Wherein shall be guaranteed and secured to all the people of India justice, social, economic and political; equality of status, of opportunity, and before the law; freedom of thought, expression, belief, faith, worship, vocation, association and action subject to law and public morality, and (6) *Wherein adequate safeguard shall be provided for minorities, backward and tribal areas, and depressed and other backward classes...* (italics added, Ibid: 365-66).

The special provision made for positive discrimination in favour of the scheduled castes (SCs) and the scheduled tribes (STs) as well the inclusion of the 'socially and educationally backward classes' for such protection made in the Directive Principles of the State Policy flows from this formulation of the objectives of the Constitution.

Development Policies and Measures: Impact on Class and Caste

The policies and measures of social and economic development and change following the adoption of the Constitution ushered in several radical steps for structural changes in the economy and society in India commensurate with the vision that Congress had evolved through the national movement. These measures are reflected through the first three Five-Year plans from 1951 to 1966 approximately. Primacy was accorded to the structural changes in the agrarian feudal system of the rural economy, which had deeper interface with its social structure, policy and power and to a large extent the cultural institutions of the rural communities. The institutions of *zamindari, taluqdari* and the rule of the princes in widely scattered regions of India was abolished. They were all incorporated within the new institutional, economic, political and cultural framework of the Indian Republic. The impact of these radical reforms was immediate on the social structure of the rural society. Slowly, as the outcome of the reforms began to erode the centuries-old tradition of exploitation and marginalisation of the rural working classes, peasants and artisans and other categories of village population, a new equilibrium in inter-caste and class relationship began to emerge.

In addition to the abolition of *zamindari* and intermediary rights on land, several other radical reforms such as the conferment of ownership rights to peasantry over their land, ceiling on land holdings, consolidation of land and projects to ensure irrigation facilities for farmers, extending scientific innovations to the processes of agriculture, its marketing and management, etc., were undertaken on a very wide scale. The institutions of community development projects, village *panchayats* elected on civil principles (not caste) and the network of development institutions from the village upward to block and the district were introduced and established. These measures were not undertaken in isolation but formed an integral part of the industrial, technological-educational and macroeconomic policies for the nation. Massive investment in irrigation dams and canals, establishment of the agricultural universities and research institutes, petrochemical industries for fertilisers, etc., were undertaken on wider scale. Care was also taken to ensure that peasants did not suffer from distress sale of their products; so provincial governments took upon themselves to ensure a market which gave farmers a minimum profitable rate of price at which food grain were purchased. It was to ensure food availability to the state for its distribution to vast number of the urban and rural poor and consumers in the country. In this context, we may note that during this period the country faced several drought-like situations, also leading to food scarcity and had to face unexpected geopolitical problems.

The period from 1950 to 1964 could be treated with justification, despite many hurdles, as a period which laid down the foundations of the agricultural and industrial planning and its implementation. The Industrial Policy Resolution updated from time to time aimed at the autonomous economic and industrial growth of the nation. Massive public investment in heavy industries, steel, petrochemicals, mega-construction of irrigation dams and several other ventures calling for long duration gestation period to bring forth results (for which capital was also not available from the private sector during all this time) were taken up by the state on a priority basis. In addition, large scale investment was made in establishing and promoting the knowledge sector. Institutions of higher research and training in science and technology, in space sciences, medicine and management and social sciences etc., were implemented. The spheres of culture and fine arts were also brought into the domain of support by the state through creation for them of financial and institutional foundations.

The Outcome of Policies and Impact on Caste

The demographic composition of the country at this time was such that approximately more than 70 percent of the population was rural and dependent on agriculture including the landless agricultural labourers. The segment of the trading communities and artisans was miniscule indeed. This demographic feature was deeply embedded in the caste structure and its social stratification. It also had a close interface with class stratification in villages (Desai, 1959). Most of the peasants dependent on farming came from the middle segment of the caste system scattered throughout the country. An important point to be noted here is that the institution of caste had traditionally always been entirely a regional/local social phenomenon. The studies of the regional dispersal of individual caste groups measured through kinship and marriage ties (since endogamy constitutes an integral feature of caste system) have shown that beyond a distance of 200-300 miles, the nomenclature or marks of sociocultural identification of a particular caste ceases to be meaningful or understood by the people. The caste status has, therefore, to be made comprehendible through taking recourse to markers of *varna*, an ideal-typical model of caste largely, (e.g., the fourfold caste hierarchy, the Brahamana, Kshatriya, Vaishya and Shudra along with reference to the outcaste, the Panchama or the fifth category).

In terms of realities on the ground, this ideal-typical categorisation of caste hierarchy has always remained ambiguous since several borderline situations within the hierarchical notion tended to exist which, apart from other factors, were complicated by continual processes of 'passing' or claims for a social status within the *varna* scheme higher than traditionally assigned to an individual caste. This process overwhelmed the Census operation of 1931, particularly in southern and western parts of India. Many castes in these regions noticing in the Census operation an opportunity to claim a higher status, as they thought a new legitimacy was being provided by the state as it was being enumerated. M.N. Srinivas in his sociological analysis of the processes of caste dynamics calls it the process of 'Sanskritisation', since the claim to higher caste status was generally preceded also by imitation of the cultural and social (sanskritic) attributes of the higher caste to which the claim was made.

How this claim for Sanskritisation saw a reversal following Independence when the Constitution made special provisions for positive discrimination for a large number of traditionally marginalised castes leading to an opposite process, named 'de-Sanskritisation' which generally denotes an attempt to discard upper caste cultural markers adopted earlier in favour of reassertion of one's traditional caste identity. This process has been increasingly reinforced both by increase in cultural and social self-consciousness (for instance, Dalit consciousness) among the castes traditionally lower in hierarchy as well as the provisions for their political and economic empowerment guaranteed by the Constitution. (Singh, 1973).

Nevertheless, the regional and local anchorage of caste in the landscape of our nation leads to a host of consequences which have become meaningful as the momentum of development and change has gained strength. It became visible as the consequence of development policies in agriculture and land reforms began to take root in the village society and the policies of positive discrimination in favour of the scheduled castes, tribes and backward castes/classes began to show results. It introduced not only a new dimension of internal changes in the caste dynamics at several levels but in course of time, impacted significantly on party politics and governance in our country.

Emerging New Dynamics of Caste

The development policies that the Congress Party pursued as outlined above, began to show both economic and sociological consequences for the society and polity by the end of 1970s. The period from 1964 to 1970 could roughly be treated as an indicator when several and momentous new changes took place with far-reaching consequences. With the passing away of Jawaharlal Nehru, the Congress Party entered an altogether new phase of its internal dynamics. Lal Bahadur Shastri took over as prime minister in June 1964. In 1965, India was confronted with aggression from Pakistan which had to be dealt with and its consequential problems resolved. It was also the period when Indira Gandhi entered into the cabinet as precursor to her initiation to power. This consequently led her to assume the responsibilities of prime minister's office at a very difficult period of country's economic, geopolitical and social conditions. But a significant and positive turn of events for the country was that this period inaugurated the process of a breakthrough in agriculture since the investments in technological and infrastructural investments the country had made so far began to show results. This momentous change has rightly been termed as the 'Green Revolution' in agriculture which eventually made India self-sufficient in matters of food production.

As a consequence of Green Revolution and other investments in agriculture the structural features of the rural society in all parts of India began to manifest a new dynamics of caste which slowly began to crystallise. Its social impact began to be felt on the nature of empowerment and consolidation of caste identities which triggered also a new class dynamics in villages. The impact was enlarged when the social outcome of the Green Revolution evolved its interface with the previous policy measures implemented on positive discrimination in favour of the depressed castes. The decade, 1950-1964 provided impetus to political, social and economic empowerment to the SCs, STs and backward classes/castes (BCs) in the states. Commensurate with caste demography in the states it had already impacted upon the electoral and political empowerment of these castes in most of the southern states of India, where the Brahmins largely comprised the upper caste but had only about three percent share of population. Here, power overwhelmingly shifted to the BCs and SCs/STs. But in this shift, the BCs had a comparative advantage both because of their peasant tradition and substantial land ownership and also because of the advantages they had of their numbers in the population. In the north and other parts of India the comparative advantage of Green Revolution largely went in favour of the peasant backward castes.

The major factor in this process of empowerment of the middle and lower castes in most regions was the result of electoral empowerment. It was further reinforced by investment in a large number of social policies oriented to achieve the goals of accelerating the processes of economic and social mobility among these categories of castes. The substantive base for initiatives from within these castes, particularly from the BCs for such mobility and growth was provided by the Green Revolution. It gave rise to the emergence of a new countrywide dynamic with far-reaching social and political implications which have been widely analysed. The period of 1960s in India was when the country suffered from acute food shortages due to failures of monsoon and very low productivity on land. Throughout this period the country depended upon food aid from the USA on deferred payment basis. The Congress leadership was acutely conscious of this critical situation, and as we have mentioned above the policies in the domains of agriculture, industries, science and technology and rural management, etc., were orchestrated to make a new breakthrough in agricultural productivity. This began to happen slowly as peasants haltingly in the first instance (particularly in Punjab and Haryana) and then on a wider scale in the country started adopting the new technological and managerial innovations in agriculture. New varieties of wheat and rice were introduced which yielded production many times higher than in the past. Interestingly, the peasant castes which took the lead in bringing Green Revolution to success comprised about 20 percent of their population possessing approximately a size of landholding ranging from 5 to 15 acres on the average. The social and economic consequences of this breakthrough in agriculture had the potential, therefore, to impact both on the class and caste structure, its power relationships within the village and its much wider political roles later in the states and the nation. A new middle class in villages slowly began to emerge whose population size varied from region to region in the country. But in no region did it form a minority in the rural community, not being less than about 25-30 percent of the population. It formed a very substantial single electoral constituency of the 'backward classes' (Singh, 1993). The success that came through the green revolution had a wider social impact on the rural social system not all of it being of positive consequence. While it augmented economic growth, food security, social mobility and political empowerment of the middle castes, it also led to displacement of women from work, gender marginalisation and high incidences of conflict between the middle peasant and lower Dalit segments of castes in villages. This added to the intensity of emerging caste dynamics and its social and political impact upon society.

The new technological imperatives of farming required very precise schedules of irrigation, fertiliser uses, and linkages with market, banks and community development structures of support. It had a significant impact on the role of gender, and traditional system of authority in the peasant families. Studies show that Green Revolution technologies displaced women from work on farming in many social and economic sectors having negative consequences for ecological sustainability. In families, it brought about a change in the traditional pattern of authority, because new innovations in agriculture empowered the younger male adults who had to assume responsibilities of negotiating with markets, banks, authorities of governance and development sponsored by the state. Authority in several domains, particularly in the economic and political sectors thus shifted from the traditional control of the elderly parents to the new generation of youth. However, in areas of kinship, marriage and rituals, etc., the elders in the family continued to have decisive voice. This brought about a major change in the village-centric traditional pattern of negotiations in matters political and economic within the community of castes and families and linkages of the village slowly spread wide and became centrifugal. In fact, in course of time following the period of 1970s this process led to slow erosion of the nature of traditional village communities as they increasingly were converted into political communities (Singh, 2009). It has to be realised, however, that most of these changes were a consequence of the policies of development that the country followed under the leadership of the Congress and Jawaharlal Nehru.

New Turning Points and the Congress Party

As Indira Gandhi assumed the office of the Prime Minister after the sudden demise of Lal Bahadur Shastri, a new turning point in the social, economic and political spheres began to slowly take shape. This could be discerned during the period 1970-1977 when some innovative policies and priorities were introduced. The Congress Party under Indira Gandhi's leadership announced and began to implement some radical new measures, such as the nationalisation of banks, abolition of the privileges and privy purses of the rulers, and a shift leftward in policies sidelining the long enduring control of the conservative regional Congress leaders in states. The new emphasis was on removal of poverty or 'Garibi Hatao' as it came to be known. The bank nationalisation released enormous financial facilities to the hitherto denied sections and sectors of marginalised parts of society, such as the villages, tribal regions and small towns, etc. It reinforced the outward linkages of the rural agrarian economy with markets and institutions outside.

It may also be worthwhile to mention here that this period had also to bear a variety of social, political and economic pressures on the polity. The regional geopolitical atmosphere was hardly conducive, the 1965 conflict with Pakistan and its troubles later on with East Pakistan where India had to intervene decisively despite alienation from the western powers led by the USA had its economic and political costs which the nation had to bear. Indira Gandhi led the country through these difficult times with élan and the national consensus was in her support by and large. Nevertheless, these events also had serious long-term political repercussions.

The emerging new dynamics of caste in politics had the tendency increasingly to augment regional political pressures as the emergent rural middle classes from the ranks of peasantry began to exert their politics of identity. Sociologically, this process coincided with the increasing consolidation and assertion of the SC self-consciousness and its manifestation in a variety of forms of demand politics (Punalekar, 2010). It is noteworthy that Congress Party's investment in SCs' economic and social liberation from their traditional state of marginalisation, its policies of positive discrimination and special efforts for their economic and educational development, etc., had brought about a measure of social, economic and political empowerment and upward mobility discernable in their communities. It threw up a new structure of leadership and elite formation in their midst. It contributed also to the spread of the identity politics adding new energy to the long enduring SC or Dalit movement in the country. No doubt, the development policies in favour of the Dalits and its 'spread effect' had largely contributed to this process.

The cumulative impact of most of the steps that India had to take to overcome the crisis following the Bangladesh war, looking after the millions of refugee from East Pakistan during the period of conflict and political rebellion, taking care of about 90,000 prisoners of the Pakistan army who had surrendered to the Indian armed forces during the conclusion of the conflict in addition the need for coming to terms with the rising aspirations of the new peasant middle classes, BCs to further extend policy of positive discrimination in their favour in the Central services and its institutions and the continuing stress on the economy in general due to adverse capital resources, etc., contributed to two significant consequences: first, the momentum for regionalisation of political leadership enmeshed with caste politics increased in the northern states where the caste demography, though complex, gave numerical advantages to the BCs and SCs. This led to strident competitive demand politics. Secondly, the voices of the conservative Congress leaders whom Indira Gandhi had isolated through her own party craftsmanship began to reassert itself as this section saw the opportunity in the new crisis situation to reemerge as a powerful force. The call by Jayaprakash Narayan, a Gandhian-Sarvodaya leader, for a 'total revolution' galvanised this discontentment. Most of these social and political processes emerged slowly and in stages to culminate to a point of a major national crisis by 1975. To overcome the crisis Indira Gandhi declared a state of Emergency annulling most of the democratic rights of the citizens guaranteed by the Constitution.

It led to a serious crisis of consensus and reconciliation in the democratic republic, the two basic principles for the success of democracy. There was a sudden and preemptive arrest of political leaders of the opposition, the liberal activists and most of those who were supporters of Jayaprakash Narayan's call for 'total revolution'. It was an extremely controversial decision which led to major disenchantment of most people, particularly in the northern states of India. The impact was less intensely felt in the south as most of the action plans of the new policy engineering were localised in the urban and rural settings of the northern India. Ironically, some of the policies, such as the population planning and slum clearances and urban planning, etc., were such that its victims were the poor people, slum dwellers and small vendors and trader. The policy to introduce force in population planning in villages also generally targeted the poor. These policies were most ill-advised and badly implemented. The result was massive disenchantment in northern India particularly from the Congress rule.

Its net result was that most of the political leaders from the opposition who were in jail evolved a consensus to come together and joined together not only to overwhelmingly denounce the declaration of emergency but to merge together to form one united party. They gave it the nomenclature of Janata Party. Ironically, the state of emergency was declared by the President in exercise of the discretion provided by the Constitution to declare emergency in rare cases of national crisis. Whether the prelude to declaration of emergency had given reason enough to take such a radical measure remains controversial. There is some allegation that a few exhortations from prominent leaders of the opposition amounted to a call for rebellion, even from those who were an organic part of the instruments of national governance. The issue, however, remains controversial and a holistic sociological inquiry is required. Particularly we need to investigate as to how emergent new dynamics of caste of BCs and middle class peasantry provided energy to new political processes.

An interesting aspect of the entire episode of emergency declaration which has not been fully researched is its possible linkages with the dynamics of caste in the northern states of India, particularly by the middle class/caste peasant leaders from Bihar and Uttar Pradesh in addition to those in states such as Gujarat, Madhya Pradesh and Rajasthan. Is the social dynamics of caste, such as the rise of the middle caste BCs in the north as a consequence of the Green Revolution and social policies of state level positive discrimination, empowering them socially, economically and politically not contributory to a crisis of aspirations contribution to discontentment which added fuel to the demand politics and politics of opposition parties during the periods interim to emergency declaration? Is it ironically not etiologically linked to the outcome of the economic and social policies implemented and carried out by the successive Congress governments during the previous decades of its rule which under the sudden and unexpected pressures led to a political 'blow up'? Was the declaration of emergency a response to contain the political discontent and social discordance through an extraordinary provision provided in the Constitution taken in haste, a firefighting measure without due regard to its wider and long-term consequences? Answers to most of these questions do merit systemic and in-depth historical explorations.

Aftermath of Emergency and New Dynamics of Caste

The aftermath of the Emergency declaration was, as we have mentioned above, felt most intensely in the north Indian states where the complexity of caste structure was already giving fillip to consolidation of the caste consciousness of the SCs and BCs torn by its own contradictions. In addition, the measures taken for population planning and other policies generally targeted the poor. Hence it offered an opportunity which led to the unity of interest and wider disillusionment commonly felt by both the peasant middle castes as well as the Dalits and other marginalised castes. A unity which did not exist earlier as we have already mentioned. As the duration of the emergency in steps marched forward its acute contradiction even in the structure of governance became glaring. These internal and external pressures on the Indira Gandhi regime led the Congress to annul emergency and declare general elections in 1977. These elections went overwhelmingly against the Congress in the northern states of India, although in the southern states the party did better. This could be due to the fact that the negative perception of emergency and the sufferings it caused to the people were felt not in equal measure between the two regions of India. Its political fallout was almost radical. Most leaders from the opposition parties, with the exception of the Left were imprisoned and, as already mentioned, they evolved a consensus on merging together against the Congress forming a united new party called the Janata Party to contest the elections. It included, the former Jana Sangh, a national party enjoying sympathy of the Rashtriya Swayam Sewak Sangh (RSS) professing the ideology of *Hindutva*. This coming together of a new political formation with the merger of Jana Sangh, which was considered to profess communal ideology for its links with RSS, had an inbuilt contradiction within the new formation and soon it became a bone of contention.

After its victory in the General Elections of 1977, the Janata Party came to power with Morarji Desai, a former Congress leader with conservative leanings as Prime Minister. The members from the former

Jana Sangh now merged into Janata Party were given responsible ministerial positions. But as soon as the new government started functioning, some prominent members coming from other political parties, professedly opposed to RSS demanded that all former Jana Sangh members within the new party who also were members of RSS must renounce their RSS membership. It came to be known as the conflict on dual membership within the new united party. This being not acceptable to the members of former Jana Sangh, led to a split within Janata Party as the Jana Sangh members split from the Janata Party, renounced political offices and formed a new party naming it as the Bharatiya Janata Party (BJP). Even with support from the BJP on issues from outside the ruling party became seriously disabled, its internal contradictions became unbearable and Morarji resigned as prime minister. Charan Singh, a leader of the peasant castes replaced Morarji Desai.

The Mandal Commission

Despite many fragilities, the Janata Party took two controversial decisions: one, they moved a privileges motion in the Parliament against Indira Gandhi for declaring Emergency, and since they had majority she was held guilty and (as a token gesture to make a point) jailed for a very short duration. This was a political blunder and in the next General Elections the party had to pay a very heavy cost. Consequently, Indira Gandhi came back to power. But their second step, setting up of a Commission for reservation for the BCs in Central services and institutions was, despite being contentious, indeed a step with implications of long-term process of social engineering for inclusion policies adding new dimensions to caste dynamics. The party in power set up a Backward Class Commission in 1979 to determine the policy and quantum of reservation for the BCs/OBCs in the Central services etc., and make recommendations accordingly. The Commission had B.P. Mandal, a senior backward class leader, as its Chairman and most of its members were drawn mainly from the BC/SC categories; a senior civil servant was appointed as the member-secretary.

Its report constitutes a landmark towards the culmination of the policies of positive discrimination in favour of the traditionally marginalised BC castes. The Commission realised that its recommendation about the percentage of reservation for the BCs will have to be within the limit of 50 percent set by a decision of the Supreme Court of India. To determine the number of BCs in the country due to lack of Census data it arrived at an estimate based on the data generated by the Backward Class reports at state level in addition to extrapolation of 1931 Census data which included the enumeration of castes.

On the basis of these estimates it determined the number of BCs in the country to a figure of about 56 percent of the total population. In the light of the Supreme Court ceiling for reservations at 50 percent and considering that 7.5 percent reservation was already made for STs and 15 percent for SCs, it recommended a quantum of 27 percent of reservations in favour of the BCs/OBCs since it was the residuary figure available for reservation. It may be mentioned, however, that the Commission realised the fact that unlike the cases of the STs and SCs on which there existed a general consensus on their uniform backwardness deserving positive discrimination, the 'social and educational' backwardness among the BCs was not uniform; its levels varied from region to region, within the region from caste to caste. Indeed, several backward castes in parts of India were internally differentiated in terms of economic, social and educational status, many among them being substantial landowners or even former landlords. With the intention to overcome this difficulty the Commission rightly thought of conducting surveys of one village each in every district of the country. An Expert Panel of social scientists was invited to help the Commission in this process and on related issues. The Panel finalised the operational tools for the survey; even a sub-committee of the experts from the Panel was constituted to process the data. It was left to the Government and the Commission to complete the survey and generate the required data. For various reasons, however, the survey could not be completed and the Commission recommended the quantum of percentage for BC/OBC reservation on the principles outlined above. This did cause disappointment among several members of the Expert Panel as they looked forward to using the statistical data thus generated to determine the quantum of reservation with statistical support and objectivity at a more convincing level to avoid dissensions and help in building a national consensus on the policy.

The Janata Party government fell while the work of the Commission was in process. The Commission submitted its report around 1980 and before the action could be initiated, the government fell. In the next General Elections it lost power to the Congress as it was widely rejected even in the north Indian states. Indira Gandhi once again became the Prime Minister. She did take some initiative on the Mandal Committee report but the government through its wider consultation and its own internal evaluation of the report could not come to a conclusion. It probably realised the level of complexity in building a national consensus on the issue of BC/OBC reservation and of the need to evaluate its operational aspect further. After her tragic assassination in 1984 following which Rajiv Gandhi took over as Prime Minister the implementation of the recommendations of the Mandal report remained in abeyance until around 1990s. V.P. Singh, a former senior minister in Rajiv Gandhi's cabinet who had broken away from him leading to fall of Rajiv Gandhi government, formed a new coalition of opposition called Janata Dal and fought the elections and came to power. He became Prime Minister and announced implementation of the Mandal Commission recommendations without any modification. As anticipated by most of the members of the sub-committee of experts invited to advise the Commission, this step caused violent reaction in the north, particularly from the upper caste youth. Several cases of self-immolation as a mark of protest took place. As a consequence, those opposed to this took legal action in 'public cause' and the matter was placed before the Supreme Court. It gave its historical verdict, most important among these being that in providing the benefits of reservation, the BC/OBC (the OBC category was introduced by the Commission) castes which belonged to higher categories of income, or the 'creamy layer' of the empowered sections among them may be identified and excluded from the privileges of reservation. To operationalise its recommendations it proposed setting up of the Backward Commissions at the Centre and states on a standing basis. Thus, at least in policy, the degree of dissonance and lack of consensus on the recommendations of the Mandal Commission was minimised. Nevertheless, this phenomenon marks a vital aspect in the chain through which caste dynamics in the Indian polity has found manifestation. It highlights how the caste dynamics that received fillip from the policies of development which Congress had implemented led to growth in economy and to social mobility. But it also caused increasing contradictions of mismatch between aspirations and desired degree of inclusion. By the time Indira Gandhi regime ended around 1984, these contradictions were building up and peaked eventually.

Summing Up

Our analysis makes an effort to review the dynamics of caste in the perspective of history. Congress as a political party since its emergence as a party from its journey through the national movement for independence had its anchorage in the ideology of nation building, democracy, secularism and policies of development and modernisation of India based on the cardinal principles of civic liberty with justice to the traditionally deprived sections of India. Nehru's focus on nationalism and nation building even though rooted into the specificity of India's problem had simultaneous commitment to values of cosmopolitan and universalistic humanism. He was manifestly against the policy of enduring the divisive and fragmentary aspects of social structure, such as religion, caste or regionalism, etc., which had imperilled India's growth through centuries. He favoured preference for minimising their role eventually towards their obsolescence. Yet, as mentioned above, adaptive adjustment of policies had to be made. This legacy of normative liberalism was also in consonance with Gandhi's emphasis on purity of means to achieve goals and his emphasis on placing the problems of the poor and the exploited in the forefront of the endeavours towards nation building. We find a remarkable degree of convergence on this point between the approach of Nehru and Gandhi on the philosophy and worldview of the vision for a future India.

This vision, however, had to be converted into paradigms of social, economic and cultural policies taking into consideration the concrete social realities of India—caste, religion and ethnicity and the regional and pluralistic characteristic of the social structure of the country necessitated creative and tactical accommodation of these realities within the framework of a republican Constitution with commitment to values of civic liberty, equality and secularism. We have observed how these two contending values, that is, constitutional universalism on the one hand, and on the other, the urgent necessity to address demands for removal of poverty, injustices and exploitations of the traditionally marginalised castes, tribes and ethnic communities had to be reconciled and addressed with equal emphasis. The articulation of the demands for providing special provisions for the overall development of the scheduled castes, tribes and backward classes, we notice, finds a sustained voice in the Constituent Assembly debates. Hence, the provision for the SCs/STs scheduling and reservation for them in the Constitution. In addition, the Directive Principles of the Constitution further refer to the fact that socially and educationally backward classes deserve 'protective discrimination'.

The Congress Party right from the time of Jawaharlal Nehru sustained a policy of creative and adaptable balance between the objectives of developing India into an industrially and technologically advanced and prosperous democracy, on the one hand, and on the other, it paid special attention for the prosperity and empowerment of the scheduled castes, tribes and backward sections of society through policies of positive discrimination. States of the union were granted enormous autonomy in this regard under the Constitution and apart from the Centre SCs/STs and BCs obtained large benefits through reservation policies within the states. The Congress as the national party supported reservations for castes and classes as per the provisions in the Constitution and it also in accordance with its basic normative principles could not legitimise caste as a defining or determinant principle of political and social discourses of the nation and its vision of its future transformation. The policies that the Congress Party pursued through the period 1964-1984 led by Indira Gandhi, reflect this approach.

We have to recognise that caste as a social structural and cultural phenomenon represents local identities. In the process of nation building demands of the sections representing local identities have to be integrated with the national development perspective and vision. The Congress Party had employed this criterion throughout and Indira Gandhi's policies during her tenure as the Prime Minister affirms the sustenance of this policy. In fact, her call for 'Garibi Hatao' or removal of poverty, reflects her commitment to all inclusive approach to removal of social and economic disparities which took care of the issues of distributive justice both at the specific level of castes and tribes as well as for all communities and classes deserving special attention. The Congress Party's policies on caste and positive discrimination throughout 1964-1984 show a consistency and continuity of approach in tune with its past history and its vision for India's future.

References

Batabayal, Rakesh (ed.) (2007). *The Penguin Book of Modern Speeches—1887 to the Present*. New Delhi: Penguin Books of India.

Bose, N.K. (1977). *Culture and Society in India*. New Delhi.

Chandra, Bipan (1979). *Nationalism and Colonialism in Modern India.* New Delhi: Orient Longman.

Davis, Kingsley (1958). *Population of India and Pakistan.* New York: Free Press.

Desai, A.R. (ed.) (1959). *Rural Sociology In India*. Bombay: Popular Prakashan.

Government of India (1980). Mandal Commission Report.

Punalekar, S.P. (2010). "Dalits, Dalit Consciousness and Sociology", in Yogendra Singh (ed.), *Social Sciences, Commucation, Anthropology and Sociology*. Pearson Longman.

Srinivas, M.N. (1966). *Social Change in Modern India.* Berkeley: California University Press.

Singh, Yogendra (2009). "Social Praxis, Conceptual Categories and Social Change: Report from an Indian Village", in *Sociological Bulletin* 58(50).

———. (1986). *Indian Sociology: Social Conditioning and Emerging Concerns.* New Delhi: Sage-Vistar Press.

———. (1973). *Modernisation of the Indian Tradition*. New Delhi: Thompson Press.

Chapter X

The Tribal Issue: 1964-1984

Sanjukta Das Gupta

The tribal population in India today, numbering 83,580,634 in the 2001 Census, accounts for about 8 percent of the country's total population. According to the 1971 census, the numerical strength of the Scheduled Tribe Population in the country was 38,015,162, i.e., 6.93 percent of the population. Taking into consideration their historical, ethnic and sociocultural relations, the tribal communities can be divided into four territorial groups. The first comprised the northeast Indian states of Assam, Arunachal Pradesh, Manipur, Meghalaya, Mizoram, Nagaland, and Tripura. The second consists of the sub-Himalayan region of north and northwest India which include Himachal Pradesh, the sub-mountain districts of Uttarakhand, West Bengal and Sikkim. The third group, the most populous and accounting for about 80 percent of the tribal population, are to be found in the central part of India in a belt stretching from Gujarat and Rajasthan in the west, across Maharashtra, Madhya Pradesh, Chhattisgarh, Andhra Pradesh, Bihar and Jharkhand, to West Bengal and Orissa in the east. A fair number are also to be found in the southern states of Kerala, Tamil Nadu and Karnataka and in the Union Territory of Dadra and Nagar Haveli, Andaman and Nicobar Islands and Lakshadweep.

The very dimension of tribal society in India made tribal issues one of the main points in the Congress agenda ever since independence. The colonial administration had no plan of tribal development, although it professed itself, time and again, to be the protector and liberator of the tribals. It was the popular Congress ministries in the 1930s which formulated the first tribal welfare programmes. The Constituent Assembly itself broke new ground with its emphasis on universal adult franchise for tribals and welfare policies for the speedy development of tribal areas. Once the Congress government took office after independence, it sought to implement those elements of the colonial discourse that it found useful, while adopting policies that would ensure development. The tribal policy that came to be adopted after independence was, thus, based on development and protection in

Table 1

Size and Distribution of Tribal Population, 1981

State/Union Territory	Population	Percentage of Tribal Population with respect to	
		Total Tribals	Total Population
INDIA	51,628,638	100.00	7.76
1. Andhra Pradesh	3,176,001	6.15	5.93
2. Bihar	5,810,876	11.26	8.31
3. Gujarat	4,848,586	9.39	14.22
4. Himachal Pradesh	197,263	0.38	4.61
5. Karnataka	1,825,203	3.54	4.91
6. Kerala	261,475	0.51	1.03
7. Madhya Pradesh	11,987,031	23.22	22.97
8. Maharashtra	5,772,038	11.18	9.19
9. Manipur	387,977	0.75	27.30
10. Meghalaya	1,076,345	2.08	80.58
11. Nagaland	650,885	1.26	83.99
12. Orissa	5,915,067	11.46	22.43
13. Rajasthan	4,183,124	8.10	12.21
14. Sikkim	73,623	0.14	23.27
15. Tamil Nadu	520,226	1.01	1.07
16. Tripura	583,920	1.13	28.44
17. Uttar Pradesh	232,705	0.45	0.21
18. West Bengal	3,070,672	5.95	5.63
19. Andaman & Nicobar Islands	22,361	0.04	11.85
20. Arunachal Pradesh	441,167	0.85	69.82
21. Dadra & Nagar Haveli	81,714	0.16	78.82
22. Goa, Daman & Diu	10,721	0.02	0.99
23. Lakshadweep	37,760	0.07	93.82
24. Mizoram	461,907	0.89	93.55

Source: Census of India (1981). *Primary Census Abstract: Scheduled Tribes*. Series I, India, Part II B (iii), pp. xix-xxiii.

the form of positive discrimination. It introduced reservation of administrative and educational places and also of legislative seats for scheduled castes and tribes, where only persons from designated caste or tribal groups could contest.

This paper will explore the basic assumptions of the Congress tribal policy, as well as its gradual evolution over the decades. It will analyse the nature of the welfare projects undertaken by the Congress governments and its impact upon the tribal people. It has three sections: the first traces the formulation of the tribal policy in India and the changes over time, the second studies the developmental activities undertaken by the Congress governments and the third examines the insurgencies and movements in the tribal regions. Although it was initially based on a model of national integration and development, at a later stage the Congress government realised that a diverse tribal reality required a diverse approach in terms of development programmes. The initial Nehruvian policy came to be replaced by a more nuanced multiplicity of plans. However, ultimately, the needs of industrial development of the country which was given precedence by policymakers resulted in a slow pace of development among the tribal people, who still remain marginalised in the economic, cultural and political spheres.

The Framing of a Tribal Policy in India

The Colonial Background

Prior to colonial rule most of the tribal people had lived in relative isolation, with their distinct traditions, cultures and ways of life. Since the mid-19th century, the British popularised the notion of the total isolation of the tribal groups in many parts of the sub-continent in a bid to legitimise their rule and to project themselves as their protectors and guardians. Contrary to the colonial discourse, however, most of these communities had linkages with the wider polity and economy and were part of a complex regional system that had arisen out of specific historical processes, which imparted to different tribal groups their distinct identities. Colonial rule was in fact, invasive and all-pervasive, ending the relative isolation of tribal societies which were brought within the 'mainstream' through the new administrative set up and programmes. Initially drawn to the tribal regions by the need to maintain 'law and order', the colonial government attempted to extend its authority through building up a framework of rule which was based on a system of collaboration with local allies. At a later stage, they claimed for themselves the role of 'liberators' of the tribals from the 'oppressions and exploitation' of the indigeneous rulers. Together with the twin strategies of protectionism and isolation, the paternalist colonial government also sought to civilise the 'wild' tribals and to induce them to give up their former 'predatory' way of life. Many tribal regions were declared to be 'non-regulation' areas, where the usual regulations of the Empire did not apply. The integration of the tribals within the British administration and the penetration of the market forces unleashed a process of disintegration of the earlier village based community life. The new system of political control came to redefine the status of different groups of tribals and to categorise the people and their privileges. There was also a greater influx of outsiders into these regions as well as migration of tribal people to far-off plantations and mines in search of a livelihood, all of which had significant economic and cultural implications. The tensions arising from the intrusion of colonial authority thus found expression in acts of rebellion throughout the 19th and 20th centuries, as the different tribal groups in India sought to adjust to the new stresses and strains.

The Scheduled Districts Act of 1874, which was based on the principle that normal laws should not automatically apply to tribal areas, also informed the notion of 'backward areas' in the Government of India Act of 1919. In these areas, the responsibility of administration lay with the governors and not on elected governments. Financial allocations for these areas were, therefore, not subject to voting in the legislatures. The policy of segregating different communities was continued through the Government of India Act of 1935 which provided for excluded and partially excluded areas for the administration of tribal regions and was criticised for perpetrating isolation and status quo. T.G. Rutherford, the last British Governor of Bihar, for instance, stated that the protective legislation under British rule could only function effectively in the hands of sympathetic, paternalist officers, and with the aid of missionaries.[1]

The need to provide adequate safeguards for the tribals was discussed extensively in the Constituent Assembly. The Advisory Committee on Fundamental Rights, Minorities and Tribal and Excluded Areas of the Constituent Assembly argued against the policy of having excluded/partially excluded areas stating that, 'partial exclusion or exclusion has been of very little practical value. There has been neither educational nor economic development on any appreciable scale. The object of special administration has not been achieved, and it is clear that if the hill tribes are to be brought up to the level of the rest of the population the strongest measures are now necessary.'[2] During the 1940s, the 'tribal question' was debated at length by 'assimilationists' and 'isolationists'. Reacting to the handling of the tribal issue by the British government, which had laid stress on the pluralistic tendency of Indian society and asserting that tribals were a segmentary polity and could not be assimilated into the mainstream Indian society, the nationalists took the position that tribes were an essential component of the Indian civilisation. G.S. Ghurye, a vocal proponent of this theory believed that the indigeneous peoples of India, whom he termed 'Backward Hindus', were part of mainstream Hindu culture and needed to be totally assimilated.[3] In stark contrast was the isolationist approach of Verrier Elwin who held both colonial rulers and Hindu moneylenders and landlords responsible for uprooting tribals from their indigeneous production system and placing them within the peasant production network. As a result, they could neither benefit from the mainstream economic growth nor go back to their subsistence based primitive production system. The conditions of the tribals, according to Elwin, were worse where they lived in a Hindu majority area. Elwin insisted on what came to be known as the 'national park' approach for the development of the tribals.[4]

Both these approaches were criticised by Jawaharlal Nehru in the following words:

> I find that so far we have approached the tribal people in one of two ways. One might be called the anthropological approach in which we treat them as museum pieces to be observed and written about. To treat them as specimens of anthropological examination and analysis...is to insult them...The other approach is one of ignoring the fact that they are something different requiring special treatment and of attempting forcibly to absorb them into the normal pattern of social life. The way of forcible assimilation or assimilation through the operation of normal factors would be equally wrong.[5]

Rejecting both the isolationist and assimmilationist approaches towards tribal development, Nehru favoured an approach whereby the tribal people would 'progress in their own way', with no imposition or compulsions from outside, with measures for progress being 'worked out by the tribals themselves.'[6] Such a policy which approached tribal life and culture with respect and affection would bring to them the advantages of modern life, but in such a way that they would not destroy the traditional way of life, but instead would help to enhance and develop all that was good in it.

Nehru's notions of tribal development came to be reflected in the Indian Constitution. Embodying the Fabian concept of the State as 'redeemer/provider', the Directive Principles of State Policy provided for active state support for economic and social groups which suffered from exploitation and discrimination.[7] According to Article 46 of the

Constitution, the State had to promote the educational and economic interests of the tribal people and protect them from social injustice and exploitation, while Articles 330, 332, 334 dealt with the issue of reservation of seats in the legislatures[8], and Article 335 provided that the claims of the members of the Scheduled Castes and Tribes had to be taken into consideration for appointment in the administration services. In order to facilitate tribal welfare, Tribal Advisory Councils were set up in the states containing tribal areas and, according to the provisions of Article 338 a Special Officer (later named the Commissioner for Scheduled Castes and Scheduled Tribes) was to be appointed by the President to ensure that the safeguards for them were being followed. The Constitution also undertook to specify the categories of people who were to be defined as 'Scheduled Caste or Scheduled Tribe' (Articles 341, 342). Specifying the rights and privileges of the tribal communities, the Fifth and Sixth Schedules of the Constitution provided a degree of protection for tribals in the 'partially excluded areas' of middle India and autonomy to the 'excluded areas' of the northeast respectively. Thus, the Constitution provided a framework with a three-pronged strategy to improve the situation of scheduled castes and scheduled tribes, consisting of protective arrangements (i.e., measures to enforce equality, to provide punitive measures for transgressions, to eliminate established practices that perpetuate inequities, etc.), affirmative action (which provides positive preferential treatment in allotment of jobs and access to higher education as a means to accelerate the integration of the scheduled castes and scheduled tribes with mainstream society) and development. It was hoped that such a strategy would help to bridge the wide gap in social and economic condition between the scheduled castes/ scheduled tribes and other communities.

The Congress Programme during the Nehruvian Era

After Independence, the Congress government, therefore, replaced the old policy of status quo and adopted the policy of development and tribal integration, while preserving the tribal people's distinct social and cultural heritage. To Nehru, as the first Prime Minister of the newly-independent country, the task of integration and consolidation had the first priority. Together with political and economic integration, Nehru also laid emphasis on psychological integration: the tribal people had to feel that they were, above all, Indians. In a speech delivered at the opening session of the Scheduled Tribes and Scheduled Areas Conference held in New Delhi in 1952, he stated:

After the achievement of independence, the basic problem of India, taken as a whole, is one of integration and consolidation. Political integration is now complete, but that is not enough. We must bring about changes much more basic and intimate than mere political integration...The greatest problem of India today is not so much political as psychological integration and consolidation. India must build up for herself a unity which will do away with provincialism, communalism, and various other 'isms' which disrupt and separate. As I said, we must approach the tribal people with affection and friendliness and come to them as a liberating force. We must let them feel that we have come to give and not to take something away from them. That is the kind of psychological integration that India needs."[9]

Towards the close of the 1950s Nehru enunciated the five fundamental principles of this policy, which came to be regarded as the Panchsheel of tribal development.

1. People should develop along the lines of their own genius and we should avoid imposing anything on them. We should try to encourage in every way their own traditional arts and culture.
2. Tribal rights in land and forests should be respected.
3. We should try to train and build up a team of their own people to do the work of administration and development. Some technical personnel from outside will, no doubt, be needed, especially in the beginning. But we should avoid introducing too many outsiders into tribal territory.
4. We should not over-administer these areas or overwhelm them with a multiplicity of schemes. We should rather work through, and not in rivalry to, to their own social and cultural institutions.
5. We should judge results, not by statistics or the amount of money spent, but by the quality of human character that is evolved.[10]

Thus, the new approach came to be informed by two apparently contradictory principles, that of protection of the tribal population as well as their integration in the national society. However, as B.K. Roy Burman points out, 'protection of the tribals in the real sense of the term did not mean maintaining status quo. What was aimed at was creating conditions in which tribal societies could grow naturally, free form both external impositions and internal inhibitions.'[11] Specific schemes were initiated for the tribals which included setting up of training-cum-production centres and the grant of subsidies for the development of cottage and village industries in tribal areas to provide employment, resettling the tribals who practised shifting cultivation, providing educational facilities—scholarships, free studentships and other educational aids and legislating against the exorbitant rates of interest charged by moneylenders.

Post-Nehru Developments

While subscribing to the Nehruvian idea that development was the main task of a government, Indira Gandhi showed more determination and pragmatism than her father in putting that idea into practice.[12] If Nehru, the builder of a new nation state had streaks of romanticism in his statesmanship,[13] Indira lived in times when the state itself was coming under different kinds of threat, and problems had to be solved efficiently and fast. Her awareness of ground realities helped her on many occasions to get an immediate grasp of the situation. Coming close to leftist positions, she made development and eradication of poverty the main points in her government agenda. These were not only ends to themselves, but would also serve to ensure social justice in a bid to neutralise the growth of Naxalite and other radical movements in different parts of the country which were deriving strength from the high inflation rate and the impact of rising prices on the poor.

In this context, even Indira Gandhi's tribal policy became part of her overall effort to formulate an integrated approach to economic and social issues. The poor and the marginalised were, in her opinion, only two sides to the same coin, and she believed the problems of scheduled castes and scheduled tribes would be best addressed in a common perspective with those of India's poor. This attitude became even more pronounced after the Congress split in 1969, when Mrs. Gandhi became the leader of one faction of the party and could implement her policies free from internal opposition. In some of her speeches after reelection, she reiterated her concern for the poor and the minorities:

> In India we have poverty and it is necessary that we implement our development programmes speedily to eradicate poverty and create conditions conducive to these changes.[14]
>
> We have to build a society in which each individual can enjoy full freedom—economic, social and political.[15]
>
> Forget about who belongs to which caste. We all belong to the larger Indian family and we all have equal opportunity. Naturally, until that day when there is real equality of opportunity, we must help those who are underprivileged so that they can compete on a more equal basis with the more privileged sector.[16]

In her speech at the first UN Conference on the Human Environment at Stockholm in June 1972, for instance, she stated that the humanity had to find a solution to the problem of unequal access to wealth and knowledge if the earth was to remain habitable. She pointed out:

> Are not poverty and need the greatest polluters? The environment cannot be improved in conditions of poverty. Nor can poverty be eradicated without the use of science and technology. For instance, unless we are in a position to provide for the daily necessities of tribal people and those who live in and around the jungles, we cannot keep them from combing the forests for their livelihood, from poaching and despoiling the vegetation. When they feel themselves deprived, how can we urge the preservation of animals?[17]

With the same fundamental pragmatism, Indira Gandhi considered the atrocities committed on scheduled castes and scheduled tribes in different parts of India as the main source of evils which these communities were suffering from. As a first step, she tried to tackle this problem through legislation and in April 1972 presented some amendments to the Untouchability (Offences) Act of 1955. The Parliament, however, did not respond as speedily as she had expected and took more than four years to pass the reforms, which were finally approved as the Protection of Civil Rights Act of 1976. Meanwhile, she came to realise that social justice could not be ensured only by an act of Parliament, it also, and foremost, required a general change in the attitude of the people. Thus, she observed, 'Atrocities on harijans, casteism, that is, something that cannot be removed by the government decision or action—it has to be a people's movement'. In her opinion, scheduled castes and scheduled tribes had to contribute on their own to equality and social equity by giving up their ghetto like attitude which was in itself a factor of marginalisation. In 1975 she stated, 'I personally will be happy if SCs and STs also start forgetting that they are SCs and STs...they are entitled to these opportunities (reservations) and we are doing our best but to give them. But if we try to perpetrate the caste system, then it is very difficult to ask other castes not to give way to their own feelings.'[18]

The Tribal Developmental Programme of the Congress

Developmental Schemes under the Five-Year Plans

For the Indian state the pressing need of the hour was the speedy implementation of developmental policies and the Congress came to adopt an industry based model of development for this purpose. There were three key issues that the Congress wished to address through the industrialisation programme, namely, the need for heavy industries, the needs of defence and the question of ownership and control of industry.[19] For the rural population, the strategy adopted was that of community based development. The First Five-Year Plan, which was started in 1951, initiated a comprehensive programme of community development, aiming at an all-round development of the rural areas. In the Second Plan Period (1956-1961), the model of community development blocks (CDBs) was adopted which was expected to create a new thrust for development in the rural areas and to bring about self-sustained growth. All aspects of community life were brought within the purview of this programme and the CDBs covered a wide spectrum of activities in agriculture, animal husbandry, education, health, communications, social services, rural industries, *panchayats* and so on. Since the detailed programmes were to be formulated in consultation with the people, block advisory committees and district advisory committees were constituted to ensure a dialogue between the administration and the people. The programme was also extended to the tribal areas as tribal uplift was considered to be a part of the process of rural development. Special Multi-Purpose Tribal Blocks (SMPTBs) were set up on the lines of the CDBs in tribal areas and by selecting specially undeveloped but compact areas for multisided development, the programme aimed at engendering rapid improvement in the socioeconomic standards of the tribal people and to make development more intensive.

The community development programmes encountered certain specific problems in the tribal areas. The task was rendered more difficult because of the hilly and forested terrain, poor communication and lack of institutional infrastructure. It was thus decided to supplement the community development programme by 43 (SMPT) development projects which started in 1954. Finally, a less intensive model of tribal development block (TDB) was evolved. The TDB was envisaged as an area of 150-200 square miles having a population of about 25,000. These were first introduced in regions with the highest tribal concentration. The Ministry of Home Affairs provided a sum of Rs. 6.45 crore under the Second Plan for the establishment of 43 such blocks, at the rate of Rs. 15 lakh each, in addition to Rs. 12 lakh each provided in the budget of the CDB.[20] Even though the blocks were unable to spend the amount of Rs. 27 lakh allotted to them, they had been sufficiently successful to justify their extension to the areas of tribal concentration which had not been covered by them earlier. By the Third Five-Year Plan (1961-1966) period there were 500 blocks covering 40 percent of the total tribal population in the country. However, it was seen that only those areas with concentrated tribal population (constituting more than two-third of the total population) derived the benefit of this programme up to the end of the Fourth Five-Year Plan (1969-1974) period. These developmental schemes were not extended to the dispersed tribal zones where the tribal people were scattered in little pockets in the remote hills and forest.

The tribal development programmes were reviewed from time to time by the Planning Commission through the Social Welfare Division to ensure a pragmatic and critical review of the programmes and their implementation. Commissions were appointed in accordance to the constitutional provisions for examining tribal problems and welfare and suggest remedial measures. The Verrier Elwin Committee, which had been appointed on 1 May 1959 to review the performance of the SMPTBs, noted the far-reaching changes introduced in tribal areas by the development process in its report of 30 March 1960, stating that:

> Great schemes for development are bringing and, by the end of the Third Plan, will have brought to every tribal village new ideas, new techniques and new contacts. Roads are everywhere pushing their way into places which have hitherto been virtually inaccessible. Education, as it spreads, is revolutionising the social and economic conditions of the tribal villages and is creating new demands as it generates new skills. In many of the hills and forests where the tribals live, there are vast resources of minerals, raw materials and hydraulic power...In other tribal areas great changes are taking place as a result of industrial development. The short-term and long-term consequences of the industrial invasion of the tribal areas, at any rate in the central belt, have, of course, an enormous significance. They raise the issues of rehabilitation, land possession, education, training and equipment...
>
> All these things will make demands for extensive psychological and physiological adjustments. They will affect the code of tribal life, and especially social discipline, the integrity of the family, the integrity of the village community (may even in some places cause the disappearance of the village community), the general culture and spiritual and aesthetic values. The new way of life may lead also to the spread of certain social vices which generally accompany urbanisation.[21]

Regarding the performance of the SMPTB scheme, the Verrier Elwin Committee noted that in many blocks the proportion of non-tribals to tribals was far too high and that they had received complaints that the developmental programme of the multipurpose block areas had primarily benefited the non-tribals. Conceding the fact that all economically distressed people in a block needed assistance, the Committee however asserted that the tribes needed to have their proper and special share. It also noted that the schematic budget had come to stand in the way of adaptation of the programme to tribal needs. In order to meet local requirements state governments had been authorised to transfer funds from one head to another within the same block, but they failed to do so with 'sufficient knowledge and imagination'. Consequently the schematic budgets tended to set a rigid pattern, resulting in lopsided expenditure. The Committee thus called upon the state governments to take up the matter for developing their tribal areas more seriously, with advance planning and organisation. The Committee also observed that in almost all the blocks the majority of the benefits of the development schemes were being received by the most progressive and prosperous among the tribal people. It therefore recommended that block officials target the poorest people living in the more remote areas.

As the tribal situation in the country was becoming a rising social and political concern, in 1959 the Central government decided to implement Article 340 of the Constitution by appointing a new commission, called Scheduled Areas and Scheduled Tribes Commission. In 1961 its Chairman, U.N. Dhebar issued a report which highlighted the unsatisfactory results of State policies till then, and recommended the adoption of a new legislation aimed at protecting the lives and interests of all tribal communities in India through an integrationist and developmental approach. With respect to integration, the report stated that:

> Apart from [this] basic approach, there is the problem of integration, and development activity is its psychological aspect ...There are other aspects of the problem. They can be summed up as "protective aspects" and "development aspects". The protective aspect relates to the protection of the rights of tribals in the forests and the right to be safeguarded from usurious and exploitative elements. The development aspect relates to positive welfare schemes.[22]

The social and the economic aspects of the tribal problem, the report claimed, went hand in hand with the overall advancement of the country. If the State wanted to create 'a social order based upon the equality of status and opportunity and a fraternity', the diverse stages of development to which the tribals belonged had to be replaced by a full integration with the mainstream Indian society and economy.[23] In order to achieve this aim, the Dhebar Commission favoured intensive development of tribal areas extending beyond the areas specified in the Fifth Schedule, where the tribals enjoyed the benefit of legislative protection in relation to their land etc. The proposed 'area of development', which was defined in terms of the area of tribal concentration where tribals accounted for 66 percent of the population, therefore became larger than the 'scheduled area'. True to the Nehruvian tenets of industrialisation and national integration, the Dhebar Commission made an effort to locate the factors which hindered industrial development among tribals, without questioning whether that development model was actually suitable to them. At the same time, it also recommended a vast range of protective measures related to the tribals' right to land, forest, rehabilitation etc., in an attempt to implement constitutional safeguards. However, despite such constitutional safeguards, the progress and welfare of tribals remained slow and, except in the northeast, tribals continued to be poor, indebted and landless, largely due to the poor execution of well-intentioned schemes.[24]

In 1966, the Planning Commission set up a Study Team on the Tribal Development Programme under the Chairmanship of P. Shilu Ao, the former Chief Minister of Nagaland, with the object of appraising the tribal developmental programmes during the Third Five-Year Plan and making recommendations regarding schemes to be carried out during the Fourth Five-Year Plan. It submitted its report to the Prime Minister Indira Gandhi on 19 September 1969. Besides the all-India Report, the Committee also prepared 20 reports on the tribal situation in the different states and union territories. According to the Shilu Ao Committee, one of the chief problems of tribal development related to the categories as to who were to be identified as 'scheduled tribe'. This problem had arisen largely because the Indian Constitution had failed to define the concept of a 'tribal'. In the absence of a precise working definition or clearly-defined principles governing the classification of 'tribe', or for that matter, 'scheduled tribe', the term came to signify different connotations to different people. The Shilu Ao Committee recommended descheduling the more advanced tribal communities on the one hand, and, on the other, excluding communities which should not have been included in the list of scheduled tribes in the first place.[25] It identified the imposition of a uniform pattern of development, irrespective of the stage of development of the community and ignoring the special conditions of the region concerned as being the chief reasons for the non-implementation of developmental schemes in tribal areas. The Committee noted that although there had been an increase in the overall expenditure on the welfare of scheduled tribes from the First to the Third Plan, the per capita expenditure during the Third plan was far less than that of the previous plan. This was because the tribal population had risen to about 30 million according to the 1961 census as against the population of 22.5 million recorded in the 1951 census.[26] Similarly it was shown that the ratio of expenditure on tribal welfare to the total plan expenditure declined progressively over the three plan periods: from more than 1 percent in the first plan, it declined to 0.94 percent in the second plan, to 0.62 percent in the third.[27] While agreeing with the general conclusion and approach of the Dhebar Commission, the Shilu Ao Committee concluded that the blocks were inadequate for dealing with the complex problems of tribal development. These were too small to function effectively as a basic unit for planning. The main problems of tribal communities, according to the Committee, were related to indebtedness, debt bondage, land alienation, educational backwardness and poor communications, which were not provided within the framework of the TDB.

The idea itself of tribal development, however, continued to form the backbone of Congress tribal policy, though the latter took a distinctly different path in the following years. On the eve of the 1971 parliamentary election, Mrs. Gandhi had coined the slogan 'Garibi Hatao' (remove poverty). After the elections the Congress embarked on a project to promote 'with special care the educational, employment and economic interests of the weaker sections of the people, particularly the scheduled castes, scheduled tribes and backward classes' and the recommendations of the Shilu Ao Commission were put into practice. When a Task Force on 'Development of Tribal Areas' was formed in 1972 in order to formulate proposals for the Fifth Five-Year Plan (1974-1979), its suggestions were based on the assumption that all over India the main problems of tribal communities were the economic backwardness of the areas they inhabited, and the limited social integration with Indian society. To these, regional problems added to their unfortunate lot: remoteness and climatic hardship in the north; economic disruption due to the formation of East Pakistan in the northeast; demographic pressure, indebtedness and low productivity in the western, central and eastern zones; unproductive agricultural techniques in the south. The solution to all these problems, according to the Task Force, had to take into account the specific situation of each tribal group, which had to be clearly identified on the basis of social, ecological and occupational parameters. For the first time, it was suggested that the main thrust of development policies had to be on agriculture and forestry, rather than industry. As to the protection of tribals, the Task Force's recommendations were related not to the lofty principles of constitutional safeguards, but to very concrete issues, such as land alienation, indebtedness, credit and marketing and excise policy.

This innovative approach was implicitly reaffirmed by the Expert Committee on Tribal Development headed by S.C. Dube, which was constituted by the Central Department of Social Welfare in late 1972. While defining the new strategy for tribal development to be included in the Fifth plan, the committee recommended that development programmes should focus on minimising exploitation and helping tribal communities to build up their own strength by giving due attention to their specific situations and difficulties. If necessary, special programmes had to be devised to deal with remote or particularly backward tribal areas. The Dube Committee also indicated the different roles that the Central government and the states would play in the formulation and implementation of area-integrated projects.

As a result of these recommendations, the Fifth plan adopted the Integrated Tribal Development Programme (ITDP), which was to be implemented at the block and district level in areas with a sizeable tribal population. Where tribal society was of a primitive character, a Modified Area Development Approach (MADA) was envisaged and states and union territories were entrusted with the formulation of Tribal Sub-Plans. This, however, did not apply to states and union territories, where scheduled tribes formed the majority of the population. The aim of this complex structure was to come in close touch with tribals in their specific situation, especially those communities which had not been reached by government initiatives so far on account of their living in scattered pockets or remote areas. With this ear-to-the-ground approach, the Fifth plan marked a fundamental departure from the past, and influenced the following plans as well. It was recognised that the previous schematic, undifferentiated policy had proved ineffective because it had not duly taken into account the variety of tribal situations in India and the need to devise specific measures in order to help them solve their problems. In a way, the Nehruvian framework, where the social components had to be absorbed into the unitary reality of the state, was replaced by a situation where the state adopted an integrated, differentiated approach to assist communities and devise development plans on the basis of their actual social, cultural and economic situation. Another important innovative aspect of the Fifth plan, and especially of the Sixth Five-Year Plan (1980-1985) was the attention they gave to poverty alleviation and economic assistance to particularly backward communities. The Sixth plan, for instance, set the target of enabling at least 50 percent of tribal families below the poverty line to rise above that line. This was to be effected through area-specific projects aimed at providing infrastructure, spreading education and removing exploitation. Therefore, the major objectives in tribal development policy under the Sixth plan were as follows:

1. Taking up family-oriented beneficiary programmes through raising the productivity level of the beneficiary families in the fields of agriculture, horticulture, animal husbandry, small industries, etc.
2. Elimination of exploitation of tribals in the spheres of alienation of land, moneylending, debt-bondage, access to forest resources, etc.
3. Human resource development through education and training programmes; and
4. Infrastructure development.

The limited resources made available for the actual implementation of this set of targets eventually resulted in only a small number of families being able to rise above the poverty line.[28] By the late 1970s, however, the principle had gained ground once for all that tribal development policies could only be effective if they showed a perception that: (a) the intensive exploitation of the natural resources in tribal regions had had a deleterious effect on the local tribal communities; (b) loss of land, indebtedness and the transformation from peasants into landless labour had increased the incidence of tribal poverty, particularly in zones of intensive industrial activity; and (c) the diverse situations of tribal communities called for a differentiated approach to development and to area-specific, community based programmes. In this way, the State moved away from the schematic pattern of the earlier plans to the formulation of an integrated approach to the tribal problem.

Taking stock of tribal diversity also produced a modification in the size and composition of what was considered as 'tribal society'. More backward communities were identified as tribes and areas of tribal concentration were enlarged. For instance, the 'area of development' under the Tribal Sub-Plan of the Fifth plan was enlarged to include blocks of more than 50 percent tribal concentration, thus bringing under its coverage an area of 4,33,952 square miles, accounting not only for 60 percent of the tribal population within the Sub-Plan area, but also 63 percent of the total tribal population in the country.[29]

As K.S. Singh points out, this was also the result of the Scheduled Castes and Scheduled Tribes Orders (Amendment) Act of 1976, which added many communities, identified in terms of 'primitive traits', distinctive culture, geographical isolation and 'backwardness', to the old list of the scheduled tribes. As a result of the scheduling of new communities, new tribal pockets were identified, the overall tribal population went up by about three million, and Uttar Pradesh was brought, for the first time, on the tribal map of India.[30] The Fifth plan further introduced, as suggested by the Dube Committee, 'areas of tribal dispersal' where the tribal population lived in small pockets and accounted for 30-40 percent of the tribal population, and 'zones of primitive communities', about 50 in number, where tribals lived in relatively isolated habitats. These communities were identified as 'tribal' in terms of their practice of a pre-agricultural technology, their subsistence on the forest, low level of literacy, numerical smallness, and a population of slow or little growth rate.

Table 2

Enumerated and Revised Population of Tribals, 1971

(in thousands)

State Population	*Enumerated Population*	*Revised*	*Difference*
Andhra Pradesh	16.58	22.26	5.68
Gujarat	37.34	37.57	0.23
Karnataka	2.31	2.62	0.31
Kerala	2.69	1.93	(-)0.76
Madhya Pradesh	83.87	98.15	14.28
Maharashtra	29.54	38.41	8.87
Orissa	50.72	50.75	0.03
Rajasthan	31.26	31.35	0.06
Tamil Nadu	3.21	4.50	1.38
West Bengal	25.33	26.03	0.70

Source: Commissioner for Scheduled Castes and Scheduled Tribes (1977). *Report 1975-76 and 1976-77 (Part I)*, New Delhi: Ministry of Home Affairs, Government of India. p. 16.

Despite the emphasis on tribal welfare and development, the budget allocated for the purpose had not been substantial during the first four plans as the table below shows.

Together with the change in the fundamental assumptions behind government policies in the 1970s, there was also an attempt at increasing the resources earmarked for the implementation of development programmes and plans. While funds allocated to tribal development by successive government since independence had not been commensurate with the proportion of the tribal population, the Fifth and Sixth plan marked an increase up to, respectively, 3.01 and

4.37 percent of the total plan expenditure. In fact, the Sixth plan registered a spectacular investment in tribal development of the order of Rs. 5,535 crore, i.e., 5 percent of the planned outlay. About 40 lakh tribal families were thus assisted under poverty alleviation programmes.[31] However, the problem remained of the non-utilisation of funds allocated to scheduled areas. The Seventh Five-Year Plan (1985-1990) was still formulated on the basis of diversification of tribal development, but subsequently the focus shifted to collateral programmes of rural development—for instance, generation of purchasing power, development of infrastructure, etc.—which benefited, among others, a high percentage of tribal population. Tribal development, thus, lost much of its distinct status and largely became part of more encompassing rural development projects. This has reproduced the initial shortage of funds allocated for the assistance to tribal families.[32]

Table 3

Review of the Supplemental Outlays for Tribal Development

(Rs. in crore)

Plan Period	*Total Plan Size*	*Tribal Development*	*Percentage*
First plan (1951-1956)	1,960	19	0.89
Second plan (1956-61)	4,672	41	0.87
Third plan (1961-66)	8,577	51	0.60
(1966-69)	6,756	35	0.52
Fourth plan (1969-1974)	16,160	84	0.52
Fifth plan (1974-1979)	39,322	1,182	3.01

Source: P.K. Bose (1990). "Congress and the Tribal Communities in India", in Ramashray Roy and Richard Sisson (eds.), *Diversity and Dominance in Indian Politics*, Vol. 2: *Division, Deprivation and the Congress*. New Delhi: Sage. p. 65.

If we analyse the schemes for tribal development implemented under the various five year plans, we find that certain basic issues like providing food security and nutrition, improving health services and checking mortality, and education were given priority in all the plan periods. Apart from these, a wide range of schemes were floated, ranging from infrastructure building to tribal empowerment, from collective welfare to family and beneficiary-oriented development schemes, from solitary area development to integrated area development. All in all, it appears that the five year plans have achieved a certain degree of success in their tribal development programmes, etc. A significant increase in agricultural production and in the marketing of produce in tribal areas resulted, for instance, from the creation of separate TDBs in the Second plan and of a Tribal Sub-Plan within the state plans in the Fifth plan, as well as from the formation of Large Agricultural Multi-Purpose Societies (LAMPS), Tribal Development Corporations, the Tribal Cooperative Marketing Development Federation of India (TRIFED) and other similar institutions. In the fight against malnutrition and in the creation of employment among tribals a distinct role was played by crash special nutrition programmes and crash employment programmes in the Fourth plan.

The ultimate target, however, of removing the disparity in social and economic conditions between tribal and non-tribal populations, has remained largely elusive.[33] The gap in the standard of living between those living in tribal and non-tribal areas did not decrease and, in fact, studies have shown that it began to increase after 1974.[34] To mention but a few examples, in 1999-2000 the number of landless people among scheduled tribes was 7 percent, second only to scheduled castes (10 percent). Increasingly, tribal people lost control over their land and the size of their cultivated holdings got steadily smaller. Large landholdings (more than four hectares) are owned mostly by non-tribals, while scheduled tribes only account for 3 percent. Legislative attempts to reverse these trends proved to be ineffective.[35] The problem of land alienation remained endemic in tribal areas. The different commissions cited various reasons to explain the phenomenon, namely, manipulation of records, *benami* transfers, developmental projects like the construction of dams, power plants etc., and loss of land through mortgage and encroachment. The National Commission on Backward areas noted that in many region tribals were never legally recognised as owners of the lands which they cultivated; they were simply considered to be occupiers till the enforcement of superior claims.[36] The illegal occupation of large areas of tribal land by non-tribals could not be prevented even in states which introduced a ban on the transfer of immoveable property in scheduled areas to non-tribals. The process of industrialisation in tribal areas also led to the pauperisation of the tribals, many of whom became landless workers after industries acquired land from them with minimal compensation. Furthermore, the construction of dams also adversely affected the tribals. Government figures suggested that for the 18 dams being constructed in 1980, 67 percent of the people who would be displaced were tribals.[37]

Interestingly, while tribes have less chronically unemployed persons than the non-tribals, in both rural and urban areas their monthly per capita expenditure (MPCE) is lower than that of the scheduled caste populations (Rs. 387.69 in rural India and Rs 690.52 in urban areas). As far as education is concerned, school attendance rate (5-14 years) among the tribal people is quite low in comparison to others.[38] It also appears that State policies have not uniformly affected all tribal regions, but have favoured development in certain areas more than in others. The tribals of Nagaland, Meghalaya and Mizoram have shown better results than other tribal areas on all available indicators of socioeconomic development. MPCE is higher among the tribes of Nagaland, Mizoram and Lakshadweep, followed by Andaman and Nicobar Islands, Arunachal Pradesh, Daman and Diu, Tripura, Sikkim, Meghalaya, Kerala, Tamil Nadu and Himachal Pradesh, but it is lower among the tribes of Orissa, Madhya Pradesh, Bihar, Jharkhand, West Bengal and Andhra Pradesh. The percentage of literacy among the tribal population, according to the 1981 census, was 60 in Mizoram, 40 in Nagaland, and 31 in Meghalaya which compare very favourably with corresponding tribal literacy figures for Rajasthan (10 percent), Madhya Pradesh (nearly 11), Orissa (14 percent) and Bihar (17 percent). Taking the percentage of the tribal population in a state living in urban areas as an indicator of tribal development, census data shows that Mizoram (with 24 percent), Meghalaya (with 12 percent) and Nagaland (with 10 percent) is better situated than Rajasthan and Madhya Pradesh (with 4 percent), Orissa (with 5 percent) and Bihar (with 6 percent).[39] A recent study has also shown that in comparison to the tribals of central India, the northeastern tribal states of Nagaland and Meghalaya could attract more funds on a per capita basis through effective political leverage over the financial disbursement mechanism of the Central government.[40] Thus it would appear that the tribes of the northeast, followed by the island territories surpass the tribes in other parts of India in many aspects of development. Among the eight states of the northeast, Nagaland holds the top position in more than one developmental indicator.

The Impact of Forest Policies

A major section of tribal communities today are still dependent on forests for their livelihood. Although the larger and more progressive tribes are mainly cultivators, many of the smaller groups have an essentially forest based economy and almost all tribes have a dual economy of agriculture and forestry. Their relationship with the forest is not only economic in nature. Forests had, for long, been central to their specific way of life, the core of their material, spiritual and mental world. Through its forest acts, colonial government had sought to regulate rights and restrict privileges previously enjoyed by the inhabitants in the neighbourhood. At the time of independence, it was hoped that the new nation would redress the injustices that tribals had suffered in colonial times. Nehru's principles of tribal development had recognised the significance that forests held for the tribal communities and had stated that tribal rights in land and forest had to be respected. Although such concerns came to be reflected in important policy documents, including the Indian Constitution, there remained to be a wide gulf between policy and implementation.

The claim of the State to exclusive control over forest protection and production came to be reinforced in the revised National Forest Policy of 1952 that chose to prioritise the need to meet the 'paramount needs' of the country. After independence forests came to be seen as national assets. Regulating forest rights was therefore considered essential for developing agriculture, industry and communications. This orientation of the forest policy is reflected in the following passage:

> Village communities in the neighbourhood of forests will naturally make greater use of its products for the satisfaction of the domestic and agricultural needs. Such use, however, should in no event be permitted at a cost of national interests. The accident of a village being close to a forest does not prejudice the right of the country as a whole to receive the benefit of a national asset. The scientific conservation of a forest inevitably involved the regulation of rights and restriction of privileges of users depending upon the value and importance of the forest, however irksome such restraint may be to neighbouring areas...Therefore, while the needs of the local population must be met to a reasonable extent, national interest should not be sacrificed because they are not directly discernable.

By identifying shifting cultivation as one of the main threats to state forestry, the forest policy of 1952 laid stress on the importance of persuading tribal people to give up this 'baneful' practice. It sought to increase the efficiency of forest administration through adequate forest laws, controlling grazing, providing facilities for forest management and for conducting research in forestry and forest products utilisation. Although the tribal communities were granted certain concessions like collection of minor forest products, grazing of cattle, etc., the policy of 1952 effectively curtailed the rights of the tribals on forests in the wake of national interest. It set out to evolve a system of balanced and complementary land use under which each type of land would be utilised in such a manner so that it combine maximisation of production with the minimum deterioration. Among its other goals were the need to check denudation, establish tree-lands, provide *nistar* rights (i.e., the rights of the forest dwellers over some minor forest products), and organise defence and industrial uses of the forests.

In the years that followed, the Congress government appointed several committees to study the situation and make proposals as several developments called for a review of the forest policy. As a result of the increase in population and the concomitant increase in the pressure on land, there was a substantial loss of the forest cover on the one hand and a rise in the demand for forest products on the other. Moreover, there was a growing consensus of opinion that emphasised on the necessity of involving tribals as active partners in forest operations such as afforestation, harvesting, collection and processing of minor forest products, in order to counter the alienation between forest managers and forest dwellers. For instance, the Verrier Elwin Committee of 1960, recommended issuing *pattas* in the predominantly forest areas to all tribals who did not have them. Where land was insufficient, the less valuable parts of the protected forests should be given exclusively to the landless tribals. It also called for modifying hunting rules in order to promote greater freedom for the tribals. While permitting ceremonial hunts, it recommended the organisation of vigorous propaganda to educate the tribal people about the value of preserving game and of hunting only during the open season. In fact, it further stated that the forest should not be managed primarily for profit or for conservation, but with a view to furthering tribal interests. Arguing that forest protection could only be effective when there was 'a mutual sense of trust and even affection between the forest staff and the tribal people'[41], the Committee suggested that the tribal people must have a direct share in the profits of the forest through tribal cooperative societies. Unless this was done they would not identify their interests with those of the forest management. The Dhebar Committee in 1961 had similarly recommended a reconsideration of the policy of 1952. It proposed that subject to safeguards, tribals should be allowed forestlands for cultivation, their needs should be met from the outlying areas in the reserve forests, and their requirements for grazing and shifting cultivation should be conceded. In tune with the recommendations of the Verrier Elwin committee, the Dhebar Committee was also of the view that the forest department should consider themselves responsible for both the betterment of the tribals and the development of the forest. The forest department, together with the agriculture, industries and development departments of each region should prepare a time schedule with the intention of providing work to the tribals all the year around.

In practice, however, such recommendations remained a dead letter. Within the parameters of the State forest policy and forestry operations, the tribal economy has figured little, by and large, being regarded as revenue earners for the State and the private sector. The National Commission on Agriculture (NCA), 1976, put almost the entire blame for deforestation on the forest dwellers, thereby minimising the role of industry in the loss of India's tree cover.[42] It recommended further restriction of the rights and privileges given to the people, particularly the regulation of the *nistar* rights, as a pre-condition to improving the forest cover. Betraying an inadequate understanding of the socioeconomic and psychological situation of the tribals and other forest dwellers, it attributed unemployment and under-employment in the rural areas to be the main cause of encroachment and suggested the creation of more employment opportunities in forest operations.[43] Based on the recommendations of the NCA, the Draft Forest Bill was prepared by the Congress government in 1980. Significantly, the Draft Bill sought a stringent redefinition of forest offences and proposed to vest forest officers with full powers to directly deal with the new offences. However, the Congress government decided to shelve the bill as it was strongly criticised by social activists, environmentalists and others.

A new approach that served the interests of both the forest and the forest dwellers, was suggested in 1982 in the 'Report of the Committee on Forests and Tribals in India', prepared under the chairmanship of B.K. Roy Burman. It stated that for any forest policy to be successful it was necessary to accept that, 'the development of forests and well-being of tribals are interdependent...or sound management of the eco-system the relationship should not only be properly understood but should also be made the bed-rock of the operational policy.[44] Arguing that vast potential for serving national, regional as well as local developmental goals to do so, the '"intimate complementarity of forest development and tribal development" had to be recognised in policy and in action.'[45] Instead of policing the forest, the responsibility for their preservation should be cast on the people. By making the involvement of the people an indispensable feature in its formulation and implementation, the B.K. Roy Burman Committee called for a conscious shift in the orientation and approach of the forest policy. During the period discussed in this chapter, yet another committee, the Committee for the Review of Rights and Concessions in the Forest areas in India (the Chaudhury Committee), had been appointed by the Congress government. In contrast to the Roy Burman Report, the Chaudhury Report of 1984 once again held forest dwellers responsible for the destruction of the forests, making only cursory references to industries which swallowed large chunks of the forest. Some concessions were, however, provided to the forest dwellers.

The continuing denial of their rights brought the tribal in conflict with the forest department. As early as 1957 the Kharwars of Madhya Pradesh rebelled against forest regulations by refusing to pay rent to revenue collecting agents, utilising the timber and forest produce without making any payments, and flouting the forest laws which violated the tribals' customary rights. The movement dissipated only after the arrest of its leaders. Forest grievances arising out of restrictions on shifting cultivation, the oppression of forest officials and the state's reluctance to allow forest labourer cooperatives, also played a part in the tribal revolt organised by Maoist revolutionaries in Srikakulam district of Andhra Pradesh.[46] In central India, the state's attempts to convert the mixed forests into monocultural plantations met with stiff resistance. For instance, in August 1979 the Hos, Mundas and Santhals of Chota Nagpur Plateau opposed the Bihar Forest Corporation's policy of replacing *sal* and *mahua* forests with teak. The tribals cut down the newly planted teak saplings, demanding their replacement with species which were more useful to the local economy.[47]

With the growth of commercial forestry, many forest-dependent communities, both hunter-gatherers and shifting cultivators, have been forced to accept the new system of forest management and have been transformed to the status of wage labourers in the forest. Large scale deforestation largely due to various developmental projects and extension of cultivation by reclamation of land and forests affected the tribals the most. A persistent grievance of the tribal forest dwellers is the operation of the contractor system in the forest. Although the forests are state property, the state itself has a limited direct role in the actual extraction of timber and other forest produce. Selected trees are auctioned to the highest bidder under contract with the state. The responsibility for organising labour, conducting felling operations and transporting the log lie with the contractors. A similar system prevails in the case of minor forest products. The contractor system has led to corruption and waste, a fact that has been noted in successive policy documents which have stressed the need to replace contractors by forest labour cooperatives. During the period under review, the government did not take the initiative to replace the contractor system, which has led to militant movements of forest labourers. Consequently the distribution of the benefits bypassed the tribals who received only a fraction of the profits that commercial forestry engenders. However, as the Commissioner of Scheduled Tribes discovered, the tribals did not benefit either in regions where government cooperatives replaced the auction system in forest management.[48] Another problem related to the encroachment of non-tribals within the forests. Crispin Bates has shown that between 1951 and 1971 nearly a million non-tribals from Bihar migrated into the tribal areas in Chota Nagpur, either as cultivators taking over tribal lands or as wage labourers in the iron and coal mines in the region. Some of the resettlement schemes following the Partition, such as the *Dandakaranya* project in Bastar, also adversely affected the tribal cultivators. Thus, in sum, despite well-intentioned schemes, the process of marginalisation of a large section of the tribal people in their own habitat could not be stemmed.[49]

Tribal Insurgencies and Movements

Thus, it can be seen that much of the protective legislation for the tribals came to be ignored in practice and that the process of marginalisation of the tribals continued in spite of the developmental schemes and protective measures, thanks to the extensive exploitation of the rich natural resources of their habitat, the decline in their traditional activities, the lack of any viable alternative, continuing land alienation and exploitation of cheap labour. With the general rise in population, the pressure on land increased and non-tribal peasants moved into tribal regions in search of a livelihood. As industries developed, based on the exploitation of forest and mineral resources, there was an increase in the migration of labourers and other job seekers. The outmigration of the tribals, on the other hand, was much less and alienation of tribal lands occurred on a large scale.[50] The inequitable economic and political situation of the tribals have been attributed by some scholars to the progressive erosion of their territorial base through mass immigration of non-tribals from surrounding areas and also to the administrative fragmentation of its constituent parts into several large states which were dominated by non-tribals.[51]

Not surprising, the period under review witnessed several tribal movements as they sought to grapple with the fast-paced changes affecting their world. Most of these movements remained in an incipient stage during the Nehru era and only became prominent in the late 1960s, 1970s and 1980s. They were not only motivated by backwardness and deprivation, though. In fact, protest often emerged among more politically and economically advanced tribal communities which sought to assert their identity and fought for secession or the official recognition as a separate state. Unevenness in rates of social change among different social groups and imbalances in their relative access to jobs, educational advantages and political power explain why some groups could mobilise and not others. Studies conducted by the

Anthropological Survey of India (ASI) suggest that tribal unrest assumed an organised character only among the larger, homogeneous landholding tribal communities, who had a relatively strong economic base. Tribal communities with a higher degree of literacy and a higher rate of participation in the democratic processes could react more strongly to issues concerning land and forest. The new urban middle class agitated both about reservation of jobs and also against the exploitation of tribal labour in agriculture, mining and industries.[52] Such are the cases of the unrest in Meghalaya, Mizoram and Nagaland insurgencies and the Jharkhand movement for political autonomy.

Some of these movements were directly connected with the process of linguistic reorganisation of states in India. This was a prolonged and divisive affair, raising fundamental questions of Centre-state relations. Although several new states had been carved out in response to tribal demands in the northeastern part of the country, such reorganisations have not always satisfied the people. In course of the linguistic reorganisation of the states, Paul Brass argues, the Central government developed certain formal and informal rules, the first and most significant being that the Central government would not recognise groups which made secessionist demands, but would suppress them by all means necessary, including armed force.[53]

The hill tracts of Assam are home to over a hundred tribal groups, which for a long time had had only a very restricted contact with the rest of the country. As Nehru had once pointed out, '... they never experienced a sense of being in a country called India and they were hardly influenced by the struggle for freedom or other movements in India. Their chief experience of outsiders was that of British officers and Christian missionaries who generally tried to make them anti Indian.'[54] This moved Nehru to single out the northeast within the constitutional framework of the newly independent state. The Sixth Schedule of the Constitution, thus, which offered a degree of self-government to tribal peoples by providing for autonomous districts and creating district and regional councils, was made applicable only to Assam. Fearing that such provisions might ignite separatist movements in that area or elsewhere, Nehru made it amply clear that they did not in any way entail secession from India or independence in any region.

In addition to the special status conferred on Assam in the Constitution, in 1948 a union territory was created in the border areas of Assam, called North-East Frontier Agency (NEFA). The British had maintained a close control over the northeastern frontier tracts, treating them as 'excluded' areas and sending out expeditionary missions whenever occasion demanded. When the British left, the network of communications built by them consisted only of 168 km of mostly fair-weather roads along the foothills. After independence when the Government of India decided to carry the administration into the interior of the hills in 1950, the conditions were favourable for the application of Nehru's ideas as enunciated in his five principles. In view of the strategic importance of the area, the NEFA was administered by specially trained officers who were entrusted with the task of implementing carefully designed, low-impact developmental policies, so that the local communities could maintain their age-long customs and traditions and live in peace. Tribal institutions of village councils like the *kebang* of the Adis (Abors) and *buliang* of the Apatanis were reactivated. Tribal interpreters were employed to serve as intermediaries between the administration and the local people and a simple form of administration called 'Single Line Administration' was introduced.[55] The pace of transformation in NEFA was rapid and by the end of the Third plan the entire territory was covered by CDBs. The Chinese incursions of 1962 quickened the pace of administration. The NEFA Panchayat Regulation was introduced in 1967 at the instance of the Ering Commission (1965).[56] Development since then has been even more spectacular and in 1972 NEFA was replaced by a union territory under a Chief Commissioner. The Agency Council was converted into a Provincial Legislature in 1975 and the first General Elections, on the basis of adult franchise, to the state legislature held in 1978. The Chief Commissioner was made the Lieutenant Governor of Arunachal Pradesh, the new name for the union territory and the first elected government came to power in 1978.[57]

Contrary to Nehru's fears, however, the trouble arose not among the poor and illiterate tribes of the NEFA, but in other areas of the northeast which had been included in the state of Assam. These areas were inhabited by non-Assamese tribes who felt threatened by the cultural and political predominance of the Assamese and Bengali communities, which had resulted in their growing marginalisation in the political and economic life of the state. More than economic grievances, however, it was the identity question which gave rise to their demand for a separate state, i.e., a state where they could escape what they considered as a policy of Assamisation. When Assamese became the only official language of the state through the Assam Official Language Act of 1960, various political parties in the hill areas decided to join hands and formed the All Assam Parties Hill Leaders Conference (APHLC) which renewed the demand for a separate state. After almost a decade of debates and negotiations, the Assam Reorganisation (Meghalaya) Act was passed in 1969, and came into effect on 2 April 1970. In its somewhat unique provisions, it created Meghalaya as a state within the state of Assam, endowing it with full administrative autonomy except for the maintainance of law and order, and a legislature of its own, as per the Sixth Schedule of the Constitution. Only a few months later, in 1971 the Parliament passed the North-Eastern Areas (Reorganisation) Act, which came into effect on 21 January 1972. It granted full statehood on the autonomous state of Meghalaya, as well as on the former union territories of Manipur and Tripura.

In another autonomous district of Assam, Mizo, the separatist demand of local tribes acquired a more militant character. The movement originated in the 'rat famine' of 1959, which moved tribals to form a Mizo National Famine Front (MNFF) to call for economic assistance from the government. This organisation was rechristened as Mizo National Front (MNF) in 1961 after the passing of the Assam Official Language Act, which made the identity issue the main focus of the movement. In March 1966, shortly after Indira Gandhi's rise to the office of Prime Minister, the MNF leader Pu Laldenga launched an uprising with arms obtained from the military regime in East Pakistan and declared independence from India. Soon the revolt was crushed by the Indian army, but despite the apparent resumption of government control, guerrilla activity continued for a few years. Only in 1973 there was a rapprochement between Delhi and some of the less radical Mizo leaders, who agreed to the concession of union territory status for Mizoram instead of full independence. This did not put an end to the Mizo insurgency, though, which resumed in the late 1970s and required again a military intervention from the Centre. Following this, the Congress-led government offered terms of amnesty to the rebels and began negotiations for peace, which culminated in the formation of Mizoram as a separate state in 1986-87.

Even more violent in character was the Naga insurgency, which had occurred ever since Independence. The Naga tribes firmly opposed the central policy of integrating them within the state of Assam, and in 1955 a section of the Naga leadership under A.Z. Phizo launched an amred insurrection and declared the formation of an independent government. The Indian army was deployed to suppress the uprising, after which the Central government opened up negotiations with the more moderate leaders headed by Dr. Imkongliba Ao. As a result, in 1963 the new state of Nagaland was formed within the Indian Union. Insurgency, however, continued, particularly in the jungle areas and occasionally in urban centres, with attacks on the army and mainstream politicians.

Indira Gandhi's visit to Kohima on the occasion of the tenth anniversary of Nagaland's statehood in December 1973 had the effect of bringing about reconciliation with a section of underground insurgents, who accepted her offer to allow them to freely participate in the state elections of February 1974 in exchange for their giving up the revolt. After the elections brought to power a coalition government which included several former rebels, it was hoped that the allocation of funds by the Government of India for education, employment and economic development in Nagaland would put Naga resistance to a final end. To this effect, the Shillong Accord was signed in November 1975 on the basis of the following terms: (a) the representatives of all the underground organisations would convey their decision, of their own volition, to unconditionally accept the Constitution of India; (b) the rebel groups would surrender their arms and deposit them at appointed places; (c) the representatives of the underground organisations should have reasonable time to formulate their demands to be incorporated in the final settlement.[58] Moreover, the Accord resolved that 'all forms of violence and bitterness shall have to be brought to an end'[59], since it was the 'non-combatants who were suffering more than the combatants' as a result of the 20-year long war in the Naga country. Many members of Phizo's Naga National Council (NNC) laid down their arms following the Shillong Accord, while other radical leaders rejected what they considered as a betrayal of the Naga cause. Among the latter was T. Muivah, who had sought the help of China in the 1960s; in the 1980s he and Isak Swu started a new phase of the insurgency by setting up the National Socialist Council of Nagaland (NSCN) which received support and assistance from other rebel groups in India's northeast and Burma.

The most politically articulate movement took place in Chota Nagpur. Here a Jharkhand Party was formed in 1949 to give vent to the demand for tribal autonomy. The party acquired influence particularly in the period between 1952 and 1957, but began to decline since the 1960s, when the relatively advanced Christian tribals and the relatively backward non-Christian tribals entered into a competition for education and employment facilities, thereby dividing the movement front. This was reflected in the debacle of the Jharkhand Party at the election of 1962, when it lost half of its 1957 votes to the Congress and the Jana Sangh. This was mostly due to a shift of political affiliation among non-Christian tribals. In order to counter these developments, in 1963 a major section of the leadership of the party, including its founder Jaipal Singh joined the Congress claiming that by 'working from within the Congress' it stood for a better chance of getting its demand for a separate state accepted by the government. Between 1963 and 1980 the Jharkhand movement continued but without a unified political leadership, as the Jharkhand Party got fragmented into a range of smaller parties built on ethnic lines.[60] At the same time, political life in Jharkhand witnessed a growing radicalisation, due to the influence of the Naxalite movement and the entry of leftist parties in the region, on the one side, and on the other, to the rise of urban pressure groups led by educated tribals, mostly Christian, demanding jobs for tribal youths in administration and industrial undertakings.

It was in this period that the Jharkhand Mukti Morcha (JMM, founded in 1972) was started with the objective of: (a) forming a separate Jharkhand state, (b) ending exploitation of tribals by non-tribals, and (c) securing the preferential treatment of the 'sons of the soil' in matter of employment. The JMM pragmatically recognised the fact that nearly two-third of the population of Jharkhand was non-tribal and a movement that only appealed to the tribal sentiment could not gain in political strength. It therefore asserted that all the older residents of the Jharkhand region, whether tribal or non-tribal, were exploited and discriminated against and dominated by north Biharis and new migrants. It was claimed, for instance, that even though the region accounted for 28 percent of minerals, it availed of only 15 percent of the state's budget for development. By mixing together terms and ideas drawn from different political areas—leftist, regional, industrial and tribal—JMM ideologues described Jharkhand as an internal 'colony' whose 'peasants and workers' were being exploited by 'outsiders', and asserted its right to become a separate state. The JMM soon emerged as a major political force in the industrial and mining belt of Chota Nagpur and in Bihar state politics after the 1980 General Elections. By formulating a common political platform for tribals and non-tribals as objects of economic exploitation, in theory it discarded the notion of tribal ethnicity which had formed the ideology of the Jharkhand Party, although in practice, however, the JMM largely remained a tribal party.

In central India, there had been other demands for statehood by tribal groups during the period under review. The desire to set up a separate raj had been voiced by Gonds and Bhils under colonial rule. Furer-Haimendorf writes that Kumra Bhimu of Adilabad had demanded a Gond raj in 1941.[61] Following independence, raj-gond leaders, demanding a separate tribal state to be carved out of the tribal areas of Chhattisgarh and the contiguous districts of Rewa and Vidarbha, submitted a memorandum to the States Reorganisation Commission. The demand for the formation of a Gondwana state, consisting of the Gond and other tribal regions of Chhattisgarh and Vidarbha was reiterated on 19 May 1963 by Narain Singh Uikey, the President of the Gondwana Adivasi Seva Mandal. There were also tribal autonomy movements in south Gujarat where the Dangis demanded the formation of an autonomous state. The movement received widespread support, particularly of the CPI (M).[62]

Besides movements for political autonomy, there have been several other movements among the tribal people in the post-independence period. K.S. Singh has categorised these as: (i) agrarian and forest based movements, (ii) sanskritisation processes, and (iii) cultural movements based on script and language.[63] As Brass argues, state recognition in both the pre- and post-independence periods has been a critical factor in the explaining the rise of some ethnic and cultural movements.[64] Land alienation gave rise to movements in Tripura, among the Kharwars of Madhya Pradesh, the Gonds of central India and in Andhra Pradesh and Maharashtra. The Bhils of the Dhulia district in Maharashtra, for instance, were organised in a protest against landlessness by a Sarvodaya worker, Ambarsingh Suratwant in 1967. The movement succeeded in restoring to the tribals 1,872 acres of land in 31 villages between February and April 1972[65] and in July 1975, the Maharashtra government issued an ordinance prohibiting the alienation of tribal lands and providing for the restoration of lands that had been alienated in contravention of the law. Tribal and non-tribal peasants were also mobilised by the Naxalites in their movement against the rich peasants, moneylenders and local officials. This occurred in two phases, the first was from 1967 to 1972 and the second phase was from 1978 onwards. The movement was particularly active in north Bengal, in the Srikakulam-Adilabad region in Andhra Pradesh, the Chota Nagpur-Santhal Pargana region and among the Bhils in western India.

Two patterns thus have been identified as having emerged from the historical development of the tribal regions.[66] On the one hand, in the northeastern parts of India, the formation of the states in the 1960s and 1970s in accordance with the principles of ethnicity indicate the development and transcendence of the concepts of 'exclusion' and autonomy of local institutions' enshrined in the Sixth Schedule. On the other hand, in central India and other parts of the country the concepts of 'scheduled area', 'area of development', 'area of tribal dispersal', 'zones of primitive tribes' have been developed within the structure of the existing states. Thus, in the period under review, it was only in the northeast that tribal regions could develop into full-fledged states or autonomous territories organised on the basis of the principles of ethnicity. In other parts of the country they developed within the framework of states which had been reorganised in the mid-1950s according to language.

Conclusion

In the Nehruvian period, the Central government pursued pluralist policies, but avoided direct involvement on regional conflicts among different ethnic and language groups. In the post-Nehruvian period, however, the Central government has played a more directly interventionist role in regional conflicts between opposed ethnic, communal and caste groups.[67] Local crises were nationalised and the coercive power of the state was increasingly called into safeguard national integration.[68] To Indira Gandhi, the nation state was of central importance. And, as her tribal policies reveal, her commitment to the nation state transcended all other calls.

Ian Talbot argues that the Congress Party was as crucially important as the formal institutions of the state in providing the 'steel frame' for national integration[69], a role that it could play because of its historical prestige, its heterogeneous base of support, its broad based ideological appeal, its access to patronage and its accommodationist political stance which enabled it to become the voice of regional interests at the state level.[70] Because of its flexibility, the Congress in the first two decades of independence could ensure stability for India, yet, on the flip side there was an inability to redress social inequalities, despite its commitment. Nehru's goals could not be realised during his lifetime. According to Judith Brown, this happened as many reforms relied for their implementation both on administrative services schooled in the conservative ways of the Raj, and on state governments that represented the vested interests of the locally powerful.[71] There were also distortions over time in some of the constitutional provisions for tribal uplift. Critics argue that, from 1954 onwards, the Commissioner for Scheduled Castes and Scheduled Tribes became more concerned with the examination of grants-in-aid received from various state governments and non-official agencies, rather than in reviewing the actual welfare work accomplished. As a member of many government committees he became closely associated with the formulation and implementation of several schemes, which stood in his way of becoming an impartial evaluator of government policies. He had become more a policymaker than a neutral evaluator.[72] Organisational changes further reduced the powers of the Commissioner as is reflected in the debates on the 'Report of the Commissioner for Scheduled Castes and Scheduled Tribes.' The members not only pleaded for strengthening the office of the Commissioner, but also deplored the lack of cooperation from state governments in giving necessary information. The main criticism of the members centred around the 'inordinate delays' in discussing the reports and over the fact that the recommendations were not always adopted. Another factor behind the non-implementation of reforms was that the majority of the poverty-stricken tribals lacked both the knowledge of their constitutional rights and the power and resources to fight for them through the courts.

The Congress has been critiqued for being influenced more by 'proprietary classes' while seeking to represent the interest of the nation, a charge that is not entirely valid. The Congress functioned as the national platform of different social categories. Nehru's socialist commitments had greatly widened the Congress's social base, promising progress to India's downtrodden. During the succession struggle that developed after Nehru's death, especially after the split in the Congress in 1969, and during and after the 1971 elections, the Congress led by Mrs. Gandhi, intensified its appeal to the disadvantaged groups in order to counter the power of the state party bosses. Electoral support from these disadvantaged groups was of critical importance in Mrs. Gandhi's triumph in the 1971 elections.[73] The loss of support from the scheduled castes and other disadvantaged groups was a major factor in the heavy defeat of the Congress in the post-Emergency 1977 elections. In the 1980 elections, Congress again drew heavy support from the scheduled castes and scheduled tribes.[74]

Has the tribal policy of the Congress in the post-independence been a total failure? For a balanced judgement we may summarise as K.S. Singh has done, the achievements of successive Congress governments with regard to the tribal issue:

> While the Indian experiment with tribal development is comprehensive in the world perspective of the treatment of indigenous people, one has to take a balanced view of its processes. On the positive side the tribals who are full citizens have, barring a few islandic communities, maintained their demographic growth rate. They have also maintained their identity, their distinct way of life, although they have not remained unaffected by the storms blowing around their country. They have also remained in good parts in the north-east and a large part of middle India an agrarian community in possession of their lands, even though the incidence of land-alienation has sharply increased in and around urban areas. From almost the zero levels in the 1930s, progress in education and literacy, health care and communication has been remarkable, though critical gaps exist in the utilisation of these facilities by tribals as compared to non-tribals. They have also participated in the democratic processes and have their share in the control of the apparatus of political power.[75]

An important aspect of tribal uplift was positive discrimination or the reservation policy, a policy that has created controversy and conflict. However, alternative proposals for tribal uplift have not been very satisfactory.[76] A variety of benefits, protections and programmes for the scheduled castes and tribes, including reservation of seats in legislatures, places in educational institutions and posts in government departments was provided by the Congress government since independence. As a consequence of the latter, the representation of scheduled castes and scheduled tribes in public employment has begun to approach their proportion in the population. Reservation of seats in the legislatures ensured the election of a fixed proportion of scheduled caste and scheduled tribe representatives to Parliament and the state legislatures. However, 40 years after the adoption of such reservations, scheduled castes and scheduled tribes remained, much less well represented in the higher classes of government service than in the lower ranks.[77]

On the negative side, however, tribal communities remain backward and underdeveloped, and next only to scheduled castes, the most exploited community in India. Although it has advanced hugely, the Congress, even when it had the political will, could not succeed in overcoming the problems of poverty and backwardness still endemic in 'tribal' or scheduled areas.

Endnotes

1. Singh, K.S. (1985). *Tribal Society in India: An Anthropo-Historical Perspective.* Delhi: Manohar. p. 248.
2. Government of India (1947). *Interim Report of the Excluded and Partially Excluded Areas (Other than Assam) Sub Committee.* New Delhi. p. 5.
3. Ghurye, G.S. (1943). "The Aborigines—'So Called' and Their Future", Gokhale Institute of Politics and Economics, Poona, India, *Publication No. 11.*
4. Elwin, Verrier (1941). *The Loss of Nerve: A Comparative Study of the Contact of Peoples in the Aboriginal Areas of the Bastar State and the Central Provinces of India.* Bombay: Wagle Press. Such an approach to tribal development grew out of his studies particularly of the Baigas in course of which he observed that despite extreme exploitation and poverty, they still dreamed of having a Baiga Raj in which they would have their own king and no exploitation by outsiders. Much later, however, Elwin wrote that, 'Although in the earlier years I thought in terms of preserving tribal culture, I came later to think in a less static way. Culture obviously must be a living, moving thing, always subject to change, and Nehru's formula of developing the tribal people along the lines of their tradition and genius seemed to put what was needed in a nutshell'. Elwin, Verrier (1964). *The Tribal World of Verrier Elwin.* London: Oxford University. p. 295.

5. Nehru, J. (1973). "The Tribal Folk", in *The Tribal People of India*. Delhi: Ministry of Information and Broadcasting. pp. 6-7.
6. Nehru, J. (1959). "Foreword", to Verrier Elwin, *A Philosophy for NEFA*. Shillong, 2nd edition.
7. For a detailed discussion see, Corbridge, Stuart (2004). "Competing Inequalities: The Scheduled Tribes and the Reservation System in Jharkhand, India", in Stuart Corbridge, Sarah Jewitt and Sanjay Kumar (eds.), *Jharkhand: Environment, Development, Ethnicity*. New Delhi: Oxford University Press. pp. 180-182.
8. Originally provided for 10 years, they were extended by the Constitutional Amendment Acts in 1959, 1969, 1980 and 1990.
9. J. Nehru, "The Tribal Folk", pp. 4-5.
10. J. Nehru, "Foreword" in *A Philosophy for NEFA*.
11. Roy Burman, B.K., "Perspective and Programme for the Development of Adivasis", in *The Tribal People of India*: 180.
12. Gandhi, Indira (1975). *The Years of Endeavour: Selected Speeches of Indira Gandhi (1969-1972)*. New Delhi: Publication Division of Ministry of Information and Technology. p. 187
13. Singh, K.S. (1990). *Ethnicity, Identity, Development*. Delhi: Manohar. p. 13.
14. Gandhi, Indira (1975). *The Years of Endeavour*. p. 185.
15. Ibid: 186.
16. Gandhi, Indira (1984). *Selected Speeches and Writings 1972-1977*. Delhi, pp. 216-217.
17. Gandhi, Indira (1983). "Man and His World". Speech at the UN Conference on the Human Environment, Stockholm, June 14, 1972, in Indira Gandhi, *Our People and Problems*, London: Hodder and Stoughton, pp. 60-67.
18. Lok Sabha Debates, March 13, 1980.
19. Chaudhuri, Pramit (1988). "Origins of India's Economic Development Strategy", in Mike Shepperdson and Colin Simmons (eds.), *The Indian National Congress and the Political Economy of India 1885-1895*. Aldershot: Avebury. p. 276.
20. Singh, K.S. (1990). *Ethnicity, Identity and Development*. p. 10.
21. Government of India (1960). *Report of the Committee on Special Multi-Purpose Tribal Blocks*. New Delhi: Ministry of Home Affairs. March. pp. 192-3.
22. Bhanage, N.P. (1961). "Report of the Scheduled Areas and Scheduled Tribes Commission", October 14, in *Tribal Commissions and Committees in India*. Bombay: Himalaya Publishing House (1993).
23. Government of India (n.d.). *Report of the Scheduled Areas and Scheduled Tribes Commission*, 1960-61, volume 1, New Delhi.

24. Chandra, Bipan, Mridula Mukherjee, Aditya Mukherjee (1999). *India After Independence, 1947-2000*. New Delhi: Penguin Books. p. 109.
25. Bhanage, N.P. (1993). "Report of the Study Team on Tribal Development Programmes", September 19, 1969, in *Tribal Commissions and Committees in India*. p. 217.
26. Ibid: 218.
27. Ibid.
28. Chaudhuri, Sarit Kumar (2004). *Constraints of Tribal Development*. Delhi: Mittal Publications. p. 22.
29. Singh, K.S. (1990). *Ethnicity, Identity and Development*. p. 33.
30. In his demographic study of Indian tribes, Arup Maharatna corroborates this statement. The proportion of tribal people rose from about 5 percent in the 1951 census to more than 8 percent in 1991. The enumerated size of the tribal population—an Indian minority group—is nearly 70 million according to the 1991 census. Maharatna explains this increase thus: in the first place, the substantial enlargement of the list of scheduled tribes, especially between 1971-1981, as well as the removal of area restrictions in 1976 contributed to the relative swelling of the enumerated tribal population. There has also been an increasing demand for recognition of tribal identity among several hitherto unidentified tribal communities, especially in some regions where local level activism and state support was relatively more pronounced in assuring tribal rights and privileges. Of course, the most significant factor was that of a higher real natural growth of the tribal population. Maharatna, Arup (2005). *Demographic Perspectives on India's Tribes*. Delhi: Oxford University Press. pp. 22-23.
31. Government of India (1981). *Report on Development of Tribal Areas—National Committee on the Development of Backward Areas*. New Delhi: Planning Commission.
32. Singh, K.S. (1990). *Ethnicity, Identity and Development*. p. 37.
33. Rath, Govinda Chandra (2006). *Tribal Development in India: the Contemporary Debate*. Delhi: Sage Publications. p. 17.
34. Nayar, V. and S. Prasad (1984). "On levels of living of Scheduled Castes and Scheduled Tribes", *Economic and Political Weekly* 19(30), 28 July.
35. Dubey, S.N. and R. Murdia (1977). *Land Alienation and Restoration in Tribal Communities in India*. Bombay: Himalaya Publishing House.
36. Government of India (1981). *Report on the Development of Backward Areas: National Committee on the Development of Backward Area*. New Delhi: Planning Commission. p. 50.
37. Bose, P.K. (1990). "Congress and the Tribal Communities in India", in Ramashray Roy and Richard Sisson (eds.), *Diversity and Dominance in Indian Politics: Division, Deprivation and the Congress Volume 2*, New Delhi: Sage. p. 67.

38. NSSO 55th Round, Report No 469 (55/10/17) of National Sample Survey Organisation, Ministry of Statistics and Programme Implementation, Government of India, 2001, cited in Govinda Chandra Rath (2006). *Tribal Development in India: the Contemporary Debate.*

39. Saha, Suranjit (1988). "The Territorial Dimension of India's Tribal Problem", in Mike Shepperdson and Colin Simmons (eds.), *The Indian National Congress and the Political Economy of India 1885-1895*. Aldershot: Avebury.

40. Saha, Suranjit and Kavita Srivastava (1983). "Federalism and Inter-Regional Resource Allocation Policy in India", *Third World Planning Review* 5(1): 37-56. February.

41. Bhanage, N.P. (1960). "Report on the Committee on Special Multipurpose Tribal Blocks", in *Tribal Commissions and Committees in India,* March 30. p. 68.

42. Bhanage, N.P. (1976). "Report of the National Commission on Agriculture, in *Tribal Commissions and Committees in India.*

43. Ibid.

44. Bhanage, N.P. (1982). "Report on the Committee on Forests and Tribals in India", in *Tribal Commissions and Committees in India*. September. p.338.

45. Ibid: 353.

46. Singh, K.S. (ed.) (1983). *Tribal Movements in India*. Vol. II, Delhi: Manohar.

47. Guha, R. (1994). "Fighting for the Forest: State Forestry and Social Change in Tribal India", in Oliver Mendelsohn and Upendra Baxi (eds.), *The Rights of Subordinated Peoples*. Delhi: Oxford University Press. p. 32.

48. GoI (1988). "Report of the Commission for Scheduled Castes and Scheduled Tribes for 1986-87", 28th Report. Delhi.

49. Bates, Crispin (1992). "Congress and the Tribals", in Mike Shepperdson and Colin Simmons (eds.), *The Indian National Congress and the Political Economy of India 1885-1895*. p. 241.

50. Singh, K.S. (1986). "Agrarian Dimensions of Tribal Movements", in A.R. Desai (ed.), *Agrarian Struggles in India after Independence*. New Delhi: Oxford University Press. pp. 147-148.

51. Saha, Suranjit (1988). "The Territorial Dimension of India's Tribal Problem". p. 253.

52. Singh, K.S. (1985). *Tribal Society in India: An Anthropo-historical Perspective.* New Delhi: Manohar. p. 264.

53. Brass, Paul R. (1990). "The Politics of India since Independence", *The New Cambridge History of India* 4(1). Cambridge: Cambridge University Press, p. 171.

54. J. Nehru, *Letters to Chief Ministers,* vol. 3, Delhi. p. 150.

55. Chowdhury, J.N. (1989). "Two Visonaries, Nehru and Elwin, in the Context of India's Tribal Policy since Independence, with Special

Reference to India's North-East Frontier", in K.S. Singh (ed.), *Jawaharlal Nehru, Tribes and Tribal Policy*. Calcutta: Anthropological Survey of India, 1989. p. 45.

56. Daying Ering, who headed the Commission was a tribal from the Adi community. He was first made a Parliamentary Secretary and then a Deputy Minister under Nehru.
57. NEFA was granted statehood in 1987 and renamed as Arunachal Pradesh.
58. Shillong Accord, signed on 10 November 1975. Weshokhrolo Lasuh (ed.) (2002). *The Naga Chronicle*. New Delhi: Regency Publications. p. 333.
59. Ibid: 335.
60. Singh, K.S. (1985). *Tribal Society in India*. p. 272.
61. Christopher von Furer-Haimendorf (1945). "Aboriginal Rebellions in the Deccan", *Man in India: Rebellion* 24.
62. Singh, K.S. (1985). *Tribal Society in India*. pp. 270-271.
63. Ibid: 269.
64. Brass, Paul R. (1990). *The Politics of India since Independence*. p. 152.
65. Singh, K.S. (1985). *Tribal Society in India*, p. 279.
66. Singh, K.S. (1990). *Ethnicity, Identity and Development*.
67. Brass, Paul R. (1990). *The Politics of India since Independence*, p. 153.
68. Talbot, Ian (2000). *India and Pakistan*. London: Arnold. p. 182.
69. Ibid: 181.
70. Rajni Kothari terms this overarching predominance of the Congress Party in the political process as 'the Congress system' in (1964). "The Congress System in India", *Asian Survey* 4: 1161-73.
71. Brown, Judith (1999). *Nehru*. London. Ch. 5.
72. Narayana, G., "Rule Making for Scheduled Castes: Analysis of Lok Sabha Debates, 1962-71", *Economic and Political Weekly* 15(8): 435.
73. For a discussion of how tribal constituencies in India voted, see Weiner, Myron and John Osgood Field (1975). "How Tribal Constituences in India Vote", in J.N. Bhagwati *et al*., *Electoral Politics in the Indian States: Three Disadvantaged Sectors*. Delhi: Manohar. pp. 78-165.
74. Brass, Paul R. (1990). *The Politics of India since Independence*. p. 248.
75. Singh, K.S. (1985). *Tribal Society in India*. pp. 253-254.
76. The Rane Commission suggested that scheduling should be dropped altogether and reservations be allocated on the basis of income.
77. Brass, Paul R. (1990). *The Politics of India since Independence*. p. 250.

Chapter XI

Congress and Women

Aparna Basu

The roots of the women's movement in India can be traced back to the early 19th century when social reformers beginning with Raja Rammohan Roy (1772-1833) who began to focus on women issues. He condemned *sati, kulin* polygamy and spoke in favour of women's rights. He held the oppression of women as one of the factors responsible for the degraded condition of Indian society. If Rammohan Roy is remembered for his anti-*sati* campaign, Ishwarchandra Vidyasagar championed the cause of widow remarriage (1856). Following them, Jyotiba Phule, Maharshi Karve, the leaders of the Prarthana Samaj such as Narayan Ganesh Chandavarkar, Mahadev Govind Ranade and R.G Bhandarkar in Pune, Mahipatram Rupram Nilkanth in Gujarat, Behramji Malabari in Bombay, the Arya Samaj in North India, reformers such as Pantalu and the Theosophists in South India all worked for improving women's status and denounced early marriage, the condition of widows, enforced seclusion and lack of education.

The first organisations for women were started by men. These male guided and male inspired organisations did valuable work in educating women and giving them their first experience with public work. By the end of the 19th century, women from reformed families began forming associations first at the local and then at the national level. Swarnakumari Devi, the sister of Rabindranath Tagore, founded the Sakhi Samiti in 1882 in Calcutta for educating and imparting skills to widows and poor women to make them economically self-reliant. In the same year, Pandita Ramabai Saraswati started the Arya Mahila Samaj in Poona also to educate and teach skills to women, particularly widows. In 1910, Saraladevi Chaudhurani, the daughter of Swarnakumari Devi, founded the first national women's association, Bharat Stree Mahamandal but it proved to be a short-lived venture.

In the inter-war years between 1917 and 1945, the two main issues that women's associations took up were political rights of women and reform of women's personal laws. The Women's Indian Association

(WIA), the first all-India women's association, was established in 1917 by Annie Besant, Margaret Cousins and Dorothy Jinarajadasa, all three Irish Theosophists and ex-suffragettes, with the clear objective of obtaining suffrage for women. Indian women, among them, Ammu Swaminathan, Malati Patwardhan, Mrs. Dadabhoy and Mrs. Ambujammal joined the WIA. At this time petition politics was the main way of pressurising the government to grant voting rights to women. A delegation of WIA members led by Sarojini Naidu met the Secretary of State, Lord Edwin Montagu and the Viceroy, Lord Chelmsford to plead their case. After considerable lobbying by the WIA in India and in England, the British Parliament ultimately agreed to remove sex disqualification but left it to the provincial legislatures to decide how and when to do so. The princely state of Travancore-Cochin was the first to grant votes to women in 1920 followed by the provinces of Madras and Bombay in 1921.

The National Council for Women (NCW) was established in 1925 and the All India Women's Conference (AIWC) two years later. The latter was started on the initiative of Margaret Cousins with the objective of promoting women's education but it soon took up social issues such as child marriage and *purdah*. It launched a vigorous campaign for raising the age of marriage leading to the passing of the Sarda Act in 1929 and for the reform of Hindu personal law. While on the one hand, women formed organisations to fight for political, economic, legal and social rights, with the coming of Mahatma Gandhi on the political scene, women from all castes and classes, regions and religions started participating in the freedom struggle.

Indian women are not a homogeneous category and as there are vast variations across social, economic and cultural spaces, it is difficult to give a generalised picture of Indian women or to capture their contributions, struggles, concerns and achievements and despairs.

Indian National Congress and Women

'The women of India should have as much share in winning *swaraj* as men. Probably in this peaceful struggle woman can outstrip man by many a mile. We know that she is any day superior to man in her religious devotion. Silent and dignified suffering is the badge of her sex and now that the government has dragged the woman into the line of fire, I hope that women all over India will take up the challenge and organize themselves.'[1] It was in words such as these that Mahatma Gandhi appealed to women to enter the struggle for India's freedom. 'If non violence is the law of our being, the future is with women.'[2] If the women of India arose, he said, no one could stop the country's march to freedom.

From the very inception of the Indian National Congress, its membership was open to women. At its first session, Allan Octavian Hume asked political reformers, 'of all shades of opinion never to forget that "unless the elevation of the female element of the nation proceeds *pari passu* (with an equal pace) with their work, all their labour for the political enfranchisement of the country will prove vain."'[3] The National Conference was founded at the third session of the Congress in 1887 to provide a forum for the discussion of social issues. The Bharat Mahila Parishad was the women's wing and this was started in 1905 and focussed on child marriage, condition of widows, dowry and other 'evil' customs.

Ten women attended the fourth session of the Congress in Bombay in 1889. Among them was Swarnakumari Devi, sister of Rabindranath Tagore. Also present were Kadambini Ganguli, one of the first two women graduates of Calcutta University and the first woman doctor of Bengal, Pandita Ramabai, a social reformer, educationalist and noted Sanskrit scholar and Shevantibai Trimbak, Shantibai Nikambe, Kashibai Kanitkar and Miss Manekjee Cursetjee. The following year, when the Congress met in Calcutta, both Swarnakumari Devi and Kadambini Ganguli attended as delegates. In 1901, a chorus of 56 girls representing all regions of India performed a song, 'Hindustan' written by Swarnakumari's daughter, Saraladevi. The following year, in Ahmedabad, the National Congress anthem 'Bande Mataram' was sung by Vidyagauri Nilkanth and her sister Sharda Mehta, the first two women graduates of Gujarat. In 1917, Annie Besant was the first woman to be elected President of the Congress. And in 1925, Sarojini Naidu became the Congress President; the next woman President was Indira Gandhi in 1959-60.[4]

While women delegates in small numbers attended the annual sessions of the Congress and had taken part in the *swadeshi* movement in Bengal (1905-1911), and in the Home Rule Movement (1917-1919), the involvement of really large number of women in the Indian national movement began with Mahatma Gandhi. Women took part in the Borsad (1923-24) and Bardoli satyagrahas (1928), Non-Cooperation movement (1921-22), Salt Satyagraha, Civil Disobedience movement (1930-31), and in the Quit India movement (1942). They held meetings, organised processions, picketed shops selling foreign cloth and liquor and went to jail. The Congress recruited women volunteers or *swayamsevikas* and trained them to help out at its annual sessions.

The participation of women in the freedom movement shaped the struggle for women's rights. It legitimised their claim to a place in the governance of India. Gandhi declared, 'I am uncompromising in the matter of women's rights. In my opinion, she should labour under no legal disability not suffered by man'.[5] If Gandhi drew Indian women out of the four walls of their house to join the freedom struggle, Jawaharlal Nehru recognised the need to formally grant equal rights to women in all respects reflected in the Resolution on Fundamental Rights drawn up at the Karachi Congress in 1931.

To Nehru, women's participation in large numbers in the national struggle in response to Gandhi's call was a kind of social revolution. It gave women a new cause and a sense of commitment. He wrote in the *Discovery of India*,'...a remarkable thing happened. One woman came in the front and took charge of the struggle,...Here were these women, women of the upper or middle classes, leading sheltered lives in their homes—peasant women, working class women, rich women—pouring out in their tens of thousands in defiance of government orders and police lathi.'[6]

To Jawaharlal Nehru, the participation of women in the freedom struggle was the beginning of a larger process whereby women would find their identity and enjoy equal rights with men. 'I have the greatest admiration...for the women of India today. I have faith in them. I am not afraid to let them grow, because I am convinced that no amount of legal constraint can prevent society from going in a certain direction. And if you put too much legal constraint, the structure breaks'.[7] But he held that women themselves had to fight for their rights. As he put it, 'no people, no group, no community, no country has ever got rid of its disabilities by the generosity of its oppressor...the women of India will not attain their full rights by the mere generosity of the men of India. They will have to fight for them and force their will on the men folk before they can succeed.'[8] While Nehru condemned India's male dominated society where man treated a woman 'as a chattel and a plaything to be exploited for his own advantage and amusement,'[9] he was equally aware that change would have to be brought about gradually—that mindsets do not change so easily.

The Congress Manifesto in the 1937 provincial elections stated:

> The Congress has already declared that it stands for the removal of all sex disabilities whether legal or social or in any other sphere of public activity. It has expressed itself in favour of maternity benefits and the protection of women workers. The women of India have already taken a leading part in the freedom struggle, and the Congress looks forward to their sharing, in an equal measure with the men of India, the privileges and obligations of citizens of a free India.[10]

In 1937-38, the Indian National Congress set up a National Planning Committee under the chairmanship of Jawaharlal Nehru. One of the 29 sub-committees was on 'Women's Role in a Planned Economy'. Its President was Rani Laxmibai Rajwade and Mridula Sarabhai was the Secretary. The terms of reference of the committee were very comprehensive and dealt with every aspect of women's life and work—'their socio-economic and legal status, their right to hold property, carry on trade, professions or occupation and remove obstacles or handicaps in the way of realizing an equal status and opportunity for women'. The sub-committee worked very hard and came up with some extremely radical recommendations.[11] It held that women's position must be in a footing of absolute equality with men in all respects.

Mridula Sarabhai was among the women members of the Congress who pressurised the male leadership to start a women's wing of the Congress. She approached Vijayalakshmi Pandit asking for her and Nehru's support for she felt that without it nothing could be achieved. Both Mrs. Pandit and Mridula issued an appeal to Congress women workers to approach Nehru and Sarojini Naidu and suggested that Sucheta Kripalani should be put in charge of the Women's Department. Finally, in April 1940, it was decided to open a women's wing with Sucheta in charge but it never really took off.

Post-Independence

The Indian Constitution declared equality a fundamental right. It also guaranteed equal protection of the law, equal opportunity in public employment and prohibited discrimination in public places. Adult suffrage gave women the vote.

The Hindu Code, passed as separates Acts between 1955 and 1956, rewrote for Hindus the laws of marriage, divorce, succession, adoption and maintenance. The founding fathers of the Constitution had only a few years earlier passed the Constitution which gave equal rights to women and prohibited discrimination between sexes but a large number of them, including many Congressmen, now opposed the changes proposed in the Hindu Code Bill. Their opposition revealed age-old superstitions, deep-rooted prejudices and patriarchal attitudes towards women. The passage of the Bill was possible because of the support it received from Jawaharlal Nehru. Rajkumari Amrit Kaur was right when she said that, 'The social reforms that are now in the Statute Book would...have been talked out if it had not been for Jawaharlal's powerful advocacy of and insistence on them.'[12]

Many women who had participated in the freedom struggle and in working for social reform and women's education in the 1920s, 1930s and 1940s were naturally pleased with the constitutional provisions and legal reforms in the years after independence. There was a belief, especially among women belonging to the upper and middle classes of society, that with the end of foreign rule, women's position was bound to improve.

Some women dissatisfied with the status quo joined struggles for the rural poor such as the Tebhaga movement in Bengal, the Telangana movement in Andhra Pradesh or the Naxalite movement. Shahada, which acquired its name from the area in which the movement occurred, in Dhulia district in Maharashtra, was a tribal landless labourers' movement against landlords. Women played a prominent part and led demonstrations, invented and shouted militant slogans and mobilised people. As women's militancy developed, gender based issues were raised. There was an anti-alcohol agitation as men used to get drunk and beat their wives. Women went round villages breaking pots in liquor dens.

There were some women followers of Gandhi who held that social and economic change was more important than constitutional and legal rights. Many of them focussed their attention on constructive work projects in rural areas.

The Indian National Congress at its annual sessions continued to pass resolutions emphasising the importance of allowing women to play their due role in the development of the country. In the second sitting of the Plenary Session of the 69th session in 1965 supporting the resolution on 'Task Before Congressmen', Savita Behn (Punjab) said that, 'the resolution was important and a necessary one but there was no reference to women who were more than 50 percent of the country's population and who play a significant role in the development and reconstruction of the country. There was a reference to youth in the resolution but none to women.'[13] In 1966-67, a National Women's Committee with Nandini Satpathy as chairperson was set up for coordinating responsibilities at the national level of the state level committees and the *pradesh* committees. These committees had to work in coordination with the women's department of the All Indian Congress Committee (AICC).[14]

Training-cum-work centres were set up to provide a means of livelihood to needy and displaced women. The party also wanted to provide special training to its own members who could play a leadership role in voluntary women's organisations. Efforts were made to train women librarians to provide employment for educated women. An AICC Women's Front was started and its Convener toured several provinces to discuss the situation of women workers and their role and start branches of the Front. A Central Women's Advisory Council was formed in February 1970 by the Congress president for creating a sense of participation and involvement among women members of Parliament and state legislatures. Among other activities, the Front started two monthly journals *Women on the March* in English and *Mahila Pragati Ke Path Par* in Hindi.[15]

The Pradesh Women Conveners' Conference was convened in Simla in October 1971. A resolution was passed claiming the revival of 15 percent representation for women in all the organisational and other elected bodies represented by the Congress. The Congress Working Committee (CWC) endorsed the resolution.

In 1974-1976, the main activities of the Women's Front were connected with the International Women's Year and a number of Front members went to the Mexico Conference. A National Forum of Women was constituted with Pramilabai Chavan, MP as its President and Tara Devi Saxena as its General Secretary. This Forum constituted several sub-committees, such as on culture, women's employment, social and civic consciousness, self-defence training, etc.

In its Election Manifesto of 1977, the Congress reiterated its commitment to enlarging the equality of opportunity for women in all walks of life—political, economic, educational and cultural. It promised to work intensively to remove every form of discrimination against women and pledged to ensure that women enjoy dignity and equality so that they can make their due contribution for building a strong and prosperous India. These sentiments were reiterated in the Election Manifesto of 1980.

At its annual session at Calcutta in 1983, the Congress recognised that despite improvement in women's working conditions and in opportunities open to them in various walks of life, they continue to face problems. The meeting strongly deplored the inhuman crimes against women and urged the government to pass effective anti-dowry legislation. It resolved to eradicate social evils such as child marriage and work for an equal and honoured status for women in society.

The All India Mahila Congress was set up in 1984 and a two-day National Convention was held, attended by about 20,000 delegates. The new constitution of the Mahila Congress was adopted at this meeting. A 'law' wing was started which organised conferences of lawyers and social workers to discuss inadequate legal provisions in respect of women. An All India Society for the Welfare of Women and Children under the umbrella of the Mahila Congress was registered in May 1984. In its Election Manifestos of 1984 and 1985, the Congress promised to continue its fight against dowry and other social evils, initiate a programme to improve the educational status of women and improve economic opportunities for women.[16]

Towards Equality

After Independence, most women believed that their position was improving. In 1971, the Ministry of Education and Social Welfare appointed a committee 'to examine the constitutional, legal and administrative provisions that have a bearing on the social status of women, their education and employment and also assess the impact of these provisions.'[17] There had been a demand for this from within the country but the actual timing was in response to a United Nations request to all countries to prepare reports on the status of women for the International Women's Year scheduled for 1975.

Dr. Phulrenu Guha, Union Minister for Social Welfare, chaired this committee with Dr. Vina Mazumdar as member secretary. The other nine members were either academicians or women who had worked with women's organisations or were involved in politics. In order to write this report, the committee commissioned a number of studies and interviewed about 500 women from each state. The report, *Towards Equality*, published in 1974, was a major effort to understand the extent to which constitutional guarantees of equality and justice had been achieved for women. It put women forcefully on the agenda by arguing that the position of Indian women had not improved, in fact, in many areas declined.

> The review of the disabilities and constraints on women, which stem from socio cultural institutions, indicates that the majority of women are still very far from enjoying the rights and opportunities guaranteed to them by the Constitution...The social laws, that sought to mitigate the problems of women in their family life, have remained unknown to a large mass of women in this country, who are as ignorant of their legal rights today as they were before Independence.[18]

The revelation, that social change and development in India had adversely affected women shocked many Indians. Whereas the advances made by a small number of Indian women were indeed inspiring, the overall progress was not at all satisfactory. The majority of Indian women had not benefited from the economic, technological, political or social changes that were taking place in the country.

Towards Equality can be regarded as a landmark in the women's movement in post-Independence India and its publication had considerable impact on subsequent programmes and policies for Indian women.

Women and Politics

Indian women have occupied an unusual position at an elite level of Indian politics. During these 20 years, Indira Gandhi was Prime Minister for 13 years. Apart from a woman Prime Minister, we had women as members of Parliament, Governors, Chief Ministers, Ambassadors, members of the Cabinet and Deputy Ministers. At the same time, the involvement of women in politics fell short compared with their participation in the freedom struggle and the equality granted to them in the constitution.

Women in India got the right to vote for the provincial legislative assemblies in the mid-1920s after the introduction of the Montagu-Chelmsford Reforms and for the central legislature by the Government of India Act of 1935. The first woman to stand for election to a provincial legislature was Kamaladevi Chattopadhyaya from Mangalore who lost by a narrow margin. The first woman nominated to a provincial legislature was Dr. Muthulakshmi Reddy, a social worker and a medical doctor, in Madras in 1926. Of course, franchise was very restricted and only a small percentage of women with the qualifications of wifehood, education and property could exercise this right. The 1935 Act relaxed these qualifications but it was only after Independence that all adult women got the right to vote and stand for elections. It has been found that women vote in almost the same proportion as men but few women stand for elections. In the 20 years under consideration, women never had more than 7 percent seats in the Lok Sabha.

Year of Election	*Total No. of Seats*	*No. of Women Who Contested*	*No. of Women Who Won*
1967	520	67	29
1971	542	70	19
1977	542	143	28
1980	542	143	
1984		42	

The small proportion of women in the Lok Sabha is replicated in the state legislatures as well.

The Lok Sabha elections of 1984 saw a large turnout of women voters and candidates. The *Hindutan Times* of 25 December of 1984 wrote, 'If the large number of women who exercised their franchise yesterday is anything to go by, then Indian women seem to have come of age—at least as far as political consciousness is concerned.' Forty-two women were elected to the Lok Sabha, the largest so far and with 22 in the Rajya Sabha, there were 64 in the two Houses combined.

It is often asked as to why Indian women who played such an important role in the freedom struggle have not entered electoral politics. This is largely because they have lacked party backing. Political parties pay lip service to women's equality but are reluctant to give seats to women. Women from political families, wives, widows, daughters of politicians are usually given seats. The presence of mafia and criminal elements in politics and the expenses involved in fighting elections makes women unwilling and unable to fight elections. Women also often have to face sexual harassment and sordid gossip in politics and prefer to do social work.

Only a few women who joined politics in these years focussed on women's issues. Among them were Mrinal Gore, a Member of the Maharashtra Legislative Assembly in the 1970s and a member of the Lok Sabha in the 1980s. She took up the issue of shortage of water and price rise both of which affected women. In 1973, she and Ahilya Rangnekar of the CPI-M, together with many others formed the United Women's Anti Price Rise Front, which demanded consumer protection and distribution of essential commodities at prices fixed by the government. Ordinary housewives joined the movement by marching on the streets beating *thalis* (metal plates) and *belan* (rolling pins).[19] Renuka Ray and Phulrenu Guha who had been associated with the women's movement in the pre-independence era, continued to articulate women's concerns in Parliament as did MPs such as Sushila Gopalan and Pramila Dandvate.

India had a number of distinguished women in politics during these years, such as Rajkumari Amrit Kaur, Union Minister of Health, Sucheta Kripalani, Chief Minister of UP, Renuka Ray, Minister for Refugee and Rehabilitation in West Bengal, Vijayalakshmi Pandit, India's Ambassador to UK, USA and USSR, or Durgabai Deshmukh, member of the Planning Commission. There were women who did not hold official positions but were involved in the political process such as Mridula Sarabhai. While it is true that most of the women who attained positions of power belonged to 'political families', this was not always true and they did not all belong to a wealthy elite. There was a vast difference between Amrit Kaur who came from the princely family of Kapurthala and Durgabai Deshmukh or between Vijayalakshmi Pandit and Phulrenu Guha.

The most important political woman in India during these years was, undoubtedly, Indira Gandhi, India's first woman prime minister, whose long tenure in office, from 1966 to 1977 and 1980 to 1984 ended with her assassination on October 31, 1984. Mrs. Gandhi consistently denied that she was a feminist. Addressing the Silver Jubilee celebrations of Miranda House college Delhi on March 7, 1973, she said, 'I am not a feminist and I do not believe that anybody should get preferential treatment merely because she happens to be a woman.[20]... Yet in my concern for the underprivileged, how can I ignore women who, since the beginning of history, have been dominated over and discriminated against in social customs and in laws. How insidious and all pervasive is this attitude of male superiority is revealed in the vocabulary of the language the world over'. Women, she said, '...were doubly underprivileged, because they had their own prejudices and superstitions plus those of the men.'[21] But at the same time, she was aware of the problems Indian women faced such as child marriage or dowry, and referred to women as 'the biggest oppressed minority in the world.' Indian women, she said, faced many different types of problems. For the vast majority of them, the question was not of rights but of basic decencies, basic requirements. 'In India, there has been an impressive increase in the number of women in the liberal professions. Yet there has been little change in the drudgery to which the large minority of women in the villages and of the weaker sections are subject.' In her speeches, she frequently referred to the importance of women's education, health and family planning. 'Countless women have been compelled to live a life of ill health, little energy and poor fulfillment by frequent child bearing but too little time for child rearing. Family planning corrects this. It makes for healthier women who can make fuller use of their mental and emotional capacities. In this respect, family planning is akin to education for women.'[22]

Indira Gandhi recognised that, 'the human race can prosper only on the basis of equality. Equality does not mean identity of form or function or a denial of biological differences. But to be a woman should not come in the way of a person developing her talents and receiving her due.'[23] 'Women are not weak by themselves but because they are so handicapped from birth, by customs and social attitudes, that they have no chance of developing their innate strength'.[24] '"Our education system" she said, "has evolved in a way which tends to perpetuate inequality between man and woman as also unfortunately between man and man. A recent survey of textbooks has shown that they promote the impression of a passive, supporting role for women and that action, leadership, dynamism, artistic creativity and intellectual genius are male prerogatives..."'. She repeatedly said that women must have equality of opportunity and there should be programmes for their health, education and employment and better conditions of work.

When asked by a foreign correspondent as to what she wanted to do immediately to improve the condition of women, she replied that much greater stress should be laid on women's education as well as girls' education. In a radio interview from Sarajevo, Yugoslavia in March 1980, she was asked, 'As the leader of the largest democracy in the world elected by men and women alike who have traditionally worshipped woman as goddess but neglected her in day-to-day life, how do you envisage woman's role in a progressive society like ours?' She replied, 'Women comprise half our population. How can we neglect their talent and capability in nation building? How can women themselves lead full lives if they remain aloof? And finally can man be complete without the full support of woman? Woman in India has a special role. She is the upholder of tradition and she must also be the usher for modernity. Her task is to be a vehicle for social reform and the bringing in of a new society.'[25] These concerns were reflected in the policies of her government. While Indira Gandhi did not specifically focus on women's issues, she was a role model for women across the country and having a woman Prime Minister made Indian women feel proud.

The Women's Movement

The publication of *Towards Equality* in 1974 and the United Nations Declaration of 1975 as the International Year of Women, beginning with the First World Conference on Women in Mexico, generated a new interest in and debate on women's issues which found expression both in activism and the academia. During the next 10 years, seminars, publications, projects, documentation of literature and research proliferated. Conferences focussing on different aspects of women's life were held, campaigns were launched to highlight significant issues. Numerous women's groups, collectives and organisations emerged focussing on specific issues and sometimes undertaking the task of making women conscious of their oppression. Political parties activated their women's wings or started new ones. The media started discussing women's issues. The Government launched programmes and policies for women's development. Numerous pro women laws were passed. This period is often referred to as the second phase of the women's movement in India as well as globally. The women movement is multipolar and influenced by different political ideologies but on many issues women's associations do come together and launch a common campaign cutting across party lines.

One of the features of the post-1975 women's movement was the rise and proliferation of autonomous women's groups such as the Stree Shakti Sangathan and Progressive Women's Organisation (POW)

(Hyderabad), Sakhi Kendra (Kanpur), Forum Against Women's Oppression (Bombay), Stree Sangharsh (Delhi) and Pennuramai Iyakkam (Madras), to name a few. They called themselves autonomous, as they were not affiliated to any political party. Not all members were non-political, many of them belonged to political parties and adhered to political ideologies such as Marxism, radical or liberal feminism or Gandhian *sarvodaya* but they found that while some of these organisations were sensitive to the problems of the peasants and workers or denounced casteism and communalism, they were insensitive to the oppression of women. Hence they decided to form autonomous women's organisations that would exclusively concentrate on women's issues. These groups were joined not by formal links but through connection of their leaders who took up issues such as dowry deaths, bride burning, rape, *sati*, alcoholism, deforestation, and focussed on violence and various forms of oppression against women. They attacked patriarchy and stressed the humiliation, torture and violence suffered by women within the family.

Women's issues entered fields of culture, religion, and law, of family and community structures, of official responses to population, health, literacy and labour and of new socials movements of Dalits, environmentalists, tribals, anti-dam activists, peasants and trade unions. In all these discourses, gender began to figure as an issue and category of analysis. Data on gender discrimination in employment, education, land distribution, inheritance, health and nutrition could not now be ignored.

Women's groups adopted various methods for mobilisation. They issued pamphlets, collected signatures in support of their demands, wrote articles in journals and newspapers, tried to get media coverage, organise protest rallies and demonstrations. They also organised street corner plays, skits and songs, poster exhibitions and tours.

The Campaign against Dowry

In the late 70s and early 1980s, reports of rising numbers of dowry deaths in Delhi brought together 35 organisations of women, students and trade unions to form a joint front called the Dahej Virodhi Chetna Mandal (organisation for creating consciousness against dowry) to oppose the evils of dowry. This involved *padyatras* (marching on the streets), and meetings in colleges, market places and residential areas. The anti-dowry campaign attempted to bring social pressure to bear on offenders so that they would be isolated in the community in which they lived. The campaign culminated in a massive rally at the Boat Club in Delhi. Speakers included Sushila Gopalan and Pramila

Dandavate, both Members of Parliament and many other women leaders.

The campaign against dowry cut across boundaries of religion and language and included students and teachers of the colleges and universities in Delhi, housewives and members of women's organisations. Experience in the campaign revealed that women were ignorant of the laws and that there was the need for creating legal awareness, counselling, and legal aid. It was in response to this that women's organisations set up legal aid and counselling centres in different parts of the country. As the campaign against dowry deaths increased, political parties also condemned this. Pramila Dandvate introduced a Private Member's Bill in 1980 to amend the laws against dowry.

Increasing number of cases of young brides being set on fire for not bringing enough dowry, a phenomenon that came to be known as 'bride burning', forced the Supreme Court to justify the death penalty in such rare cases. In 1980 Sudha Goel, a 20-year old pregnant girl, was burnt for dowry by her in-laws. The Additional Sessions Court Judge had imposed the death penalty on the in-laws. The verdict of the Sessions Court was reversed by the Delhi High Court and led to protests by women's groups across the country. Women of the Dahej Virodhi Chetna Manch courted arrest outside Parliament. Among the participants were Sushila Gopalan and Kanak Mukherjee, both MPs and many members of parliament came out in support of the protestors. The Supreme Court reversed the judgment of the High Court and held Sudha's husband and his mother guilty of murder, sentencing them to life imprisonment. This was indeed a great victory for the women's movement in its struggle against crimes of violence against women.

A Joint Committee of both Houses of Parliament was appointed, chaired by Krishna Sahi, a Congress MP, to examine the working of the Dowry Prohibition Act and it presented its report to the Lok Sabha. The Law Commission held several hearings on which women from different groups participated and gave evidence and presented its report 'Dowry Deaths and Law Reform.' In 1984 the Dowry Prohibition (Amendment) Bill was passed by Parliament. It introduced section 498-A to the Indian Penal code. Under this, cruelty to a wife was made a cognisable, non-bailable offence, punishable by up to three years' imprisonment and a fine. Cruelty was redefined to include mental as well as physical harassment. Section 113-A was also amended so that the court could draw an inference of abetment to suicide. Both these changes in law were what the women's movement wanted. Finally the Act amended Section 174 of the Criminal Procedure Code, making a post mortem examination compulsory on the body of a woman who died within seven years of her marriage. In November 1980, the Central government had ordered compulsory investigation and post mortem in cases of married women dying under unnatural circumstances during the first five years of marriage.

The anti-dowry campaign drew in a number of journalists, writers and filmmakers. Meera Dewan made a film called *Gift of Love*, which carried the dying declaration of a woman who had been burnt for not bringing enough dowry. Dina Mehta's controversial play *Brides are not for Burning* was also a response to the shocking statistics of bride burning and abuse. The play sponsored by the Institute for Development Education won the BBC Play of the Year Award. Women's groups used street theatre to create consciousness about the spread of dowry.

The Agitation against Rape

Women's groups took up the struggle against rape in 1980. This was triggered by the case of a minor tribal girl, Mathura who was detained at the police station though she had not committed any offence and raped repeatedly through the night. The Sessions Judge refused to convict the two policemen. However, the High Court indicted them but the Supreme Court dismissed the case on very flimsy grounds. Four eminent lawyers, including two women, Professor Lotika Sarkar of Delhi University and Professor Vasudha Dhagamwar of Pune University as well as Professor Upendra Baxi and Raghunath Kelkar addressed an open letter to the Chief Justice of India protesting against the 'patent' injustice of this decision and asked him to review the case. When the Supreme Court rejected their petition, women in Bombay and Delhi protested on the streets.

In Bombay, a group of women formed the Forum Against Rape and decided to campaign for the reopening of the case and wrote to feminist groups all across the country to hold demonstrations on the International Women's Day, March 8, to demand a retrial.

Several other rape cases such as those of Santhal women and of Rameeza Bee, a poor woman from Hyderabad, were also taken up and became part of this campaign. Women demanded better conditions in police stations, more gender-sensitive judges and changes in the outdated rape law. Government asked the Law Commission to study the problem and suggest amendments to the existing law. The government responded to the demands of the women's groups and Section 375 of the Indian Penal Code relating to rape was amended. In the amended law, as in all cases of custodial rape, or rape by a person in authority of someone in his employment or care, the onus of proof was placed on the accused, not the victim. The amended law also provided for trial 'in camera' in order to protect the woman and lay down that a woman's past sexual history could not be taken into account in judging cases of rape.

Shah Bano Case

There were several campaigns in the 1980s relating to women's rights. Among them was the one in 1985 in support of the Supreme Court judgment in the divorce case where Shah Bano, a Muslim woman, had petitioned the Court for maintenance from her husband under Section 125 of the Criminal Procedure Act and the Court granted her demand. The orthodox Muslim *ulema* protested and in 1986, the Muslim Women's Protection of Rights in Divorce Bill denying Muslim women redress under Section 125 was introduced. Women's associations protested against this outside Parliament.

Pro-Women Legislation

All these campaigns resulted in new legislation and these years saw extraordinary pro-women legislation. In terms of legislation, India has taken far-reaching steps to counter social injustice. As we have noted above, since the adoption of the Constitution in 1950, the legislature passed a Maternity Beneift Act (1961), legalised abortion (1971), passed a Dowry Prohibition Act (1961) which was amended in 1984, legislated equal pay (1975) and amended the law against rape. Laws have changed but the ground reality has not! Without political will and enhancement of women's ability to claim and assert their legal rights, laws have existed largely on paper and rarely enforced. However, these laws have created an awareness of sex inequalities reflected in the number of books and articles written by Indian scholars on Indian women. Laws have deeply affected the lives of individual women but these individual changes have not led to an improvement in the social and economic situation of women as a whole.

Sex Ratio

One of the most disturbing features of contemporary Indian society is the declining sex ratio. Sex ratio is defined as the number of females per 1000 males and is an indicator to measure the equality between men and women. Sex selection technology was developed in the 1970s and amniocentesis or abortion of the female fetus is a recent phenomenon. A medical entrepreneur, New Bhandari Clinic in

Amritsar, advertised abortion of the female fetus, arguing that daughters were a liability to the family and it was better to spend a few hundred rupees on a sex selection test and abortion than thousands on dowry. The Centre for Women's Development Studies, Delhi, convened a meeting of women's organisations condemning the misuse of scientific technology. Present at this meeting was the then Joint Secretary to Government of India, in charge of women's issues within the Ministry of Social Welfare. He had seen the advertisement by the New Bhandari Clinic Laboratory that had appeared in the morning's newspaper and was shocked. He obtained copies of the resolutions adopted at the meeting and promptly sought the intervention of the Union Health Ministry. A conference of State Ministers of Health took place and the Union Minister made a strong statement expressing deep concern over the 'highly unethical, unjust and immoral practice'. The Government of India issued circulars to state governments making use of technology of prenatal sex determination for the purpose of abortion a penal offence. The ostensible reason for these tests is to identify genetic disorders but 95 percent of the clientele is anxious to find out the sex of the unborn child. An analysis of abortions performed during 1984-85 in a Bombay clinic revealed that nearly 100 percent abortions had followed sex determination tests.

Environmental Sustenance and Women

Women also took up environmental issues which came into prominence in the 1970s. In the 1972 Conference on Environment in Stockholm, Indira Gandhi, then Prime Minister, emphasised the relationship between poverty and environmental degradation as a major problem She drew attention to the situation of women, the poorest of the poor, with less than one percent of the productive resources of the world. In rural India, 96 percent of households use biofuels, 39 percent of fuel wood is collected from forests, 62 percent of households collect water from lakes, hand pumps or wells, and 90 percent lack toilet facilities. Women have been traditionally responsible for subsistence and survival tasks, which include collecting fodder, fuel and water.

For centuries women have managed forests and forest resources. As users, women have direct contact with the natural environment as they collect fuel, food and forest products for their everyday needs. As such, they have a close relationship with trees and forests. The Chipko movement got its name from the word '*chipko*' which, in Hindi means to cling. This clinging to trees was the particular action people used to save trees, which were crucial to their lives, from being felled. The

Chipko movement began in 1973 in the remote hill town of Gopeshwar in Chamoli district of Uttarakhand, when representatives of a sports goods factory arrived to cut ash trees. The villagers requested them not to do this, but when the contractors refused, the villagers came up with the idea of hugging the trees. The movement was initiated by a group of Sarvodaya workers led by two men—Chandi Prasad Bhatt and Sunderlal Bahuguna but women soon joined the movement.

Within a few years the Chipko movement spread all over Chamoli district and parts of Tehri Garhwal, with women taking the lead in many places. With the help of the Dasholi Gram Swarajya Mandal (DGSM), an organisation headed by Chandi Prasad Bhatt, women formed Mahila Mangal Dals (women's groups) in many villages and began to claim the right to decide what was to be done in forests and fields. In 1980, in Dongri Paintoli village, while the men in the village council, wagered to the forests being cut for building a school, a cemented road a new hospital and electricity for the village, the DGSM members were for preservation of the forest. The women came out in large numbers and held a demonstration to save the trees and avoid moves which threatened their survival and continuity. The government, thereupon, ordered the stoppage of the forest felling in that area.

Twelve years after the inception of the Chipko movement, several areas of Uttarakhand were in ferment. On this occasion, it was the sale of liquor, legal and illegal that was being challenged. Originating in Almora, the movement spread to many districts and women participated in this agitation in a big way.

Women's Studies

Women's Studies as a distinct area of research and teaching emerged in the United States of America in the late 1960s with what we call the second phase of the women's movement which grew out of student radicalism in Europe and USA, the anti-Vietnam war agitation and the civil rights movement. This provided the impetus for the growth and establishment of women studies centres. The First World Conference of Women in Mexico in 1975 led to a worldwide interest in women's studies.

Shreemati Nathibai Damodar Thackersey Women's University (SNDT) University, in Mumbai, had started a Women's Studies Research Centre under Dr. Neera Desai's directorship in 1974. It was the first university in India to use the term women's studies for activities connected with women's issues—academic and action oriented. This was a new project to equip women to fight for their rights and build a positive self-image. SNDT Research Unit set up a small information cell providing material on various issues to scholars, journalists, student and activists. At the World Conference for Women in Copenhagen in 1980, as part of the Forum of Non-Government Organisations, a series of women's studies seminars and workshops were conducted under the joint sponsorship of the Feminist Press, the National Women's Studies Association of USA, the Simon de Beauvoir Institute, Canada and SNDT University, Mumbai.

Dr. Hemlata Swarup, Vice Chancellor of Kanpur University, wanted a Women's Studies Center in her University. Dr. J.P. Naik, Secretary of the Indian Council of Social Science Research (ICSSR), suggested that a Women's Studies Conference should be called. Dr. Madhuri Shah, Vice Chancellor, SNDT was appointed Chairman of UGC and with her support and the support of ICSSR and the Ministry a conference was called in April 1981 in Mumbai. SNDT agreed to host it and it was a resounding success. Nearly 400 delegates from all over India representing diverse areas of interest such as research, teaching, social work, trade unions and activism, attended the conference. It paved the way for legitimising women's studies in India. The delegates felt that more such meetings should be held and that there should be a body to keep the efforts growing. It took a year before the Indian Association of Women's Studies was formally started in 1981-82 to bring together those engaged in teaching, research and action programmes. Out of the Conference arose the demand for women's studies to provide an input in the system of higher education as well as in schools. Women's issues became academically much more visible. However, it was felt that women's studies should not be a separate discipline but should be included in the curricula of different subjects.

The Centre for Women's Development Studies was started in Delhi with Dr. Vina Mazumdar as its first Director. An Expert Group Meeting on Women's Studies in Asia sponsored by UNESCO's Bangkok office was held and its Report sent to the UGC. The UGC issued a letter to all Vice Chancellors and principals of colleges in 1983 asking them to think about including 'issues relating to the status of women within their research and teaching activities.' The initial lead taken by ICSSR in 1975 was taken over by UGC which set up a cell and also units within universities and colleges selected for this programme 'to play a catalytic and co-coordinating role in promoting women's studies. The person behind these initiatives was Dr. Madhuriben Shah, then Chairperson UGC, who gave women's studies an official status and made its entry possible into the higher education system.

A national seminar on Perspectives and Organization of Women's Studies within Indian Universities was held in April 1985 and another on Education for Women's Equality in November of the same year. It stressed the need to monitor and regulate all the measures that sought to improve the role of education in women's equality and development at the Central, state and institutional level, such as in the Ministry of Education, UGC, NCERT, NIEPA, etc.

The growth of women's studies during these decades, its acceptance in institutions of higher education by the UGC and bodies like the ICSSR, ICHR and NCERT resulted in generating a new understanding and analysis of women's problems and academic research on women's issues.

The twin movements—the women's movement and women's studies movement—found allies in the media, in the academia and even in the bureaucracy, as well outside the country, all of which helped to strengthen the movements.

Civil Society and the State

India being a democracy, there has been, on the whole, a symbiotic and mutually complementary relationship between the government and the women's movement. The women's movement in India continually interacts with the government and influences public opinion and government action. From its inception, the women's movement looked for support to the state in its efforts to pass progressive legislation. Pressure created by social reformers and later women's organisations enabled or compelled the state to pass laws, which were aimed at removing injustices against women. The process began with the anti-*sati* campaign led by Raja Rammohan Roy in the 1820s which led to the Sati Prohibition Act in 1829, the Widow Remarriage Act of 1856, the pressure for which was initiated by Ishwarchandra Vidyasagar, the efforts of Behramji Malabari which led to the raising of the Age of Consent of Marriage in 1892, the Sarda Act of 1929 for raising the age of marriage and so on. The first phase of the women's movement concentrated on three issues; child marriage, enforced widowhood and property rights.

When there was a coincidence of interests between the political elites and the women's movement, the demands were readily accepted, where there was a divergence of interests, the campaign had to be of a longer duration. While the suffragist campaign was long and bitter in the United States and Great Britain, in India, women got the right to vote fairly easily because of the support they obtained from the leaders of the Indian National Congress and other political parties and because the principle had been accepted in UK. The Hindu Code Bill aroused a bitter debate but its passage became ultimately possible because of the support of Jawaharlal Nehru, the Prime Minister and Dr. B.R. Ambedkar, the Law Minister.

The Government of India in 1953 established a Central Social Welfare Board with a nationwide programme of grant-in-aid for promoting welfare and development services for women and children and under privileged groups. These government programmes, on the one hand, encouraged the growth of a large number of women's organisations and on the other, provided status and position to many of the erstwhile active women social or political workers. A large number of Mahila Mandals were set up during this period.

The series of liberal and progressive laws affecting women that have been enacted by the Indian state since 1976 are the outcome of the struggle of women's groups, gender-sensitive lawyers and democratic rights groups. Although the Indian Constitution recognised the principle of equal pay for equal work and India ratified the ILO Equal Remuneration Convention, 1951 (No.100) which required the ratifying countries to promote the application of the principle of equal remuneration for work of equal worth regardless of sex, as early as 1958, the Government of India promulgated the Equal Remuneration Ordinance in September 1975, which subsequently became in 1976 the Equal Remuneration Act. The Act provided for no discrimination on the ground of sex at the time of employment carried on by or under the authority of the Central government.

In 1978, the Law Commission introduced a highly controversial bill regarding marriage laws recommending the introduction of 'the irretrievable breakdown of marriage' as a ground of divorce. This also provided safeguards for women by empowering the courts to direct the husband to pay maintenance and alimony to his divorced wife. Unfortunately this bill did not take the form of an Act because of the opposition it aroused from certain sections.

As discussed above, the nationwide anti-rape movement during 1980 forced the government after three years of heated debate to pass the Criminal Law (Second Amendment) Act of 1983 according to which custodial rape had to be punished severely putting the burden of proof onto the rapist. The increasingly reported cases of dowry deaths and the effective lobbying by women's organisations pressurised the government to set up the Joint Committee of both Houses of Parliament in 1980 which submitted its report in 1982 and in 1984 the Dowry Prohibition Amendment Act was passed. The Criminal Law (Second Amendment) Act, 1983, made some crucial amendments concerning women in the Indian Penal Code, the Code of Criminal Procedure and the Indian Evidence Act. As per this Act, cruelty in terms of mental and physical torture, abetment to suicide of a woman by her husband or husband's relatives can be punished with imprisonment for a term up to three years and be liable to fine. This

Act also provides for a thorough enquiry by the police officer of a death of a woman within seven years of her marriage. The police officer is also empowered to order a post-mortem of the dead body to be made in such cases.

In 1984 the government conceded the demand of women to establish family courts for the speedy conduct of matrimonial disputes. It also authorised the court to seek the help of social workers, specialists, psychologists, and recognised institutions for recording disputes.

The national machinery set up after 1975 to develop policies and programmes for women consisted of a national committee, an inter-departmental coordination committee and a women's welfare and development bureau. In 1984, a special Ministry for Women and Social Welfare was formed at the Centre.

The interaction between the women's organisations and the government is also evident from the dialogue between the former and the members of the Planning Commission, particularly during the formulation of the Sixth plan, as discussed below.

Five-Year Plans

The Planning Commission defined three major areas in which they paid special attention to women's development—education, health and social welfare. The First plan (1951-1956) was informed by the vision of women's welfare. The plan document had taken notice of organisational apparatus on the part of the Central and state governments for promoting the welfare of women. However, it expected private agencies like the All India Women's Conference, National Council of Women, Young Women's Christian Association, Girl Guides Association, the Kasturba Gandhi National Memorial Trust, etc., to undertake the welfare programmes for women.

The Second plan (1956-1961) continued the welfare approach. It was explicitly concerned about the issues of social and moral hygiene and provision of after care services. It recognised women as 'workers' and their specific handicaps as industrial workers. Providing training facilities, maternity benefits, crèche for children and possibility of increasing part-time employment were included.

The Third plan (1961-1966) emphasised the expansion of education for girls and the Fourth (1966-1971) once again stressed women's education and allowed voluntary agencies to operate programmes of social welfare. The Fifth plan (1975-1980), which covered the first five years of the Women's Decade, gave priority to women and development projects and to income generating activity for rural women. Following the submission of the Report of the Committee on the Status of Women, a National Plan of Action was formulated and three working groups were set up on employment of women, adult education and village level organisation of rural women. The Ministry of Agriculture appointed a committee to look into women's marginalisation in the rural economy.

The Draft Sixth Five-Year Plan admitted that the benefits of education had failed to reach the majority of people. When the Sixth plan (1980-1985) was being formulated, there was some concern among women activists, academicians and even women administrators, that all the homework women's groups had done over the last three years would be wasted as women were mentioned only six times in the document, all in connection with education, health and welfare. There was not a word about employment. They did not want to waste the strategising of the three previous years and so decided to contact the women's organisations. As a result, all the major women's organisations were called for a discussion on women's issues in the forthcoming Five-Year Plan. Initially, they had been rather dubious, as they feared that women's organisations had never thought about five-year plans. But they felt that it was high time that they did so. So a meeting was called.

All the organisations agreed to intervene. It was at this meeting held on 10 September 1980 that a unique partnership of groups called the Seven Sisters was born. The organisations were the YWCA (of India), All India Women's Conference (AIWC), National Federation of Indian Women (NFIW)—which was the front of the Communist Party of India (CPI), the All India Democratic Women's Association (AIDWA)—the women's front of the Communist Party Marxist (CPM), the Joint Women's Programme (JWP—which was a grouping of mostly Christian women with mild political leanings), the Mahila Dakshita Samiti (with distinct socialist leanings) and the Centre for Women's Development Studies (CWDS), a research institute funded by ICSSR. This rainbow coalition represented virtually all different shades of political opinion, as well as political parties in the country. The Seven Sisters functioned as the collective voice of the second phase of the women's movement in India and played an important role in pressurising the Government of India into bringing policy changes in employment, health, population and education.

Aruna Asaf Ali belonging to the old generation of freedom fighters was present at this meeting. She suggested that they should talk to someone in the Planning Commission. Dr. Vina Mazumdar contacted Dr. M.S. Swaminathan, Deputy Chairman of the Planning Commission and told him that the women's organisations wanted a discussion with him on the Plan. He agreed to come to the meeting. Dr. Ashok Mitra, ICS, was put in the chair and through the morning the discussion went on. By the end of the day, the women were all angry. The outpouring of rage had made it an extraordinary meeting. It was finally agreed that all the concrete suggestions made at this meeting would be placed before the Planning Commission.

The document eventually prepared, which Sarojini Varadappan from AIWC undertook to print, was entitled, *Indian Women in the Eighties, Development Imperatives*. It was sent to the Prime Minister and to every ministry, the Planning Commission, etc., and it marked the start of a new consultative process with the GoI, particularly the Planning Commission.[26]

The Planning Commission held two or three meetings where Vina Mazumdar and Sushila Gopalan, a Member of Parliament, were present and they argued their case vehemently. If the women's organisations had not intervened, the chapter on Women and Development, the first in a five-year plan, would not have been included, nor would resources been allocated for this. The Sixth plan made some departures from the earlier plans in so far that it recognised women as a special category requiring urgent attention in developing strategies. It also stated that early marriage, repeated pregnancies with resulting poor health and lack of opportunities for personal development create the vicious trap in which a large number of women are caught. A positive contribution of the Sixth plan was the decision that henceforth the government will endeavour to give joint titles to husband and wife for all asset transfers such as house sites, land redistribution or facilities in economic generation or subsidies programme. It accepted the criticism that in the past, asset transfers to alleviate poverty had in fact intensified intra-household inequalities, as title credit is largely tied to land ownership. The Plan also emphasised women's employment to further their economic independence and emancipation. Acceptance of the concept of *balwadis* and crèches attached to schools—to free young girls from surrogate mother roles—and to project sites and residential colonies to enable women to participate in economic activities more freely was another important development. The Sixth plan recognised the importance of creating awareness among planners and development administrators at all levels regarding the real constraints facing women in reaping the benefits of development.

When exercises began for formulating the Plan, working groups were formed in which women were involved. For instance, the working group on employment of women included government representatives, researchers and persons from women's organisations. Successive plans have made some shifts in their policies regarding women's issues and have to a certain extent been influenced by the views of women's organisations. For example, when they protested against the family being recognised as the basic unit of development on the ground that, in doing so, planners were lumping together the least well off and better off within the household. In response to this adverse reaction, the planners attempted a compromise. Although the family was retained as the basic unit of development, attention was focussed on women as the most vulnerable members within the family. The planners began to acknowledge that economic betterment with social support was necessary if women were to benefit from economic development programmes. The plans started revealing a greater awareness of the realities of poor women's situation. Addressing the meeting of the National Development Council in 1980, Indira Gandhi said, 'Special attention must be given to Harijans and tribals, to women and our minorities. They must be enabled to live and work in safety and in dignity.'[27]

Education

Education has been seen to be a significant instrument in improving women's status and consequently right from the 19th century social reformers as well as nationalist leaders emphasised its importance. The framers of India's Constitution viewed education as an instrument of social change, individual mobility and social equality. Article 45 enjoins that the state shall endeavour to provide within a period of 10 years from the commencement of the Constitution, free and compulsory education to all children until they complete the age of 14. This constitutional obligation had been time and again deferred successively into 1970, 1980, 1990, 2000 and 2010. Article 15(3) makes a special provision enabling the state to take affirmative action in favour of women and children and Article 15(a) and (c) impose a fundamental duty on every citizen to renounce practices derogatory to women. Indira Gandhi as Prime Minister and the Indian National Congress in its manifestos continually emphasised the importance of women's education.

The first sector of education to receive attention after independence was higher education. The Indian Universities Commission (1948-49) headed by Dr. S. Radhakrishnan, reflected the persistent ambivalence between the traditional view, which supports women's education to equip them to become better wives and mothers and the modern view, which visualises education as an instrument of equality and development. It asserted that, 'Women's present education is entirely irrelevant to the life they have to lead. It is not only a waste but often a disability...The present system of women's education, based as it is upon men's needs, does not in any way make them fit for coping with the problems of daily life...The modern educated Indian woman is neither happy nor contended, nor socially useful. She is a misfit in life. She is highly suppressed and needs opportunities for self-expression. The new education must provide these opportunities.'[28]

Deriving lessons from the above report, the First Five-Year Plan stated, 'Everyone realizes the significance of the problem of women's education in the special circumstances of our country today and the need for adopting special measures for solving it. The general purpose and objective of women's education cannot of course be different from the purpose and objective of men's education. There are, however, vital differences in the way in which this purpose has to be realized.'[29] The First plan coincided with the appointment of the Secondary Education Commission headed by A. Mudaliar. Differing from the Radhakrishnan Commission, which sought to differentiate between the education of girls and boys, the Mudaliar Commission held that, 'In a democratic society where all citizens have to discharge their civic and social obligations, differences which may lead to variations in the standard of intellectual development achieved by boys and girls cannot be encouraged.'[30] The Second plan emphasised the need for creating public awareness on the importance of girls' education.

In 1958, a committee was appointed under the chairmanship of Durgabai Deshmukh to deal exclusively with women's education. It recommended that more funds should be allotted to girls' primary education, a national council for girls' and women's education be set up and that a special unit dealing with girls' education be created in the Ministry of Education. State governments were asked to take greater interest and enlist the cooperation of voluntary organisations and the public in the promotion of women's education. It suggested a campaign to remove the traditional prejudices against women's education, appoint women teachers, establish separate schools for girls, if required, provision of free books, writing material, uniforms and construction of hostels for girls.[31]

In 1963, a Committee on Differentiation of Curriculum for Boys and Girls proposed a common curriculum up to the primary stage. It recommended a core curriculum of home science for both boys and girls at the middle stage and inclusion of crafts or handiwork or productive work in the general courses at the secondary level.[32] A year later, the Bhaktavatsalam Committee was appointed to look into the causes for lack of public support, particularly in rural areas, for girls' education and to enlist public cooperation.

The Indian Education Commission, under the chairmanship of Dr. D.S. Kothari, (1964-1966) fully endorsed the recommendations of the

Durgabai Deshmukh Committee and observed that the role of women outside the home had become an important feature of Indian life. It said that, 'education of women should be regarded as a major programme for some years to come and bold and determined effort should be made to face difficulties involved and to close the existing gap between the education of men and women in as short a time as possible...'[33] The National Education Policy Resolution of 1968 rejected a gender differentiated approach to the content of education and stated that, 'the education of girls should receive emphasis not only on the grounds of social justice but also because it accelerated social transformation'.[34]

Despite all these Commissions and their recommendations, the Committee on the Status of Women (1971-1974) found that in the Census of 1971, about 68 percent women in the age group 15-25 and 87 percent of women in the age group 25 years and above was illiterate. In classes I to V, one out of three girls in age group 6-11 was out of school and only one girl out of every five in age group 11-14 was in school. The drop out rate among girls was higher than that among boys. Out of every 100 girls enrolled in class I, only about 30 reached class V. The committee recommended a common curriculum for boys and girls, pre-school education, coeducation, part-time education for girls who could not attend full time, free education for girls up to the secondary stage and multi-entry for girls among other things.

The Sixth plan admitted that the benefits of education had not reached the majority of people. The Sixth plan emphasised the eradication of illiteracy, universal primary education and job-oriented courses. It said that efforts should be directed towards enrollment and retention of girls in schools, income generating activities for girls outside school hours for supplementing the family income, increase in the number of female teachers, etc

Female literacy rate has, no doubt, increased since independence. In 1951, it was 7.9 percent in 1961, 13 percent in 1971, 18.70 percent and in 1981, 24.81 percent in 1991. Kerala has consistently had the highest rate and Arunachal Pradesh, Bihar, UP and Rajasthan the lowest. There has been a spectacular growth in the number of schools, colleges, universities and enrollment in them. Girls' enrollment has increased faster than that of boys but the drop out rate of girls is also higher. In 1985-86, while 60.70 percent boys dropped out between classes I-VIII, 70.04 girls dropped out. The reasons for this are well known. Poverty compels girls to help with household work such as cooking, fetching water and fuel, looking after younger siblings, as well as earn an extra income by working outside the home. Early marriage is also a deterrent. Schools often do not have toilets. Poor facilities in government schools, teacher absenteeism, irrelevant curriculum and dim prospects of employment after schooling all contribute to girls leaving school early.

A strong sex bias was noticed in school textbooks. In order to address this problem, NCERT along with the A.N. Sinha Institute of Social Science sponsored a national seminar in 1975 on 'Identification of Values Commensurate with Status of Women' for incorporation in school textbooks. Since then continuous efforts have been made by NCERT to remove sex bias from schoolbooks and the curricula and gender-sensitise teachers.

The higher education system has also grown steadily since independence. From 35 universities in 1947 and 700 colleges for general and professional education (1951), there were nearly 200 universities by the 1980s. There was only one women's university, the SNDT, at the time of Independence, by the 1990s, there were five women's universities and 800 colleges catering to about 50 percent of girls enrolled in higher education. Though the total number of girls enrolled in science and technology has increased, the percentage has not significantly changed.

The only professional course considered suitable for women earlier were teaching, nursing medicine and law. Today, there are innumerable professional and vocational courses available to girls ranging from management, computer science, information technology, mass communications, fashion technology, architecture, etc. A recent study by the University Grants Commission on 'Women and Research' spanning the six decades since Independence shows that more and more women are opting for professional courses once considered 'masculine' in place of disciplines like teaching and the arts. Instead of Bachelors in Arts and B.Eds, women are going for Bachelors in Engineering, LLB and M.Com, apart from pure science. But this is truer of girls from the more affluent urban middle class families[35].

While access to schools, enrollment and retention are important; the content of education is equally crucial. Education must improve women's skills so that they are not confined to low-paid and semi-skilled jobs. It must also give the girl child a positive self-image and build up her self-confidence. Textbooks have to reflect these values and teachers as well as administrators in schools and universities have to be gender-sensitised. Investment in women's education shows useful returns as it has a positive impact in improving women's health care, immunisation, reducing infant and maternal mortality, lowering the birth rate and raising the age of marriage. But education is also important as it enriches a women's personality and gives her greater self-confidence, economic independence and ability to take part in decision-making. Education opens up new horizons, creates new opportunities and empowers women.

Women and Work

There are many who would argue that the key to women's status is their economic position. Regardless of the indices consulted—ownership of land, control of resources, wages earned, food consumed, access to medical care or sex ratio—Indian women are not the equal of men. Economic independence, the ability to earn one's livelihood is a means to empowerment!

The Constitution of India had proclaimed certain far-reaching concepts to promote equality and prevent sex discrimination. This was long before the various ILO and UN conventions to promote equality and prevent sex discrimination were adopted. And yet, the continued deeply entrenched existence of sex discrimination at the Indian workplace reflects what Justice Krishna Iyer described as 'the distance between Constitution in the Book and Law in Action'.[36]

Article 14 of the Constitution guarantees equality before law. Article 15 prohibits discrimination on grounds of sex. Article 16 ensures equality of opportunity in matters relating to employment. Article 39 guarantees equal pay for equal work. Article 42 says that it is the duty of the state to provide maternity benefit. Despite these constitutional guarantees, on the ground women have faced discrimination as is illustrated by the following three instances. While women were allowed to join the Indian Foreign Service, they were required to take permission before marrying. The government also had the right to ask any married woman officer to resign if it was felt that her family responsibilities would interfere with her efficiency. Married women were denied employment. In 1979, C.B Muthamma, India's first woman IFS officer, filed a writ petition in the Supreme Court that these rules violated Articles 14 and 16 of the Constitution. As soon as the petition was filed, the government itself withdrew the rules. The second much publicised case was that of the air-hostesses of Air India and Indian Airlines in 1981. They were fighting against discriminatory service conditions and demanding parity with the male cabin crew. They won some gains but lost out on other issues. The third case was in 1983 when the Kerala High Court held that denial of jobs to women in class IV government service was discriminatory and unconstitutional.

India is one of the developing countries where women's participation in the workforce continues to remain quite low, both in absolute and relative terms. According to the Census of 1971, after careful standardisation of the definition of 'worker' the female work participation rate (FWPR) in India dropped from 28 percent in 1961 to 14.2 percent in 1971 and rose to 21 percent in 1981 Census. Thus, a little more than one fourth of women in India participate in the work force. It is important to add, however, that FWPR varies considerably not only across states in India but also between regions and social groups within states as well. While Mizoram and Himachal Pradesh have a high FWPR, Kerala and UP have low rates. FWPRs are consistently higher in rural than urban areas.

Occupation wise agriculture is the major field for women's employment in rural areas with about 87 percent of the economically active women engaged in this category in 1971 and 1981 although the economically active were only 11 and 14 percent of the rural female population in these two census years.[37]

While the number of educated women who are employed outside the home has no doubt risen since independence the number is surprisingly small. The work participation rate of urban women is significantly lower than that of rural women and that of literate women significantly lower than that of illiterate women.

The majority of Indian women work in the unorganised or informal sector. In Gujarat, what was probably the first attempt at a women's trade union was made in Ahmedabad by Gandhian socialists attached to the Textile Labour Union (TLA) founded by Mahatma Gandhi. Formed in 1972 at the initiative of Ela Bhatt, who worked in the women's wing of TLA, the Self-Employed Women's Association (SEWA) was an organisation of women who worked in different trades in the informal sector, but shared a common experience of extremely low earnings, very poor working conditions, harassment from those in authority and lack of recognition of their work as socially useful labour. The aims of SEWA were to improve the conditions of work through training, technical aids and collective bargaining, as well as to 'introduce the members to the values of honesty, dignity and simplicity of life goals reflecting the Gandhian ideals to which TLA and SEWA subscribe'.

SEWA's first cooperative, a credit society formed through the collective efforts of 4,000 women, who contributed Rs.10 per share in 1974 is now a full-fledged flourishing cooperative bank. Mahila SEWA Bank, the first women's bank of its kind in the country, works with and for poor, illiterate, self-employed women.

A number of NGOs have shifted their agenda from simple literacy classes towards programme of self-help through which women could acquire skill and get gainful employment and financial independence. They have started functioning in villages where women's groups are formed and their activities included literacy classes, health training, programmes to prevent female infanticide and campaign against child marriage, illicit *arrack,* dowry and violence against women.

The visionary microcredit movement led by Muhammad Yunus in Bangladesh aimed at removing the disadvantages from which women suffer because of the discriminatory treatment in the rural credit market, by making a special effort to provide credit to women borrowers. In India also the formation of self-help groups (SHGs) has encouraged women to save and take loans to start small entrepreneurial ventures. Teaching poor rural and urban women new skills, upgrading their existing skills, facilitating their access to loans and giving them information about marketing are means by which women can be moved out of poverty.

Women's Health

Women's health status is basic to their advancement in all fields. While women's health has been a key area for state intervention, in the initial years after independence, the emphasis was on reproductive health and family planning. The family planning programme was launched with the objective among others, of improving the health of the mother, the care of the child, economic stability of the family, reducing the birth rate to the extent necessary to stabilise the population at a level consistent with the requirements of the national economy. Maternal care, antenatal, prenatal and postnatal care of mother and child, together with nutrition and immunisation received some attention. These measures contributed to a decline in the death rate bringing it down to 19.0 percent during the decade 1961-1971.

The Family Planning Association of India was functioning actively but was officially registered in October 1954 with Lady Rama Rao as President, Mithan Lam as Vice President and Avabai Wadia as General Secretary. The Indian branch of the International Planned Parenthood Foundation was established at the Third International Conference of Planned Parenthood, which met in Bombay in 1952 and was inaugurated by Dr. S. Radhakrishnan who was then Vice President of India and Jawaharlal Nehru sent a message.

During the 1970s, the Government took a number of steps to improve the health of women. Primary health centres and sub-centres were expanded throughout the country. During 1975-76, the Integrated Child Development Services (ICDS) was launched.

Research has shown that in India the girl child suffers from discrimination in terms of nutrition and medical care. Her poor health status is further exacerbated with early marriage and child bearing. Due to discrimination from birth, unequal access to health care, socio-cultural and economic conditions and lack of autonomy regarding health, women have high mortality and morbidity rates.

Despite the various schemes and measures taken by the government in these 20 years, women's health continues to be a cause of major concern. Unfortunately data regarding maternal mortality in our country is not very reliable. According to a UNICEF Report of 1984, maternal mortality in India ranged between 376 to 418 per 1,00,000 live births in 1970-1972. Corresponding figures for Sweden (1979), USA (1978) and UK (1980) were reported to be 1, 10 and 11 respectively. Unlike in developed countries where male death rate exceeds female death rates (maternal mortality rate, MMR), in India, death rates of women in the reproductive period exceed those of men in corresponding ages. Low longevity of women, high infant mortality rates (IMR) and high birth rate are hallmarks of poor social development. The concern for the reduction of MMR and IMR by the Government dates back to the Bhore Committee Report (1943) and the Mudaliar Committee Report (1961), which laid emphasis on nutrition, health education, maternal and child health, among other health issues. The maternal and child health programmes outlined in the various five-year plans are based mainly on the Bhore Committee Report.

Life expectancy for women, which was 40.55 per 1000 of the population in 1961, rose to 55.7 in 1981-1985. Death rate of girls in the age group 0-4 declined from 55.1 per 1000 population to 40.4 in 1985. Death rate of women in all ages declined from 15.6 per 1000 population in 1970 to 11.8 in 1985. Despite these improvements, the fact that after six five-year plans, we were still plagued in 1985 with massive problems of ill health and undernutrition of women and children implied that the measure taken were not enough and a great deal had still to be done for women's health.

Conclusion

Twenty years is a short period in the history of a country but the years between 1964 and 1984 were crucial in the struggle for women's rights in India and globally. As discussed above, during these decades conscious efforts were made to understand the specific problems of women and systematic attempts to create awareness of these problems among women in particular and citizens in general was made all over the world.

The International Women's Decade, which began in Mexico in 1975, ended with the Second World Conference on Women in Nairobi in 1985 to review and appraise the achievements of the UN Decade for Women. From the last quarter of 1984, a series of meetings and seminars were held in India to appraise the achievements and limitations of the women's movement. A workshop was organised under the auspices of the AIWC, YWCA and NFWI, which were attended by about 175 delegates from different organisations all over India. Copies of the report were submitted to the Prime Minister and Minister of State,

Ministry of Social Welfare and Women's Welfare. SNDT, Mumbai also organised a workshop. A 12-member official delegation from India led by Maratha Chandrasekhar, Union Minister of State for Social Welfare attended the Nairobi Conference where 370 delegates from 158 countries were present. A parallel NGO Conference was organised where over 14,000 women came from all over the world. The hall could accommodate only 6,000, as the organisers had not expected so many delegates. Five hundred had attended the first Conference in Mexico and 8,000 the Mid-Term Review Conference in Copenhagen in 1980. The overwhelming response showed the growing interest in women's issues. The Nairobi Conference computed the gains and losses of the past decade and came out with a document—The Forward Looking Strategies.

While these two decades created a growing interest in women's issues both among academics and activists in India, they also highlighted the obstacles in the path of women's development. In terms of numbers, few women were involved and the impact of the movement should not be exaggerated. Despite the long history of women's struggle, the majority of Indian women were still illiterate, lacked basic health care, nutrition, employment opportunities, safe drinking water, sanitation; they faced discrimination and violence within the family and outside. Thus women still had a hard and long way to go to achieve the goal of equality.

Endnotes

1. Gandhi, M.K. (1921). *Young India*, 15 December.
2. Ibid, 10 April, 1930.
3. Murdoch, J. (comp.) (1898). *Twelve Years of India's Progress, Extracted from the Indian National Congress: The Resolutions of its Thirteen Sessions*. Madras. p. 36.
4. Basu, Aparna (1974). "The Role of Women in the Indian Struggle for Freedom" in B.R. Nanda (ed.), *Indian Women: From Purdah to Modernity*. New Delhi: Vikas.
5. Gandhi, M.K., *The Role of Women*, (ed.) by Anand Hingorani.
6. Nehru, Jawaharlal (1982). *Discovery of India*. p. 41.
7. Speech during the third reading of the Hindu Marriage Bill, 5 May 1955. Lok Sabha Debates 1955, Vol. IV, Part II.
8. *Selected Works of Jawaharlal Nehru*, (SWJN), Vol. 8.
9. SWJN, Vol. 8.
10. Zaidi, A.M. (ed.), *Election Manifestos*.
11. Basu, Aparna, Mridula Sarabhai (1998). *Rebel With A Cause*. OUP.
12. Kaur, Amrit. 'A Friend Without Friends', in R. Zakaria, (ed.), *A Study of Nehru*.

13. Zaidi, A.M. (ed.) (1983). *The Encyclopaedia of the Indian National Congress,* Vol.19. 1965-67. New Delhi: S. Chand & Co.
14. Idem.
15. Zaidi, A.M. (ed.) (1984). *The Encyclopaedia of the Indian National Congress,*Vol. 20, 1970-71, *The Split and the Aftermath.* New Delhi: S. Chand & Co.
16. Zaidi, A.M. (ed.) (1987). *The Encyclopedia of the Indian National Congress.* Vol. 26: 1983-1985, Full Circle, New Delhi: S. Chand & Co.
17. GoI (1974). "Towards Equality", Report of The Committee on the Status of Women in India, New Delhi, Ministry of Education and Social Welfare. p.xii.
18. Ibid: 359.
19. Kumar, Radha (1993). *History of Doing: An Illustrated Account of movements for Women's Rights.* Kali for Women.
20. GoI (1984). *Selected Speeches and Writings of Indira Gandhi,* Vol.III, September 1972-1977. New Delhi: The Director of Publications Division, Ministry of Information and Broadcasting. p.481.
21. Ibid: 525.
22. Ibid: 605-6.
23. Ibib: 606.
24. Ibid: 719.
25. GoI (1985). *Selected Speeches and Writings of Indira Gandhi,* Volume IV, January 1980-December 1981, The Director of Publications Division, Ministry of Information and Broadcasting, p. 416.
26. Mazumdar, Vina (2010). *Memories of a Rolling Stone.* New Delhi, Zubaan. pp. 105-107.
27. *Selected Speeches and Writings of Indira Gandhi, Vol.IV, op.cit.* p. 230.
28. Report of the Universities Commission, (1948). p. 394.
29. Govt. of India (1951). *The First Five-Year Plan,* Chapter xxxiii, Para 102, p. 357.
30. Govt. of India (1953). *Report of the Secondary Education Commission,* Chapter iv, p. 56.
31. Govt. of India (1959). *Report of the National Committee on Women's Education,* Chapter XVI.
32. Govt. of India (1964). *Report of the Committee on the Differentiation of Curricula for Boys and Girls,* Chapter IV.
33. The Indian Education Commission Report, (1964-1966).
34. Govt. of India (1966). The National Policy Resolution on Education.
35. *Indian Express,* May 17, 2010.
36. Balasubramanyan, Vimal (1985). "Biology and Gender Bias, Some Issues in Discrimination against Women at the Work Place", *EPW* xx(20): 876. May 18.
37. Ghosh, Bahnisikha and Sudhir K. Mukhopadhyay (1984). "Displacement of the Female in the Indian Labour Force", *EPW* xix(47): 1008. November 24.

Chapter XII

The Environmental Challenge 1947-1984

Challenges to the Polity

Shekhar Singh[1]

Essentially this paper is an attempt to document and analyse the evolution of environmental policy and its implementation by the Congress Party while it was in power at the national level in India. The paper specifically covers the period from 1947 to 1984.

Preamble

Though the paper only deals with the post-independence period, in order to place the approach of the national government towards the environment in its proper perspective, there has to be at least a cursory understanding of traditional environmental practices, and environmental policy and its implementation in the colonial period prior to independence. Towards this end and for the purpose of this paper, Indian environmental history is divided into three phases, pre-colonial (before the advent of the British), colonial, and post independence.

The Pre-Colonial Era

Much before the birth of the Congress Party, or of the modern nation states and the centralised systems of governance that we know today, India had a rich history of environmental consciousness. However, given the scope and purpose of this paper, only a very brief and general account of this period is attempted here.

Pre-colonial India, compared with much else of the world at that time, was marked by a very complex attitude towards nature and a relatively sophisticated system for the management and conservation of nature and natural resources. Nature was, for the most part, feared, worshipped and revered, wilderness areas were variously considered to be the abodes of Gods, of the souls of ancestors, and of evil spirits.

Among the strategies adopted for its conservation were the recognition of sacred sites, where there were restrictions for exploitation, desecration and sometimes even of entry. Certain species were recognised as sacred and treated accordingly, and other species had taboos attached to them.

> Stretching into prehistoric times, the concept of the sacred grove in India has its roots in antiquity, even before the era of the Vedas which presents the only recorded remains of the thoughts of the ancient Aryans who migrated into the sub-continent. In their migration from the steppes of Central Asia, through Balkh in Khorassan[2] to the Indian sub-continent, the ancient Vedic people of prehistoric times assimilated new environmental values system of the original inhabitants of the Indian sub-continent.[3] Though many traditional societies value a large number of plants species from the wild for a variety of reasons such as for food or medicine, sacredness attached to species in Indian is perhaps a more recent aspect of post-Vedic Hindu rituals. Thus the existing concept of sacred groves at the landscape or ecosystem level of the original pre-Vedic inhabitants of India was interpreted by the migrants of the Vedic age down to the level of particular species.
>
> Buddhism and Jainism, which initially branched out as revivalistic off shoots of Hinduism,[4] also led to a renewal in practices with conservation value. One branch of this religious revival was the creation of a sect of Jains (the Digambara Jains) implacably set against killing any living organism. Another branch was the concept of the 'sacred landscape' represented by the holistic ecological philosophy of Sikkimese Buddhists. (Ramakrishnan, 1996)

It is a moot question whether the ecological value of conserving certain sites was recognised by the wise people of that time and the depiction of sacredness followed as the most effective way of conserving these areas, or whether fear and awe of nature was primordial and the consequent strategies just an ecologically fortunate option. Most likely, it was a bit of both!

However, lest the impression be created that all conservation imperatives were based on a fear of the supernatural (with roots in superstition), it is important to note that there were numerous community practices recorded from all over India that clearly showed a concern for the sustainable use of natural resources. There was also public participation in the management of common resources, of a kind that is almost impossible to find today, except in a few isolated tribal areas.

Pre-colonial India was also characterised by an extraordinary public compassion for animals—even those species that often attacked human beings and their crops and livestock. There was also a concern for public and personal hygiene and especially for the integrity of drinking water sources: something that unfortunately became imbedded into the repressive caste system prevalent in India.

The Colonial Era

The British brought in an entirely different approach towards nature. By the time they came to India, much of the natural forests in Britain had already been destroyed and most of their large mammals had become extinct. They saw the natural resources of India as a renewed opportunity to carry on, with a few modifications, the policies and practices of exploiting natural resources that had helped them to become a world power, albeit while depleting their own forests and wildlife.

The British replaced the traditional systems of managing nature and natural resources with an extractive ethos and a centralised management system, with a stress on selective regeneration of commercially valuable timber species, stocking of hunting and fishing compartments, and 'scientific' management and classification.

The evolution of the traditional Indian methods of conserving nature and natural resources was thus interrupted by the British and especially by their setting up a forest department in India in 1864[5], and enacting the Indian Forest Act in 1865[6], soon to be replaced by a more comprehensive act in 1878, and finally the Indian Forest Act of 1927, that survives till today.

The Impact of Technology

Arguably, with the growth of forest based industries new systems of managing the forests had to be developed. Also, with the rapid growth of technology, new and more effective methods of accessing (and destroying) forest resources became available and had to be put to use. The progress from hand-held stone tools, to the axe and then to the hand saw, the pit saw, the power saw, right up to bull-dozers and specially designed machinery that could clear hundreds of hectares of forests in a day, had an inevitable impact on the time frame, the quantum and the economics of extracting timber and other natural resources.

Similarly, implements for hunting went through a rapid transformation, especially with the invention of gunpowder and of precision rifles, and finally machine guns and explosives.

As technology grows in a sociopolitical ethos and not in isolation, the nature of colonialism encouraged the growth of technology designed to destroy nature and extract natural resources, without the concomitant growth of technology aimed at protecting and regenerating nature. Unfortunately, even after the colonial bond was broken, nature remained external to the politico-economic systems and continued to be treated as a free commodity.

Institutional Structure for the 'Management' of Nature

With the setting up of a forest department, the forests also began to be viewed more as a source of raw material, especially timber for the construction of ships and railway tracks, rather than as sacred sites or sustainable sources of raw materials for local communities. An element of 'scientific' forestry was introduced, mainly to increase the production of commercially valuable timber species (like the Indian teak) often at the cost of other 'less valuable' species. Large tracts of forests were converted into single species plantations, invariably with an adverse impact on other species and on the biodiversity.

The Indian Forest Act of 1878 prescribed a process by which rights of local people over the forests that were now being appropriated were recorded and either allowed, settled, or extinguished. Though at least for a while this meant that all access of the people to forest resources was not denied, in most parts of the country only land owners were considered to have rights over forests. Besides, even in those forests where people were allowed to retain their rights, all the existing rights were not allowed.

Wildlife

As the British settler's population increased in India, there was also an increasing demand for *shikar* or animals to hunt, the most prized among them being the tiger, unique to Asia, followed by the lion, the cheetah, and the elephant. The one horned Indian rhinoceros were also hunted, as were 'edible' species of deer, antelope, wild boar, pheasants, fowls, and partridges, among others.

Fishing was also a favourite 'sport' of the British, and there was an increasing demand for well stocked fishing streams, especially with preferred species like *mahasheer*. Even exotics, like the trout, were introduced into the rivers and streams of India as preferred 'game fish'.

Though, from all accounts, wildlife was plentiful during the early 1800s, by the dawn of the 20th century there was a marked decline in populations of the preferred game species, especially large mammals. Accordingly, from the early 1900s the British started setting up a network of sanctuaries and game reserves, culminating into the passing of the Hailey National Park Act of UP in 1936, by which the Hailey (later renamed Corbett) National Park was created in the then United Provinces. Subsequently, similar laws were passed in Madhya Pradesh, Maharashtra and Assam.

The British also seemed to have inspired the princely rulers in India, many of whom took to the British way of hunting, which essentially involved the mass slaughter of animals, mainly for trophies, with each dignitary trying to outdo the others by shooting or catching the biggest, the longest and of course the most. Many of these princes set up their own hunting preserves, like Bharatpur, Sariska, Bandhavgarh, Madhav (Scindia), most of which survive till today, though mercifully now as national parks and sanctuaries, rather than as hunting preserves.

A plethora of laws were passed, ostensibly to protect threatened species, but mainly to ensure that they were only accessible to those who had the patronage of the government. Such laws included the Elephant Preservation Act of 1879, the Wild Birds and Wild Animals (Protection) Act 1912, and the Bengal Rhinoceros Preservation Act of 1932.

Growth of Population

Along with all this bonhomie among the 'sahibs' and the 'brown sahibs', there were other conflicts brewing. The growing population and the demand for increased production of food, especially to support the various wars that the British were perpetually engaged in, meant that the area under agriculture also multiplied drastically. This coincided with British policies aimed at creating a market in India for British industrial goods. By suppressing the indigeneous artisanal sector (and its associated guilds) the British ensured its collapse all over India, and many of the erstwhile artisans lost their markets and were consequently forced back to the land to eke out a living. All this added to the pressure on land, and ultimately on the forests.

The livestock sector was also expanding rapidly. Though accurate national statistics before 1950 are not available, the sense was that the number of livestock, especially cattle, goats and sheep was growing exponentially, with a parallel rise in demand for fodder and grazing areas.

Given the reducing forests, the expanding area under agriculture and the rapidly rising number of livestock, it was not surprising that conflicts between wild animals and the rural population increased, primarily as a result of animal attacks on livestock and people, and because of crop depredation. Interestingly, historical records show that the forest department and the civil administration were very alarmed at this conflict and a host of measures were set in motion to both prevent incidents and pay compensation where such attacks or depredation were not prevented.

On the Eve of Independence

Therefore, by the eve of independence, the British had succeeded in colonising almost all of the forests of India, bringing these under the control of a forest department, regulated by the Indian Forest Act, to be managed 'scientifically' in order to maximise production of commercial species and provide game for hunting. This was done after dismantling most or all of the traditional systems of conservation and management that existed for hundreds of years in much of India, and mainly at the cost of conservation values, especially biodiversity conservation, and to some extent at the cost of the basic needs of the rural people, especially the poor and the landless.

The British had not only damaged our political system, which we could repair after independence, but had also begun to change our relationship with nature and natural resources, a change that we could have arrested at Independence, but failed to do so. This changing relationship, and our reluctance to challenge it, perhaps lost us some of the unique advantages our history and tradition had provided us in the battle to conserve nature and secure a sustainable future while tackling the problems of poverty, starvation and underdevelopment that afflicted us as we gained Independence from British rule.

INDEPENDENT INDIA

Evolution of Environmental Policy in India: 1947-1984

Government policy is the fundamental statement of government perspective and intent regarding various public issues. From policy follows legislation, schemes and programmes, financial allocations, and even institutional structures. However, if one was to seek to understand government policy from only the formal policy statements that the government issues, then much of the actual policy would go unnoticed. Government makes policy statements in many ways, and unfortunately there is no one place where all the elements and nuances of government policy can be easily found, even for one aspect of governance.

Rather than cluttering this paper with numerous references to policies, circulars, Parliamentary speeches and undertakings, affidavits before courts of law, and various other instruments of government that implicitly or explicitly enunciate government policy, it was thought that perhaps the best compilation of government policy is the Five-Year Plan document of the Planning Commission. Though it might not be comprehensive, it almost always contains all the main elements of the policy of the government, with a brief and perhaps rosy description of the practice of these policies during the period under review. Therefore, what follows is an account of the evolution of environmental policy in India through an analysis of the Five-Year Plan documents.

For many years after independence, the only two aspects of what is today thought of as the 'environment sector' that got any attention were forests, and wildlife. These two, however, were viewed as a part of the agricultural sector, perhaps given the predominant preoccupation with 'harvesting', and therefore did not get the kind of attention they deserved. Though even at independence there was, as earlier mentioned, an understanding of the role forests played in regulating water regimes and preventing soil erosion, little else of their contribution to the health of the earth was recognised.

Though the management of other natural resources, especially land and water, should very much have been a central part of the environment agenda, nearly for the first 30 years they were looked at more as an economic resource that needed to be exploited more fully, rather than a natural resource that needed to be conserved and regenerated.

First Five-Year Plan Period (1951-1956)

As already mentioned, when India became independent there was recognition of some of the ecological services that forests played and of their value as a source of raw material for industry. Accordingly, the chapter on forests in the First Five-Year Plan document states:

> Forests play a vital role in India's economy. They are an important source of fuel and also of raw materials, such as, timber, bamboos, lac, gum, katha, useful for domestic, industrial and agricultural purposes. They also provide materials for defence and communications as well as grazing for cattle. Forests help in the conservation of soil fertility and play an important part in the maintenance of the water regime of the land. ... Thus forests protect

> the hilly areas against excessive soil erosion. Similarly, they protect flat lands against desertification and erosion caused by winds. (First Five-Year Plan, Planning Commission, Chapter 21)[7]

However, despite such sentiments in the opening sections of the chapter on forests, the thrust of the plan was on the exploitation of forest 'resources', and the philosophy was clearly enunciated in the first chapter: 'An underdeveloped economy is characterised by the co-existence, in greater or less degree, of unutilised or underutilised manpower on the one hand and of unexploited natural resources on the other.' (Emphasis added; *The Environmental Challenge* 1947-1984; First Five-Year Plan, Planning Commission, Chapter 21; Planning: Economic and Social Aspects)

This tendency of paying lip service to the ecological functions of forests while actually devising schemes and methods for extracting as much timber and 'minor forest produce' as possible, especially for industrial use, and to convert forest land to agriculture, as a part of the 'Grow More Food' programme, was continued in the Second Five-Year Plan.

A new forest policy was announced in 1952, but apart from setting the target of 33 percent forest cover for the country, it added little to the existing policy and practice.

Second Five-Year Plan Period (1956-1961)

The Second plan also saw a mention of the value of wildlife and (as it became subsequently known) biodiversity. The plan document specifically stated that:

> The conservation of wild life is an intergral part of forest management, especially in view of the imperative need for protecting India's rich heritage of wild life, which is now finding its last refuge within the limits of the reserved forests of the country. Such notable animals as the lion and the rhinoceros are in danger of extinction. In order to serve the cause of wild life, forestry programmes in the second plan include the establishment of 18 national parks and game sanctuaries, besides a modem zoological park in Delhi. (Second Five-Year Plan, Planning Commission, Chapter 15).

However, the lack of understanding of what biological diversity really was—the recognition that plants were as much a part of biodiversity (and of wildlife) as animals, especially large mammals, and that the survival of the one was inextricably linked to the other—did not seem to have been understood till then. Earlier in the same chapter, for example, it is lamented that the Indian forests had too many 'inferior' and 'low value' species:

> Reference has already been made to the disadvantages arising from the mixed character of the tropical forests, with the valuable species forming a mere sprinkling in them. This causes serious difficulties in the effective regeneration and management of the mixed forests. In the case of teak, these difficulties could not be overcome in many areas except by resort to clear-felling and artificial regeneration in compact areas. A similar solution will have to be found for the production of wood required for industrial purposes....

Third Five-Year Plan Period (1961-1966)

It was only in the Third plan that there was a mention of the notion of environmental sustainability, though even then from the perspective of extracting forest resources. The plan document, for the first time, had a chapter on natural resources (Chapter 12) that talked mainly about forests but also about the approach to natural resources in general.

> The productivity of India's forests can be greatly increased. Forests are among the few renewable resources in nature which, if properly managed, could go on yielding at undiminished rate and for an indefinite period. There is shortage of timber and fire-wood, of raw materials for drugs, paper and pulp and of fodder for cattle. (Emphasis added; Third Five-Year Plan, Planning Commission, Chapter 12 – Natural Resources).

There was also, for the first time, recognition of the need to conserve both the flora and fauna of the nation. In Chapter 22, on 'Forests and Soil Conservation', the document states:

> Nature conservation is an important aspect of forest development and includes the protection and proper management of indigenous flora and fauna. Where fauna have been greatly depleted due to human interference, animals and birds will be re-introduced. (Emphasis added; Third Five-Year Plan, Planning Commission, Chapter 22 – *Forests and Soil Conservation*)

Fourth Five-Year Plan Period (1969-1974)

In the Fourth plan, for the first time, there was recognition of the dependence of the poor on the forests. In a section titled 'The Problems of Weaker Sections', as a part of the first chapter of the plan document laying out the approach and policy, there is an assertion that the weaker sections of society must be enabled 'to participate in and benefit from the growth of the economy.' The document goes on to state that, 'A similar approach will have to be adopted for the numerous miscellaneous producer classes as of migratory shepherds or those living on the exploitation of forest produce.' (Emphasis added). Perhaps not the most elegant way of putting it, but it was, at the very least, recognition that the forests were critical for the survival of some of the weakest segments of the Indian society.

However, the approach continued to be somewhat paternalistic with an assumption that the rural people needed to be 'educated' about the value of nature and its conservation. A telling prescription reads as follows: 'In the ultimate analysis problems such as those of improving the conditions and status of scheduled castes and tribes or conserving forest wealth or vegetation cover cannot be solved unless local communities understand the significance and importance of national objectives and participate actively in the programmes for their attainment.' (Emphasis added; Fourth Five-Year Plan, Planning Commission, Chapter 1—Approach and Policy)

However, later in the document (Chapter 8), there was again an explicit acknowledgement of the linkage between rural communities and forests. While enunciating the objectives of the forestry sector, the document states that, 'In the sector of forestry, there are three main objectives namely, to increase the productivity of forests, to link up forest development with various forest-based industries and to develop forests as a support to rural economy.' (Emphasis added)

The Fourth plan was also the first plan to acknowledge the overall concern for the environment, which had already been echoing for many years in other parts of the world, especially in the industrialised nations. This being a dramatic change, at least in the rhetoric of Indian policy towards the environment, the section on the 'Quality of Environment', in the chapter on 'The Long Term Perspective' (Chapter 2), is worth quoting in full.

> Most countries face in varying degrees problems of pollution of air and water, erosion of soil, waste of natural resources, derelict lands, loss of wild life, ugly landscape, urban sprawl and city slums—generally a progressive deterioration in the quality of environment. There is growing concern about the matter in India also. A healthy environment is vital for good life. It is an obligation of each generation to maintain the productive capacity of land, air, water and wild life in a manner which leaves its successors some choice in the creation of a healthy environment. The physical environment is a

dynamic, complex and inter-connected system in which any action in one part affects others. There is also the inter-dependence of living things and their relationships with land, air, and water. Planning for harmonious development recognises this unity of nature and man. Such planning is possible only on the basis of a comprehensive appraisal of environmental issues, particularly economic and ecological. There are instances in which timely specialised advice on environmental aspects could have helped in project design and in averting subsequent adverse effects on the environment, leading to loss of invested resources. It is, therefore, necessary to introduce the environmental aspect into our planning and development. Along with effective conservation and rational use of natural resources, protection and improvement of human environment is vital for national well-being. It is particularly important that long-term basic considerations should prevail over short-term commercial considerations, the social costs and benefits be used as the yardstick rather than private gains and losses. At present there is no point in the structure of Government where the environmental aspects receive attention in an integrated manner. Nor are there sufficient numbers of experts who can analyse environmental problems and examine developmental projects from this angle so as to be able to give balanced advice. These deficiencies have to be overcome before any advance can be made. Meanwhile, it is proposed to make arrangements to provide for environmental expertise in teams constituted for planning major projects so that environmental aspects are not left out or misjudged. (Emphasis added)

It might be pertinent to mention here that the UN Conference on the Human Environment was held during the Fourth plan period (1972), in Stockholm. This conference not only focussed the attention of the world and its leaders on the growing environmental crisis, but also on the cost that much of humanity, especially the weaker and poorer among them, had already started paying as a result of environmental degradation. It was also at the Stockholm Conference that Mrs. Indira Gandhi, the then Prime Minister of India, made her famous statement that, 'poverty was the greatest polluter'[8], thereby once and for all altering the tenor of the global debate on the environment, but also, perhaps unintentionally, providing an alibi for continued environmental neglect in India.

During the Fourth plan, various significant initiatives were taken to give effect to the long-term perspective described above. The first was the enactment of the Wildlife (Protection) Act, 1972, and the Water (Prevention and Control of Pollution) Act, 1974. In 1973, the Government of India, with the help of international groups, designed and launched 'Project Tiger', to protect critical tiger habitats and all the other faunal and floral species that formed the habitat, and use the tiger as a symbol for widespread conservation of wilderness areas and biodiversity.

In February 1972, a National Committee on Environmental Planning and Coordination (NCEPC) was set up in the Department of Science and Technology. The NCEPC functioned as an apex advisory body in all matters relating to environmental protection and improvement.

Fifth Five-Year Plan Period (1974-1979)

The Fifth plan period marked a continuation of the new perspective and awareness that had emerged during the fourth plan period. The National Commission on Agriculture submitted its report in 1976 and, perhaps for the first time, there was a recognition that the forests of India were not doing very well. The finalisation of the Fifth plan document was delayed and it was only completed towards the end of 1976. Perhaps as a response to the findings and recommendations of the National Commission, the plan document was even more focussed on ensuring conservation of nature and natural resources. The document started with an exhortation that: 'Concentration on development should focus more pointed attention on its long-term effects. We must inculcate in our engineers and all our people a deep reverence for Nature. Forests must not be recklessly cut down, nor air and water polluted. Technology should work in resonance with natural forces.' (Foreword: Being the address of the Prime Minster to the National Development Council, 24 September 1976)

In a later chapter it is stated that: 'Taking note of the fact that forestry development has assumed a significant dimension as a source of timber and fuel and for the maintenance of the natural ecological system, special programmes for social forestry and economic plantations have been given high priority. Accordingly, for the remaining two years of the plan, the provision made is almost double the outlays provided for in the first three years of the Plan. Adequate provision has also been made for 'project Tiger' and for the development of National Parks and for strengthening the research programme in the forestry sector.' (Chapter 5, *Plan Outlays and Programmes of Development: Forestry*)

The National Commission on Agriculture, in its 1976 report, highlighted the rapid destruction and degradation of forests—something that was some years later verified by remote sensing imagery. It identified the hiring of private contractors for extracting forest resources as one of the main factors contributing to the degradation and recommended the reorganisation of the forest departments and the setting up of forest development corporations, to be exclusively in-charge of extracting forest resources.

The National Commission also identified the growing demand for fuel wood and fodder as another important factor behind the degradation of forests and recommended the plantation of fuel wood and fodder plantations in non-forest land, especially in wastelands and degraded common lands, as a part of what it called social forestry.

These two recommendations of the National Commission were accepted by the government and contractors were banned from Indian forests. Each state formed a forest development corporation and initiated social forestry plantations.

Subsequently, the government also passed the Constitution (42nd Amendment) Act of 1976 whereby they introduced articles 48-A and 51-A (g), as part of Directive Principles of State Policy, and of the Fundamental Duties, respectively. The amendment provided for the following:

- Article 48 A: 'The State shall endeavor to protect and improve the environment and to safeguard the forest and wildlife of the country'.
- Article 51-A (g): 'It shall be the duty of every citizen of India to protect and improve the natural environment including forests, lakes, rivers and wildlife and to have compassion for living creatures'.

The Constitution (42nd Amendment) Act of 1976 also inserted, in the Seventh Schedule of the Constitution:

'17A. Forests.

17B. Protection of wild animals and birds.'

Thereby bringing forests, and wild animals and birds, into the concurrent list on which both the Central government and the state governments could legislate.

Towards the end of the Fifth plan period, the NCEPC in the Department of Science and Technology started doing some assessments of proposed projects, thereby laying the foundation for the environmental impact regime that was soon to follow.

Sixth Five-Year Plan Period (1980-1985)

The Congress Party lost the General Elections in 1977, and was out of power till 1980. With the return of Mrs. Indira Gandhi as Prime Minister, in 1980, there was a sudden focus on environment conservation and sustainable development, the likes of which had never before been seen in India, or in the rest of the so called developing world.

A Committee for Recommending Legislative Measures and Administrative Machinery for Ensuring Environmental Protection was set up in 1980 (under Mr. N.D Tiwari, the then Deputy Chairman of the Planning Commission). Based on its recommendations, a Department of Environment was created in 1980, which took over the environment related functions of the NCEPC and the Department of Science and Technology.

In the 1980s the government enacted The Forest (Conservation) Act (1980), the Prevention and Control of Air Pollution Act (1981), the Environmental Protection Act (1986), and made many other rules and legislations. Also set up was a system of environmental appraisal for all development projects, and finally (in 1985) a full-fledged Ministry of Environment and Forests[9].

In the Sixth plan document there was, for the first time, an attempt to address all the major areas and issues relating to nature and the natural environment. There was also recognition that environmental concern must be an underlying factor in all activities and programmes. The chapter on the environment declared that: 'The environment must not be considered as just another sector of national development. It should form a crucial guiding dimension for Plans and programmes in each sector. This becomes clear only if the concern for environmental protection is understood in its proper context.' (Chapter 20)

Broadening the approach taken during the Stockholm Conference, the plan document recognised that, 'Environmental problems in India can be classified into two broad categories. A. Those arising from conditions of poverty and under-development. B. Those arising as negative effects of the very process of development.' (Paragraph 20.2)

In the chapter on environment there were sections on land and water, soil, forests, marine ecosystems, water pollution, air pollution, land pollution, and even noise pollution. There were separate sections, in the chapter on environment, on human habitation, urban environment, rural environment, and on environment impact assessment.

Also for the first time there was an explicit statement of the need to conserve genetic resources, and of the value of wild relatives of domesticated animals and cultivated plants.

As a result, India very quickly became one of the most legislated nations among the 'developing countries' and began to compare favourably with many 'developed' countries. However, implementation remained a major problem.

Implementation of Environmental Policy in India: 1947-1984

Even though we were somewhat late starters and reacted to disasters, rather than proactively anticipating them, few would dispute that by the mid-1980s India had an impressive array of policy and legislation relating to the environment. Therefore, judging only by the 'evolution of policy', we were home safe. However, when we examine the implementation of these laws and policies, the institutional capacity built up around them and how seriously they were taken, then the picture that emerged was depressingly different.

Sectors of the Environment

The broad environment 'sector' can be divided into various sub-sectors. Traditionally there were the 'green' issues, which comprised the conservation, sustainable use, and regeneration of natural resources like forests, grasslands, water and land resources, wetlands, coastal and marine areas, wildlife and, as much of this is now described, biodiversity. There were the 'brown' issues, related mainly to the prevention and control of pollution, including water, air, land, and noise, and the prevention of chemical and other hazards.

SOME ENVIRONMENTAL MILESTONES

1857	The Oriental Gas Company Act (was enacted to prevent or reduce atmospheric pollution in and around Calcutta.)
1864	The British set up a Forest Department
1865	First Indian Forest Act
1871	The Cattle Trespass Act (For preservation of forests)
1878	New Indian Forest Act
1879	The Elephant Preservation Act
1882	The Indian Easements Act (guaranteed property rights of riparian owners against 'unreasonable' pollution by upstream users.
1893	The Shore Nuisance (Bombay and Kolaba) Act (was enacted to prevent marine water pollution)
1897	The Indian Fisheries Act
1905	The Bengal Smoke Nuisance Act (was enacted to prevent or reduce atmospheric pollution in and around Calcutta)
1912	The Bombay Smoke Nuisance Act (was passed to check smoke nuisance in Bombay area)
1912	The Wild Birds and Wild Animals (Protection) Act

1927 Amended Indian Forest Act

1932 The Bengal Rhinocerous Preservaion Act

1936 The Hailey National Park Act

1948 The Factories Act (provides that the liquid effluents, gases and fumes should be treated)

1951 The Industries (Development and Regulation) Act

1952 New Forest Policy

1954 The Prevention of Food Adulteration Act

1956 The River Boards Act

1957 The Mines and Minerals (Regulation and Development) Act

1968 The Insecticides Act

1972 The Stockholm Conference and Mrs. Gandhi's 'poverty is the greatest polluter' remark

1972 The Wildlife (Protection) Act

1972 Setting up of the National Committee on Environmental Planning and Coordination (NCEPC)

1973 The launch of Project Tiger

1974 The Water (Prevention and Control of Pollution) Act

1974 Setting up of the Central and few State Pollution Control Boards

1976 The report of the National Commission on Agriculture

1976 The Constitution (42nd Amendment) Act of 1976 (whereby they introduced Articles 48-A and 51-A (g), as part of Directive Principles of State Policy, and of the Fundamental Duties, respectively).

1977 The Water Cess (Prevention and Control of Pollution) Act

1980 Forest Conservation Act

1980 Setting up a Committee for Recommending Legislative Measures and Administrative Machinery for Ensuring Environmental Protection (the Tiwari Committee)

1980 Setting up of the Department of Environment

1980 Rejection of the Silent valley Project

1981 Shelving of the Tehri Project

1981 The Air (Prevention and Control of Pollution) Act

1982 Inclusion of social forestry in the restructured 20-Point Programme

1983 The National Wildlife Action Plan

The Government of India maintained this distinction for many years, in fact right up to 1980, by giving the mandate for the 'green' issues mostly to the Ministry of Agriculture, and of the 'brown' issues partly to the Ministry of Science and Technology, and partly to the Industries and the Urban Ministries. It was only in 1980 that a Department of Environment was set up and took over some of the 'brown' issues, along with wildlife and the relatively new concern for an integrated approach towards sustainable development. And it was only in 1985 that the Ministry of Environment and Forests was formed and took over both the green and the brown issues, along with the process of environmental impact assessment.

Given the period covered by this paper, and the way policy evolved and was implemented, for the purpose of this section we can divide up the environmental area into four different segments: forests, wildlife, pollution and hazards, and the overarching sustainable development.

Constraints of length inhibit a detailed analysis of the implementation of each of the policies and their many objectives. Also, a detailed analysis of the various factors that supported and inhibited success can at best only be cursorily touched upon here. The best that can be done is to identify one or two of the major objectives in each segment of the environment and then judge implementation of the policies of each segment based on how fully, effectively, and sustainably these objectives were achieved.

Forests

Objectives and challenges: As discussed earlier, at the time of independence, policy relating to forests was more developed than policy relating to any other segment of the environment. There was recognition of the many different and critical roles that forests played and the consequent need to conserve and regenerate them. Therefore, the primary objective of the forestry sector could be seen as the conservation and protection of the existing natural forests and the regeneration of the degraded forests to finally ensure that 33 percent of the land area (60 percent in hilly areas and 20 percent in the plains) was under good forest cover.

The challenge was to do this while providing timber and other forest based raw materials for industry, non-timber forest produce (then known as minor forest produce) to local communities, and allowing various development and infrastructure projects and urban centres to come up on forestland. There was also the concurrent pressure to grow more food and convert forestland to agricultural use. This was clearly a tall order!

Fortunately, at independence there already existed a large and professional forest department in most of the states. There were also various laws and policies in existence, and a fair amount of survey and inventory work had already been completed.

History of Implementation: Initially, the forest area of the country seemed to increase. This was because along with independence came the abolition of the princely states and, therefore, the amalgamation of the forests of the erstwhile princely states with the national forests. In addition to this, there was the enactment of a law abolishing *zamindari* and this also brought into the national forest kitty some amount of forests that were a part of the *zamindari* holdings. Consequently, the legal forest area went up in the first few years of independence.

However, these notional gains were shortlived. With the resurgence of the 'Grow More Food Programme' in the early 1950s, a lot of forests were cut down and the land brought under cultivation of agricultural crops.

As the population and economy grew there was increased demand for forest produce and a consequent increase in the felling of timber. Development projects, especially the construction of river valley projects and of roads, also took their toll on the forests. In fact, the new and rapidly expanding network of roads opened up a lot of inaccessible forest areas, further facilitating their destruction.

Deforestation was particularly acute in the mountainous regions of the Himalayas, where populations were sparse and traditionally poor communications and a lack of industrial development had ensured that the forests stood almost untouched. Increasing demand for high value timber (like deodar) and the expanding road and transport network soon reversed this trend, and even where the road network was inadequate, timber began to be floated down on all the major mountain streams and rivers, not only depleting the forests but also disrupting the river ecology. Hill slopes started destabilising and the frequency of landslides, aggravated by the construction of sometimes badly designed roads, went up sharply.

Soil erosion also increased manyfold and mountain streams, which had perennially carried sparkling blue water for thousands of years became muddy seasonal streams, carrying the rich soils of the mountains and depositing it on the river beds in the plains. This started the eternal vicious circle of floods in the monsoons and drought in the dry season.

However, despite all this, there seemed to be no sense of alarm at the national level, especially as most Indian statistics were about 'forest-land', which was just a legal classification indicating the area that had been declared as forest under the Indian Forest Act or other similar state acts. In actual fact much of this 'forestland' had no forest or other vegetation cover. There were no statistics at the national level on how much of this forestland actually had forest cover, was this cover increasing or decreasing, and at what rate.

Recognition of the Crisis: As earlier discussed it was only in 1976, when the report of the National Commission on Agriculture highlighted the alarming state of India's forests, that there was a glimmer of recognition that the current policies and practices were not working and something drastic needed to be done.

The government launched, in 1979, a social forestry programme, with support from the World Bank and various other bilateral and multilateral donor agencies. However, forests continued to decline and, these social forestry programmes, apart from being only marginally successful, caused major distortions in the forestry sector.

Meanwhile, remote sensing, false-colour imagery had made it possible to assess the actual extent of forest cover in the country (see table 1).

These estimates by the National Remote Sensing Agency, made public in 1984, suggested that India was losing 1.3 million hectares (ha) of forest cover each year—a truly alarming picture which, if true, would have meant that the 46 million odd hectares of forests that was remaining in India in 1982 would have all disappeared in 30 years or so. Fortunately, this has not happened.

In 1981 the Government of India set up the Forest Survey of India, with the express purpose of monitoring the state of the forests in India. Their first report, produced in 1987, showed that good forest cover had further declined to just 36 million hectares. In the foreword to the 1987 report, the then Union Minister for Environment and Forests wrote:

> According to interpretation of satellite imagery, good forest cover extends over 36 million hectares only, which is about one third of the extent of forest cover envisaged in the National Forest Policy... There is now a marked thrust in the Government policies to protect what is left, nurse back that has been degraded and bring new area under tree cover, wherever possible. It would not be an exaggeration to say that the country has entered into an area of ecological "renaissance".

Table 1

Forest Cover in the Country

State/UT *1972-1975*	*Forest Area (sq km)* *1980-1982*	*Forest Area (sq km)*	*% Change*
Andhra Pradesh	49049	40435	-17.6
Assam	21055	19796	-6.0
Bihar	22687	20139	-11.2
Gujarat	9459	5057	-46.5
Haryana	757	401	-47.0
Himachal Pradesh	15075	9130	-39.4
Jammu & Kashmir	22335	14361	-35.7
Karnataka	29480	25655	-13.0
Kerala	8611	7376	-14.3
Madhya Pradesh	108568	90215	-16.9
Maharashtra	40682	30350	-25.4
Manipur	15090	13572	-10.1
Meghalaya	14390	12458	-13.4
Nagaland	8154	8095	-0.7
Tripura	6330	5138	-18.8
Orissa	48383	39425	-18.5
Punjab & Chandigarh	1120	499	-55.4
Rajasthan	11294	5972	-47.1
Tamil Nadu	16676	13187	-20.9
Uttar Pradesh	25869	21022	-18.7
West Bengal	8347	6483	-22.3
Sikkim	1761	2883	+63.7
Arunachal Pradesh	51438	58104	+13.0
Delhi	18	10	-44.4
Goa, Daman & Diu	1221	1139	-6.7
Mizoram	13860	11971	-13.6
Total	**551709**	**462873**	**-16.1**

Source: National Remote Sensing Agency (1987). *Evaluation Report on Social Forestry Programme*. New Delhi: Programme Evaluation Organisation, Planning Commission, August.

Box - 1

Social Forestry in India during the Sixth Five-Year Plan

A shortage of adequate fuel wood for rural communities was perceived during the 1980s, and the consequent destruction of forest areas to meet these shortages was recognised. It was also noted that when fuel wood was in short supply cattle dung, which was far more useful and important as a fertiliser, was used in its stead, leading to lower soil fertility. In response, the government of India developed the Social Forestry Programme, launched during the Sixth Five-Year Plan and included in the 20-Point Programme when it was restructured in 1982. In addition to meeting the demand for fuel wood in rural areas, the Social Forestry Programme was also designed to meet fodder and small timber requirements, and fuel the drive towards afforestation. The programme received a great deal of foreign funding, with funds from the World Bank, US Aid, SIDA (Sweden) and CIDA (Canada) being allocated to various states.

The Social Forestry Programme was believed to be the most efficient way to raise plantations of quick growing species on all available private and community wasteland outside forest areas. Designated areas were to be as close to consumption points as possible, so as to minimise the energy needed for transportation purposes. The newly afforested regions were expected to be ecologically beneficial as well. The Fuelwood Study Committee in its 1982 report (*Report of the Fuelwood Study Committee, Planning Commission, Government of India, New Delhi, March 1982)* further emphasised the importance of meeting the requirement for fuel wood among the rural and urban poor, while protecting existing forestland.

The programme was initially launched in 101 select districts in the country, where acute fuel wood shortages had been documented, and was later extended to an additional 56 districts to ensure wider coverage. Nurseries were set up to provide saplings free of cost, and programmes like 'A Tree for Every Child' aimed to encourage farmers and children to plant trees in their farms and in the backyards of their homesteads. In addition to fuel wood and fodder-specific species, where tenable, commercial species like Eucalyptus, Poplar and Bamboo were also planted, as were fruit trees.

Though widely initiated, the programme was only somewhat successful. It was found that the government did not sanction enough additional staff for the project, and the brunt of its implementation was borne by already overworked Forest Department staff. Further,

contd...

...contd...

the nurseries set up were, in most cases, rather small and yet appeared to meet the requirement for saplings, indicating that the demand was quite small. There were also shortcomings in the drive to motivate people to participate in the programme, with local *panchayats* particularly uninterested and uninvolved. Additionally, there was a tendency to plant trees on land meant for agricultural use, especially in the case of commercially valuable trees like Eucalyptus.

Source: Planning Commission (1987). *Evaluation Report on Social Forestry Programme*.

Performance: Therefore, in 1984, the forest cover in India was just a little over 40 million hectares, and declining fast—reaching 36 m ha in 1987. Given that the land area of India is over 340 m ha, 40 m ha was less than 12 percent of the area—while the policy required a minimum of 33 percent forest cover.

Further, the assessment done through remote sensing could only capture the density of the canopy cover; it could not reveal the health of the forests. In actual fact, some of this forest, though its canopy was relatively intact, was dead or dying as there was heavy pressure on the undergrowth and regeneration was badly affected. Clearly, the implementation of the forest policy was not a success.

Wildlife

After independence, several states promulgated wildlife laws modelled after the British acts, specifically the Bombay Wild Birds and Wild Animals (Protection) Act 1951. However, hunting was still rampant in most parts of the country and the last of the Cheetah was reportedly shot dead in the mid-1950s and has never since been seen in India. Populations of almost all the species began to decline, partly as a result of hunting but mainly due to the destruction of their habitat.

Though a network of wildlife protected areas existed at the time of Independence, and a few more areas were added later, in 1960 there were just 65 wildlife protected areas (national parks and sanctuaries) in India, covering less that 0.5 percent of the land area, and many of these were under great pressure. The bulk of India's wildlife was outside these protected areas and had virtually no protection. It was hunted, legally and illegally, and also became victim to the destruction of forests and other wilderness areas, the expansion of agriculture and human habitation, and to the disruption of its migratory routes by roads and other infrastructure projects.

However, this rampant destruction of wildlife went unnoticed once more, as did the extinction of many species of birds, plants and insects. It was only in the late 1960s, with international attention becoming focussed on the fast disappearing Indian wildlife, especially the enigmatic tiger that, for the first time since independence, there was an effort to review policy and step up implementation.

Accordingly, in 1972 the Wildlife (Protection) Act was promulgated and, in 1973, Project Tiger was launched. The website of Project Tiger describes the events leading up to the launching of Project Tiger as follows:

> An estimate of the tiger population in India, at the turn of the century, placed the figure at 40,000. Subsequently, the first ever all India tiger census was conducted in 1972 which revealed the existence of only 1827 tigers. Various pressures in the later part of the last century led to the progressive decline of wilderness, resulting in the disturbance of viable tiger habitats. At the IUCN General Assembly meeting in Delhi, in 1969, serious concern was voiced about the threat to several species of wildlife and the shrinkage of wilderness in the country. In 1970, a national ban on tiger hunting was imposed and in 1972 the Wildlife Protection Act came into force. A "Task Force" was then set up to formulate a project for tiger conservation with an ecological approach.

Apart from launching Project Tiger and setting up various Tiger Reserves, the government also rapidly increased the number of wildlife protected areas (national parks and sanctuaries) and by 1984 the number had crossed 200, tripling the number from the 65 in 1960.

Though the trend of destruction had not been fully reversed, the rate of depredation had been significantly slowed down and some of the more threatened species, including the Tiger, the Lion, the Elephant, and other such had been given special protection under the law.

Pollution and Hazards

Despite the fact that India was rapidly industrialising, urbanising, and adding emissions from motor vehicles and thermal power stations to its atmosphere, its regime for the prevention and control of air and water pollution remained very weak.

Water Pollution: Though a national law to prevent and control water pollution was enacted in 1974, and the Central Pollution Control Board set up the same year (along with corresponding state pollution control boards), our rivers and water bodies continued to be polluted, both by industrial effluents and by municipal wastes. In the 'green revolution' areas this was supplemented by runoffs of chemical pesticides and fertilisers from agricultural fields.

However, the bulk of the water pollutants were from domestic sources, essentially household waste. The polluted water caused a host of waterborne diseases, including diarrhoea and dysentery and killed millions of people, mostly children.

Unfortunately the industrial and agricultural pollutants, though smaller in quantity were by far the more deadly. Chemicals and heavy metals released by industries persisted in the environment and there was a process of bio-accumulation of heavy metals in the human body that led to a buildup of dangerous levels of mercury in people living in and around industrial and urban areas. Research suggested that many inexplicable and often fatal 'major organ failures' were a result of the chemicals and heavy metals accumulated in the body, which killed slowly but surely.

There was widespread contamination of fruits, vegetables and grains by pesticides and chemicals. Fruits, like grapes, were saturated in chemical pesticides. Shockingly, in order to cater to elite urban tastes, vegetables were being bleached white or dyed green, all using toxic chemicals. Wheat and rice grains were being contaminated by pesticides and residual chemical pesticides in the soil were being picked up even by those vegetables which were not the intended targets.

Random studies of people living in and around the capital, and other 'green revolution' areas, showed that concentrations of chemical pesticides accumulated in their fat reserves were many times the maximum prescribed limit.

Air Pollution: In 1981 a national law to prevent and control air pollution was added to the statute books. Though the Central and state pollution boards were given the added responsibility of implementing this law, our cities and industrial areas continued to be polluted, with the air getting worse each year.

Leaded petroleum continued to be used, despite it being phased out in many parts of the world. It was only in 1998 that unleaded petrol was finally introduced in the capital of India, Delhi, but by that time Delhi had already become the fourth most polluted city in the world!

Indian coal, which is the staple for the power industry, has very high ash content—nearly 40 percent. Though there was a legal requirement that the ash that rose up the chimney of the power plant (called fly ash) must be trapped in the chimney and safely disposed of, most power stations did not follow the law. In Delhi itself, till the 1980s, the Indraprastha Power Station and the Rajghat Power Station, both located in the heart of the city surrounded by millions of people, spewed most of the fly ash they produced into the atmosphere. Badarpur Power Station, located on the outskirts of Delhi was similarly polluting. It was, therefore, no wonder that the suspended particulate matter in Delhi's air was often five to six times the maximum prescribed limit, leading to severe rampant ailments amongst the city's population.

The proliferation of vehicles without any check on emission levels, especially of diesel vehicles, trucks and buses in particular, ensured that the level of respirable suspended particulate matter (rspm), which got imbedded in the respiratory system and was suspected to be carcinogenic, was many times higher than the safe limit.

The situation in other towns and cities, and in industrial areas, was even worse. Air pollution levels in towns like Korba, which was a centre of power generation, could not be measured, as their values crossed the capacity of the measurement instruments!

Hazards: The growth of the chemical industry, and of nuclear power plants, raised the specter of chemical and nuclear hazards in India. Unfortunately, this was never adequately acknowledged at the policy level, and there were hardly any policies or laws relating to hazardous substances and processes in existence, and no effective institutional structure at all. The country paid a heavy price for this in 1984 when a highly toxic gas, MIC, leaked out of the Union Carbide plant in Bhopal.

Sustainable Development

As mentioned earlier, it was only in the Fourth Five-Year Plan period (1969-1974) that for the first time there was a talk of sustainable development and the need to integrate environmental planning and economic planning. The Fourth plan document specifically stated that:

> There is also the inter-dependence of living things and their relationships with land, air, and water. Planning for harmonious development recognises this unity of nature and man. Such planning is possible only on the basis of a comprehensive appraisal of environmental issues, particularly economic and ecological. ...It is,

> therefore, necessary to introduce the environmental aspect into our planning and development. ...At present there is no point in the structure of Government where the environmental aspects receive attention in an integrated manner. (Fourth Plan document, quoted earlier)

However, though these pious intentions were expressed as early as 1969, it was only in the next (Fifth) plan period that preliminary steps to do an environmental impact assessment began. The first recorded instance seems to be in 1976, when the Planning Commission asked the Department of Science and Technology (there was no department of environment then) to assess the environmental impacts of river valley projects. Subsequently such assessments were done for other projects requiring the clearance of the Public Investment Board of the Government of India.

Even then, the process was formalised only in the late 1980s and, even then through an administrative order. It was only in 1994 that it became a legal requirement.

The Department of Environment came into being in 1980, but it was only 10 years later, in 1990, that the Planning Commission, which had the primary responsibility for integrating environmental concerns into economic and development planning, formed an integrated division for environment and forests.

In the 1980s there were two major decisions of the Government of India that reflected its growing concern for the environment. The first was the scrapping of the proposed Silent Valley Hydro-Electric Project (SVHEP), in Kerala, as it submerged a very valuable biodiversity area. The second was the shelving of the Tehri Hydro-Electric Project, in 1981, as it was judged to be environmentally non-viable and had major safety concerns. Unfortunately, the Tehri Project was subsequently reinstated and is now operational.

Meanwhile, Carter Brandon and his team, from the World Bank, estimated that the cost of environmental degradation for selected environmental parameters was between 2.64 percent and 6.41 percent of the GDP (see Table 12.2). This was without taking into consideration loss of biodiversity, among others. Clearly a country whose growth rate was under 5 percent could hardly lose up to 6 percent in natural resources and still pretend to be growing sustainably.

Discussion

In 1984, would the Indian government's effort at conserving and regenerating the natural environment been considered a success or a failure? There are no absolute standards to judge against. We can either compare our own performance with those of other countries, or perhaps measure ourselves against our own expectations and potential.

Table 2

Summary of Major Annual Environmental Costs in India

Problem	*Impacts on Health and/or Production*	*Low Estimate (million US$)*	*High Estimate (million US$)*
Urban air pollution	Urban health impacts	517	2,102
Water pollution (health impacts)	Urban and rural health impacts, esp. diarrheal diseases	3,076	8,344
Water pollution (production impacts)	higher incremental costs for clean water supply	not estimated	not estimated
Industrial hazardous waste	Long-term health impacts, esp. cancer	not estimated	not estimated
Soil degradation	Loss of agricultural output	1,516	2,368
Rangeland degradation	Loss of livestock Carrying capacity	238	417
Deforestation	Loss of sustainable timber supply	183	244
Coastal and marine resources	Unsustainable harvesting of marine resources	not estimated	not estimated
Loss of biodiversity	Loss of use, option, and existence values	not estimated	not estimated
Tourism	Decline in tourism revenues	142	283
Total costs of environmental degradation		5,672	13,758
Total cost, % of GDP		2.64%	6.41%
Average Cost—US$ % of GDP		9,715	4.53%

Box - 2

Some Environmental Impacts of Economic Activities

Essentially the understandable push for growth and modernisation of Agriculture had a series of impacts on the environment. Some of the main ones included:

- Expansion of land under cultivation, especially as a part of the 'grow more food' programme, the resettlement of refugees, and the later Green Revolution. This resulted in the cutting down of large tracts of forests to bring the land under agriculture.
- This also resulted in the reduction of numbers of many threatened species of wildlife and an increase in the conflicts between wild animals and people.
- The introduction of chemical fertilisers and pesticides, especially as a part of the Green Revolution, which resulted in extensive water and soil pollution and the contamination of foodstuff and milk, thereby affecting human wellbeing and the health of plants and animals.
- The introduction of hybrid varieties of crops and livestock, which also led to the extinction of traditional crop varieties and domesticated species of livestock, and the traditional practices associated with them.
- The expansion of the irrigation network, especially the construction of large irrigation projects that submerged large areas of forests, destroyed natural habitats and the species found in them, and often waterlogged parts of the command areas. They also displaced a large number of people.
- In many parts of the country expanding agriculture also meant the overexploitation of ground water resources.
- The rapid growth of livestock for milk production, goats and sheep for meat and for other purposes, put unsustainable pressure on the forests and the grasslands.
- The growth in fisheries resulted in the overexploitation of the commercial species, both in inland and marine areas. This also sometimes resulted in the introduction of exotics or the manipulation of populations of certain species, resulting in loss of biodiversity.
- The shortage of fuel wood resulted in the further degradation of forests, and in the diversion of biomass like cow dung and green

contd...

...contd...

manure from the soil to the rural kitchens, thereby impoverishing the soils.

Similarly, the inevitable growth of Industry also had serious environmental consequences, some of which were:

- Exploitation of forests for wood based raw material for the paper, match, rayon and veneer industry, and for timber for construction and for development of infrastructure, especially railways.
- Conversion of green areas, especially in and around towns and cities, into industrial belts, and the resultant loss of green cover.
- Air and water pollution, and the dumping of toxic and hazardous wastes, and the resultant impact on human health and on the environment.
- Overexploitation of ground and surface water sources and the consequent degradation of the ecosystem.

To fuel the growth of industry and to service the growing urban population, there was the need to supplement Energy generation. This resulted in:

- Extensive mining for coal, with the attendant environmental problems, especially the impact of the dumping of overburden on land and rural habitations, the poor working and living conditions of miners, and the depletion of ground water.
- The diversion of water, especially in the rural areas, from agriculture and domestic use to meet the requirements of power plants.
- Thermal pollution of rivers and coastal areas by release of heated water.
- Pollution of the air, especially by fly ash and sulphur dioxide, and by coal dust.
- Contamination of land and of ground water because of the dumping of fly ash.

The growth of towns and cities, as part of the Urbanisation of India, took its toll, especially in terms of:

- Conversion of forest and other productive land for urban use.
- Use of topsoil (for bricks), stone, sand and other construction material and the resultant environmental destruction in their extraction.

contd...

...contd...

- Water and air pollution.
- Consumption of water and energy.
- Municipal waste.

The growth of the Transport network in India, especially the construction of roads and railway lines, had many impacts including:

- Destruction of forests for accommodating roads and railway tracks.
- Disruption of water drainage due to roads and railway tracks.
- Construction material extraction, especially wood for rail sleepers.
- Blasting in mountain regions, destabilising the hillsides.
- Air pollution by steam, diesel and petrol engines.
- Destruction of forests due to easy access through newly constructed roads.

Global Comparison

If we compare ourselves to Western Europe or North America then, of course, we come up short. By the 1980s, though Western Europe had lost most of its natural forests it had managed to regenerate secondary forests in vast areas and had stabilised the area that was under forest cover. Though many fauna and flora species had been lost in the early phases of industrialisation and urbanisation, what remained was well protected. Water and air pollution was, by and large, within prescribed limits. Though new issues relating to climate change and depletion of the ozone layer had started emerging, in all the conventional parameters they were well ahead of India.

North America, mainly the USA and Canada had lower population densities than Europe and had managed to preserve much of their wilderness areas intact. They had also managed to keep pollution in check, though perhaps not as effectively as Western Europe had done. They were also yet to appropriately deal with new and emerging issues, including threats from genetically modified organisms, but they had otherwise stabilised their environment and their use of natural resources.

However, is a comparison between India and these countries fair? These were colonial and neocolonial nations who had options of resource management that were not available to India. The Western European nations had exploited the natural resources of their many colonies in Asia, Africa and South America to build up their infrastructure and their economies. They, along with their North American counterparts, had the buying power to continue to use, even after the dismantling of the political colonies, the resources of the erstwhile colonies while conserving their own.

Therefore, the timber for the houses and furniture in these countries came from Asia and Africa, and the beef for their hamburgers was grazed mainly in South America. The minerals for their consumption were mined in other parts of the world, and their polluting and hazardous industries operated in lands where human life was cheap, and regulations and standards less stringent. For many years the need to attract foreign investment, especially to provide employment, and the need to export whatever possible in order to earn foreign exchange, perpetuated a systematic degradation of the environment in countries of the South, thereby allowing the countries of the North to protect and regenerate their own natural environment.

The wealth that the erstwhile colonialists had accumulated as a result of exploiting the natural resources of their former colonies had allowed them to achieve a level of economic wellbeing that immunised them from the adverse environmental impacts of poverty. They no longer had large proportions of their population foraging in their forests for fuel wood, fodder and raw materials. They did not have impoverished people being forced to commit ecological suicide by over-cultivating their lands, overexploiting the water resources, or congregating in slums and shanties, in order to survive another day. There were enough surpluses in their system to allow a comfortable lifestyle for themselves without degrading their own environment, especially as they had the money power to transfer their environmental costs to others.

India, on the other hand, was an impoverished nation on the eve of independence, where food was scarce and poverty was rampant. Indian agriculture and industry were both in need of rapid growth and development. Agricultural development was critical to move towards self-sufficiency in food, which was essential for true political freedom. There was also the constant fear of famines and the resultant human misery and civil unrest. Industrial development was critical if India was to become self-sufficient in industrial goods and also in order to provide employment to a large and growing population. Would it, then, be fair to compare ourselves to those who had used, and continued to use, the natural and other resources of the rest of the world to set themselves up in a position where they could afford to conserve their own, without any grave risks to their economic or social wellbeing?

Our Own Expectations and Potential

What should have been our own expectations from our government, and how best could our own potential have been actualised to conserve nature while establishing a firm path towards sustainable development.

The Historical Perspective

At Independence, the Congress Party chose to unquestioningly follow the objectives and structure of the British system of resource management. It can be argued, with some merit, that the Indian leaders, and the world as a whole, were too distracted by what seemed then to be the predominant and enduring problems of humanity: poverty and starvation, disease, colonialism, and war—to even be aware that there was another looming issue, that of conserving the natural environment. They were most certainly unaware that it was inextricably linked to the problems of poverty and starvation, of disease, and of war if not to the threats of political sublimation.

Perhaps the adoption of the colonial systems of 'managing' nature and natural resources was also a result of the belief, among a large majority of the leadership of that time, that India needed to break away from the dark ages that clouded her past and emerge as a modern, scientific and democratic society. The chains of casteism, superstition, feudalism and colonialism needed to be shed, and there was a very strong sense of this transformation even in Nehru's famous 'Tryst with Destiny' speech when he said: 'The moment comes, it comes but rarely in history, when we step out from the old to the new, when an age ends... .'

Unfortunately, as we have discovered in the years since Independence, there were some bits of 'the old' that needed to be understood, resurrected and amalgamated into 'the new'. This never really happened.

The Contemporary Perspective

In 1984, where this narrative stops, the options on how to deal with the environment were still not fully exercised. We were still some years away from the collapse of the Soviet Union and the burying of the socialist dream, and India had not yet transformed into a globalised, privatised and liberalised market economy. Therefore, if one looked back from 1984, perhaps one would have said that though India was a slow learner, it was no different from all the other countries of the region and, indeed of the world, who were trying to catch up with the erstwhile colonisers of the planet, while making sure that they did not in the process sink into political or humanitarian chaos.

One would also say that when India did get going, in the 1980s, whatever its reasons were, it was moving fast and though down a narrow path, it was preserving its options to broaden its approach at a later date. In this, it was ahead of most, perhaps even all, of its peers.

1947-1977: The first 30 years after Independence could, at best, be described as a 'reactive' period as far as the natural environment was concerned. The government seemed to move slowly and nothing much changed till there was a crisis or a wake-up call. So, the forest policy and the practice of forestry remained almost unchanged from independence till 1976 when, partly as a result of the rapidly growing numbers of floods and droughts, and partly as an outcome of the alarm call given by the National Commission on Agriculture, the government set up forest development corporations in most states, and initiated an ambitious social forestry programme. However, as we have seen, neither of these measures had a very profound impact and we kept losing forests and forest land, as became obvious from the remote sensing findings that started becoming available. This second wake-up call resulted in the government enacting the Forest Conservation Act, which took away the power of state governments to convert forest areas to non-forest use, and vested this with the Union government.

1980-1984: It is generally acknowledged that when Mrs. Gandhi returned as Prime Minister in 1980, after being out of the government for three years, she seemed to have a renewed interest in the environment and many laws and policies were formulated or initiated at that time. On her becoming the Prime Minister, she immediately set up a committee to recommend the institutional measures required to protect the environment (the N.D. Tiwari Committee), set up the Department of Environment, enacted the Forest Conservation Act, and undertook various other policy and legislative measures.

There has been much speculation on why Mrs. Indira Gandhi's priorities *vis-à-vis* the environment suddenly changed—Mrs. Gandhi was always known for her compassion towards animals, but the environmentalists still remembered her remark that, 'poverty was the greatest polluter'. This was a remark that had often been used by the system to ignore environmental concerns.

Perhaps one explanation is that she felt a need to rehabilitate herself internationally after the ignominy of the emergency, and what better way to do it, now that she had restored democracy, than by becoming a champion of a cause that was at that time the western world's favourite—environmental conservation. On the other hand, perhaps her time out of office had given her the opportunity to look around and recognise that the environmental crisis, that was overtaking the country, required urgent attention.

Despite the new-found zeal and urgency, in some instances too much time had been lost and this became painfully obvious when, in December 1984, less than two months after the assassination of Mrs. Gandhi, a disastrous gas leak occurred in the Union Carbide plant in Bhopal. The fact that the country had not been able to anticipate or prevent it was disastrous, but what was worse was its inability to comprehend and contain it. Many lives were needlessly lost because there was no preparation, no awareness, and not even basic information about the nature and impact of the gas—Methylisocyanate (MIC).

Looking Back at 1984

How would one have judged, in 1984, the performance of the Government in fulfilling national expectations regarding the environment? Though there seems to be no easy way to answer this question, perhaps one could ask and answer three specific questions that both reflect the essence of what was the emerging thrust of Indian environmental policy, and capture the constraints and opportunities inherent to India.

The three specific questions are:

1. Had we achieved, or were we on the right track to achieving, a sustainable pattern of use and regeneration of nature and natural resources.
2. Was our pattern of use and regeneration equitable, or did it put a disproportionate and unfair burden on the poor, the marginalised, the disempowered, and promoted regional disparity and a rural-urban divide in the access and use of nature and natural resources.
3. Was our approach to nature compassionate to other living creatures and sensitive to the value of maintaining the diversity of living forms.

Sustainability[10]

However tempting it is to restrict one's evaluation and analysis to the three or four 'environmental' sectors, like forests, wildlife, pollution and hazards, and the management of land and water resources, such an evaluation would be misleading. What happens to the 'environment' affects and is affected by many other sectors of the economy and governance. Just as what happens to our forests or our land and water resources and our fauna and flora, affects many other things, most importantly our health and the health of our economy; so do many other sectors impact upon the environment.

Therefore, though the financial allocations made for protection, conservation and regeneration of the environment have a grave impact on it, perhaps even more important are the subsidies we give, or do not give, the land uses we promote, our fertiliser and pesticides policy, our energy policy, our irrigation policy, our agricultural policy, our transport policy, the dams and roads we build, our patterns of urbanisation, the location and nature of our mines and, perhaps most important, the determination of who uses whose resources, for what, and why. Concern for the environment cannot be seen in isolation of the lifestyles that a society is propagating, and the political reality that will determine who enjoys that lifestyle and who pays for it.

Though much that had happened before was clearly unsustainable, in 1984 it seemed as if finally, after much indifference and blundering, the country was beginning to take stock of the natural environment and start turning things around. A Department of Environment had been set up, and would soon become a part of a full-fledged ministry, most major aspects of the environment now had legal protection and there were the beginnings of an effective regulatory regime. The government was talking about sustainability and though we had lost large amount of forests and many species, and our water and air was polluted, it all still seemed retrievable.

The environmental movement in the country was growing and the Centre for Science and Environment (CSE) had just brought out their influential *State of the Environment Report*, highlighting national failures in conservation but also showcasing the pockets of hope where individual or group action was conserving and regenerating nature. This and subsequent reports were extensively covered by the media and Rajiv Gandhi, when he became Prime Minister, invited the then Director of the CSE to address the Union Cabinet on the environmental crisis facing the government.

At local and regional levels, the Narmada Bachao Andolan, the Anti- Tehri movement and the Chipko movement were all growing in influence and size, forcing the government to take another look at their development strategies at least in so far as they impacted the environment. A major hydroelectric project, the Silent Valley Project, was shelved because of environmental concerns, becoming perhaps the first major project being shelved for such a reason.

The National Wastelands Development Board (NWDB), which promised to afforest India by planting five million hectares of forests each year through a people's movement, was optimistically launched soon after, as was the Ganga Action Plan which promised to once and for all cleaning up the Ganga and return it to its pristine glory. It was a time of hope and anticipation. Never had the natural environment received so much attention or appeared to have had so much support at the highest levels of the government.

Equity

The rapid growth of population, the slow and somewhat skewed economic growth, and the diversion of natural resources for urban and industrial use had put increasing pressure on local communities, especially those primarily dependent on nature and natural resources for their livelihood and survival needs. Areas where industry, power stations and other infrastructure had come up had lost much of their green cover, making access to fuel wood, fodder, and non-timber forest produce increasingly difficult for the local communities. Pollution levels had also gone up and water resources had come under increasing pressure.

Mining areas were sometimes even worse off, with much of the agricultural land in the region being degraded because of the careless dumping of the overburden. In some such areas ground water became scarce as mining operations often involved the pumping out of ground water that could threaten the safety of the mines. Urban areas also swallowed up forests and fertile land, and became bottomless sinks for energy, water, stone and other building material, and a source of air and water pollution. Large dams not only submerged large tracts of forests and fertile land but invariably displaced thousands of families.

However, on the other hand, areas that did not get industry or infrastructure remained 'backward' and 'underdeveloped'. It was famously, and not inaccurately, demonstrated that if you overlaid a map of India's forest cover over a map of all the economically developed regions, you would find a perfect inverse correlation. Therefore, for the common Indian the option seemed either to be polluted, alienated from nature, and ecologically impoverished, or be marginalised, isolated and economically impoverished.

This was the pattern of development that seemed prevalent in 1984, and there were no signs that this was about to change in the near future. So, even if the environmental destruction wreaked by commercial and development projects was minimised, there was little or no hope that it would be more equitably distributed. And even though there were many benefits generated by these projects, there was little hope that these would go primarily to those who paid the major costs. The battle for ecological justice had still to be fought.

Concern for Life Forms and their Diversity

India had a proud and ancient heritage of compassion to other living creatures. Though this did not stop a section of Indians hunting animals, and others eating meat, the common Indian was loath to kill or otherwise harm most animals and even some plants. This was partly a result of the historically prevalent notion of the sacredness of nature, but also partly an element of the Indian culture. Therefore, to formalise a code that involved compassion towards other living creatures was not a difficult task and the hunting of most wild animals was effectively banned in the early 1970s. The ban has been successful in most parts of the country, for most species. Poaching of commercially valuable species (like the tiger, the elephant, or the rhinocerous) still continues, but mainly for demand from China and other countries rather than because of rampant domestic demand.

However, compassion for animals and plants did not automatically lead to an understanding of the value of biodiversity. It was business as usual till 1970, with wildlife being regularly and extensively hunted, and deprived of its habitat, food and water. This led to a rapid decrease in the population of many species. The realisation, in the early 1970s, that the Tiger was on the verge of extinction was the wake-up call that the country needed, and this, finally, led to serious efforts at protecting what remained of the wilderness areas and wildlife in India.

By 1984, the Government of India was well aware of the threats to India's biodiversity, and of the ecological, social and economic imperatives for protecting it. Perhaps the main strategy adopted was limited, for it primarily involved the setting up of national parks and sanctuaries (wildlife protected areas) where the habitat and all the species comprising it would be protected from all or almost all use and impact. In addition, certain species were declared as protected species (protected to varying degrees), and stringent penalties prescribed for those who sought to hunt or collect them, or in any other way harm them.

Unfortunately, there was little or no involvement of the local affected communities in this strategy. Most of the areas identified as potential national parks and sanctuaries either had human populations, very often tribals or other disempowered groups, living within them. In many cases, even where there were no populations living within these protected areas thousands of people living in peripheral areas were dependent on their forest and other resources. The sudden expansion of the wildlife protected area network, as took place in the 1980s, resulted in the social and economic dislocation of a large number of rural families.

Therefore, though strong measures were taken to protect biodiversity and, in 1984, it seemed that we might finally be able to halt and turn around the rapid loss of wildlife species and populations, which had been the trend since Independence, the measures were somewhat restrictive and did not take into consideration the legitimate needs of the local communities. This resulted in growing conflicts around national parks and sanctuaries, between forest officials and the local people, making it increasingly difficult to protect the biodiversity. Unfortunately, this increased protection to our biodiversity resources was planned and implemented with little concern for the local communities living in and around the wilderness areas, and many of them had to pay a heavy social and economic cost that could have been avoided with better planning and some sensitivity.

Conclusions

Therefore, in 1984 it would have been understandable to believe that, as far as halting the headlong rush towards environmental destruction was concerned, we were for the first time in an era of hope, where the criticality of the issue had been recognised, been understood, and remedial action had started. The same could have been said for biodiversity conservation. The equitable distribution of the costs and benefits still remained a major worry.

Perhaps the leaders of India had missed a historical opportunity, at independence, to reinforce some of the progressive traditional strategies of conservation, especially the community protected sacred sites and species. However, they had weathered the storm and managed to wake up in the nick of time. Perhaps our leaders were reactive, rather than being proactive, and needed crisis after crisis—the near disappearance of the tiger, the satellite based estimate that we were losing over a million hectares of forests each year, or the rapidly growing cycle of floods and droughts—but at least they reacted before it was too late and reacted decisively. In 1984, there were very few other nations that faced the sorts of challenges that India did and moved even half as far.

However, there would have been another equally credible viewpoint. From the perspective of an environmentalist, the writing was on the wall much before the 1980s, and certainly by the early 1970s. Yet we did nothing till there was a crisis. And even then, perhaps too little too late. Surely the time had come to change our model of development and switch to one that was truly sustainable, both ecologically and socially, being inclusive and equitable.

But from the perspective of a Prime Minister the question could well have been: where is this model? Who has adopted it and shown that it is workable. Would it not be unforgivable adventurism to embark on an untested and vague model of development when failure could mean millions of starvation deaths and the worsening of acute poverty?

In 1984, one could have been forgiven for saying that this was yet an unresolved debate and only time would tell who was right. However, if one was to look back from 2010—as fortunately one is not required to—one might not have an excuse to defer judgment!

Endnotes

1. I have been greatly assisted while writing this paper by Ms. Misha Singh, who researched for information and edited the final draft.
2. Dandekar, R.N. (1979). "Vedic Mythological Tracts", *Select Writings I & II*. Delhi: Ajanta Publications.
3. Vannucci, M. (1994). *Ecological Readings in the Veda*. New Delhi: D.K. Printword.
4. Berreman, G.D. (1993). *Hindus of the Himalayas: Ethnography and Change*. New Delhi: Oxford University Press.
5. Though there was a forest department set up in Madras in early 1800s to study the plantation of teak in the Malabar.
6. Though in 1855, Lord Dalhousie framed regulations for conservation of forest in the entire country, these were not codified into law till 1865.
7. Copies of Five-Year Plans accessed from *http://www.planningcommission.gov.in/plans/planrel/fiveyr/index9.html*
8. 'Are not poverty and need the greatest polluters? The environment cannot be improved in conditions of poverty. Nor can poverty be eradicated without the use of science and technology. For instance, unless we are in a position to provide for the daily necessities of tribal people and those who live in and around the jungles, we cannot keep them from combing the forests for their livelihood, from poaching and despoiling the vegetation. When they feel themselves deprived, how can we urge the preservation of animals?'
9. Till 1980, when a separate department of environment was set up, environment was under the Department of Science and Technology. Till 1985, forests were under the Ministry of Agriculture.
10. In a fundamental sense, environmental sustainability can be understood to involve extracting from nature only that much that can be regenerated, and dumping into nature only that much (and only such substances) that can be assimilated.

Chapter XIII

The Naxal Challenge

Shantha Sinha

Introduction

On July 16, 2010, in the meeting of the Chief Ministers of the states affected by naxals, P. Chidambaram the Home Minister of India stated that, 'during the period January to June 2010, there have been 1103 incidents of violence. 97 extremists were killed and 1342 apprehended, while 209 members of the security forces were martyred. The Naxals have been attacking people by projecting them as "police informers". The real objective is to eliminate anyone who stands in the way of their objective—an armed "liberation struggle."'[1] Further, he stated that, 'the Central government would provide more helicopters for logistics support, troop movement, supplies and evacuation; fund the establishment/strengthening of 400 police stations in the affected districts at the rate of Rs. 2 crore per police station on 80:20 basis over a period of two years; sanction additional SPOs to the States; and requested the State Governments of Chhattisgarh, Jharkhand, Orissa and West Bengal to create a Unified Command for anti-naxal operations; appoint a retired Major General of the Army as a member of the Unified Command and appoint an IG as IG (anti-naxal operations) for that State; and to appoint an IG, CRPF as IG (Operations) for that State to work in close coordination with the IG (anti-naxal operations) of that State.'[2]

As of 2010, naxalites are active across approximately 160 districts in 10 states of India namely Andhra Pradesh, Bihar, Chhattisgarh, Jharkhand, Karnataka, Madhya Pradesh, Maharashtra, Orissa, Uttar Pradesh and West Bengal prompting Indian Prime Minister Manmohan Singh to describe the naxals as the biggest threat to country's internal security while addressing the Conference of Chief Ministers on 7th February 2010. Naxals have penetrated into a large tract of land and its people with armed cadre strength of 20,000 in addition to 50,000 regular cadres from among the areas where they are present.[3] Of these

160 districts are those amongst the most backward areas in the country with a large tribal population. These areas also coincide with the rich mineral resources such as coal for 75 percent of India's electricity generation is from the five of the states of Andhra Pradesh, Bihar, Chhattisgarh, Jharkhand and Orissa. These states are also rich in bauxite and iron ore, and are attracting major investment plans in steel and in oil refining. It is reported that the Chhattisgarh, Jharkhand, Orissa and West Bengal governments have already signed hundreds of MoUs with corporate houses for steel plants, sponge iron, power plants, aluminum and bauxite reserves, dams and mines. Whether there is a systematic plan to clear the forest areas of tribal presence as they come in the way of investments of large corporations—both national and multinational prospecting for rich mineral resources and wealth is hard to tell. It is true however that the tribal populations are totally unprepared to use these investments that are coming in their areas to their advantage. It is certainly a situation over which the tribals have no control.

In its present form where it has evolved into a militarist outfit on an offensive against the government through the People's Liberation Guerilla Army (PLGA) the Naxals have been in operation since the formation of the CPI (Maoist) in September 21, 2004. The CPI (Maoist) is the coming together of the People's War Group (PWG) which had its presence in Andhra Pradesh, Bastar area in Chhattisgarh, West Orissa and parts of Bihar and the Maoist Communist Centre (MCC) which was concentrated in Jharkhand, Chhattisgarh, and Bihar and eastern UP. This area is also known as the 'Red Corridor'. The word corridor is a misnomer as there are several districts that separate the areas of naxal presence and in actuality there is no contiguity in their areas of operation. Their support in the areas where they have a presence is uneven ranging from tacit consent of the local population to fear of being crushed between police and the Maoists.

The naxals have been in existence since the 1960s. Although they never had a continuous presence of 40 years in any area they have had continuity in history, with an institutional memory that developed over this period enabling Maoist parties to mature as an extremely secretive party to combat State through armed struggle. There are several splinter groups among the naxals, who differ in their understanding of methods for bringing about change in the society. Yet there are factors specific to their politics over the years that characterise them as naxals, the important one being that it is only through armed struggle that power can be seized and revolutionary transformation of society is possible. All of them describe themselves as Maoists and thus the words naxals and Maoists are used interchangeably.

This paper has four parts. The First part traces the beginning of the Naxal politics in India, the debates and discussions that took place in the process of formulation of 'armed struggle' as a strategy for seizure of political power and the modalities of its practice by Charu Majumdar and others. It also deals with the contours of the movement and its different streams. It elaborates the direction Charu's line took in practice in Andhra Pradesh where mass politics and village level activities of the tribal poor and the community was substituted for squad (*dalams*) actions, and in turn how squads were substituted for a 'virtual squad' and individual actions of annihilation of class enemies.

In the Second part, faced with state repression and weakening of the movement, and intense intra-party squabbles, it traces how the movement still survived in the post-Emergency context in the late 70s and early 80s. It shows the attempts at building of alliances among the various factions of Maoists and their expansion to new areas and States with a clear militarist strategy. In the Third and Fourth parts, it tries to understand the extent and depth of Maoist activities and the implications of armed struggle for both the community as well as the State. Finally, it offers an explanation of why they have been able to continue in spite of losses and the challenge they pose.

I

First Phase: Splits in CPI, CPI(M) and the Maoists

Critique of Peaceful Transition to Socialism

The naxal politics as it emerged in the 1960s is embedded in the larger political context of protest movements and disillusionment with the existing political regime in the country during the 1960s. It was an era characterised by rise in regional political parties who formed governments in eight states after the fourth General Elections in 1967 which had an unprecedented voter turnout[4] and weakening of the one-party dominance of the Congress. Those were the times marked by popular uprisings, student riots and agrarian unrest, industrial strikes, *gheraos* and *dharnas* in several cities. It was also a period where the increase in defence expenditure due to the Indo–Pak war burdened the exchequer, and correspondingly there was a decline in public expenditure on capital goods, railways, power and metals and mining and industrial stagnation due to narrow home market, unemployment and the economic downturn compounded by food crisis and drought. Indeed the 1960s were the times of vibrant political expressions outside the institutional frameworks of the Parliament and the state assemblies adding substance and content to India's democracy.

More specifically the naxal politics in India can be traced to the Communist Party of India (CPI) and its own dynamics as it evolved in the early 1960s. This included the larger ideological and programmatic framework of the CPI at a national level, and also the diverse trajectories of the CPI, its organisational strengths and its history in all the states where it led agrarian movements, and trade unions. When elections were held once again in 1957 the Communists were reduced to a non-entity even in the two states of Andhra Pradesh and West Bengal where they had always had a considerable support. To the members of CPI in Andhra Pradesh this was particularly mortifying after the tremendous public sympathy and support they had received in the wake of the Telangana People's Armed Struggle of 1948-1951. They were inclined to strengthen the agrarian struggles on the ground.

The 'Amritsar thesis' of CPI in 1958 decided to abjure violence and participate in elections, and accept parliamentary democracy and constitutionalism to make a peaceful transition to socialism.[5] This stand led to its alignment with the 'national bourgeoisie'—a class that had progressive sections, was against imperialism and an ally of the working class which could defeat the monopoly groups, landlords and wholesalers.

The shift in CPI's stand to support constitutionalism and parliamentary action coupled with support given to specific policies of Indian National Congress in post-independent India could not fit into the mood of the left at the grassroots level. They were concerned about the somewhat indifferent attitude that the CPI had towards agrarian and tribal struggles in the Khammam and Warangal districts as well as in Srikakulam which were led by district level CPI leaders, replete with sacrifices and gains. Likewise there were other areas, more importantly Naxalbari in West Bengal where a tribal movement for land was in progress.

Many party members felt that the CPI was lending support to Congress and Nehru because the government was getting close to the Soviet Union. They saw this as a dilution in the programme of agrarian struggles that were developing in early 1960s. Therefore several of them supported China in the Sino-Indian war in 1962 claiming that it was a conflict between a socialist and a capitalist state. Hundreds of CPI leaders, accused of being pro-Chinese, were detained without trial. The differences between the two factions simmered and at a CPI National Council meeting held on April 11, 1964, 32 Council members walked out in protest, accusing S.A. Dange and his followers of 'anti-unity and anti-Communist policies.'

Split in CPI, CPI(M) and Maoists

While there were differences amongst themselves in their opposition to CPI, yet together they formed the 'Communist Party of India (Marxist)' [CPI(M)]. P. Sundarayya was elected general secretary of the party at the Calcutta Congress in 1964 claiming that they represented 104,421 CPI members, 60 percent of the total party membership. The Conference did not allow any dissidence especially those representing the Maoist line and path of agrarian struggles. Parimal Das Gupta's alternative draft programme from West Bengal[6] was not circulated at the Calcutta conference. Souren Bose, a delegate from Darjeeling questioned why there was no mention of Mao nor was of his portrait there along with other communist stalwarts. His intervention met with huge applause from the delegates of the conference indicative of a pro-Maoist strand in the opposition to CPI but was not included in the Party agenda.

Throughout 1964-1967 the pro-Maoists of CPI(M) in the country continued with their propaganda on an alternative line. In Andhra Pradesh, publicity was given to Peking's views[7] on all important issues through articles published in *Janashakti*.[8] In Kerala, Sengadi was the forum for Peking's views. In Bengal, 'The Revolutionary Council' led by Parimal Das Gupta, the 'Chinta group', of Amulya Sen and the 'Marx—Engels group' of Sushital Roy Choudhary were actually carrying out Maoist propaganda. However, by far the more active proponent of Maoist line was Charu Majumdar. Between the years 1965-1967, Charu wrote eight letters laying down the strategy for carrying out the revolution in the country. He also formed the 'Siliguri Council' along with Kanu Sanyal, Jangal Santhal, and several other Maoists from Bengal calling for an instant armed peasant revolution. This was a period where alignments and realignments of the groups and factions within and outside CPI(M) occurred emphasising a Maoist perspective. This reinforced the tribal and agrarian struggles in Siliguri in West Bengal and in several districts in Andhra Pradesh.

CPI(M) Split and West Bengal Maoists

After winning the election and forming the United Front government in West Bengal in 1967 the CPI(M) spelled out its party line to strike a difference in their stand with both the Maoists and the CPI through the Madurai Draft. The Madurai Draft characterised the epoch as that of weakening of imperialism but still required the armed might and diplomacy of socialist camp, forces of national liberation movements in colonial and neocolonial countries, proletarian revolutionary movements in advanced capitalist countries and peace movements to defeat imperialism. It criticised Soviet Union for transforming dictatorship of proletariat to dictatorship of Party but felt that the unity of socialist countries was essential for success of revolution in any place and to this extent it advised China to 'unite in action' with Soviet Union in giving aid to Vietnam. They differed with the Chinese view that India was a stooge of imperialism and held that the Congress Party continued to hold considerable influence despite weakening economic situation. On the other hand the revolutionary party was far from being properly organised and as such to talk about immediate revolution at this stage amounted to neglecting the realities of the situation.

The reaction of the Bengal Maoists to the Madurai document among other issues was to give a call to overthrow the leadership of CPI(M) which was now in the government as it supported 'peaceful transition to socialism' and refused to lead country wide mass upsurge and mass movements. The Maoists in Bengal severed its links with CPI (M) and formed the All India Coordination Committee of Communist Revolutionaries (AICCCR) in May 1968. It was essentially an organisation of Bengal Maoists under the leadership of Charu Majumdar and Kanu Sanyal and in a course of one year formed a new party, CPI(ML) in May 1969 taking several radical Maoists such as Kunnikal Narayanan from Kerala, the Srikakulam group and others from Andhra Pradesh, and also from Punjab and Tamil Nadu. They were in agreement on Soviet Union having become revisionist, necessity of armed struggle and non-participation in elections in India. A high prestige accrued to them with the recognition and open support of Communist Party of China (CPC) and also support of middle class urban youth, artists, and other cultural groups and intellectuals especially in Kolkata who were not directly associated with the CPI(M) or CPI.

CPI(M) Split and Maoists in Andhra Pradesh

The Andhra unit of CPI(M) which had a large group of Maoists too criticised the Madurai document and unlike the Bengal Maoists held the view that that prolonged armed revolution is the only path left open to all backward countries for social emancipation. They did not object to the CPI(M)'s formulation that legal and illegal work must be combined and so must parliamentary work with mass struggles. However, they denied that their stand on elections was the same as that of CPI(M) on the ground that they were pursuing it as a tactic to expose the illusory nature of the parliamentary party and not as an alternative strategy to armed struggle.

Further, even after the Bengal Maoists broke away from CPI(M), the Andhra Maoists continued with the CPI(M) since the state committee in Andhra Pradesh was dominated by Maoists. This continued until it became fully evident that there was no meeting ground between the CPI(M) and the Maoists used its platform and took away a very large section of party cadre when they finally split in 1968 and formed the Andhra Pradesh Coordination Committee of Communist Revolutionaries (APCCCR). The movement in Srikakulam and also the revolutionary fervor of the Naxalbari movement also pressurised them to break away from CPI(M). Both these movements were facing severe repression from the police as well as attacks of the local landlords.[9]

APCCCR reorganised its activities after July 1970 around a programme of popular agitations, political education and land occupation though the programme of creating armed squads and liberated zones remained the long-term objective. The leaders were Chandra Pulla Reddy, Tarimela Nagi Reddy, Devulapalli Venkateswarlu and Kolla Venkayya. At the same time there were dissenting voices among the Maoists in Andhra Pradesh who represented the Srikakulam movement and also Kondapalli Seetharamaiah and K.G. Satyamurty who were inspired by Charu's basic premise of the existence of revolutionary upsurge everywhere and that the setbacks were seen as only being temporary and as arising out of organisational and operational weaknesses which could be overcome.

Beginnings of Armed Struggle

Darjeeling

In the Siliguri division of Darjeeling district the communists under the leadership of Charu Majumdar, Jangal Santhal, and Kanu Sanyal started mobilising the tribal community on issues of occupation of land that belonged legally to them. Charu formulated the Maoist line as early as 1964, and was the first to circulate the Chinese documents, among members of CPI, set up a parallel committee within the CPI (M) to propagate Maoism. As early as 1966 they formed a parallel party centre of the CPI(M) where they launched a struggle not for land or crops but for political power.

It drew the attention of CPC who hailed in the editorial of *People's Daily*, July 5, 1967 that, 'A peal of spring thunder has crashed over the land of India' and added that the 'revolutionary group of the Indian Communist Party has done the absolutely correct thing' by adopting the revolutionary line advanced by Chinese leader Mao Zedong, which involved 'relying on the peasants, establishing base area in the countryside, persisting in protracted armed struggle and using the countryside to encircle and finally capture the cities.' The editorial concluded that, 'a single spark can start a prairie fire' and that, 'a great storm of revolutionary armed struggle will eventually sweep across the length and breadth of India.'

With CPI(M) winning elections in West Bengal in 1967 and forming the ministry they tried to persuade the local leadership of Naxalbari to withdraw their plans for struggle, but failed miserably to win them over. In March 1967, a tribal youth who had obtained a judicial order, went to plough his land. The local landlords attacked him. Enraged at the retaliation to a legitimate claim over land, tribals under the leadership of the Maoists started recapturing all their lands determined to set Naxalbari as an example of implementation of the political line backed by the Chinese moral support. Under these circumstances, the United Front Government of West Bengal led by CPI (M) ordered full scale police action in which thousands were arrested including Kanu Sanyal and other leaders. The Darjeeling District Committee was dissolved and Charu Majumdar and Souren Bose were expelled from the party.[10]

The Maoists in Bengal severed its links with CPI(M) and formed AICCCR in May 1968 under the leadership of Charu Majumdar and Kanu Sanyal. They were in agreement on Soviet Union having become revisionist, necessity of armed struggle and non-participation in elections in India.

Kolkata

The context of the Bengal group was provided by the growing self-activity of the working class in terms of *gheraos, dharnas* and strikes, the enormous problems of city of Calcutta, enthusiastic support of youth and students, the hunger riots of 1966 and above all the experiences of Naxalbari.

In the words of Mohit Sen, 'In Calcutta, it was a more murderous business. The poorer students coming from lower middle-class families formed the bulk of the activists. Presidency College, though, was an exception. It was an elitist institution in both the good and the bad sense of the term. Some brilliant students became Naxalites and engaged in mayhem and murder. Statues of Rammohan Roy, Ishwar Chand Vidyasagar and Rabindranath Tagore were beheaded or vandalised. Books by reputed authors were burnt on the grounds that they reinforced the rule of the exploiters. Colleges and schools were closed down on the premise that it was foolish to study. The young participants had been taught to kill first those who were easiest to kill, i.e., traffic constables, milkmen, doctors going out on calls, smaller landlords who did not have private security, etc. Those who had received their baptism in murder were sent off to the villages. It became dangerous to move about by oneself in deserted streets and lanes after dark. There has been far too much romanticising about the Naxalites especially by some Communist writers, themselves disillusioned and with guilty conscience. It has to be recorded, however, that the police and special task forces set up to seek out and destroy the Naxalites dealt mercilessly with them. This is true of the CPI(M) as well as the Congress Governments. State terrorism was more brutal than the Naxalites. Public opinion turned against both and by and large watched helplessly waiting for the nightmare to end. It did end leaving hardly any traces of the movement behind. Some of the leaders later participated in the elections. Others, including the infamous Charu Majumdar, were betrayed by their colleagues."[11]

Naxalbari's importance in the history of Maoist movement is based not on the intensity of the movement or its success (both of these were quite limited) but on symbolic significance and theoretical value. It had a symbolic value in the sense that it came to represent idealism and revolutionary ardor for many young people. To the Indian communist movement it posed the question of seizing political power and directing all struggles in that direction. Also, theoretically it aimed at the implementation of agrarian, peasant based guerilla struggle in rural areas with the specific intention of destroying the existing power structure. It was also the first recent example of the practice of Maoist path in India.

Formation of CPI(ML)

The internal debates amongst the factions within the Maoists crystallised their different positions and paved the way for the formation of the CPI(ML) and its party line. It was believed that people were ready and the immediate aim of the struggle was to seize political power and that it was simply a matter of the armed forces of the people destroying the armed forces of the ruling class. The immediate task was to destroy State power, liberate people for completion of agrarian revolution. Thus, for example, the direct attack of Kunnikal Narayanan on police stations of Tellichery and Pulpally in Wynad forests in Kerala by 300 people was commended by Charu and the Peking Radio as well. Participation in elections was also seen as abandoning of revolutionary path for parliamentary path.

The CPI(ML) implemented its line of unleashing Naxalbari type of struggles in various areas in 1969 with varying degrees of success. The line as it was implemented in early 1968 had extremely limited success, that too only in Srikakulam, Musahari and Lakhimpur. Even in these areas the movement was ultimately suppressed by police forces. In those circumstances the choice before the CPI(ML) was either to abandon the basic assessment of the situation—as being favourable to immediate armed activities for capturing State power or to make certain tactical innovations which might enable them to continue with armed struggle. The CPI(ML) chose the latter alternative and as a result fell prey to self-accelerating extremism, i.e., by persisting with their original assessment of the situation they had to shift from armed mass uprising of the Naxalbari and early Srikakulam type to limited guerilla actions and then to individual annihilation and abandonment of peasant struggles and finally to terrorist activities.

Importance of Srikakulam

It is in Srikakulam that the theoretical formulations of the Maoists through the AICCCR and subsequently the CPI(ML) were actualised into practice in Srikakulam. The movement here began in 1958 where the communist workers organised *sanghamas* and over the years led series of agitations and movements against forced labour, for higher wages, against forest contractors against corruption and high handedness of revenue, forest and excise officials and finally against landlords for fair rents. They succeeded in large measure in instilling a sense of self-respect, dignity and self-confidence among the tribal people. However, the movement in Srikakulam entered a stage of stagnation. It faced intense repression by the police; one evidence of it was the involvement of over 600 *sangham* members in police cases in 1964 and the killing of some 70 activists from 1952 to 1968 in Srikakulam and Telangana areas. How was the movement to overcome this impasse? The dominant tendency was to opt for greater militancy.

Breaking the impasse the Naxalbari Solidarity Committee which had students from Guntur Medical College along with the Srikakulam communist leaders established direct contacts with Charu Majumdar and joined the CPI(ML). Charu ignored the losses due to police action in Srikakulam and instead gave a call to raise the movement to the higher stage of armed guerilla struggle by guiding them to start armed squad action for seizure of crops of the landlords and occupation of temple lands, etc., and through this they hoped to create a people's army and a liberated zone. Faced with further isolation from tribal and police suppression, the CPI(ML) leadership would not give up its framework of armed struggle but introduced the tactic of individual annihilation of class enemies, i.e., landlords, moneylenders, police informers and policemen. Finally, during 1969-70 the Government was able to suppress the movement wiping out most of its leaders. However as we will see, while the movement in Srikakulam was effectively suppressed it could not efface the basic perspective that armed struggle is the only method for seizure of political power.

II

Second Phase—Splits among Maoists: Triumph of Armed Struggle

The decade of the 1970s was marked by the Congress Party coming back to office. Capitalising on the euphoria in the country subsequent to emerging victorious in the war with Pakistan and the accomplishment of Bangladesh liberation, Indira Gandhi steered the Congress to a landslide victory in 1971. Campaigning on the slogan of 'Garibi Hatao' (remove poverty), she returned to Parliament with 352 seats, an improvement from the party's poor show of 283 in the previous polls. This should have led to greater political stability, but it was followed by a period of unrest and pressure of movements especially those led by Jayaprakash Narayan leading to the declaration of Emergency.

More particularly, it was marked by the Congress coming back to office in 1972 in West Bengal and the fall of CPI(M) and a hard stand by the government to combat the naxal offensive in Kolkata and other districts amidst the challenges of resettling over a million of Bangladeshi refugees. And in Andhra Pradesh, as home minister Vengal Rao took a firm stand to wipe out naxal politics before he became its chief minister in 1973. During his tenure as the chief minister from 1973-1978, which also coincided with the phase of Emergency, the government took steps to contain Maoists. He replaced local officers with officers from far away districts so that a naxalite-police nexus could not be formed. Even more, during the Emergency many 'encounter deaths' occurred.[12]

For the Maoists, it was a period of splits, alignments and re-alignments following Charu's death in 1972, and crushing of the movements in Srikakulam and West Bengal through police action. The police repression became even more severe after the declaration of the state of emergency. In fact the Maoist activists in the field have always been under police surveillance but with Emergency in operation several Maoist sympathisers and their front organisations such as the Andhra Pradesh Civil Liberties Committee (APCLC) were forced to go underground. Unable to withstand the pressure many activists also abandoned their support to the Maoists. This had an adverse impact on their networks and also functioning. In spite of this the CPI(ML) held its second Congress in February 1976 at Gaya in Bihar and resolved to continue its armed guerilla struggles and work for an anti-Congress United Front.

In a way in the early 1970s most of the Maoist groups were working independently in Andhra Pradesh, West Bengal, Bihar, Punjab, Maharashtra, Kerala and Tamil Nadu and their ideological stands were defined by their understanding of whether to carry out armed struggle immediately as people were ready, or build a mass base and in the process go for an armed struggle.

One set of groups took a moderate line and propagated the need for a mass base, participation in multiple forms of struggles with armed struggle being one of the forms, contesting the elections at the *panchayat* level, even if it was in the Maoist framework of armed agrarian struggle. These were CPI(ML) CP group which had joined the Satya Narayan Singh's Party the CPI(ML) Coordination Committee in 1977 but split from them in 1980, the Unity Centre of Communist Revolutionaries of India (UCCRI) group of Devulapalli that was formed in 1975 which aligned with Moni Guha but this did not last even one year; the Central Organising Committee (COC) led by Sharma and Suniti Kumar Ghosh which aligned with Kondapalli Seetharamaiah in Andhra but even this alignment did not last as the latter chose to take a more radical stance; and the Organising Committee of the Communist Revolutionaries (OCCR), a group formed in the Visakhapatnam jail by Kanu Sanyal and Nagabhushan Patnaik.

The groups that took a pro-Charu line were the anti-Lin Piao group led by Vinod Mishra, based in Bhojpur, Bihar which later evolved into CPI(ML) Vinod Mishra group, the CPI(ML) CRC Venu group which was coming together of a section of Kerala pro-Charu faction and a splinter group from Andhra; and the PWG of Andhra that was formed in 1976 and evolved into the CPI(ML) PWG by 1980. Since then the CPI(ML) made several attempts to forge unity between the rival groups and factions in Tamil Nadu, Bihar, Assam and Maharashtra and Andhra and even contacted activists in Punjab but these did not yield any lasting result.[13]

There was yet another group called the Maoist Communist Centre (MCC) led by Amulya Sen and Kanhai Chatterjee that did not fall into either of the positions. This had an independent presence. Thus there was a maze of splits and realignments in this decade. Over a period of time those who took a moderate line gradually dissipated. And those for whom a call for armed struggle was an immediate task stayed on.

People's War Group in Andhra Pradesh

On the other hand the CPI(ML) PWG spearheaded by Kondapalli Seetharamaiah in 1980 was the party that consolidated its position particularly in Bihar and Andhra Pradesh and it was in continuity with Charu Majumdar's line of armed struggle.[14] Going against the groups of Chandra Pulla and Tarimella Nagi in Andhra Pradesh that emphasised preparation of the people and nurturing front organisations as pre-requisite to armed struggle, PWG was of the opinion that the people were already fully prepared for armed struggle. The group went on to state that one need not wait for large areas to be liberated before starting the armed struggle as some others had claimed. According to them, to postpone or avoid armed struggle on the plea that sufficient area was not available even when people were prepared was tantamount to a revisionist manifestation. Thus, every form of struggle including annihilation would ultimately transform into a higher form as the struggle intensified. Till such time as this actually happens annihilation would continue as one of the forms of struggle.[15]

The cornerstone of PWG was the mobilisation of students through the Radical Students Union (RSU) by a campaign called 'Go to villages' to integrate the student activists with the rural masses. The students took part in the movement as members of the squads in Adilabad, Jangaon, Karimnagar and Khammam. Batches of 5 to 10 students were sent to villages to stay with the Dalits and the poorest in the village. In these villages groups of youth were mobilised by singing and teaching revolutionary songs and attempts to educate them on the policies of seizure of power through armed struggle, as also on the need for an agrarian revolution were made. They also collected statistics of existing land distribution in villages and with the help of these concrete statistics proved the inevitable necessity of redistribution of land according to the principal of 'land to the tiller.' The campaign was strictly in consonance with the party's line that all organisations must ultimately serve the party's task of ushering in the democratic revolution. The RSU was indeed a recruitment ground for full-time party cadre.

The activities of the RSU and the Radical Youth League (RYL) triggered massive land occupation programmes of the peasants as well as tribal communities. They took courage to reclaim the land that was assigned to them with support from CPI(ML) PWG in Karimnagar and Adilabad districts. People's courts were organised by them for instant justice and trials, some of them resulting in violence and crime. The Andhra Pradesh government declare several areas in Karimnagar district as 'disturbed areas' giving police draconian powers.

Squad Action and Armed Struggle

Squad action of the PWG met with severe police action and pressure on the cadre more so in the plains areas. As a response 'annihilation of class enemies' continued to be a form of struggle. In addition a 'modified' form of squad action was introduced. In this the squad was not a fixed one and members from different places collected at a point just prior to the action to carry out the attack and as soon as the action was completed the squad dispersed. With this form of operation the element of secrecy was very high and it was difficult for the police to isolate the entire squad at one time. In fact tracing the identity of the members of the squad became a difficult proposition and therefore it was generally not necessary for the participants to go underground and to this extent the party's responsibility towards their maintenance was reduced.

In the forests, the squad members were in a better position to defend themselves against police attacks working as a group. The squads were given extensive training both in methods of offence and defence. The weaponry used also gained a certain amount of sophistication. Over a period of time the main fighting force of the PWG was a platoon comprising 25 to 30 highly trained guerrillas organised into sections and sub-sections. There were two types of platoons—the military platoon and the protection platoon which were located in the guerrilla zones. The *dalam* or armed squad comprising 5-7 cadres was the secondary-fighting unit. The strength of a squad was varied, as is its type. Mostly, it was in the form of a local guerrilla squad (LGS) and in some areas it functions as a central guerrilla squad (CGS).

PWG and Expansion to Other States

In view of the intense suppression by the State police force of the PWG in Adilabad and Karimnagar districts of Andhra Pradesh, the PWG armed squads came to Bastar area in Chhattisgarh and the Gadchiroli area in Maharashtra, in the 80s. They claimed a string of bases in remote and inaccessible areas with a virtual parallel government in some 'liberated zones', particularly in the tribal areas in the Dandakaranya belt.[16] Beginning from a stage of suspicion the cadre was treated by the villagers as one among them. The local tribal communities gave them respect, won their trust and instilled confidence in them to take to collective action. Consequently the tribal communities confronted forest guards on their corruption, questioned forest contractors and demanded better rates for *tendu* leaves and bamboo. While there were remarkable gains, these actions invited police repression. It was decided to learn from earlier experiences in Andhra, and consolidate their gains. Undeterred by police force, the PWG moved in the direction of creating a base and a guerilla zone with a view to creating a people's army with people's support.

After the late 1980s there has been a turnover of leadership, with younger cadres[17]. They renewed their strategy emphasising the importance of revolutionary armed struggle. Class struggle and armed struggle were to be led by armed cadres. The strong party organisation of PWG had a clear distinction between the political and military wing. On the political side the PWG consisted of the Central committee at the apex, regional bureaus, zonal or state committees, district or division committees and squad area committees. In the military sphere, the Central Military Commission (CMC) headed by the General Secretary Ganapathi stood at the top. And there were military commissions parallel to the political committees at each level. At the bottom was the village defence squad, consisting of a handful of people in a village, organised as a people's militia, and possessing basic training in handling small arms. At the political level, there were the village governance committees.

Maoist Communist Centre (MCC)

The MCC founded in October 1969 was led by Amulya Sen and Kanhai Chatterjee. It was never a part of CPI(ML) and indeed criticised Charu Majumdar's line of annihilation of class enemies[18.] It held the view that, 'it is only through agrarian revolutionary guerilla struggle and the establishment of people's army that a red base area can be built up. Again through this work alone can the revolutionary high tide be accelerated throughout the country, and depending on the base area and with the help of People's Army, the agrarian revolution can be consolidated, deepened and expanded'.[19] During 1967-1969 it started its interventions in Kolkata, Howrah, Midnapur, Burdwan, Bardhaman, Birbhum, 24 Parganas in West Bengal, Gaya in Bihar and also in Assam and Tripura. Through the Krantikari Kisan committees of the peasants, they took up demands for wage increase, fertiliser problem, seizure of crops, confiscation of grains and even punished 'notorious' landlords and distribution of land to landless peasants in Kanksha block in Bardhaman district in West Bengal which was suppressed.

Between 1979 to 1988 the MCC focussed its activities in Bihar. A Bihar–Bengal Special Area Committee was established and was successful in building their squads whom they called the Red Defense Corps and the Youth and Women Fronts. Thereafter they extended their activities from Gaya to Dhanbad, Bokaro, Aurangabad,

Hazaribagh and Giridh in Jharkhand. It is reported that they had raised their squads and squad action, built people's trust and confidence in them for redistribution of lands, off-loading trucks full of grains and its distribution, conduct People's courts and settle disputes in favour of the tribal communities and so on. In the process many villages came under their control which they could call as base area. Undoubtedly this invited repression. The MCC developed its militia in a systematic fashion to take to offensive action which would eventually contribute to the building of the PLGA.

Since the early 80s the CPI(ML) PWG has been contacting likeminded Maoist groups to form an all-India alliance with the objective of overthrowing 'the bureaucrat comprador bourgeois and big landlords classes who control state power in collusion with imperialism' and 'to establish in its place the New Democratic State under the leadership of the proletariat' with the ultimate aim of establishing socialism and communism. This was especially so with the MCC.[20] Due to turf issues and internecine squabbles and violence this effort did not yield any result. There were attempts to join Kanu Sanyal and the PWG, but this got aborted with death of Amulya Sen and Kanhai Chatterjee in 1982, and arrest of Kanu Sanyal, Pramod Mishra and Sanjay Dusadh emerged as the most formidable leaders of the MCC.[21]

It became clear that those Maoists who viewed armed struggle as an ultimate stage of the movement, something of a grand finale, which was to be carried out only after the people had all been sufficiently motivated and their level of political consciousness raised did not continue with the same fervour and soon were gone. On the other hand those who emphasised Charu's line of armed struggle—here and now and the need for raising people's political consciousness and participation as a part of the process of armed struggle continued, even when in an area the police could totally suppress the movement. The Maoist politics that has become a challenge in the 21st century is a continuation of this line of armed struggle.

III

Why Maoists?

There cannot be any one explanation for the origins and continuation of naxal politics. The overall explanation is the relentless work of the local cadre and their ability to establish contact with the poor and the tribal communities in the struggle for dignity. More specific factors could be the limited reach of the State, its programmes and policies in spite of special provisions governing tribal areas; inability of the CPI to guide the movement in preparing the community to engage with the various departments of land and revenue, forest and police and also the development sector and pressurise the State to democratise its system, structures and procedures; the growing institutional memory of the naxal politics to evolve ways of surviving police and para-military attacks and in building a party organ that is secretive and centralised to carry out the strategy of armed struggle; and the legitimacy it gains for taking up the cause of the poorest and most vulnerable sections in the society.

Role of Cadre: Emphasis on Dignity of the Poor

In this period from 1964-1984, the naxal interventions were most accepted among the poorest and the most deprived in our country. The Maoists developed skills to recruit local cadre without much difficulty. Young boys and girls fired with the imagination that they could play a role in bringing about equity and justice in the lives of the poor were given sufficient training and a world-view that enabled them to defy all authority, sacrifice and take risks. Having seen no other way of fighting for justice, they become the true foot soldiers of the movement.

The local cadres of the movement have been the actual backbone of the struggle over the years. The dedication and sacrifice of the cadre and their faith in the capacities of the tribal community brought them close to the community. They have had an advantage over the State functionaries because they have known how to treat the poor with dignity. In spite of losses and sacrifices of the youth for the movement; they become legendary figures and local heroes inspiring each new generation to join the Maoist politics. Indeed this was not easily replicable by the functionaries of the government, with a few exceptions.

State Deficit and Maoist Presence

It is seen that most of the areas where the naxals were active the presence of the State has been negligible if not totally absent. They have all the indicators of backwardness for example illiteracy, ill-health, lack of water and sanitation, malnutrition and non-availability of infrastructure, connectivity and so on. There is lack of clarity on entitlements to land and other resources and have left the tribal and the marginalised rural population disempowered and helpless. In addition their experience with State machinery, usually the forest, revenue and police officials, have seldom been positive. The distance between the State functionaries and the poor as well as the tribal groups was wide and manipulated in favour of local landholders and authorities. The concerned officials have been corrupt and are not known to have addressed the community as equals giving them respect and dignity.

In fact it is also an area that has coincided with rich mineral resources enabling flight of mineral wealth at the cost of backwardness and underdevelopment in these areas. It has also caused devastation of forests as well as ecology. While the markets have penetrated and exploited the natural resources, the tribal communities have lost their livelihoods. They have never been given the capacity to engage with either the market or the public institutions to their advantage.

It was in the context of State deficit that the naxals have been able to win over the tribal community, gain their acceptance and trust and give them confidence to seek a path that would liberate them through armed struggle. While the poverty arguments as well as the backwardness have been true to fuel the politics of naxals in the area, the broader issues relating to absence of the State as well as treating the tribal community as unequal citizens have a role to play in creating popular support for the Naxal activists.

Fifth Schedule and the Constitution of India

Most of the areas with a predominant presence of the naxals, *viz.*, Andhra Pradesh, Bihar, Madhya Pradesh, Maharashtra and Orissa come under the Fifth Schedule of the Constitution of India. Much of the tribal unrest could have been prevented if only due attention was paid to instruments in the Constitution as contained in this schedule.

Even in the pre-independence period, there were many heroic battles fought by the tribals against the British colonial regime. Tribal revolts were suppressed and the tribal dominant areas were declared as non-regulation areas. In 1874, the Scheduled District Act was enacted and all non-regulation areas were designated as scheduled districts. The policy for the administration of tribal areas finally culminated in the 1935 Government of India Act. While framing India's Constitution there was the recognition of the fact that these scheduled areas with predominantly tribal population required special attention; therefore the Fifth Schedule in the Constitution under Article 244 enabled a framework of administration to concretise the directives contained in Article 46.[22] The Governor was responsible for the peace and governance of scheduled areas and had the power to make regulations for the welfare of the tribals and secure their rights over tribal land. He was also required to draw up annually a report on the administration of the scheduled areas and submit it to the President. The schedule also provided for a Tribal Advisory Council which the governor had to consult, of whom three-fourths had to be representatives of scheduled tribes in the legislative assembly of the state. The Constitution has given only tribal people this privilege according to which they are constitutionally mandated to participate in their policymaking. These provisions are so strong and comprehensive that the Fifth Schedule has been termed by some legal authorities as 'Constitution within the Constitution.'

It is only due to the pressure of naxal politics and tribal revolts that legal and policy measures were introduced under the Fifth Schedule. For example, the enactment of The Andhra Pradesh (Scheduled Area Ryotwari Settlement) Regulation, 1970 Act which prevented sale and transaction of land under possession of a non-tribal in the scheduled areas to another non-tribal. Also in 1986, after the blasting of Central Reserve Police Force (CRPF) truck by PWG in Adilabad district, the Government of Andhra Pradesh reserved 100 percent of jobs in 26 departments such as school teachers, auxiliary nurse and midwife (ANMs), and so on for local tribals.

Communist Party and its Role

An analysis of the history of CPI suggests that it seems that they are partly responsible for the development of the line of armed struggle in the country. When there were growing mass movements in the country either in Naxalbari or in Srikakulam the CPI did not offer any support to them. They did not give guidance to them or even engage with the government either at the state level or national level, raise administrative as well as policy demands on behalf of their own cadre and the people who were struggling for their legitimate share in the resources and their entitlements. It did nothing to utilise the mass pressure to strengthen the capacities of the State to deliver services. According to Mohit Sen, 'the CPI had not worked out the strategy of the democratic transition to the next stage of the revolution while CPI(M) denounced such strategy as revisionist betrayal of the revolution.'[23]

In the initial stages of the movement, i.e., in the 1960s the State had little capacity to respond to the petitions made by the community on legitimate demands. Neither did the CPI have a strategy for supporting the local movements and guide them to engage with the system in bringing about democratisation of public institutions as part of its strategy for 'peaceful transition to socialism' in accordance with the Amritsar Thesis. Thus by the 1970s the Maoists saw the State as the enemy of the people. The movements were perforce allowed to come to a dead end. The leaders who did not want to give up the battle chose to follow the armed struggle line of Charu Majumdar.

The Idea of 'Armed Struggle'

Over the years the Maoists evolved a conscious strategy of giving the tribal community and local youth confidence to confront the existing power structures and fight against injustice. This is especially so in those areas where their experience of the community with the State functionaries had been negative and the State presence was in deficit.

Subsequently, the path of armed struggle became the trait of militant and radical left wing movements. It was bound to develop a logic of its own and as we have seen from a small beginning of developing squads for self-defense over the years the Maoists have evolved into a party with sophisticated arms and ammunitions, building strategies to take on the State military and armed forces. Their expansion to newer areas and states was in spite of severe police repression where several cadres and leaders lost their lives; the movement was virtually finished in many areas and districts and as in the instance of Andhra Pradesh, splits amongst Maoist groups for leadership and turf battles. They could also merge with all groups overcoming deep fissures and violent differences, developed more numbers of local cadres and in a relatively short span of time acquired skills in mobilising communities and obtaining their confidence and trust. This was in addition to the sophistication they are constantly achieving in directly attacking the CRPF, paramilitary forces and the police.

All those Maoists that had a moderate stand on armed struggle did not survive. Somewhere the clear cut strategy of 'armed struggle' without any nuances sent simple and straightforward messages. We have seen that these youth have been able to mobilise the tribal communities through songs, literature, meetings and mobilisation strategies that focus on impoverishment and exploitation of the tribal community and the forces responsible for their vulnerability. The message that gets across is that it is only violence and through armed struggle that justice will be rendered. It is in consonance with the mythical stories of triumph of the good over the evil where that *rakshasa* is killed once and for all. A more complicated line becomes difficult to transact and negotiate at all levels from the village to the State.

Levy and Maintenance of the Party

As of late 1980s the naxals[24] had a huge network of whole timers, party cadre and bosses, squads and supporters. They had poets and singers, and a network of men and women from the community to cater to. Plus they had links with their sympathisers and service providers like couriers and providers of arms and ammunition, printers and suppliers of all their commodities. More important were the thousands of cadre who emerged through community mobilisation and were inducted in the process of participating in raids and their constant training to be part of the party organisation and the military wing. All these had to be sustained.

The survival of Maoists is thus linked to their capacities to raise money over the course of time through extortion from government contracted workers, politicians, and investment project developers and also by levying taxes on *tendu patta,* the leaves used to roll unfiltered Indian cigarettes known as *beedis*[25]. This has evolved into a fairly systematic procedure of levies to be paid by contractors of public works such as roads, bridges and buildings, petrol pump owners, pharmacists, groceries stores, shoes and textile shops, land owners and so on. They have also demanded money from industries functioning in the areas 'as and when they need' and even issue receipts for the same.[26]

It is quite ironical that all these companies have paid a handsome levy to the naxals in return for protection and safety from them. It is their contribution that went into the coffers of the Party, to maintain them and their cadre, even if in frugal conditions and enable them get their supplies of sophisticated arms and ammunitions. It is difficult to tell how either the corporates or the Maoists find this partnership ethical. While the corporates get the required protection, the Maoists are able to sustain themselves. In the short run it is a win-win situation and helps the naxals perpetuate themselves.

Support for Naxals and Legitimacy

It is stated that the naxal politics in its earlier phase was infused with idealism and romanticism and over a period of time, it has lost this spirit. Stated differently, the Maoists were on a correct path earlier but have become a terrorist outfit now. It must be recognised that their justification of violence is the same as when they started out in the 1960s. The idealist phase paved the way for making the idea of using violence an acceptable form of seizure of power. Their politics has remained consistent and its development over a period of time into such a militarist programme has its roots in its original understanding of armed struggle and its necessity.

At times even those in bureaucracy, intellectuals and politicians trace naxal politics to poverty and backwardness. Overwhelmed by the heroic sacrifices and dedication of the naxal cadre in bringing forth the issue of justice to the poor, even as they condemn the naxal violence, they see that the cause is a genuine one. Thus they lend their voices to bring legitimacy to the politics of the naxals. The fact that the naxals have worked for the poor and marginalised does not automatically make their politics acceptable. We have seen the consequences of their politics of violence and under no circumstance can their path be justified. Therefore there is no question of having an 'understanding approach' to the Maoists and even if it is characterised by sacrifice it is still action that is devoid of political solution in the direction of deepening of democracy. The support to naxal politics gives them legitimacy and fosters their continuance.

IV

State Response

Increase in Police and Armed Forces

In the Maoists' understanding an unjust war was imposed by the comprador bureaucratic bourgeoisie, feudal forces of this country and imperialists, particularly America. 'This all out war (was) unleashed by the enemy...principally against the Maoist movement but also aimed against the movement of the oppressed communities, and nationalities in India. Therefore it was inevitable that an armed struggle had to be waged to take on the might of the police and armed forces of the Indian state.'[27]

Once a war has been declared by the Maoists, there is no space for civil liberties or human rights. The state governments have massacred tribals and anybody suspicious of having links with the Maoists. It has dealt with the naxal challenge in a combative manner by stepping up its forces. It has increased the budgets for the police and paramilitary forces over the years and procurement of arms and ammunition for warfare of this nature. It is convinced that a hard stance and use of brutal force to suppress the movement as in the case of the action by the Greyhounds in Andhra[28] would alone be able to squash the movement once and for all. There is a greater clarity on how to enhance the police forces and their capacities.[29]

All Maoist action was based on the assumption that there were no democratic spaces in the existing system and it was futile to engage with the state which was actually an enemy of the people. According to them, the state used the might of force such as the police, paramilitary force and the army to repress any legitimate demand made by the poor. Their politics, therefore, compels the state response to be that of brutal use of force. The State response is a mirror image of the manner in which it was constructed by the Maoists. As we know, the State expresses itself through ideology, structures and processes that are dynamic and requires political ingenuity to engage at all levels of the state apparatus. Maoists had neither the patience nor the capacity for such politics.

The increase in police presence has not actually curbed the Maoists over the years. They have been effective in Andhra but in driving the Maoist leaders to other areas have fostered the Maoist politics of armed struggle in newer areas. Indeed it has provoked more combative skills and abilities and greater militarisation of the Maoists. This begs the question whether a militarist solution to combating Maoists is a real solution.

Development Programmes

There has seldom been a similar ambitious programme mooted by concerned departments of welfare and development demanding resources with equal force and conviction as the police and para-military forces have done. Most often the development agenda seems like tokenism. The development sectors are unable to compete for funds as they are seen to be plagued by corruption and inaction in any case. On the other hand the police sacrifice their lives to maintain law and order and protect the nation and so there is a greater justification for investments in police.

At the same time it is important to recognise the programmes undertaken by the State in response to naxal politics to bridge the State deficit. One of the most important interventions has been that of the land reforms programme initiated by Hare Krishna Konar who was the land and revenue minister under the United Front government in West Bengal. Between 1967 and 1970, one million acre of *benami* land i.e., land held in excess of ceiling were identified and vested in the state for redistribution. This was done through a strict legal procedure 'which ultimately stood the scrutiny of the courts of appeal. It broke the backbone of economic power and social dominance of landed aristocracy of West Bengal.'[30]

It is reported that the land reforms of the government were effective because of the large scale mobilisation of the peasantry by the CPI(M) to stake their claims against the local landlords. Subsequently when the Left Front government was formed once again in 1977, the

West Bengal government initiated land reforms giving share croppers their entitlement to land under the 'Operation Barga'. Since most share cropping contracts are oral, a clear protocol for verification of land based on oral testimonies was allowed and followed up with verification on the field by the administrative machinery. Consequently over 1.2 million sharecroppers were recorded between 1978 and 1981 and about 65-70 percent of sharecroppers got their entitlement to land. It is reported that this move had even broken the years of stagnation in agricultural production and increase in resources for the poor peasants[31].

As a result of the naxal politics the Andhra Pradesh government brought an amendment to the LTRA in 1970 which is popularly called the 'One of 1970' Act. According to this Act, all land transactions in the scheduled area were restricted to be entered into only with tribals or the government. Earlier, non-tribals who possessed land in the tribal areas could enter into transactions with non-tribals. This enabled land distribution to the tribal communities in several tribal areas and more particularly in the Khammam and East Godavari districts. Development projects were also introduced in the tribal areas under the Integrated Tribal Development Authority. It constituted a Tribal Welfare Advisory Committee with a tribal leader as its chairperson. It emphasized the principles of decentralisation and involvement of tribal leaders in executing the various schemes through the Village Tribal Development Agency (VTDA). A heavy investment in roads, electricity, irrigation, and infrastructure was made in the area along with development projects and schemes. These schemes were not exactly lacking in wastage and corruption. However it monetised the economy and brought in systems where the rent seeking middlemen and contractors no longer fleeced the tribal population but graduated to take their share from the State and its programmes. Further there was an increase in the residential schools for girls and boys in the tribal areas creating literacy and a new layer of school graduates who could be absorbed as school teachers and other functionaries of the government.

In spite of such initiatives the deficit in terms of its functionaries reaching out to the tribal community and the poor still remains unresolved. The development programmes and schemes, land reforms and other efforts are introduced in response to the naxal challenge and gain legitimacy and not so much as to involve the poor in nation building task that is inclusive and democratic. Rarely are the tribal communities taken into confidence nor is their participation sought. The crux of the issue is that in the naxal areas the State interventions and delivery of services are regarded as programmes to bring legitimacy to the State and an end in themselves and not as entitlements for attainment of dignity and self-respect and deepening of democracy.

In areas where Maoists have abandoned their activities and the police too have withdrawn, there still remain some blocks in a situation of statelessness. In such areas there is no antipathy to the naxals as the memory of police harassment is still strong.

Response of Central Government

Whilst the issue of maintenance, law and order is a state subject, most development programmes come under both State programmes and centrally sponsored programmes. They are also governed by policies and legal reforms that are framed by the Central government. The Congress Party was in office between at the Centre from 1966-1977 and 1980-84 under Indira Gandhi as the Prime Minister. During the first tenure of her leadership, progressive economic steps were taken as in the case of nationalisation of banks, abolition of Privy Purse that enabled the Congress Party recover from the debacle in the General Elections of 1967. It came across as as a party inclined towards the poor. In its preface to the Fourth Five-Year Plan Indira Gandhi clearly spelled out that, 'The basic aim is to raise the standard of living of the people, especially of the less privileged sections of society. Our planning should result not only in an integrated process of increased production, but rational distribution of the added wealth. The overriding inspiration must be a burning sense of social justice. While increased production is of the utmost importance it is equally important to remove or reduce, and prevent the concentration of wealth and economic power. The benefits of development should accrue in increasing measure to the common man and the weaker sections of society, so that the forces of production can be fully unleashed. A sense of involvement, of participation by the people as a whole, is vital for the success of any plan of rapid economic growth. This can only be evoked by securing social justice, by reducing disparities of income and wealth, and by redressing regional imbalances. A reorientation of our socio-economic institutions in this spirit is accordingly, a first necessity'[32]. Further it stated that in implementing the Plan there would be 'advanced yet another stage towards our goal of a prosperous, democratic, modern, socialist society.'

Under the Fourth Plan, six pilot projects were set up in the Central sector in Andhra Pradesh, Bihar, Madhya Pradesh and Orissa. A separate Tribal Development Agency was established for each project and Rs. 2 crore was allotted to these agencies.

In 1971, General Elections the Congress Party's electoral agenda was 'Garibi Hatao' and creating a base for the party amongst the poorest of the poor through announcements of anti-poverty programmes.

The culmination of socialism as the objective to be attained found expression in passing of the Constitution (42nd Amendment) Act, 1976 where in the Preamble to the Constitution the words 'Sovereign Democratic Republic' was substituted with the words 'Sovereign Socialist Secular Democratic Republic'.

Abiding by the principles of equality and social justice, bonded labour was abolished by law with the enactment of the Bonded Labour System Abolition Act, 1976. With the insertion of Article 39(A) in Directive Principles of State Policy that read 'equal justice and free legal aid. The state shall secure that the operation of the legal system promotes justice, on a basis of equal opportunity, and shall, in particular, provide free legal aid, by suitable legislation or schemes or in any other way, to ensure that opportunities for securing justice are not denied to any citizen by reason of economic or other disabilities', it envisaged access to legal entitlements for the poor.

Thus during the Emergency, Indira Gandhi's 20-Point programme promised to liquidate the existing debts of landless labourers, small farmers and rural artisans. The programme planned to extend alternate credit to them, abolish bonded labour and implement the existing agricultural land ceiling laws. It provided house sites to landless labourers and weaker sections and it revised upwards minimum wages of agricultural labour. The programme also provided special help to the handloom industry by bringing down the prices, preventing tax evasion and smuggling, increasing production and streamlining distribution of essential commodities. It increased the limit of income tax exemption up to Rs. 8,000, and liberalised investment procedures.

Indeed, it was quipped that the constituency of Indira Gandhi and the naxalites were both the same—the poorest of the poor, marginalised and scheduled caste and scheduled tribe communities. It is not fair to state that the pro-poor polices of the Congress Party were directly in response to the naxal challenge, but the naxalite politics had influenced the government to the extent that if the core issues of social justice and equality were not addressed by the government it could result in greater violence and mass upsurge.

Conclusion

What started as a movement of the local tribal communities and peasants confronting the rapacious moneylenders, landlords, forest and revenue officials and impacting local power structures, the naxal or the Maoist challenge is now no longer confined to remote tribal pockets or villages questioning local authorities. It is now compelling a national response and coordinated action of states that share the borders. This has inevitably changed the character of naxal response too, and it is now operational on a national scale.

V

From Community Support to Armed Struggle

The entire Maoist politics developed a vested interest in perpetuating itself in their business of seizure of power and they depended on the poor tribal population and their loyalties for their own survival and continuance. Their intervention in any new area started with building trust and confidence of the people in taking charge of their lives. To a large extent they were successful because the cadres started on the firm belief that people are ready for armed struggle. Communities' indignation against all the forces that were pitted against them is built, to be followed up with local actions against the corrupt officials and all those who cheat them on a daily basis. They begin to enjoy their new-found strength taking decisions to stand against injustice. This often invited retaliation from the police. The movement is stepped up by the Maoist leaders and takes a violent form, involving killings of landlords or raids and attacks on police forces.

People are subjected to police violence and untold suffering for giving shelter to the cadre, sharing their woes with them, and taking part in joint actions. Many were forced to go underground and seek protection of the Maoists. They soon joined the cadre as whole timers. The Maoist leadership anticipates the consequences of their actions and is fully aware that their actions would lead to a greater presence of the police, paramilitary forces and repression of the poor. In their view, redemption of inequities and injustice meted out to them would happen only after seizure of power. It seems that for the Maoists entry into a new area and engaging with the poor becomes necessary for creation of a cadre force for joining the 'people's army' and carrying out armed struggle.

Violence, Armed Struggle and Consequences

Considering the challenges faced by the poor, their landlessness, marginalisation and increasing impoverishment and vulnerability there is often a justification of the violence meted out by the Maoists as being an answer to the structural violence. What else is available to the poor when they are being repeatedly insulted and humiliated and have reached a point of hopelessness, they ask. How can one fault them for taking to arms? The answers to these questions are at multiple levels ranging from issues of ethics and politics.

It is important to recognise that violence is an integral characteristic of the Maoist politics. Conceding to the principle that using violence is a legitimate form of action to bring about change, it has been used not only to 'annihilate class enemies' but also in inter-group squabbles, resolving leadership and turf issues, against one's own party members if found suspicious or as informers, and also against women and children, and all those who dared to defy and not comply. There are endless reports on the public trials of the Maoists through the People's courts that issued dictats to chop off limbs and even behead someone for being an oppressive landlord, cutting of tongues and eliminating the person in public for being police informers, killing local tribals and their leaders if they defied their orders like for instance not offering their sons to be recruited by the Maoists, cutting of thumbs for participation in elections and the like. Maoists could certainly kill unarmed persons on trains that are bombed, buses and ordinary people stepping on improvised explosive devices (IEDs). Thus once the principle of violence is adhered to there is no bar to its use. This was justified as revolutionary violence and at times mistakes could occur in use of violence.

The worst affected in this warfare are women and children. There have been incidents where women cadres were subject to sexual exploitation, forced separation from children and infants and taking up of menial chores with little say in the decision-making processes within the party. It has also been reported that children have been forcibly taken away from homes and recruited as child soldiers. They have been trained in handling of arms, making of bombs, planting IEDs. They have been used as couriers, spies, head load carriers and graduates to join as full-time Maoist armed cadre. The violence meted out on children too is justified where in Ganapathi the supreme commander in chief of CPI (Maoist) stated, 'Making fuss over age makes no meaning in a situation where the enemies of the people are targeting children too without any mercy. If the boys and girls do not resist with arms, they will be eleminated completely. The intellectuals of civil society should understand and not raise idealistic objections (to recruitment of children).'[33]

Such a stand on violence has been to their advantage causing damage to ordinary people and their lives. Families and the lives of the people have been fractured leaving behind debris of hatred. It has forced the poor out of their habitations, and thousands were displaced making them most vulnerable caught between the violence of both the naxals and the police. While some sought shelter in the camps as in the case of Chhattisgarh, several migrated to neighbouring states or stayed as refugees in their own forest lands. It is found that there is a breach of trust and the society is enveloped in mutual suspicion and insecurities. Taking sides and being pro-Maoist or pro-police becomes necessary even as a large number of villagers wish to remain neutral. They find little space for expression of neutrality. The Maoist politics have created conditions of gross violation of human rights in all these areas. For the Maoists this is an inevitable consequence of the war against the State.

The actions of the Maoists and their politics may have won over the tribals, but in the long run have left them totally disempowered. They have not built their capacities or knowledge to grapple with the State, engage with it and partake in the process of development as equal citizens. It does not give them any confidence to deal with the government. It creates a hiatus between the State and the people.

The inherent violence in its functioning has defined the nature of the Party organisation, which is secretive and centralised. Most decisions are made by the Maoist leadership outside the realm of the community. Being a secretive organisation it generates politics and actions on behalf of the people and not people themselves. The community is unprepared and has lost the capacity to exercise agency and is never consulted nor is in the knowledge of the important decisions taken by the Party. In a way, use of violence imposes secrecy and exclusion contrary to the fundamental principles of democracy that is open and inclusive.

Also the logic of violence results in increasing State violence and weakening of State provisioning of its services.

Way Forward

Living precariously, the poor hope for a change as subjects and not as objects of reality being manipulated both by the Maoists and the government. They hope to participate as citizens, engage and deal with all the forces that matter in a manner that accords them the power to take sides or even be neutral and live without fear. At the moment it seems that all paths for normalcy in their lives have been sealed.

What is needed is to inspire the local youth and the community to engage with the system and reopen public spaces for debate, discussion and deepening of democracy. In the process of enabling the community gain access to all their entitlements, they must start engaging with the State and its institutions. The State too must respond with sensitivity and give a timely response to this act of faith of the people who have given the State one more opportunity to deliver its responsibilities. There are undoubtedly several initiatives in the country that can take up precisely such activities, in full faith that a non-violent movement alone could build a sound basis for democracy in the country. It is for the State and its functionaries to strengthen such agencies in the civil society and treat them as equal partners in rebuilding societies. This is not an easy process, but certainly more sustainable.

Endnotes

1. *pib.nic.in/release/release.asp?relid=63222*
2. Ibid.
3. According to India's external intelligence agency, the *Research and Analysis Wing,* 20,000 armed cadre Naxalites were operating in addition to 50,000 regular cadres[4].
4. The voter turn out in 1952 general elections was 45.7%; in 1957 it was 47.8%; in 1962-55.4% and in 1967 it was 61.3% v. Large houses obtain licenses in excess of demand and under utilisation of the same; Industrial stagnation due to narrow home market, dependence on foreign technology, decline in capacities to use import substitution, decline in public investments that hit railways, electricity, metals and mining, intermediate and capital goods.
5. Fic, Victor (1963). *Peaceful Transition to Communism in India.* Nichiketa.
6. He proposed that the party should adopt a class analysis of the Indian State of the 1951 conference.
7. Mention the Articles in *Peoples Daily* from Peking exhorting and hailing armed struggle.'
8. Janashakti-a news letter in Telugu of CPI in Andhra Pradesh.
9. Between 1952 and 1968 some 70 activists had been killed. 1000'S of activists were jailed with cases being foisted on them.
10. This was followed by State wise expulsions of Maoist leaders like Sushital Roy Choudhary, Ashim Chatterjee, Parimal Das Gupta, Asit Sen, Suniti Ghosh, Saroj Dutt and Mahadeb Mukherjee.
11. Sen, Mohit (2003). *A Traveler and the Road-The Journey of an Indian Communist.* Rupa & Co. pp 286-87.
12. Interim Report of Civil Rights Committee (1977). "'Encounters' are Murders", *Economic and Poltical Weekly* 12(21): 827-829. May 21.
13. In September 2004 Communist Party of India (Maoist) was formed with the coming together of the Communist Party of India (Marxist Leninist) (CPI (ML) , CPI (ML) –Party Unit (PU) and Maoist Communist Centre

(MCC). This signified a culmination of 35 years of resistance to police, their tribulations and lessons learnt to combat the State. All these parties traced their roots to Charu Majumdar and Kanhai Chatterjee and the Maoist tradition of armed agrarian uprising. At present i.e., in 2010 it is active in parts of, Madhya Pradesh, Maharashtra, Chhattisgarh, Andhra Pradesh, Orissa, Jharkhand, West Bengal and Bihar. It has been making attempts to establish and expand its presence in several other States such as Tamil Nadu, Kerala and Karnataka in Southern India, Uttar Pradesh, Haryana, Punjab and Rajasthan in Northern India.

14. The CPI (ML) developed out of Central Organizing Committee, CPI(ML) (which had been dissolved in 1977) in Andhra Pradesh.
15. Quoted in Sinha, Shantha (1989). *Maoists in Andhra Pradesh*. Gyan Publications. p. 283.
16. *http://www.satp.org/satporgtp/countries/india/terroristoutfits/CPI_M.htm*
17. Until then the CPI (ML)-PWG was active in Andhra Pradesh but weak in Tamil Nadu. Its Central Committee was limited to these two states alone. The MCC had its presence in Bihar and quite weak in Bengal and Assam. Kobad Gandhi from Maharashtra joined PWG at that time.
18. Rajat Kapur (2008). *Naxal Movement in India: A Profile IPCS Research Papers,* September, p. 3.
19. Thakor, Harsh (2009). "Legacy of Com.Amulya Sen and the Maoist Communist Centre", September 9 *http://indianvanguard.wordpress.com/2009/09/09/legacy-of-com-amulya-sen-and-the-maoist-communist-centre/*. The MCC were also known as the Dakshin Desh Group.
20. The first ever meeting between the PWG and MCC was held in 1981, when Kanai Chatterjee of the MCC and Kondapally Seetaramaiah of PWG met for over 12 days. Both leaders, though belonging to different streams of the Naxalite movement, stated that the grounds to merge are strong as both were pursuing a similar end. The PWG and MCC subsequently set out the procedure for a possible merger. However, such possibilities were premature, as in 1982 Chatterjee died of illness and Seetharamaiah was arrested in the Secunderabad conspiracy case.
21. At present in 2010 the MCC has merged with PWG to form the CPI (Maoist) and has a presence in Bihar, Orissa (Sundargarh, Keonjhar) and Jharkhand. In Bihar, the MCC is primarily active in Gaya, Aurangabad, Camoor (Bhabhua), Rohtas, Darbhanga, Muzaffarpur, Bettiah and Sitamarhi districts. In the newly created State of Jharkhand, the group is active in Chatra, Daltangonj, Hazaribagh, Palamu, Giridih, Dhanbad, Bokaro, Ranchi, Garhwa, Lohardaga, Gumla, East Singhbhum, West Singhbhum and Latehar districts.
22. Article 46 of Constitution of India under the Directive Principles of State Policy stipulates 'To promote with special care the educational and economic interests of the weaker sections of the people, especially the Scheduled Castes and Scheduled Tribes'.

23. Sen, Mohit, *op cit.* p.285
24. *http://www.massline.info/India/Indian_Groups.htm*
25. Banerjee, Sukanya (2008). *Mercury Rising: India's Looming Red Corridor. http://csis.org/files/media/csis/pubs/sam_oct08_naxalite.pdf* Number 123 October 03.
26. *http://www.defenceforum.in/forum/showthread.php/2402-Naxalism-A-Rs-1500-crore-red-corridor-menace*
27. Myrdal, Jan and Gautam Navlakha (2010). "In Conversation with Ganapathy General Secretary of CPI (Maoist)", See *http://southasiarev.wordpress. com/2010/02/14/jan-myrdal-interviews-cpimaoist-leader-ganapathy/*
28. 'Greyhounds is a commando force in Andhra Pradesh that are imparted specialised training in fields craft and weapons handling. More emphasis is given to developing high standard of physical fitness and mental alertness. Greyhounds started to give commando training since June 2000 to Police Personnel from other states of Maharashtra, Madhya Pradesh, Bihar, Chhattisgarh, Jharkhand, Orissa and West Bengal'. *http://www.aponline.gov.in/apportal/departments/departments.asp?dep=17&org=100&suborg=102&category=Faq*
29. 'The core of the police strategy of response over the past two years in Tripura is to dominate the most remote areas in the State, and to minimize the reaction time for counter-insurgent operations. As many as 386 camps of police and security force personnel are now being maintained in the interior areas, providing immediate access to the people in the event of militant movement, and reducing operational and reaction time to a minimum. In addition, 2,600 Special Police Officers (SPOs) in another 105 'Special Police Pickets' (SPPs) have also been located in the strategic interior. This network of camps and pickets is backed by the existing network of 37 police outposts and 55 police stations in the 20 police sub-divisions that control the States four districts. Each of these police stations, posts and camps has been upgraded in terms of arms, communications, and where possible, vehicles and bullet-proofing, improving response capacities and reducing response time to a minimum, and placing a very substantial, dispersed but coordinated force at the command of each District's Superintendent of Police.' Tripura shares a long border with Bangladesh and affected by the cross border insurgency. *http://www.satp.org/satporgtp/sair/Archives/4_7.htm# assessment1*
30. Bandhopadyay, D. (2000). "Land Reform in West Bengal-Remembering Hare Krishna Konar and Benoy Chaudhury", *EPW* 35. May 27-June 2.
31. Ibid.
32. *http://planningcommission.nic.in/plans/planrel/fiveyr/4th/4ppre.htm*
33. 'Mao's Children' *OPEN*, June-July 2010. p.22.

Chapter XIV

The Left in India: 1964-1984

Girish Mishra

The period, ranging from 1964 to 1984, occupies a very crucial position in the history of post-independent India. In the year 1964, Jawaharlal Nehru, one of the greatest freedom fighters and the second in command in the national movement passed away. He, publicly nominated as his heir by Mahatma Gandhi, led the country as its prime minister till his death. He laid down the foundations for building a self-reliant modern economy and polity so that not only the newly-won political freedom was secure but also meaningful to the vast masses of the people. This was no easy task. To appreciate this, let us look back.

At the time of Independence, the Indian economy was dependent in character and lopsided in development because, during the two centuries of foreign rule, it was made to serve the needs and interests of the British economy. It was geared to supplying raw materials and minerals to British industries and be a market for British manufactured products and an outlet for British capital. The British policies and approach were based mainly on these considerations.

In 1947, agriculture was the mainstay and it and accounted for more than half of the GDP. Only 17.1 percent of the GDP originated in mines, manufacturing and small industrial enterprises. Almost 70 percent of the working population was engaged in agriculture while the industrial sector provided work only to 9.6 percent. Agriculture was technologically primitive in character and its productivity was extremely low. Between 1931 and 1947, agricultural productivity had actually declined. Agriculture was shackled by feudal and semi-feudal relations of production, which did not allow the development of productive forces and resulted in a continuous decline in the purchasing power of the rural masses, and restricted the size of the home market.

In the arena of manufacturing, agro-industries were in a dominant position. Light industries contributed 78 percent of the gross output of the manufacturing sector. Textiles alone accounted for 46.2 percent of the gross product of the manufacturing sector while the share of capital goods industries was 22 percent. But, here also, most of these capital goods enterprises were geared mainly towards catering the needs of transport and civil engineering. Consequently, most of the Indian industries were dependent on imported machines and spare parts. Heavy machines, machine tools, aluminum, power transformers, electric motors and heavy chemicals had negligible production.

The infrastructural facilities were inadequately developed and were insufficient to sustain the building of a modern Indian economy. Investment in human capital was very little. Illiteracy was extremely high and the system of education was geared towards producing the clerks to man the lower rungs of bureaucracy. Technical education was given very low priority and only a few branches of engineering with a limited number of technical institutions were available in the country.

Mortality rate ranged between 4 and 5 percent per annum till 1921 and then between 3.7 and 3.1 percent during the rest of the post-independence era. More than 40 percent of the people died before attaining the age of 20. The average life span was 32.1 years, while for the female population, it was only 31.7 years. Health care facilities were extremely meagre and epidemics such as cholera, smallpox, *kala-zar* ravaged the country at regular intervals and took a heavy toll.

Country suffered from regional economic imbalances, largely, as a result of certain policies of the British government. Industrial and commercial activities got concentrated in and around port cities and some other places. Over the years, market forces accentuated the regional imbalances.

Indian society was fragmented. Regional, religious, linguistic and caste based barriers and differences obstructed the emergence of a unified and homogeneous Indian society. A few sections of the society got all or most of the benefits of education and economic development. The disparities in the distribution of wealth, incomes and employment opportunities had gone on increasing over the years. While a few lived in riches, the overwhelming masses lived a life of semi-starvation and misery. Most of these economically miserable people belonged to socially discriminated castes and tribes.

Soon after Independence, notwithstanding all the political opposition by vested interests and all the theories decreeing that the country was fated to remain a backward agricultural economy, the Indian National Congress under the leadership of Jawaharlal Nehru came out with a strategy to build a self-reliant modern economy. It was in the form of an ever-expanding public sector, central planning, a strong basic and heavy goods sector, and institutional reforms. India declared in the mid-1950s the establishment of a socialist society as its goal, which meant that social and economic justice would inform the policies and actions of the government.

Radical agrarian reforms were introduced, doing away with oppressive land systems. Tenancy reform and land ceiling laws were enacted and the consolidation of holdings carried through in most parts of the country despite a stiff resistance from the vested interests.

Indian peasantry responded to increased market demands for agricultural produce, and the government made sufficient quantum of better inputs, scientific and technological guidance besides the guarantee of remunerative prices. The result was self-sufficiency in food grains by the 1970s. The production tripled. Days of famine were gone.

The policies of the Nehru government were continued and strengthened by the Indira regime by doing away with bonded labour, strengthening the socioeconomic infrastructure in villages and alleviation of rural poverty. Major commercial banks were nationalised and their activities expanded rapidly in rural areas. NABARD was set up and *grameen* banks were established to cater to the needs of rural industries and agriculture.

Industrialisation was an important feature during the Nehru-Indira Gandhi dispensation. Under Industrial Policy Resolutions of 1948 and 1956, state was to play a pioneering role in this. Looking back, one finds that, apart from quantitative increase in output, industrial structure underwent great diversification. India developed a whole range of basic and heavy industries. Its dependence on capital goods import declined. This was reflected in the composition of country's foreign trade. The share of manufactured items in imports went down while their proportion in export increased. The rapid progress of industrialisation was accompanied by a corresponding growth in technological and managerial know-how. The country set up modern institutes of science and technology. All these things were done in the face of a stiff opposition from certain external and internal forces.

All along the Americans exerted pressures on India to make it change its goals and priorities in the economic sphere. They were supported by the right wing political parties and intelligentsia in India. Swatantra Party, Bharatiya Jana Sangh and the Forum of Free Enterprise were most vociferous opponents of the Nehruvian approach.[1]

The Third Five-Year Plan was to be launched in 1961 and Nehru wanted to add one more steel plant during it. He was given the impression by the Americans that they would be willing to help. Then it turned out that they wanted a heavy price for it. They wanted a change in the priority given to the public sector besides acceptance of US nuclear umbrella over India and the facilities for Voice of America to broadcast from the Indian soil. Seeing India's reluctance, they backed out of their commitment to build a steel plant at Bokaro. India then had to turn to the Soviet Union.[2]

With the Chinese invasion of India in October 1962, it became clear that it was able to resist the invaders and withstand the American pressures, thanks mainly to the soundness of the Nehruvian strategy of development. The strains caused by the Chinese invasion and American machinations put a heavy pressure on Nehru's health. He suffered a mild stroke at Bhubaneswar in January 1964 and passed away on May 27 that year. With this, a long chapter in India's fight for political and economic independence came to an end. Nehru, however, left a precious legacy of ideas and a grand vision of a modern nation, besides firm foundations for an independent modern economy.

II

It will be interesting to look at how the two major left political streams viewed Nehru's ideas and strategy and actions to transform the socio-economic scene during his life time and after his death. These two streams were communist and socialist.

Let us begin with the communist stream. The Communist Party of India (CPI) as a unified all-India Party came into being in 1925 (though this date was pushed back to 1920 after the split of the CPI and the CPI(M) sticks to it in its documents) and continued as a unified entity till 1964 when a split took place. The group that came out of the parent party named itself as the Communist Party of India (Marxist) [CPI(M)]. Even before the formal split, the party remained virtually divided into several groups and carried on, what is called, IPS or inner party struggle for their respective lines of thinking.

There were, prior to the birth of the CPI, several small groups that were working for marrying anti-imperialism with a future based on socialism. The Non-Cooperation movement of Mahatma Gandhi had radicalised the masses, especially the youth and intelligentsia who were struggling to devise a socioeconomic perspective of independent India. The Bolshevik Revolution had stirred them and they wanted to emulate its perspective. A significant proportion of the youth and intelligentsia, influenced by the writings of Marx and Lenin, was impatient to go quicker than the Indian National Congress and its great leader and was not convinced of the need of sticking to non-violence.

From the very beginning, the question whether Communists should simultaneously fight both foreign rule and Indian class enemies dominated. One view was that in a colonial country like India, the nature of revolution would be different from the Bolshevik one. Here it was bound to be a national revolution, and all classes must unite, notwithstanding their conflicts and differences, against the foreign rule. The foreign rule was the main enemy. It was a revolution to free the nation as a whole from foreign rule and domination and not against capitalism as such.

M.N. Roy and those under his influence did not accept this line and opposed the very concept of a multiclass national revolution. Roy asserted that the fight against imperialism could succeed only when the working class, led by the Communist Party, strove, on the basis of worker-peasant alliance to break the hold of Gandhi and the Congress over the masses. Gandhi and the Congress were regarded as representatives of the bourgeoisie and were bound to succumb to imperialist pressures. Thus Roy and his followers rejected the idea of the multiclass national revolution and any truck with the Indian National Congress, led by Mahatma Gandhi. This position which was critiqued strongly nevertheless got crystallised with the official sanction of the Sixth Congress of the Comintern in 1928 under Stalin's influence.

This proved restrictive to CPI's activities among the masses and inside the Congress. It did not leave much scope for collaboration with the Congress, i.e., the mainstream of the national movement. Though the Congress and its top leaders like Mahatma Gandhi and Jawaharlal Nehru had soft corner for the Communists as became obvious through their sympathies during the Meerut Conspiracy Case involving prominent Communists, the Comintern line prevented the Communists from coming out with any positive response. Comintern's understanding was that, without destroying the hold of the Congress, the CPI could not advance. As a result of the adoption of this line by the Communists of India they were cut off from the Congress and the anti-imperialist national movement.

The CPI could revive itself only from 1934 onwards. It began to set up its units in various parts of the country and front organisations among students, writers, artists and so on. The realistic approach and dynamic personality of the general secretary P.C. Joshi was a key factor. The change in the Comintern line proved to be a catalyst. The victory of fascism in Italy and Germany and Japan forced it to change its approach. The change began with the adoption of the Popular Front Thesis, propounded by Georgi Dimitrov on August 2, 1935 at the Seventh Congress of the Comintern (The Fascist Offensive and Tasks of the Communist International in the Struggle of the Working Class against Fascism).

The CPI took part in General Elections in 1952 and 1957. Thus began the process of learning the real character of India's secular, parliamentary and democratic polity. In the course of time it became a part of it. The realisation dawned on it that it could capture power through the ballot box when, in 1957, it along with its allies won the Kerala assembly elections and formed the government with E.M.S. Namboodiripad as chief minister.

In spite of all this, streaks of sectarianism continued and the CPI touted this while contesting the first assembly elections of the newly formed Andhra Pradesh in 1955. The people rejected the CPI's contention that Indian freedom was fake and the Congress had betrayed the nation. It faced a devastating rout while the Congress was returned with a thumping majority.

This opened an intense ideological-political debate inside the Party. Three contending lines emerged. The first was the Joshi line whose chief protagonist was P.C. Joshi. It stressed that India's independence was real and democratic and further consolidation of this development must take place on the basis of Indo-Soviet cooperation and the formation of a national front. The cooperation between the Congress and the Communists was indispensable to the formation and progress of this front.

The second line of thinking was promoted by P. Sundarayya, B.T. Ranadive and Promode Dasgupta. It asserted that India was not really an independent country. It was a dependent entity with a bourgeoisie-landlord government led by the big bourgeoisie, collaborating with imperialism. The Congress was the representative of the big bourgeoisie and the main task of the CPI was to overthrow such a government and replace it with a government of people's democratic front, headed by the working class and its party, the CPI.

The third line was the result of a compromise between the two and it was sponsored by Ajoy Ghosh. It was adopted at the Fourth congress of the Party at Palghat. It contended that the internal policies of the government were, by and large, anti-people. Thus, the Communists had to remain in opposition to the government and there was no possibility of a united front with the Congress. At the same time, it was admitted that the Congress was engaged in building an independent capitalist economy which quite often brought it in conflict, on the one hand, with imperialism and feudalism and, on the other, with the people at large.

Notwithstanding the shortcomings, there was a definite improvement in CPI's understanding of the Indian situation. This enabled it to extend its mass base and improve its public and parliamentary performance. It became the main opposition party in parliament and could, along with its allies, capture power in Kerala and initiate some progressive steps.

In 1958, the CPI had its Fifth Party congress at Amritsar. Here it was decided that peaceful transition was a possible form of the advance to socialism in India. It adopted a preamble to its constitution wherein it was stated that in its concept of socialism full civil rights including right of opposition to the socialist government would be granted provided the Constitution of the country was respected. Significantly, the phrase 'dictatorship of the proletariat' was replaced by 'socialist statehood'.

It took note of the growth of the forces of Right reaction in the country as well in the Congress. To defeat this menace, the CPI advocated the unity of all patriotic elements wherever they might be. At that time, Swatantra Party and Bharatiya Jana Sangh were the main parties of Right reaction.

The CPI congress underlined the possibility of some sort of unity of the Congress and the Communist Party to defend and popularise country's foreign policy, for realising the aims of the Second Five-Year Plan and seeing to it that maximum benefits of economic growth reached the people at large. It welcomed the growth of democratic forces in the Congress and called for adopting a friendly approach to them. It vowed to unite all patriotic and democratic forces, irrespective of their party affiliations. These were some of the positive shifts in the strategy of the CPI, though anti-Congressism was not altogether given up. Its commitment to the replacement of the Congress government by a people's democratic government remained.

Around this time, differences surfaced in the international Communist movement that impacted the CPI in a big way. The CPI got vertically divided into two factions, one subscribing to the Soviet understanding while the other toeing the Chinese line. While the former supported the break with Stalinism, the latter opposed it and dubbed it as revisionism. The Chinese media and the Communist Party opened a front against both the new line of the Communist Party of the Soviet Union (CPSU) and Nehru. They called Nehru a bourgeoisie leader, collaborating with imperialism. This propaganda got magnified when border clashes between China and India became more frequent and bloody.

Internationally, the CPC became isolated. Except for Indonesian and Albanian Communist parties, no one else came forward to lend support to it. The CPI stood against Maoist chauvinism at the world conference of the Communist and Workers' Parties held in Moscow in 1960. The CPC, fearing its further isolation, pledged to return to negotiating table to sort out border disputes and declared that it would not cross the McMahon line even though it did not recognise it.

Against this background, the Sixth congress of the CPI took place at Vijayawada in April 1961. Two important formulations emerged from it. First, the contradictions between India and imperialism had sharpened and, simultaneously, the contradiction between the Congress government and the masses had aggravated. Second, the CPI would pursue the line of unity and struggle with the Congress but would not go in for a united front with it.

It was obvious that there was no clear-cut answer as to which of the two contradictions was primary. Besides, the aim of the line of unity and struggle was not spelled out. The lack of clarity allowed dogmatic-sectarians to pursue their line of anti-Congressism.

During the year 1962, two events took place that had far-reaching impact on the CPI. First, in the beginning of 1962, Ajoy Ghosh passed away and a new arrangement under which S.A. Dange came to occupy the newly-created post of chairman and E.M.S. Namboodiripad becoming general secretary was nothing but a compromise between the two factions operating in the Party. Second, the Chinese launched a massive aggression on India in the third week of October that weakened the leadership of Nehru and emboldened American imperialism. While the CPI officially condemned the Chinese aggression and stood by Nehru, the other faction denied the act of aggression by saying that it was unthinkable in the case of a socialist country like China.

The Chinese army crossed the McMahon line and pushed back the Indian army which was not prepared for such an action from a country, regarded 'friendly' by the government. It was a great shock to Nehru who had always done his best to end China's international isolation. To the Indian Right wing's reaction it came as a big opportunity to attack Nehru and his policies. His close associate V.K. Krishna Menon had to resign, owning up the responsibility for unpreparedness.

The dogmatic faction in the CPI not only refused to condemn the Chinese aggression but also tried to give it a rational cover. It did not utter a single word of protest when the Chinese called upon Indian Communists to rise against their government. The general secretary, Namboodiripad, stood by the sectarians while the chairman, S.A. Dange rallied the Party in support of Nehru and against Right wing's reaction.

The dogmatic faction became so frustrated because of its failure to capture the CPI that it began a malicious propaganda against Dange and gathered 32 out of 101 members of the National Council to announce the formation of a new party on April 11, 1964. This new entity came to be known as CPI(M).

III

Since 1964, there have been two major Communist parties, besides numerous splinter groups of the people walking out of the CPI(M) from time to time. Both the CPI and the CPI(M) have been recognised as national parties by the Election Commission of India and have been represented in Parliament and most of the state assemblies.

In spite of the commonality in names, there have been lots of differences in their perception of the Indian and international situations, and the class character of the Indian National Congress that has led most of the governments since Independence. Their aims and the paths to travel towards them have also been different. To understand them, let us begin with their basic documents like their programmes.

The CPI held its Seventh Party congress in Mumbai from December 13 to 23, 1964 and adopted its programme, running into 60 pages. It opened with a review of the Indian situation since Independence, which, according to it, 'opened a new epoch in the history of our people.' It went on to add: 'The achievement of Indian independence was a historic event not only for our own people but for all mankind. The vast millions of our people, whose labour, wealth and freedom had been subjected to long years of foreign domination and plunder, were now free to remake their future in the midst of a new world that was rising at the end of the Second World War.'[3]

It had words of appreciation for the Indian National Congress that had led the freedom struggle and formed the first government of Independent India. The Congress had frustrated the attempts by imperialists to subvert independence and integrity of the country. Among other major achievements to the credit of the Congress were the merger of native states including Jammu & Kashmir, initiation of planning, Industrial Policy Resolutions of 1948 and 1956 and the nationalisation of the Imperial Bank and airlines. The Congress had launched the country on to the path of independent economic development. It had not swerved from this path despite pressures and machinations from imperialist quarters. Bold efforts to develop basic and heavy industries and a strong public sector were made with the help of the Soviet Union and other socialist countries.

The country was, however, facing problems of grim poverty, unemployment and multidimensional backwardness. Vested interests had tried to sabotage land reforms and slow down the pace of economic development. The CPI programme underlined that the root cause of all this was the very character of the state. To quote: 'The state in India is the organ of the class rule of the national bourgeoisie as a whole, which upholds and develops capitalism and capitalist relations of production, distribution and exchange in the national economy of India.'[4] But, in the formation and the exercise of power, it was the big bourgeoisie that wielded considerable influence. The bourgeoisie as a whole compromised with landlords made them its partner in running the state machinery. Consequently, the progress of land reform measures remained tardy and slow.

Notwithstanding all these shortcomings, the character of the state remained democratic and it was definitely 'a historic advance over the imperialist-bureaucratic rule over our country.'[5] Further, 'The Constitution of the Republic of India provides for a parliamentary democracy based on adult franchise and certain fundamental rights for the people and directive principles for the state.'[6]

It underscored that, in spite of being:

> ...a form of class rule, India's present parliamentary democracy has enabled the people to a certain extent to fight the distortion of that class rule in the direction of autocracy in the service of reactionary monopoly and landlord interests. India's Parliament has provided a forum for the people to intervene in the affairs of the state in a measure and to voice the cause of peace, national freedom and democracy, to counter imperialist conspiracies and for demanding social transformations in favour of the people such as land reforms, working class rights, curb on monopolies, etc. Within the national bourgeoisie itself, as the top monopolist groups get more and more differentiated from the rest of the bourgeoisie, a struggle grows among the various sections to get hold of parliamentary machine in order to wield power over the budget and other economic measures, laws and policies to shape them in their own particular group interests.
>
> The influence of foreign monopoly interests is also felt in these developments, in which they generally support those monopoly groups and princely feudal circles who demand measures that facilitate the entry of foreign capital in the country, who demand curtailment of the state sector and the abandonment of nonalignment.
>
> The monopolist groups and feudal circles represent the main anti-democratic forces of reaction in the country.[7]

Thus the CPI contended that the bourgeoisie was not one homogeneous whole and there were conflicts and contradictions in it. The monopoly layer, quite often, aligned with foreign multinationals and was more anti-people than other sections of the bourgeoisie. Thus the CPI did not lump the entire bourgeoisie together declare its enemy. This was inherent in its slogan of 'unity and struggle' with the Congress.

It vowed to fight for the rights and interests of tribal and backward people, to break the grip of foreign monopoly capital on the economy, to strengthen the state sector, to restrict the activities of Indian monopoly groups and to eliminate the hold of landlords and feudal remnants.

To achieve and realise these aims, a national democratic front of the working class, cultivating peasants, rising class of urban and rural intelligentsia and non-monopoly sections of the national bourgeoisie was to be formed. The CPI resolved to strive for establishing National Democratic Front (NDF) in government. The leadership question of the NDF was to remain open. In fact, as we shall see presently, though the CPI had a positive understanding of the Congress with which a strategy of 'unity and struggle' was possible, in practice the CPI tended to slip into anti-Congress alliances in the late 1960s, coming close to the theory and practice of the CPM.

Now let us turn to the programme of the CPI(M), adopted at its Seventh Congress held in Calcutta, from October 31 to November 7, 1964 and updated at its special conference at Tiruvananthapuram that took place during October 20-23, 2000, and see the differences.[8]

The CPI(M) pushed back the year of the birth of the organised Communist movement by five years to 1920 and declared itself the sole inheritor of 'progressive, anti-imperialist and revolutionary traditions of the Indian people. Since its formation in 1920, by a small group of determined anti-imperialist fighters inspired by the October Socialist Revolution in Russia, the Party had set before itself the goal of fighting for complete independence and basic social transformation. The Party pledge to work for the establishment of socialist society in India, free from class exploitation and social oppression.'

The CPI(M) demarcated itself from the CPI when it asserted that, notwithstanding a broad mass participation in the freedom struggle, its leadership remained 'in the hands of big bourgeoisie that refused to complete the basic tasks of the democratic revolution.' How did it happen? Why did not democratic masses rise against this? Why did the predecessors of the CPI (M) fail to convince them and encourage them to rise in revolt against the Congress and its big bourgeoisie leadership? How was it possible for the socalled conjurors like Gandhi, Nehru and others who led the Congress to have their way in spite of Communist leaders whom CPI(M) reveres? The CPI(M) then goes to say that the big bourgeoisie forged an alliance with landlords and compromised with imperialism. The Congress rulers' policies reflected this bourgeoisie-landlord alliance. Surprisingly, no objective assessment based on reliable data was put forth in support of this contention. Thus this did not carry conviction outside a select band of people who regarded these assertions which were regarded as axiomatic. Thus the CPI(M) programme was just like some religious text carrying the words of God almighty.

It went on to underline: 'The present Indian State is the organ of the class rule of the bourgeoisie and landlords led by the big bourgeoisie, who are increasingly collaborating with foreign finance capital in pursuit of the capitalist path of development. This class character essentially determines the role and function of State in the life of the country.'

From this it followed that there was 'no hope of emancipation of the people from backwardness, poverty, hunger, unemployment and exploitation under the present bourgeoisie-landlord rule.' The prime task of the Party was thus crystal clear: overthrow the bourgeoisie-landlord government, collaborating with foreign finance capital. Anti-Congressism flowed from it. The main enemy was Congress and its overthrow must be accomplished by uniting and collaborating even with the devil. Whatever the Party might have said occasionally, communalism, casteism and obscurantism and the parties championing them were not the prime targets. This explained its attitude to Indira Gandhi who succeeded Nehru and various measures and policies adopted by her government. Unlike the CPI, it remained lukewarm. When a big broad anti-Congress front led by Jayaprakash Narayan came into being in the 1970s, the CPI(M) found itself nearer it. Even during the Bangladesh liberation, the CPI(M) did not show any enthusiasm for the oppressed of that country.

The programme declared 'The Communist Party of India (Marxist) firmly adheres to its aim of building socialism and communism. This... cannot be achieved under the present State and bourgeoisie-landlord government led by the big bourgeoisie. The establishment of a genuine socialist society is only possible under proletarian statehood. While adhering to the aim of building socialism in our country, the Communist Party of India (Marxist), taking into consideration the degree of economic development, the political ideological maturity of the working class and its organisation, places before the people as the immediate objective, the establishment of people's democracy based on the coalition of all genuine anti-feudal, anti-monopoly and anti-imperialist forces led by the working class on the basis of a firm worker-peasant alliance. This demands first and foremost the replacement of the present bourgeoisie-landlord State by a State of people's democracy. This alone can complete the unfinished democratic task of the Indian revolution and pave the way for putting the country on the road to socialism.'

It was emphatically underlined that, 'The people's democratic front cannot successfully be built and the revolution cannot attain victory except under the leadership of the working class and its political party the Communist Party of India (Marxist). Historically no other class in modern society except the working class is destined to play this role and the entire experience of our time amply demonstrates this truth. The core and basis of the people's democratic front is the firm alliance of the working class and peasantry.'

How far all these assertions are valid in the contemporary world is beyond the purview of this paper.[9]

During the 1970s, several events took place in quick succession that brought more confusion than clarity. In 1972, India helped liberate Bangladesh from the tyrannical rule of Pakistani army dictatorship. The USA stood by General Yahya Khan and tried to intimidate India to fall in line with it. Indira Gandhi rebuffed the Americans and stood like a rock. This boosted the prestige of her government and the country. But soon inflationary pressures and the decision of the Allahabad High Court setting aside her election encouraged the anti-Congress forces, led by Jayaprakash Narayan, to launch a nationwide agitation for her overthrow. Except the CPI, all political forces from the Left to the Right and communal to secular forces joined hands. The situation became so critical that National Emergency had to be imposed and civil rights had to be suspended. Agitating leaders and their supporters were detained under MISA (Maintenance of Internal Security Act) in 1971. The government came out with a 20-point programme to calm the dissatisfied masses by looking after some of their grievances. It seemed, for a while, people's anger was subsiding, but, in the meantime, Sanjay Gandhi came out with his own 5-point programme and began implementing it with a great hurry. The two of these five points angered people. They were compulsory sterilisation and uprooting of hutment dwellers in order to make urban settlements decongested and orderly.

In the early months of 1977 when General Elections took place, the Congress was completely routed in North and East India. A hurriedly cobbled Janata Party with anti-Congressism as the binding thread formed the government at the Centre. Its vindictiveness towards Indira

Gandhi and her associates started getting expressed in persecution. The economy and polity soon became a mess. In-fights paralysed the administration. Governance became a casualty as a result of a perpetual tug-of-war between secularists and communalists. Ultimately the government collapsed and Indira Gandhi returned to power with a thumping majority.

During 1974-1980, while the CPI(M) remained with anti-Congress front, the CPI supported the government, but it became lukewarm and then frustrated after the ascendancy of Sanjay Gandhi. The CPI became so demoralised that, without looking into the changes in the ground reality and international factors, took to the line of anti-Congressism. At its Eleventh Party congress at Bhatinda, it almost gave up all its old positions. It found that the national scenario had undergone a sea change since its Tenth Congress, held in Vijayawada in January-February 1975. However, it still maintained that the Janata Party government, headed by Morarji, 'in which reactionary and communal forces predominate'[10] was far worse than the preceding Congress government. India was not an isolated case in the world where such a change had taken place. Reaction had been able to capture power in several countries of the world including South Asia.

Talking of the Congress, the CPI was now of the view that the capitalist path of development pursued by the Congress government brought in acute crisis notwithstanding certain policies of economic self-reliance and assistance from the Soviet Union and other socialist countries. The government 'tried to solve the capitalist crisis at the expense of the people through "hard" decisions. It sought to impose a wage-freeze on the workers and middle class through merciless suppression of their movements and struggles, for instance, the heroic strike of 14 lakh railway men. It imposed heavy tax burdens on the common peasants and refused to make remunerative prices for their produce available to them.'[11]

The CPI found the US imperialists trying to profit by the growing difficulties and weaknesses of the Indian government. 'They wanted a complete reversal of the nationally-accepted progressive economic and political policies and the installation of a regime fully amenable to their diktat.

'The reactionary Hindu communal and fascist forces which rallied under the banner of JP's so called total revolution tried to utilise the mass discontent against the Indira Gandhi government and attracted big sections of the middle class, students and upper sections of peasants.'[12]

The CPI's assessment at the Bhatinda Congress was that, from 1974 onwards, the government began succumbing to the US pressure and accepting the World Bank strategy of 'export-oriented' economic growth and diluting the Industrial Policy Resolution of 1956. What the CPI did to resist this trend was not made clear. The only thing was its confession that its assessment and understanding of the government and emergency was faulty. It was aware of the fact that RSS and Jana Sangh had set up a struggle committee with Nanaji Deshmukh as its convener soon after the Allahabad High Court decision setting aside Indira Gandhi's election to Lok Sabha was announced on 12th June 1975. Jayaprakash Narayan openly gave a call to the army, police and bureaucracy to disobey the orders of the government. The danger of a Rightist takeover of the government was obvious. Viewed against this background, the imposition of internal emergency appeared as inevitable. While on the one hand, steps were taken to provide benefits to the rural poor, curb inflationary pressures, check smuggling and improve the economy, on the other hand, large scale arrests of political opponents, steps to reduce dearness allowances of the employees, denial of bonus to workers, bringing in of compulsory deposit scheme, press censorship, and the imposition of Sanjay Gandhi's 5-point programme washed away popular sympathy and alienated the masses. The CPI in its Bhatinda document talked of numerous acts of the Opposition to excesses and policy deviations of the Congress but this was nowhere effective. It appeared that the CPI was bewildered and, to an extent, demoralised. Consequently, in its own words, 'our party's image was blurred and it became identified with the then ruling Congress Party. For this we had to pay heavily in the post-emergency Lok Sabha electon.'[13]

It admitted that it failed to grasp the real motives behind the imposition of the Emergency and opposed it once its negative features became obvious. Instead, it rushed to support it. 'On the other hand, the party leadership came to the mistaken understanding that a split has taken place between the anti-imperialist, democratic sections of the bourgeoisie and the pro-imperialist, most reactionary, pro-landlord, anti-Communist sections and the emergency could be used to bring about progressive shifts in the correlation of forces and state power in a national-democratic direction. Thereby the progressive potentialities of the national bourgeoisie and Indira Gandhi's government, and the capacity of our party and other democratic forces to bring about these positive shifts in the situation were overestimated. The potentialities of the favourable international situation and the progressive foreign policy in relation to its impact upon the international situation were understood in a very mechanical manner...our support to the emergency was wrong from the beginning.'[14]

The CPI confessed that its policy to build the unity of left and democratic parties got reduced ultimately to the Congress-CPI unity. 'The fact that CPI(M) joined hands with the rightist parties in the name of fighting Indira Gandhi government's authoritarianism was no reason why our party should not have paid serious attention to building left and democratic unity.'[15] Further, it admitted that it was a mistake not to protest against indiscriminate arrest of political opponents by the government. Besides, it was not correct to support the postponement of Lok Sabha elections.

In spite of all these mistakes, it reiterated that its basic understanding as embodied in its programme was correct. It must strive to build a national democratic front. In this front, primacy was not to be accorded, any rate, to the national bourgeoisie. It was a deviation from the understanding of the programme and undue importance was given to the Congress. It was argued that the Party followed a correct line till 1974 but deviations occurred afterwards and that sapped its mass base.

Thus the Party went back to its earlier practice of anti-Congressism, which was seen during the 1960s when it joined hands with all sorts of elements, communal and remnants of feudalism not excluded, and participated in Samyukta Vidhayak Dal (SVD) governments in Punjab, UP, and Bihar. In its manifesto, issued on the eve of the fourth General Elections in 1967, it declared that the situation demanded overthrow of Congress power because 'Under Congress rule the plunder of India's wealth by imperialistic exploiters continues. Foreign private investments in our economy [is]...a source of this loot.[16]

It suggested that a united front of left and democratic forces be formed to replace the Congress in power and categorically stated: The Communist Party of India...cannot agree to make any electoral front with the Swatantra Party and the Jana Sangh.'[17] However, after the election results came and the Congress lost power in northern and eastern states and the question of forming alternative governments came up, the CPI forgot its allergy to the Swatantra Party and communal outfits like the Jana Sangh and the Akali Dal and participated in SVD governments. This decision was rationalised by it as follows: 'The National Council of the Communist Party of India fully shares the urge of our people for the removal of the reactionary Congress government from power at the Centre. This, in fact, is a logical corollary to the great popular upsurge at the time of the general election for a radical change.'[18]

It was so emboldened that it gave a call for a non-Congress democratic coalition government at the Centre. An article in the *New Age* by a top CPI leader discovered democratic and non-democratic factions even in the Jana Sangh, the former led by Atal Bihari Vajpayee and the latter by Balraj Madhok! It declared: 'It becomes the duty of all those who genuinely stand for progress, especially the left and democratic parties, to rally to this urgent central slogan. The Communist Party of India pledges to do all in its power for the realisation of this urgent task.'[19]

It went on to say that the non-Congress popular governments could play a greater role in not only offering much-needed relief to the common people but also attracting other sections of the society. It visualised the end of the Congress rule once and for all because the people so desired. Thus it was following the masses and not leading them as visualised by traditional Marxist-Leninist understanding.

Soon, its expectations came to naught and the bickering and opportunism marred the image of the newly-formed governments. There were defections in Bihar, leading to the fall of the government. The CPI failed to abolish the *zamindari* rights of the Tatas and finish the unfinished tasks of land reforms.

By 1969, the situation in the country radically changed and Indira Gandhi came to have an upper hand. Her decisions to nationalise coal mines, big commercial banks, general insurance and abolish the privy purses endeared her to the people at large. India's decision to stand by the Bangladeshis in their struggle for liberation from Pakistani army rule and the 15-year Indo-Soviet Treaty for Friendship and Cooperation and the visit by the Soviet President Leonid Brezhnev, rubbished all the CPI analysis of the character of state power and correlation of class forces. The split in the Congress and the victory of V.V. Giri in the presidential elections led to a mass upsurge for Indira Gandhi. Even though she lost majority in the Lok Sabha, the Communists were left with no alternative but to support her. The CPI at its Tenth Congress admitted that the Left was in disarray. 'The Socialist Party continues headlong with its policy of unabashed opportunism and open alliance with the forces of reaction and counter-revolution in the name of the bankrupt policy of anti-Congressism. It has virtually become the tail of the right at this critical juncture....

'The CPM presents a woeful picture of confusion and opportunism. It talks of building a left and democratic alternative to the ruling party, but in practice concentrates fire on the CPI, progressive Congressmen and joins up either openly or through convergent action with right-reaction.'[20] The CPI was now once again poised for a strategy of united front with the Congress. A pendulum like flip-flop which had become a habit with the communist movement in India virtually since its inception in the 1920s.

What we have discussed above shows that neither of the two Communist Parties formulated their policies and programmes on a solid basis of scientific analysis of the Indian situation, polity, economy and class-correlation of forces. No data or case studies were ever presented. The terms like bourgeoisie, peasantry, feudalism, worker-peasant alliance were loosely defined and subjectivism and the needs of the situation influenced the interpretation rather than any in-depth research. The result was they and, in particular, the CPI behaved like weathercocks and indulged in slogan mongering. Notwithstanding all their claims of struggles and championing the cause of the people at large, their influence declined and those of communal and reactionary forces increased.

IV

Now let us turn our attention to the socialists to whom we have, till now, made only passing references. The Congress Socialist Party (CSP) was founded on May 17, 1934, at Anjuman-e-Islamia Hall, Patna by a group of, mostly young, people who wanted to give a definite direction to the Congress policies and make it clear that the Independence, whenever it came, would work for the common people as against the propertied. To begin with, it was to work as a pressure group inside the Congress, bound by its discipline. This organisation had the blessings and moral support of Jawaharlal Nehru. Prof. Abdul Bari, speaking on behalf of the reception committee, underlined that the fight was not for political freedom only; it must be accompanied by far-reaching institutional changes in the economy so that all forms of exploitation were ended and equal opportunities were given to each and every Indian for moral and material progress. Acharya Narendra Dev who presided over the meeting emphasised the need to bring in a big way industrial workers in the fight for freedom. It was decided that the Congress Socialist Party (CSP) would remain a part of the Indian National Congress and persuade it for the acceptance of a socialist programme. The CSP declared 'the establishment of socialist society' as its main objective. There was, however, no ideological clarity about CSP's concept of socialism. Some wanted it to be a Marxian one while others had their own ideas.

Soon after the 'Quit India' movement was over and independence seemed to be round the corner, the differences between the CSP and its parent body began surfacing. The CSP leaders, miscalculating their influence on the basis of the popular appreciation of their role in the movement, thought their organisation to be more important than the

Congress. They refused to join the Constituent Assembly because it was not up to their expectations.

Jayaprakash Narayan (JP), general secretary of the CSP, declared: 'The only way is to renew the demand of 'Quit India' and to mobilise the people in a final challenge with the foreign power. It is that power which is our primary enemy and which instigates and supports the reactionary forces in this country. It is that power which has to be destroyed first.... I believe that in the fire of revolution alone can be burned down the edifices of imperialism together with the supporting edifices of communalism and feudalism.'[21]

JP opposed the Cabinet Mission Plan and asked the Congress to reject it and not to take part in the Constituent Assembly. Mahatma Gandhi, however, rejected this demand. He told the Socialists: '... you are all seasoned and veteran fighters. A soldier is never afraid of danger.... If there are shortcomings in the proposed Constituent Assembly, it is for you to get them removed. It should be challenged to combat, not be a ground for rejection.' He went on to add: 'I was not prepared to hear such defeatist languages from the lips of a tried fighter like Jayaprakash.... A satyagrahi knows no defeat.'[22]

The CSP conference took place on February 26-28 at Kanpur where two important decisions were made, namely, dropping the prefix Congress from the party's name and rejecting Marxian socialism of the Soviet variety and accepting democratic socialism.

In March 1948, the Socialists gathered at Nasik where they decided to come out of the Congress and constitute themselves in a separate and independent identity known as Socialist Party (SP). Earlier the Congress had told them that there was no possibility of continuance of a party within party with dual membership. After the decision to leave the Congress, the struggle for power or supremacy began in the Socialist Party. It became evident in the context of the Korean War. A powerful faction, led by JP and his associates tilted towards the American line.

In the 1952 General Elections, the Socialists received the shock of their life and all their hopes to capture power in a number of states and emerge as the main opposition in the Parliament collapsed. With 10.6 percent of the votes, they could capture only 12 seats in Lok Sabha and 126 in assemblies while the Communists with only 3.3 percent of votes secured 16 seats in Lok Sabha and 162 in assemblies. Most Socialist candidates lost their security deposits. They were far behind the Congress which, with 45 percent votes had 364 seats in the Lok Sabha and 2,293 in assemblies.

In order to boost the morale of the workers and paint a better picture of the future, The Socialists decided to merge with the KMPP (Kisan Mazdoor Praja Party) of Acharya Kripalani, a splinter group of the Congress, which had secured 5.8 percent votes, 9 and 77 seats in Lok Sabha and assemblies respectively. Thus a new party PSP (Praja Socialist Party) came into being in the second half of 1952. Dr. Rammanohar Lohia was instrumental in bringing about this merger to ward off the growing danger of either going back to the Congress or seeking alliance with the CPI. He outmanoeuvred both the pro-Congress and the Marxist lobbies inside the SP.

In 1953, the talk of cooperation between the PSP and the Congress began when Nehru invited JP for a meeting and also held talks with Acharya Narendra Dev and Acharya Kripalani to explore the possibilities of cooperation at both governmental and organisational levels. Asoka Mehta supplied theoretical justification for cooperation between the two. A beginning was made in Travancore-Cochin and Andhra Pradesh.

In the course of his talks with Nehru, JP put forth a 14-point programme as the basis of cooperation. Nehru did not agree to condition based cooperation and the talks collapsed. The PSP was badly divided on the issue of cooperation with the Congress. Lohia was a staunch opponent. So much so that he did not even attend the meeting of Socialist leaders in Delhi on March 1, 1953 for formulating their approach to this issue. To resolve the differences, a special convention was held at Betul on June 14-18, 1953. Asoka Mehta presented a paper, 'Economic Compulsions of Development'[23] in order to underline the urgency of co-operation between the PSP and the Congress.

Even before the debate could come to any conclusion, Asoka Mehta, JP and a few others resigned their official positions in the PSP. This created an unprecedented crisis. Somehow or the other a temporary patch up was done. In 1954, the situation worsened and Lohia on the one hand and JP and Mehta on the other traded charges and made personal attacks. Lohia's use of vulgar language against Nehru was severely criticised by JP and Mehta. Lohia, in turn, charge JP and Mehta of collaborating with the CIA and named two CIA-backed and funded outfits like Democratic Research Centre and the Congress for Cultural Freedom, with which they were associated.

In the meantime, an incident of police firing in Travancore-Cochin took place. Whether the chief minister of the minority PSP government should resign ultimately led to a split in the Party. Lohia formed his own separate party—Socialist Party which became an unrestrained opponent of the Congress and could go to any extent to destroy it. To give an instance, when the Congress adopted a 'socialistic pattern of society' as its goal at its 60th session at Avadi, Madhu Limaye, the stormy petrel of Lohia's faction termed it as a 'colossal fraud' on the people of the country.[24] A group of nine PSP members from Bombay challenged the contention of Limaye. Worst kinds of abuses were traded between the two factions.

Ultimately, Lohia and his supporters formed a new party—Socialist Party (SP)—in January 1956. Lohia gathered a band of youngmen whom he trained in a particular kind of anarchic approach to national and international problems. His Nehru-phobia reached its climax when he unsuccessfully contested against Nehru in 1962 and, later, entered Lok Sabha through a bye-election. His speeches in Lok Sabha were full of vituperations against Nehru and his daughter. This put him in a unique position as an uncompromising ideologue of non-Congressism. An impression was created that he alone could bring together disparate political forces from the extreme right to the left adventurists to uproot the Congress regime.

In the meantime the process of the disintegration of the Socialists was in full swing. Prominent leaders like Mrs. Aruna Asaf Ali, Mrs. Kamaladevi Chattopadhyay, Achyut Patwardhan, Ramanandan Mishra, Minoo Masani and JP left. Acharya Narendra Dev died in 1956.

During 1957, efforts were made by JP who had 'retired' from active party politics, after delivering his 'Parting of Ways', and had joined Sarvodaya movement and was busy propagating his thesis on partyless democracy and eulogising dictatorial and autocratic regimes in neighbouring countries, to unite the two parties—PSP and SP, but the talks failed. Lohia wanted the PSP to bend on its knees and was confident that, sooner or later, it would have to yield to him.

In 1962 there started fresh efforts to unite the two parties and they gained momentum when Asoka Mehta was thrown out of the PSP on his accepting vice-chairmanship of the Planning Commission. With Mehta and his followers going over to the Congress, the PSP too fell for Lohia's anti-Congressism.

In June 1964, the process of reunification started and Samyukta Socialist Party (SSP) came into being. A foundation conference was held at Varanasi on January 29-31, 1965 where a small section, led by H.V. Kamath, belonging to erstwhile PSP, walked out and revived it. Most of the PSP including top leaders like S.M. Joshi, Karpoori Thakur, Ramanand Tiwari, etc., remained with the SSP.

Non-Congressism witnessed its crowning glory when it united most of the non-Congress parties in northern states and defeated the Congress in assembly elections. A party like the CPI which had fought elections independently too fell in line and joined SVD governments.

Under Lohia's leadership, Socialists came to believe that real socialism would come only after the stranglehold of the Congress on India was eliminated for all time to come. This could be possible only when all non-Congress parties came together to sink their political and ideological differences and put up one agreed candidate in each constituency. In a somewhat detailed exposition of his strategy of non-Congressism, Lohia made a number of formulations: [25]

First, no single party was in a position to match the Congress in strength, and there was no possibility of overthrowing it from power, even though it got less than 50 percent of the votes because there was no system of proportional representation.

Second, all the opposition parties worked for the overthrow of the Congress in their own separate ways. So long as they continued to go their own way, the Congress rule would continue with all its attendant evils. It was certainly possible that those who vote against the Congress could combine and give a tough fight. Parties should try to allocate seats among themselves on the basis of their performance in the previous elections.

Third, ideological and political divides among the non-Congress parties were much less real.

Fourth, the old theory of equidistance from both Communists and communalists must be buried. In fact, Communists and communalists were less dangerous than the Congress. Ties must be forged with the CPI, Jana Sangh, Swatantra and so on to destroy the Congress forever.

Fifth, the Congress won at the elections not on its merit but by the default of its rivals. Other political parties quarrelled among themselves and divided the non-Congress votes. Consequently, the Congress won even though it polled much less than 50 percent of votes.

Sixth, the non-Congress parties should consolidate their strength and give the people a chance to displace the Congress from power. This consolidation could be done in various ways, ranging from merger to agreeing not to divide their votes by forging adjustments.

Last, a common minimum programme could be the basis for electoral adjustments.

This thinking was tested in a limited way in the fourth Lok Sabha when a floor coordination committee was formed. Then Swatantra

Party had emerged as the main opposition group in Lok Sabha. Soon, when the presidential elections came, attempts were made to extend the scope of this opposition consolidation. The combined opposition put up K. Subba Rao as its candidate against Dr. Zakir Hussain, the Congress nominee. It was forgotten that Subba Rao had delivered a very reactionary judgment in the Golaknath Case, creating great hurdles in the way of further measures of land reforms. Lohia, the tallest Socialist leader in active politics declared: 'Dr. Zakir Hussain's victory would most definitely mean the victory of continuity of famine, rising prices, dynastic politics, national shame and disintegration. Mr. Subba Rao's victory would stir things up and would affect change.'[26]

In UP, Lohia and Nanaji Deshmukh, the Jana Sangh-RSS leader worked in tandem to pull down the Congress government, led by C. B. Gupta. Charan Singh with 17 Congress MLAs were lured away and the Gupta government fell. Charan Singh was made chief minister. Obviously, no ethical considerations troubled Lohia and his Socialists. Even Madhu Limaye, his staunch follower, could not swallow it.[27]

It appeared, after 1969, that non-Congressism had received a grave setback and it would not arise again. The Congress under the leadership of Indira Gandhi seemed invincible. The Congress split and a number of steps like bank nationalisation, nationalisation of coal mines, abolition of privy purses, steps to complete the task of unfinished land reforms, etc., broadened its mass base. The success of the Bangladesh liberation struggle increased the popularity of Indira Gandhi.

However, the situation changed after the Allahabad High Court Judgment against Indira Gandhi, success of reactionary Nav Nirman movement in Gujarat and the declaration of national emergency and its excesses which we have already referred to. JP had come back from his retirement from politics. Acharya Kripalani too had returned from obscurity. All the non-Congress parties except the CPI and the CPI(M) combined, formed a single entity called Janata Party and wrested power in 1977 and the first non-Congress government, headed by Morarji Desai was formed at the Centre. It needs to be noted that this conglomerate soon disintegrated, but in this process the separate identity of Socialists was lost for ever. Even now, in spite of attempts by certain Socialist intellectuals like Surendra Mohan, the late Kishan Patnaik, Vinod Prasad Singh, Yogendra Yadav, Mastram Kapoor, etc., and the followers of Lohia like the late Janeshwar Mishra, nothing tangible has been gained.

V

Our survey underlines a few important things. First, the two major streams of the Left gradually lost their relevance because they had failed to grasp the fact that the situation in India as well as the world had been constantly changing and they had not been able to update their analyses and strategy and tactics. Till now, there is no convincing analysis as to why the Soviet Union collapsed and disintegrated and why there is no attraction for Marxian socialism unlike the days of the Great depression, even though the world faced the severest recession since the Second World War in 2008. Second, Communist influence has failed to extend beyond its traditional strongholds; on the contrary, it has been on the decline even there. Third, both the Communists and the Socialists failed to grasp that non-Congressism could not be a long-term strategy though it might appear to be succeeding for a short time. Fourth, even though the Congress influence and mass base have shrunk, it remains the only true all-India Party with the potential to regain its lost ground. What we have in India are a number of small regional or caste based parties with no real interest in wider issues whether national or international. Their time horizon is extremely limited and their future uncertain. The contribution of Lohia and Kanshi Ram in encouraging caste polarisation is immense. While Lohia encouraged the neo-rich of the OBCs especially Yadavas, Kurmis and Koiries (Kushwahas) in Bihar and UP, Kanshi Ram patronised the newly emerging middle class of the Dalits. How long this will yield political dividends is not clear.

Both the Communist parties have been talking of worker-peasant alliance as the basis for revolutionary transformation in India. But they have failed to realise that 'workers' and 'peasants' of their conception have been fast vanishing. It became obvious during 1964-1984 when the *kisan sabhas* became just paper organisations. After the introduction of land reforms, abolishing intermediaries, most of the tenants began transforming themselves into farmers rather than remaining peasants. The answers to the three vital questions: What, how and for whom to produce?—were increasingly dictated by market forces. They were rapidly sucked into the vortex of capitalism and they began thinking of improving both their economic and social status within its parameters. While Lohia socialists responded to this situation by mobilising the neo-rich of the OBCs under their banner by demanding 60 percent of government jobs for them and a share in political power, the Communists failed to grasp the realities and revise their strategies and tactics. In West Bengal, for a while 'Operation Barga' did help increase the mass base and influence of the CPI(M), but once this task was partially completed, the stagnation set in. In Bihar, UP and elsewhere, the CPI could not do anything substantial on agrarian front beyond shouting slogans periodically before government buildings. During the first half of the 1980s, the two Communist Parties tried unsuccessfully to win over the rich farmers by demanding higher prices for their produce. The rich farmers rallied round Charan Singh, Mahindra Singh Tikait, Sharad Joshi and the Lohiaites.

The Communist parties failed to grasp the changing character and significance of a industrial worker. Changing technology and the nature of products rapidly rendered jute, textile and other traditional industries irrelevant. Textile mills in Maharashtra, Gujarat, MP, Delhi and UP and the jute mills in West Bengal and Bihar had to put down their shutters. Similarly, most of the sugar factories in Bihar and UP (especially in its eastern districts) were shut down. The number and significance of factory workers declined, rendering the mass base of the Communists smaller and less effective.

The Communists and their trade unions failed to grasp the changing concept of work place in view of the forces of free market and globalisation that had started penetrating India, though globalisation could descend in full force only after the collapse of the Soviet Union and the world socialist system. The ascendancy of Margaret Thatcher and Ronald Reagan to power and the emergence of New Labour in Britain had begun pushing back socialist thinking by making it much less attractive. The two decade-long uninterrupted prosperity and economic progress in the West had made the Chicago School of Economics and its leaders like Milton Friedman and Friedrich Hayek more influential. John M. Keynes and his theories were sought to be discredited by pointing to stagflation, supposed to be the result of pursuing Keynesian prescription.

The changes in the thinking in the CPSU and CPC besides their economic stagnation and inner party ideological struggle began impacting the orientation and approach of Indian Communists. The emergence of Naxal movement and China's changed attitude to the US and growing indifference to the CPI(M) brought in no less confusion. It appeared that one of the reasons for splitting away had collapsed and it could not convince its cadres and followers of the justification of its separate existence.

The fast expansion of the financial sector after the nationalisation of major commercial banks and general insurance did expand the influence of the Communists among bank and insurance employees but these employees, being in the grip of economism, had a limited perspective and they were not much interested in radical socioeconomic transformation. Bank nationalisation and the efforts at financial inclusion of the rural population, artisans, small traders and so on besides the growing success of Green Revolution extended the influence of the Congress and Indira Gandhi became an idol in the interiors of the country. Women especially in the tribal areas became her devotees.

During 1964-1984, the Indian economy aroused new hopes and expectations in lower as well as middle classes and they began entertaining the dream of rising up in socioeconomic hierarchy. Thus the subjective factors made them drift away from the Communist circuit of influence. As far as West Bengal was concerned, with the collapse of old industries like jute and engineering, job opportunities fast declined and people began migrating westward in search of sources of livelihood. The CPI(M) leaders failed to grasp and come to terms with these changes. The two Communist parties did not realise that their influence was declining and the mass base shrinking and they could not survive for long on the staple diet of anti-Congressism and hollow slogan mongering. They also forgot the Leninist teaching that there could not be two main enemies at any particular point of time and the Congress could not be the main enemy when communal and separatist forces posed greater dangers. In fact, their blind anti-Congressism led them to the camp set up by Lohia. The CPI(M) became an important constituent of the anti-Congress front. It convened a conclave of anti-Congress political parties in Kolkata in the name of fighting for 'legitimate' rights of the states against the dictatorial Central government, led by Indira Gandhi. This did not go well with the people at large. And it contributed to the decline in their influence and prestige.

A very important shortcoming of the Communist movement, more so of the segment, led by the CPI(M) was the neglect of the Hindi belt and its problems. The CPI(M)'s politbureau seldom gave representation to the Hindi region. Its social, economic and cultural problems never merited any serious attention. Consequently, the CPI(M) failed to extend its base there while the CPI's declined. Besides, throughout 1964-1984, the leadership of both the formations remained dominated by old people with not much capacity to come to grip with new realities and hardly any appeal to the younger generations. This was a big hurdle in attracting the fresh blood. As against this, lot of young leaders joined the ranks of leadership, led by Indira Gandhi, especially after the split in the Congress.

Endnotes

1. Dasgupta, Biplab (1971). *The Oil Industry in India*. London. p.141.
2. See, Rangnekar, D.K. (1963). *Bokaro: A Story of Bungling*. New Delhi.
3. CPI, Proceedings of the Seventh Congress of the Communist Party of India, Bombay, 13-23 December 1964 Documents, New Delhi, 1965, p. 1.
4. Ibid: 25.
5. Ibid: 26.
6. Ibid.
7. Ibid: 27.
8. File://*C:/Documents and Settings/abc/Des12top//party-programme1.htm*
9. If one has interest one may see my article "Vam ka Bhavishya", in *Samayantar*, July 2010, pp.21-24.
10. CPI (1978). *Political Review Report Adopted by the Eleventh Congress of the Communist Party of India, Bhakna Nagar, Bhatinda*, 31 March to 7 April, New Delhi. p.5.
11. Ibid.
12. Ibid.
13. Ibid.
14. Ibid.
15. Ibid.
16. CPI, *Election Manifesto of the Communist Party of India, 1967*, New Delhi, December 1966, p.2.
17. Ibid: 17.
18. CPI, *Post-Election Situation And Our Tasks*, Resolutions adopted by the National Council of the Communist Party of India, Calcutta, 23-30 April 1967. New Delhi, 1967, p.9.
19. Ibid: 10.
20. CPI, *Documents of the Tenth Congress of the Communist Party of India, Bhowanisennagar, Vijayawada*, 27 January to 2 February, 1975, New Delhi, 1975, pp.95-96.
21. *Janata*, 26 January 1947.
22. Pyarelal, *Mahatma Gandhi: The Last Phase*, Vol. I, Ahmedabad, pp.244-45.
23. Included in Mehta, Asoka (1953). *Politics of Planned Economy*.
24. *Free Press Journal*, December 24, 1955.
25. Rammanohar Lohia, *Note and Comments*, Vol. II, pp.36-47.
26. *Mankind*, March-April 1967.
27. Limaye, Madhu (1988). *Birth of Non-Congressism: Opposition Politics, 1947-1975*. Delhi. p.139.

Chapter XV

The Hindu Communal Challenge: 1964-1984

Rakesh Batabyal

All human solidarities claim a telos of virtue and a moral horizon. Substantive freedom and good life is invoked for such moral communities. The evolution of societies in India too has seen the emergence of such solidarities organised to expand human freedom. In more recent times, communalism has emerged as an idea invoking such solidarity to be organised within the boundaries of a community defined by religion (and sometimes, culture). The politico-historical horizon of such a community, it is claimed, would help expand the political and social wellbeing of the people.

The operation of the logic of invocation of communal solidarity, however, has brought serious impediments to human life and wellbeing in the sub-continent. It is therefore very significant that the claims of communalism have been seriously analysed by the political leadership and intellectuals in India, and have also been seriously contested. The context of democratic space within which the claims were presented and countered provided the contest with a character of deep ideological and hegemonic character. The period between 1964 and 1984, in many senses, seems to be most crucial for determining the contours, particularly of the Hindu variant of the communal challenge.

I

The phenomenon of communalism in India has been studied from two different traditions of scholarship.[1] There is the one in which the communal phenomenon is examined, explored and explained to test certain models already developed in the academia, particularly outside India.[2] Which model of governance induces more violence than others? Is inducing communal violence electorally more profitable, or for that matter whether religious conflicts are inherent in plural societies?

These are the questions that are tested with social scientific models, and certain conclusions are derived. Recently, the question whether the rise in communal conflict in the cities is related to the decline in associational civic life in the same way as it has induced urban violence has been explored using large scale samples from a couple of dozen Indian cities.[3] This analysis however begs the question as to why the civic life did decline in the first place. Communal violence or the rise of communalism has been linked with the decline in the civic life in most of the cities that have been examined and not the other way round, as the premise was set. With the rise of a voluntary sector linked to the global policymaking entrepreneurship, such models are then applied back to the societies by the global NGOs. Therefore, for example, the newly circulating idea in certain intellectuals circles that we should have proportional representational system instead of the presently working representational system comes from the argument for 'consociational model' of governance proposed by political scientist Arend Lijphart way back in 1977 in which he had argued that, '...in societies where minorities and groups are represented in the governments, religious conflict are less than where they are not represented.'[4] He had put India as one of the exceptional cases where conflict had nothing to do with representation. But with the rise of conflicts in the 1970s and 1980s, he had come back on the issue by including India in his model, suggesting that India also satisfies conditions of his model.[5] The conflict in India was less in the 1950s and 1960s, when the communities were richly represented in Nehru's government, while later their representation had been reduced and this had a direct correlation with the new spate of violence.[6] The model has been countered on the basis of the fact that as far as minority representation is concerned, it is the other way round: the period after Nehru, i.e., the post-1964 period, is precisely when the minorities had more representation (consociational) and the number of conflicts too were large in number.[7] Significantly, no counter-point is presented. The idea of communal representation that the 'superior' British colonial policymakers had introduced (well before this model was developed by the academia in recent years) which had led to the development of communalism in many colonised countries including India, is not addressed by both sides. Nor is it recognised that people in these societies have been trying to not only get out of these policies but also the deeply entrenched dividing ideas of proportional representation, in a manner specific to their own context. The argument then is proposed that societies with plurality may not be, for all practical purposes, conducive to democracies.[8] Incidentally, proponents of such arguments for other societies have come primarily from the United States, a society that prides itself on its plurality. It was for these scholars initially a factional fight (between the Hindus and Muslims in India), which led to conflicts—a methodology developed in the 1950s and 1960s in America to study the native Indians and African tribal polity, and then tested in studies on Indian society.[9] The old 'factions' theory has, with time, become outdated with the Political Science peer group, and been replaced with the idea of 'fights over religions'. Now clashes were read as pogroms—the Russian term used for killing the Jewish people in tsarist Russia.[10] There are also richly documented works, which begin by accepting the original claims of the communalists with regard to certain definitional criteria, and then use these definitions to conform to the academic currency and western European models of nation building.[11] In these works, concepts of religious or communal conflict or Hindu and Muslim nationalism have been generally applied without much disagreement with the claims of the communal groups. They serve as rich documents of the times but they somehow fail to give us a sense of the deep and intense contestation that had existed or continues to exist, which would establish the claims or contest those claims about the concept, ideologies and politics of the communalists.

The second tradition, prominently visible in the writings of Indian intelligentsia, locates communalism in the historical processes in Indian society and polity, and its implications for the democratic polity and the historical evolution of a civilisation.[12] There is a sense of urgency in these writings as communalism is seen as an idea and a phenomenon to be seriously engaged with. It is with this understanding that many contemporary historians have approached the idea of communalism. The period during the 1960s has been seen by historians primarily in terms of the evolution of the nation, through trials and tribulations. The nascent nation state is seen as trying to solve, and to some extent as solving, the intricate issues of the demand for the formation of linguistic states, separatist and secessionist movements, dealing with violent political opposition to the governments in the states, and finally trying to secure an equal and just national and international social order. The nation building and nation making exercise has been captured by locating the process in colonial, national and communal contexts.[13] The colonial past and the struggle to gain freedom, and the framing of a democratic and just path of evolution of a large society have also informed the larger body of modern and contemporary historians.[14] While this gradual evolution of the process of the nation-in-the-making has been recorded by historians, there have also been contestations from the colonial and also what is known as communal historiography. The former, most often, is seen as emanating from the Imperial centres of knowledge; while the latter has largely been an indigeneous product taking recourse to the intellectual presuppositions derived from 19th and 20th century scholarship. In European history, the nation has more or less been coterminous with either language or religion, and there had been no tolerance for religious or linguistic diversity during the long history of the continent, and this is best exemplified by the rise of the Nazis. This anathema to heterogeneity and the premising of the nation state on religion becomes the inspiration for the communal historiographical trends.

Nation and nationalism have been deeply contested concepts in these historiographies. While the Indian nation, theorised by a large section of intelligentsia, is understood as having grown out of the people's struggle against the colonial rule and therefore a wholly modern phenomenon, which is not yet fully developed, there has been a historical trend which believed that India has always been a nation—nation being defined in terms of the religiously defined community, i.e., the Hindus. Thus the Hindus constituted a nation and since they were living here since ancient times, India was always a nation. Only its freedom was snatched by foreign rule—here, the Muslims, against whom the fight has been going on for centuries. This historical trend has no quarrel with the British colonial rule. The broader ideology of Indian nationalism, which had guided the national movement has been seen by this historiography as not a real nationalism but false nationalism. The former's understanding of secularism is denounced as pseudo secularism. Significantly, the premises of the section denouncing the national movement have been interpreted by historians as communal, and most often lacking historicity since it is based on the communal projection of the present into the past.[15] The colonial historiography, on the other hand, sees Indian nation and nationalism as merely a Hindu upper caste manipulation of self-interest. It therefore sees nothing new in the communal or caste assertions, but would rather recognise them as representing real historical processes rather than the false pretenses of nationalism by the Congress and its leaders.[16] There is yet another trend of historical scholarship, which too saw the nationalist intelligentsia, including Nehru and the latter day nationalist and Marxist historians, as propagating this false nationalist history by suppressing the voice of the real community or people's history. For them, this history has been all lies ('*sab jhoota hai*').[17] Since the 'nationalist elite' needed to project the 'other' as bad to glorify themselves they imposed the term 'communalism' on events which were, as these historians tried to show, manufactured communalism, and creating communal stereotypes to denigrate 'genuine popular assertions' as communal assertions.[18] This they did by taking recourse to the colonial knowledge, colonial sociology and the power derived from the colonial authority. For a real and genuine history of the people, terms like communalism have to be rejected along with the politics of nationalism too, according to this view.[19] In this reading of history, therefore, an incident like communal conflict, in fact, should be celebrated as it reflected popular assertions, and what instead needed to be rejected was the language of western liberal knowledge imbibed by the nationalist intelligentsia.

Communalism has been a political phenomenon and the ideologues of the communal groups too have been arguing for the last century in much the same way as the 'subaltern' scholars, that the terms of discourse used by the modern nationalists in India have been false and they needed to be discarded. The authentic language of the community, which constituted the true 'nation', should be accepted.[20] The communal groups and parties have been not merely articulating this idea, but trying to act upon it by changing the contours of not only the intellectual discourse but of politics and society. It is quite important to locate here another set of writings, as we would see, that has emerged from this deep contestation between the challenge of communalism and those who are opposed to it in India.

Synchronising with a new economy, which celebrates markets without borders, these historians too celebrate society without nation and valorise a community life. Nationalism and also its attendant idea of Secularism, for these scholars, are both authoritarian ideas as they impose their authority over other categories like community or communalism. What for them seems most important is to attack the idea of nationalism as it obtains in India, and reexamine the notion of secularism by placing it on the same discursive plane as communalism.[21] Therefore, historiographically the targets of their criticisms have been the nationalist and Marxist historians, and not the communal or colonial historians. It is in this milieu that there is a new saliency of historical writings with a strong colonial stereotype, which has gained currency with a new intellectual fringe, in fact sharing its new found prosperity, aiming at throwing off the struggling past of the nation as something to be discarded as a bad dream. While the communal history wants to unite the present with a mythical Hindu and Muslim past, this history tries and unites with the good British past.[22] The communal project goes completely unchallenged.

II

The Turbulent 1960s: Struggle of the Communalists to Enter the Mainstream

The Chinese army launched a major offensive against India in 1962. Beginning around 10 October and ending with the unilateral ceasefire by the Chinese on 21 November 1962, this war left behind a completely shattered Indian army and a humiliated leadership. At the same time, coming as it did merely 17 years after Independence; the nation was in a flux and tried to mobilise itself afresh.[23] The Chinese attack made the Congress and Nehru particularly, the focus of attack by the Opposition. It brought the Socialists, and the Jana Sangh which articulated a Hindu communal position to come together in their attack on Nehru. [24] The aggression was caused by the changes in both the internal changes in China and the international situation. By 1956, India had emerged as the leading voice for the third world, and this was so particularly after the Suez Crisis in which Nehru played not only a crucial role for his bold stand but also a role for moderation and did not allow the crisis to become anti-west. In fact, he found the USA too against the move by the French and the British. It appears that China wanted to take on the leadership of the third world and give it an anti-American slant. The attack on India may be seen not just as an effort to humiliate India but to finish off India's moderating role in third world affairs. While India withdrew for the time being, the American drive against the Communists worldwide, but closer to home, in Indonesia, was to completely destroy the communist movement as well as governments with a nationalist legacy, by killing almost three million Communists there and ushering in the military regime.

Established by the efforts of Shyama Prasad Mukherjee, the Jana Sangh was given its organisational strength by the Rashtriya Swayamsevak Sangh (RSS), and by 1954-55, it virtually took over the party by bringing all the latter's organisers in the party fold.[25] Sunder Singh Bhandari from Rajasthan, Jagannath Rao Joshi from Mysore, popular Hindu Mahasabha leader Bhai Paramananda's son Bhai Mahaveer and Balraj Madhok from Delhi, Nanaji Deshmukh and Deen Dayal Upadhyaya and his younger colleague Atal Bihari Vajpayee from Uttar Pradesh and Madhya Pradesh were among its members. Jana Sangh was formed with the core ideas of the Hindu Mahasabha, that it was the spokesperson of the Hindus, and that Congress and particularly Jawaharlal Nehru's secular nationalism has been the bane of the Hindus not only in India but also in Pakistan. The Indian state must be a strong (read belligerent) state and the final aim should have been to reclaim the old territory of united India (Akhand Bharat).[26] Therefore, Nehru's policy of evolving friendly relations with Pakistan and encouraging it to respect the minorities inside its territory through the initial Nehru-Liaqat Ali pact in 1950, a matter on which Shyama Prasad Mukherjee resigned from Parliament, had been the target of attack by the Jana Sangh. It concentrated on the treatment of the Hindu minority in eastern Pakistan, which it thought would be better done with a dominating Indian presence and in fact, threat of action.

Alternatively, it also talked of complete transfer of the Hindu population to India, and the Congress Party and particularly Nehru was blamed for not executing this. Thereafter, it was the attacks on Nehru and his foreign policy in Parliament, which gave the party some much needed visibility. On 21 August 1959, for example, Atal Bihari Vajpayee moved a resolution in the Lok Sabha to refer the Tibetan issue to the UN. Thus, by the time the Chinese began a full-scale attack, there were already very powerful attacks on the government.

On the other hand, this also gave the Jana Sangh a handle to target its other political enemy, the communist flank, in the newly surcharged nationalist upsurge. The communist position that the boundary questions were created by the colonial masters and should be solved by mutual discussion could no longer be voiced, as it would be construed as supporting the Chinese position at the time of a massive nationalist upsurge. Taking advantage of the situation, the right wing and communal parties targeted the communists throughout the country but the democratic core of the nation, represented by Nehru, saved the Indian polity from becoming anti-Communist, the way it happened in Indonesia, Malaysia, and in many other places, quite often with the active support of the Western democracies. The Parliament and the leaders, both Communist and non-Communist alike, saw to it that while the sentiments found expression, the nationalist upsurge did not lead to a tyrannical regime.

While these attacks on Nehru were aimed at projecting Jana Sangh as a strong 'nationalist' articulator, it was the attack on the Communists which was strategic, as the party needed a physical enemy to establish its own 'nationalist credentials'. This nationalism, as has been discussed by many scholars in great detail, is what has been defined in the Indian intellectual tradition and political leadership as communalism.[27] Communal idea of a nation as developed by the Hindu Mahasabha and the Muslim league was in direct opposition to a nationalism, which had developed in the course of countering colonial rule. The communal idea was that a community of religious people sharing the same cultural attributes, language and world view would constitute a new nation—this became the basis for the demand of a new nation of Pakistan by the Muslim League, while the Hindu Mahasabha began advocating that India needed to establish a Hindu nation. Both of these ideological and political strands, by the end of the 1930s began to attack pan-Indian nationalism. On the other hand both these strands, theorised as communal and the politics as communalism, were not only shown to be reactionary politics, but as having a false history and false notion of Indian society and nation. However, since Pakistan was created much to the chagrin of the nationalists, Hindu communalists retained their self *raison d'être* to ideologically consolidate for a future real Hindu nation, as opposed to, and also in many ways to complete, the phenomenon of what has been articulated in many circles as the civilisation fault line of the Hindu-Muslim division. Thus, in self-definition Hindu communalism has always been Hindu nationalism, while Indian nationalism to it has been Congress nationalism—false and unreal, based on ideas like pseudo secularism. The RSS founded in the 1920s became the ideological and cultural centre for propagation of this 'real nationalism', while initially it was the Hindu Mahasabha (1915), and from 1951 onwards it was the Jana Sangh which became its political face, attempting to entrench itself into the democratic polity.[28]

On the other hand, in the situation that obtained across the world in the 1960s, where the cold war saw the western world trying to contain Communists everywhere and by all means, arguing that the biggest ideological opponents and enemies of the Indian state were the communists, at a time when Nehru was following the policy of political engagement, would have been disastrous even for the polity. In fact, the presence of Nehru was, in many ways, the sole guarantor of the survival of democracy, as Nehru had been warning that democracy and nationalism could be throttled in the newly independent countries in the name of suppressing Communism. As mentioned earlier, this is what finally happened in many parts, i.e., large scale massacre of the communists as in Indonesia in 1964-65 followed by other countries in the region.[29] Had they been more powerful than what they were, the Hindu communalists could have seriously affected the nascent democracy.

III

The Aligarh University: Creating an Enemy Metaphor

In 1965, the then education minister M.C. Chagla sent a renowned educationist and Indian diplomat Ali Yavar Jung as the new vice-chancellor of Aligarh Muslim University (AMU), to raise the university to the level of a world class centre of excellence in scholarship on Islamic history and culture. However, things moved in a direction that could not have been predicted by the minister or by the vice-chancellor. On April 25, the university was having its court meeting when a big clash took place between the students and police, leaving many injured. But before the police came in, the students had already disrupted the court meeting and attacked the vice-chancellor to the extent that he had to be hospitalised for serious injuries, and as it later came to be known resulted in his loss of hearing. This was the beginning of a long haul, which saw the University completely losing out academically; and more importantly the University became the metaphor of communal politics.

The students apparently were protesting against the academic council's decision to allow 50 percent of the seats in the technical institutions of the university to students who had done their prior studies outside the University of Aligarh, as compared with 25 percent previously allocated to them. They regarded this as unjust to deny University of Aligarh students special consideration. The practice of the University previously was to allow 50 percent seats to outside students but the recent vice-chancellor had reduced their quota to 25 percent. The University Grants Commission (UGC), on the other hand, in the interests of admission on the basis of merit had favoured allowing 25 percent to students already enrolled in the Aligarh Muslim University. It was the effort of the admission committee to restore the balance between the home students and outside students which was the occasion for the outbreak of the violence.

The event angered M.C. Chagla, the education minister, who announced in Lok Sabha on 2 May that, 'the violence was organised by the illiberal, rowdy and communal elements inside the campus'. Secularist to the core, Chagla was in the process of bringing changes to the Aligarh and Banaras universities through two separate bills. The BHU Bill, which was being discussed in the final round during 3 -12 November 1965, and was almost on the verge of being passed, had proposed to change the name of the University from Banaras Hindu University to Madan Mohan Malviya Kashi Vishwavidyalaya, and drop the 'Hindu' from its nomenclature.[30] He was planning a similar move in Aligarh too. The Hindu groups under the leadership of RSS and the local vested interests in Banaras began to campaign against the bills and the minister. Soon, it was violently opposed by the Jana Sangh members in the House and a complete mobilisation was in place. The BHU had been the scene of incidents for some time as the vested interests were aligned closely with the local RSS members and the caste network had been organising violence, which very soon made the university the site of strikes and processions. The senior Socialist leader and professor of Political Science, Prof. Mukut Bihary Lal, was garlanded with shoes by the Hindu elements. Thus, the proposal to change the names of Aligarh and Benares saw the mobilising of Muslim communal elements as well as Hindu ones. Incidentally, Chagla was portrayed as a Hindu communalist in Muslim garb by Muslim communalists, while there were ferocious attacks on him for intervening in the Banaras Hindu University. The RSS had in fact saved the University for itself, while at the same time it had saved the Aligarh to keep brandishing it for future onslaughts.

A new organisation called All India Muslim Majlis-e-Mushawarat (AIMMM) came into existence to apparently save the interests of the Muslims in the light of the attacks on the community's interests in Aligarh.[31] On the face of it, it looked like a simple issue and one could argue that Muslim communalists were the real actors in Aligarh. And a committed nationalist, Chagla also drew the same conclusion. However, on looking at the overall picture one soon realises that the Muslim communal position had got strengthened in the university at a time when a progressive section was beginning to assert itself, precisely because there was a Hindu communal mobilisation constantly targeting the university. Four years back, in 1961, Jana Sangh and the local RSS led a vicious campaign against the university, in what was essentially a student affair, leading to violence. Aligarh University, which had become the intellectual centre of the Pakistan movement, was limping back to normalcy after partition under the soothing hands of its vice-chancellor Dr. Zakir Hussain. However, since the 1950s it was beset with problems like mass migration to Pakistan, and a visitorial enquiry which killed in some sense the life of the University for some time to come. It had, by the mid-1950s, begun to get back to its academic moorings when the RSS and the Jana Sangh began to make Aligarh, Muslim and Urdu the metaphors of the enemy of the nation. Significantly, the chief target was the un-nationalised Muslims and the 'communists' in Aligarh. In fact, the Communists in Aligarh were a new breed, and their presence was in some ways helping the University to connect to the larger life of the nation in a serious manner. Obviously, from the Hindu communal viewpoint, this was not to be encouraged at any cost.

The police firing in Aligarh in 1961 during the students' disturbance, in which a couple of students died, found the Jana Sangh leaders from the local to provincial to the national level very well linked, and the attack against the University was well orchestrated. It was soon to prove that the Aligarh issue was part of the 'separatist act'. Vajpayee claimed that, 'as long as the university was not emancipated from the clutches of the communalist-cum communist incubus, the danger of recrudescence of communal trouble in western UP would always persist'.[32] Jana Sangh appointed its own enquiry committee under Pitamber Das and Shiva Prasad, and gave its verdict: 'there seemed to have been a tacit collaboration between Pakistan agents and communists in creating the trouble'. Jana Sangh in its national general council in the same year in Varanasi came out with the demand that the AMU should be Indianised.[33] Soon Vajpayee and Balraj Madhok moved a resolution in the Parliament demanding that the time has come to 'nationalise and Indianise'[34]. Both terms were interchangeably used by Madhok and Vajpayee. The term *Bharatiyakaran* was used for Indianisation. Jana Sangh's clamour was if there was any enquiry, it had to be only into 'the communal and anti national character of the university', because as Madhok declared, 'The two nation theory was born and cherished in the Aligarh University. They say they have a separate culture. When you have a separate culture, separate language, separate history, then you are a separate nation. It is this talk of separate nation, separate culture and separate history which goes against Indian nationalism'.[35] It also talked about a mentality of anti-nationalism, of which Aligarh was the symbol. The leaders declared that:

> By and large Aligarh University still continues to be the centre of that very mentality which resulted in the partition of this country. We are not against any individual, a particular person (sic) or professor, but against this mentality. So long as this mentality continues, we will continue to raise our voices against this university, because we think it continues to be a plague spot of India. Until and unless this plague spot is cleared of its plague symptoms and made a national organisation, there will be danger. Let the professors be all Muslims, let the students be all Muslims, but let nationalism be taught there.[36]

Now there was no confusion among the rank and file of Indian intellectuals and political class about the Jana Sangh's proclamations of nationalism. The freedom struggle was afresh in people's memory, and the inglorious part played by the Hindu Mahasabha and the assassination of the Mahatma were too fresh not to understand the ideas of the Jana Sangh and RSS. The party had also articulated its idea of nationalism when Madhok and Vajpayee along with Bhai Mahaveer, Deen Dayal Upadhyaya, Golwalkar and Deoras spoke on the issue at various platforms. Madhok in fact was representing them when he wrote in the RSS mouthpiece, the *Organiser*:

> Nationalism as conceived and preached by the Congress and its allies had given a new lease of life to Muslim separatism and has become the biggest ally of communism. It has still failed to draw inspiration and sustenance from the ancient roots of Indian national life which has stood the test of time. It is neither national nor secular. It is based on compromises with separatism and communalism which it seeks to employ for the political gain of the Congress. But in doing so it is

> cutting at the roots of Indian nationalism. It is un Indian, un Hindu and un Bharatiya.[37]

This is the Hindu communal idea which had been attacked by generations of leaders and intellectuals in India since the 1920s. Its ambition to replace the newly evolving nation is what has been the telos of the RSS and communal parties. While the opposition parties opposed Nehru on many counts, there was a template of unity with regard to their social philosophy. Even the Marxists who had an ambivalent position on the nation and had declared Indian independence as false (*yeh azaadi jhoothi hai*), debated more on the social questions. Jana Sangh notwithstanding its bold proclamations was intellectually and politically on the fringes. Therefore, there was an extra amount of sensitiveness within the University, which felt under siege in the current crisis. It was therefore an opportunity for the vested interests and the Muslim communal elements to take the lead in such a situation.

The evolution of the Aligarh Muslim agitation to a Muslim communal agitation gave fillip to the Hindu communal groups to target the Muslim separatist trends in an atmosphere of fear and suspicion, as Pakistan was involved in the aggressive posturing along the western borders in 1965. A major violent upsurge of a sub-continental level had erupted in 1963 which soon took the shape of Hindu-Muslim conflict over the issue of the theft of the 'prophet's hair' from the Hazratbal Mosque in Srinagar in Kashmir on 26 December 1963. From January to March 1964 series of riots starting from Khulna (East Pakistan) soon travelled to Calcutta and then back to Dacca (East Pakistan) and afterwards to the steel cities in eastern India, namely Jamshedpur and Rourkela.[38] It was a ground which could have reaped a rich sectarian harvest, as the bruised national psyche after the Chinese war could have been mobilised to assuage itself by targeting one physical enemy of the nation. This was the reason for the stridency of the RSS and its various organisations, who were trying to make anti-Muslim pronouncements, linking the AMU to Pakistan. The Muslims, feeling the loss of Nehru as the big protector and the agitation going on around the Aligarh crisis, must have felt insecure. It is in this situation that the escalation of Indo—Pakistan conflict began to take place, which ended up in a full-scale war in 1965. Now the second part of the nationalisation thesis unfolded itself, when there was talk of the pro-Pakistan elements within India, and therefore the need to Indianise was very important. The Jana Sangh in its Delhi meeting of the Central committee resolved that, 'There should be no political bargaining with Indian Muslims. They must be guaranteed all constitutional rights due to them in this secular state. But all separatist tendencies and attitudes betraying a pro Pakistan bias must be curbed and the outlook of Indian Muslims must be nationalised'.[39]

It was to cater to these insecure times that orgnisations like AIMMM etc., came up, which further made easy the task of the communal groups to paint the Muslim community as having such separatist tendencies. Throughout the 1970s while the University was trying to secure its autonomy from the bureaucratic and administrative imprisonment that it found itself in after 1966, the communal attack on it by the Hindu communalists strengthened the Muslim communal groups' claims as the defender of the University. Both these forces attacked the intellectuals and those who wanted the University to find its way to fulfill its intellectual promise and align with the larger intellectual and historical forces operating in the outside world. From the 1970s, the groups fought over the possible university act, which finally came into place in 1981. The more the communalists reigned inside, the easier the Hindu communalists found it to keep the University as the metaphor of the essential Muslim separatist psyche, which was un-Indian, and needed to be Indianised but how this was to be done was never spelt out.[40] Those who fought those elements inside and forged a linked with the larger Indian political and cultural life were attacked by the Muslim communalists within the University, and provided the fodder for the Hindu communalists from outside.[41] While the Muslim communalists were shouting that the University symbolised the identity of the Muslims in the subcontinent and required protection as a minority institution, the Hindu communal attack on this further entrenched their position. The political class however, did not come out successfully from this conundrum as it increasingly saw in Aligarh, as the Hindu communalists had planned, a political and not an educational issue. Therefore, only the administrative and political solutions for the University's character was sought to be attended to, leaving the academic needs and demands unsatisfied. In this sense, the Hindu communal effort to attack the University since the 1950s resulted in a front ranking university becoming a stultified place, groping in the dark for a glimmer of hope.

IV

Language and Other Divisive Tactics

While Urdu, for the Jana Sangh, was a language which was artificial and a symbol of separatism, and henceforth should be resisted and in fact rejected, Hindi was the language which it thought was the only source of Indian unity, and thus any opposition to its imposition in the wake of the language agitations of the 50s, it claimed, was an anti-national act:

> People who demanded the continuation of English for the sake of unity were no lovers of Indian unity. It is only a clever ruse to beguile the innocent people of the country. In fact when they say so they give a veiled threat that if you do not continue the use of English, we shall secede. This veil must be cleared. National unity is an article of faith and not a matter of compromise. If there are some people who can think of disrupting unity simply because Hindi comes or English does not remain, they definitely have no faith in unity.[42]

The Socialists and the Jana Sangh were the two anti-English and pro-Hindi political formations, most vocal in the 1960-1965 anti-English agitation which precipitated the anti-Hindi agitation in southern India and partially in Bengal. This stand was tested in Punjab where the Akalis began to demand for the Punjabi Suba movement, which took an immediate turn in late 1966. Here the Hindi-Punjabi controversy and agitation saw the Jana Sangh campaign for Hindi, and for the united state. Now the whole agitation was a significant test for democracy, with regard to change in policies by acceding to people's wishes. The Jana Sangh, however, was clear in one thing—its stand on Hindi was firm. Hindi had made the nation, while Urdu was unmaking it. In Punjab, there was another dimension that began to come into sharper focus—the Jana Sangh was in a dilemma while dealing with other communal groups. The Akalis were bent on having their demand fulfilled *vis-à-vis* the Jana Sangh and RSS demand. The Jana Sangh could not take any stand against the Akalis for two reasons: one, because its only electoral successes in the region were dependent on an alliance with the Akalis, and second, the success of the Akalis would lead to Hindus, whom the Jana Sangh wanted to mobilise, gravitating towards the Congress.

In November 1966, with the new Prime Minister at the helm, it appears that the RSS and other organisations wanted to use the political flux to further strengthen the Hindu consolidation. While it may be true it was a Hindu communal party, there were few signs that Hindu religious organisations had any enthusiasm for the politics of Jana Sangh. It is therefore with an issue, which was sentimental and sensitive that a front could be galvanised. In a move, which would become characteristic of the Hindu communal organisations in later years, there was a mobilisation of its ranks and blackmailing of the system with big processions. On 7 November, a meeting of *sadhus* and thousands of people was organised as the culmination of a month-long agitation demanding the ban on cow slaughter. The meeting was prompted by a Member of Parliament, Rameshawaranand. The Jana Sangh leader Atal Bihari Vajpayee was on the improvised stage set up on Parliament Street in Delhi. It was reported that an incendiary comment led to the crowd bursting barricades, indulging in arson and damaging property in the area. Later on, the Jana Sangh and Vajpayee in particular tried to disassociate from the whole incident. It is from this point that the RSS and its organisations were mastering a new form of mass action, which went against the tradition that was initiated and organised by the Indian National Congress during its agitational phase from the 1920s onwards. At the core of the latter was the principle of the leadership taking the responsibility for mass actions, while there was a complete guideline for action for all the participants.

Another dimension of the party's behaviour became obvious, its diversionary strategy. While it completely dissociated itself from the event by claiming it was not organised by the party, it also attacked the government and in fact charged that there were provocateurs who incited the mob. However, it was soon revealed that the Jana Sangh and RSS senior activist Kedar Nath Sahni had sought permission for the meeting, exposing the fact that the Jana Sangh was hand in glove with the whole incident and this was a ploy to evade the responsibility of the party for the incident.[43] The argument given by the Jana Sangh was that the government was jealous of the Jana Sangh's popularity.[44] The *modus operandi* of the RSS, which was clear even in the 1940s, made for an interesting read again, as it worked through different formations and at times of crisis disassociated itself from all the responsibility.

Democratic polity as it was evolving worldwide, required the institutional rooting of its machinery. This fact was shown by the leaders and intelligentsia of the nationalist movement since the 1880s and came to fruition when the post-Independence government tried to institutionalise democratic practices. The disavowal of responsibility reflected Jana Sangh's attitude to democracy. One sees the point of the arguments that many voiced, particularly those who premise their arguments from the Nazi experience that democracy is the system which allows the anti-democratic forces to hijack democracy.[45] The forces ranged against the democratic and secular forces in many parts of the newly independent world have later even been used by outside forces to derail the experiment of any kind of democracy.[46]

Consolidation of the Communal Ground

The war with Pakistan in 1965 had a protracted timeframe as Indo-Pakistan hostility had been there for some time already, creating a war like situation. The anti-Muslim communal propaganda at this time was reaching its most vulgar level, when a person of the stature of

President Zakir Hussain was also made the object of such propaganda, when he was rumoured to be under house arrest. The propaganda began to implant now the idea of a 'fifth columnist'—a Muslim being a potential Pakistani inside Indian territory. Pakistan, Muslim, Urdu and Aligarh now formed the template for the potential Hindu consolidation. However, ideological consolidation required time and space. Jana Sangh and the RSS, even at this juncture, did not have the respectability and reach. Seen by the Indian middle class and in regions other than northern region as merely the representative of the small town shopkeepers and semi-literate intellectuals of north Indian towns with a large refugee population, it tried to gain respectability by accepting a philosophical core. In its 1965 meeting, it accepted what was called 'Integral Humanism', a collage of few Indian philosophical ideas woven into some kind of political doctrine. It was neither philosophically deep nor politically elating for the youth, to attract them to the party's programme, particularly at a time when the youth all around the world were looking for new ideas. However, the nomenclature itself bore resemblance to the philosophical basis of fascism, integral humanism. The philosophy of integral humanism needed a political definition of the self through a comparison with the outsider. And it is here the template of Muslims as other came into operation, and the RSS was quick to use this in many regions for propagating its own ideas.

The 1967 elections had brought a coalition ministry in Bihar where the Jana Sangh had a presence precisely due to the RSS ground work in parts of the state.[47] Ranchi was the headquarters of the largest district in the country at that point of time, in the heart of the tribal belt of central India. A new industrially developing township with high rate of literacy and chain of missionary educational institutions, Ranchi had been the centre of RSS propaganda both against the Christian missions as well as against the sizeable Muslim population settled there for centuries. It also had a sizeable business community from Rajasthan and the Punjabi and Bengali refugee business community, which could have played host to the RSS.

But in reality, the RSS and other Hindu communal groups still had a minuscule presence, and were primarily engaged in an ideological war game by targeting Indian Muslims. In 1964, news of communal riots in East Pakistan saw communal violence in Calcutta, Jamshedpur, Rourkela and tensions in other places in the rich industrial belt of Chota Nagpur. The new industrial development already had seen new populations moving into the area, taking away the land and livelihood of the local population who also were in a quandary. Communal polarisation therefore also suited a segment of these new migrants into the area. The 1965 war with Pakistan had allowed it to carry out extremely insensitive propaganda against the substantially high Muslim population. The ideological penetration of the propaganda launched on Aligarh and Banaras were also reaching the region, as not only were these places geographically close but also Aligarh was a centre of education for hundreds of Muslim students of the region.

It was in this climate that the political demand for Urdu being the second language of the state came up. There were processions demanding this to be implemented. However the RSS and Jana Sangh had shown its displeasure with Urdu long back in UP and this time the demand by the Muslims suited them well to connect it with the ongoing project of creating an 'enemy'. On 12 August, the Jana Sangh organised a procession and meeting in Ranchi opposing the demand. It distributed hand bills referring to the undesirablity of making Urdu the second official langauge of the state. The hand bill announced that participation in the procession and the meeting would save the country from further partition and the claws of Pakistan. It claimed that the question of language which had led to the partition 20 years ago had been raised by some Pakistani and anti-national forces.[48] Significantly the opposition was not a one stop matter, and was well-coordinated. Golwalker, the chief of the RSS, speaking in the Ramlila ground at Delhi declared:

> The Indian Muslims are trying to organise themselves around the slogans of Urdu. Any status or recognition to Urdu would help the process of the separatist Muslim organisations, which would result in another partition of the country.[49]

Very soon a massive riot took place in Ranchi, leaving many dead and resulting in a dreadful communal polarisation. The Hindu communal mobilisation was led by the local business community. The administration initially showed its lethargy and the army was called in quite late; by that time many Muslims had lost their lives. The Raguvir Dayal Comission enquiring into the riots found that the weakness and compromising character of the coalition ministry in the state was one of the most important reasons for the violence.

Post-1967 Ranchi increasingly became a kind of nerve centre of Hindu communal mobilisation, and a kind of headquarters for the RSS penetration into the tribal region of central India. The Muslim insecurities resulting after the riot also led to the ghettoisation of the localities and this gradually changed the shape of the city and its culture, which had evolved over a century in a predominantly tribal milieu with its own kind of freedom and relaxed atmophere. The work of the Hindu communal consolidation however proceeded at pace and within 10 years another site in the vicinity witnessed a similar demonstration of the penetration of this ideological group. This was Jamshedpur, barely 230 kilometres away from Ranchi, and more cosmpolitan in nature with a prosperous Muslim community engaged in different occupations in the relatively rich economy of the industrial city.

The Ranchi riot was meant to create a communal core in eastern and central India. In the west, it was the series of riots beginning from the prolonged Ahmedabad riots in 1969, followed by riots in Bhiwandi and Jalgaon in Maharashtra, which would create the communal core of the region. While the riots demonstrated the organisation, both physical and ideological, that had gone behind each of these riots, they also showed the depth of the new cultural codes that were scripted at the sites of this violence. Madon Commission enquiring into the Bhiwandi and Jalgaon riots had stated that, 'communal tensions does not spring up over-night. It is built up over a period of time, suckled on communal propaganda, nursed on communal incidents and fed on rumours, until men's hearts are filled with hatred and their thoughts turn to violence.'[50] The enquiry commission also gave detailed accounts of how and when the riots began to take shape in the minds and hearts of the organisers and the people. Bhiwandi branch of Jana Sangh was established in 1964, and in October Bhagwan Prabhashanker Vyas was elected the president of the Bhiwandi Branch. On 10 March 1968, Bhiwandi district Jana Sangh convention was organised coinciding with Bakra-Id (sic).[51] It was therefore a predictable progression of events by the time the final riots began in 1969. The way people were provoked and others threatened have been diagnosed by the commission and it listed 27 common themes of communal propaganda.[52] They include, decrying of the religion, customs and traditions of the other community; the charge that Muslims, with a few exceptions, are anti-national and harbour extra-territorial loyalty to Pakistan; the appeasement of the Muslims by the Congress government with a view to secure their votes by upholding their so called unreasonable demands in detraction of the rights of the Hindus; the atrocities committed by the Muslims at the time of partition; the atrocities committed by Pakistan against Hindus residing in their country; the destruction and desecration of Hindu temples and idols of Hindu gods by Muslim rulers in the past; the forcible conversion of Hindus by the Muslim rulers; the charge that a Muslim has publicly slaughtered a cow; the charge that a Muslim has desecrated and offered insult to a Hindu temple or the idol of a Hindu god; the charge that a Muslim has kidnapped or raped a Hindu girl or outraged her modesty;

advocating sending away all Muslims to Pakistan; advocating the Indianisation of Muslims, by which is really intended the Hinduisation of Muslims; the charge that the Hindu majority is out to crush the Muslim minority and to wipe out its religion, culture and language; the Muslim in a minority will never get justice or fair play in India—the charge that the Muslim in a minority are discriminated against in service, employment and other matters; the charge that Muslims are persecuted in India.[53] In fact the exhaustive list had their full play in all the riots in Maharashtra, where the RSS and Jana Sangh have been joined by another formation, which had come into the field by first beating up the south Indians and which now found the Muslims as its new enemies.

The Ahmedabad riots in 1969 was for all practical purposes one of the most organised instance of communal violence, notwithstanding the denials of the RSS and Jana Sangh.[54] The ideological aim of the riot was to obliterate Mahatma Gandhi's philosophy, which formed the political core of Indian nationalism. It was organised in Ahmedabad, which was to be the centre of the nationwide celebrations of Gandhi's birth anniversary. However the Parliament saw some of the most powerful repudiation of communal politics and violence by the Congress and Communist leaders. People like Bhupesh Gupta, Hiren Mukherjee and many others tore into Jana Sangh and its ideology as did many Congress leaders. Unfortunately, Gujarat had also become the centre of the Swatantra Party, which did not have any core political ideology to argue against the Jana Sangh's politics, and hence could not even identify the danger to its own existence in the province.

VI

Communalism Confronted: The Creation of a New Milieu

1969-70 also saw the coming together of the three different ideological cores to the forefront—the aggressive Hindu communalism, split in the Congress organisation and thereby a kind of flux in the whole polity, and the newly emerging trend of the Indira Gandhi government moving towards populist and socialist policies thereby attracting the intellectuals, the left and Socialists to its ambit. The Hindu communalism, in a rearguard action, heightened its rhetoric of 'Indianisation' of the Muslims. Significantly, the anti-communal attack this time was spearheaded by a large intellectual front, which had come up, with a strong counter to the communal propaganda.

From March 1970 onwards, there was a definite combative tone adopted by the Congress leadership towards the RSS and Jana Sangh leadership. The debate on the Ahmedabad, Bhiwandi and Jalgaon riots had given rise to a very aggressive Jana Sangh and RSS leadership. Atal Bihari Vajpayee spoke of how the Hindu will become *'ugra'* or aggressive if the Muslims were communal. Challenging his assertions, Indira Gandhi took the floor and countering his theory of Indianisation, doubted that *'bhartiyakaran'* was a very innocent or obvious slogan. 'If therefore Shree Vajpayee wants every Indian to love his country and to be patriotic, nobody can quarrel with that and I certainly do not do so; nor is any special theory of Indianisation required. But I think his theory is not quite innocent. Shri Vajpayee would not waste his energy in stating something which is so obvious. He and those of his way of thinking have a very definite purpose.'[55]

She argued that the Hindu communal groups are evidently taking upon 'themselves to be the judges of who is Indian and who is not.... That is what I think, most sinister. Whenever any group sets itself up to decide who is an Indian and who is not, there is bound to be trouble.' She further wondered: 'If this task of Indianisation was so simple why should it arouse fears in the minds of some sections of our people?'[56] Vajpayee countered by saying that it was Mrs. Gandhi and her party that was 'carrying on a deliberate propaganda to mislead the minority. I am sorry to say that the Prime Minister does not stand for national integration. She wants division in the society.'[57] Madhok came in by saying even she needed to be 'Indianised.' Indira Gandhi countered by saying that she considered 'every child who is born of mother India is a good Indian. There is the law of treason and there are competent courts to decide if anyone is guilty of treason. This cannot be left to be decided by any political group or party. No oratoreal devices can hide the real intentions of those who advocate Indianisation of their fellow countrymen.'[58] Therefore she concluded that either '"Shri Vajpayee's doctrine means the obvious" and needs "no reiteration, or it is hiding something."' She in fact pointed out how 'Vajpayee's colleague Shri Madhok is a better guide. He bluntly says what he means and the house is aware of his numerous utterances on the subject.'[59] She continued taking on Vajpayee's aggressive tenor by counter aggression when on 14 May, in reply to Vajpayee's speech on riots where he mentioned that Hindus are retaliating the Muslim communalism, she argued:

> Some hounourable members shouted that Vajpayee's remarks should be expunged. I am glad that the deputy speaker did not expunge it. I would like those remarks to remain on record and be read by future generations and by the people so that they could see what is really

> in their minds, not the sweet sounding beautiful Hindi that he paraded before us, from time to time, but what is really behind those words. And today we saw behind those words naked fascism. This is what fascism has been.[60]

The lead taken by the leadership now seems to be more coordinated. When the All India Congress Committee met on 13-15 June 1970, the party president Jagjivan Ram talked about the urgent need of 'the party to fight the communal tendencies'. Significantly, a resolution attacking the idea of Indianisation was moved by the Congress veteran Kamalapati Tripathy, who described it as 'anti-national, anti-Indian and anti-Hindu'.[61] He went on to say that, 'if anybody needed Indianisation, it were the RSS and Jana Sangh who were guilty of falsifying our history, our tradition, our culture in the cruelest manner.'[62] The resolution which was moved was against communalism and communal organisations and there was a hint that there were voices demanding a ban on these organisations. The resolution said,

> Para military communal organisations like the RSS and Jamat-e-Islami have no place in our secular society. The government should seriously consider whether such organisations should be allowed to continuously poison our society with communal violence and hatred.

Indira Gandhi, speaking on 14 June made it clear that the priority was providing security to life as the recent riots had shown that it was the security of life which was in peril. If a man is not going to be alive, she said,

> what does it matter to him what kind of economy you have or you don't have, what does it matter to him what kind of social system you have or you don't have. Therefore, the first necessity is to give security of life to our people regardless of what religions they practice or what caste they happen to belong, what language they speak or what area they live in.[63]

At the same time however she tried to underline the ideological fight against the communal forces. '"The government cannot be wholly successful unless we have people in every village", she argued, "in every street, helping us in this task. The police can help, but the police by itself cannot be as effective as our party could be if it geared itself to this task. Because the task is not merely of hitting back or punishing; that should certainly be done. The task is to try and remove this poison from people's mind, to try and create an atmosphere in every neighborhood where a citizen can feel he can live in peace,"'[64] Now many in the party thought the groups such as these must be banned. However the Communist leaders who had been in the forefront, fighting the communal groups, did not think so. Sripad Amrit Dange, the leader of CPI, argued that bans are not going to help. 'They will go underground.' He on the other hand was of the view of letting 'those who have democratic values to push forward in this country through both parliamentary struggles and defending the exploited class. Let them come together and launch a new movement of democratic unity in this country.' He also berated the National Integration Council in which he said, 'there are members who themselves riots because they are represented in this house and committee must be composed of all parties in the House.' Dange was advocating a united battle. The close cooperation between the communist leaders of the CPI with the Congress on the economic front could be seen, and now on the communal question it was realised that a movement needed to be launched.

The coming together of these two forces was also the result of the substantial intellectual climate that had been created by the assertive intelligentsia. Some of the most creative and respected cinema artists, for example, visited Bhiwandi and Jalgaon riot sites and condemned the communal groups. Some of the respected members of the film fraternity, namely, Dilip Kumar, Balraj Sahni, Khwaja Ahmad Abbas, Sahir Ludhianvi, Rajinder Singh Bedi, Krishan Chander, Gulabdas Broker, Mahendranath, Gajanan Jagirdar, Pragji Dosa, Shri Premji Manmohan Krishna, issued a statement in those crucial days intervening in the issue. It said:

> we the following artistes and writers, were deeply shocked at the shameful and tragic happenings in Bhiwandi and Jalgaon. We unequivocally condemn the orgy of rioting, arson, incendiarism, regardless of who was responsible for it. This brutal violence and the senseless destruction negates our traditional humanitarian values. These horrifying massacres which arise from the gospel of hate and intolerance which is being preached on all sides are a cancerous communal outgrowth that is spreading fast, as is retarding our efforts to usher in an era of just and egalitarian society and to evolve a healthy, national, secular set up. It is imperative to stamp out this monster of communalism, and it is high time for all secular, non communal and humanitarian forces to unite in all out efforts to maintain peace based on tolerance, goodwill, coexistence and secularism.[65]

The period which is generally seen by some political scientists and outside observers as the breaking up of the centrality of the Congress, in fact can be seen as a transition of the party to a different ideological sphere. It could be a paradigm shift. While it had almost no solid organisational structure in place, and it had only ideology left to itself to energise its workers, the period beginning with 1969 saw the party acquiring a new 'ideological umbrella'. For the first time since Independence, the party was accepted as an agent of radical change by the Communist party as well as the intellectuals in the hot radical climate of 1969-70. Coming together of the left intellectuals, anti-communal activists, erstwhile Socialist youth leaders and the personal ideological position of Indira Gandhi, is what coloured this new ideological field. Scholars have emphasised the role of economic policy as the basic determinant of these changes. But it seems that the communal threat to ideas and institutions may have proved to be the catalyst for this new found unity of perception.

The most important development in this regard was the coming of age of an indigeneous intellectual tradition, which used the autonomous space that freedom and democracy had provided. While the idea of 'Indianisation' and 'communal interpretation of history' came to be in direct confrontation with the intellectual developments taking place in the country, the constant attack on institutions by the communal groups must have precipitated this desire for unity among the democratic forces. Historical scholarship since the early 1960s had now matured to such an extent that there was an outright rejection of many of the ideas that the colonial historians had injected in understanding Indian history and society. Thus, the writings of D.D. Kosambi, R.S. Sharma, Satish Chandra, Bipan Chandra, Irfan Habib, Barun De, Athar Ali and many others thoroughly rejected the colonial constructions and demonstrated that the ideas the RSS was propagating stemmed from illiteracy. The Indian History Congress, the body founded in 1935, was now dominated by the ideas of such scholars since the 1960s, and had contributed to the democratisation of the discipline and the spread of new ideas and scholarship. By the time the Aligarh University historian, Prof. Nurul Hasan, became the Education minister, the Indian historians had already changed the academic historical discourse to an advanced level. An issue which generally escapes analysts' eyes is the fact that it is from the mid-1970s that there was a sharp decline in the standard of education and particularly of the centres of excellence in most of the universities and colleges in the country. Therefore it is very interesting that the Hindu communal groups began to capture alternative and parallel spaces made available in the new educational establishment and the declining institutions.[66] Significantly this is the phase when many of the restrictions in the academia and intellectual world were removed, quite often with the Prime Minister's personal intervention, and many Communists got jobs and positions in universities, which in the 1960s was not open. Indian leadership was contesting the dominance of the developed world and the intellectuals were coming up with a sophisticated critique of colonialism precisely at this point of time. It was through this critique of colonialism that scholars demonstrated how Hindu communalists, as well as their Muslim and Sikh counterparts, were in fact following the trajectory laid down by the colonial politics and historiography.[67] By 1969, this intellectual section became the major bulwark against the communal ideas, and more so in the case of the Hindu communal idea of Indianisation, which it attacked as unhistorical and even undemocratic as it was concocted to attack the Muslims. They argued that the idea of India has historical underpinnings, and it is trained historians as well the democratic policy of the modern state which will be crucial elements in determining Indianness, and not communal groups like the RSS or Jana Sangh. On the contrary, they argued that these groups had a very un-Indian philosophy. Therefore, when the Prime Minister was speaking in parliament on the question of Indianness, she was not only representing the nationalist political ideology but also the intellectual tradition which had come to fruition in the post-independence culture.

VII

The War with Pakistan: 1971

The elections of the 1971 saw a major drubbing for the Hindu communal groups. However the crisis in eastern Pakistan provided these groups with a new front to open its activities. The demand for the partition of India was based on the two-nation theory propagated by the communal parties, particularly the Muslim League which under the leadership of Mohammad Ali Jinnah made the demand for a separate nation state of Pakistan its sole political plank.[68] The Hindus and Muslims constituted, according to him, two nations defined by their religion and could not cohabit the same nation state. Thus, religion was argued to be the basis of the nation, and the Muslim majority districts were partitioned off from India and combined to form one nation state of Pakistan.

Not very long after Independence, difference began to crop up within the two physically distant zones, the East and the West Pakistan. To make matters worse, Mohammad Ali Jinnah, now the Governor General of Pakistan, on his official visit to East Pakistan, declared that Urdu was going to be the national language, an announcement which not only made the Bengalis angry but also apprehensive. There appeared also strong communal hatred and violence almost sponsored by the Pakistani state against the strong Hindu minority. There were official efforts at purifying the cultural profile of East Pakistan, of what was called the Hindu element. By late 1950s and 1960s, the problem took a serious turn when there was apparent and perceived discrimination by the West Pakistan elements against East Pakistan, heightening the popular resentment against the West Pakistani domination. The military take over of the Pakistan government after 1955-56 and its tightening grip over the polity and society, also meant a control of the west over the east as the Pakistan military was more or less Punjab dominated. Thus, in a crude sense it began to be seen as the Punjabi domination over the Bengalis. In the 1970s, elections to the Pakistan Parliament were provided in the new constitution and the demographically dominant as well as politically more conscious and mobilised eastern part sent the party of Mujibur Rahman who had emerged by this time as the most respected leader of East Pakistan, to the Parliament with a huge majority. In terms of the overall seats in the Parliament, Mujibur Rahman should have been invited to form the Government, which the West Pakistan establishment including politicians like Bhutto, would not allow to happen. Seeing this completely unjust behaviour, the East Pakistan rose up in anger and there was a popular upsurge. General Yahya Khan, who had appointed himself President in 1969, had given the job of pacifying East Pakistan to his junior, General Tikka Khan. The later ordered a general crackdown on the Bengalis on 25 March 1971, leaving thousands of Bengalis dead. Mujibur Rahman was arrested the next day. There were also massive attempts to disarm the Bengali troops in the army. All of this led to the exodus of the Bengalis—almost 10 million (more than half of them Hindus) crossed the Indian border and entered into West Bengal, Tripura, Meghalaya, etc. The burden of sustaining such a vast number of refugees fell upon the Indian government, which appealed to the international community to help solve the situation so that the people could go back home.

The international community was not very forthcoming and in fact United States began to show openly its bias towards Pakistan, which was its closest ally at the time. The American President Nixon was trying to use Pakistan to improve its relations with China. China too was Pakistan's ally, and India was in some sense isolated.[69] On the other hand, within the country the Jana Sangh and the RSS began to use this opportunity of a crisis to bring the language of communalism into the open. The Muslim communal propaganda was actively making it a Muslim *versus* Bengali issue, while there were those who made it a

Bihari *versus* Bengali issue. But more dangerous was the Hindu communal angle which directly impinged on the diplomatic action of the government. The show of intransigence towards Pakistan in the speeches and propaganda of these parties had the effect of making the issue get a communal colour. The Government was equally concerned that its mobilisation of public opinion around the world was towards solving the East Pakistan crisis, and it was not aiming at dismembering Pakistan. From mid-1971, the Jana Sangh more than any other party began to push the government for immediate action to punish Pakistan. It is to the credit of the leadership that it never allowed this issue to erupt into a Hindu-Muslim conflict, as perceived by the communal groups. It was in such a tense situation that the Pakistan air force triggered the first apparently pre-emptive attack. The actual war began at about 5.40 pm on 3 December 1971, when Pakistan Air Force (PAF) combat aircraft struck nine Indian airfields along the Western borders.[70] Prime Minister Indira Gandhi's speech on 3 December 1971 scotched any communal agenda:

> I speak to you at a moment of grave peril to—our country and to our people. Some hours ago, soon after 5.30 p.m. on December 3, 1971, Pakistan launched a full-scale war against us. ... Since last March, we have borne the heaviest burden and withstood the greatest pressure, in a tremendous effort to urge the world to help in bringing about a peaceful solution and preventing the annihilation of an entire people, whose only crime was to vote for democracy. But the world ignored the basic cause and concerned itself only with certain repercussions. The situation was bound to deteriorate and the courageous band of freedom fighters have been staking their all in defense of the values, for which we also have struggled, and which are basic to our way of life.[71]

In another address to the army she did not invoke belligerence but larger principles, 'The people of all regions, all languages, all religions, and all political parties are united as never before. They are determined as you to defeat the aggressor. They are imbued with boundless faith in their cause and in your capacity to meet any challenge.... You and we are fighting in defence of the great principle that people of all religions are equally our brothers. We are defending the great ideals of equality and brotherhood, which are life and blood of our democracy.'[72] Significantly enough, the Jana Sangh leaders at this time were found speaking in a podium where the backdrop was the map of United India. The ideology lives on.

The mobilisation by and coming together of the democratic and left groups, which had begun in late 1969 and early 1970s, assured that the largest number of political leaders, intellectuals, artists and left leaders who campaigned not merely for the war but on behalf of the struggling people of East Pakistan and the democratic and popular dream of those people. They also highlighted the plight of the people through their poetry, their plays and their songs, and in this way the crisis which began to be used by the communal groups to propagate communal ideas was turned into a popular and intellectual engagement. The crisis was soon over with the establishment of Bangladesh. But the mobilisation against the communal forces that was steadily coming to the fore could not takeoff, as the polity soon began to slump due to the onslaught of the student movements, which rapidly escalated into what is called the JP movement, first in Gujarat and then in Bihar, from where it engulfed a large part of North India.

This movement saw the coming together of diverse political formations like the Socialists, the Jana Sangh, RSS, and others. The Communist parties had divisions. While the radical and more sectarian Communists (Marxists) were decidedly against the Congress and remained opposed to Indira Gandhi, the Communist Party of India joined hands with the Congress. The movement demanded Indira Gandhi's resignation. The chief mobiliser, Jayaprakash Narayan's slogan of 'partyless democracy' however, was unheard of in any democratic theory and hence, created doubts among even those who did not support the Congress.[73]

The more concrete result was that the movement allowed the communal groups to amalgamate their communal and very personalised opposition to the Congress leader Indira Gandhi, and provide a cordon sanitaire to their communal agenda.[74] It is therefore not merely political posturing that in defence of the emergency, Indira Gandhi was talking about the communal forces operating along with others and posing a threat, for even the Communist Party members were aware of the danger. The banning of the Ananda Marg and the RSS during the emergency had the short-term effect of denying the communal parties visibility, but it also produced the result that Dange had warned of. Not only did they go underground, they also earned respectability. It is thereof quite significant that more than any other party, it is the BJP which is likely to portray the Emergency as the most important phase of its history. This was the best opportunity for the Hindu communal groups to acquire respectability by claiming to lead some sort of secular movement. The Government that was formed in the post-Emergency period saw Jana Sangh come back as part of the ruling coalition, which had the support of the Communists (Marxist) who were now in ascendancy in Bengal, Tripura and Kerala, and the Akalis who would be in government in Punjab.

VIII

Communalism Enters a New Milieu

Communalism came to be part of the consciousness of sections of the Indian people during the 19th and 20th centuries as a result of the political, social and economic restructuring of the Indian society. Colonialism had a major role in this restructuring. Creation of a national community to counter the colonial exploitative practices and bring about a modern and developed society saw another development along with this—the emergence of sections of communities that felt at odds with the principles and ideology of nationalism, which championed the cause of the newly emerging democratic ethos, universal values and a notion of freedom from the authoritarian constraints of traditions, communities and above all the overarching presence of colonialism. It is not surprising that the Hindu and Muslim communal sentiments were primarily directed against any extension of this ethos through the national movement.

Communalism was against this notion and spirit of nationalism, and its fight was therefore against nationalism and not against colonialism. While one communalism defined the Indian nation as existing even before the British arrived at the scene, the other tried to define a religious community as entirely different in existential terms from other religious communities, and therefore constituting the basis of a nation. Thus all shades of communalism bypassed any critique of colonialism. The clash was always against the other religiously defined community. This was a product of a new history that came to be written by the British who characterised the History of India into Hindu, Muslim and British phases. Where the Hindu was a glorious period, Muslim was a dark age, and Modern was a period of development under the British aegis.[75]

The early Indian nationalist also argued that India witnessed a glorious history in the ancient period, thereby agreeing with the historiographical presuppositions of the colonial writers. This created a problem, which still lingers in the commonsensical understanding of history, and this is resurrected in the Hindu communal as well as the Muslim communal histories. The early nationalist historians argued against the colonial assertions that India never had a democratic experience and it never had any sense of popular participation, science, technology and in sum, it was always a backward authoritarian society steeped in spiritualism. This was countered by evidence to show that ancient India had democratic institutions, science and technology. It was the golden age of Indian history. Then the obvious question was, how did this vanish? The trap was clear and obvious: the Muslim period was characterised as the dark ages. Though the nationalist historians did not want to enter into this period, the teleological understanding of history in this way entrapped them. The idea of a golden age of ancient India remained strong, which became the cornerstone for many a fantastic and fabulous stories.

As mentioned earlier, the Marxist historiography, beginning in the 1960s, was the first major breakthrough which tried to take Indian scholarship as well as historical understanding out of this labyrinth into what one would call a processual history, which tried to argue that history is about people and not kings and soldiers, and that in this history what matters is larger historical processes. In these processes, what mattered most was how people lived their lives, what was the nature of society and what sort of practices were followed in order to legitimise political authority. Here, colonialism was found to be a major exploitative system, while at the same time the exploitative social system of medieval and ancient India was seriously looked into. The notion of a pan-Indian Hindu community was recognised as a construction of the Colonial historiography as much as the notion of an all-India Muslim community.[76] These scholars along with many non-Marxist new generation scholars were in fact making the field of history wide, and opening up many important issues related to caste, community, politics and religion for historical analysis, which went against the grain of the communal groups who looked for legitimation and justification of their present day claims in history. By 1977, however, the communal formations were sharing power with the Janata Party. One could see the basic and perceptible shift in the Indian state's policies, relating to the offices that the Jana Sangh and RSS members held. The foreign ministry with Vajpayee at its helm displayed a rapid change of policy towards Israel. India always had been in sympathy with the Jewish predicament after Hitler's arrival. However, at the same time India did not endorse the Israeli treatment of the Palestinian population. The Hindu communal groups interestingly had admired Hitler. But ironically they also looked towards Israel as a strong state, to be admired and befriended. Here, the Jana Sangh injected a communal perception into India's foreign policy, because the Hindu communalists perceived the Israel-Palestinian conflict in terms of its own anti-Muslim prejudice.[77] The other minister from this group, Lal Krishna Advani, was given the information and broadcasting portfolio, which meant the media was under his control. But the most opportune moment that the Hindu communalists got as part of the state apparatus was in the shape of directly intervening in the education sector: it succeeded in getting certain textbooks removed from the school reading lists. This was part of the larger attack on the institutions of historical scholarship, which included making non-academic appointments in institutions, and awarding projects and fellowships not necessarily of a high standard that were meant to advance the communal historiography.

That Indian schools should have textbooks written by Indians had been an issue since the early 1940s. The Colonial government had kept a strict control over the textbooks and significantly by the 1940s and 1950s, a few British publishers monopolised the publications scenario. Talking about education, the communist leader Dange had argued way back in 1947 in the Maharashtra Legislative Assembly that some British publishers had monopolised the textbook publication.[78] Mahatma Gandhi too gave importance to books written by those who taught students directly. By the 1960s, Indian schools and college system had all sorts of textbooks of varying standards. There were therefore two crucial issues before a perceptive education minister. First, to introduce textbooks written by Indians which would provide a national perspective rather than the current textbooks. Second, to ensure the printing of books within India, which would be available to all sections of society. M.C. Chagla, the Education Minister, was very alert to this and he argued that, 'it was high time that books are written and printed in India.'[79] However, school education was in the hands of the states and not the Centre, and education was a state subject. Hence, a national consensus was gradually evolved, where the model textbooks were written with great care and after detailed discussions, so that the states, even if they did not adopt these, could model their textbooks on these texts. Organisations like Sampradayikata Virodhi committee, under the dynamic leader Subhadra Joshi, played a key role in the campaign for new textbooks which were not communal.

On the basis of a note that emanated from the Prime Minister's office in 1977, the Education Minister, Pratap Chandra Chunder, himself a literateur from Kolkata, took the decision to remove four of these model textbooks, which were written by eminent historians for the schools, namely the textbook on *Medieval India* (Romila Thapar), *Modern India* (Bipan Chandra), *Freedom Struggle* (Bipan Chandra, Amales Tripathy and Barun De) and *Ancient India* (R.S. Sharma). However, as we have seen, several intellectuals had been at the forefront of the political battle for some time now and the communal design behind this move was immeditely understood. Very soon, an all-India movement against the removal began, which found its reflection in the media as well. Beginning in the early 1960s with a critique of Nehruvian policies, the majority of these intellectuals had developed their own sophisticated analysis of colonialism and communalism in the newfound freedom of the collective space in the Universities, rare in any of the other third world countires, which gave them the confidence to do that. The leadership's independent stance against major powers during the nascent stage of the nation's independence had also emboldened them and provided them with the self-assurance and respect required for intellectual engagement. By the 1970s, when the emergency was imposed it was this trust in the democratic vision of the leadership which was badly bruised. Yet, this also provided the intellectuals with the confidence to fight their own battles when the textbooks were removed. This act was seen not only as an attack on their scholarship, but was perceived as the continuation of the communal attack in the garb of what was earlier referred to as Indianisation. Very soon a stiff resistance ensued. Significantly, a fringe segment of intellectuals now came out in the open to attack these historans as well as the intellectual tradition that they had developed. They argued that the revoking of textbooks was not wrong as these intellectuals were patronised by the Congress regime, and it was natural that the new regime would be patronising a new set of intellectuals.[80] Such arguments were made to normalise the communal aspect of the attack.[81] Secondly, this idea falsified the rich intellectual traditon that had evolved quite independently of the state.[82]

While the attack on the past was organised by having the state apparatus at hand, attacks on Muslims also were organised, due to the confidence emanating from the wielding of state power. This time it was in Jamshedpur, the most modern, most developed industrial township in Bihar. The historian's call on the planned nature rather than the spurious argument about the spontaniety of riots is vindicated by the circumstantial evidence, which even the State's Commissions of Enquiry highlighted.[83] The riots began on 11 August 1979, and by the time journalists toured the city that was still simmering on the 25-26 August, the pulsating cosmopolitan city was dead and a communal city had been born.[84] The way the riot was organised, the brutality unleashed and the clear hand of larger organisations makes the Jamshedpur riot an important case-study to understand the communal polarisation across the Chota Nagpur and eastern Indian landscape. The communal clash began on the question of passing of a procession on the occasion of the Hindu festival of Ramnavami, through road number 14, a non-descript small street inhabited by poor Muslims and close to the tribal colonies. It appears that the heat generated by the passing of the procession was more because of the new-found confidence of the RSS and Jana Sangh leaders in the area, working in close tandem with the Central leadership. On 31 March, the divisional meeting of the RSS was organised in the premises of the big cooperative college—a clear violation of the sanctity of educational institutions. On 1 April, Balasaheb Deoras, speaking in the regal ground in the city reportedly said that, he was sad that, 'Hindus in their own country were not allowed to take out religious processions freely, while the number of mosques were increasing day by day. In the Arabian countries on the other hand, Hindus were not allowed to construct temples. The RSS divisional *'shakha'* had created with their drills and formations a military like situation. The anti-Muslim rhetoric of the ordinary *'shakha'* goer and the communal rumours must have vitiated the atmosphere. Now, all of this created an atmophere of confidence among the communalists. The administration seemed to have acted in a fair manner. But the local MLA, who had just returned from Patna, played truant and went back on the original promise of letting the procession pass on the scheduled route. He demanded the release of one Mahant Trivedy, who had been arrested earlier as a precautionary measure. This was not accepted by the administration and soon after the riot broke out. It began around 10.45 am and raged on for the next fortnight. The Bihar military police, which had earlier played quite a commendable role, now did not seem immune from the communal ideology. Except for the first company, composed of Gorkhas stationed in Ranchi, other companies showed their communal colours. In many place, there was indiscriminate shooting of Muslims. For example, in one place, when the Hindu mobs were chased and apparently driven out, 108 rounds were fired in a Muslim *basti*. No Hindu was killed while nine Muslims were found dead.[85]

In many senses, Jamshedpur was the commmunalists' dream city. Here, the historical memories of a riot earlier in 1964, when Muslims were butchered by Hindus excited by real and imagined torture of their brethren in east Pakistan, remained. The riot brought another dimension of the working of the communal groups—the use and spread of lies and rumours. This was reported by the journalists touring the riot-torn city. *Adivasis* were told, and they believed, that *adivasis* had been attacked in Delhi, and so they should take revenge in Jamshedpur. Hindus were told that the administration, which was more or less playing by the rules, had not allowed the procession despite the permission granted by the High Court. The Muslims were supposed to have been armed with bullets made in America, China and Pakistan; in other words the community was seemingly in touch with all the forces, which in public perception were seen as not favourable to India. The rumour was that Pakistani guns had been discovered, thereby substantiating the communal argument that Muslims were the agents of Pakistan.[86]

The communal violence that erupted in organised fury and completely polarised the atmosphere brought out the worst in ordinary people. Sukhdev Prasad complained to the journalists that his nephew Anil Prasad was killed 'when he was runing away from the approaching crowd to save himself, he was overpowered by the Muslims and shot dead and his body was hacked to pieces.'[87]

IX

A Violent Decade for the Democratic State

The year 1979-80 was a crucial phase in Indian politics. The Janata phase came to an end with the clash on the issue of ministers surrendering their RSS membership. However, it may also have been the strategy of the Jana Sangh to save itself from the unpopularity of the Janata regime and carve its own niche separately. It refurbished the organisation as the Bharatiya Janata Party, in its first national convention in Bombay in December 1980.

It is here, in the beginning of the 1980s that the most excruciating phase of the history of communalism began. This phase also marked the return of the Congress to power and a new and gradually changing economy. The most visible aspects of the latter were the changing urban landscape, the rise of small scale enterpreneurs and increasing industrial unrest, and the big industries resorting to violent and 'extra-legal' means against the workers and agricultural poor (particularly the scheduled castes). It was against this background that during the elections of 1980, there was a personal communal attack against Mrs. Gandhi. The most frightening result of the communal campaign of the previous decade was the sense of insecurity generated in the cities with a substantial Muslim population. The prolonged communal campaign had its effect in some of the crucial areas of governance and on the police. One had seen it in Jamshedpur but the worst demonstration of this was the firing of the police on the crowd offering '*namaz*' (prayers) in Moradabad on 13 August 1980.

On 13 August 1980, more than 50,000 Muslims had gathered at the Idgah (the festivity grounds) of Moradabad. It was during the '*khutba*' (reading) that a pig wandered into the Idgah. A dispute arose between the people and the locally posted policemen as to how the pig wandered inside, with the policemen arguing that it was not their job to stop pigs. Altercations took place where the congregation was tapering off.[88] Then suddenly there was firing by the police and their were dead bodies all around. Children, old men and youth—the firing was indiscriminatory. Thus, the Idgah became almost a graveyard. The local MLA Hafiz Mohammed Siddique shouted from the loudspeaker at the police to stop.[89] But the police had gone berserk. It was its own master.

An angry Muslim mob then torched the police station in the locality that night. And now begins the new story of communalism in modern India. The administration and particularly the police tried to pass off the issue as a communal one, and in fact tried to provoke a communal diturbance. This is what characterises the new phase of communal violence, where the administration and political lack of direction now allowed the communal ideology to dictate the administration. Taking place just a year after the communal violence in Jamshedpur, where too the stories of the Bihar military police's completely partial role in attacking Muslims had brought a sense of injustice and anger, Moradabad was in a perverse way a vindication of that anger. While the communalised instruments of governance required a strong anti-communal and secular political class and intelligentsia to counter attack and restore harmony, the politics of the 1980s tell a different story. The Moradabad riots also resulted in the Hindu communal groups launching their new missive of Hindu enrolment, by asking people to proclaim with pride that they were Hindus: '*Garv se kaho ham Hindu hain*'. Moradabad violence would now create a backdrop of the communal mobilisation in which the Central government and the Congress Party would find itself lacking support, with the development of autonomous political segments by the communities feeling insecure.

It was around this time that the Assam movement came up, where the students, literateurs and common people from across the state began to be mobilised on the issue of foreigners. By 1979, people could see that a volcano was about to erupt.[90] By the time the Congress came to power, the Assam issue had become explosive and it revealed many more dimensions of a sensitive and delicate nature. This related to cultural sensitivity about language—Assamese identity and the linguistic issue were important historically.

The RSS entered the race to capitalise on this issue, by focussing on the question of demography, a question it was deeply concerned about. It is significant that the first sponsored book that the RSS got published through the auspices of the ICSSR by the Centre for Policy Studies in Madras in 2000 was on religious demography.[91] The issue of demography goes back to 1909 when Col. U.N. Mukherjee published his book entitled *A Dying Race,* which talked about the possibilities of the extinction of the Hindu race, as indicated by statisticians on the basis of Census figures in 1909. In the aftermath of the communal award of 1930, the issue of comparitive demography of the Hindus and

Mulsims became very important, particularly in Bengal, and the political discourse, both Hindu and Muslim, began to take on deeply communal undertones with demographic elements in the backdrop. The partition demand of the Muslim League too was based on the idea of demographic majority of the Muslims in those areas. The rise of the Jamat-i-Islami in the 1970s saw the return of the demographic argument by the Muslim communalists, and significantly the forced sterilisation during the Emergency was attacked in the later period by the Jamat members in terms of deliberate reduction of the Muslim population, which would reduce it to a smaller minority community.

The Hindu communalists' concern with the issue of demography was stirred to a rousing pitch by the Meenakshipuram conversion. Meenakshipuram district is located in southern Tamil Nadu, and it was reported that an entire community belonging to the untouchable caste had embraced Islam.[92] This created a sensation and it was soon raised as a public issue. The issues raised by the conversion were primarily related to caste atrocities. But in the hands of the the religious groups and communalists, this came to be perceived as a threat to the Hindu community, because of the demographic change that was wrought. The Hindu communal groups tried to build a conspiracy theory showing how the new-found money from Arab lands was being channelled into the region to convert people. This argument of inducement had already been levelled against the Christian missionaries. Incidentally, the Meenakshipuram incident proved to be a catalyst for the Vishwa Hindu Parishad (VHP) to rapidly transform into a major communal force and be seen as the more active agent of propagation of the new and militant Hindu consolidation movement.[93]

Coming back to the Assam question, Indira Gandhi had visited Tejpur in 1962 during the worst of the Indo-China war, when the Indian forces were driven back. The situation was almost one of surrendering to the Chinese forces, and some Assamese intellectuals have recently argued on this basis that the Indian leadership had actually surrendered Assam, i.e., Assam was dispensable. While the 1980s witnessed a critical situation, this time it was not the invading Chinese army but a completley non-violent 'democratic' movement that had to be dealt with. It was at this time that there were indications of RSS activity in the region. The leftist Assamese intellectuals could see the efforts at penetration of the movement and came out strongly against this, particularly after the VHP had its session in Gauhati in 1982. The VHP had been very active after the Meenakshipuram conversion debate, and at this point in Assam it gave the slogan that Hindus were in danger and under seige. There were attempts by the AASU (All-Assam Students' Union) to counter the RSS presence. The apparent success of the RSS in entrenching itself in the movement at this stage could have been because 'Assam has rejected political parties and the RSS offers some kind of an alternative to a society divided bitterly along communal lines.'[94] Indira Gandhi attempted to attack this aspect rather than the AASU, with whom she was ready to negotiate. She visited the province and tried to reassure the minorities. The Hindu communal propaganda seized the opportunity to counter her strategy, by attacking her for saying '*Khuda hafiz*' at a meeting. The RSS and its other associates in this manner vitiated the atmosphere by trying to divide the targetted population into Hindu and Muslim. However, soon the communal potents of the movement culminated in the Nellie and Gohpur massacre. Nellie, where about 3,300 people, mostly Muslim villagers were killed mercilessly and what was worse—there was no sense of remorse and the local Assamese administration as well as poltical class showed their bias, in fact, robbed the movement of its innocence.[95] The Nellie massacre showed the depravity of the communal penetration that had touched the people in the provinces. The AASU tried to dissociate itself from this, but it was too late. The movement lost its sheen among many who had seen in the democratic nature of the movement a new hope. One could see the spiralling effect of the movement in neighbouring Tripura, where the Upajaiti mercilessly killed the Manadai in 1980.[96]

While the Assam movement was giving the RSS a much needed all-India platform, the stint in the government and a new profile gave all its organisations a new boost, and the push towards forming a new organisation. The party was now on its way to recreate the formation of the Congress Party in the previous century. In December 1980, the Bharatiya Janata Party had its first national convention in Bombay. For all practical purposes, it was a grand conclave of about 56,000 delegates showing the new strength and confidence in the party.[97] The party leader Vajpayee did not talk about Indianisation at this point but of how 'capitalism was on its way out and hence the new party will work to usher Gandhian Socialism. Its fight was with capitalism.' The efforts by those who celebrated the Mahatma's death earlier, to now own Gandhi as well as present themselves as pro-poor were revealed.[98]

The same argument of Arab money was used when riots broke out in Meerut, situated close to Moradabad, in August 1981. The tension in Aligarh University, also close to Meerut, had again reared its head to distort the overall atmosphere. The communal elements in the university and outside appeared to have the upper hand, a result of the continuous polarisation and communalisation of the atmosphere. The voice of Syed Shahabuddin, (an Indian bureaucrat who had now joined politics and began to take a strong Muslim communal position) 'crying crying for

Moradabad' appeared to be booming, whereas Irfan Habib who had been fighting against Hindu and Muslim communalism for years was now physically attacked inside Aligarh University.[99]

All of this contributed to reigniting the communal mobilisation, and now it was the turn of Biharsharif in Central Bihar where over a petty altercation, the riot that began on 3 May soon became a nightmare as the RSS lynchpin in the area was found roaming around freely organising and attacking the villages. The fury of the communal anger soon left 52 dead in which 50 were Muslims and there were 12,733 Muslim refugees. The Prime Minister had to force the Chief Minister (who was enroute to Delhi) back to his state and she herself rushed to the place to be on the spot as it was realised that the edifice of civilised administration was collapsing. By the end of 1981 one heard the Jamat-i-Islami voices even as the RSS was engineering a push, aggravating the insecurity and helplessness of the Muslims.

The increasing fury and helplessness were two side of the same political phenonmenon, and the results were the same. Within a year, now in Meerut, this mobilised communal anger gushed out in November 1982. Meerut riot was dastardly in its expanse and timeframe, as also the direct collusion of the RSS activists. The Meerut riot revolved around claims related to a place of worship. Again, it was noticed that there were slogans about Hindusim in danger, how the Muslims were breeding fast to take over the country, and how people were being converted. The touring Minority Commission members found that the local population, obviously under Hindu communal hegemony, felt that the Commission itself should be scrapped. In overall terms, the demographic logic was used to shut out the democratic life. The campaign also gave the space to other communal groups to operate in their respective zones, and this was at the cost of the expanding social and cultural capital at a time when the economy was changing silently. In Meerut, for example, there were reports that the Congress Hindu MLA behaved like the Hindu communalist and Congress Muslim MLA behaved like a Muslim communalist. The whole episode had nothing to tell the civilised world except that the edifice of secular India had collapsed in the bylanes of Meerut. An articulate journalist wrote these poignant lines while reporting from Meerut:

> My generation has seen the brutal killings of Mulsims at Moradabad, the ugly face of Hindu fanaticism in Jamshedpur, the bloody ravaging hands of Muslim communalism in Sambhal and the ridiculous communal wars between these two sections in Meenakshipuram and Kerala. My generation had till now, known the tense atmosphere of 1947 only through hearsay. But we can feel it now, in the city of Meerut.[100]

What is further significant is that the Moradabad and Meerut riots were the beginning of the two new phenomena, namely administrative collapse and communal enrollment, which would go a long way in defining the communal map of the country. The autonomy of the communal situation also indicated that in every town where communal riots took place or where the insecurities were aggravated, the new phenomemon of local, individual protectors of the communities became visible. Incidentally, these individual protectors were linked to the larger ideological and political organisations like RSS, BJP and Jamat-i-Islami or other new political formations that were coming into shape. The relation was however of a contract; the nature of the contract would change in the years to come when protectors of larger groups would appear with state power in their hands. It is in this sense that the local caste politicians and the Hindu communalists offered themselves as protectors of the communities feeling under seige. The romance of Hindu communalism was that it had succeeded by the early 1980s to convince the biggest majority that it was living under a constant seige. The government of Indira Gandhi, with no organised party in shape and depending on ideological sway as well as political skills, was finding it difficult to counter the communal ideological attack which was trying to consolidate a Hindu monolithic psyche of seige.

It is to confound the situation that the communalisation and the violence in Punjab contributed in a big way. Punjab, since the days of Partition itself, had been witnessing a clash between its own variants of communal interests. The Akali Dal, a unique formation of a political party based completely on religious identity and appeal, could be seen as a model case for an Indian communal party that had been demanding in one way or the other its autonomous space of rule. However, in a democratic order it had to contest with the Congress and other formations, which too commanded the electoral support of the Sikhs and other components of the population, on whom the Akalis were trying to assert their claim. In the 1960s, the Akalis began demanding a Punjabi Suba, a separate province, which had a Punjabi speaking majority, thereby dreaming of extending its own political life. The Central leadership, despite hesitation and prolonged agitation, finally conceded the demand. However, typical of the communal demands, the scope went on increasing until by the 1970s, there were further demands in the name of autonomy but in reality for a monopoly of the Akali Dal dominance in state politics. The Hindu communal parties too played their part by aligning with the Akalis. They were in a piquant situation since they were in no position to attack the Akalis as they would have done to Muslim or Christian communal parties. This was because the Hindu communal organisations viewed Sikhs as part of the larger Hindu community, an idea which the Akali political formation began to attack in the 1980s. Frustrated by their inability to attack the Akalis, the RSS and Jana Sangh began attacking Indira Gandhi for the partition of the province.

In a bid to cut down the Sikh communal party's base, the Congress leadership encouraged the introduction of a more virulent element, Bhindranwale. The intra-party fight in the Punjab and the new combination of forces which very soon became conspicuous by 1981-1982, began creating a deep communal hiatus.

X

Call for a National Consensus

Notwithstanding differences of the Congress Party with the local politics and the sectarian rhetoric of the communist left, the intelligenstia, which had been in the forefront in critiquing the communal interpretation of society and politics in the early 1970s and had withstood the communal attacks in 1977-1979, was still there to counter communalism in its most widespread and violent phase. Significantly, this was the time when historians were developing a complete theory of communalism, which was not merely a binary of Muslim and Hindu commuanlism, but a complete ideology and world view that the long evolution of modern Indian history had seen developing. The Sikh communalism too could be explanied within this frame.[101] Punjab in its earlier years, saw quite a serious intellectual and political critique of the Akalis but by the end of 1983-1984, voices were either silenced or threatened, except for a few like Satyapal Dang.[102]

It is to realign itself ideologically by invoking the intellectuals and the other democratic political sections that Indira Gandhi called for a national consensus in such a communalised social milieu. She was trying her best to prevent a Hindu consolidation by not allowing the communal groups to keep projecting her as anti-Hindu, while at the same time would not allow the minorities to feel insecure in the face of such a massive communal attack. While the bigger left party, the CPI(M) took a position of equidistance between the BJP and Congress, its attack on the systemic failure would hurt the Congress more, and the other parties were now looking for fresher pastures. The normalisation of the BJP as a political force began to be accelarated at this juncture.

It was at this juncture when sensing the crisis that the Congress made efforts to invoke the conscience of the nation. It organised a conclave of intellectuals, including some of the finest scientists, historians, political scientists and journalists to deliberate on the increasingly volatile communalisation, which had been instrumental in disseminating ideas, information and ideology based on spurious, false and what has been spoken of as 'unscientific' data. The conclave brought out a 'document on scientific temper'. This was a major effort in the direction to recoup the intellectual strength of the nationalists, and the forces of reason, modernity and development, which were the core of the national movement and the ideas that had sustained the nation-making process this far. It appealed to the people not to give into the unsceintific ideas and slogans in circulation. The signatories were all established in their fields, and the document was well prepared.[103] Significantly, and also predictably, opposition to the document came from the section which was against the nation state, development and science. However, the criticism of the document was more of an abusive attack on the individual signatories, and confused but polemical: for instance, collapsing science and technology, and then attacking science as technology.[104] This comes close to almost endorsing the later day Hindu communal intellectual position of glorifying indigeneous sciences and rejection of what is called 'alien sciences'. However, a more positive criticism came from the CPI(M) general secretary EMS Namboodiripad who saw the continuance of outmoded social institutions as the impediment to a more scientific and humane social milieu. Most of the signatories would perhaps have tended to agree with the arguments.[105] While nation and nation making was the locii around which communalism has been attacked, the intelligentsia had not left its credo of a social transformation as the basis of the Indian nation-making efforts. Thus, one of the first theorisations of communalism which came out during this time was that commuanlism was a complete ideological system and could be countered only by nationalism as the counter ideology, where the telos was to be a socialist transformation of the society.[106] The magazine *Sunday* brought out a special issue on communalism in 1983, and the left and secular historical trends identified and attacked with new vigor the advancing Hindu communalism.[107]

XI

The Second Communal Assassination

The Assam attack and later events saw the Hindu communal propaganda projecting the Congress and particularly Indira Gandhi as an appeaser of Muslims, and any gesture she made such as rushing to the site of communal unrests or riots was immediately portrayed as a sign of minority appeasement and as anti-Hindu. This is where perhaps we can locate a new element in Indira Gandhi's political strategy to counter the sense of seige and insecurity that was being fostered among minorities and the majority alike. It is also possible that she wanted to disarm the Hindu communalists from attacking her. In this context it may be wrong to describe her visits to Hindu shrines as her turning towards religion. Kuldip Nayar, the eminent journalist, who had been a severe critic since her early days, commented:

> There was a time when she would rush to places of communal riots. During this spell of power, she did not go to even Meerut, 50 kilometers from Delhi, where communal fires burnt for weeks. True she is not communal but she had gone out of the way to visit a temple as if she was trying to redeem some promise.[108]

It would be equally incorrect to argue, in a manner that struck like a cliché, that she had turned towards the Hindu side, or professed a 'soft *Hindutva*', a term made popular by the western academia in later years. The communal challenge to the polity had come from different directions, and it required very delicate handling of the polity as well as the sociopolitical aspirations of the people affected by it, while at the same time it was necessary to develop the mature frame of the nation. The evidence from Punjab indicated that religion definitely was the core of the identities around which a community had been defined, and the life of a community, imagined or real, lived. It so happened that the identity of the nation that had been conceived did not follow the pattern of, say, the Serbians or the French.[109] A close look reveals that the Hindu communal groups, which wanted to supplant the secular nationalism, were actually confused as to how to configure the Indian diversity within the confines of a unified nationalist conception that they carried. There seems to be a confusion in the Congress ranks. They, it seems were very well conscious of the large uncontested spaces which has developed due to the riots, institutional apathy and partisan attitude of the police and local administration, and was helping the entrenchment of communalism. However, a deep cynicism and doubt about the leadership's ability to protect them against the onward march of Hindu communal attacks too was becoming a new belief system. This sense was confounded when one saw the rise of the vocal and articulate voices which talked about Muslim insecurities in the language of Muslim communalism. The rise of individuals like Syed Shahabuddin could be explained by this. The Congress leadership therefore gave a call for a national consensus. It also tried to mobilise the intellectual support agaisnt communalism. However, the situation had changed as the Emergency had taken its toll and many intellectuals were not willing any longer to come to the Congress platform. Thus, instead of directly attacking the communal front, a more sophisticated and slightly broad platform was organised by the party, which tried to garner support against communal ideological onslaught, by invoking scientific temper.

The call for consensus came from other sources as well. The disheartened Janata intellectuals were calling for 'unity of secular, democratic and egalitarian forces' in order to regroup themselves.[110] The many shades of the Janata parties, on their way to position themselves as opposition to the Congress, now began to mobilise the autonomous communal and caste formations in states, which were witnessing the most virulent Hindu communal propagation, and a deteriorating law and order situation. The coming together of caste and communal elements and the projection of Syed Shahabuddin as the Janata Party candidate from Punia was one of the early indications of these trends. The CPI(M) began to articulate its tactical line of equidistance from both the Congress and the communal BJP. The line derived its inner logic from its political understanding of Congress being supported by the big bouregoisie and the big landlords, leading to intensified crisis as the leadership has surrendered itself to the bureaucracy.[111] Strategically too, the party saw the Congress as its major oppostion in the provinces where it had somehow begun to entrench itself after the 1977 elections. The ramification is best seen on the Punjab front, where instead of attacking the increasing communalisation and the Akali militancy the party was trying to organise its cadre against the Congress ministry and a large section of the intellectuals were targetting Indira Gandhi, in a manner akin to the attack by the Hindu communal party, BJP, as well as the Akali Dal.[112] Thus, one could see that by 1983-84, during the Punjab crisis, as it happened in the case of Assam, the intelligenstia and media now began to link Indira Gandhi's responses to the crisis with that of the Hindu commuanl response. On the other side, a Hindu communal polarisation must have been happening inside and outside the province, fed by the regular news of the killing of Hindus in Punjab.[113] The broad intellectual as well as political support for a secular anti-communal and democratic consensus was no longer available, as it had been in 1969-1970. It is this missing of the woods for the forest that can be seen in the attack against Indira Gandhi for the increasing communalisation of the Punjab crisis by sections of journalists, intelligentsia and larger political class. The culmination of the crisis was the administrative decision to attack the heart of the whole extremist movement—the militants in the Golden temple.

The individualisation of the state response culminated in the plot to assassinate Indira Gandhi, because she was constantly being projected as personally responsible for and aggravating the Punjab crisis. The Prime Minister was killed by her Sikh bodyguards. She was apparently warned and was advised to change her guards—an advice she had scoffed off by saying that this is a secular society. Interestingly enough, it was she who inserted the word 'secularism' in the Preamble of the constitution through the Constitution amendment, an act which was seen as an act of sheer artificiality. In hindsight provided by historical moments, one may like to change one's views seeing the urgency of her act in the backdrop of the Hindu communal aggression.

The response to the assasination was a large scale attack on the Sikhs across the country led more often than not by the local Congress Party leaders. It further underlined the fact that communal ideology when it becomes a hegemonic presence will create a situation where violence against a chosen community will seem to be a normal affair. The increasing commual pressure on the society for the last couple of years had taken its toll. Identification along communal lines was present, violence was normalised in the name of communal political interests, and the worst of all, people were ready to be led to the attack as if it was a normal affair to kill. Killing of Sikhs seemed normal—almost banal, to use Hannah Arendt's now famous term in the context of anti-semitism in Germany.[114] By 1984, it was Hindu communalism which was on the ascendance.

Endnotes

1. I acknowledge with thanks hundreds of teachers from across the country with whom I have been interacting at the Academic Staff College in JNU and with whom I have discussed issues of contemporary India at great length. Interaction with them offers me a rare opportunity to know perspectives from across the country with their myriad differences and nuances.
2. For a discussion on the historiography of communalism in modern India see, Chandra, Bipan (1984). *Communalism in Modern India*. Delhi: Vikas; Panikkar, K.N. (ed.) (1991). *Communalism in India: History, Politics, and Culture*. Dehi: Manohar; Habib, Irfan, *History an Interpretation—Communalism and Problems of Historiography in India*, (*www.sacw.net/India.../IhabibcommunalHistory. html*); Batabyal, Rakesh (2005). "Communalism in Bengal From Famine to Noakhali 1943-47", *Sage Series in Modern Indian History*. New Delhi: Sage Publishers. pp.1-43.
3. Varshney, Asutosh (2002). *Ethnic Conflict and Civic Life: Hindus and Muslims in India*. New Haven: Yale University Press.
4. Lijphart, Arend (1977). *Democracy in a Plural Society*. New Haven: Yale University Press.
5. Lijphart, Arend (1996). "The Puzzle of Indian Democracy", *American Political Science Review* 90(2): 258-268. June.

6. Ibid.
7. Wilkinson, Steven I (2003). *Votes and Violence*. Princeton University Press.
8. See arguments of inevitability of violence in plural society are approvingly cited by Wilkinson, It says, ' The Plural Society, constrained by the preferences of its citizens, does not provide fertile soil for democratic values or stability.' Rabuska, Alvin and Kenneth A. Shepsle (1972). *Politics in a Plural Societies: A Theory of Democratic Instability*. Charles E. Merrill, Columbus. p. 92, cited in Ibid: 236, Fn.1. Sri Lankan anthropologist Stanley Tambiah also reaches such a conclusion at the end of his political commentary, quite unlike his regular ethnographic work, that ethnic violence is the destiny of democracy in (1996). *Levelling Crowd: Ethnonationalist Politics and Collective Violence in South Asia*. Berkeley: University of California Press.
9. Brass, Paul (1965). *Factional Politics in an Indian State: Congress Party in Uttar Pradesh*. University of California Press; and (2003). *Production of Hindu Muslim Violence in Contemporary India*. Seattle: University of Washington Press.
10. Brass, Paul (ed.) (2003). *Forms of Collective Violence, Riots, Pogroms and Genocide*. Gurgaon: Three Essays Collective.
11. Hansen,Thomas Blom (1999). *The Saffron Wave, Democracy and Hindu Nationalism in Modern India*. NJ: Princeton University Press; See also (2004). *Hindu Nationalism and Indian Politics*. Delhi: Oxford University Press; Jaffrelot, Christophe (2007). *Hindu Nationalism: A Reader*. NJ: Princeton University Press. After collapsing the categories, historians would then search for Hindu nationalism everywhere and try and prove mainstream nationalism as Hindu nationalism, see Bhagwan, Manu (2008). "The Hindutva Underground: Hindu Nationalism and the Indian National Congress in 40s and 50s", *Economic and Political Weekly*. September 13; see also Bhagwan, Manu (2003). "The Historical Context." in *In Understanding Contemporary India*, Sumit Ganguly and Neil DeVotta (ed.). Boulder: Lynne Rienner. pp. 17-40. (There is no wonder why contemporary India is so little understood)
12. Shakir, Moin (1970). *Khilafat to Partition: A Survey of Major Political Trends Among Indian Muslims During 1919-1947*. Delhi: Kalamkar; Dixit, Prabha (1974). *Communalism- A Struggle for Power*. Delhi: Orient Longman; Chandra, Bipan (1984). *Communalism in Modern India*. Delhi: Vikas; Singh, Randhir (1988). "Theorising Communalism: A Fragment—A Note in the Marxist Mode", *Economic and Political Weekly*, 23 July; Engineer, Asghar Ali (1989). *Communalism and Communal Violence*. Delhi; Pannikar, K.N. (1994)."What Is Communalism Today", *Selected Writings on Communalism*. Delhi; Vanaik, Achin (1996). *Communalism Contested*. London: Verso, Batabyal, Rakesh, *op.cit.*
13. Chandra, Bipan (1979). *Nationalism and Colonialism in Modern India*. Delhi. (1980). "Stages of Colonialism", *Journal of Contemporary Asia*; Chandra, Bipan, Mridula Mukherjee and Aditya Mukherjee (2008). *India Since Independence*. New Delhi: Penguin; Damodaran, Vinita and Maya

Unnithan (2000). *Postcolonial India: History, Politics and Culture*. Manohar; Bhambri, C.P. (2009). *Indian Democracy*. New Delhi: NBT; Frankel, Francine (2006). *India's Political Economy*. Delhi: Oxford University Press.

14. See for example the writings of Mahajan, Sucheta (2008). *Education for Social Change*, MVF and Child labour, National Book Trust; and Chandra, Bipan and Sucheta Mahajan (eds.) (2007). *Composite Culture in a Multicultural Society*. Delhi: Pearson publishers and National Book Trust; Kudaisya, Gyanesh (2006). *Region, nation, "heartland": Uttar Pradesh in India's body-politic*. Delhi: Sage Publications, Thousand Oaks and, London; Virmani, Arundhati (2008). *A National Flag for India. Rituals, Nationalism, and the Politics of Sentiment*. New Delhi: Permanent Black; Pai, Sudha (2002). *Dalit Assertion and The Unfinished Democratic Revolution: The Bahujan Samaj Party in Uttar Pradesh*. Delhi: Sage publications, Thousand Oaks and, London; Mishra, Salil (2001). *A Narrative of Communal Politics: Uttar Pradesh 1937-39*. Delhi: Thousand Oaks and London; Menon, Visalakshi (2003). *From Movement to Government, From Movement To Government: The Congress in The United Provinces, 1937-42*. Delhi: Sage Publications, Thousand Oaks and London.

15. Though there are not many well-trained historians who will apply all communal political digits into a complete historiographical treatment, the communally coloured history writing has been quite popular as it is simplistic and does not involve much rigour and analysis of historical evidence as also certain basic presuppositions on which the historical understanding is premised upon. The school text books, which the premier educational body for primary and secondary education, the National Council for Educational Research and Training (NCERT), published in 2002, can in fact be seen as the first complete set of historiogrpahical enterprise to be placed at the heart of pedagogic discussion.

16. One of the classic works in this genre is that of Anil Seal. See Seal, Anil (1968). *The Emergence of Indian Nationalism: Competition and Collaboration in the Nineteenth Century*. London: Cambridge University Press. This was followed by a further elaboration of the colonial thesis in Anil Seal's collaboration with Gallaghar and Johnson. See Gallaghar, John, Gordon Johnson and Anil Seal (1973). *Locality, Province and Nation: Essays on Indian Politics 1870 to 1940*. Reprinted from Modern Asian Studies. London: Cambridge University Press. The contemporary follow up of the same thesis is Chatterjee, Joya (1994). *Bengal Divided: Hindu Communalism and Partition, 1932-1947*. USA: Cambridge University Press, Cambridge (the Indian Imprint, Delhi, 1994). On a more expansive scale for normalising colonialism by making the colonised the agents of colonial expansion see Bayly, C.A. (1975). *Local Roots of Indian Politics, Allahabad 1880-1920*. Oxford: Clarendon Press; (1983) *Rulers, Townsmen and Bazars North Indian Society in the Age of British Expansion, 1770-1879*. NY: Cambridge University Press; (1988) *Indian Society and the Making of the British Empire*. NY: Cambridge University Press.

17. See, Guha, Ranajit (1982). *Subaltern Studies: Writings on South Asian History and Society*. Vol. 1. OUP. Acknowledgment and p.1.
18. Thus Gandhi became an assortment of rumours, which is what constituted him as Mahatma according to Amin, Shahid (1995). *Events, Metaphor and Memory: Chauri Chaura 1922-1992*. Princeton University Press. Popular assertions in the late 19th century Eastern UP were depicted as communal riots by the British ethnographers, and then taken over by the nationalist writers as communal riots in Pandey, Gyannedra (1990). *Construction of Communalism in Northern India*. Oxford University Press.
19. Partha Chatterjee (1986). *Nationalist Thought and Colonial World: A Derivative Discourse*. London: Zed Books. For a detailed discussion as to how communalism could have 'arrived', see Pandey, Gyanendra (1990). *Construction of Communalism in Northern India in the 19th Century*. Oxford University Press.
20. Significantly one of the early contributors to this historiography has been Swapan Dasgupta, who later became (and continues to be) the chief intellectual spokesperson of Hindu communalism. See, Dasgupta, Swapan, "Adivasi Politics in Midnapore, c.1860-1924", *Subaltern Studies* 4: 101-135. Oxford University Press.
21. For a recent representative example, see Bhattacharya, Neeladri (2010). "Predicaments of Secular Histories", *Public Culture, An Interdisciplinary Journal of Transnational Culture Studies* 20(1): 58-73. This new advocacy for transcending "'nation' 'nationalism' and 'secularism'", significantly is in alignment with anti-modern, anti-secular and anti-nation treatments so characteristically resonating the academic trends, which philosophically advocate a hedonistic celebration of the new consumer world with no larger commitment except to the body and the self. Communities are invoked—but not equality, justice or larger libratory premises. See for instance, Nandy, Ashis (2010). "Coming Home: Religion, Mass Violence and the Exiled and Secret Selves of a Citizen-Killer", *Public Culture* 22(1): 127-47. Intellectual criticism of secularism also has other contributors like sociologist T.N. Madan. See Madan, T. N (1993). "Whither Indian Secularism?" *Modern Asian Studies* 27: 667-697. July, Interestingly, critique of secularism has been a burgeoning academic enterprise. See Bhargava, Rajiv (1998). *Secularism and its Critics*. Oxford University Press for such an intellectual enterprise. Significantly this enterprise has coincided with the rapid rise of the communal forces which see Indian secularism as its chief target.
22. Typifying this is Desai, Meghnad (2009). *Rediscovery of India*. Delhi: Penguin. For a critical review of the work see, Aiyar, Mani Shankar (2010). "The Supple", Spine, *Outlook*, 1 March. (*http://www.outlookindia.com/article.aspx?264331*, accessed on 29 July, 2010)
23. With the conclusion of the Chinese revolution in 1949, China emerged as the second biggest Communist country in the world, after the Soviet Union, with the erstwhile nationalist forces of Chiang Kai Shek confined

to the island of Formosa. However, China's emergence in the new world coincided with the heightening of the Cold War, where the United States and the western bloc bitterly posed themselves against the communist powers led by the Soviet Union. The People's Republic of China, which was the Communist China, was considered as the satellite of the Soviet Union and was not allowed to occupy a seat at the United Nations, while its permanent membership at the Security Council which remained being occupied by the Taiwanese representative with the active support of the West. United States of America did not give political recognition to the People's Republic of China. It was India, and particularly Jawaharlal Nehru, who advocated granting of China its rightful place in the comity of nations. India fought for China's inclusion in the United Nations. Nehru constantly reminded the world of the independence of China from the Soviet position, and that Chinese communism was not merely an onward march of World Communism that, as the Cold War theoreticians proclaimed, had to be contained. Nehru had discerned nationalism rather than communism in the expansionist drive of China a fact which finally demonstrated itself in the late 1950s. Nehru's policy thus seems to be correct.

24. On its way to consolidate its territorial boundaries, Communist China, just after the revolution, looked towards Tibet, the region which was strategically extremely important and which it considered a region under its sovereign control and had tried many a time in the past to capture. Not only that it began to push claims by defeating the Tibetan army at Chambdo in 1950 and forcing Lhasa to recognise Chinese sovereignty in 1951, the Chinese were in control of the area by 1951. With these changes and the territorial boundaries now coming under close scrutiny, the Indian and the Chinese representatives met at Beijing in 1953-54 and at the conclusion of the series of meetings, the Chinese premier Zhou Enlai and Pandit Nehru in their joint communiqué in June 1954 recognised the five principles of coexistence (Panchsheel or Pancha sila) as the foundation for their future relations. The principles were, *viz.*, mutual respect for each other's territorial integrity and sovereignty; mutual non-aggression; mutual non-interference in each other's internal matters; equality and mutual benefit; peaceful co-existence. Later on, in the Bandung conference of Asian and African nations, this was popularised and Panchaseel became widely recognised and adopted as principles of international and inter-state relations. In fact, on the conclusion of the 1954 meetings China seemed to be in agreement with India, and did not object to many of the Indian positions on the border, which later became the point of objection. Nehru, at the conclusion of this Beijing conference, joyously coined the slogan, 'Hindi-Chini Bhai Bhai' (Indians and Chinese are brothers). However, it was soon after this, that the Indian intelligence came to know that the Chinese were developing infrastructure in the Aksai Chin area. They planned a road from China to Tibet and from there via Karakoram Range to Sinkiang and Mongolia, and back to China. Aksai Chin obstructed this road and soon China began publishing maps

showing the area as belonging to China. Chinese claims now came along with assertions that it had never accepted the McMahon line demarcating the Indo-China border. Couple of meetings between Zhou En lai (1898-1976) and Nehru failed to resolve the situation. To further impel the dynamics of the situation, the Dalai Lama, the temporal and spiritual leader of the Tibetan people, crossed over to India in March 1959 with 20,000 of his followers. The Indian Government provided him with appropriate hospitality. This apparently was construed as humiliation of the Chinese leadership, and they attacked Nehru as a tool in the US led anti-Communist and particularly anti-Chinese bloc trying to sabotaging their position in Tibet, which the CIA, the American secret agency, they claimed was engaged in. This made the situation grave and the visit of Zhou Enlai in 1960 to Delhi proved to be of no help. By August 1959, the Chinese army incursions inside India became frequent. However, it was only from September 1962, when a massive incursion of 600 Chinese soldiers who crossed Thagla Ridge at Leh surrounding the Dhola post occurred, was there an indication of a serious and impending aggression. By 10th October, the war was a fact, and on 20 October 1962, the Chinese army launched full scale major offensive at the Chip Chap valley in Ladakh, which almost wiped out two regiments, i.e., Rajputs and the Gorkhas positioned there. In the North eastern sector also its attack and advance were fast, and by 18 November, Chinese forces penetrated deep inside the North-east and reached Tezpur, a major frontier town in Assam. Indian soldiers fought bravely but were no match for the well prepared, strategically located and well equipped Chinese army.

25. For a detailed understanding of the circumstances of its origin and the course of its evolution, see, Baxter, Craig (1969). *The Jana Sangh: Biography of an Indian Political Party*. Philadelphia: University of Pennsylvania Press; Puri, Geeta (1980). *Bharatiya Jana Sangh: Organisation and Ideology: Delhi A Case Sudy.* Delhi: Sterling; Graham, Bruce (1993). *Hindu Nationalism and Indian Politics: Origins and Development of Bharatiya Jana Sangh.* Cambridge University Press; Goyal, D.R. (1979). *Rashtriya Swayam Sevak Sangh*. Delhi: Radha Krishna.

26. 'There is one fundamental feature of our party's programme which differentiates it from others. This relates to the post-partition problems affecting the peace and welfare of the country at large… The Jana Sangh feels that the partition of India was the biggest tragedy that could fall on the country.' Therefore Akhand Bharat was the political slogan of the groups: 'The Jana Sangh believes that the future welfare of the people of India and Pakistan demands a reunited India, and it will work towards this end, keeping this as its goal and aim. 'Mukherjee, Shyama Prasad (1951). "The Bharatiya Jana Sangh", *Statesman*. Delhi, 21 December. p.4, cited in Graham, Bruce (1993). *Hindu Nationalism and Indian Politics*. Delhi: Foundation Books. p. 31. For a treatment of Hindu Mahasabha and Syama Prasad Mukherjee before 1947-48 see Batabyal, Rakesh, *op.cit.,*

27. See for example Nehru's views on communalism, Gupta, N.L. (ed.) (1965). *Nehru on Communalism*. Delhi: SVC. For the vision of many other leaders

see Batabyal, Rakesh (2007). *Penguin Book of Modern Indian Speeches.* Delhi: Penguin.

28. The best work on the RSS remains that of D.R.Goyal. See Goyal, D.R. (1979). *Rastriya Swayamsevak Sangh.* Delhi: Radha Krishna.
29. Crib, Robert (ed.) (1990). *The Indonesian Killings of 1965-66, Studies from Java and Bali.* Center for Southeast Asian Studies. Victoria: Monash University; Brackman, Arnold C. (1969). *The Communist Collapse in Indonesia.* NY: WW Norton. See for recent engagement with the issue, Alatas, Syed Farid (1997). *Democracy and Authoritarianism in Indonesia and Malaysia: the Rise of the Post-Colonial State.* NY: St. Martin's Press. Rocamora, Jose Eliseo (1977). *Nationalism in Search of Ideology: The Indonesian Nationalist Party, 1946-1965.* Cornell, 1974. microfilm.
30. The name was in fact suggested by those likes of Prof. Tara Chand who had been close to Malaviya who argued that the name of the university according to even Malaviya too should have been Kashi Vishwavidyalaya. Dr. Tara Chand, Banaras Hindu University Amendment Bill, Rajya Sabha, 3 November, 1965, Rajya Sabha Debate, 3 November, p. 168.
31. Qureishi, Zaheer, Masud (1964). "Electoral Strategy of a Minority Group: The Muslim Majlis-e-Mushawarat," *Asian Survey,* p. 976.
32. *The Statesman,* Delhi, 5th February 1961, p.1; 9th February p.1; 10th February, p.1. cited in Graham, Bruce, *op.cit.,* p.125, Fn. 73.
33. Central General Council, Varanasi, 10th October 1961, BJS, iv, pp. 121-22.
34. *Lok Sabha Debates,* 20 June, 1961, Vol.l ix,
35. *Lok Sabha Debates,* Second series, LVI, 11 August, 1961, p. 1722.
36. Ibid: 1722-23, 120-129
37. *Organiser,* 18 October, 1954, pp. 5 and 12. Graham, Bruce, *op.cit.,* 98
38. Feldman, Herbert (1969). "The Communal Problem in the Indo-Pakistan Subcontinent: Some Implications", *Pacific Affairs* 42(2): 148. See also Chakrabarti, Gargi (2005). *Coming Out of Partition, Refugee Women of Bengal.* Shristi Publications for a detailed treatment of some aspects of the 1964 riots in Calcutta.
39. Central Working Committee, Delhi, 15th August 1965, Bharatiya Jana Sangh resolution passed by Bharatiya Pratinidhi Sabha, 17-18 August 1965, and Working Committee on 27-28 September 1965, pp. 9-12. BJS documents iv, 77-79, cited in Graham, Bruce, *op.cit.,* p.88, fn.89. (Graham indicated some discrepancy in the wordings of two documents and says that the statement is attributed to Central General Council of 17 August.
40. There were attacks on the students who wanted to join any political event anywhere. Their political acts were always construed as Muslim communal acts and there was deliberate communal suppression in this. See, attacks on them on 10-11 May 1979, Sengupta, Vivek (1979). "Aligarh: Back to Violence", *Sunday.* p.21. May 20.
41. The best example of the former has been Prof. Irfan Habib, the foremost historian of medieval India. He was attacked grievously in the 1980s by

the Muslim communalists inside the University. See Akbar, M.J. (1981). "Aligarh's Communal Student Leaders", *Sunday*, pp.10-14. 1st February. The intellectual community too rose up against such attacks on him. See, Chandra, Bipan (1981). "AMU and the Communalist: Dangerous game of Appeasement", *Mainstream*, March 7. The Hindu communalists have always found Habib the first target to attack as a communist historian. Prof. Habib on the academic side, however, is an anti colonial scholar par excellence. This shows how close the communal position is to the colonial position historiographically.

42. Upadhyaya, Deendayal, Political Diary, *Organiser*, 22nd February, 1965, pp. 13, 14, as cited in Graham, *op.cit.*, p.135, Fn. 101
43. Kedar Nath Sahni, the Secretary of Delhi state Jana Sangh had applied for permission to hold the rally, Jaisukhlal Hathi, Minister of state for Home affairs' statement, Parliamentary Debates, Rajya Sabha, Vol. LVIII, 10 Nov. 1966, c. 817
44. Vajpayee, 16th November 1966 : 'Why are these people being arrested? Again, why are those opposed to the Jana Sangh defaming us? Is it because the leaders of the Congress are disturbed by the increasing popularity of the Jana Sangh', Parliamentary Debates, Rajya Sabha, Vo. LVIII, 10 Nov. 1966, cc.1449-57.
45. In fact many of the exiled intellectuals from Germany in the 30s had seen how Hitler emerged from the democratic Weimar Republic, and hence were very suspicious of democracy. The best example is of Theodor Adorno. See Bernstein, J.M. (1994). *Frankfurt School, Critical Assessment*. London: Routledge.
46. Best example is the overthrow of many democratic governments by the CIA operatives, using the most authoritarian and undemocratic parties and groups throughout the world. The US Political Scientists had given two preemptive policy frames for such actions in the new independent states. One, the most modernised institutions should be brought to govern the country as they were to be the best guarantor of stability and possible modernity, (Read Military the most modernising institution as influential political scientist like Lucien Pye would advocate, see Pye, Lucien V. (1966). *Aspects of Political Developments*. Boston: Little Brown and Co. and second, a counterpoint which Samuel Huntington proposed, is to slow the growth rate in these countries as a foreign policy objective of the United States. See, Gilman, Nils (2003). *Mandarins of Future: Modernisation Theory in Cold War America*. Baltimore: Johns Hopkins University Press. To propagate such Political Scientific ideas, the group of Political Scientists received liberal funds to start and train workers for 'Developing societies' in the third world countries. Many institutions and intellectuals in the third world were the product of such benevolent grants.
47. 1967 elections were very keenly watched as it was to provide solutions to the enigma of Indian democracy to many political and policy analysts. See such keen analysis, Palmer, Norma, D. (1967). "India's Fourth

Elections", *Asian Survey* VII(5): 275-291, May. There were however interesting counter point by other political scientists who saw the Indian elections as raising the political consciousness and not necessarily to the instability of the system as such, see, Verma, S.P. and C.P. Bhambhri, (eds.) (1967). *Election and Political Consciousness in India*. Meerut: Meenakshi Prakashan. See also some contemporary studies on the elections, Pattabhiraman, M. (ed.) (1969). *General Elections in India, 1967.* Bombay: Allied Publishers. (1968). "Navaneeth, Congress Debacle in Bihar", *EPW* 3(34) 24 August.

48. Secular Democracy (hereafter SD) September 1980, p.21.
49. Ibid: 21.
50. Madon, D.P., *Report of the Commission of Enquiry into the Communal Disturbances at Bhiwandi, Jalagaon and Mahad.* Vol. 1., Part II, pp. 60-61
51. SD, September 1970, p. 23.
52. Ibid: 63-64
53. The Vythayathil commission report and Justice Jaganmohan Reddy commission report on the Ahmedabad riots also give details regarding the way in which the communal riots were organised by the RSS and Jana Sangh.
54. See, the relevant proceedings of the Parliamentary Debates on the issue.
55. Speech in Parliament, SD. June 1970.
56. Ibid.
57. Ibid.
58. Ibid.
59. Ibid.
60. Ibid: 20
61. Ibid.
62. Ibid.
63. Ibid.
64. Ibid.
65. Ibid.
66. Here the debates on education in the sixties and low performance of the school education helped the communal organisations, Hindu, Muslim and others. In 1966-67 the Universities were allowed to switch over the vernacular medium. Without any preparation, without any sound literature available in translation, the universities and colleges were soon filled with locally written and published text books, without any check on the standard and facts. Such curricula soon would be the breeding ground for hundreds of graduates with no proper grounding in many disciplines. This was virtually an open field for the communalists to proliferate in. The situation would deteriorate in the eighties when most of these graduates in many states would start teaching in colleges and universities.

67. Thapar, Romila, Bipan Chandra and Harbans Mukhia (1969). *Communal Interpretation of Indian History*. People's Book House.
68. The interesting argument recently voiced about Jinnah being secular and not wanting partition voiced by a member of the successor to the Jana Sangh—the BJP, Jaswant Singh, was significantly a rehash of the thesis of Jalal, Ayesha (1985). *The Sole Spokesman: Jinnah, the Muslim League and the Demand for Pakistan*. Cambridge: Cambridge University Press. For her, Jinnah never wanted Pakistan, it was basically thrust on him by the Congress. See for a critique of Jaswant Singh's position, Misra, Salil (2009). *Jinnah: India-Partition-Independence*, Biblio, Delhi, September-October, pp. 3-4 For a detailed historiographical treatment of the issue of partition see Mahajan, Sucheta, *op.cit*. The new turn to partition studies, actually stems from an interesting politics that wishes to undermine and suppress the very idea of independence. With a few interviews or oral testimonies of some individuals many of such studies present themselves as counter to events and processes analysed historically with the weight of evidence.
69. The most illustrative account of the whole diplomatic angle from the side of the United states has been the Foreign Relations of the United states; *South Asia*, Volume 1971.
70. Indira Gandhi launched a diplomatic offensive in the early fall of 1971 touring Europe, and was successful in getting both the United Kingdom and France to break with the United States, and block any pro-Pakistan directives in the Unted Nations Security Council. Indira Gandhi's greatest coup was on 9 August when she signed a 20-year treaty of friendship and co-operation with the Soviet Union, greatly shocking the United States, and providing India with insurance that the People's Republic of China would not be involved in the conflict. China, an ally of Pakistan, had been providing moral support, but little military aid, and did not advance troops to its border with India.
71. The Year of Endeavour, Selected Speeches of Indira Gandhi, August 1969-August 1972, Publication Division, pp. 490-491
72. Message to the Armed Forces, Selected Speeches of Indira Gandhi, August 1969-August 1972, Publication Division, pp. 610-611.
73. The idea of forcing the Prime Minister to resign, and the call to the army and police to revolt went against the principles of democracy which were adhered to by the constitutional system established. The limits of protest in a democratic structure remains an issue to be debated when analysing such a movement. Bipan Chandra has raised this question in his book (2000). *In the Name of Democracy, Emergency and the JP Movement*. Delhi: Penguin.
74. I have tried to use the term normalisation and sanitisation in my Batabyal, Rakesh, *op. cit*.
75. The classic work of this genre is James Mill's History of India. A detailed critique of this communal view of history can be found in Romila Thapar, Bipan Chandra and Harbans Mukhia (1969). *Communalism and the Writing*

of Indian History. People's Publishing House. More recently, a further communal assertion of historiography has been substantively critiqued by Mukherjee, Aditya, *et al.* (2003). *History in the New NCERT Text Books: A Report and an Index of Errors; Indian History Congress.*

76. For example, the researches of Kosambi, RS Sharma and many others brought out many sides of ancient India, repudiating the claim of a unified Hindu India. Irfan Habib, Nurul Hasan and others demonstrated how the medieval and Muslim rule was as exploitative for the peasants, be they Muslim or Hindu, as any other systems were. Bipan Chandra recreated the milieu of the early Indian nationalists, who were the first to document and analyse British Imperialism and its debilitating and impoverishing role. In their critique of the colonial system, he showed, the early intelligentsia was founding the basic principles of the later day Indian nationalism.
77. Significantly such a communal interpretation has entered many scholarly works. Interestingly, these works are critical of both India's 'anti colonial sentiments' as well as what it sees as the voice of its 'Muslim minority' echoing the Hindu communal historiographical positions. For such recent works, see Kumaraswamy, P.R. (2010). *India's Israel Policy*. Columbia University Press.
78. Bombay Legislative Assembly Debates, 1947, pp. 1668-1675.
79. Chagla, M.C. (1973). *Roses in December*. Bharatiya Vidya Bhawan.
80. Some individuals and groups took advantage of the communal attack, and launched tirades against the historians concerned. The argument was that the Marxists have themselves used state patronage earlier, and hence have no right or authority to counter the communalists who were now using the state to subvert the earlier regime. See, from the supposed position of the radical left, Banerjee, Sumanta (1978). "Devaluation of Marxism by Leftist Academics", *Economic and Political Weekly* XIII(14), April 8; and from the right, Nandy, Ashis (1978). "Self Esteem, Autonomy and Authenticity", *Seminar* 222, February. These attacks were countered by many, including one of the maligned scholars Chandra, Bipan (1978). "Devaluation: of What and by Whom", *Economic and Political Weekly* XIII (19), May 6.
81. See Nandy, Ashis, Ibid.
82. While some scholars took this opportunity to attack Marxist historiogrpahy, by avoiding the role of communalism they ended up seeing this as merely reflecting a different cultural policy—another sanitised version of history, See Llyod, Rudolph R. and Susanne Hoeber Rudolf (1983). "Rethinking Secularism: Genesis and Implications of the Text Book Controversy, 1977-79", *Pacific Affairs* 56(1): 15-37. Spring.
83. Excerpts from *Jitendra Narain Commission Report*, SD, September 1981, pp. 9-23.
84. Ibid.
85. Ibid.

86. Akbar, M.J. (1979). "Jamshedpur a Brutal War", *Sunday*, 29 April. pp.10-22.
87. People, Saumitra Banerjee and Tirthankar Ghosh, Ibid: 20
88. Visit to Moradabad, a Draft Report by the Minorities Commission, Secular Democracy, March Annual, 1981, pp. 24-28; Akbar, M.J. (1980). "Id: Day of Death", *Sunday*, 24 August 1980. pp.6-11.
89. Ibid: 7.
90. *Sunday*, 25 November 1979.
91. Joshi, A.P., M.D. Srinivas and J.K. Bajaj, (eds.) (2003). *Religious Demography of India*. Centre for Policy Studies.
92. See for a report of the conversion, Sunday, June 7, 1981; a full report by Kuldip Nayar, Sunday 17 November 1982. Also see Shakir, Moin and H. Ghani (1981). "The conversion Phenomenon", *SD*, October, pp.15-21.
93. See Katzu, Manjiri (2003). *Viswa Hindu Parishad and Indian Politics*. Hyderabad: Orient Longman.
94. *Link*, 21 December 1980, p.13.
95. See a new book by Diganta Sharma on Nellie 1983: Asom Andolonor Borborotom Gonohatyar Postmortem Report (Nellie, (1983): *A Postmortem Report into the Most Barbaric Massacre of the Assam Movement), Eklabya Prakashan*, (2007). See also, the T.D.Tiwary Commission Report.
96. "Mandoi Massacre", *Sunday*, June 24, 1980.
97. 'Bharat's new party Convenes, RSS coexists with Gandhian Socialism', Sunday, 4 January, 1981, p.40. Here one of the most significant events in the whole affair was first, the active participation of the RSS organisers who looked after the whole preparation of such a huge gathering, and second, the speech by M.C. Chagla who thought that the BJP was going to be real secular party. A full blooded secularist of the Nehruvian mould, Chagla had little experience of the realpoltik and hence the rusty politics of the 1960s left him disillusioned with the Congress on many accounts. He was angry and sad when Indian government quite unwisely sent its delegation to the Islamic Countries' conference in Rabat in 1969. He was also disillusioned with the emergency. See Chagla, M.C. (1980). *Roses in December*, Bombay.
98. "Capitalism is on its Way Out" (Interview with Vajpayee), *Sunday*, 4 January. 1981. p. 41.
99. Syed, Shahabuddin (1980). "Let me cry for Moradabad", *Sunday*, 28 September. pp.18-20.
100. Sharma, Udayan (1982). "Meerut A Divided City", *Sunday*, 14-20 November. The city of Meerut, which had a historical persona, was a different city after the 1982 riots, and never recovered from this.
101. Chandra, Bipan (1984). *Communalism in Modern India*. New Delhi: Vikas.
102. Dang, Satyapal (2000). *Terrorism in Punjab*. Delhi: Gyan Publishing House.
103. "Document on Scientific Temper", *Mainstream*, July, 1981. The signatories included, Prof. Amit Bhaduri, Dr. P.M. Bhargava, Prof. Bipan Chandra,

Prof. V.K. Damodaran, P.N. Haksar, V.G. Kulkarni, Dr. Dinesh Mohan, Dr. M.N.V. Nair. Prof. H. Narasimhaiah, Bakul Patel, Rajni Patel, P.K. Ravindranath, Mohit Sen, B.V. Subbarayappa, Tara Ali Baig, Shyam Benegal, Satish Dhawan, Prof. Y. Nayudumma, Ashok Partasarathi, Prof. K.N. Raj, Dr. Raja Ramanna, S. Ramshesan, Prof. C.N.R. Rao, Dr. A.K.N. Reddy, Dr. Anand Sarabhai, Prof. B.M. Udgaonkar, Dr. M.G.K. Menon, Dr. Rais Ahmed, Prof. Romila Thapar. See P.N. Haksar Papers, Installments I-II, for some details regarding the Conference.

104. Nandy, Ashis (1981), "Counter-Statement on Humanistic Temper", *Mainstream*, 10 October. pp.16-18.

105. Namboodiripad, E.M.S. (1981). "Part of Struggle Against Outmoded Institutions", *Secular Democracy*, November, pp.28-29. See also Bhargava, P.M. "Why statement on Scientific Temper", Ibid: 29-31; Chattopadhayaya, "Defense of Scientific Method", Ibid: 31-32.

106. Significantly, historian Bipan Chandra was to speak at this time about the danger of communalism swamping any socialist project and therefore the immediacy and urgency of an ideological fight against communalism. See his *Communalism in Modern India*; and also other writings at this time brought together in (1993). *Essays on Contemporary India*. Delhi: Har Anand.

While, politically the Indian state was encountering a violent challenge from communal forces supported by international actors, there were vitriolic intellectual attacks on Indian state and Indian nationalism - many emanating from Imperial centers. These works, if not supported, legitimised the communal arguments. See, (1982). *Subaltern Studies* Oxford University Press, the first volume of a series that appeared in 1982.

On the other hand, many scholars, who work on India, began to hedge the issues, by either confusing the terms of reference or rather obfuscating the concepts such as communalism for various reasons. See, for example, this piece of information by a celebrated historian:

> The Bharatiya Janata Party, BJP, is the reincarnation of the Jana Sangh and the only former constituent of the Janata Party that was not the product of the "Congress culture." The party's close association with the Hindu nationalist Rashtriya Swayamsevak Sangh (RSS) has led to its being denounced as "reactionary" and "communal" by Congress and opposition critics alike. The party's leadership—notably Atal Bihari Vajpayee and L.K. Advani—is neither reactionary nor communal, but in taking the party on a more secular course, it has alienated the RSS cadre who form the core of the party's organisational strength and deepened dissension within the party.

Hardgrave Jr., Robert L. (1984). "India on the Eve of Elections: Congress and the Opposition", *Pacific Affairs* 57(3) : 414 (Autumn).

The conflation and normalisation of concepts such as communal with 'fundamentalism' 'reactionary' etc. would not be of great help. One such concept which began to dominate the intellectual horizon at this stage was 'Islamic Fundamentalism'. Intellectuals who were the product of the Indian political tradition could immediately sense the problems and perils of such conceptual borrowings. Girish Mathur, a senior journalist, prophetically wrote:

> Some editors and commentators have borrowed the concept of Islamic Fundamentalism from Imperial brains trust of the Contemporary world, the US Council on Foreign Relations, which employs it to find scapegoats for the debacle of American Foreign Policy in the west Asia, South West Asia and countries of South Asia. The Indian borrowers use the concept to analyse and seek explanations for certain developments in the thinking and behavior of a section of Muslims in the country. But their analysis ends in a search for the hidden hand and the involvement of foreign money in recent events in which Muslims have played an activist role. If such analysis finds acceptance at official and political decision making levels, the result can be disastrous if public opinion comes to link Muslim behavior in India with external factors.

Mathur, Girish (1980). *Mainstream,* 18 October. pp.13-16.

One can now see how Hindu communalist arguments drew sustenance from this conceptual borrowing and it helped it to strengthen its claims of representing cultural nationalism.

107. "The Rise of Communalism", *Sunday,* 3-9 April, 1983. pp.15-45.
108. Nayar, Kuldip (1983). "Mrs. Indira Gandhi: A Mid term Assessment", *Sunday,* January, 1, p.14. For his views on Indira Gandhi during her initial years as Prime Minister—*India: The Critical Years*. Delhi: Vikas Publications, 1971.
109. Dasgupta, J.N. (1970). *Language Conflict and National Development: Group Politics and National Language Policy in India*. Berkeley: University of California Press; Nayar, Baldev Raj (1966). *Minority Politics in Punjab.* New Jersey: Princeton University Press.
110. Limaye, Madhu (1979). "Unity of Secular, Democratic and Egalitarian forces", *Secular Democracy* II: 4-5. March.
111. Ranadive, B.T. (1980). "Intensified Crisis of the System", *Social Scientist* 9(100): 36-54. Naboodiripad, E.M.S., "India 1980: The Political Developments", Ibid: 11-21. Also see Namoodiripad, E.M.S. (1981). "What Is This call for "Cooperation?" *People's Democracy,* February 1, pp.1-3.
112. See, (1981). "Punjab: Successful Assembly Gherao", *People's Democracy,* 1 February, p.1-2; "The Joint Movement in Punjab", Ibid., 15 February, pp.6-8. For the overall perceptions and role of intelligentsia during the Punjab crisis see, Chandra, Bikas (1993). *Punjab Crisis: Perceptions and Perspectives of Indian Intelligentsia*. Delhi: Har Anand.
113. Saari, Anil (1982). "The Punjab Riots", *Sunday,* 16-22 May, pp. 32-39.
114. Arendt, Hannah (1963). *Eichmann in Jerusalem: A Report on the Banality of Evil*. New York: Viking Press.

References

I. Primary Sources

Manuscripts: Private and Institutional Papers

Nehru Memorial Museum and Library, New Delhi

All India Hindu Mahasabha Papers

All India Congress Committee papers

N.C. Chatterjee papers

S.P. Mookerjee papers

Documents of Socialist Parties(Samyukta and Praja Socialist Parties)

P.C. Joshi Archives of Contemporary History, Jawaharlal Nehru University, New Delhi

Documents of the Communist Party of India

Documents of Bharatiya Jana Sangh, (JNU Library)

Published Sources

Parliamentary Proceedings, Lok Sabha Debates, Rajya Sabha Debates

Journals, Magazines and Newspapers

Nehru Memorial Museum and Library, New Delhi

Dinman (Hindi)

Sunday (English)

Link (English)

Jawaharlal Nehru University Library, New Delhi

Mainstream (English),

Desh (Bangla)

Dharmayug (Hindi)

Ravivar (Hindi)

Organiser (English)

Janata (English)

People's Democracy (English)

Secular Democracy (English)

II. Secondary Sources

Books

Alatas, Syed Farid (1997). *Democracy and Authoritarianism in Indonesia and Malaysia: The Rise of the Post-Colonial State.* NY.: St. Martin's Press.

Amin, Shahid (*1995). Events, Metaphor and Memory: Chauri Chaura 1922-1992.* Princeton University Press.

Anderson, Walter K. and Shridhar D. Damle (1987). *The Brotherhood in Saffron: The Rashtriya Swayamsevak Sangh and Hindu Revivalism*. New Delhi: Vistaar Publications.

Banu, Zenab (1980). *Politics of Communalism*. Bombay: Popular.

Batabyal, Rakesh (2005). *Communalism in Bengal: From Famine to Noakhali: 1943-47*. New York, London, Delhi: Sage.

———. (2007). *Penguin Book of Modern Indian Speeches*. Delhi: Penguin.

Bayly, C.A. (1988). *Indian Society and the Making of the British Empire*. NY: Cambridge University Press.

Bhambhri, C.P. (1980). *Janata Party: A Profile*. Delhi: National.

———. (2003). *Hindutva: A Challenge to Multi-Cultural Democracy*. Delhi: Shipra.

Brass, Paul (2003). *Production of Hindu Muslim Violence in Contemporary India*. Delhi: OUP.

Chagla, M.C. (1980). *Roses in December*. Bombay: Bharatiya Vidya Bhavan.

Chandra, Bipan (1984). *Communalism in Modern India*. Delhi: Vikas.

———. (2003). *In the Name of Democracy JP Movement and the Emergency*. Delhi: Penguin.

Chandra, Bipan, Mridula Mukherjee and Aditya Mukherjee (2008). *India Since Independence*. Delhi: Penguin.

Chandra, Bipan and Sucheta Mahajan (eds.) (2007). *Composite Culture in a Multicultural Society*. Delhi: Pearson Publishers and National Book Trust.

Chandra, Bikas (1993). *Punjab Crisis: Perceptions and Perspectives of Indian Intelligentsia*. Delhi: Har Anand.

Chatterjee, Partha (1986). *Nationalist Thought and Colonial World: A Derivative Discourse*. London: Zed Books.

Dang, Satyapal (2000). *Terrorism in Punjab*. Delhi: Gyan Publishing House.

Dixit, Prabha (1974). *Communalism: A Study in Power*. Delhi: Orient Longman.

Engineer, Asghar Ali (1995). Communalism in India: A Historical and Empirical Study. Delhi: Vikas.

Gallaghar, John, Gordon Johnson and Anil Seal (1973). *Locality Province and Nation: Essays on Indian Politics 1870 to 1940*. London: Cambridge University Press.

Graham, B.D. (1990). *Hindu Nationalism and Indian Politics: The Origins and Development of the Bharatiya Jana Sangh*. Cambridge: Cambridge University Press, (Mass.).

Gupta, Dipankar (1983). *Nativism in a Metropolis: Shiv Sena in Bombay*. Delhi: Manohar Publishers and Distributors.

Dasgupta, J.N. (1970). *Language Conflict and National Development: Group Politics and National Language Policy in India*. Berkeley: University of California Press.

Jaffrelot, Christophe (1996). *The Hindu Nationalist Movement and Indian Politics: 1925 to the 1990s: Strategies of Identity-building, Implantation and Mobilisation*. (with special reference to Central India). Delhi: Viking.

Jalal, Ayesha (1985). *The Sole Spokesman: Jinnah, the Muslim League and the Demand for Pakistan.* Cambridge: Cambridge university Press.

Kaviraj, Sudipta (ed.) (1998). *Politics in India.* Delhi: Oxford University Press.

Kohli, Atul (1990). *India's Growing Crisis of Governability.* Cambridge: Cambridge University Press (Mass.).

Kumar, Pramod (ed.) (1992). *Towards Understanding Communalism in India.* Chandigarh: CRIID.

Kochanek, Stanley A. (1969). *The Congress Party of India: The Dynamics of One-Party Democracy.* New Jersey: Princeton University Press.

Lijphart, Arend (1977). *Democracy in a Plural Society.* New Haven: Yale University Press.

Mahajan, Sucheta (1999). *Independence and Partition: Erosion of Hegemony in Colonial India.* New York, London, Delhi: Sage.

Menon, Visalakshi (2003). *From Movement to Government: The Congress in the United Provinces, 1937-42.* Delhi: Thousand Oaks; London: Sage Publications.

Misra, Salil (2001). *A Narrative of Communal Politics.* New Delhi: Thousand Oaks; London: Sage Publications.

Mukherjee, Mridula and Aditya Mukherjee (ed.) (2002). With Introduction, *Communalisation of Education: The History Textbook Controversy.* Delhi: Historians' Group.

Mukherjee, Aditya, (*et al.*) (2003). History in the New NCERT Text Books: A Report and an Index of Errors. Indian History Congress.

Mukherjee, Aditya, Mridula Mukherjee and Sucheta Mahajan (2008). RSS, School Texts and *The Murder of Mahatma Gandhi: The Hindu Communal Project.* London: Thousand Oaks; New Delhi: Sage Publications.

Nayar, Baldev Raj (1966). *Minority Politics in Punjab.* New Jersey: Princeton University Press.

Nayar, Kuldip (1971). *India: The Critical Years.* Delhi: Vikas Publications.

Pandey, Gyanendra (1990). *Construction of Communalism in Colonial North India.* Delhi: Oxford University Press.

Panikkar, K.N. (ed.) (1991). *Communalism in India : History, Politics, and Culture.* Delhi: Manohar Publishers and Distributors.

Pattabhiraman, M. (ed.) (1969). *General Elections in India,1967.* Bombay: Allied Publishers.

Puri, Geeta (1978). *The Jana Sangh.* Delhi: Sterling Pubishers.

Rocamora, Jose Eliseo (1977). *Nationalism in Search of Ideology: The Indonesian Nationalist Party, 1946-1965.* 1974, Microfilm: Cornell University.

Sardesai, S.G. (1970). *Fascist Menace and Democratic Unity.* Delhi: People's Publishing House.

Seal, Anil (1968). *The Emergence of Indian Nationalism: Competition and Collaboration in the Nineteenth Century.* London: Cambridge University Press.

Shakir, Moin (1983). *Khilafat to Partition: A Survey of Major Political Trends among Indian Muslims during 1919-1947.* Delhi: Ajanta Publications.

———. (1972). *Muslims in Free India.* New Delhi: Kalamkar Prakashan.

———. (1970). *Jamat –E-Islami Hind: Theory and Practice.* New Delhi: Kalamkar Prakashan.

Shakir, Moin, Alam Khundmiri, Hafeez Malik, N.A. Kurundkar and S.A. Ansari, M.N. Massod (eds.) (1970). *Azad, Islam and Nationalism.* New Delhi: Kalamkar Prakashan.

Spencer, Jonathan (2007). *Anthropology, Politics, and the State : Democracy and Violence in South Asia.* Cambridge: Cambridge University Press, (Mass.).

Tambiah, Stanley (1996). *Levelling Crowd: Ethnonationalist Politics and Collective Violence in South Asia.* Berkeley: University of California Press.

Thapar, Romila, Bipan Chandra and Harbans Mukhia (1969). *Communalism and the Writing of Indian History.* Delhi: People's Publishing House.

Vanaik, Achin (1997). *Communalism Contested: Religion, Modernity and Secularisation.* London: Verso.

Varshney, Ashutosh (2002). *Ethnic Conflict and Civic Life : Hindus and Muslims in India.* New Haven: Yale University Press.

Virmani, Arundhati (2008). *A National Flag for India. Rituals, Nationalism, and the Politics of Sentiment.* New Delhi: Permanent Black.

Vorys, Karl von (1976). *Democracy Without Consensus: Communalism and Political Stability in Malaysia.* Singapore: Oxford University Press.

Verma, S.P. and C.P. Bhambhri (eds.) (1967). *Election and Political Consciousness in India.* Meerut: Meenakshi Prakashan.

Wilkinson, Steven I (2003). *Votes and Violence.* Princeton University Press.

Articles

Akbar, M.J. (1979). "Jamshedpur a Brutal War", *Sunday,* Calcutta, 29 April, pp.10-22.

———. (1980). "Id: Day of Death", *Sunday,* Calcutta, 24 August, pp.6-11.

———. (1981). "Aligarh's Communal Student Leaders", *Sunday,* Calcutta, 1 February, pp.10-15.

Bahuguna, H.N. (1970). "What is Indianness", *Secular Democracy.* Delhi. June.

Bhambhri, C.P. (1990). "State and Communalism", *Social Scientist* 19(207-208): 22-26. Delhi.

Batabyal, Rakesh (1999). "The Debate on Conversion", *The Hindu,* 9 February.

———. (1997). "Communalism, the Noakhali Riot and Gandhi", *Studies in Social Sciences and Humanities* IV(2): 135-170. Shimla: IIAS.

———. (2001). "The Essence of a Nation: India", in Samir Banerjee and Sanjeev Ghotge (eds.), *Contribution to the Agenda of a future India.* Shimla: IIAS and Dindigul: Gandhigram Rural University, pp. 34-56

Chandra, Bipan (1981). "AMU and the Communalist: Dangerous Game of Appeasement", *Mainstream,* March 7.

———. (1990). "Communalism and the State: Some Issues in India", *Social Scientist* 19(207-208): 38-47. Delhi.

Feldman, Herbert (1969). "The Communal Problem in the Indo-Pakistan Subcontinent: Some Current implications", *Pacific Affairs* 42(2): 145-163. Vancouver. Summer.

Goyal, D.R. (1980). "The Communal Jamaat-e-Islami Jamaat is the Mussalmans' RSS", *Sunday*, Calcutta, Delhi, 21 September, pp.16-19

Gopal, S. (1978). "Fear of History", *Seminar* 221, Delhi. January.

Habib, Irfan, Iqtidar Alam Khan and K.P. Singh (1976). "Problems of Muslim Minority in India", *Social Scientist* 4(47): 67-73. June. Delhi.

Haksar, P.N. *et al.* (1981). "Statement on Scientific Temper", *Mainstream*, Delhi, 25 July.

Hasan, Zoya (1990). "Changing Orientation of the State and Emergence of Majoritarianism in India", *Social Scientist* 18(207-208): 27-37. Delhi.

Hardgrave Jr., Robert L. (1984). "India on the Eve of Elections: Congress and the Opposition", *Pacific Affairs* 57(3): 414. Vancouver. Autumn.

Kamath, Ashok (1982). "Kerala's Communal Politics", *Sunday*, 7-13 March. pp.28-29.

Kothari, Rajni (1964). "The Congress System in India", *Asian Survey* IV(2): 1161-1173. December.

———. (1974). "The Congress System Revisited: A Decennial Review", *Asian Survey* XIV: 1035-1954. 12 December.

Katju, Manjiri (1998). "The Early VHP, 1964-1983", *Social Scientist* 300-301: 34-50. Delhi.

Limaye, Madhu (1979). "Unity of Secular, Democratic and Egalitarian Forces", *Secular Democracy* II: 4-5. Delhi, March.

Madan, T.N. (1993). "Whither Indian Secularism?", *Modern Asian Studies* 27(3): 667-697. July.

Mathur, Girish (1980). "Islamic Fundamentalism", *Mainstream*, Delhi, October 18, pp.13-16.

Mendelsohn, Oliver (1978). "Collapse of the Indian National Congress", *Pacific Affairs* 51(1): 41-66. Vancouver.

Mukherjee, Aditya (1991). "Colonialism and Communalism", in S. Gopal (ed.), *Anatomy of a Confrontation: The Babri Masjid-Ram Janmabhumi Issue*. Delhi: Viking (1991); Penguin (1992). pp. 164-178.

Namboodiripad, EMS. (1980). "India 1980: Political Developments", *Social Scientist* 9(100): 11-15. Delhi.

Nandy, Ashis (1981). "Counter Statement on Humanistic Temper", *Mainstream*, Delhi, October 10.

———. (1978). "Self Esteem, Autonomy and Authenticity", *Seminar* 222. Delhi. February.

Narain, Iqbal (1970). "Democratic Politics and Political development in India", *Asian Survey* X(2): 88-99. February.

Raj, K.N. (1981). "Irfan Habib and Basic Issues", *Mainstream*, Delhi, XIX, August 29.

Ranadive, B.T. (1980a). "The Intensified Crisis of the System", *Social Scientist* 9(100): 36. Delhi. November.

———. (1980b). "Meeting Threats to National Unity", *Mainstream*, Delhi, Annual Number, p.35.

Rudolph, Llyod and Susane H.Rudoph (1983). "Rethinking Secularism: Genesis and Implications of the Text Book Controversy, 1977-79", *Pacific Affairs* 56(1): 15-37. Spring.

Sharma, Udayan (1982). "Meerut A divided City", *Sunday*, Calcutta, 14-20 November.

———. (1980). "Kashmir's Anti-National Jamaat-e-Islami", *Sunday*, Calcutta, 21 September, pp.10-14.

Shashankan, R. (1975). "Kerala Congress", *India Today*, Delhi, 15 January, p.6.

Singh, L.P. (1971). "Political Development or Political Decay in India?", *Pacific Affairs* 44(1): 65-80. Spring.

Shahabuddin, Syed (1980). "Let Me Cry for Moradabad", *Sunday*, Calcutta, 28 September, p.18-20.

Talib, Rashid (1980). "Can Mrs. Gandhi Provide a National Consensus", *Sunday*, Delhi, July 27.

Chapter XVI

JP Movement and the Emergency

Bipan Chandra

I

Two crises of an unprecedented magnitude rocked India during the years 1974 to 1977. From January 1974 to June 1975 the country went through a turbulent period marked by a series of agitations—*bandhs* and gheraos, strikes and shutdowns, closures of colleges and universities, two massive movements in Gujarat and Bihar. The Movement in Bihar, popularly known as the JP Movement (after its leader Jayaprakash Narayan, popularly known as JP) soon spread, especially in North India, and developed into a movement for the ouster of Prime Minister Indira Gandhi. This was followed by the second 'watershed' in India's recent history: the imposition of the Emergency by Mrs. Gandhi on 26 June 1975. Any analysis of the Emergency, its causes, its historical significances, as well as consequences, has to be in the context of the JP movement.

The effort here is to understand what actually happened during those crucial years and why and with what consequences. The main justification given by JP for his movement was to defend democracy which was threatened by Mrs. Gandhi's authoritarian personality, policies and style of politics. Mrs. Gandhi's primary defence of Emergency and her main criticism of the JP Movement was that its disruptive character endangered India's stability, security, integrity and democracy.

II

The economic and political crisis facing the nation discussed in another chapter turned into a virtual crisis of the political system with the two movements in Gujarat and Bihar against the faction-ridden Congress governments, dominated by those who had little authority or influence over the people. The leadership provided to the movement in Bihar by Jayaprakash Narayan further deepened the political crisis.

Severe drought and the failure of two crops in succession had caused a rise of more than 100 percent in the prices of food grains and cooking oil in Gujarat during 1973. Simultaneously, essential commodities started disappearing from the market. The people, in general, and students, in particular whose hostel bills had increased by nearly 40 percent in the month of December alone, blamed the price rise and the scarcity of essential goods on the collusion between traders, blackmarketeers and the politicians in power. Consequently, an intense and spontaneous political upheaval occurred in Gujarat in January 1974 when popular anger now exploded across cities and towns of the state, taking the form of a violent student movement.

The students gave a call for an Ahmedabad *bandh* on 10 January, it was supported by the opposition parties, a large number of Sarvodaya workers, the powerful college and school teachers' associations, white-collar employees of banks, insurance companies, and the city and state governments, and middle classes in general. Soon the protest and attendant rioting spread to Baroda, Surat and nearly all cities, other towns and cities of the state.

On 11 January the students formed the Navnirman Yuva Samiti, NYS (Youth Organisations for Regeneration). The movement now took a new turn. It now sought the resignation of the government, which had the support of 140 members in a house of 168, and the dissolution of the state assembly. Finally, on 9 February, the Central government was forced to ask the state government to resign and suspend, not dissolve, the state assembly, and President's rule was imposed. The students, however, with the active support of the Congress (O) and Jana Sangh, continued their agitation for another five weeks demanding the dissolution of the state assembly and fresh elections. It was at this stage, on 11 February that Jayaprakash shifted to Ahmedabad. Lauding the students, he said that he was inspired by their movement. He advised the students to give up studies for a year, devote themselves to the eradication of corruption and work for a 'Youth Revolution'.

One of the tactics adopted by the agitators was to persuade or compel members of the assembly and municipal corporations of the big cities to resign. Mrs. Gandhi finally surrendered. She dissolved the assembly and announced that elections would be held six months later. The students now went back to their studies and the NYS soon disintegrated and broke up into warring groups. In this agitation over a hundred persons were killed, over 3,000 injured and over 8,000 arrested.

The Navnirman movement was to become a model for similar agitations in other parts of the country in which popular discontent was to be harnessed by political opponents to demand dismissal of ministries and dissolution of elected legislatures, irrespective of constitutional niceties. On the heels of the Gujarat agitation, and inspired by its success, an agitation on the same lines and with similar objectives was started by students in Bihar in March 1974. For years, conditions were ripe for a mass movement in Bihar. Bihar was economically more backward and politically far worse governed as compared to Gujarat. Even the pretence of combating crime and corruption had been given up by the administration. People were badly affected by galloping prices, shortages of essential commodities and high unemployment and the rampant casteism, corruption and nepotism in administration and politics. The people in general, and the students and youth, in particular, felt that there was no other way to get grievances redressed than demonstrations, strikes, gheraos, *bandhs* and street violence. A conference of more than 300 student leaders from colleges all over the state set up on 18 February the Bihar Chhatra Sangharsh Samiti (BCSS). The objective of the Samiti was to wage a struggle for student demands which included the lowering of prices of food grains and other essential commodities, reduction in tuition fees and prices of textbooks, exercise books and cinema tickets, better food in hostels, students' participation in university management, jobs for the educated unemployed, Bharatiya education, and action against hoarders, profiteers and blackmarketeers.

The Bihar students' movement attracted all-India attention when on 18 March, the BCSS organised a gherao of the Governor and the assembly on its opening day. The gherao, resisted by the police, led to large-scale violence and riots and arson in Patna. Five people died in police firing. The agitation immediately spread to other Bihar towns. Moreover, as in Gujarat, the opposition parties quickly joined forces with the student agitation and, in fact, took it over. They also added the demand for the resignation or dismissal of the state government and the dissolution of the assembly.

A new dimension was added to the Bihar movement by Jayaprakash Narayan agreeing to take over the leadership of the student movement in April. JP was to stress the revolutionary role of students and youth throughout 1974 and 1975 during his political campaign. One of his major points of advice to students, to give up studies for a year to 'save democracy', was, however, aired earlier in the third week of December 1973 while addressing an Akhil Bharatiya Vidyarthi Parishad (ABVP) meeting, and was again repeated on 22

January 1974. Later, in June 1974, he also asked the students to boycott the coming examinations.

Jayaprakash came to believe that, with people's disillusionment with Mrs. Gandhi and the government, a revolutionary situation had arisen in Bihar and was building up in India as a whole, that only a spark was needed to ignite it, and that the student movement in Bihar would provide this. Throughout 1974 and 1975, he repeatedly expressed the sentiment that the country was ripe for a revolution and the movement that he was leading had the potential of becoming one.

On 6 April, the President of the Patna University Students' Union and some other student leaders of the ABVP met JP and requested him to guide and assume the leadership of the student movement. While accepting their pleas, JP made it clear that he would be in full command of the movement: While announcing that he had no interest in changing the government for that would be 'like replacing Tweedledum with Tweedledee'. He advised the students to carry out their struggle in a peaceful manner, to function in a politically non-partisan manner and not to get involved in the game of toppling governments—this last piece of advice would be ignored by the students and even him almost immediately. From now on the students' movement in Bihar, as also its wider all-India extension, came to be generally known as the JP Movement (JPM).

This was followed by a five-week programme of *dharnas*, more silent processions, observation of black days and so on. Also the demands of the protest movements were widened to include the dissolution of the elected Bihar assembly. Later JP gave a call to students and the people to paralyse the government at every level, close the universities and colleges for a year, gherao the state assembly and government offices, and set up parallel governments all over the state. In order to paralyse the government, in July, JP asked the people not to pay land revenue and other taxes. They were in turn to set up Janata Sarkars (People's Governments) from village to the block and district level. Very soon, the primary objective of the entire mass movement narrowed down to changing the Bihar government and the dissolution of Bihar assembly.

For the first time JP also called upon Mrs. Gandhi to resign. On 17 October, he specifically announced that his objective was the removal of Indira Gandhi from office. It is important to note that the Jana Sangh and its student wing, the ABVP, came to occupy a dominant position in the movement.

An important feature of the situation was the firm refusal of Mrs. Gandhi to give way to the JP movement. Having reached an impasse on the question of the dissolution of the Bihar assembly, JP felt that to exert adequate pressure on the Central government it was necessary to widen the base of the movement beyond Bihar's borders to the entire country, by uniting all political parties other than the Congress and the CPI. From June 1974 onwards, he repeatedly toured the country, addressing large and receptive crowds. JP got the backing of nearly all the non-left political parties and groups, consisting of such disparate political formations as the RSS, Jana Sangh, Anand Marg, Congress (O), BLD (which later came to include Swatanta Party), DMK, Akali Dal, SSP and Naxalites. These political formations saw in JP, what they most needed, a popular leader. JP also realised that without the organisational structures and cadres and workers of the opposition parties he could not hope to face Mrs. Gandhi and Congress at the all-India level, in the streets or at the polls.

Though Jayaprakash retained much of his popularity, the Bihar movement gradually lost its spontaneity as well as appeal by the end of 1974. It had also failed to establish itself outside Bihar. By the end of 1974, most of JP's student followers had gone back to their classes. Of course, there was nothing surprising about the movement declining after a few months. This was inevitable, for a popular movement like the JPM, could not be carried on for a long time at a fever pitch. What was surprising was Jayaprakash's belief that he could do so. The response to the JPM in other regions was also disappointing. The JP Movement had also failed to garner enough support of the left. By September-October 1974, the JP Movement had reached a dead-end.

Mrs. Gandhi challenged JP to test her government's legitimacy and his popular support throughout the country, in the coming general elections, due in February-March 1976. Elections and not unconstitutional means were the best means of finding out the will of the people, she said. JP readily accepted the challenge. He agreed to let the fate of the Bihar movement be decided by elections. The movement now took a critical turn and entered a new phase. JP continued to tour the country, one state after another. He also asked the police not to 'obey orders that were illegal or went against their conscience'. Regarding the Army he said: 'If the rulers do venture to use the army to suppress a peaceful revolution, the army should not allow itself to be so used. On such occasions the leaders of the revolution may call upon the army to come over to their side.'[1] However, despite his massive efforts, the JPM did not at any stage make much of a dent in South India and Maharashtra. In fact, it remained as a whole confined to the Hindi-speaking regions of North India.

Still, by the middle of 1975, the situation had got defused and was not beyond repair and the capacity of the political leadership to manage it within the normal political process. Also, both sides had accepted the role of elections in determining the will of the people. But this was not be, for a fortuitous event intervened.

III

An unexpected turn in Indian politics occurred when on 12 June, Justice Jagmohan Sinha of the Allahabad High Court gave a hard blow to the moral and political authority of Mrs. Indira Gandhi. Giving a judgment on the petition filed by Raj Narain, the candidate she had defeated in the election to the Lok Sabha. He convicted Mrs. Gandhi of having indulged in corrupt campaign practices and declared here election to be invalid. The conviction also meant that she could not stand for election to the Parliament and to hold an elective office, such as that of the Prime Minister, for a period of eight years. She was, however, allowed to appeal to the Supreme Court. Most observers at that time noted that Justice Sinha had dismissed the more serious charges against Mrs. Gandhi such as bribery, lavish election expenditure, etc., but convicted her of two mere technical and trivial charges. The two charges were of illegal use, during the election campaign, of the services of Yashpal Kapoor, a gazetted government servant, who resigned from the government service but his resignation had not yet been accepted by the President and the erection of a dias (platform), from which Mrs. Gandhi spoke, by a police official and the supply of electricity to the rallies of her election speeches.

In fact, the latter two were long-standing practices for the sake of the Prime Minister's security. Moreover, UP was at the time of elections in 1971 being ruled by an opposition party. A gazetted government servant's leave or resignation becoming effective as soon as it was sanctioned by the high officials, without waiting for the President's approval or being gazetted was a long-standing practice in the government.

Another set-back to Mrs. Gandhi came when the results of the Gujarat Assembly came on 12 June. The opposition—combination of the Congress (O) and Jana Sangh (BLD led by Morarji Desai and backed by Jayaprakash Narayan)—won 87 seats as against 75 by the Congress in a house of 182.

The Allahabad Judgment and the Gujarat Assembly result revived the opposition moment. Its leaders felt that in the eyes of the people Mrs. Gandhi's legitimacy had been completely eroded and she had lost the moral right to continue as Prime Minister. They were no longer willing to wait for the result of Mrs. Gandhi's appeal to the Supreme

Court, and for the General Elections due in eight months. They decided to make a bid for power. And to lead a country-wide campaign to force her to resign. In the meanwhile, JP had announced on 15 June, that is after 12 June, that he would go to Bihar and concentrate on the movement for total revolution. Mrs. Gandhi decided to appeal to the Supreme Court against Justice Sinha's judgement. She believed that the opposition had no popular mandate to rule.

While the Supreme Court was to hear Mrs. Gandhi's appeal against the Allahabad Judgment on 14 July, Justice V.R. Krishna Iyer, the vacation judge of the Supreme Court, created further confusion by a ruling delivered on 24 June. Krishna Iyer, while holding that Mrs. Gandhi had not been convicted of 'any of the graver electoral vices', gave her only a conditional stay of the High Court order on the ground that the High Court ruling, until upset, holds good, however ultimately weak it may prove. He decided that till the final disposal of her appeal by the full bench of the Supreme Court her electoral disqualification 'stands eclipsed' and she could continue as Prime Minister and participate in Parliament's proceedings but she could not vote or draw salary as an MP. Both the opposition parties and the Congress claimed Iyer's decision as a victory. The Opposition argued that the conditional stay was a snub to Mrs. Gandhi, that the 'stigma of corruption continues' and 'her credibility stands destroyed' and that she could no longer function as a Prime Minister. The Congress, on the other hand, pointed to the court's permission to let her stay and function fully as Prime Minister and said that the judgment as a whole had virtually exonerated her and fully vindicated her stand.

Both sides now decided to throw all their forces into battle. The Opposition's call for Mrs. Gandhi's resignation was renewed even more vociferously after Justice Iyer's ruling. The opposition would not wait for the final judgement of the full bench of the Supreme Court. In a mammoth rally, held in Delhi on 25 June, under the auspices of Jan Morcha, the opposition leaders declared that Mrs. Gandhi having lost the moral right to rule, they would not let her function as Prime Minister, and that to dislodge her from office and to force her to resign they would organise a nation-wide one week-long campaign of mass mobilisation, demonstrations and civil disobedience. Batches of volunteers would go daily to the Prime Minister's residence and hold demonstrations. The campaign would be intensified after one week and end with the gherao or an encirclement of the Prime Minister's house by lakhs of volunteers who would permit no one to enter or leave the house.

In his speech at the Delhi rally, JP who had returned to Delhi, denounced Mrs. Gandhi's continuation in office as illegal and unconstitutional. He said a time might come when he would ask the people to '"derecognize the government", withdraw cooperation from it, refuse to pay it taxes and in general make it impossible for it to function. He once again appealed to the military, police and government servants not to take orders from "a disqualified head of a discredited government" and to refuse to obey the government's orders that they considered wrong or "illegal" or that were "repugnant to their conscience"'.[2] In an interview that very evening with the Italian journalist Oriana Fallaci, Morarji Desai described Mrs. Gandhi as a '"second-rate" leader who "boasts no capacities except for intrigue, maneuvering, craft... lacks culture, learning", and who "is a fascist and that I, thanks to Mrs. Gandhi, have discovered that a woman is unsuited to head a government or rule a country"'.[3]

Indira Gandhi took serious note of the agitational and civil disobedience plan of the Opposition and of the plan to gherao her house as well as of the call to the armed forces, the police and government servants to disobey government orders, regarding it as a call to them to mutiny. She was not willing to let Delhi or a few other large cities decide the political fate of the government, since she felt that her rural political base, especially in the southern and western parts of the country, was as a whole still intact. Mrs. Gandhi was also not willing to concede the demand for her resignation. She believes the opposition was planning to seize power or install a puppet Congressman as the Prime Minister.

Consequently, in a lightening response to the projected campaign that was anticipated neither by her opponents nor by her supporters she declared a state of Internal Emergency under Article 352 of the Constitution on 26 June, arrested a large number of opposition leaders and several Congress dissidents, imposed a strict censorship on the Press, and suspended all other fundamental rights, thus stifling all opposition to the government. She promised to return to normalcy as soon as the conditions warranted it. In the bargain, she put an end to JP's movement for Total Revolution.

How and why did the Emergency come about? What was its legitimacy? What did it mean in practice? And why was it lifted in the end and with what consequences? We will try to answer these questions though definitive answers will come only when Mrs. Gandhi's private papers are thrown open to scholarly scrutiny.

Indira Gandhi justified her action in imposing the Emergency in two consecutive broadcasts on 26 and 27 June, in several speeches, and in innumerable interviews to Indian and foreign press persons during 1975 and 1976. Consistently maintaining that the Indian political system had not failed. She repeatedly asserted after 25 June that the stability, security, unity, the 'fabric' and the very survival of the nation were in danger due to national and international threats. Furthermore, she said that 'Some political parties with fascist leanings had combined with a set of frustrated politicians to destroy the country's self-confidence.'[4]

Mrs. Gandhi's justification of the Emergency was based on the agruments that India's stability, security, integrity and unity—'its very freedom'—as also its democracy were in danger from the disruptive character of the JPM.

Interestingly, Mrs. Gandhi did not accuse JP of being anti-democratic or a votary of violence, either before or after the Emergency. He had, however, she said, because of his lack of mass support and organisation, started to lean towards, align himself with and organisationally depend on organisations and parties which opposed non-violence and favoured both violence and dictatorship. The JPM included parties like the RSS which were communal, anti-minority, had a secret constitution and believed in violence.

Mrs. Gandhi also charged the Opposition with unwillingness to 'abide by constitutional and legal obligations'. The threat, in June, she argued, could not be met without the imposition of the Emergency.

Similarly, referring to JP's speeches, she accused the Opposition of attempting to 'undermine the loyalty of the police and military' and of 'inciting our armed forces to mutiny and our police to rebel.' But, we may note that, in fact, she was quite cautious in this respect. She did not involve the armed forces in the Emergency at any stage.

In fact, at the particular historical conjuncture, both the JPM and Mrs. Gandhi were at fault; there was in the stand of both some elements of truth as well as many half-truths. To a certain extent both masked the real reasons for the positions they adopted and the actions they undertook.

JP's and others' critique of the Bihar government and of the Central government headed by Mrs. Gandhi, the working of the political and administrative system and the political parties, and the decline in public political morality was justified in part. They did not, however, have a ghost of an idea as to what to do to cleanse the system of its evils.

Mrs. Gandhi's crucial weakness as a political leader lay in the absence of any strategic design and long-term perspective around which her economic, political and administration policies were framed. But it would be incorrect to say that Indira Gandhi was undemocratic by nature or tried or even wanted to impose an authoritarian regime. Till June 1975, she functioned within the parliamentary framework.

I will later take a critical look at both positions, those of the JPM and the Emergency—in the case of the JPM of its potential, and in the case of the Emergency of its actuality. But, at the same time, both the JPM and the Emergency had the potential from, even the opposite of, what they were believed to be or desired to be by their proponents.

IV

The JP Movement gathered force on its claim, following JP, of fighting corruption and distortions in the political system, especially in the electoral system, and to make democracy more effective. It had, however, many facets that were contradictory; in many respects, in its composition, actions, and potential consequences or the personality traits, outlook and thought of its leader. The JPM acquired a large part of its political strength and popularity from the moral authority and political appeal of Jayaprakash Narayan, who was widely respected by people and the intelligentsia for his integrity, indomitable spirit and high moral stature. He became a symbol of protest because of people's widespread disillusionment with politicians.

Undoubtedly, JP took up certain very important issues for agitation during 1974-75. Throughout his campaign, JP repeatedly highlighted electoral malpractices and emphasised the urgent need for reforms to ensure a free and fair exercise of the vote. Throughout his agitation, JP emphasised the need to defend our existing democracy. Question was what were to be the limits of the forms of popular protest? How was democracy to be deepened? JP had only confused answers, if any, to such questions. One of the major objectives of the JPM, he said, was to cleanse politics of the accumulated moral grime and bring about 'a moral regeneration of our politics'. What becomes apparent from JP's writings and speeches of the period is that he was unable either to diagnose the ills of the Indian polity or suggest effective remedies for them. It was because of this basic weakness, that it was possible for communalists and other tainted political leaders and parties to appropriate his ideas and movement and popular appeal for their own purposes. In his case, quite often rhetoric took the place of thought in the discussion of the causes and remedies of the social malaise or the conduct of the movement—a fatal flaw in the sole leader of a mass movement. In fact, sometimes it becomes difficult to distinguish between his naivete and political opportunism. This is evident, above all, in the varied positions he adopted towards political parties. Before 1973, JP had argued vigorously for a partyless democracy.

Yet, despite his strong critique of the opposition parties, very soon, by November 1974, he accepted their support, irrespective of their character and composition, invited them to join and fight along with his movement. In the Gujarat elections of June 1975, he completely surrendered before political parties and actively aided the organisation of the Janata Morcha, a coalition of the opposition parties. JP's failure to see through the motives and character of his allied parties also revealed a certain naivete in his understanding of parties and their dynamics. These political parties effectively discarded him after March 1977 once they had achieved their objectives.

The hazy and unrealistic thinking of JP was most evident in his concept of Total Revolution. He was convinced that a revolutionary situation was developing in the country and that the people were ready for a revolution that would determine India's fate for decades to come. What was JP's conception of Total Revolution? Often describing it in the broadest of terms, this was, 'a continuous process of revolutionary changes.' It implied the total transformation of the social and political system. The revolution would do away with 'the continuing injustice of the present structure of property, polity and bureaucracy.'[5]

The most important aspect of the Total Revolution was a change in the political system and political institutions. He did not, however, spell out the new, more desirable political system and political institutions. In general, JP spoke and wrote in favour of ending all forms of exploitation and social and economic inequality, and 'break-up of the power structure in the rural and urban society so that the domination of a few over many may end.'[6]

How was the Total Revolution to be ushered in and who were to be its agents or instruments? JP had no faith in elections or the Parliament. Instead, he talked of the revolution being made by the people and of relying upon people's power. Subsequently, the concept of Total Revolution remained at best a romantic notion or a matter of mere rhetoric. When JP did try to define the objectives of Total Revolution, it was in such general and vague terms as 'a change in the structure of society,' 'a fight against the system.' 'a new way of life', 'a classless and casteless society', 'welfare of the people', 'fulfillment of the people's desires and needs', 'an all-round revolution, political, economic, social, educational, moral and cultural'. As these terms or slogans were not assigned precise meanings, or were defined in broad strokes, they could be interpreted in such diverse ways that the right-wing and communal parties had no difficulty in joining JP's crusade for Total Revolution.

On 6 March 1975, the million-strong opposition marched on the Parliament, led by JP, and presented the famous charter of demands.

Except for the right of recall, there were quite within the existing structure of politics. The right-wing opposition parties could easily accommodate vague and non-specific radical demands and rhetoric. Consequently, though the inchoate concept of Total Revolution remained JPM's goal, its only concrete and effective demands were, till October 1974, the resignation of the Bihar ministry and the dissolution of the state assembly and later the dislodging of Mrs. Gandhi from power. In any case, the opposition parties did not agree with JP or even among themselves on any other political objective except removing the Bihar government and Indira Gandhi from power.

But, in fact, even for JP, well before June 1975, Indira Gandhi's being in power was a part of the chief contradiction of Indian politics. His entire all-India campaign had acquired an anti-Indira Gandhi edge and the immediate, as also the main, goal of the JPM had become 'breaking the Congress monopoly of power' and the replacement of the Congress as the ruling party by some other party both in Bihar and at the Centre. Also quite serious was JP's repeated incitement to the army, police and civil services to rebel. He repeated this advice on several occasions.

An important, perhaps critical, question in any movement, apart from its ideological orientation, is that of its organisation. A fatal flaw of the JPM, especially in its later, all-India phase, was its organisational dependence on RSS-Jana Sangh, which, along with their front or constituent organisations, had a strong well-knit structure, trained cadre and branches all over the country, especially in northern and central India, and were in a position to provide muscle to the movement.

Disciplined and trained on paramilitary lines, the RSS cadres were brought up from their adolescent years on a communal and basically authoritarian ideology. RSS was clearly neo-fascist in its origins. Its organisational structure was centralised, non-democratic and authority based. As is the case with fascist organisations the world over, it had no detailed ideological, programmatic or policy documents. Elements of its ideology and its politics were conveyed to its members only orally in the *shakhas* or branches in which they met daily or periodically. The only written and published guidelines to its thought and politics were the 100-page pamphlet, *We, Our Nationhood Defined,* written by M.S. Golwalkar, its supreme leader, and published in 1939,[7] and *Bunch of Thoughts*, a collection of Golwalkar's speeches after 1945.[8] As examples of the thinking of the founders of the RSS can be cited in the following extracts from these two books. In *We*, after pointing out that the fascist Italy and Nazi Germany were two countries where 'the ancient Race spirit' had 're-risen' and that 'Even so with us: our Race spirit has once again roused itself, thus conferring on Hindus 'the indisputable right of excommunicating from its Nationality all those, (i.e., Muslims) who having been of the Nation, for ends of their own, turned traitors and entertained aspirations contravening or differing from those of the National Race as a whole', Golwalkar went on to add: 'German race pride has now become the topic of the day. To keep up the purity of the Race and its culture, Germany shocked the world by her purging the country of the Semitic Races—the Jews. Race pride at its highest has been manifested in her. Germany has also shown how well-high impossible it is for Race and cultures, having differences going to the root, to be assimilated into one united whole, a good lesson for us in Hindusthan to learn and profit by.'

RSS' communalism was open and unabashed. Taking a cue from Germany's 'purging the country of the Semitic Races—the Jew's, declaring Muslims to be the old enemies of Hindus, Golwalkar condemned the nationalist leaders for spreading the view by which Hindus 'began to class ourselves with our old invaders and foes under the outlandish name—Indian—and tried to win them over to join hands with us in our struggle.' He went on to add: 'We, Hindus, are at war at once with the Moslems on the one hand and British on the other.'

JP did not oppose the RSS-Jana Sangh penetration and domination of the JPM and, instead, gladly accepted their active participation, even though he had been all his life a staunch opponent of communalism and communal organisations as also a sharp critic of RSS-Jana Sangh. During 1974-75 JP not only ignored the anti-secular, communal and anti-democratic character of RSS-Jana Sangh and sought their active support in his movement but also gave them good chits and lent them an aura of respectability. Replying to those who criticised him for relaying upon RSS-Jana Sangh cadres, he said: 'The Jana Sangh and RSS are neither reactionary nor fascist. How can any party which had lent its support to Total Revolution be called reactionary or fascist?' And, then, he went to the extent of saying: 'if the Jana Sangh is fascist, then I too am a fascist.'[9]

With the effective leadership of the JPM passing into the hands of RSS-Jana Sangh and leaders such as Morarji Desai and Charan Singh, the political character of the movement and the political conjuncture also underwent a major shift. After November 1974, its chief goal was not to change the policies of the Central government or to change the Bihar state government but the removal of Mrs. Gandhi from office.

The opposition movement, after being initiated on 29 June, was to be rapidly accelerated and brought to completion on 5 July. The finale of the movement would come on Sunday, 5 July in Delhi, with a huge rally at the Prime Minister's house in defiance of a ban. The Prime Minister was then to be gheraoed, making it impossible for her to function. In other words the opposition plan had all the hallmarks of a non-military *coup d'etat*.

JP's neglect of ideology was not accidental. He was conscious of the need for a programme qualitatively different from Indira Gandhi's, but he could not evolve one because of the mixed bag of parties he was carrying. The essential weakness of the JP Movement was captured at the time by Sham Lal, certainly the most well-read and perceptive of the contemporary journalists. In an editorial in *The Times of India* of 29 May 1975, he wrote 'Total Revolution', far from being a revolution, was merely 'a poly to beat the Congress at its own game.' Total revolution was, he said, 'a phrase so empty of content that it brings at least the sceptics among us face to face with the void at the heart of our real life.' He went on to add: 'What kind of revolution can it be which can dispense with a strategy, a vanguard and even cadres?...What are the new weapons with which he (JP) intends to fight entrenched communal and caste interests? And what are the new sanctions he plans to forge against all the elite classes which have come to acquire a stake in corruption of one kind or another?... The talk of "Total Revolution" doesn't even permit a search for an honest answer.' The opposition's movement would 'only replace what is in fact a comparatively well-knit coalition of interests with a loose federation of interests.' The danger was that the movement would 'only create a political climate propitious not for a revolution but for anarchy.'

Let me add a caveat. JP himself was not the stuff of which dictators are made. The danger of authoritarianism did not come from him. However, there were, as pointed out earlier, others around him who were so inclined, and who increasingly coming to dominate the movement organisationally, and only too willing to capitalise on JP's ideological woolliness, political confusion. So long as it lasted, the JPM did not become authoritarian or fascist. Nor can it be said that it would necessarily have ended up as such. It was, however, capable of creating a space for those of its constituents that were authoritarian or fascist; it carried the possibility of being transformed in that direction.

V

At midnight of 25 June 1975, President Fakhruddin Ali Ahmed, acting on the advice of the Prime Minister, signed a proclamation that would come into effect the next morning, declaring a state of Internal

Emergency on the grounds that, 'a grave emergency exists whereby the security of India is threatened by internal disturbances.' The Cabinet had no inkling of the deed; its members were woken up and gathered at a dawn meeting and asked to meekly endorse the decision retrospectively. As a result of the declaration, the normal political processes were suspended, immense powers were conferred on the central executive, seeking to alter the basic, democratic character of the Indian state for the duration of the Emergency. The basic federal provisions of the Constitution and fundamental rights and civil liberties were curbed. From them on the rule of law was severely curtailed; protest from any quarter was declared illegal and suppressed. Later, in January, the government suspended the right of citizens to appeal to the courts for defence of their fundamental rights.

In the early hours of 26 June, hundreds of prominent leaders and activists of the Opposition were arrested, mostly in northern states, where the JP movement was strong, under the Maintenance of Internal Security Act (MISA). Among those taken into custody were Jayapraksh Narayan, Morarji Desai, Charan Singh, Asoka Mehta, Atal Bihari Vajpayee, and nearly 30 MPs including dissident Congressmen such as Chandra Shekhar and Mohan Dharia. However, several prominent opposition leaders such as Nanji Deshmukh, George Fernandes and Balraj Madhok evaded arrest. Several teachers, newspapermen, trade unionists and student leaders were also jailed. None of the top leaders of the CPM or DMK were arrested. A few days later, extreme communal organisations such as the RSS, Jamat-i-Islami and Ananda Marga and the groups affiliated with them were banned. Several far-left Naxalite groups were also banned. The leading cadres of the banned organisations were arrested.

Arrests continued throughout the period of the Emergency which lasted for 19 months. However, most of those arrested were set free after a few days or months. JP was released on 12 November 1975 on grounds of health. Others including Asoka Mehta, Atal Bihari Vajpayee, Charan Singh and Piloo Mody were set free during 1976. In all nearly 1,10,000 persons were detained under MISA and Defence of India Rules (DIR) all over the country during the period of the Emergency. The Emergency provisions were also used by the government to take strong action against 'anti-social elements' and arrest of a large number of smugglers, foreign currency or *hawala* operators, hoarders, blackmarketeers and known *goondas*. Some of the detained were also ill-treated in the overcrowded jails. Through a series of presidential ordinances, strict censorship, and in many cases pre-censorship, was imposed on newspapers, magazines and other publication in order to control the news and their views. Editors were instructed by the censoring authority as to what they could print. Any news, cartoons, photographs or advertisements which were seen to be even slightly critical of the government were censored. The government also imposed censorship over the reporting of all parliamentary and court proceedings. Some periodicals, for example, the *Janata* of the Socialist Party, the *Mainstream*, and the *People's Democracy* of the CPM, suspended their publication for varying periods.

The government tightened its control over the Press and other publications through several steps. The government forced a merger of the four independent news agencies, Press Trust of India, United Press of India, Samachar Bharati and Hindustan Samachar, into a single news agency, Samachar, which functioned under effective government control. The All India Radio and Doordarshan were now used to disseminate a one-sided version of the news. Even the pro-government *The Patriot*, controlled by Aruna Asaf Ali and friendly to Mrs. Gandhi was at one stage denied government advertisements for its refusal to praise and report the activities of Sanjay Gandhi. Individual journalists too came under pressure. The accreditation of some of them was withdrawn or they were refused permission to go abroad, or were even dismissed at the government's behest. Several foreign correspondents were expelled from the country for not accepting censorship or violating the censorship rules.

The government could, of course, offer one justification for Press censorship: control of the Press was a key feature, the very essence of the Emergency, without which it could have little practical meaning! As pointed out earlier, many student and teacher political activists, mostly belonging to the banned organisations or involved in the JP movement in Bihar and UP, were arrested in the initial days of the Emergency, though most of them were soon released. Intelligence agents also kept tabs on teachers and students in most of the university campuses. The proceedings of the Parliament were to be censored; the speeches of the MPs, who spoke against the Emergency proclamation, were not allowed to be reported in the Press. Later, in 1976, the Parliamentary Proceedings (Protection of Publication) Act was passed, putting a total ban on the publications of parliamentary proceedings.

Angry with these steps and with the arrest of 30 of their fellow members, all the non-CPI opposition members of the Lok Sabha and Rajya Sabha voted against the resolution approving of the Emergency and, then, most of them walked out and announced their decision to boycott the remainder of the Parliament's proceedings.

In January 1976, the Parliament passed a resolution postponing elections to the Lok Sabha scheduled in February-March 1976. Elections to the Lok Sabha were again postponed for a year in November 1976.

To eliminate the existence or emergence of rival centres of power, the state governments were rigidly controlled throughout the period of the Emergency. The Congress Party also came to be even more strictly disciplined and controlled by Mrs. Gandhi, this was especially so after the rise of Sanjay Gandhi, when the Youth Congress led by him became more important than Congress, the parent organisation. Senior leaders like Rajni Patel and Siddhartha Shankar Ray, who had some political base of their own, were sidelined, while upstarts, like Bansi Lal, gained influence relying only on the personal popularity of Mrs. Gandhi. A series of ordinances, laws and constitutional amendments drastically reduced, in fact virtually nullified, the power of the judiciary to check the functioning of the executive. The MISA was also made non-justiciable; that is, the right of a *detenu* to appeal to the courts for protection against undue arrest or the misuse of the act was taken away. Nor could a court enquire into the grounds of detention. The citizen was thus left completely defenseless against the harassment by or malice of officials, high or low.

Very soon the government went on a constitutional amendment spree that could have changed the basic structure of the Indian Constitution. Mrs. Gandhi also amended the Constitution itself to suit the act of the Government. The Supreme Court, in a 5 to 4 majority judgment delivered on 7 November, accepted the changes in the election law of 1951 as constitutionally valid and in the light of the changed law upheld Mrs. Gandhi's election to the Parliament in 1971. This spree ended with the 42nd amendment in November 1976, which became an important landmark of the Emergency. This amendment will be discussed at length later.

Sanjay Gandhi and his cronies like Bansi Lal, Minister of Defence at the time, were keen on postponing elections and prolonging the Emergency by several years. Taking advantage of the current talk of constitutional reform they came up with the proposal for convening a fresh Constituent Assembly to 'radically transform the Constitution'. To avoid fresh elections for the purpose, their proposal involved the conversion of the existing parliament, with its large Congress majority, into a Constituent Assembly. Whatever else this Constituent Assembly might or might not achieve, it was hoped that it would lead to the Emergency being extended for a long time.

In October-November 1976, an effort was made to change the basic civil libertarian structure of the Constitution through the 42nd Amendment to the Constitution. The 59-clause bill for the purpose was placed before the Lok Sabha on 1 September, taken up for discussion on 25 October and was approved both by the Lok Sabha and the Rajya

Sabha and by 13 states. The President gave his consent on 18 December 1976.

While the new description of India in the Preamble to the Constitution as 'a Sovereign Socialist Secular Democratic Republic' and some of the changes suggested by the amendment were unexceptional, this was not the case for most of the amendments. The most important changes were designed to strengthen the executive at the cost of the judiciary, and thus disturb the carefully crafted system of constitutional checks and balance between the three organs of the government. Several amendments put an end to the judicial review of Constitutional Amendments. The 42nd Amendment laid down that there would be no limitation whatever on the power of Parliament to amend the Constitution in any of its aspects, and that on no grounds would any amendment of the Constitution be called in question in the courts. Several clauses of the amendment were designed to whittle down the power of the judiciary to review Parliament's legislation. One of its most regressive and dangerous clauses enabled Parliament to pass legislation banning 'anti-national activities and associations' without giving reasons for doing so. Moreover, anti-national activities were defined in a strange way. These included not only advocacy of secession from the Union and questioning the sovereignty and integrity of India but also 'creating internal disturbances' and threatening and questioning 'the security of the state.'

The amendment was openly opposed by a large number of intellectuals apart from the opposition parties. Despite the protest, the 42nd Amendment was passed by the Parliament in November, but the opposition parties boycotted these sessions of the Parliament.

In conclusion, it can be said that the Emergency centralised and concentrated unlimited state and party power in the hands of the Prime Minister, Mrs. Gandhi, to be exercised in an authoritarian manner through a small coterie of the politicians and bureaucrats around her. Moreover, the institutions of the political system, as evolved since 1950, were, 'partly dismantled and greatly weakened.'

A very important aspect of the imposition of the Emergency was the reaction of the people. While a section of the intelligentsia were markedly hostile to it, the large majority of Indians did not immediately understand what this unprecedented step meant. They responded to it with apathy and passivity, acquiescence and obedience; in some cases they even welcomed and supported it. Only some sporadic, though sometimes heroic, instances of protest by word or deed were registered. Most of the votaries of Total Revolution however went quiet and the JP Movement just 'melted away'. Of course, the passive acceptance of the Emergency and even its slight popularity among some lasted through only its early phase. With the passage of time, the Emergency regime became increasingly unpopular and opposition to it began to take root in large parts of the country.

Why were the people reconciled to the Emergency and the hard steps that went with it so readily? Why did democracy collapse so easily? And why was there no significant resistance to the government for a considerable period of time? There are no simple answers to such questions. A few easy explanations suggest themselves. The JPM was less popular and Mrs. Gandhi not that unpopular outside or even in Bihar than JP and many of his followers believed. Also, the lightning arrests of 26 June had paralysed the leadership of the JPM. Apart from the arrest of JP and some other opposition leaders, the main edge of the Emergency's repressive measures seemed to be almost entirely directed against anti-social elements or against the extreme communal right. All the 26 organisations banned, for example, were communal or left extremists. No action as such was taken against the major secular or left opposition parties. Moreover a large number of people were impressed by the immediate positive outcome of some of the well-publicised measures of the Emergency. Some of these 'gains of Emergency' were appreciated by the poor, who believed that Mrs. Gandhi was working for their welfare; others were appreciated by the middle and upper classes. Most of the 'improvements', however, as we shall see, proved to be short-lived and were overshadowed by the 'excesses' of the Emergency.

Also suddenly, with the imposition of the Emergency, peace and public order were restored. Crime and hooliganism in the cities came down. Strikes, *bandhs*, sit-ins and gheraos and mass demonstrations and rallies ended. Calm was restored on the campuses as students and teachers went back to classrooms, and examinations were held on time. After the turmoil of previous years industrial peace prevailed. Many felt relieved that the country had been saved from the spectre of 'disorder', 'chaos', instability', 'anarchy' and 'destabilisation'. At another level, some felt that Mrs. Gandhi had saved the Indian state from instability and disintegration.

There was also an immediate and general improvement in administration—in government departments and public services. Many corrupt and inefficient government officials were dismissed or forced to take premature retirement. Quick, well-publicised and stern action was taken on a large scale and in a determined fashion against smugglers, hoarders, black marketeers, illegal traders in foreign exchange and tax evaders. The economy registered a major, dramatic improvement, though only partially due to steps taken under the Emergency for streamlining and accelerating the pace of economic development and improving production. Most welcome was the dramatic improvement in the prices. Public distribution system (PDS) also showed improvement. The rate of inflation, which was running as high as 30 percent in September 1974, turned negative, with wholesale prices declining by 11.6 percent by March 1976 and food prices by 20 percent.

Popular expectations having been raised, the Emergency was sought to be legitimised and made further palatable by the announcement of specific steps to speed up the process of social and economic change and to implement the promise to eradicate poverty made in 1971. On 1 July, Mrs. Gandhi announced the omnibus 20-Point Programme, which was designed to appeal to various sections of the people. Its edge was, however, the socioeconomic uplift of the vast mass of the rural poor, the landless and the marginal farmer. The Programme, which in a way was 'the economic rationale' of the Emergency, promised to liquidate rural indebtedness and put a moratorium on the recovery of the existing debt of landless labourers, small farmers and rural artisans and provide for the extension of alternate credit to them; abolish bonded labour; strictly enforce agricultural land-ceiling laws passed earlier and speed up distribution of surplus land to the landless, provide house sites to landless labourers and weaker sections on a scale much larger than hereto; revise minimum wages of agricultural labourers upwards; provide special help to handloom industry; bring down prices; raise the income-tax exemption level from an annual income of Rs. 6,000 to Rs. 8,000; and provide cheap textbooks and stationery to students.

There is no doubt that though the 20-Point Porgramme was not part of a well-thought out scheme of structural reform of the economy, if implemented, especially its agrarian component, it would have brought real relief and benefit to the rural poor and the urban middle classes as also promoted economic growth. In fact, it would have increased the social and economic power of the landless labourers and poor peasants and led to a virtual rural revolution.

Mrs. Gandhi had, as she acknowledged, now got the power and the opportunity to implement her left-of-centre developmental agendas.

Serious efforts were made to implement the 20-Point Programme. At the heart of the programme was its agenda for the upliftment of the rural poor and social change in the villages. Some immediate progress was made even in these respects, though nowhere near as much as the exaggerated claims of the government. On the whole, the rural part of the 20-Point Programme soon ran out of steam as its progress was stymied by the resistance of the rural rich. In fact the achievements in the rural sector remained insignificant and far short of the promises made.

A major reason why the Indian people accepted the Emergency and did not immediately protest against it was its constitutional and legal character. The Emergency was proclaimed under Article 352 of the Constitution and was assented to by the President and legitimised by the Supreme Court. In 1974, 15,000 political *detenus*, mostly Naxalites, were in jail. It may also be remembered that both MISA and the DIR were already in place before 1975. From the beginning, Mrs. Gandhi proclaimed her full commitment to the Constitution and assured the people that she had no intention of changing India's political system.

The people also expected that the Emergency was going to be of short duration. To them, it represented an interim measure. Many expected the Emergency to be lifted before February 1976 and elections to be held on the due dates. Mrs. Gandhi consistently and publicly emphasised this temporary nature of the Emergency throughout its duration. Mrs. Gandhi also repeatedly stressed that the Emergency had been imposed to save democracy from being destroyed by the Opposition and to save the country from 'anarchy and chaos' and protect its 'unity, its integrity, and its very freedom'.

The people took Mrs. Gandhi at her word and were willing to go along with her. For the poor, she not only as Jawaharlal Nehru's daughter, but also their champion with regard to land reforms, removal of poverty and struggle against caste oppression. Likewise, women and minorities also looked up to her. The people were willing to give Mrs. Gandhi time to sort out a messy and difficult situation and to bring order and discipline into a turbulent society and recalcitrant administrative institutions. On the other hand, was the fear of perfunctory arrest, or various kinds of harassment, of the omnipresent CBI spies noting down what one said or did, of widespread telephone tapping.

The other side of the paradox, as to why was not much opposition to the Emergency in its initial months, was its comparatively mild character, as repressive regimes go, despite the fear aroused. There was also no deployment either of the Army or on a significant scale even of the police, or violation of the letter of the Constitution, or disobedience of the courts. Moreover, most of the prominent opposition leaders, including JP, were released during the period of the Emergency itself. To make this point is not to ignore or condone the excesses and some of the crimes committed during the Emergency, including in its earlier phase, but to retain an analytical balance.

A year into the Emergency and the mood of the people began to change. By mid-1976, there was considerable discontent at the level both of the masses and the intellectuals. Many, including the Congress's ally the CPI, had begun pressing to call off the Emergency. Despite the official easing of the Emergency regime—easing of press control, release of most of the political leaders and a large number of the *detenus*, public discussion of the constitutional amendments, permission to opposition leaders to meet, negotiations with JP, even subdued criticism of the government and its policies—people were unwilling to go along with the Emergency any more. Relief provided by the Emergency to the people did not last long and most of 'the gains' turned out to be very short-term.

Economic growth in the first year of the Emergency was not sustained. The corrupt, the blackmarketeers and smugglers resumed their activities as the initial shock wore off. People also began to realise that the tall promises of social change made at the beginning of the Emergency were not being kept. Very little progress was made towards the advancement of the social and economic goals that Mrs. Gandhi had herself set forth in the 20-Point Programme designed primarily to appeal to the rural poor. There were also other discontents. The middle classes and intellectuals were unhappy with the loss of liberty and lack of faster economic development. In fact, reliance for the implementation of the 20-Point Programme and other developmental and welfarist policies was placed exclusively on the same old bureaucracy, manipulative and discredited politicians and the rural elite. Importantly, since the Press was gagged they could not ventilate the people's discontent.

Even the common people, and not merely intellectuals and political workers, began to live in an atmosphere of fear and insecurity. The poor discovered that they too required civil liberties and freedom and, therefore, missed having them. Having emasculated the Congress Party and having no other organisation to rely upon, Mrs. Gandhi and the Central and state governments depended almost entirely on the bureaucracy and the police both for routine administration of the 20-Point and family planning programmes.

With the silencing of all forms of protest, the police and bureaucracy set out to abuse their newly-acquired power in various forms. An inherent defect of an authoritarian regime is its inability to control arbitrary behaviour of its instruments, especially at the lower levels. Gradually the rule of law virtually disappeared and the Emergency rule became in time a bureaucracy-cum-police raj. Mrs. Gandhi and others, who might have been serious about implementing the new ameliorative and developmental measures, were now completely cut off from public sentiment or reliable information as all lines of communication except those of intelligence agencies and sycophants got blocked. Mrs. Gandhi's total domination over the party and the government had one other consequence. It not only eroded the power of her cabinet colleagues, chief ministers, party president and other senior party leaders, but left no institutional or personal breakwaters for sharing the blame for failures in policies or administration. Also because the people knew that what appeared in the Press or on the radio was heavily censored, they no longer had faith in it. Every government source or statement became suspect and people increasingly disbelieved anything given out by the government. Rumours and gossip were circulated freely and became major sources of information.

The denial of civil liberties gradually began to pinch common people as it started to impact their daily lives by way of harassment and corruption by petty officials and police. Also as the political consciousness of the people and their perception of the Emergency began to undergo a change, it began to lose legitimacy and arouse alarm and hostility instead.

That Emergency might become a permanent feature seemed a possibility with the rise to power of Sanjay Gandhi and his coterie, their assumption of extra-constitutional authority, and further concentration, subversion and misuse of power, together with the increasing eclipse of institutions and the accompanying 'excesses'. We may turn next to this last aspect.

VI

A major reason for the growing unpopularity of the Emergency regime was the predictable development of a parallel apparatus of governance at the Centre. This was bound to happen once checks on the executive's exercise of powers diminished; the regime began to act more and more outside the constitutional, administrative framework and the law. This process reached its zenith with the emergence of an extra-constitutional centre of power associated with the rise to political and administrative power of Mrs. Gandhi's younger son, Sanjay Gandhi, who held no office in the government or the party.

Born on 14 December 1946, Sanjay had hardly any political or administrative experience, or academic or any other achievement to his credit, except his sudden emergence in 1970 as the head of Maruti, the company he set up to manufacture the first wholly Indian car—a project which had been grounded from the beginning. As the political crisis facing Mrs. Gandhi deepened after the Allahabad judgement,

Sanjay Gandhi emerged as her close confidant and adviser and became a major influence over her. Sanjay Gandhi assumed importance from the outset of the Emergency. His political and administrative power grew over time, and by April 1976, he had emerged as a parallel authority. Despite not having any official position in the government or the party, he interfered at will in the working of the government and administration, had access to cabinet papers and other government files, and often participated in decision-making in the name of his mother.

Sanjay was courted, consulted and obeyed by cabinet ministers, Congress Party leaders, chief ministers, chief secretaries and other senior and junior civil servants, and business magnates. Large rallies were organised for him. Sycophancy of Congress leaders sometimes crossed all bounds of decency. Very soon, the personality cult built around Mrs. Gandhi began to be rivaled by that of the son. Radio, television, the Films Division and newspapers gave him enormous coverage and publicity, fostering his personality cult. Sanjay wielded this immense extra-constitutional power, both in government and the party, through a coterie that soon came up around him. Mrs. Gandhi had no worthwhile political organisation to implement the Emergency and its programmes—the Congress Party was neither equipped to perform the task nor did she and Sanjay Gandhi trust the average Congressman who remained a mere spectator. Instead, she relied almost entirely on the bureaucracy.

The development of extra-constitutional power at the Centre was also manifested in the growth of the non-official institution of Prime Minister's House (PMH), which comprised a small caucus consisting of Sanjay Gandhi, Bansi Lal and R.K. Dhawan, aided by a small, carefully chosen secretariat. Dhawan's official position was that of additional private secretary to the Prime Minister. He enjoyed the favour and trust of Mrs. Gandhi and worked in close collaboration with Sanjay Gandhi. PMH was Sanjay Gandhi's power base. Domination of politics and administration by a caucus was also possible because most of the avenues of information and redressals were blocked, so far as the higher echelons of the government were concerned.

Within the Congress, Sanjay Gandhi emerged as the leader of its youth wing, the Youth Congress. Even in that body he had no official position, at least not until December 1975 when he was made a member of its Executive Committee. He soon emerged as the *de facto* head of the Youth Congress, which became his main political vehicle. Gradually, the Youth Congress began to be built up as a rival centre of political power *vis-à-vis* Congress. It was in the Youth Congress that lay its orientation towards dictatorship. Sanjay Gandhi was right-wing, anti-communist and authoritarian in his outlook.

In August 1975, Sanjay created quite a public sensation by giving a long interview to Uma Vasudev in which he aired his right-wing views, criticised the government's earlier economic policies and the public sector, praised private enterprise and advocated giving it a freer hand.[10]

One result of Sanjay Gandhi's rise to power and eminence was that the 5-Points he put forward in July 1976 gradually rivalled and then became more important than the official 20-Points. His 5-Points were: abolish the dowry system and refuse dowry at the time of marriage; practice family planning and birth control and limit families to only two children; plant trees; promote literacy—each literate person to teach an illiterate one; and end caste distinction and give up belief in the caste system. Sanjay Gandhi was also determined to clean up and beautify the cities and relieve the intense congestion by clearing slums and demolishing encroachments and unauthorised structures that were impediments on roads, bazaars, parks, monuments, etc.

In themselves the 5-Points were quite sound and socially relevant, though far less radical and egalitarian than the 20-Points. Still, because they dealt with some of India's important problems, these steps, if even partially implemented, would have helped transform Indian society in a significant manner. However, family planning and to a certain extent slum clearance and city beautification were sought to be implemented as crash programmes, in an illegitimate, ham-handed, authoritarian and coercive manner, especially in North India where Sanjay Gandhi and his coterie could operate with impunity. This led to some of the worst excesses of the Emergency and contributed significantly to the unpopularity of the regime. His other four points remained on paper. There is no doubt that the birth rate needed to be brought down. All efforts of the last 20 years to control population having proved inadequate, the government rightly decided to promote family planning more vigorously and to reduce the annual birth rate from about 35 to 25 per thousand by 1984. A new population policy based on more stringent measures was therefore adopted in April 1976. In addition to stronger incentives and disincentives for not having more than three children, the new policy mainly aimed at persuading people to limit their families by undergoing voluntary sterilisation, vasectomy in the case of men and tubectomy in the case of women, with greater emphasis on the former. The minimum age of marriage was also raised to 18 for girls and 21 for boys.

Some negative factors intervened at this stage. First, the quota system or the system of setting high targets for sterilisation was put in place for every state and district. Compulsion was thus built into the target-oriented approach itself. Very soon Sanjay Gandhi took over the programme and made it his own. Under his guidance and direction the voluntary nature of the programme, including relying on incentives and disincentives, education, propaganda and persuasion, was replaced especially after July 1976, by compulsion and coercion, usually by cruel methods. This was especially the case with Punjab, Delhi and Haryana and to some extent with UP and Bihar.

Family planning was now sought to be aggressively promoted, above all through compulsory sterilisation. Government servants, village officials and municipal employees, school teachers, doctors and family planning and other health workers and even government contractors were assigned arbitrarily fixed quotas of the number of persons they had to 'motivate' to undergo sterilisation and 'deliver' to the sterilisation centres. The police was widely used to harass, coerce and intimidate people to make up the prescribed quotas. Quite often in the cities, the police would pick up persons from their homes or waylay the homeless and the vagrants on streets and drag them to sterilisation clinics and camps where vasectomies were performed on them despite their protest. Very often, the victims, both in cities and villages, were picked up, irrespective of their age or marital status.

A significant aspect of the sterilisation programme was that those worst affected were the rural and urban poor and low-level government employees and school teachers. Moreover, as was inevitable in view of press censorship and total ban on any criticism of the family planning programme—and criticism or opposition to forcible sterilisation made a person liable to be arrested under DIR (Defence of India Rules)—stories, true or false, of forcible vasectomy operations, of police brutality and violent resistance by the people or police firing on protesting crowds, started circulating by word of mouth and were believed. The family planning programme during the Emergency was an example of a vital national issue being handled in an insensitive, heartless and inhuman manner. It brought out the concept of family planning itself into disrepute.

Far less significant, but equally controversial, was the Sanjay Gandhi-led programme of slum clearance, demolition of unauthorised structures and removal of congestion in bazaars and around historical monuments and, in general, of the beautification of cities largely confined to Delhi, though it did to some extent extend to a few other cities and towns such as Bombay, Jaipur, Varanasi, Agra and Lucknow, but with far less severity. The elements of Delhi's slum clearance-cum-resettlement programme had been worked out much earlier—in case of some of its parts as early as 1958. It could not, however, be fully or properly implemented. Sanjay Gandhi and DDA authorities saw the

Emergency as providing an opportunity to make Delhi a modern, non-congested city, above all, free of slums. The resettlement colonies were ill-prepared, unhealthy and disease-ridden and lacking in all amenities, including drinking water.

What is surprising, and to an extent inexplicable, is why someone as sensitive, imaginative and politically-shrewd as Mrs. Gandhi failed to perceive the gravity of the situation and did not provide a healing touch, especially when the poor, her major political power base, were being alienated. Ignorance is, in any case, a handmaiden of an authoritarian regime. In this case, ignorance was also enhanced by the Sanjay factor. Finally, when she did come to realise the enormity of the misuse of the family planning programme, she tried during November and December 1976, to stall the campaign. She stopped the enactment of the bill on compulsory national sterilisation for those having two or more children.

Balasaheb Deoras, head of the RSS, who was detained in Yervada jail, Pune, made a major overture to Mrs. Gandhi in a letter on 22 August 1975. Praising the speech that she had made on the Independence Day as appropriate and well-balanced, he asked her to utilise the 'power of the Sangh for the upliftment of our country.' In another letter to Mrs. Gandhi on 10 November 1975, Deoras congratulated her on the successful election appeal before the Supreme Court, asserted that the RSS had no connection with JP Movement, refuted other charges against his organisation, repeated, as in 1948-49, the assurance of its non-involvement in politics, and appealed to her to lift the ban on the RSS and release its workers. He also suggested that she use RSS's strength to implement government's programmes. RSS's Hindi organ, Panchajanya, also welcomed in December 1975 the emergence of Sanjay Gandhi as a youth leader.[11]

VII

In as sudden and dramatic a manner as she had declared the Emergency, Mrs. Gandhi, sprung another surprise and announced on 18 January 1977 that the existing Lok Sabha stood dissolved and fresh general elections would be held in March. The government simultaneously released political prisoners, lifted press censorship and removed other restrictions on political activity such as holding of public meetings. The opposition parties could now function normally and freely undertake electioneering.

Prodded by JP and faced with a situation where their survival was at stake, the opposition leaders left behind their personal and ideological differences and lost no time in forming a single party. The Janata Party was born on 20 January 1977 when the Congress (O), BLD, Jana Sangh, and Socialist Party decided to merge and form a party, the Janta Party and fight the coming elections with a common election symbol and with Morarji Desai as their head.

Another dramatic development took place when, on 2 February 1977, the senior Congress leader, Jagjivan Ram, resigned from the cabinet and the party, condemned the Emergency, and along with H.N. Bahuguna, ex-chief minister of UP, Nandini Satpathy, ex-chief minister of Orissa, and several other Congress leaders announced the formation of a new party named Congress for Democracy (CFD). Another immediate fallout was that a large number of Sanjay Gandhi's nominees were dropped from the list of Congress candidates and replaced by older MPs and Congress leaders.

Very soon an electoral pact was signed between the CFD and the Janata Party to share seats and to fight on a common election symbol. In fact, the entire Opposition closed its ranks when the new combination entered into seat adjustment with the CPM, Akali Dal and DMK, in order to give a straight fight to the Congress and its allies, the CPI and AIDMK. Mrs. Gandhi, too, carried on a whirlwind campaign around the country, claiming credit for having put an end to violence, indiscipline and political disturbances, saving the country from political disaster, improving the economic situation, and setting the country on the path of progress. The Opposition concentrated on authoritarianism, deprivation of democracy and loss of civil liberties, and the excesses of the sterilisation and slum-clearance campaigns.

From the very outset, a Janata wave swept the whole of North India. When elections were held between 16 and 20 March, like the election campaign, they proved to be quite free. When the results came in, it became clear that Congress had suffered a comprehensive defeat. The Janata Party, along with the CFD, swept North India, winning 43.2 percent of the total all-India votes and 298 out of 542 seats. Of its allies, the CPM won 21 seats, Akali Dal 8 and DMK 1. The Congress trailed far behind with 34.5 percent of the votes and 153 seats. Of its allies the CPI got 7 seats and AIDMK 19. Both Indira Gandhi and Sanjay Gandhi were defeated by large margins.

Mrs. Gandhi promptly resigned, asked the President to formally end the Emergency, and issued a dignified statement accepting the verdict of the people 'unreservedly and in a spirit of humility' and offering her 'good wishes' as well as 'constructive cooperation' to the new government.

It is interesting to see what reasons Mrs. Gandhi herself gave for the decision to hold elections. In conversations with Mohit Sen[12] she pointed out that she had declared the Emergency to prevent a coup by a small but well-organised group and the imposition of a dictatorial regime. But she had no ideological objection to being defeated in elections by a democratic party even if she disliked the party, for the resulting regime would still be a democratic one. To Dom Moraes she emphasised that fear of foreign penetration was a major factor in her 18 January decision. The following extract from Dom Moraes's interview with Mrs. Gandhi is illuminating: 'She had this feeling when she decided to suspend the Emergency and declare elections: something awful would happen unless she did. "To you, ma'am?", I inquired. "No", she said. "Not to me. To the country. I had this sense that more and more foreign influences were seeking for excuses to disrupt, perhaps even to destroy, this country."'[13]

VIII

There are several conclusions to be drawn and lessons learnt from the JP Movement. JP made an attempt, however well-intentioned, to change the government through an extra-parliamentary and extra-constitutional movement. Mrs. Gandhi, faced with the Hobson's choice of total surrender or fight to the finish, responded with an authoritarian regime. India however, escaped both outcomes.

The Emergency also did not lead to alteration of the basic structure of the Indian polity. The government continued to function within the constitutional framework. What is also significant is that elections were postponed twice but were not abandoned or rigged and, in the end, they were held in a free and fair manner within a year of their being due.

The Emergency was also not an effort to bolster a failing system threatened by a movement which was opposed to the existing social or political system. The JP Movement also had no such design or content despite the talk of Total Revolution. The Emergency was thus purely political in origin and character and was imposed to meet a specific situation.

Nor was the JPM authoritarian or fascist in character to begin with or became so in practice at any stage. However, the JPM as it was developing, particularly with the formation and programme of the Lok Sangharsh Samiti in June 1975, had the potential of bringing about a *coup d'etat* that could lead to an authoritarian sociopolitical order.

The organisational muscle of the movement was provided by the cadres of the RSS and those of the Jana Sangh and its student wing, the ABVP, and to a certain extent by the activists of the rich-peasants based BLD in UP and the communal Akali Dal in Punjab. Consequently, while JP remained the movement's chief mobiliser and public face, organisationally it came to be increasingly dominated by the RSS-Jana Sangh. JP's inadequacy as its leader constituted a major shortcoming of the movement. Revolutionary rhetoric without ideology, organisation and cadres could have been a recipe for disaster. The threat to democracy did not, however, come from JP himself.

No doubt that Mrs. Gandhi's decision to virtually revoke the Emergency and to hold free and fair elections, her defeat and the opposition's victory that followed, and her acceptance of that defeat and easy surrender of power were a remarkable achievement, 'a veritable triumph', of Indian democracy. The years 1975-1977 have been described as the years of 'the test of democracy'; there is no doubt that the Indian people passed the test with distinction if not a perfect 10. The resilience of democracy in India stood proven.

Thus the democratic system in India not only survived the JP Movement and the Emergency, it emerged stronger. Paradoxically, even the Emergency experience strengthened democracy. It inoculated Indian people not only against another bout of authoritarianism but also against an irresponsible movement like the JPM. Democracy, freedom and parliamentary form of government were further entrenched. Since 1977, there has been little talk of the need to scrap or change the existing political system and replace it by military rule or dictatorship or some sort of non-party democracy in order to have faster economic development or to end corruption, even though corruption has vastly increased since 1974-75.

Thus, the lifting of the Emergency and the announcement and holding of elections were to a certain extent a defining moment in the history of modern India.

IX

Democracy was the key word that both JP and Mrs. Gandhi used to appeal to the people. Each accused the other of endangering it, held the other responsible for the 'rising menace of fascism', and justified their own political actions in the name of safeguarding democracy 'from the assault mounted on it by the other.' Ironically, neither of them took the democratic way out or advocated the adoption of the basic constitutional remedy of appealing afresh to the electorate, and, therefore, of holding fresh elections to the Lok Sabha. These elections were in any case due in February-March 1976 (i.e., eight months later) and could have been preponed to October-November 1975. By adopting this course, JP and Indira Gandhi could have provided in June 1975 a practical, democratic alternative to both a civil disobedience campaign for Mrs. Gandhi's ouster and declaration of the Emergency. After all, this was the course JP had agreed to follow in November 1974, when he had accepted elections as the means to resolve the political conflict.

The imposition of the Emergency by Mrs. Gandhi was also flawed. Mrs. Gandhi, too, had another real democratic option which she could have pursued. Apart from appealing to the Supreme Court against the Allahabad judgement or asking the Opposition to wait and test its support among the people till early 1976 elections she could have declared that the Lok Sabha would be dissolved and fresh elections to it held in October-November, with her fighting elections subject to the Supreme Court or the Parliament, through fresh legislation with retrospective effect, lifting the ban placed on her by the Allahabad High Court.

If JP and the Opposition accepted this offer, the door to a democratic resolution of the political impasse through an appeal to the electorate would have been opened. If they did not, and stuck to their demand for her resignation and to their declared methods to bring it about, she could legitimately declare that in view of the Opposition's rejection of the democratic option she was imposing an Internal Emergency or prime ministerial dictatorship till elections as the only viable and available option of meeting their extra-constitutional challenge. She could at the same time announce that the Emergency would be lifted as soon as the Opposition gave up its demand for her resignation, agreed to adhere to the Supreme Court's judgement, and accepted the test of elections. There was a good possibility that JP and the majority of the Opposition would have had to respond positively to her offer; but if they had not, they would have committed political harakiri, for then the charge against them of being at least undemocratic if not also neo-fascist would have been credible to the people.

Endnotes

1. Jayaprakash Narayan, *Towards Total Revolution,* Vol. IV, p. 146.
2. *Times of India* (Bombay) 26 June 1975.
3. Fallaci, Oriana (1975). "Mrs. Gandhi's Opposition—Morarji Desai", *New Republic,* 2 and 9 August. p. 18.
4. Official summary of the *White Paper,* in Puri, Balraj (1978). "Revolution Counter—Revolution", Appendix 1: 130-1, 136. New Delhi.

5. Narayan, Jayaprakash, "A Long Battle', A Revolutionary's Quest",– *Selected Writings of Jayaprakash Narayan,* (ed.) Bimal Prasad, 1980, p. 369.
6. Narayan, Jayaprakash, *Towards Total Revolution,* Vol. IV, p. 166.
7. Golwalkar, M.S. (1939). *We, or Our Nationhood Defined.* 4th edn. 1947, Nagpur.
8. Golwalkar, M.S. (1966) (1996). *Bunch of Thoughts.* Bangalore.
9. *Times of India,* 6 March 1975.
10. Quoted in Vasudev, Uma (1977). *Two Faces of Indira Gandhi.* New Delhi. The entire interview has been reproduced in her book as an Appendix.
11. The following three paragraphs are based on Limaye, Madhu (1994). *Janata Party Experiment—An Insider's Account of Opposition Politics : 1975-77,* Vol. 1; and (1991). *Socialist—Communist Interaction in India.* Madhok, Balraj (1980). *Stories of Decade (Indian Politics) 1970-80;* Dutt, Brahm (1978). *Five Headed Monster—A Factual Narrative of the Genesis of Janata Party.* Appendix 4.
12. Interview with Mridula Mukherjee, *Archives on Contemporary History,* JNU.
13. Moraes, Dom (1980). *Indira Gandhi.* New Delhi. p. 264.

Chapter XVII

The Punjab Crisis

Mohinder Singh

While the long drawn struggle for Indian freedom triumphed with India attaining its independence on 15 August 1947, the nation had to pay a heavy price for its freedom. The long cherished secular values of the freedom struggle were compromised with Mohammad Ali Jinnah putting a spanner in Mahatma Gandhi's dream of independence for a united and secular India. Through his rhetoric of two-nation theory he succeeded in creating a theocratic state of Pakistan. Thus the man who talked of uniting Muslims in the name of Islam, ultimately divided them into three different regions of the sub-continent—India, Pakistan and later Bangladesh. Partition of India also resulted in partition of two of India's important provinces—Bengal and Punjab. The people of Punjab, especially the Sikhs, had to pay a rather heavy price when they had to suddenly leave their rich canal colonies and also places of historical importance including Nankana Sahib, birth place of Guru Nanak. As a result of partition, an unprecedented migration in human history took place with communal violence taking large number of lives of innocent people on both sides of the border, including rape of women, and looting and burning of properties by frenzied mobs.

As Prime Minister of the independent India, Jawaharlal Nehru had to perform a formidable task—rehabilitation of the refugees, economic development, and national integration. In Nehru's scheme of development Punjab occupied a special place because of its agricultural importance in independent India. To settle the uprooted refugees from western Punjab, Nehru designated two of the most competent men of the Indian Civil Service—Tarlok Singh and M.S. Randhawa.

Immense suffering during the migration also created a sense of solidarity and bondage among the Sikhs, who, for the first time got concentrated in eastern Punjab. By another administrative measure Sikh princely states were integrated in a larger unit called Patiala and East Punjab States Union (PEPSU) with Maharaja Yadavindra Singh of Patiala as its *Rajpramukh*. In these two developments Master Tara Singh[1] and other Akali leaders saw the possibilities of reviving their dream of creating a Sikh state.[2] The situation in Punjab was further complicated by writings and speeches of Kapur Singh,[3] a civil servant turned Akali advisor, who popularised the thesis of 'betrayal of the Sikhs by the Congress'. Kapur Singh was equally critical of the Akali leaders, particularly Master Tara Singh and S. Baldev Singh, for their inability to tactfully handle the issue of a Sikh state during various parleys for transfer of power from the British. Unfortunately, others in the line of Kapur Singh's thinking continue to promote this thesis in their popular accounts without verifying sources of Kapur Singh's information. Non-realisation of Sikh dream and the frustration it caused to the community is best described by Robin Jeffrey:

> The Sikhs were more sinned against than sinning. They had been abandoned by the British, tolerated by the Congress, taunted by the Muslim League, and above all, frustrated by the failure of their own political leadership.[4]

A careful study of the *Selected Works of Jawaharlal Nehru* and his other writings of Jawaharlal Nehru show that Nehru, who was committed to building a strong and secular state, was unwilling to accommodate any demands with communal overtones. He was opposed not only to the demand for Punjabi Suba by Master Tara Singh and his lieutenants but also that of the Maha Punjab put forth by the Hindu communalists. To put it in Nehru's own words, 'The objectionable feature in the demand for linguistic provinces is not that demand but rather the background and the manner it is put forward.'[5] He expressed similar reservations for the division of the then Bombay state into Maharashtra and Gujarat. During a heated debate in the Lok Sabha, on 7 July 1952, Nehru said:

> ...Speaking for myself, I have been overburdened by the thought that in these critical days or years we must give topmost priority to developing a sense of unity in India and that anything that might come in the way of that unity might perhaps be delayed a little, till we have laid that strong foundation. Because of that I have, frankly—and I should be quite frank with this House—not taken any aggressive or positive step for my own part in regard to the formation of these linguistic provinces.[6]

Conversely, Nehru opposed the formation of Karnataka and did not approve of the agitation for creation of a separate state of Telangana. The Maithali movement in Bihar and Urdu movement in Uttar Pradesh met similar fate. While Nehru was not opposed to the creation of linguistic states *per se*, he was keen that the process of consolidation in independent India should take priority over all other demands. Nehru had more pressing problems at hand—getting rid of unemployment and poverty by raising the standard of living, setting up of a Planning Commission for planned development in different fields, preparing five-year plans and resolving problems with neighbouring countries. While addressing the Congress workers in Kurnool, on October 1, 1953, Nehru said:

> The emotional integration of the people is one of the biggest tasks. I do not understand the business of linguistic provinces and, more particularly, the uncontrolled intensity to which these agitations go. The Congress has not fulfilled its purpose or its historic destiny of integrating the country emotionally, with a view of facing the economic and other problems...[7]

In an address to the Congress legislators and workers in Chennai on 2 October 1953, Nehru said:

> I am not prepared to consider linguistic provinces singly... Reorganization of states can be carried out keeping in mind all factors, and keeping in view linguistic, cultural and other matters...[8]

In his writings and speeches, Nehru emphasised that in reorganisation of states the primary concern should be unity and security of the country. It was in this context that Nehru expressed his apprehensions about the creation of a small state in Punjab right on the Indo-Pak border. Irresponsible statements of Master Tara Singh and other Akali leaders added to Nehru's opposition to the Punjabi speaking state. In an interview to the *Dawn* of 12 July 1950, Master Tara Singh talked about the 'inevitability of war between India and Pakistan' and added that, 'this will be an opportunity to re-establish Sikh rule in the land'.[9]

After the partition of Punjab in 1947, the Sikhs, who constituted 13 percent of the population of the undivided Punjab, got concentrated in one place because of their *en masse* migration to East Punjab, especially in the princely state of Patiala. Merger of other Sikh princely states and creation of PEPSU with Maharaja Yadavindra Singh as its *Rajpramukh*, (head of state) created an area where Punjabi in Gurmukhi script was the official language and where Sikhs formed 40 percent of the population and felt cultural affinity. Master Tara Singh rejoiced at this development and felt that this was perhaps the first step towards the creation of the 'Sikh Homeland' of his dreams. He tried to exhibit his strength in the newly created PEPSU by organising a demonstration.

But the Punjab government pre-empted his move by arresting him on 24 February 1953.[10] However, this dream proved a short-lived one. As a result of the factional fights among the Akali groups, the first non-Congress Ministry in PEPSU headed by Gian Singh Rarewala, was dissolved. President's Rule was imposed in PEPSU on March 5, 1953, and fresh elections announced.

On the invitation of Maharaja Yadavindra Singh, Jawaharlal Nehru agreed to visit Gurdwara Fatehgarh Sahib on 27 December 1953, to participate in the *Shahidi Jor Mela*, organised to observe the martyrdom of the two younger sons of Guru Gobind Singh. When Nehru stood up to pay homage to the *sahibzadas*, on the instigation of Master Tara Singh, activists of the Sikh Students' Federation[11] raised slogans—'Master Tara Singh Zindabad' and 'Pandit Nehru Go Back'. They prevented India's first Prime Minister from making any speech in the Gurdwara which, perhaps, was the first public protest that Nehru faced as the Prime Minister of India. In his letter to Maharani Mahinder Kaur of Patiala, Nehru wrote that the scene created at Fatehgarh Sahib was 'most unfortunate'. The Maharani criticised the irresponsible action and described this as a 'slur on the *Panth*'.[12]

When Master Tara Singh was debating ways and means to broaden the scope of his agitation, he got support from rather strange quarters in the far-off Southern parts of India. The death of Potti Sriramulu, the Telugu leader, who had gone on hunger strike for the creation of Andhra Pradesh, on 16 December 1952, compelled the Government of India to set up States' Reorganization Commission (SRC) in December 1953 with Justice Fazal Ali as chairman and Dr. H.N. Kunzru and Sardar K.M. Panikkar as members.[13]

In response to Commission's notice inviting suggestions from interested citizens and political parties, the Shiromani Akali Dal prepared and submitted a Memorandum to the Commission suggesting inclusion of the following areas of PEPSU, Punjab, and Rajasthan in the proposed Punjabi speaking state: [14]

(i) Punjab—The districts of Gurdaspur, Amritsar, Ferozepore, Ludhiana, Jullundhur, Hoshiarpur, Ambala, Karnal (except Panipat tehsil) and the tehsils of Sirsa and Fatehabad, and sub-tehsil of Tohana in Hissar district;

(ii) PEPSU—The districts of Patiala, Barnala, Bhatinda, Kapurthala, Fatehgarh Sahib and Sangrur (except Jind and Nirwana *tehsils*); and

(iii) Rajasthan—Ganganagar district.

To counter the Akali demand for Punjabi Suba, several Hindu organisations offered an alternative proposal by suggesting merger of

Himachal Pradesh in the Punjab and thus creating Maha Punjab. After going through various proposals and meetings with several organisations, the Commission recommended removal of the distinction of A, B & C states and suggested reorganisation of the boundaries by creating or dissolving some states. The Commission suggested division of the country into 14 states, not necessarily based on language. The advocates of the Punjabi Suba were in for a surprise. The Commission noted that both demands—Punjabi speaking state with Sikh majority and Maha Punjab with Hindu majority—were based on communal considerations and hence rejected. Besides, the Commission did not find any logic in the Akali Dal's demand for inclusion of Ganganagar area of Rajasthan 'which never formed part of the Punjab'[15]. According to V.P. Menon, this decision was taken on the advice of Giani Kartar Singh and S. Baldev Singh. Menon writes that the decision of the merger of PEPSU was `applauded' by national Sikhs as well as Akali leaders, including Master Tara Singh and Giani Kartar Singh. However, in a statement published in the `Spokesman' Master Tara Singh denied giving his acceptance for the merger of P.E.P.S.U. and described this act of the Commission as 'a decree of Sikh annihilation.' [16]

While in the reorganised state, Sikh majority was reduced from 40 to 30 percent the principle of linguistic states based on Punjabi language was indirectly conceded with the division of Punjab into three zones—Punjabi speaking zone, Hindi speaking zone and bilingual zone where both Hindi and Punjabi got equal status. Since this new arrangement was made under the leadership of Bhimsen Sachar, Chief Minister of Punjab from 1952 to 1956, this came to be popularly known as the Sachar Formula. Under this dispensation, the area comprising six districts of Punjab—Amritsar, Jalandhar, Gurdaspur, Ferozepur, Ludhiana and Hoshiarpur—alongwith Ropar and Kharar *tehsils* of Ambala district, constituted the Punjabi speaking zone. The Hindi speaking zone comprised districts of Rohtak, Gurgaon, Karnal, Kangra, and Hissar. The remaining areas—Shimla, Ambala, Chandigarh and Sirsa, were declared bilingual. The arrangement indicated tacit understanding about division of Punjab on linguistic basis. It was not surprising therefore that when formation of Punjabi speaking state was announced on 1 November 1966, Haryana was carved out of the Hindi speaking area and Chandigarh, being bilingual area, became the joint capital of the new states of Punjab and Haryana.

In the Akali-Congress relations a positive development took place in 1956 when the Congress leaders convinced the Akalis that they had more in common with the Congress rather than the Jana Sangh and encouraged them to merge with the Congress. While Master Tara Singh did not join the Congress Party himself he permitted prominent Akali leaders like Giani Kartar Singh[17], S. Hukam Singh[18], and others to join the Congress Party in Punjab. The Congress reciprocated the gesture by inducting Giani Kartar Singh as a minister in the Gopichand Bhargava's Cabinet and S. Hukam Singh as Deputy Speaker of the Lok Sabha.

The Congress was fortunate in so far as it succeeded in making Partap Singh Kairon,[19] a dynamic and forward looking Jat leader with a Master's degree in Political Science from the University of Michigan, as the Chief Minister of Punjab. Kairon had the longest tenure as Punjab's Chief Minister (1956-64) and put the state on the path of development. In Kairon, Jawaharlal Nehru found a like-minded state leader, who could successfully check the communal designs of the Akalis and the Jana Sangh.

With prominent Akali leaders joining the Congress, Master Tara Singh soon realised that he was left alone to fight the battle for Punjabi Suba. Master Tara Singh's dilemma is thus described by Inder Malhotra, 'As his frustration increased, Tara Singh upped the ante. His movement became more and more violent, even militant. And then he gave it unabashedly secessionist overtones, confirming the opinion of those who had always said that Punjabi Suba was but a cover for a Sikh-majority state as a prelude to an independent Sikh state.'[20] Master Tara Singh's lieutenants stirred the Sikh sentiments by popularising slogans like *'Dhoti, Topi Jamuna Par'* (meaning those wearing *dhotis* and *topis,* i.e., Hindus, will be sent across Jamuna). The Jana Sangh leaders and RSS. retorted by giving a call—*'Hindi, Hindu, Hindustan'* and demanding repatriation of the Sikhs to Pakistan by popularising the slogan—*'Kachha, Kara te Kirpan ehna nu bhejo Pakistan'*.[21] A period of intense agitations and communal riots followed. Unmindful of the consequences, Master Tara Singh continued his campaign for the Punjabi Suba.

The results of the General Elections of 1957 indicated that the popularity graph of the Punjabi Suba was going up slowly but steadily. It was in this triumphal mood that on 30 April 1960, Master Tara Singh gave a new call 'now or never'. The government pre-empted his move by immediately arresting him. While he was in jail Master Tara Singh appointed Sant Fateh Singh,[22] hailing from Ganganagar district of Rajasthan, as his successor for carrying on the agitation for the Punjabi Suba. While Sant Fateh Singh managed to organise powerful agitation in support of the demand for the Punjabi Suba, success eluded him. Fateh Singh tried to pressurise the government by going on fast unto death, which was called off on 9 January 1961, on assurance from the government that genuine grievances of the Sikhs would be looked into. Later Master Tara Singh also went on fast unto death. Like Sant Fateh

Singh, he also gave up his fast without achieving his goal. Master Tara Singh saved his life but killed his political career and joined the line of fallen idols. It will be interesting to note that almost a decade later, Darshan Singh Pheruman,[23] a Congress leader, who had gone on fast unto death for transfer of Chandigarh to Punjab, put the Akalis to shame by refusing to break his fast and meeting his end.

With a view to resolving the deadlock created over the issue of the Punjabi Suba, Jawaharlal Nehru invited Sant Fateh Singh for a meeting in February 1961. During the meeting, Nehru made it clear that while his government was willing to redress all genuine grievances of the Sikhs, he was not prepared to meet any demand based on communal considerations. Nehru further told Sant Fateh Singh that when Master Tara Singh met him at Bhavnagar he said he wanted a 'state for the protection of the *Panth*. Here language was a secondary issue'. Nehru was equally critical of the Jana Sangh's agitation for promoting Hindi at the cost of Punjabi. In his letter to Swami Atmanand, President of Hindi Raksha Samiti, Nehru wrote, '... this agitation whatever his motivations could only be a communal one and would raise communal passions.'[24] Nehru exposed the double standards of the Jana Sangh leaders saying, 'they talked of Akhand Bharat and then follow a policy which will break up India into pieces.' Nehru voiced his concern when he noticed that Jana Sangh, RSS and the Hindu Mahasabha usually 'function on the violent plane.'[25] He noticed with concern that opposition to Punjabi language, which was spearheaded by the Arya Samaj, was now being guided by the Jana Sangh leaders. Nehru was shocked to note that during their agitation against the Punjabi speaking state Jana Sangh leaders, especially Mangal Sen, MLA from Rohtak, provoked the followers saying 'the Sikhs should be looted and killed.'[26]

While in the case of other states issues of statehood did not take communal colour, in the case of Punjab it became so. The Punjabi language, which is in fact the language of the people of the Punjab, willy-nilly got associated with the Sikhs and the Akalis, since they spearheaded the agitation for Punjabi Suba. While a section of the Punjabi Hindus are to be blamed for disowning their mother tongue for political reasons, some of the Akali leaders should also share the blame for confusing the Punjabi Suba agitation with the call for a Sikh-majority state. It is strange that while Master Tara Singh was always talking of creating a Sikh-majority state, the area mentioned by the Shiromani Akali Dal in their Memorandum to the States Reorganisation Commission could not have created a Sikh majority state of their dreams. As the Commission members had already been prejudiced as a result of Akali leaders' irresponsible statements, the Akali demand for a Punjabi Suba was summarily rejected. Punjabi Hindus' opposition to the Suba was used by the Commission to argue that, 'The case for a Punjabi speaking state falls firstly because it lacks the general support of the people inhabiting the area and, secondly, because it will not eliminate any of the causes of friction from which the demand for a separate Punjabi speaking state emanates.'[27]

The Commission not only rejected the Akali demand but also questioned the validity of Punjabi in Gurmukhi script as the language of the people of Punjab. Nothing could have been more unfortunate than the communalisation of the language in the process of reorganization of India with Hindi being associated with the Hindus; Punjabi with the Sikhs and Urdu with the Muslims. Religious colour was also provided to the scripts by supporters of the languages—Gurmukhi in which Punjabi was written was mystified as a script coming from the 'mouth of the Gurus', and Devnagari, in which Hindi was written, was legitimised as coming from 'the Abode of the Devas'. Now onward fate of the language got linked with the fate of the religious groups supporting that language.

It was during the Akali agitation for the Punjabi Suba that a major shift in leadership took place and marked a change from the traditional non-Jat urban leaders to the newly emerging rural Jat Sikhs. Master Tara Singh, a middle-class educated non-Jat leader, who had emerged on the scene during the Akali agitation for Gurdwara reform in the 1920's and dominated Sikh politics for nearly four decades, was ousted by once his *protégé*, Sant Fateh Singh, a Jat leader from Ganganagar area of Rajasthan.

Backed by a powerful Jat peasantry, Sant Fateh Singh introduced a secular tone into Akali politics by presenting the Punjabi Suba demand based on purely linguistic consideration. 'We do not seek a Sikh majority area,' the Sant declared. 'We are not concerned about percentages. We want the Punjabi Suba to comprise an area where Punjabi language is spoken regardless of the fact whether the Sikhs are in a majority or minority.'[28] This shift in stand weakened Hindu opposition to the demand for the Punjabi Suba. By another tactical move the Sant and his lieutenants succeeded in creating a wedge between the opponents of the Punjabi Suba by demanding Haryana and Punjabi Suba in one and the same breath. The new slogan had an electrifying effect in the Hindi-speaking districts, with the result that some of the Punjabi Hindus, who had been blocking the creation of a Punjabi Suba, were quickly isolated from the Haryanvis, who, for their own interests, became supporters of the demand for the Punjabi Suba.

Another positive development that occurred at this juncture was that a group of secular Punjabis like Balraj Sahni, Satpal Dang, Sant Singh Sekhon, and others organised a serious campaign to remove the misgivings among the Punjabi Hindus which weakened the resistance being offered by the Jana Sangh in Punjab. Sahni chided the Punjabi Hindus and Arya Samajis for abandoning their mother tongue. 'If the Arya Samaj had the wisdom to adopt Punjabi in the Punjab as its medium of cultural and religious activity the dangerous chasm that yawns between Sikhs and Hindus in the Punjab today would not have appeared', Sahni wrote in a letter to P.C. Joshi. [29]

In the meantime, significant developments took place which brought about a major change at the national and provincial level. On the death of Jawaharlal Nehru on 27 May 1964, Lal Bahadur Shastri succeeded him as the Prime Minister of India. In Punjab, Partap Singh Kairon, the powerful Chief Minister, who alone could contain the agitation for the Punjabi Suba, was replaced by a rather weak non-Sikh Congress nominee, Comrade Ram Kishan[30]. With this change in leadership at almost all levels, opposition to the Punjabi Suba demand started dwindling. Soon a Cabinet sub-committee was appointed under the chairmanship of Indira Gandhi to consider the question of formation of a Punjabi-speaking state. Ironically enough, Punjabi speaking state came into being on 1 November 1966, when Indira Gandhi, generally projected by the Akali leaders as anti-Punjab and anti-Sikh, was the Prime Minister of India. Sant Fateh Singh, a bachelor, greeted the new state saying: 'A handsome baby has been born into my house.'[31]

Jana Sangh, which had been consistently opposing the formation of Punjabi speaking state, described the Congress resolution for the creation of Punjabi speaking state as 'a blow to the forces of unity and integration in the country'.[32] However, what surprised everyone was the speech which Sardar Kapur Singh, generally considered to be the leading exponent of the Akali-Khalistani think tank, made in the Parliament of India while taking part in the debate on the resolution for the creation of the Punjabi speaking state. Comparing the new state being offered by the Congress leadership to 'curate's egg', Kapur Singh mentioned that though 'it might be edible, it is devoid of nutritional qualities and since its putrefaction is far gone, it is really unfit for human consumption'. Kapur Singh opposed the creation of Punjabi speaking state on the grounds that: (i) it is conceived in sin, (ii) it has been delivered by an untrained midwife, and (iii) it is opposed to the best interest of the nation as it would almost certainly lead to weakening of national integration...'[33]

In a long speech, Kapur Singh traced the 'history of betrayal of the Sikhs' by Jawaharlal Nehru and Congress leadership. He also blamed Master Tara Singh and Maharaja Yadavindra Singh of Patiala for having refused the 'offer' of a Sikh state made by Jinnah through the British officials. Kapur Singh declared that as a representative of the Shiromani Akali Dal on the Constituent Assembly, he did not accept the sanctity of the Indian constitution as S. Hukam Singh, representative of the Shiromani Akali Dal had refused to append his signatures to it. While Kapur Singh gives enough evidence of his intellect and erudition he seems to have conveniently forgotten that Hukam Singh, who refused to append his signatures to the Constitution as Akali Dal's representative, happily swore in by the same Constitution when, after joining the Congress, he was elected as Deputy Speaker in 1956 and later Speaker in 1962. Same was the case of Kapur Singh himself as he entered the Parliament after being sworn in by the same Constitution which he described as 'an is invalid document'.

Since the issue of a Sikh state being offered by the British has been often repeated by those supporting Kapur Singh's line of thinking and hard liners among the diaspora it would be worthwhile to refer here to the exchange of correspondence between Sir Stafford Cripps and the Sikh leaders. Giani Kartar Singh, who was one of the members of the Sikh delegation that met Cripps to present the Sikh point of view prior to the partition of India, pleaded that the Sikhs would not feel safe in either a united India or Pakistan. He suggested that they should have a province of their own where they would be in a dominant or almost dominant position. In reply to Sir Stafford Cripps, who asked what would be the area of the proposed Sikh state, Giani Kartar Singh suggested that it should be the whole of Jalandhar and Lahore divisions together with Hissar, Karnal, Ambala and Shimla districts of the Ambala division and Montgomery and Lyallpur districts. Sikhs in the proposed area would have been a very small minority. It would be naive to believe that the majorities from the proposed area would have migrated to India and Pakistan to allow Sikhs to have a dominant position.

While some of the middle-rung British officials, especially Major Short and Penderel Moon, had genuine sympathy with the Sikhs either because of their contribution to defence or for larger strategic reason of having a friendly buffer state between India and Pakistan they could not help much because there was no Sikh concentration and contiguity in the areas demanded by the Akali leaders for inclusion in the 'Khalistan'. This is also confirmed by perusal of the correspondence between the British officials in Punjab and the higher echelons in Delhi and London. For instance, in one of his letters to the Viceroy of India, Sir Bernard Glancy, the Governor of Punjab, wrote:

> The Sikhs, although, as I have recently told you, are undoubtedly relieved by the rejection of the offer brought by Sir Stafford Cripps, are still feeling distinctly restive. Master Tara Singh and his lieutenants have found it an easy matter to stir up communal feeling

> at the alleged danger of the Sikhs being subjected to Muhammadan rule in the Punjab, and they are loath to cease from exploiting this opportunity. They will no doubt derive some degree of comfort from the sympathetic references made to Sikhs in the debates which have just taken place in Parliament, but it is to be hoped that these expressions of sympathy will not go to their heads and lead them to believe that "Khalistan" is regarded in responsible quarters as a practicable proposition. As you are well aware, the practical objections to "Khalistan" are even greater than those which lie in the path of Pakistan. Apart from the upheaval that would be caused by tearing out a large section of territory from the vitals of the provincial body politic, it is worth remembering that there is not one single district in which the Sikhs command a majority. Another illustration of the complexity of the problem can be placed on the results of the last census [of 1941] owing to the determination of all the communities to inflate their own figures, but it is true that a few years ago, though there are half a dozen Sikh States in the agency, there was only one state, the Muslim state of Malerkotla, where the majority of the population were Sikhs.
>
> The obvious course for the Sikhs to pursue is to seek a satisfactory basis for combining with the major community in the Province.[34]

This expression of sympathy and goodwill for the Sikh community was clearly evident from Lord Mountbatten's broadcast to the nation on the night of June 3, 1947:

> We have given careful consideration to the position of the Sikhs. This valiant community form about an eighth of the population of the Punjab, but they are so distributed that any partition of this province will inevitably divide them. All of us who have the good of the Sikh community at heart are very sorry to think that the partition of the Punjab, which they themselves desire, cannot avoid splitting them to a greater or lesser extent. The exact degree of the split will be left to the Boundary Commission on which they will of course be represented.[35]

When the Sikh leaders realised that transfer of power was imminent and they could not get the Sikh state of their dream, they dreaded the idea of Muslim domination over the Sikhs. According to Lord Mountbatten, 'I found that it was mainly at the request of the Sikh community that Congress had put forward the resolution on the partition of Punjab'. According to Lord Mountbatten: 'On the basis of that resolution which the Sikhs themselves sponsored, that this division has been provided for.' Mountbatten could have never imagined the realities on the ground. When he called for a map and studied the distribution of the Sikh population he was astonished to find that the plan that the Sikh leaders submitted divided the Sikh community of Punjab into two almost equal parts. Mountbatten mentions that he spent great deal of time in India and England to find some way out by which division of Sikh community, their rich lands and historic Gurdwaras, could be avoided without departing from the accepted principle of contiguity. In sheer frustration he had to give it up saying, 'I am not a miracle worker and I have not found the solution.'[36]

In demanding the inclusion of leftout areas of the 'Sikh Homeland' within the union of India and in demanding an autonomous and constitutional status for the 'Sikh Homeland' or later on the analogy of Jammu and Kashmir, Kapur Singh was clearly suggesting the issues which could be taken up by the Akali leaders to continue their struggle after the formation of Punjabi speaking state. Kapur Singh has also been accusing the 'Hindu dominated Centre' of calculated discrimination against the Sikhs. In a lecture delivered in Vancouver on October 7, 1974, and published under an interesting title of *Stupid Sikhs,* Kapur Singh says,

> And ever since 1947, persistent calculated well planned and regular attempts have been made on the cultural, on the political and on the economic levels, not only to disintegrate the *Khalsa*, the collectivity of the Sikh people, once and for all, but to weaken the Sikh citizens economically in such a manner that they are reduced to the status of what is known as peonage so that the highest ambition of a Sikh citizen after some time might remain delimited only to become a peon, a night watchman at the palatial door of a rich Hindu industrialist, a driver of his commodious foreign-imported car, and a mere lowest rank soldier in the army, so as to provide cannon-fodder whenever the rulers of Delhi wish to pick up a quarrel with somebody.[37]

Portrayal of the Sikhs as a persecuted community in the popular history written by S. Kapur Singh and his likes is not supported by ground realities and empirical data. Apart from the fact that Sikhs did very well in the fields of agriculture, business and defence they also occupied highest positions in independent India, with Giani Zail Singh occupying the highest office of the President of the Indian Republic (1982-1987) and Dr. Manmohan Singh being twice elected as the Prime Minister of India, Sikhs have occupied other high positions as well. Baldev Singh, the first Defence Minister of independent India, Surjit Singh Majithia, Deputy Defence Minister of India, Swaran Singh as the Minister for Defence and later External Affairs, Hukam Singh as

Deputy Speaker and later Speaker of the Lok Sabha, Gurdial Singh Dhillon as Speaker of the Lok Sabha, Giani Zail Singh and Buta Singh as Home Ministers, M.S. Gill as Minister for Youth and Sports Affairs, Preneet Kaur as Minister of State for External Affairs, Montek Singh Ahluwalia, Deputy Chairman of the Planning Commission of India, and many other Sikhs as governors, ambassadors and members of the Parliament, chairpersons and members of various Constitutional bodies, could not have occupied these positions if there was a 'calculated attempt in free India to weaken the Sikhs economically and politically', as claimed by Kapur Singh and his tribe. Again it was in independent India that Bhai Mohan Singh and Raunaq Singh emerged as captains of Indian industry and M.S. Oberoi and other Sikhs almost monopolised the hotel industry. While India had two Sikhs as chiefs of the Indian Air Force—Arjan Singh and Dilbagh Singh—Gen. J.J. Singh became the first Sikh Chief of the Indian Army in 2004. It is pertinent to note that all this happened under the Congress-ruled Centre.

While the Congress can be accused of being anti-Akali, because of the clash between Nehru and Tara Singh and between Mrs. Gandhi and Badal, especially because both parties have been fighting against each other for political supremacy in the Punjab, the Congress cannot be accused of being anti-Sikh and anti-Punjab.

In a well argued case Gian Singh Sandhu writes:

> ...I am extremely hesitant to buy the theory that Sikhs in India were minority in need of protection or special rights. Similarly the notion that Punjab as a state is subjected to systematic discrimination does not stand scrutiny. In 1977-78 the per-capita real income in Punjab was Rs. 1965 as compared to a national average of Rs. 1190 only. From 1960-61 to 1977-78 the per-capita real income in Punjab rose at a compound rate of 3.17 compared with 1.21 percent of India as a whole. Economic grievances from every state are far too common and Punjab's grievances are not towering amongst those. To the extent Punjab's complaints coincide with the process of development biased in favour of urban and against rural population they are a part of the national problem crying for correction.[38]

As we have seen the root cause of the crisis in Punjab was, and unfortunately still is, Akali Dal's quest for power and Congress's unwillingness to offer power to the Akalis on a platter. In the competitive power politics while Akalis have been working on the thesis of 'Panth in Danger' by claiming to be 'sole spokesman' of the Sikhs and holding them promises of protection from the other. The 'other' has been changing in different situations—the British and the Mahants during the Akali movement for Gurdwara reform, Muslims during transfer of power and partition riots and the `Hindu dominated Centre' in independent India. The tragedy of Punjab politics is that, in the competition for votes both the Congress and the Akalis have started making emotional appeals to the Sikh electorate by taking up communal issues as was done by Giani Zail Singh. This politics of vote-bank is fast eroding the secular space in the political arena in Punjab which is a dangerous signal.

While the creation of Punjabi Suba put an end to the long Akali agitation, the later history shows that it created more problems while solving one. The new Punjab was not the one the Akali Dal had demanded and hoped for. Since the division was made on the basis of the 1961 census, wherein a section of Punjabi Hindus had been returned as Hindi-speaking for political reasons, a large area which in reality was Punjabi-speaking, was left out of the new Punjab. Chandigarh, which was built on the Punjab territory and out of the resources of Punjab as its new capital, was put under Central control and declared a Union Territory and also joint capital of Punjab and Haryana. Also, control of the Bhakra Dam, Madhopur and other water headworks was taken over by the Centre. All this gave the Akali leaders enough cause to whip up anti-Congress sentiments to launch powerful agitations whenever it suited their political interests.

It is interesting to note that when elections were held for the newly created Punjabi Suba in February 1967, the Akalis could not come to power on their own. They had to form a United Front along with Jana Sangh, staunch opponent of Punjabi speaking state, and the communists. Gurnam Singh[39], who headed the government, had to accommodate Dr. Baldev Parkash of Jana Sangh and Satyapal Dang, the Communist leader of Punjab as Ministers. Master Tara Singh's faction was not happy with Gurnam Singh, whose Ministry was toppled after it had been in office for nearly eight months. Lachhman Singh Gill, a protégé of Master Tara Singh, replaced Gurnam Singh as the Chief Minister of Punjab and ruled for nearly nine months. After a brief spell of Governor's rule, Gurnam Singh formed the coalition government for the second time in 1969. He was succeeded by Parkash Singh Badal[40], a rich landlord from the Malwa region of Punjab, who also formed a coalition government with the help of Jana Sangh.

In the Punjab Assembly elections in 1972, Congress recovered most of the ground it had lost soon after the creation of the Punjabi Suba. After emerging as the largest party in the state assembly, with 67 seats, the Congress formed government in Punjab with Giani Zail Singh[41] as the Chief Minister. Deeply rooted in Sikh tradition and having understood the psyche of the Sikhs much better than his predecessors, Giani Zail Singh took wind out of the Akali sail by hijacking most of the Sikh issues on which Akalis have been getting electoral support. By introducing a religious tone to Punjab politics, Giani succeeded to a great extent in weakening the Akalis. But the result—growing communalisation of provincial politics—was disastrous. In an attempt to secure Sikh votes for the Congress, Giani organised one of the biggest religious processions, commemorating the march of Guru Gobind Singh, from Anandpur, near Bhakra Nangal, to Damdama near Bhatinda. The march started after the state level function at Anandpur Sahib on 10 March 1973, where Dilbagh and Amolak, two horses believed to be in the pedigree of a famous horse of Guru Gobind Singh, were specially brought from far-off Takhat Hazur Sahib, Nanded, and accorded special 'reception' with D.C. Pavte, the Governor, Giani Zail Singh, the Chief Minister of Punjab[42], presenting them traditional shawls. Interestingly apart from Congress, Akali Dal and Jana Sangh, RSS workers also participated in the state level function in a big way. Many other important Sikh festivals were also arranged by the 'secular' government of Giani Zail Singh including tercentenary of the martyrdom of Guru Tegh Bahadur in 1973. Mohali, a satellite town of Chandigarh, was renamed as Sahibzada Ajit Singh Nagar, after Guru Gobind Singh's eldest son. All state functions started with Sikh invocation and were organised at state's exchequer.

On the completion of five years of Giani Zail Singh's rule, elections were held for the Punjab Assembly. As the Akalis returned to power in June 1977, Parkash Singh Badal formed the government in Punjab. It was during the Akali *morcha* against the internal emergency imposed by Mrs. Indira Gandhi in 1975 that the Akalis came closer to the leaders of the opposition at the national level. Parkash Singh Badal built a personal rapport with the prominent leaders of the opposition when he shared jail with them after being detained during the Emergency. It was not surprising therefore when the opposition formed a government at the Centre in March 1977 with Morarji Desai as Prime Minister, Badal was invited to join as the Minister of Agriculture. Later he had to resign from this position to take over as the Chief Minister of Punjab in June 1977 as the Akalis got majority on their own during the elections to the State Assembly. If at all the Akalis were serious about getting their demands accepted this was the right time to act. Rather than raising any demands for which they had been fighting all these years they contented themselves by reinterpreting the controversial Anandpur Sahib Resolution by calling it as a document supporting state autonomy and federal system. However, some members in and outside the Akali Dal, made no secret of their desire of establishing a Sikh state of their dreams. Ambiguities on different terms mentioned in the resolutions passed on different platforms were interpreted by different groups to suit their convenience. The first draft was prepared by Kapur Singh who declared that the Sikhs were a *Raj Jatti,* the chosen ones, predestined to rule. Since the draft prepared by Kapur Singh was in English and Fateh Singh did not know the language he nodded his approval to whatever was verbally explained to him. The draft was formally adopted in a meeting held at Anandpur Sahib, on October 16-17, 1973. That is why it came to be popularly known as Anandpur Sahib Resolution. Not much was heard about the Resolution till Giani Ajmer Singh, Secretary of the Shiromani Gurdwara Prabandhak Committee, released another version from Amritsar which also included a draft of New Policy and Programmes of the Akali Dal. This version was presented at the All India Akali Conference held at Ludhiana on 28-29 October 1978. [43] Shifting paradigms of the Akali politics are best described by Khushwant Singh:

> When the Akalis were in power as they were when the Anandpur Resolution was formally passed, and again during that Janata regime, they did not exert much pressure on the central government to have it accepted. They kept it as not-too-secret weapon in their archives, to be brought out and brandished when they were out of power and use its non-acceptance as grievance justifying agitation. Also, when it suited them they put it across as no more than a demand for more autonomy, just as the communist parties, the Janata and the regional parties like D.M.K., the A.I.D.M.K and Telegu Desam were doing.[44]

After the fall of Janata government at the Centre, General Elections were held in 1980 in which Indian National Congress headed by Mrs. Indira Gandhi secured clear majority with 353 seats out of 529. When Indira Gandhi became the Prime Minister again, Parkash Singh Badal, who was then heading the Akali government in Punjab, let it be known that if left undisturbed he would extend full cooperation to the Congress government at the Centre. Mrs. Indira Gandhi, nursed a grudge against Badal for his having joined hands with the Opposition and launching Akali *Morcha* against the Emergency. And this the Akalis did in spite of the fact that while banning RSS and other communal organisations, Akali Dal remained untouched. Repeating the Janata government's experiment of dismissing properly elected governments in the states, Indira Gandhi also dismissed some state governments including the Akali government in Punjab. Results of the election in the Punjab gave clear majority to Congress which formed government in the province with Darbara Singh[45] as the Chief Minister.

Out of power, the Akalis quickly retrieved their list of grievances and did not hesitate in making a common cause with pro-Khalistani elements abroad. It was in this fluid situation that Ganga Singh Dhillon, a US based supporter of Khalistan, tried to gain cheap publicity in the Sikh Educational Conference held at Chandigarh from 13-15 March 1981, by forcing on the organisers a resolution describing 'Sikhs as a separate Nation' and demanding 'Associate Membership' of the United Nations. The organisers of the Conference, belonging to the Chief Khalsa Diwan, a moderate Sikh organisation, quickly realised the trap and disowned Ganga Singh Dhillon and his slogan of 'Sikhs are a Nation'. The mission of Sardar Kapur Singh was carried forward by Dr. Jagjit Singh Chauhan and others among the Sikh diaspora. *The New York Times* of October 12, 1971, carried an advertorial signed by Dr. Chauhan:

The Sikhs Demand an Independent State in India ...
The Only Guarantee for Peace on the Sub-continent.[46]

In his statement Dr. Chauhan made many exaggerated remarks which caught the popular imagination and romanticised the Sikh past but were far from the truth. In the opening paragraph of the statement he mentions, '... Another 6 million of us live abroad in alienation and exile for the day of deliverance'. It seems the diasporic Sikh leaders were working on the analogy of the Jewish idea of a homeland, a sense of persecution, an idea of exile and the idea of eventual return to the homeland. The facts of life both in India and abroad however were far away from the rhetoric of the Sikh diaspora. While Sikhs migrated to UK, Canada, US, Australia and other countries of the pacific rim much before the idea of Khalistan popularised by Ganga Singh Dhillon and others, it would be wrong to describe that the Sikhs in these countries are living in 'exile'. Because of their being an adventurous and hardworking migrant group most of the members of the Sikh diaspora have done well for themselves. While Dalip Singh Saundh became the first Sikh Congressman in the United States, Ujjal Singh Dosanjh created history when he became the first Sikh Premier of the state of British Columbia in Canada. We all know too well the stories of those of our compatriots who have managed to get the status of `exile' to escape from being deported because of their illegal entry in the western countries. Similarly Dr. Chauhan's statement that Sikhs constituted 80 percent of the Indian armed forces is far from the truth. As is well known, the number of Sikhs in the Indian armed forces was 13 percent at the time of partition and has come down drastically since then because of opening of fresh avenues to the Sikh youth.

Like Sardar Kapur Singh's lecture in Vancouver this advertisement also made many assertions which do not find any confirmation from the extant records on the subject in India and abroad. Again without quoting any historical document or evidence the advertisement mentions that:

> In 1848 [sic. 1849], under the Lahore Treaty, the British Government became the caretaker of the Independent Sikh state and gave an undertaking to the Sikhs for eventual self-determination. During the mid 19th and early 20th century, the Sikh people supported the British on the express understanding that when a final dispensation of power was made on the sub-continent, they would be treated as a nation in their own right and given sovereign control of the area over which they had once ruled.[47]

The Treaty referred to above by Dr. Chauhan, was signed in 1849 and does not anywhere mention any 'eventual self determination' by the Sikhs. On the contrary Clauses 2 and 3 of the Treaty specifically mention:

> ...All the property of the State, of whatever description and wheresoever found, shall be confiscated to the Honourable East India Company, in part payment of the debt due by the State of Lahore to the British Government, and of the expenses of the war. The gem called the *Koh-i-Noor,* which was taken from Shah Shuja-ul Mulk by Maharaja Ranjit Singh, shall be surrendered by the Maharaja of Lahore to the Queen of England.[48]

While this rhetorical pitch was increasingly becoming popular and making many local convert among the Sikh youth and intellectuals, the Akali leadership in control of the Shiromani Gurudwara Parbandhak Committee (SGPC) and the Golden Temple complex failed to assert its authority and knowingly allowed the Guru Nanak Niwas adjacent to the SGPC headquarters to be occupied by Jarnail Singh Bhindranwale and his men. Again when the situation became rather volatile Bhindranwale was allowed to occupy the Akal Takhat Complex. It is rather unfortunate that G.S. Tohra, a senior Akali leader, who was President of the SGPC for the longest tenure of 27 years, did not play any constructive role in diffusing the volatile situation. Patwant Singh squarely blames Tohra:

> The central fact which emerges out of a careful reading of Punjab's politics is that Mr. Tohra is the one who has woven the many webs in which the state and central governments have so frequently been trapped. By allowing Jarnail Singh Bhindranwale to use the shrine for his inflammatory politics, Tohra helped to place the Golden Temple, that sacred and exalted emblem of Sikhism, in the very eye of the political storm. It is entirely likely that its eventual destruction formed a part of his calculations, for he seems to have foreseen that an attack on the temple would do more to drive the Sikhs and the rest of India apart than any other event. What makes him doubly suspect is that he seems prepared to enact this scenario once again.[49]

If one has to look for one solid reason for creating greater confusion in the recent Punjab politics, it was the passage of little versions of the Anandpur Sahib Resolution and their exploitation by the Akalis and their critics alike. While the Akalis might have devised the Resolution to embarrass the Congress government at the Centre and to seek the support of the non-Sikhs, particularly in those states which are up against the Congress hegemony at the Centre, the Resolution seems to have boomeranged on the Akalis. While the Resolution could have posed a real threat to the Congress monopoly over all states under the existing unitary system, the Akalis, and particularly those claiming to be 'the Sikh intellectuals', failed to explain the basic spirit underlying this Resolution. Rather than carrying non-Sikhs and non-Congress parties with them, men like Kapur Singh, who were the main spirit behind the drafting of this controversial Resolution, blew hot and cold in the same breath. While the major part of the Anandpur Sahib Resolution deals with autonomy on various political and economic issues which could make strong appeal to various other regional parties and non-Congress governments in various states, by branding it as a 'Sikh' and 'Akali' document and by launching it from the Gurdwara platform the drafters of the Resolution limited its appeal to the Sikhs alone.

A careful perusal of the articles and editorials of various national dailies shows that leading journalists responded unevenly, sometimes in a knee-jerk manner to these developments. Editors of some Indian dailies seemed to have coloured the Sikh past on the basis of the generalisations of irresponsible actions of some misguided individuals. *The Hindustan Times,* [50] an English daily founded and nurtured by the Akalis in the early 20s, became a great critic of the recent Akali agitation. In one of the issues, its Editor, N.C. Menon, wrote:

> What was so special about Punjab and the Akalis? The centre had tackled with fortitude and firmness a number of regional crises—student revolt in Gujarat, Telengana, separatist demands by DMK, parochialism in Assam and insurrection in the North East. So why should the Akali agitation alone loom larger than life? Why should the centre project an image of weakness regarding issue after issue, even as the Akalis kept raising the ante?[51]

Menon and others argued that the myth of the 'superdom' of the Punjabis and everything great about Punjab being ascribed to the Sikhs needed to be demolished. Strangely Menon went to the extent of suggesting that government could even explain to the public the 'occasional need for a temporary suspension of some human rights.'[52]

Another prominent journalist who was greatly instrumental in reconstructing the Sikh past according to his own perception of Sikh history was Girilal Jain, long time Editor of the *Times of India*. With the major thrust of his editorials and writings being that the Sikhs were reformed Hindus, he argued that, 'the Sikhs had much to gain and little to lose if they had accepted the Devnagri script.'[53] This he felt would have been consistent with national integration and would have allayed Hindu fears of Sikhs dominating them which formed the basis of Hindu opposition to Punjabi Suba. Mr. Jain was very critical of those who suggested that the disowning of Punjabi by the Hindus was one of the major causes of the present crisis. In one of his articles published on 7 March 1984, titled 'Only An Hour Before Midnight' he called upon the Akalis to immediately call off their agitation and warned them of the growing danger of Hindu backlash.

Arun Shourie, Editor of the *Indian Express*, also wrote a series of articles on the Sikh problem, entitled 'Politics of Pandering' wherein he questioned the Sikhs' role in the freedom struggle and casually mentioned their occasional participation in the freedom movement. The articles provoked great resentment amongst the Sikhs. In addition to various letters to the Editor, Devinder Singh Duggal of the SGPC reacted in a serious and scholarly way by writing a rejoinder entitled 'The Heroic Sikh Tradition'. In one of his articles Shourie wrote, 'the national leadership has perceived only two ways of securing support: first, by fomenting communal, caste and other divisions; second, by buying it with concessions.' His accusation was that, 'the policy of purchasing concessions to whichever was the more aggressive group had rendered one group, the Hindus, fearful as they saw each concession (Punjabi Suba, allowing the Sikhs to carry *kirpans* on the aeroplanes, etc.) as a sign that the state would not be able to protect them, while the other group, the Sikhs, became convinced that they could snatch whatever they wanted.'[54]

Bhajan Lal, Chief Minister of Haryana, added insult to injury by issuing instructions to the Haryana police to frisk all Sikhs passing through Haryana on the eve of 1982 Asian Games in New Delhi. Apart from ordinary Sikhs the Haryana police did not hesitate in humiliating some of the highly decorated service officers including Arjan Singh, now Marshal of the Air Force, General Jagjit Singh Aurora, hero of Bangladesh's liberation. Incidentally Mrs. Amarjit Kaur, a Congress Member of the Upper House of the Indian Parliament, was also not spared by the Haryana police. In this overall context where Bhajan Lal, Giani Zail Singh, P.S. Badal and Bhindranwale were settling scores with each other Dr. S.D. Sharma, a veteran Congressman, who occupied the august office of the President of India, played the role of a statesman.

In spite of the fact that his daughter and son-in law (Geetanjali Maken and Lalit Maken) had been gunned down by the militants, he made a statement with far reaching consequences for the Sikhs and the nation. A scholar of standing and well-versed with the Sikh scripture, he asserted that the Sikh tradition does not permit killing of innocent citizens and clarified that militants have no religion and as such irresponsible actions of a few individuals should not be generalised as actions of the Sikh community as a whole. Not only this he also made conscious efforts in appointing a Sikh as his A.D.C., he also continued the tradition of celebrating Guru Nanak's birthday in the Rashtrapati Bhavan with great sense of devotion and enthusiasm.

The confusion created by different versions of the Anandpur Sahib Resolution and entry of the diaspora in the 'proxy war' in Punjab weakened the Akali leadership's hold over the Sikh masses. In the meantime, Jarnail Singh Bhindranwale, [55] originally planted by Giani Zail Singh to weaken the Akalis, had grown out of his shoes. A simple village preacher, by this time Bhindranwale had become a law unto himself. He had developed contempt for the traditional Akalis whom he successfully marginalised in Punjab. After shifting to a safe haven in the Akal Takhat in the holy precincts of the Golden Temple, Bhindranwale ridiculed the state and state machinery and used contemptuous language both for the Congress and the Akali leadership. In his daily sermons, he preached ideology of hate which inspired his gun-trotting young followers, popularly called *Kharkus,* who killed all those whom they perceived as enemy of Khalistan. Bhindranwale and his men became self-appointed moral police and started prescribing dress codes for school boys and girls, norms of behaviour for police and bureaucracy. Khushwant Singh has beautifully described the cultural transformation which Bhindranwale and his moral police was trying to seek:

> To Bhindranwale modernity was evil; the Sikhs must return to the simple ways of their warrior forefathers. They must look like them: wear their beards loose and not rolled up and tied under their chins; they must wear long shirts, below knee-length breeches (*kucchas*) covering their shins. Likewise, Sikh women should not drape themselves in *sarees* which were Hindu, but in *salwar-kameez* (baggy trousers and long shirts) which are Punjabi, nor wear *bindis* (dots) on their foreheads.[56]

With the help of Major-General Shahbeg Singh,[57] Bhindranwale succeeded in fortifying the Golden Temple complex to pre-empt any move to eject him from his safe haven. After having fortified himself, Bhindranwale sent instructions to his men, to eliminate all those who dared to oppose his ideology and actions. It is unfortunate that Mr. Tohra and his lieutenants in the SGPC, the supreme body for the control and management of the Akal Takhat and other historic shrines[58], did not stop Bhindranwale and his gun trotting young men from occupying Guru Nanak Niwas and later occupying and fortifying the Akal Takhat complex both of which were under the control of the SGPC. It is ironical that those who talked of upholding the Sikh tradition became instrumental in their violation.

A campaign for defiance of the established law was jointly launched by Bhindranwale and splinter groups of Akali Dal, All India Sikh Students Federation led by Bhai Amrik Singh and protégés of Dr. Ganga Singh Dhillon, Dr. Jagjit Singh Chauhan and other self-proclaimed promoters of Khalistan abroad. Beginning with hoisting of *Kesri* flag, a symbol of the Republic of Khalistan during the Hola Mohalla festival in Anandpur in March 1984, issuing of Khalistan Passports and currency, these groups together created chaotic conditions where Bhindranwale and his supporters started challenging the authority of the State. [59]

Editors and correspondents of newspapers opposing Bhindranwale, became special targets of the terrorist groups patronised by Bhindranwale. To attract media attention aeroplanes of government-owned Indian Airlines were hijacked. Country-made bombs and hand grenades were thrown at strategic places. Buses were stopped by terrorists, members of a particular community were forced to come out and shot in cold blood. The situation reached its nadir when A.S. Atwal, DIG of Punjab Police, was shot dead at the main entrance of the Golden Temple soon after his return from the sanctum sanctorum after offering his morning prayer. Rather than taking prompt action at this stage the situation was allowed to deteriorate both by the state and the Centre. It seems that rivalry between Union Home Minister Zail Singh and Punjab's Chief Minister Darbara Singh, stood in the way of prompt action.

It is believed that soon after the incident, Darbara Singh recommended to Mrs. Gandhi immediate intervention to avoid further deterioration of delicate law and order situation but Zail Singh seems to have prevailed over Mrs. Gandhi not to take any drastic action in haste.

Things were further complicated with Akali leaders launching *Dharma Yudh Morcha* to get their grievances redressed. Mrs. Indira Gandhi did not take the Akalis and their 'Holy War' seriously. Darbara Singh, the Chief Minister of Punjab, who had reversed Giani Zail Singh's policy of compromise with communal forces, thought he would be able to contain the Akali agitation through constitutional means.

Mrs. Indira Gandhi, who disliked the communal politics of the Akali Dal, supported Darabara Singh's line of action.

In sheer frustration, the Akalis organised a series of agitations throughout Punjab and at the same time kept on adding to their charter of demands[60] which had by now gone up to 45. It is interesting that when the Akali leaders were asked to come to the negotiating table with their serious demands, their number was quickly reduced to 15. The revised list had an interesting item under the head 'Political Economic and Cultural Demands, which relates to permission for opening of a Private Bank by Dr. Inderjit Singh, who lost his job as chairman of Punjab & Sind Bank because of nationalisation of major banks in 1969. Mrs. Indira Gandhi tried to accommodate the Akalis to whatever extent she could. But Indira, like Nehru, was not willing to negotiate on the unity and integrity of India and accept challenge to the constituted authority of the state. Rather than coming out with a clear-cut plan to take the state out of the *impasse*, Sant Harchand Singh Longowal, President of Shiromani Akali Dal[61], called upon the Sikhs to 'launch a countrywide non-cooperation movement by refusing to pay land-revenue, water and electricity bills and prevent the movement of food grains out of Punjab.' Worried over the outcome of the latest move of the Shiromani Akali Dal, coupled with the fact that Bhindranwale had already fortified himself in the Akal Takhat, Mrs. Gandhi made an appeal to the Akali Dal leaders 'to call off their threatened agitation'.

It seems, by this time, Akali leaders were no longer in control of the situation. Rather than immediately responding to Mrs. Gandhi's call, Akali leaders decided to follow the policy of inaction which resulted in the tragic events of June 1984, known as 'Operation Blue Star'[62]. Whether this was a 'pre-meditated plan', 'an act of vengeance', 'failure of intelligence' or a 'fatal miscalculation', the action greatly disturbed the common Sikh masses who were neither interested in the Akali agitation nor Centre's tactics to handle them. The army action invited flood of protests from the Sikhs and their supporters and well-wishers at home and abroad. Dirty electoral politics and use of religion for political ends clearly boomeranged both on the Akali and Congress leadership with disastrous consequences for the Sikh community and the Indian state. The attack on the Golden Temple (and later, the massacre of innocent Sikhs in the aftermanth of the killing of Mrs. Indira Gandhi) did great damage to the psyche of the Sikhs.

Realising the gravity of the situation Mrs. Gandhi tried her best to assuage the hurt feelings of the Sikhs. In an exercise of damage control, the Government got the Akal Takhat quickly repaired through Baba Santa Singh, the Nihang chief. In keeping with the wishes of the devotees, army was withdrawn from the Golden Temple complex as soon as there was some semblance of normalcy. Mrs. Indira Gandhi visited the Golden Temple escorted by Beant Singh, among others, her Sikh bodyguard whom she refused to drop from her inner security ring against advice from the concerned quarters as she believed this would have been against the secular principles of the Indian State. It is rather ironical that while she trusted Beant Singh and other Sikhs in her inner security ring in spite of all that had happened in recent past, they betrayed her trust. On the morning of October 31st Beant Singh (38) and Satwant Singh[63] (21) opened fire on Mrs. Gandhi and 'pumped eighteen bullets into her frail body.'[64]

The assassination of Indira Gandhi, like that of Mahatma Gandhi, was the result of ideology of hate propagated over the years by communal forces. To check the spread of communal virus we need to launch a long-term ideological war based upon secular principles of the Indian National Congress. [65]

Three years of violence in Punjab and selective targeting of members of a particular community and the ideology of hate against the Hindu community preached by Sant Jarnail Singh and those supporting his line of thinking was bound to create violent repercussions. Though many Sikhs also became victims of the killer gangs of Bhindranwale, none of the prominent Akali leaders or for that matter any prominent Sikh intellectual condemned the violent actions of these gangs. Since Bhindranwale and his followers claimed to be devout Sikhs, their irresponsible actions were generalised by the media as the actions of the Sikh community. This also added to the growing resentment against the Sikhs. While certain amount of anger against the Sikhs and resultant violence on the 31 October 1984, is understandable what surprised every one was the systematic attacks on Sikh establishments and Sikh dominated colonies right in the national capital. H.K.L. Bhagat, who was then Union Minister for Information & Broadcasting and others like Sajjan Kumar, Jagdish Tytler and Dharam Das Shastri, were suspected of flaming the anti-Sikh passions that led to the killing of innocent Sikhs, rape of their womenfolk and looting and burning of their properties. Several prominent citizens, organisations defending civil liberties, condemned the killings of innocent Sikhs and the failure of the state. Several inquiry commissions and committees condemned the killings of innocent Sikhs and looting of their properties and censured the official machinery for the failure to maintain law and order. However, the major saving feature in this overall dismal situation was the role of average law-abiding citizens which saved many Sikh lives and properties. In Delhi, the Jawaharlal Nehru University, which upheld the secular values and condemned all forms of communalism, played a commendable role. The university not only provided shelter to those seeking refuge at the campus but encouraged its faculty and students to go out in the streets in the defence of innocent citizens. It was only appropriate that when Sant Harchand Singh Longowal came to visit Delhi to express sympathy with the members of the Sikh community, the first thing he did was to visit the Jawaharlal Nehru University wherein he started his speech by thanking the students and faculty for their commendable role before talking about other issues.

Now that Sikh history has taken a full circle—from November 1984, when the Sikhs were hiding their identity and taking shelter in safe havens, to May 2004 when Dr. Manmohan Singh, a turbaned Sikh, was elected to highest executive office of the Prime Minister of world's largest democracy—what should the Sikhs do? Rather than being carried away by the past they would do well to take a leaf from the Diary of Anne Frank:

> Who knows, maybe our religion will teach the world and all the people in it about the goodness, and that's the reason, the only reason that we will have to suffer. We can never be just Dutch or, just English, or whatever we will always be Jews as well. And we will have to keep on being Jews, but then, we'll want to be.[66]

In keeping with the spirit of Prime Minister Manmohan Singh's intervention in the Lok Sabha during Nanavati Commission's Report in the Parliament on 11 August 2005, wherein he described anti-Sikh riots 'as a great human tragedy and a national shame', the Sikhs should seek refuge in Guru Granth Sahib, their Guru Eternal:

ho-ay ikatar milhu mayray bhaa-ee
dubiDhaa door karahu liv laa-ay.

Come and join together, O my Siblings of Destiny;
dispel your sense of duality and let yourselves
be lovingly absorbed in the Lord.
(*Guru Granth Sahib,* Mahla 5, p.1185)

Endnotes

1. Tara Singh was born at Village Harial, District Rawalpindi (Pakistan) on 24 June 1885. His original name was Nanak Chand. He got his present name at the age of 17 after he embraced Sikh faith. As he started his career as Headmaster in Khalsa High School, Lyallpur, in 1908, he came to be popularly known as Master Tara Singh. He developed anti-British feelings during his college days at Amritsar. He was one of the student leaders in the demonstration organised against Sir Charles Riwas, the

Lt. Governor of Punjab, in 1907. During the Akali Movement he came to the forefront and emerged as one of its top leaders. He was an extremist and non-cooperator. He was also a member of the AICC. He supported the Congress first during the Non-Cooperation movement and later by leading a Jatha of 100 Akalis during the Civil Disobedience movement of 1930. However, during the Second World War, he developed differences with Mahatma Gandhi over the Sikh help to the British Government in the army recruitment and left the Congress to help the British government in the war efforts. While there is no standard biography on Master Tara Singh, details of his role in various movements are available in such works as Singh, Jaswant (ed.) (1972). *Master Tara Singh: Jiwan, Sangharsh te Udesh* (Punjabi) Amritsar: Harnam Printing Press); Singh, Niranjan (1968). *Jiwan Yatra Master Tara Singh* (Punjabi) Delhi: Navyug Press; and his autobiography, *Meri Yaad (1972).* (Punjabi) Amritsar: Shiromani Gurdwara Prabandhak Committee.

2. According to popular accounts the idea of Khalistan was first floated by one V.S. Bhatti from Ludhiana, in 1940, who issued a pamphlet demanding Khalistan, which was to act as a buffer between India and Pakistan. This demand also came to be known as Sikhistan and Sikh State. The proposal was endorsed in a resolution passed at a gathering of prominent Sikhs held at Lahore under the Presidentship of Master Tara Singh, which apart from other things demanded, 'In order to ensure the free and unfettered growth of the Sikh Panth, the Panth demands the splitting up of the existing province of the Punjab, with its unnatural boundaries, so as to constitute a separate autonomous Sikh State in those areas of the Central, Northern, Eastern and South-Eastern Punjab in which the overwhelming part of the Sikh population is concentrated, and which because of the proprietors in it being mostly Sikhs, and its general character being distinctly Sikh is also the *de facto* Sikh Homeland —the area, extent, the status and constitutional frame-work of such a State being left to be settled by negotiation between the accredited representatives of the Sikh Panth and the other interested parties, such as the British Government, the Hindus and the Muslims; further resolving that the above demand is the unconditional absolute and minimum demand and political objective of the Sikh Panth as a whole.' (Quoted in Gurbachan Singh and Lal Singh Giani (1946). *The Idea of Sikh State.* Lahore: Lahore Book Shop. pp. 1-3. After the visit of Cripps to India when it became clear that the British were quitting India. Fearing Muslim domination in the West Punjab, the Sikh leaders made desperate attempts to get an autonomous area which could protect their rich lands and historic shrines and also act as a buffer state between India and Pakistan. With a view to weaken Muslim League's case for Pakistan, Congress did not oppose the demand for Khalistan while Communists actively supported the demand. The British officials were quite sympathetic towards the Sikhs because of their traditional loyalty and contribution in the war effort and worked out various strategies to help the Sikhs. This became clear during Cabinet Mission's press conference

held on 17 May 1946. To a question that the Secretary of State for India had divided Indian nation into three categories: (i) General (ii) Muslims and (iii) Sikhs. The questionnaire asked that whether this was done in consultation with the parties in India? The Secretary of State for India, reply was that the statement was his own and did not necessarily represent the opinion of anybody in India. (Quoted in Menon, V.P. (1999). *Integration of the Indian States*. p. 585). As the Sikhs were not concentrated in any area where their rich lands and historical shrines were and the Labour government, which had come to power in England after World War II, was not willing to give any consideration to the special claims of the Sikh community, concerned British officials could not help the Sikhs realise their dream in spite of their genuine sympathy with the Sikhs. S. Kapur Singh and others who follow his line of thinking have been unnecessarily blaming Master Tara Singh for having 'refused' the Sikh State being offered by the British. In the recorded interview with Mallik Hardit Singh published in the *Makers of Modern Punjab* compiled by Dr. Kirpal Singh and Prof. P.S. Kapur, there is a mention of a meeting that Mallik Hardit Singh arranged between the Akali leaders and Mr. Jinnah. While Mr. Jinnah was making vague offers he was not willing to give anything in writing. Asked by S.H.S. Mallik, 'Where shall we stand if your people would not carry your word?', Jinnah replied, 'My friend, my word in Pakistan would be like the word of God.' However nothing concrete came out of the meeting. The *Statesman* next day carried the news, 'The Sikhs will under no circumstances accept the Pakistan'. Therefore, fixing blame on one leader or the other for refusing something which was not being offered would be meaningless. It is obvious that Jinnah was trying to humour the Sikhs to weaken their opposition towards creation of Pakistan. Without verifying the basis of Khalistan or Sikh State Akali politicians and supporters of Khalistan at home and abroad have been indulging in blame game to suit their political interest from time to time.

3. Born on 2 March 1909, S. Kapur Singh received his Masters degree with First Class from Government College, Lahore. Later he went to Cambridge from where he received his Tripos in Moral Sciences. He joined the Indian Civil Service under the British rule. In independent India he had serious problems with the new dispensation. After his exit from the civil service he joined the Akali politics and was responsible for drafting most of the resolutions of the Akali Dal, including the controversial Anandpur Sahib Resolution.

4. (1974). "Punjab Boundary Force and the Problem of Order", *Modern Asian Studies* 8(4): 557-62.

5. (1988). *Selected Works of Jawaharlal Nehru,* Vol. 23. New Delhi: Jawaharlal Nehru Memorial Fund. p.197.

6. Batabyal, Rakesh (ed.) (2007). *The Penguin Book of Modern Indian Speeches.* New Delhi: Penguin Books. p. 678.

7. (1998). *Selected Works of Jawaharlal Nehru,* Vol. 24. New Delhi: Jawaharlal Nehru Memorial Fund. p. 269.

8. Ibid: 233.
9. Quoted in (1993). *Selected Works of Jawaharlal Nehru*, Vol. 14, Part II, In. no. 16. New Delhi: Nehru Memorial Fund. p. 497.
10. Quoted in *Selected Works of Jawaharlal Nehru*, Vol. 21. New Delhi: Jawaharlal Nehru Memorial Fund. p. 590.
11. Three men who played active role in snatching the mike from Jawaharlal Nehru were Tarlochan Singh, Amarjit Singh and Bedi Gurbaksh Singh. Interestingly all the three supporters of the Master Tara Singh, Akali Dal later became protégés of Giani Zail Singh. Tarlochan Singh rose to be the Additional Press Secretary to the President of India in 1982. For details see Batra, Pritam Singh (ed.) (2005). *Narion Takia Itihas*, by Tarlochan Singh. Chandigarh: Unistar Books Pvt. Ltd. pp.180-83.
12. (1999). *Selected Works of Jawaharlal Nehru*, Vol.24. New Delhi: Jawaharlal Nehru Memorial Fund. p. 301.
13. For Details see (1955). *Report of the States Reorganisation Commission*. New Delhi: Manager of Publications. pp. 140-150.
14. Ibid: 140-41.
15. Ibid: 145.
16. For details see Menon, V.P. (1999). *Integration of the Indian States*. New Delhi: Orient Longman. p. 282. For Master Tara Singh's rejoinder see *The Spokesman*, 19 October 1955.
17. Born on 22 February 1902, in Lyallpur district in a Jat Sikh family, Giani Kartar Singh had a religious bent of mind. He earned the epithet of Giani. He joined politics in young age and participated in Congress's campaign for Tilak Swaraj fund. He actively participated in the Akali Movement for Gurdwara Reform and was later elected as a member of the Shiromani Gurudwara Parbandhak Committee (SGPC). Considered to be a 'brain of the Akali Dal' he played active role as Akali representative during various parleys for transfer of power in India. After migration to East Punjab Giani Kartar Singh emerged as a strong Akali leader but later shifted to the Congress and was a minister under Gopi Chand Bhargava and Bhimsen Sachar, the chief ministers of Punjab. Giani Kartar Singh led simple and honest life and was greatly respected. For details see Sandhu, Jasdev Singh (ed.) (2001). *Giani Kartar Singh: A Commemorative Volume*. Patiala: S. Jasdev Singh Sandhu Foundation.
18. Born in 1895 in Sahiwal, Montgomery district, Hukam Singh matriculated from the local Government High School in 1913 and graduated from the Khalsa College, Amritsar in 1917. He later got a law degree from the Law College, Lahore. After few years of practice he joined the Akali Movement for Gurdwara Reform and later emerged as a distinguished Akali leader. He joined the Congress in year in 1956 and was made the Deputy Speaker in 1956 and Speaker of the Lok Sabha in 1962. He was greatly instrumental in the creation of Punjabi speaking state. After his retirement from active politics he settled in Delhi and played an active role in celebrating the centenary of the Singh Sabha Movement in 1973.

19. Born in 1901, in the village of Kairon, Amritsar district, Partap Singh Kairon had his early education in the village school. While still a student of Khalsa College, Amritsar, Partap Singh left for the United States where he earned his living by working in firms and factories. Through sheer hard work he earned Masters Degree in Political Science from the University of Michigan. The prosperity of the state of California greatly impressed Kairon. Back home, he joined the Congress Party and served as Chief Minister of Punjab for the longest tenure of eight years. He had a dream of transforming Punjab into California. He successfully checked the powerful agitations of the Akalis and the Jana Sangh.
20. *The Indian Express*, 17 May 2010.
21. Quoted in speeches of Sant Fateh Singh in the Sikh Reference Library, Amritsar.
22. There is hardly any biography of Sant Fateh Singh. A small booklet in Punjabi—*Do Mahan Purakh*—by Jasbir Singh Sabar throws some light on the life and times of Sant Fateh Singh and Sant Chanan Singh.
23. Born in 1986, Darshan Singh Pheruman was active in anti-British agitations in Malaya and later in India. He spent many years in jail. He was Member and later General Secretary of the S.G.P.C.
24. (2002). *Selected Works of Jawaharlal Nehru,* Vol. 30. New Delhi: Jawaharlal Nehru Memorial Fund. pp.385-387.
25. Ibid: Vol. 33, p. 273.
26. Ibid: Vol. 39, p. 389.
27. For Details see GoI (1955). *Report of the States Reorganisation Commission.* New Delhi: Manager of Publications. p. 146.
28. Singh, Harbans (1994). *Heritage of the Sikhs.* New Delhi: Manohar Publishers and Distributors. p. 330.
29. Joshi, P.C. (ed.), *Punjabi Suba: A symposium.* Delhi: National Book Club. pp. 14-39.
30. Born in Kot Isa Shah village of Jhang district (now in Pakistan) Ram Kishan entered public life in 1929. He was secretary of the Punjab Congress Committee from 1934 to 1948. He was Deputy Minister in Kairon Government. On 6 July 1964, he was elected as the Chief Minister of Punjab and remained in this position till the formation of Punjabi Suba on 1 November 1966.
31. Singh, Harbans (1994). *Heritage of the Sikhs.* New Delhi: Manohar Publishers and Distributors. p. 340.
32. Joshi, P.C. (ed.), *Punjabi Suba, A symposium.* Delhi: National Book Club. p.36.
33. Batabyal , Rakesh (ed.) (2007). *The Penguin Book of Modern Indian Speeches.* New Delhi: Penguin Books. p.698.
34. Menon, V.P. (ed.) (1957). *Transfer of Power.* Princeton: Princeton University Press, Vol.2. p.7.

35. Singh, Khushwant (1999). *A History of the Sikhs*, Vol.II. New Delhi: Oxford University Press. p. 275.
36. Ibid: 275-276.
37. Text of Kapur Singh's public speech delivered under the auspices of All Canada Sikh Federation, Vancouver, on 7 October 1974, and published under the title *Stupid Sikhs*, (Chandigarh: Goodwin Printers, New Delhi), p. 23.
38. Singh, Amrik (ed.) (1985). *Punjab in Indian Politics: Issues and Trends*. Delhi: Ajanta Publications. p. 62.
39. Born in 1899, Gurnam Singh was first Akali Chief Minister of the reorganised state of Punjab and ruled from March 1967 to November 1967 and again from 1969 to 1970.
40. Prakash Singh Badal, born in 1927, did his graduation from the F.C. College, Lahore. A wealthy landlord, he joined the Akali Dal, and was member of the SGPC. for many years. He was first elected to the Punjab Assembly in 1957 and again in 1969. He was elected Chief Minister of Punjab on 27 March 1970. Except for a brief stint as the Union Minister for Agriculture, Prakash Singh Badal has remained the most powerful Akali leader in Punjab. Till recently he was leader of both, the Government and the Akali Party and has been wielding tremendous power in the S.G.P.C.
41. Zail Singh started his career as a village preacher but later joined the freedom struggle as an activist of the Praja Mandal Movement in the princely Sikh state of Faridkot. After Independence he became a minister in the Punjab cabinet and later rose to the position of Chief Minister of Punjab in March, 1972. In January 1980 he was inducted into the Central Cabinet as the Home Minister and later in July 1982 elevated to the office of President of India, the first Sikh to attain this exalted position in free India.
42. For details see (1976). *Guru Gobind Singh Marg: The Great Pilgrimage.* Patiala: Languages Department, Government of Punjab.
43. For the full Text of Anandpur Sahib Resolution adopted at Anandpur sahib on October 16-17, 1973 see Singh, Mohinder, *The Akali Struggle: A Retrospect*, Appendix X, pp. 246-53; For second version passed on October 28-29 1978 at the 18th All-India Akali Conference at Ludhiana see the Punjabi version written and published by Giani Ajmer Singh, Secretary, Shiromani Akali Dal, pp. 1-54.
44. Singh, Khushwant (1999). *A History of the Sikhs*, Vol. 2. New Delhi: Oxford University Press. pp. 348-349.
45. Born in 1916 in Jandiala, Jalandhar district, Darbara Singh participated in the Quit India Movement of 1942 and remained in jail for three years. He was the member of the legislature and was Home Minister of Punjab in the Kairon cabinet. He was Chief Minister of Punjab from June 1980 to October 1983.

46. I am thankful to the American Centre, New Delhi, for providing me copy of the Advertorial.
47. *New York Times,* 12 October 1971.
48. For full text of the treaty see Khullar, K.K. (1980). *Maharaja Ranjit Singh.* New Delhi: Hem Publishers. pp. 253-254.
49. *Hindustan Times,* 6 December 1986.
50. According to Sardar K.M. Panikkar it was Sardar Mangal Singh, a prominent Akali leader, who founded the *Hindustan Times* and invited him to be its Editor. Mr. G.S. Raghavan became an Assistant Editor. This paper made a singular contribution in winning over sympathy and support of the nationalist leadership for the Akali cause. It was later sold to Pandit Malaviya from whom it passed on to the industrial house of Birlas, present owner of this paper. See for details, Panikkar's (1977). *Autobiography.* New Delhi: Oxford University Press. pp. 48-54.
51. *Hindustan Times,* 3 November 1982, NMML.
52. Ibid., 22 June, 1983.
53. *Times of India,* 18 May 1983.
54. Quoted in Chandra, Bikas (1993). *Punjab Crisis: Perceptions and Perspectives of Indian Intelligensia.* New Delhi: Har-Anand Publications. pp.179-180.
55. Born in 1947, in Village Rode, district Faridkot, Punjab, Jarnail Singh was youngest of the seven brothers. He came to be known as Bhindranwale after he joined Damdami Taksal, a Sikh seminary of village Bhinderkalan. Not much was known about him till Giani Zail Singh, the Chief Minister of Punjab, encouraged him to stand as a candidate to oppose the official Akali candidate for the SGPC elections. Upon the death of Sant Kartar Singh Khalsa in a road accident in August 1977, Jarnail Singh was appointed as successor to manage the Damdami Taksal at Chowk Mehta, near Amritsar. Because of political patronage and the attention paid to his activities by the media at home and abroad Bhindranwale soon emerged an extra-constitutional authority and defied the established law with impunity till his death during the army action in the Golden Temple in June 1984.
56. Singh, Khushwant (1999). *A History of the Sikhs,* Vol.2. New Delhi: Oxford University Press. p.331.
57. Shahbeg Singh, who traced his lineage to the legendary Sikh warrior Bhai Mehtab Singh was a distinguished army officer with good knowledge of Punjabi and other languages and flair for Sikh history. He participated in the army action in Bangladesh and was in the forefront on many major operations. Somehow he fell out with the authorities and was discharged from the Indian army a day before his retirement, for which he nursed a grudge against the Indian State. Through Gurcharan Singh Tohra, Shahbeg Singh got involved with the Akali Morchas. In Bhindranwale's politics of revenge he seems to have found an opportunity to settle his score with the Indian State, which did not

recognise his services. It is believed that the Akal Takhat complex was fortified under his professional guidance.

58. For details about formation and development of the Shiromani Akali Dal and SGPC see Singh, Mohinder (1978). *The Akali Movement*. New Delhi: Macmillan. pp. 87-112.
59. For Details see pp 110-162 of Government of India's *White Paper on the Punjab Agitation,* New Delhi, dated 10 July 1984.
60. For list of demands see pp. 61-63 of Government of India's *White Paper on the Punjab Agitation,* New Delhi, dated 10 July 1984.
61. Born in 1934 in Village Gideryani of Sangrur district, Harchand Singh Longowal entered the Akali Dal under Master Tara Singh. Later he was elected to the Punjab Assembly in 1967. During the Akali Morcha against Emergency he played an active role. A moderate leader he was greatly instrumental in bringing about peace in Punjab by signing Rajiv-Longowal Accord.
62. A large number of books have come out giving details of the action. I have depended mainly on Singh, Khushwant (1999). *A History of the Sikhs,* Vol.2. New Delhi: Oxford University Press; Tully, Mark (1985). *Amritsar: Mrs. Gandhi's Last Battle.* London: Rupa and Company and Singh, Amrik (ed.) (1985). *Punjab in Indian Politics: Issues and Trends.* Delhi: Ajanta Publications.
63. Beant Singh and Satwant Singh, two of Mrs. Indira Gandhi's bodyguards, were motivated by Kehar Singh to avenge the army's attack on the Akal Takhat to flush out Jarnail Singh Bhindranwale and other militants who had taken shelter inside. Details about as to how they planned and executed their conspiracy are given in several works such as Sarin, Ritu (1980). *The Assassination of Indira Gandhi.* New Delhi: Penguin Books and Gupte, Pranay (1985). *Vengeance: India After the Assassination of Indira Gandhi.* New York: W.W. Nortan & Company.
64. Singh, Khushwant (1999). *A History of the Sikhs,* Vol.2. New Delhi: Oxford University Press. p. 380.
65. Prof. Bipan Chandra and his colleagues have suggested various strategies to fight communalism. See for details Chandra, Bipan (1988). *India's Struggle for Independence 1857-1947.* New Delhi: Viking and *(2008). India Since Independence.* New Delhi: Penguin. Also See Chandra, Bipan (1987). *Communalism in Modern India.* New Delhi: Vikas Publication.
66. Frank, Otto H. and Mirjam Pressler (2001). *Anne Frank: The Diary of a Young Girl.* New Delhi: Penguin. p. 329.

I am thankful to Prof. Bipan Chandra, Prof. Harish Puri and Dr. Rakesh Batabyal for their having gone through the draft and offering valuable suggestions and to my colleagues Dr. Navneet Kaur, Dr. Amrit Basra and Kuljeet Singh for their input for the completion of this paper.

Chapter XVIII

Jammu & Kashmir

The Troubled Course of Integration and Party Merger

David Devadas

Politics in Jammu & Kashmir was in great flux from mid-1963 until Prime Minister Jawaharlal Nehru's death on 27 May 1964. That turbulence led to some radical shifts, including the extension of many more Union laws to the state than had hitherto been applicable. Henceforth, the political and constitutional position of Jammu & Kashmir was more like any other state of India. In line with that, the dominant (and ruling) party in the state, the National Conference, converted itself into the Pradesh Congress Committee of the Indian National Congress.

The dramatic event that set the stage for such major political changes in 1964 and 1965 was the loss of the relic of the Prophet Mohammed from the Hazratbal shrine on the 27 December 1963.[1] It was one of three grave crises of the 20th century that occurred in Kashmir but jolted the world far beyond.[2] Although the relic was recovered on the 4 January 1964, its brief loss caused riots in parts of south Asia, and a fresh wave of migration from East Pakistan to India. The Union government's urgent response reflected Nehru's abiding concern for Kashmir.

Since the talks[3] that were held amid panic behind the scenes of the 'relic crisis' focused on personalities rather than a clear vision or agenda, the two major political events that followed led in opposite directions. The first was the succession of Ghulam Mohammed Sadiq to the leadership of the state government. The second was the release of Sheikh Abdullah from jail. Soon after his release, Abdullah visited Pakistan to explore the contours of a solution that might be acceptable to all. Although nothing came of Abdullah's initiative, and he was re-arrested after a few months, the 'greater Kashmir' plan[4] for near-independence that he discussed with Pakistan's President Ayub Khan and leaders of 'Azad Kashmir' became a point of reference for future discussions, at least within Kashmir. On the other hand, Sadiq's elevation led to closer integration of the state with the Indian Union, and between the ruling parties in the state and at the Centre. The state was ruled directly by the Congress for the next decade.

It was a decade of turmoil: two wars with Pakistan, the first of them directly over Jammu & Kashmir; incipient guerrilla activity; the first Hindu-Muslim riots in the Kashmir valley since 1931; and the return of Sheikh Abdullah to mainstream politics.[5] Most of these events might have taken place in any case, but the enhanced integration of the state into the Indian Union gave fissiparous tendencies greater salience. At least at the level of mass psychology, activists of the Plebiscite Front[6] and other such secessionist organisations were able to promote the idea that promises made by Nehru at the time of accession had not only been flouted, they had been reversed. Further, they were able to promote the idea that India was treating Kashmir with contempt, like a colonial power. Most dangerous for the Nehruvian foundation of the post-independence Congress, and republic, was the propaganda that a Muslim community, now sometimes posited as a nation, was being oppressed by a Hindu one.

A Change of Guard

Sadiq had been a leading Left ideologue of the Muslim Conference even before the party converted itself into the National Conference on the June 11, 1939.[7] He presided over the Jammu & Kashmir Constituent Assembly, which was elected in 1951. He was therefore not among the five members of Sheikh Abdullah's cabinet in the early 1950s. Among those that were, Mirza Afzal Beg backed Sheikh Abdullah in 1953 and was also arrested along with Abdullah. Girdhari Lal Dogra (from Jammu) and Sham Lal Saraf (a Kashmiri Pandit) had joined the deputy Prime Minister, Bakshi Ghulam Mohammed, to write to the *sadr-e-riyasat* (head of the state) that Abdullah had lost the confidence of the cabinet; Bakshi thus succeeded Abdullah as Prime Minister of Jammu & Kashmir on August 9, 1953.

Over the next few years, Bakshi was able to consolidate his position as head of the administration but Sadiq emerged as an alternative. In fact, the party split briefly after the elections of 1957, when a group led by Sadiq formed the Democratic National Conference. However, Nehru persuaded the group to reunite, even going to Srinagar to reason with them. That would have been an opportune time to encourage a two-party democratic option in the Valley's politics.

Not only was the time opportune, there was political logic to the split, given the ideological differences between Bakshi and Sadiq.

Bakshi focused on infrastructure and development while also working tirelessly for the welfare of common people. He might be described as liberal conservative. Sadiq, on the other hand, was committed to Communist principles. This difference was reflected in their respective relations with Congress leaders: Bakshi was close to Sardar Patel and later to G.B. Pant and Morarji Desai, while socialists in the Congress, including Nehru, held Sadiq in high esteem.

The United Nations' efforts to resolve the issue went onto the backburner that year; after a visit to the subcontinent, General Assembly president Gunnar Jarring reported failure to make any headway. Already, on the 10 December 1955, Soviet leaders Bulganin and Khrushchev had declared in Srinagar that the people of Kashmir had settled that Kashmir was one of the states of India.[8] China's premier, Chou En Lai, had stated on the 16 March 1956 that the people of Kashmir had expressed their will regarding accession to India.[9] And former British Prime Minister Attlee said on the 20 November 1956 that, 'Kashmir has definitely opted for Union with India.'[10] On 26 January 1957, a new Constitution had taken effect for the state. It stated that: 'The State of Jammu & Kashmir is and shall be an integral part of India.' By 1958[11], senior functionaries of the Government of India had begun to talk of turning the Ceasefire Line into the international boundary between India and Pakistan.

There was a great difference between the ways in which ideological factions functioned in the Congress and in the National Conference, however. Nehru's extraordinarily democratic sensibility provided space simultaneously for a variety of political ideologies and aspirations within the Congress Party. He allowed a great deal of autonomy to the party's regional satraps. Not only were there robust conservative and socialist groups within the Congress, the party had a fair share of both liberals and illiberal conservatives. It had space for scheduled caste politics as well as Brahmin-dominated politics.

There are key differences between India's political realities and those of most European countries. Democratic politics based on universal adult franchise took root in most countries only after they were relatively developed economically. More important, most countries where democratic political systems worked based nationhood on a single ethnic identity, a single language and a single religion. Most countries in Europe were built on the principles accepted in the 1648 Treaties of Westphalia: each was identified by its religious sect. India was built on a radically different vision. Nationhood was inclusive, predicated on religious, ethnic and linguistic accommodation; its politics were not just ideology-driven but needed to channel aspirations based on region, religion, caste and language too.

The Congress was modelled on this inclusive paradigm of nationhood. Nehru's party was flexible enough to channel aspirations felt and expressed across wide spectrums on all four axes of India's politics: ideology, region, religion and caste. In keeping with the idea that India's unity was predicated on nurturing diversity, Nehru had refused to establish a unit of the Congress party in Jammu & Kashmir, despite requests from politicians in the Jammu region during the mid-1950s[12]. With the wisdom to understand the folly of repressing Kashmiris' sense of their unique identity, he treated the Jammu & Kashmir National Conference as a sister party of the Congress; the leader of the party was a permanent invitee to meetings of the Congress Working Committee.

Particularly in the upper Chenab valley, people sometimes describe Jammu & Kashmir as mini-India—referring to the great variations of religious, ethnic, linguistic and cultural identity across the state. There are differences in patterns of co-existence, however. Since three-quarters of the state's pre-partition population was Muslim, and many Hindus were concentrated in towns in areas such as Poonch and Mirpur, cohabitation of various castes in the same village did not form the basis of interaction between separately endogamous identity groups in Jammu & Kashmir to the same extent as in some other parts of the subcontinent. Many villages, particularly in places like Ladakh, were inhabited by a single identity group. In most parts of the Kashmir valley, the Chenab basin and areas around Jammu, people of different religions and castes lived together in the same village or town. However, most villages comprised a large majority that was at least technically consanguineous, rather than an assortment of several relatively small and separately endogamous identity groups.

In such a context, minorities' fears naturally ran deep. Especially as the people of the state grappled with the lingering question of whether they wanted to adopt Pakistan's Europe-based model of nationhood or India's, the need for inclusive politics was urgent. However, the political strategies of the state government did not nurture liberal accommodation the way Nehru did on the national stage. Abdullah and then Bakshi each imposed his will on his party, his government and the polity. Intra-party dissent was not tolerated, other parties were sabotaged, and public criticism stifled. On one occasion, Abdullah took a hockey stick to Lal Chowk and beat up an editor who had criticised him in print. The state's autonomous status gave scope, and the threat of subversion by secessionists provided a pretext, for the autocracy of Kashmir's leaders. Though his tactics were not ham-fisted, Sadiq also lacked Nehru's inclusive openness. Single party dominance continued to deprive Kashmir of democratic space, contributing to frustrations that plugged in to secessionist movements.

Equally perilous, the National Conference did not adequately account for alternative political, social and economic patterns in parts of the state beyond the Valley. The value of multi-party politics—and the devolution of powers to local authorities—in Jammu & Kashmir cannot be over-emphasised, for high mountains accentuate identity differences as well as the logistical challenges of efficient administration. Although Sadiq's moves to integrate the state more closely with India were generally popular in Jammu and Ladakh, his failure to provide regional autonomy within the state caused frustration. Rising aspirations combined with differing historical memories to boost fissiparous sentiments in parts of the state.

In this context, it is ironic that Sadiq's turn as head of the state's administration came as a result of the 'Kamaraj Plan,' which ended the Nehruvian accommodation of divergent political ideologies and aspirations within Congress at the national level. A permanent invitee as leader of the National Conference, Bakshi was present when the Congress Working Committee discussed the plan for senior leaders of the Congress to resign and strengthen the party at the grassroots. Noticing that Nehru repeatedly glanced in his direction[13], Bakshi enthusiastically announced his support for the idea, and added that he would be the first to resign.[14]

His offer was accepted. Over the next few weeks, a compromise was negotiated whereby Sadiq would be the new prime minister of the state but Bakshi would recommend the majority of the cabinet.[15] However, on 12 October 1963, National Conference legislators elected a relatively unknown leader, Khwaja Shamasuddin, as the state's prime minister[16]. Bitter, a small band of Sadiq's supporters refused to join Shamas-ud-din's council of ministers. This set the stage for the political negotiations that occurred against the background of the loss of the relic.

The Politics of a Disappearance

The 'relic crisis' was perhaps the sharpest reminder until then in the short life of the republic of the dangers of religion-based politics. (Sharper jolts were to come in the late 1980s and through the events that culminated in the demolition of the Babri mosque at Ayodhya.) Particularly in Kashmir's context, one must distinguish between communal conflict rooted in the socioeconomic situations of different religious groups, or in unequal opportunities for some of them, on the one hand, and the manipulation of religious symbolism and emotions for political purposes on the other.

Although the loss of the relic caused communal conflict elsewhere, there was no violence against the minority Hindus in the Valley, despite the overwhelming outpouring of emotion and trauma among the Valley's Muslims. In fact, a message was spread through mosque preachers across the Valley that Hindus were not responsible and should not be targeted. This message was spread through word of mouth by activists of a new political formation, the Action Committee,[17] which was formed within hours of the relic's loss. The Action Committee comprised nine organisations, two-thirds of them distinctly religious. Nevertheless, even while taking steps to ensure that the highly charged response of common Muslims did not turn towards violence against minorities, the Committee used its influence over those emotions for political ends. Its posters called for the intervention of the United Nations and of Islamic countries. Its slogans focused on the need for Sheikh Abdullah, who was then in jail, and for Mirwaiz Yousuf Shah, who was in 'Azad Kashmir' (and had twice served as head of that area's administration[18]), to identify the relic.

The Committee had no elected representative status. However, Nehru readily responded to the Committee's self-projection as the popular voice of the people. Nehru, and the Congress party, had been deeply committed to democratic responsiveness and willingness to engage. Already, when Maharaja Hari Singh of Jammu & Kashmir had acceded the state to India in October 1947, Nehru had insisted that the accession be endorsed by Sheikh Abdullah on behalf of the National Conference. This was despite the fact that the National Conference had boycotted the elections that were held in the state in 1946, and so had not formally re-established its popular base in the recent past. In negotiating with the Action Committee in 1964, Nehru re-established this precedent; later, negotiations were held between representatives of the Government of India and Sheikh Abdullah and, in the new century, between the All Parties Hurriyat Conference and no less than the Prime Minister of India.

Initially, the Union Home Secretary and the Director of the Intelligence Bureau, B.N. Mullick,[19] engaged with the leaders of the Action Committee. Nehru was also telephonically in touch with the Committee's head—Maulana Masoodi, who had been a member of the Indian Constituent Assembly and then an MP. Later, negotiations were taken up by Lal Bahadur Shastri, who went to Srinagar after being re-inducted into the Union cabinet as a minister without portfolio.[20]

Many of the irate processions had raised slogans against Bakshi, who continued to control great power while Shamsuddin was prime minister. Bakshi's nephew, Bakshi Rashid was assaulted in Lal Chowk and his jeep pushed into the river. So, the issue of the state's leadership was in focus during negotiations between Nehru and Masoodi. The latter held a strong hand; the Action Committee was holding out for the authentication of the recovered relic, over which public distress persisted—fuelled in part by Radio Pakistan.[21] The relic, which had been recovered on the 4 January[22] 1964, was identified as authentic by a panel selected by Masoodi at a highly charged viewing at Hazratbal on the February 3. Sadiq replaced Shamsuddin on 29 February. Abdullah was released from jail on 8 April.

A Bold Initiative

So sound was the personal equation between Nehru and Sheikh Abdullah that, after being released from prison, the latter went to stay with the Prime Minister at Teenmurti House. Nehru agreed to Abdullah's suggestion that he take to Pakistan a proposal for the permanent settlement of the Kashmir issue. Shaken as he had been by the 'relic crisis,' Nehru was no doubt eager to back any effort to solve the Kashmir issue at the earliest. He was satisfied that Abdullah's ideological commitment to secularism equipped him to bridge the divide between India and Pakistan. He explained to the AICC that:

> Sheikh Abdullah is wedded to the principles of secularism and does not want anything to be done to vitiate these in any way. He does not believe in the two-nation theory, which was the basis of formation of Pakistan. Nevertheless, he hopes that it should be possible for India, holding on to her principles, to live in peace and friendship with Pakistan and thus incidentally to put an end to the question of Kashmir. I cannot say if we shall succeed in this, but it is clear that unless we succeed India will carry the burden of a continuing conflict with Pakistan with all that this implies. I hope Pakistan will get rid of its hatred and fear of India. She has nothing to fear from India, unless she herself attacks India. I hope that it may be possible for the two countries to develop closer and more intimate relations to the advantage of both. If Sheikh Abdullah can help in bringing this about, he will have done a great service to both the countries. We are prepared to help him in this attempt but, in doing so, we must adhere to our principles as well as our basic attitude in regard to Kashmir.[23]

With this strong vote of confidence from Nehru, Abdullah was able to put forward his proposals with confidence. According to a member of that delegation,[24] Abdullah mooted the idea that India and Pakistan could jointly manage defence, foreign relations and communication for the Kashmir valley and some adjoining areas, including Muzaffarabad. Other areas of the erstwhile princely state were to be merged into India and Pakistan respectively. Abdullah discussed the idea, which was dubbed the 'greater Kashmir' plan, with General Ayub Khan, the

President of Pakistan[25], and with leaders of 'Azad Kashmir.' A tentative plan was made for Ayub Khan to visit New Delhi in July for talks with Nehru.[26]

However, Abdullah received news of Nehru's death while he was addressing a public meeting in Muzaffarabad. He cut short his visit. Visibly distraught, Abdullah not only attended the funeral in Delhi, he accompanied Nehru's ashes to Allahabad for immersion. The initiative for peace that he had taken to Pakistan was shelved. Ayub Khan's visit was put off. Instead, shelling increased at the Ceasefire Line. The next summer, Pakistan launched another war against India.

Wars and Warnings

Under the leadership of Prime Minister Lal Bahadur Shastri, India was able to weather the 1965 war with firm determination. It was soon followed by another Indo-Pak war in 1971, at the end of which East Pakistan (earlier East Bengal) seceded from Pakistan. That secession sounded a note of caution, not only for Pakistan but also for India—particularly for the Congress Party, the standard-bearer of India's inter-regional, inter-religious and inter-caste unity in diversity. If distance and ethno-cultural differences did not allow East Pakistan to continue as a part of Pakistan, the Congress needed to work with sensitivity to accommodate, nurture and secure the various kinds of pluralities that made India such a uniquely rich nation.

In fact, dangerous fissiparous tendencies were successfully contained in Tamil Nadu almost immediately after the 1965 war—and, albeit with limited success, in the northeast during the next decade and after. Nehru had sought to contain and to celebrate within the overall rubric of Indian nationalism a variety of other ideas of nationhood. For he recognised that India's history was a unique story of accommodation and inter-dependence,[27] that this continent-sized country contained the widest pluralities anywhere in the world, and that many ideas of community and nationhood could, would and should cohere in citizens' minds. In the unsettled period following his death, violent conflicts and intense geopolitical pressures made it less easy to hold with confident tenacity to this vision. It was challenged by separate and sometimes separatist nationalisms in Maharashtra, Punjab and elsewhere. However, the causes of Pakistan's split needed to be urgently studied in India with regard most particularly with Muslim-majority Kashmir, which also had a strong nationalist sentiment. In the years after Nehru, the relationship between Kashmir and India was becoming more troubled.

Pakistan's problems with East Bengal, Baluchistan and the Pakhtoon movement were also portentous for peoples within the extraordinarily disparate state of Jammu & Kashmir. Although many in the state saw the place through the prism of its Muslim majority, the state had a substantial Hindu minority, a small but vigorous Buddhist community and, in pockets, a robust sprinkling of Sikhs. There were other sorts of differences, each of them in flux: a large Gujjar-Bakarwal community, that gradually became more assertive from the mid-1970s, the developing consciousness of a Pahari culture and identity, the cautiously modernising Balti and other often Shia peoples in the Kargil mountains, newly assertive Bhagat, Ramdasi and other scheduled caste identities in Jammu and surrounding districts, small but culturally distinct communities such as Gaddis and Sippis, the wounded but determinedly fostered identities of migrant Hindu and Sikh communities from Mirpur, Muzaffarabad and west Punjab—and minorities sprinkled among all of these communities spread across mountainous terrain that naturally emphasised differences. The impasse between India and Pakistan over the future of the state had given great salience to the Kashmiri-speaking Sunni Muslim community concentrated in the large bowl of the Kashmir valley, but conflicts among some of the other communities would gather steam over the next few decades.

A different sort of insight was to be gained from an event that paved the way for the war over East Pakistan: the hijacking of an Indian Airlines plane, named Ganga, enroute from Srinagar to Jammu on 30 January 1971. The plane was welcomed with delirious celebrations when it landed in Lahore; the garlanded hijackers were carried through the streets in huge processions. However, Gandhi's insistence on the right means to obtain any objective was in play around the hijacking of that plane—ironically, on the Mahatma's 22nd death anniversary. The plane which was burnt at Lahore airport after all 32 passengers had disembarked, cost Pakistan dear; for India suspended Pakistani aircrafts' over-flight rights between East and West Pakistan in the crucial months of civil war in East Pakistan, which led up to the Indo-Pak war of December 1971.

Pakistan's war strategies in 1965 not only continued the pattern of the past but went on into the 21st century: covert action, diversionary ruses and preparations for violent initiatives even while negotiations were underway. The fact that border shelling was stepped up within weeks of Nehru's death indicates that the use of violent coercion to make Kashmir a part of Pakistan had remained an option for Pakistan's leaders even while they engaged with Sheikh Abdullah. Pakistani strategists perceived India's political leadership as weak after Nehru's death and so brought that option to the forefront almost immediately. Alistair Lamb asserts in *Kashmir: A Disputed Legacy, 1846-1990*, that, 'planning for Operation Gibraltar may well have started as early as 1964, not long after the *Moe-i-Muqaddas* crisis.'[28]

Lamb points out that naming it Gibraltar flagged a link between this Operation and Tariq, the *nom de guerre* that Pakistan's Major Akbar Khan adopted[29] in 1947—in memory of the Moor commander who burnt his army's boats upon landing in Spain. Akbar Khan had coordinated the invasion by Waziri and other Pathan tribesmen from the North-West Frontier Province on the 22nd of October 1947, just a couple of months after the two nations came into being. That first Pakistani attempt to wrest Kashmir from India had been even more covert than the one in 1965. Although Pakistan denied official complicity in the 1947 operation, Major Akbar Khan's *Raiders in Kashmir* makes it clear that Prime Minister Liaquat Ali and the chief ministers of west Punjab and the North-West Frontier Province were involved in planning the Operation to send the tribesmen and to provide arms, transport and passage.[30] Further, Pakistani authorities told members of the United Nations Commission for India and Pakistan (which was formed in 1948), during formal meetings in the summer of 1948,[31] that regular Pakistani troops had been deployed in the battles against the Indian Army since April 1948.

Pakistan's strategists employed the option of deniability more strongly in later decades. Although units of the Pakistan army—particularly the Northern Light Infantry, which recruits soldiers from Gilgit, Baltistan and other areas of the erstwhile state of Jammu & Kashmir that are under Pakistan's control—were deployed in the icy battlefields of Kargil in 1999[32], Pakistan's leadership insisted that 'mujahideen' freedom fighters were involved in the operations. For a time, they even refused to take the bodies of slain soldiers.[33] Pakistan also denied any involvement beyond moral and diplomatic support for the insurgency that erupted in the Valley in 1989, although the various militant groups involved in that militancy were not only armed and trained in camps in Pakistan, their operations were minutely controlled by officers of the Pakistan Army.[34]

Pakistan's military engagements in 1965 too included a devious component. Early that summer, Pakistan's army attacked the Kutch region at the southern end of the India-Pakistan border. That diversionary tactic was calculated to draw Indian troops away from Jammu & Kashmir while the Pakistan Army launched the main war in Jammu & Kashmir later that year. After a surprise strike on the 5 September, it nearly severed the arterial road from Pathankot to Jammu, which was then the only road connecting the state to the rest of India. Under instructions from Prime Minister Shastri, the Indian Army responded by invading Pakistani Punjab, an attack aimed directly at Lahore. The war ended with some gains for both sides along different parts of the border (including the Ceasefire Line that had been drawn on 1 January 1949). However, when Shastri met Pakistan's President Ayub Khan at Tashkent in the Soviet Union—a meeting that the US too backed—they agreed to accept the *status quo ante*. So, the Indian Army had to return the strategically and logistically vital Haji Pir pass in Jammu & Kashmir. The pass provides a direct and short road link between Uri in the Valley and Poonch. Shastri suffered a massive heart attack while he was still in Tashkent and died there.

Although Pakistan was openly at war against India in 1965, Pakistan's strategy that year also included a major deniable, covert component. By July that year, a large number of Pakistani activists, including some regular army men disguised as civilians, infiltrated the Valley and spread out to various parts of north Kashmir and Srinagar city. Many of them found sympathetic refuge in the Batmaloo region of the city. They spread propaganda and tried to mobilise Islamist and other youth. Their purpose[35] apparently was to instigate a popular revolt in order to declare independence of the state from India even while the two armies were engaged along the Ceasefire Line and the international border.

In this context, one of the most memorable aspects of the 1965 war is that, at that stage, most rural Kashmiris were chary of falling in line with this scheme. It was from villagers in the hills around Kashmir that governmental and military authorities first learnt of the infiltration. In many villages, ordinary Kashmiris risked their lives to report the presence of infiltrators to police stations or nearby army camps. Pakistan's Air Marshal Asghar Khan noted with disappointment that, 'it was presumed that widespread support existed within occupied Kashmir to make such a guerilla campaign a success.'[36] Brigadier Shaukat Qadir (retd.), who served in the Pakistan Air Force during the 1965 war, went further: 'Pakistan undertook Operation Gibraltar without preparing the grounds for it, or seeking guarantees of local support, or even attempting to assess the mood of the Kashmiri people.'[37]

Some Pakistani strategists may have hoped that China would pincer India from the east while it engaged India on the west. Trade and military links between Pakistan and China had grown apace from 1963; Pakistan's new foreign minister, Zulfiqar Ali Bhutto, forged links with China within weeks after China's war with India ended in December 1962. Through the next two decades, the Karakoram highway through Gilgit and the Aksai Chin plateau, which China had seized during 1962, became a major artery of the China-Pakistan relationship. India's decision in 1983 to secure its territorial hold on the Line of Control atop the Siachen glacier by maintaining troops there was partly a response to the military threat it faced in the northern parts of the state from this burgeoning and potentially menacing alliance.

Aspirations Remain Muffled in the Jammu Province

By the 1960s, the people of Jammu were still struggling to emerge from the multiple traumas they had suffered in 1947. The Dogra Rajputs of the area had lost the political dominance they had enjoyed over the entire state for a century. Not only that, the land reforms that had been implemented from 1949 on had robbed the landlord classes among them of dominance over the agrarian economy, without compensation.

The demography of the area too had changed drastically. Most parts of the Jammu province, stretching as far as Kishtwar to the northeast of Jammu and Poonch to its northwest, have a proud tradition of accommodation and inter-community harmony. Jammu-ites cherish the legend that the town was established when the king Jambu-lochan passed the river Tawi and saw a deer and a tiger drinking side by side, indicating a place so virtuous that none was another's enemy. Over the past millennium and more, peoples from the plains of India, both Hindu and Muslim, have found refuge in Jammu, Kishtwar, Poonch and some of the score of other small principalities in the region.

That tradition had suffered a rude shock in 1947-48. Amid genocidal rioting and arson, an overwhelming proportion of the Hindu and Sikh populations of Mirpur, Poonch principality and Muzaffarabad were killed, raped or displaced from those areas, which came under Pakistani control. Some of them resettled in areas on the Indian side of the battle lines, leading to the establishment of at least one new town at Sunderbani. On the other hand, a very large number of Muslims were killed, abducted and expelled from the areas around Jammu, Udhampur and, to some extent, Bhaderwah.

The traditional communal harmony of some of those areas was repaired; even half a century after both leading lights of the 1940s Bhaderwah had died, people spoke of how Malik Ghulam Rasool and Kotwal Swami Raj had fallen into each other's arms in the middle of Bhaderwah's main street and wept copiously in the wake of those riots. Muslims continued to act in Bhaderwah's annual Ramlila for decades—and the tradition of Muslims and Hindus participating in each other's weddings and funerals continued into the next century, right across the upper Chenab basin.[38]

Up the river from Doda town, Kishtwar has almost equal numbers of Hindus and Muslims. It remained an island of peace in 1947—one of the boons, some proud Kishtwaris would say, of being the resting place of the 17th century seer, Shah Fariduddin Baghdadi. Poonch too managed tenuously to retain communal peace, despite being in the vortex of the India-Pakistan war through 1948.

By the time a ceasefire was declared on 1 January 1949, Jammu province on the Indian side of the Ceasefire Line had overall turned from a Muslim majority area into a Hindu majority one. A very large proportion of the populations of the rural belts around Ranbirsinghpora (south of Jammu city) and adjacent Sialkot (farther south) in Pakistan had changed places; Ranbirsinghpora, hitherto a Gujjar Muslim belt, became a largely Jat Hindu area.

These traumatic changes combined with the question marks that now hung over the future of the state to unsettle political patterns in the Jammu province for several decades. At least educated, well-settled Hindus, the only articulate classes among the area's Hindus, had felt secure as part of the Dogra establishment. So, Hindus had never mobilised politically, except in support of the regime. The Muslim Conference had represented the aspirations of a large proportion of the region's Muslims. It had articulated demands for Muslims' rights but had not sought to overthrow the Dogra Maharaja—as Sheikh Abdullah of the National Conference had, through the Quit Kashmir agitation launched in May 1946. Indeed, on 19 July 1947, Chaudhary Hamidullah, acting president of the Muslim Conference, had called for the state to remain independent under the Maharaja.

By 1949, Muslim Conference leaders had gone (or been dispatched by Abdullah's dispensation) to Pakistan. The Maharaja, hitherto the bulwark of Jammu's social and political stability, had been marginalised to the extent that he left the state, appointing his young son as regent. His ouster was soon made formal, though: monarchy was abolished soon after a Constituent Assembly of the state came into being towards the end of 1951. The Constituent Assembly elected Karan Singh, the Maharaja's son, as *Sadr-e-riyasat* (head of state) on Nehru's birthday, 14 November 1952, instead of regent of the Dogra dynasty—after Nehru persuaded the young man to accept the change.[39] All this deeply unsettled Rajput and other upper caste Hindus of the region; from being part of the establishment, they now saw themselves in the role of a dispossessed minority. Moreover, they were deeply uneasy about the possibility of the state becoming a part of Pakistan, or independent under Abdullah's Kashmiri leadership.

Led by the widely respected Prem Nath Dogra, Jammu's first *sanghchalak*, they organised themselves under the banner of the Praja Parishad from 1 November 1947.[40] The title harked back to the Praja Sabha, through which the Maharaja had granted limited democratic expression since the mid-1930s. The organisation's agitations gained momentum from October 1952. Despite their abiding loyalty to the Dogra dynasty, Jammuites boycotted the reception the government organised in Jammu for the new *Sadr-e-riyasat* on 24 November,[41] and adopted the slogan, *'ek pradhan, ek nishan, ek vidhan'* (one chief, one flag, one law). The agitation reached a peak around the visit, in the summer of 1953, of the former Union cabinet minister Shyama Prasad Mukherji, who had launched the Bharatiya Jana Sangh the previous winter. Mukherji defied the law that required non-state subjects to obtain a permit to enter the state, was imprisoned, and died in jail. Many activists spent months underground, thousands were arrested, and 16 were killed in police action against their agitation.

The political sting had already been taken from the Praja Parishad, however. After many of its candidates' nomination papers were rejected, the Parishad had boycotted elections for the Constituent Assembly, allowing the National Conference to win all the seats in the house—all but one of them uncontested. Following back-room negotiations[42] preceding that politically loaded boycott, Girdhari Lal Dogra, adoptive son-in-law of Prem Nath Dogra, was installed as the only non-Valley member in the state cabinet, which was now reduced to just five members.

Since the erstwhile dominant classes among Jammu's Hindus desired to regain lost status, they were drawn to conservative politics. However, right-wing politics lost salience, partly owing to Girdhari Lal Dogra's participation in the regime. Prem Nath Dogra nominated Sheikh Abdur Rehman as his successor, but the latter was unable to garner wide support—perhaps the RSS had succeeded in positing Jammu's aspirations too sharply in communal terms for people to accept a Muslim leader. Also, the ruling party's land reforms had benefitted lower caste Hindus the most in the Jammu province, thus undermining attempts to build a pan-Hindu support base. On the other hand, Jammu's leading intellectuals, rooted in socialist idealism, sympathised with Kashmiri Muslim aspirations.

Since elections were generally flawed, results do not necessarily reflect popular trends. However, most political leaders, including many on the right, acknowledge that Jammuites were generally happy enough to go along with the Kashmir-based ruling party for much of the period after 1953. Particularly during Bakshi's tenure (1953-1963), the Jammu province remained largely complacent, reassured both by Bakshi's decidedly pro-India position and his dynamic development and welfare-oriented administration. That calm was shattered after he demitted office. A students' agitation at the Government Gandhi Memorial Science College was brutally put down. A contingent of Punjab Police, which had been called in to supplement the local force, fired indiscriminately in the third week of October 1966, in response to stone-pelting by the students.[43] Four students died. Versions of what the students' demands ranged from inadequate facilities for students to the demand for a separate university for Jammu to discrimination against the Jammu province to the influence of other students' agitations across north Indian campuses.

The regional discrimination issue was taken up by a group of socialists under the banner of the Jammu Autonomy Forum in the late 1960s. They made little progress but at least they were able to conduct their meetings peaceably. When Asoka Mehta had visited in 1955 to attend a socialist conference, their tent poles had been uprooted in Srinagar and delegates, including leaders, had been beaten by activists of Bakshi's regime, including the notorious Peace Brigade.[44]

Mistrust between activists of the Jana Sangh and socialists stymied political mobilisation in Jammu throughout this period. This mistrust became sharpest when they tried to work together in the Janata Party from 1977 to 1979. Although most of Janata's 19 MLAs were elected from the Jammu province in the 1977 assembly elections, other potential winners were defeated by sabotage within the party, including 'rebel' candidates. The socialist ginger group within Janata ensured that Abdul Ghani Lone from the Kashmir Valley was elected leader of the legislative group.[45] There was another agitation in Jammu during 1979 and Sheikh Abdullah, who was chief minister, received a delegation. Several commissions were appointed[46] to examine Jammu leaders' complaints that the state government discriminated against their province in the allocation of funds, developmental projects and the delimitation of constituencies. Not much came of the commissions' reports.

Gradually, other dimensions of political mobilisation began to emerge in the Jammu province. Owing to the unique status of the state guaranteed by Article 370 of the Indian constitution, reservations for scheduled castes and tribes did not initially extend to citizens of the state. Bhagat Amar Nath undertook an indefinite hunger strike in Batote as part of an agitation in 1970 for the extension of reservation for the state's scheduled castes, all of them in the Jammu province. The government ignored the agitation but, when Amar Nath died fasting on June 1 that year, the resultant anger forced the Sadiq regime to extend reservations for scheduled castes. Consequent on Amar Nath's sacrifice, a scheduled caste political leader, Bhagat Chhaju Ram, secured a ministry.

Demands by certain identity groups, including Gujjars, Bakarwals, Gaddis, Sippis and several groups in the Ladakh region for recognition as scheduled tribes began to be articulated soon after. Rallying under the leadership of Chaudhary Ghulam Hassan Lasanvi of the Congress,

Gujjars began to mobilise politically. There was an agitation in the Poonch district in 1972-73.[47] State governments, focused since the beginning on providing more educational and recruitment opportunities to the politically dominant and restive Kashmiri Muslims, resisted these demands. It was only under Governor's rule that these groups were recognised as scheduled tribes in 1991, and opportunities were reserved for them in 1992. Such was the enthusiasm for social justice that a Watal-Mochi Association was formed in Doda that year to demand reserved quotas for despised classes among Muslims.[48]

Agitations for development had emerged earlier in the upper Chenab valley, focusing on the need for education, access and development in the hitherto remote area. Quite soon after taking charge in 1947, Abdullah's initial emergency administration had separated this area from Udhampur Wazarat (district under Dogra rule) as the Doda district. The area, including Kishtwar, Bhaderwah and the Seeraz stretch from Ramban to Doda, lies between the Kashmir valley and Jammu. Among the leaders of an agitation in Doda in 1968 for a college and a district court, many were also active in the Plebiscite Front.[49] Many of the agitation's leaders were embroiled in criminal cases for years. Some were arrested under the state's draconian Public Safety Act, which allows imprisonment for two years without charge. Doda, where a high school had been established in 1949, only got a college in town in 1990.

A similar agitation in Kishtwar concentrated on the establishment of a college and a separate district. Although it has a rich ancient history—Kishtwaris claim that Kashmiri is a dialect of the Kishtwari language and that the fourth Buddhist conference took place at Nagsehi 20 km along the Kishtwar-Padar road—and has drawn migrants from as far as Bengal over the centuries, Kishtwar remained backward and neglected until the road from Doda became operational while Bakshi was the Prime Minister of the state. He rode a horse 60 km from Doda and promised a public meeting that he would return on a '*chaupanja*' (four-armed vehicle) the next year.

Beginning in 1969, Kishtwar's agitation gained momentum in 1974, when there were demonstrations through the summer, and institutions remained closed for a month. The agitation was led by non-partisan organisations, the Kishtwar Welfare Front and the Kishtwar Youth Front.[50] On Friday, 13 September, the police fired from the Sub-Divisional Magistrate's residence on demonstrators on Friday, killing four young men.[51] The last rites of the two Hindus and two Muslims took place at the same spot, beside Kishtwar's main street. The two graves and two *samadhis* there stand testimony to the town's fraternal tradition, which remained until the end of the 20th century. Nothing came of another agitation in 1981-82 either. Development got a push after Prime Minister Indira Gandhi's visit in 1983, when she laid the foundation stone of the Dul Hasti hydro-electric project in the vicinity of Kishtwar.[52] The project brought employment, income through compensation, and development. The town only got a college in 1991 (Governor Jagmohan announced it when he visited during Governor's rule in 1990), and became the headquarters of a separate district—the third largest in area in the state even after being divided from Doda—in the new century. Roads to interior areas of Kishtwar (then still a *tehsil*) were built after 1990, opening up areas like Padar, Chhatru and Wadwan to the world.

Ladakh Opens to the World

Ladakh had remained cut off from the rest of India, except for an infrequent air service, until the 1962 war. The need to defend India's northern frontier drove the construction of a road to Leh over the 3,529m (11,578 ft) Zoji La pass. It was completed in 1964. This particularly served the people of Kargil, the largest town on the route from Srinagar to Leh; the largely Shia people of this less developed area had hitherto had to walk long and treacherous journeys over terrain more than 10,000 feet high.

It is not as if Ladakh had overall been neglected, though. Nehru had grappled with the political demands of Ladakhi leaders since 1947. These had at that stage been posited in terms of Buddhist identity, since Buddhists dominated the area around Leh, which had been the summer capital of the district.[53] In 1947, Rigzin Kalon had demanded the creation of a separate Buddhist nation based on the principle of the Two-Nation Theory.[54] An alternative demand was raised by Kushak Bakula, a venerated Buddhist Rinpoche, who had recently returned after religious studies in Lhasa. He asked that Ladakh be separated from Kashmir and linked with East Punjab (the area that later became Himachal Pradesh).[55] Deeply conscious of the need to make Buddhists of Ladakh feel included and safe in the Indian Union, Nehru flew to Leh in 1949. Landing on rough gravel, he rode a horse 40 km to participate in the Hemis monastery's annual festival.

Rinpoche Bakula became the MLA for Ladakh and later a Member of Parliament. Politics at this stage was primarily feudal in Ladakh; common people often bowed when the monk passed on horseback. However, although he had been born in a royal home and then been discovered as a reincarnated lama, Bakula promoted education and rights among common people. His chief lieutenant, Sonam Wangyal, was a commoner. A similarly respected Shia clerical leader of Kargil, Agha Ibrahim Shah, served as vice-chairman of the district board.

Nehru continued to visit during the 1950s, sometimes with Indira Gandhi. Both donned traditional attire and danced with Ladakhis.

Strong patriotism developed, especially among Buddhist Ladakhis. Kushak Bakula's leadership, combined with the cultural-cum-political identification of Nehru and Indira Gandhi with Buddhist Ladakh, allowed a public perception of continuity with Leh's kingdom before it was defeated by the Dogra general, Zorawar Singh, around 1832. China's annexation of Tibet in 1959 no doubt contributed to the perception of well-being within India. Tibet and the Buddhist portion of Ladakh had for centuries been independent kingdoms, but were linked by a common religious tradition (reverence for the Dalai Lama being pivotal), trade, culture and genes. The patriotism of the Buddhist portion of Ladakh expressed itself from the beginning in demands to be separated from Kashmir (which sought autonomy or secession) and more closely integrated with the Union. In the early years, Ladakhis demanded an arrangement similar to that of the North-Eastern Frontier Area (NEFA). This later metamorphosed into a demand for a Union Territory.

A deep bond developed between the people of Ladakh and the Congress party, particularly the Nehru family. So strong was this bond that when dissent against the district leadership emerged among some young, educated (at this stage, generally Buddhist) Ladakhis, they did not organise as an alternative party. They called themselves the 'B Congress' and put up independent candidates against the party's official candidates. Even that required daring: not only did they invariably lose, they often faced public wrath. For example, even after Tsering Phunsog Shunoo, the B Congress' candidate against Bakula in 1962 had been trounced, his shop was stoned and he and his workers faced a social boycott.[56] So difficult was it to win on a non-Congress ticket from Ladakh that, when Sheikh Abdullah caused fresh elections in 1977, his cabinet colleague from Ladakh, Sonam Norbu, contested the assembly general elections on a Congress ticket before getting a nod from Indira Gandhi to rejoin Abdullah's National Conference government post-election.[57]

In cultural and economic terms, Ladakh changed radically after 1974, the year it was opened to tourists. Some monasteries shifted the traditional winter dates of their annual festivals to accommodate the summer influx of tourists. Since the area was projected as a Buddhist centre, and Buddhism had by then become popular in the West, Leh benefitted far more than the Kargil area. As the consciousness of relative neglect grew there, the district of Ladakh was divided in 1979 into Leh and Kargil districts. The Iranian revolution that year gave a further impetus to the self-confidence of Kargil's Shia majority, and there was more rapid social and economic change in that district during the 1980s.

As the aspirations of Ladakhis grew, a demand for scheduled tribe status was expressed. Two persons, including a lama, were killed in police firing at an agitation over this demand at Leh's Polo Ground on January 24, 1982. So intense was the demand that Congress leaders from the district went to Delhi to convey their dismay regarding their electoral prospects after Prime Minister Indira Gandhi stated during a visit in 1983 that an appellation would not make much difference. The government had been giving a great deal for the people of Ladakh and would continue to, she had said, but this did not assuage the demand for scheduled tribe status. There was talk of local Congress leaders boycotting the assembly elections that year[58] but an announcement soon followed over All India Radio that the Centre had decided to grant scheduled tribe status for Ladakhis. The legal formalities would have to be completed by the state assembly under the terms of Article 370 of the Constitution of India, the bulletin added. The Congress won the elections hands down again. Scheduled tribe status was finally extended, to most of the people of Ladakh, in 1992.

In the Kargil area, the Congress Party had tried to repackage itself in the 1980s as a champion of the common people. It had begun by adopting the leadership of influential clerics, whose word was virtually law among the less educated people of the generally backward mountainous area. By the late 1970s, the revived National Conference had won over the council of clerics who ran the Islamic School, the nerve centre of Kargil's politics. The Congress changed track during the 1980s, backing grassroots leaders instead of feudal clerics.

Mohammed Hasan, a young Lance Naik (sergeant) of the Ladakh Scouts, had resigned from the force during the 1960s to protest an officer's injustice in awarding gallantry medals.[59] In 1968, Hasan formed a Youth Federation in Kargil. Through the 1970s, it attracted many of the area's bright, dynamic youth who went on to earn professional qualifications. Although the Congress MLA in 1983, Kacho Mohammed Ali Khan, hailed from an erstwhile ruling family, he persuaded Hasan and his young associates to join the Congress. When Indira Gandhi visited Kargil in 1983, she took Hasan on to the stage at her public meeting and announced the merger of the Youth Federation in to the Congress. Hasan won the 1989 Lok Sabha elections from Ladakh, the first candidate from Kargil district to win the seat. Although he had contested as an independent, Hasan went to meet Rajiv Gandhi and said his respect for the Nehru-Gandhi family had not wavered, nor his loyalty to the party. Two decades later, he remained a PCC office-bearer.

The Historical Context of Integration

The key marker of Sadiq's term was the series of constitutional changes that integrated Jammu & Kashmir with the Indian Union. The symbolically most significant change occurred when, on 30 March 1965, the state Constitution was amended[60] to change nomenclature—from prime minister to chief minister, and from *Sadr-e-riyasat* to governor. On the political plane, Sadiq had already brought about a radical change: on the 26 January 1965, the National Conference converted itself into the Pradesh Congress Committee of the Indian National Congress.[61]

Parties primarily representing state interests were not yet common; apart from Kerala, the norm across the country still was Congress rule. However, this was about to change—the stage having been set by the very 'Kamaraj Plan' which had brought Sadiq to power. Indeed, the Congress split quite soon after the 'Kamaraj Plan' ended the accommodation of divergent political steams within the Congress; the conservative faction separated from the one dominated by Prime Minister Indira Gandhi in 1969. However, India's political realities required consensual accommodation of various aspirations, expressed along the axes of ideology as well as of regional, religious and caste identity. So, even as the Congress prepared to split, ideologically disparate groups such as socialists and the Hindutva-based Jana Sangh came together around the 1967 elections to provide an alternative to the Congress. Non-Congress coalition governments were formed across much of the north that year. Under the veneer of ideology, they represented caste-based aspirations to some extent. In the south too, Congress dominance was about to be severely eroded—by aspirations expressed vociferously along the axis of regional identity. 1965 was the very year when language riots erupted in Tamil Nadu, leading to the victory of the DMK in 1967.

That Sadiq's move went against the grain of current political trends is made more ironic by the fact that, when the All Jammu & Kashmir Muslim Conference was first established in 1932, it had been the second party with long-term significance, after the Akali Dal, to represent local interests rather than a pan-Indian agenda. Particularly after it turned itself into the National Conference in 1939, the party was the vehicle of the deeply embedded consciousness among people in the Kashmir Valley of having inherited an ancient and unique history.

No doubt Sadiq had in mind the ideological parallels between his party and the Congress since before independence. To celebrate the Congress' golden jubilee, the party[62] General Secretary, Maulana Masoodi, had moved a resolution at a public meeting chaired by Prem Nath Bazaz at Amira Kadal on December 28, 1935: 'This representative meeting of the people of Kashmir acknowledges the services rendered to the country by the Indian National Congress for the last 50 years and requests the President of the Congress that millions of people of Kashmir are with him in his fight for the freedom of our motherland.' It was passed unanimously.

Some Srinagar-based Pandits having written to Nehru of Abdullah's fierce rejection of Islamic chauvinism, Purshottam Das Tandon had visited in August 1936 to meet Abdullah and Bazaz. Khan Abdul Ghaffar Khan and K.M. Munshi had followed in 1937. Then, in January 1938, Abdullah and Bakshi went to meet Nehru at Peshawar, and took the train with him to Banu and Kohat. Links with the Congress got a boost at the 1938 State People's Conference, which the Congress convened at Udaipur for those living in principalities. Jammu & Kashmir was one of the largest and the Muslim Conference the most effective political movement in any of them. So, although Abdullah was in jail, Nehru, the conference president, got him elected in absentia as vice-president. During the conference, Nehru had taken the Muslim Conference delegation of 55 aside for several intensive discussions on the need to open the party to all Kashmiris.[63] Addressing the 1939 session at Tripura, Abdullah had stated that the state's people would not rest until it fulfilled the Congress' ideals.

Particularly after it converted itself into the National Conference, the party avowedly stood for secularism, socialist principles and development for all the people. These principles were articulated in radical terms in the *Naya Kashmir* manifesto, which the party adopted at its Sopore session in 1944.[64] The manifesto, which included a draft constitution for the state, vouchsafed the right to education for all students, equal rights for women and men, equality of opportunity, legal remedy, of religion and of rest.

However, in order to comprehend the ramifications of the merger of the National Conference into the Indian National Congress in 1965, it is important to understand that the agitations and agenda of the Muslim Conference/National Conference had since the 1930s been regional in scope, predicated on Kashmiri aspirations. More important, the presumption that both parties were committed to secular ideals, and so were ideologically suited to each other, is not adequately nuanced. To many in the Indian National Congress, the National Conference represented and was built on a robustly maintained equidistance from every religious affiliation. However, in the perception of many in Kashmir, the National Conference was meant to represent Muslim interests, while the Indian National Conference was primarily Hindu. Indeed, despite the various secularist statements by its leaders, religious identity had played a major part in mass mobilisation by National Conference cadres.

The reason for the National Conference's self-perception is to be found in Kashmir's socioeconomic patterns. The party had struggled against the exploitation and impoverishment of the Kashmiri masses under Dogra rule. A significant aspect of this struggle is that the impoverished masses in the Kashmir Valley were generally Muslim; they perceived the Dogras as a Hindu regime.[65] Thus, the Hindu-Muslim divide in the Valley was far more a consequence of class interests than anywhere else in the subcontinent. Under Sikh and Dogra rule from 1819 to 1947, the Valley's Hindus (including Pandits and settlers of Punjabi origin) and Jammu-based Dogras had dominated the agrarian economy; they were the large majority of landlords.[66] They also dominated trade, and owned many of the shawl looms and manufactories.[67] For a balanced perspective on Kashmir's history, it must be borne in mind that all this was, broadly speaking, the reverse of Afghan rule (1756-1819). Then, a Muslim even had sanction to order a Pandit to carry him on his back.

Soon after the appointment of a British Resident in Jammu & Kashmir from 1885, land settlement was conducted by British officers, A. Wingate followed by Walter Lawrence.[68] Among the effects of the settlement was a trend towards monetisation; for, after the maharaja's regime strongly resisted British insistence that revenue be collected in cash, the settlement officers decided that revenue should be collected partly in cash and party as a share of the crop. Monetisation strengthened the power of moneylenders. Shortages of grain, sometimes artificial, simultaneously strengthened revenue officials, who were often corrupt, exploitative and given to hoarding. The settlement also created a new landless class, members of which could not simply start cultivating fallow land. Since the landless were generally Muslims, and moneylenders and revenue officials were generally Hindu, resentment was often perceived, if not yet expressed, in communal terms.

Historian Mridu Rai notes that, 'the year 1907 marked a decisive shift when a group of "Representatives of Kashmiri Mussulmans" spoke out on behalf of Kashmir Muslims.... They brought to public notice the lack of Muslim representation in the state administration and suggested that only provision of adequate education would correct this situation.'[69] After a small number of Kashmiri Muslims had been educated in the first three decades of the 20th century, competition for jobs also emerged as a reason for conflict. Since almost all the available jobs were under the control of the government, this led to a sense of grievance against the state that was felt and often expressed in terms of communal identity.

Thus, although Kashmir's mass revolt in 1931 was projected by most Kashmiri leaders as directed against the Dogra regime, many Pandits remembered it as a communal riot; Hindu shops were looted in Maharaja Bazar in the heart of Srinagar, and Pandits were assaulted in the Vichar Nag area in the north of the city. Vichar Nag was home to many Hindu moneylenders, whose records were destroyed by protesters on 13 July 1931.[70] Naturally, the political processes that followed, including the formation of the Muslim Conference in 1932 and its exercise of limited democratic rights after 1934, had to negotiate the ambivalence of 1931—over whether it was a communal conflict, assertion of economic aspirations, or a nationalist struggle for independence. These paradigms often conflated in people's minds. For the broad masses of Kashmiri Muslims, economic aspirations were perceived in terms of Muslim repression by Hindus—and this was the mass perception that Sheikh Abdullah had to deal with as he sought to establish mass politics through the 1930s.

The party was forced to walk a tightrope with regard to its image and identity. Its public stances within Kashmir were marked by ambivalence over whether it represented secular neutrality or was a champion of Muslims' interests. That tightrope walk became more demanding once the Muslim Conference re-emerged through a split a year after the original party of that name converted itself into the National Conference. In response to questions raised in the party working committee regarding his speeches around the celebration of Id-i-Milad (the Prophet's birthday) in April 1940, Sheikh Abdullah had asserted, much to the chagrin of some of his party colleagues: 'I am a Muslim first and Muslim last.'[71]

The Pandit intellectual, Prem Nath Bazaz, had collaborated with Abdullah in the mid-1930s but, around this time, became a trenchant critic. Bazaz, who considered himself secular and Leftist, asserted that many of the Hindus and Sikhs who were given leading roles in the party after it converted itself from the Muslim Conference to the National Conference 'had worked for years in different communalist Hindu and Sikh organisations and had risen to eminence by espousing the cause of obscurantism, reaction and repression.... At best from being Hindu Communalists they could take a big jump and become Hindu Nationalists. Above that they could not rise. Though all of them paid extravagant tributes to secularism in season and out of season, that noble creed still existed only in name.'[72] He also asserted that, after changing its name, 'the high command of the National Conference was a house divided against itself. While the Hindu members were actively pulling in one direction, the Muslim members were vigorously pulling the other. At every step strife ensued.'[73] While both these assertions clearly are exaggerations, these observations from a Hindu Kashmiri indicate how much deeper resentful unease may have run in many Muslim minds.

The issue came to a head in 1940, soon after the Muslim Conference converted itself into the National Conference, over the two-language formula for school education. Even though the Zakir Hussain committee had not recommended it, Gopalaswami Ayyangar, who was then the prime minister of the Jammu & Kashmir state, had introduced the option for students in state schools to write in either the Devanagari or the Persian script; the language was to be simple Urdu. Historian Chitralekha Zutshi notes that, 'The National Conference's stance on the medium of instruction issue was double-edged, and again illuminated the inability of its leadership to reconcile the "religious" and "regional" aspects of its ideology.'[74] So bitter did the debate become that several leading Muslims as well as Pandits left the National Conference over the issue. Among other issues that rankled with some Pandits was that the National Conference voted for a cut motion, moved by the rival Muslim Conference, opposing Pandits' strong hold over government jobs.

To understand the perilous consequences on the Kashmiri psyche of merging the National Conference into the Indian National Congress in 1965, one must realise that many Kashmiris had been suspicious and uneasy ever since the 1930s about the efforts of some party leaders to align the policies of the National Conference with those of the Congress. Bazaz's book—published a decade before the merger—notes with opprobrium that, even in 1939-40, the prime agenda of the National Conference's new Hindu and Sikh leaders was to bring the party in line with the Congress. He views this as unacceptable, painting the Congress as a Hindu communalist organisation: 'In trying to bring the National Conference under the hegemony of the Congress leaders, the Hindu and Sikh members were not prompted by any burning desire for freedom or even by the wish to secularise state politics. They only felt happy that by doing so they were helping the cause of Indian Nationalism which, despite the statements of the Congress leaders to the contrary, was becoming another name for Hindu Nationalism. Clearly it was the prompting of the communal mentality of the Hindus which was cleverly presented in a nationalist secular garb.' Such assertions, albeit skewed, indicate the depth of suspicion among many leading politicians in the state regarding the agenda of the Congress and their suspicions regarding hitching their politics to that of the pan-Indian Congress.

Given these misapprehensions regarding the Congress, Abdullah had quite easily been able to paint the Congress and the Indian establishment in Hindu communalist colours when, in the early 1950s, he sought a treacherously difficult path towards independence. He stated on more than one occasion that he was deeply worried about the future of the Muslim majority in his state after Nehru. In April 1952—even while the New Delhi agreement regarding the special privileges that would be vouchsafed to the state government was being tortuously negotiated between delegations led by him and Maulana Abul Kalam Azad on behalf of the Union government—Abdullah chose to make statements of this sort during a public meeting at Ranbirsingpora.[75] The venue was notable in that the border with Pakistan was a few minutes' drive away.

This sort of rhetoric set the stage for party workers to fan anti-Hindu feelings among Kashmiris on the argument that they belonged to a Muslim nation that had fallen under the suzerainty of a Hindu power. The idea of Kashmiri identity had increasingly conflated with Muslim identity in many Kashmiri Muslim minds since the beginning of Maharaja Hari Singh's reign in 1925. This paradigm of Kashmiri nationalism gained strength after Abdullah's arrest, more so after the formation of the Plebiscite Front (1955). It was repressed by state action and so remained largely undercover, but the relic crisis and the propaganda of Pakistani infiltrators in 1965 gave it greater salience—and confidence.

Although rancour was to a large extent expressed in terms of Muslim *vs.* non-Muslim, it also expressed itself along the regional paradigm—the Kashmir Valley *vs.* other parts of the state. It fanned resentment in both Jammu and Ladakh, lending strength to the Praja Parishad and (over time) the Ladakh Buddhist Association respectively. That only created a vicious cycle of communal reactions, each side seeing the expressed insecurities and resentments of the other as proof of ill-intent.

Ironically, then, political and geopolitical events post-independence had given belated salience to the rhetoric of the All India Muslim League and the All Jammu & Kashmir Muslim Conference, all of which was just taking effect around the time Sadiq merged his party into the Congress.

Communal and Inter-regional Conflict

The impression that India, and specifically the *Congress Party,* represented the old order of socioeconomic repression spurred two subliminal fears following the merger of the National Conference into the Congress. First was apprehension that the Kashmiri identity would be repressed. At this stage, this identity was seen as primarily Muslim, and linked to Pakistan. The second fear was related: a perceived threat to Muslims' recruitment to government jobs.

Kashmir's 1931 revolt had occurred when a miniscule educated class had begun to emerge among Kashmiri Muslims and compete with Pandits for jobs.[76] That competition had eased during the 1950s, when the state government made a great effort to employ and promote Muslims. An extraordinarily efficient administrator, Bakshi Ghulam Mohammed had been able to draw huge funds from the Union government in order to initiate a variety of projects and to establish new institutions, including a medical college and an engineering college. These not only educated large numbers but also provided professional and other jobs. Departments of government too expanded considerably to employ larger numbers. While the new opportunities were welcomed, resentment began to be felt in a communal framework among those who failed to get admission to educational institutions or employment in the government. As increasing educational opportunities pushed up the number of Muslim aspirants, a sense of distress had grown among many Pandits by the mid-60s. Networks of contacts and relationships in various branches of the administration had previously given the Pandit community immense influence. Competition between new, aspirant members of the middle class, many of them Muslim, and the established middle class (which was one of the causes of the revolt of 1931) returned.

Such was the conflation of religion and politics by the late 1960s, that there was at times opposition to the burial of Congress workers in Muslim graveyards. Riots had erupted in some parts of the Valley when Parmeshwari Devi, a young woman of the Pandit community eloped with a Muslim. Although she went with him to a court in Kupwara to declare before a judge that she had married him voluntarily[77], the marriage sparked violent reactions. No doubt resentment caused by competition for jobs and changing social relations (during Dogra rule, Valley Muslims had generally been obsequious in the presence of Pandits—reversing the pattern of late 18th century Afghan rule) had more to do with the violence than the elopement itself.

Ironically, the merger of the National Conference into the Congress did not pacify political insecurities in the Jammu and Ladakh regions of the state either. Those regions continued to perceive the state's ruling party and government as primarily representing the interests of Kashmiri-speaking citizens of the Valley.

Ladakh's Buddhists had backed the Congress as their link with the Indian Union as well as their bastion against domination by Kashmir. When chief minister Mir Qasim visited Ladakh in 1974, he was received with black flags. Although he belonged to the Congress Party, in Ladakh, Qasim represented Kashmiri domination within the state. The Congress central leadership did not heed the warning signal in that demonstration. By allowing MLAs elected on Congress tickets to participate in National Conference cabinets through the 1980s, Congress paved the way for the Ladakh Buddhist Association to emerge as the leading political vehicle for Ladakhi Buddhists' aspirations during the 1990s.

The resentment expressed by Leh Buddhists at this stage helped the National Conference, which Sheikh Abdullah revived a couple of years later, to wean Kargil's Muslim majority away from the Congress. The real concern in Kargil, where the tradition of communal harmony runs deep, was regional neglect within the then single Ladakh district. Again, however, religious identity was used as a vehicle of political mobilisation.

Agitations surfaced in Jammu from 1966 onward, and then in Doda and Kishtwar. The involvement of Plebiscite Front activists in the 1968 Doda agitation was spurred by resentment over integration and the merger of the National Conference into the Congress. On the other hand, protests over Parmeshwari Devi's marriage were fuelled by Jammu politicians' rhetoric about discrimination against the Jammu province. This touched a chord among people in the Jammu province and resulted in the agitation being prolonged.[78] Affiliates of the Rashtriya Swayamsewak Sangh, including the Bharatiya Jana Sangh, stirred the already seething cauldron, turning political issues and regional concerns into communal ones. Although the Jana Sangh never won a substantial number of seats in the Jammu province, except in exceptional circumstances, it persevered in its attempts to win over Jammu citizens to its ideology.

In 1968, agitations erupted, mainly in Anantnag and Srinagar, against provocative statements regarding Muslims by Balraj Madhok, leader of the Jana Sangh. That agitation brought into the limelight an Anantnag schoolboy called Shabir Shah, who was aged 14 at the time. Over much of the next quarter-century, he was an icon of Kashmiris' extra-constitutional struggle for secession, which had already begun during the 1960s.

Insurgent Reactions

Called Al Fateh, Kashmir's first guerrilla group became active from 1967. Al Fateh included some of the young men who had come into contact with Pakistani infiltrators in 1965.[79] It was led by men like Ghulam Rasool Zahgir, whose anti-India activities continued after the war with a Red Kashmir movement[80]—which specialised in marking the state red on maps and sending such maps to politicians, officials and others. A few members of the nascent group had crossed the Ceasefire Line soon after the war to seek arms and training. The Pakistan Army's General Headquarters obliged, furnishing small arms, grenades and pencil bombs for the group. The group murdered a security man on a bridge in the centre of Srinagar[81] and robbed a couple of banks,[82] but nothing much came of the group after most of its activists were arrested by early 1971. They were thus unable to damage India with terrorist attacks in tandem with the India-Pakistan war in December that year.

Al Fateh was not the only insurgent group of the time. Some were one-man armies, like Azam Inquilabi,[83] but only one of the groups formed around that time made an impact in the long term. This was the Jammu & Kashmir National Liberation Front (JKNLF), which was formed in 1966.[84] Its leading lights included several educated young men based in Muzaffarabad and other areas across the Ceasefire Line, including some Leftists. Among its founder members was Maqbool Butt, who hailed from Trehgam in the north of the Valley. He had trekked across the Ceasefire Line in 1958, aged 22, and worked for a while as a journalist. Like many others who crossed the Ceasefire Line (and later the Line of Control) passionately committed to Pakistan, he switched his preference to independence. The JKNLF stood for a secular ideology and, for the first time, openly espoused independence for Jammu & Kashmir from both India and Pakistan.

Sheikh Abdullah too had perhaps sought something approaching independence from India for Jammu & Kashmir, as is evident from his interviews to correspondents of newspapers based in Britain and the US, and a cable of US Ambassador Loy Henderson to the State Department.[85] Henderson cabled that, 'in discussing future Kashmir, Abdullah was vigorous in restating his opinion that it should be independent, that overwhelming majority of population desired this independence, and that he had reason to believe that some Azad Kashmir leaders desired independence and would be willing to cooperate if there were reasonable chance such cooperation would result in independence.'[86]

As early as 1949, Michael Davidson, correspondent for the *Observer* and the *Scotsman*, quoted Abdullah as saying that, 'accession to either side cannot bring peace. We want to live in friendship with both the dominions. Perhaps a middle path between them with economic cooperation with each will be the only way of doing it. However, an independent Kashmir must be guaranteed not only by India and Pakistan, but also by Britain, the US and other members of the UN.'[87]

Then, on the 1st of November 1951, Michael James wrote in the *New York Times* after an interview with Abdullah[88]: 'Hints have been made that once the Constituent Assembly begins to function, there is a possibility of creating an opposition to accession to India and creation of what would be a popular complete independence movement.'[89] Another indication that Abdullah's objective was independence rather than merger with Pakistan is that the Plebiscite Front, which was formed in 1955 through the efforts of Abdullah's lieutenant, Mirza Afzal Beg, did not actually demand a plebiscite; a plebiscite under the terms of the April 1948 Security Council resolution would have provided no option other than accession to either India or Pakistan. Instead, the Plebiscite Front's rhetoric was woven around an un-elucidated demand for 'self-determination'.

The JKNLF's aspiration differed from Abdullah's not only insofar as it was militant, and that its secessionist agenda was clearly stated. It also differed in its provenance. Ever since the first provisional working committee of the National Conference was announced after the party was renamed in 1939, leaders from Mirpur, Poonch and Jammu had complained that the new party represented the aspirations of Valley-based, Kashmiri-speaking people. Very few people in what Pakistan calls 'Azad Kashmir'[90] speak Kashmiri. Pathwari and Gojari are the mother tongues of many in those areas. It is in this 'Azad Kashmir' area that the JKNLF was founded and drew support.

Maqbool Butt returned to the Valley in 1968 to promote the secularist independence ideology of his new organisation. At this stage, however, sentiment in the Valley was strongly pro-Pakistan – competition for jobs, the Plebiscite Front's campaign and the recent constitutional and political integration having combined to belatedly give salience to the Two-Nation theory in Kashmir.

The organisation finally became effective after it changed its name to the JKLF in the 1980s. The word 'National' may have been dropped under the influence of the Pakistani military establishment, which was preparing at that stage to train and arm this organisation to launch a freedom struggle in the Valley. The Pakistani establishment may have wanted to leave ambiguous the issue of whether Kashmir was to be a separate nation, as per the JKNLF charter, or only to be liberated from India in order to be merged into Pakistan.

Political Challenges

Bakshi had kept a tight lid on secessionist politics. One of his strategies was adroit political management. For example, he installed a 22-year old nephew of Mirwaiz Yousuf Shah as acting *Mirwaiz* when Yousuf

Shah, who had apparently become disillusioned[91] after serving briefly as President of 'Azad Kashmir,' sent messages that he would like to return.[92] Bakshi's other strategy was suppression, harassment, torture and unreported detention by the state police and the Peace Brigade militia. This only repressed aspirations and sentiments. Resentment brewed behind the veil of public silence. The relic crisis and the propaganda of Pakistani infiltrators in 1965 helped to bring that resentment into the open during Sadiq's rule—in social conflict, political agitations and insurgent violence.

There was some limited churning within the mainstream political arena too, including political instability within the state Congress unit. Bakshi retained enough ground support to defeat the Congress candidate in the 1967 Lok Sabha elections. So potent was the challenge from Bakshi that Sadiq too resorted to rigging the assembly elections that year. Particularly in the Anantnag district, an extraordinary number of nomination papers were rejected.

There was even a revolt against Sadiq among the members of the legislative assembly. According to Mir Qasim, who eventually succeeded Sadiq, a majority of party legislators went to meet Prime Minister Indira Gandhi in New Delhi.[93] They had gone to plead that Qasim be made chief minister. However, as she sought to consolidate a Congress Party much weakened by the 1967 elections across much of north India, the prime minister was unwilling to brook factions or dissidence against the party leadership. According to Qasim, the legislators were not even asked to sit. They left her office a couple of minutes after they entered.

Two other sources of political challenge emerged during this period. First, some of Abdullah's supporters in the Plebiscite Front contested by-elections as independents—and Mrs. Abdullah campaigned vigorously for an independent candidate, Shamim Ahmed Shamim, to defeat Bakshi in the 1971 Lok Sabha elections.[94] Second, the Jamaat-e-Islami decided to contest local bodies' elections in 1969.

Units of the Jamaat-e-Islami Hind, which was formed in 1941, had separated at partition. It remained dedicated to preaching the relatively Puritanical ideas of the founder, Maulana Sayyed Abul Ala Maududi. However, it did not follow his footsteps when he led his group towards overt politics in Pakistan. A separate Jamaat-e-Islami unit was formed in Kashmir under the leadership of Saduddin Tarabali a little before Sheikh Abdullah's arrest.[95] Some of its early adherents had lost social standing with the destruction of the feudal order when radical land reforms were implemented. In the next phase, the organisation attracted some of those who were able to move from agriculture into the emergent middle class, particularly professionals such as doctors, engineers and lawyers. Having initially remained apolitical, restricting itself to preaching Maududi's ideas focused on the afterlife, the group's network of dedicated workers in different parts of the Valley had established itself strongly enough by the late 1960s to consider entering the political arena.

After debating the question in the organisation's *shoura* (council), the Jamaat-e-Islami decided in 1969 to participate in elections—beginning with local bodies' elections that year.[96] Its ground support was never strong enough to bring it victory in most parts of the state. However, its devoted cadres helped it to make a mark in election campaigns and polling in parts of the Valley such as the major apple belts in Sopore and Shopian. After back-room negotiations, five Jammat-e-Islami candidates among a total of 10 opposition candidates were allowed to win seats during the assembly elections in 1972.[97] Qari Saifuddin became the leader of the Jamaat-e-Islami group in the assembly. Sopore—which other Kashmiris sometimes referred to as 'little London' at this stage owing to the rich profits its apple orchards were earning[98]—elected the relatively younger Ali Shah Geelani. These electoral victories allowed the Jamaat-e-Islami to spread its message more openly and to establish more schools. Although Geelani was the only member of the organisation to win a seat in the next assembly, the group was able to strengthen its network of activists across much of the Valley over the next decade.

A Deal

Mir Qasim realised his ambition to be chief minister when Sadiq died at the end of 1971, but associated himself almost immediately with a project to hand over power to Sheikh Abdullah. Several factors had combined to create a conducive atmosphere for this. The third war between India and Pakistan was underway when Sadiq died, and it gave India a decisive victory. There was no possibility of Pakistani support for secessionist projects in Kashmir in the foreseeable future. Not only that, Prime Minister Indira Gandhi negotiated an agreement with Pakistan President Zulfiqar Ali Bhutto regarding Jammu & Kashmir. Under the Simla Agreement, the two countries converted the Ceasefire Line into a 'Line of Control' and undertook to settle the issue bilaterally. That seemed to rule out any further scope for mediation or intervention by bodies such as the UN.

Abdullah's stances had changed since 1968, when he had not welcomed an offer by Jai Prakash Narayan, one of the socialist icons of India's freedom struggle, to campaign across the country for renewed autonomy. Narayan had made the offer while inaugurating the State People's Convention which Abdullah, who was not strictly confined in those years, had convened in Srinagar in 1968. A range of secessionist politicians, including Mirwaiz Mohammed Farooq, Maulana Abbas Ansari and Abdul Rashid Kabuli of the Jammu & Kashmir Youth and Students' League, attended that convention. After some internal debate, the Jammu Autonomy Front also participated.[99]

Having spurned Narayan's offer in 1968, Abdullah had by 1971 nominated his chief political aide, Mirza Afzal Beg, to negotiate with G. Parthasarathi, the Government of India's nominee. Indira Gandhi also spoke directly with Abdullah. At the successful conclusion of those talks, Parthasarathi and Beg signed 'Agreed Conclusions' on 13 November 1974.[100] Sheikh Abdullah returned to power as chief minister of the state on 25 February 1975.[101]

He had been willing to take power as leader of the Congress, since the party had a commanding majority in the state assembly. He even donned a Gandhi cap, paid the subscription and took the oath of membership at a small function in the compound of the secretariat in Jammu. However, the Congress' central leadership decided at the last moment that he should lead a government with the support of the Congress Legislature Party rather than be elected as its House leader.[102] So Abdullah and Mirza Afzal Beg became independent members. The relationship between the Congress Party and the four-member cabinet was not comfortable. They took several months to sort out how many ministers the Congress leadership would nominate and how many Abdullah would select. A committee was established to review the application of central laws to the state since 1965, but its members did not agree.

Indira Gandhi declared during a visit to Srinagar in the summer of 1975 that the Congress was there to stay. The Plebiscite Front was wound up on 5 July 1975 and Sheikh Abdullah revived the National Conference in 1976. Soon after the Congress was defeated in the 1977 Lok Sabha elections, the Congress Legislature Party withdrew support to Abdullah. However, Governor L.K. Jha accepted the chief minister's advice to dissolve the house and call fresh elections. For the first time, the state was placed under Governor's rule on 26 March 1977.[103]

Abdullah now fully resuscitated his party. The veteran leaders of the Janata Party initially sought an alliance with the National Conference, but refused when Abdullah offered them only constituencies without a Muslim majority. Instead, Janata accepted some of Abdullah's leading detractors, including Maulvi Mohammed Farooq (the Mirwaiz), Ghulam Mohiuddin Kara and Abdul Ghani Lone, as Janata's leading faces in the state.[104] However, Janata leaders insisted that Maulana Masoodi, who had been a member of India's

Constituent Assembly and was the general secretary of the National Conference in its early years, should head the state unit.

The Congress was squeezed between the competitively communal rhetoric of these powerful new parties, the revived National Conference and Janata, in the state assembly elections of June 1977. Many Kashmiris responded emotionally when word spread that Sheikh Abdullah was critically ill; he won a handsome victory across the state.

Kashmir's response to Sheikh Abdullah's death on 8 September 1982 was even more emotional. Lakhs of people went to pour out their sorrow as his remains lay in state at the Polo Ground in Srinagar—and many were injured in stampedes while the body was being taken to a picturesque spot beside the Dal lake for burial. The President, the Vice-President and the Prime Minister of India all attended the funeral.

To make sense of Kashmiris' sometimes contradictory responses to Abdullah, and to the state's association with India, is a challenge. There was deep appreciation for the transformation he caused in the lives of ordinary rural Kashmiris through the land reforms he initiated in 1949—and for the self-confidence he gave to the broad mass of Kashmiri Muslims. His work earned support for his party even a quarter-century after his death. However, many Kashmiris simultaneously reviled him for having made a deal to return to power within the framework of the integration Sadiq had wrought. Coming as it did just when large numbers of Kashmiris had finally been persuaded by subversive anti-India rhetoric over the decade since 1965, Abdullah's deal with Indira Gandhi was generally seen as a 'sell out.' Abdullah's critics were most often from urban and the new professional classes in both urban and rural areas.

By and large, people had become confused and later angry over the tightrope Abdullah had walked since the 1930s on whether he stood primarily for the mass of Muslims then at the bottom of the feudal hierarchy or for secular development, or for Kashmiri nationalism or for accession to India.

An Unsettled Situation

Abdullah's eldest son, Farooq, succeeded him as chief minister. Continuing his father's policy, he refused to ally his party with the Congress for the 1983 assembly elections. In fact, some Kashmiri boys made obscene gestures while Indira Gandhi was addressing a public meeting at Iqbal Park in Srinagar. While campaigning in other parts of the state,[105] the prime minister voiced her concern about the welfare and security of Pandits' in the Valley. There was a certain degree of communal polarisation in the state, and the Congress won a large number of seats in the Jammu province. Overall, the National Conference won a handsome majority in the assembly.

Farooq Abdullah, who was re-elected leader of the ruling party on 11 June 1983, now sought to chart a course not only independent of the Congress, but antagonistic to it. In this, his political strategy differed from his father's. Although Sheikh Abdullah had not agreed to the alliance partnership that the Congress had proposed for the 1980 Lok Sabha elections, he had campaigned for the Congress that year. Farooq Abdullah, on the other hand, now began to build a relationship with parties ranged against the Congress across the country. Less than four months after the 1983 elections, the National Conference hosted a three-day conclave of leaders of the national opposition in Srinagar, from October 3. It was part of a series of joint opposition rallies that were held in places like Hyderabad and Calcutta.

Around this time, the political, geopolitical and economic resentments that had simmered in the late 1960s, but had been damped by the outcome of the 1971 war, were manifest again. Resentment against the politically and administratively inexperienced Farooq Abdullah succeeding his father dovetailed with pan-Islamist sentiments. The Iranian Revolution in 1979 and the 'jihad'-centred response, led by the US and Pakistan, to the Soviet invasion of Afghanistan, also in 1979, spurred strong sentiments regarding the resurgence of Islam, and threats to the *ummah* (global community of Muslims), in many Muslim communities, including Kashmiri society.[106]

Two classes of Kashmiris resented Abdullah's legacy. The first was the inner city population, mainly artisans concentrated in downtown Srinagar. They gained little after independence. Not only that, they watched the rural poor, whom they had hitherto treated with contempt, rise in economic and social standing—and compete with the city for white-collar jobs. Although the market for their artisanal produce—carpets, shawls, papier mache and walnut wood articles—grew, profits went largely to a relatively small number of wholesalers and retailers. Concentrated in downtown Srinagar, this class was the bedrock of the Mirwaiz' support.

The second group that became alienated was the new class of professionals and bureaucrats, often the first generation in their families to be educated and employed. They absorbed the narrative of rights denied to Muslims in a Hindu-dominated country. Many of them turned to the Jamaat-e-Islami. A faction that was influenced by Maulana Maududi's later ideas involving what has been called 'political Islam' sought to lead the branch of Jamaat-e-Islami in Jammu & Kashmir toward that path. Ali Shah Geelani, the leader of that faction, forced an election for the organisation's Amir (head) in 1985.

He was defeated after an electoral college was formed for the election; however, his political line had gained currency among a large section of the Jamaat-e-Islami cadre.[107] Already in 1982, the year Abdullah died, the Jamaat's youth wing had made an impact through its Wahadat (unity) conference at Srinagar's Jehangir Hotel.

Kashmiri society and common people's aspirations had been largely ignored in the politics and geopolitics that had occurred over Kashmir after the relic crisis—integration, the two wars, the Simla agreement, the agreement between Sheikh Abdullah and the Union government, and the choice of Abdullah's successor. There had been little effort to convince the people about the suitability of these various moves. Nor did either the state or the Union government focus on the growing socioeconomic frustrations among the people—over corruption, nepotism, stifled political dissent and, most acutely felt, the competition for jobs. The absence of a viable economic growth model caused conflict between both religious (Pandit-Muslim in the Valley) and regional (Kashmir-Jammu) communities, and would in time lead to eruptions of conflict on both axes. The perception that disproportionate numbers of Pandits—who continued to be generally better educated than Muslims—were recruited in government fuelled ire against India, which continued to be perceived as Hindu and therefore partial to Hindus.

The Indian team was heckled, abused and showered with rotting tomatoes during a cricket match against the West Indies in Srinagar.[108] A young activist from Batmaloo, where Pakistani infiltrators had received the warmest welcome in 1965, ran onto the field and dug up the pitch during lunch. In early February, 1984, JKNLF activists abducted and killed an Indian diplomat in London. Amid the public revulsion against this terrorism, Maqbool Butt was hanged in New Delhi's Tihar jail on 11 February 1984. Butt had been sentenced to death after a bank manager was killed during a JKNLF heist in 1968, in which Butt had participated. He had escaped across the Ceasefire Line but was recaptured when he returned in 1976.[109]

In such an unsettled context within the Valley and abroad, the Prime Minister considered Farooq Abdullah's participation in opposition politics at the national level untenable. Perhaps she regretted having backed Farooq Abdullah's succession, even though his sister, Khalida, wife of the rival claimant, had been her friend for years. Indira Gandhi now decided that Khalida's husband, G.M. Shah, should be given a chance to rule the state. The former Lt. Governor of Delhi, Jagmohan, became the governor of Jammu & Kashmir on 26 April 1984. That summer, the National Conference split as 14 MLAs vouchsafed their support for G.M. Shah. Farooq Abdullah's government was dismissed on 2 July and, with the support of the Congress. All 14 MLAs who had left his party were installed as ministers in a new cabinet led by Shah.

People, already feeling oppressed by a miasma of factors ranging from local maladministration to geopolitical trends, revolted. Street demonstrations were so fierce that curfew had to be imposed frequently. According to some of the advisors who were close to her at the time, the Prime Minister had realised that the change that the Congress had backed in this volatile state's administration had been ill-advised. According to one of them, she had said even before the change was brought about that one had to be very cautious in dealing with Kashmir.[110] However, she was pre-occupied that summer with the fall-out of the army's Operation Blue Star in Punjab. She was assassinated less than four months after Shah had been installed as Jammu & Kashmir's chief minister.

Endnotes

1. The Official Website of Jammu & Kashmir.
2. The other two grave crises occurred in 1931 and 1990.
3. Devdas, David (2007). *In Search of a Future: The Story of Kashmir*. Penguin.
4. The plan proposed joint management by India and Pakistan of the Valley of Kashmir and some adjoining areas, including Muzaffarabad. A version of this idea had formed the plan proposed in 1953 by UN Representative for Jammu & Kashmir, Owen Dixon.
5. The state's first Prime Minister (from March 1948) had been in prison since August 1953. He was released for a few months in 1958 and in 1964-65.
6. The Plebiscite Front was formed in August 1955 following efforts by Mirza Afzal Beg, who had been released from prison on health grounds.
7. Bazaz, Prem Nath (1954). *The History of Struggle for Freedom in Kashmir*, (first edition). New Delhi: Kashmir Publishing Company.
8. Official Website of Jammu & Kashmir.
9. Ibid.
10. Ibid.
11. Bazaz, Prem Nath (1954). *The History of Struggle for Freedom in Kashmir* (first edition). New Delhi: Kashmir Publishing Company.
12. Mir Qasim, who was chief minister of the state between 1971 and 1975 and had been an influential political worker since the 1940s, told the author in an interview in 1999 that, while Abdullah still ruled, Trilochan Dutt, who became an influential cabinet minister in the state, wrote to Nehru asking to start a Congress unit in at least Jammu, but Nehru refused even that.

13. Devadas, David. *In Search of a Future: The Story of Kashmir.*
14. Author's interview with M.L. Fotedar, who was at the time a young member of Nehru's staff.
15. Mullik, B.N., *Kashmir: My Years with Nehru.* New Delhi: Deep Publications. Mullik was at the time Director of the Intelligence Bureau.
16. The Official Website of Jammu & Kashmir.
17. After a split later in 1964, the Action Committee yielded the Awami Action Committee, the political organisation of the Mirwaiz of Kashmir.
18. Dewan, Parvez (2008). *A History of Jammu.* Manas Publications.
19. Mullick, B.N., *My Years with Nehru.* New Delhi: Deep Publications.
20. Shastri had resigned along with other senior leaders the previous summer under the decision that came to be known as the Kamraj Plan.
21. Author's interview with Mohiuddin Sofi, Masoodi's private secretary, in 2001-02.
22. The Official Website of Jammu & Kashmir.
23. Quoted verbatim in 'Autobiography' by Karan Singh, former *sadr-e-riyasat* of the state and thereafter a senior Congress leader.
24. The author interviewed Sofi Mohiuddin, who was personal secretary to Maulana Masoodi. Masoodi had been general secretary of the Muslim Conference since it was established, and then of the National Conference after the Muslim Conference converted itself in to the National Conference. This was published in Devadas, David (2007). *In Search of a Future: The Story of Kashmir.* Penguin.
25. The Official Website of Jammu & Kashmir and author's interview with Sofi Mohiuddin.
26. Author's interview with Sofi Mohiuddin.
27. *A Discovery of India,* Jawaharlal Nehru.
28. Lamb, Alistair (1993). *Kashmir, A Disputed Legacy, 1846-1990.* Karachi: Oxford University Press. Operation Gibraltar was Pakistan's code name for the '65 infiltration. Moe-i-Muqaddas refers to the Hazratbal relic.
29. Khan, M. Akbar (1975). *Raiders in Kashmir.* Islamabad: National Book Foundation.
30. Ibid.
31. Korbel, Josef. *Danger in Kashmir.* Princeton University Press
32. Entry on the Northern Light Infantry in the website *GlobalSecurity.org*
33. Swami, Praveen. *The Kargil War.* New Delhi: LeftWord Books.
34. Ibid.
35. Author's interviews with Maulana Abbas Ansari, who had become convener of the Action Commitee, and with Mohiuddin Sofi, who had been personal secretary to the National Conference's first General Secretary, Maulana Masoodi.

36. Khan, Air Marshal Asghar (1979). *The First Round.*
37. Article published in *Rediff News*, September 9, 2005.
38. Author's interview in 2010 with Kameshwar Nath Razdan, patron of Bhaderwah's Sanatan Dharam Sabha.
39. Jawaid Alam (ed.) (2006). "Jammu & Kashmir 1949-64", *Select Correspondence between Jawaharlal Nehru and Karan Singh*. Penguin.
40. Author's interview with Professor Hari Om, former head of the department of history, Jammu University
41. Bazaz, Prem Nath (1954). *The History of Struggle for Freedom in Kashmir* (first edition), New Delhi: Kashmir Publishing Company.
42. Devadas, David (2007). *In Search of a Future: The Story of Kashmir.*
43. Author's interviews with Ved Bhasin, editor, *Kashmir Times*, who was trying to negotiate peace at the spot, Manmohan Wazir, who was deputy inspector-general of police in Jammu at the time, and Prof Hari Om, Retd. Head of the Department of History, Jammu University.
44. Author's interview with Ved Bhasin, one of the leading organisers (editor of the daily *Kashmir Times* in that period, and later General Secretary of the state Janata Party).
45. Ibid.
46. Among them, the Gajendragadkar Commission and the Sikri Commission.
47. Author's interview with Poonch-based writer K.D. Maini.
48. Author's interview with Mushtaq Ahmed Sheikh, president of the Association.
49. Akbar Kichloo, one of the leaders of that agitation, told the author that the intention was to expose the top leadership of the Plebiscite Front, who were narrowly focused on self-interest and not on development.
50. Author's interview with Riaz Ahmed Zargar, one of the leaders of that agitation.
51. Sharma, D.C. *Glimpses of Kishtwar History*. Kishtwar: Chandra Bhaga Publishers.
52. Om Mehta, Indira Gandhi's minister of state for home affairs, belonged to Kishtwar. The town's people credit him for the prime minister's visit and the allocation of the project.
53. Skardu, on the Pakistan side of the Line of the Control, was the winter capital.
54. Unpublished research by Leh-based political science scholar, Shruti.
55. Unpublished research by Leh-based political science scholar, Shruti.
56. Author's interview with Ladakhi chronicler Sonam Phuntsog, author of 'Ladakh Annals.
57. Author's interview with Pintoo Norbu, Sonam Norbu's son and later minister in the state.

58. Ibid.
59. Author's interview with Mohammed Hasan, former MP.
60. The Official Website of Jammu & Kashmir.
61. Ibid.
62. Still the Muslim Conference, before it converted itself into the National Conference in 1939.
63. Author's interview in 1999 with the then non-agenarian Ghulam Qadir Ganderbali.
64. Bazaz, Prem Nath (1954). *The History of Struggle for Freedom in Kashmir.*
65. Rai, Mridu (2004). *Hindu Rulers, Muslim Subjects, Islam, Rights, and the History of Kashmir.* London: Hurst & Company.
66. Zutshi, Chitralekha (2003). *Languages of Belonging, Islam, Regional Identity and the Making of Kashmir.* Permanent Black.
67. Ibid.
68. Ibid.
69. Rai, Mridu (2004). *Hindu Rulers, Muslim Subjects, Islam, Rights, and the History of Kashmir.* London: Hurst & Company.
70. Zutshi, Chitralekha (2003). *Languages of Belonging, Islam, Regional Identity and the Making of Kashmir.*
71. Bazaz, Prem Nath (1954). *The History of Struggle for Freedom in Kashmir.*
72. Ibid.
73. Ibid.
74. Zutshi, Chitralekha. *Languages of Belonging, Islam, Regional Identity and the Making of Kashmir.*
75. *The Hindu,* April 12, 1952.
76. It was only in 1918 that Ghulam Ahmad Ashai became the first Muslim Kashmiri to get a Masters degree.
77. Devadas, David. *In Search of a Future: The Story of Kashmir.*
78. Dewan, Parvez (2008). *A History of Jammu.* New Delhi: Manas Publications.
79. Ibid. and Devadas, David. *In Search of a Future: The Story of Kashmir.*
80. Swami, Praveen (2007). *India Pakistan and the Secret Jihad, The Covert War in Kashmir, 1947-2004.* Routledge Taylor and Francis group.
81. Ibid.
82. Ibid.
83. Devadas, David. *In Search of a Future: The Story of Kashmir.*
84. Ibid.
85. The cable has since been declassified by the US.
86. Devadas, David. *In Search of a Future: The Story of Kashmir.*

87. Mullik, B.N. *Kashmir, My Years with Nehru.*
88. Ibid.
89. *The New York Times,* November 1, 1951, *www.nytimes.com*
90. This excludes the sprawling expanses of Gilgit, Skardu and other areas in the north-west of the state.
91. Dewan, Parvez. *A History of Jammu.*
92. Devadas, David. *In Search of a Future: The Story of Kashmir.*
93. Qasim, Mir (1999). *My Life and Times.* New Delhi: Allied Publishers and author's interview with him in 1999.
94. Devadas, David. *In Search of a Future: The Story of Kashmir.*
95. Ibid.
96. Ibid.
97. Ibid.
98. Ibid.
99. Author's interview with Balraj Puri and Ved Bhasin, editor of *Kashmir Times,* members of the steering committee of the convention, and Sofi Mohiuddin, private secretary to Maulana Masoodi.
100. The Official Website of Jammu & Kashmir.
101. Ibid.
102. Author's interviews with Mir Qasim, M.L. Fotedar and Ved Bhasin, editor of *Kashmir Times.*
103. The Official Website of Jammu & Kashmir.
104. Devadas, David. *In Search of a Future: The Story of Kashmir.*
105. The J&K assembly continues to be elected every six years. The state constitution was amended in 1977, following the amendment of the Indian constitution during the Emergency, but that amendment was not reversed when the amendment to the Indian constitution was reversed.
106. Devadas, David. *In Search of a Future: The Story of Kashmir.*
107. Author's interviews in 2001-02 with Jamaat-e-Islami leaders, including GM Butt and Hakim Ghulam Nabi, who served alternately as Amir-e-Jamaat between 1985 and 2002, Qari Saifuddin, Ghulam Ahmed 'Ahrar' and Syed Ali Shah Geelani.
108. Devadas, David. *In Search of a Future: The Story of Kashmir.*
109. Ibid.
110. Author's interview with Wajahat Habibullah, IAS officer in 2002.

Chapter XIX

The Challenge of the Northeast: 1964-1984

B.G. Verghese

The Northeast or Further Assam, as it was though never so called, was late in becoming part of the country's nationalist consciousness, unlike its more famous and turbulent North Western marches. Assam featured; but primarily the Brahmaputra Valley with its tea, oil and plywood and as the forward base for the Allied Army's final push against the Japanese and flying the Hump to China in the closing stages of the Second World War. Netaji Subhas Bose and the Indian National Army were part of that saga.

British power in the Northeast was not fully consolidated until the turn of the 20th century, only to be rocked by a popular upsurge in the Surma Valley over Assam being merged with East Bengal to form a new Muslim majority province following the Partition of Bengal in 1905. A swadeshi protest movement was spearheaded by Bipin Chandra Pal and bore fruit with the annulment of partition in 1911 to be followed in 1921 by Assam's graduation from a chief commissioner's charge to a full-fledged province. Assamese politics had begun to move from regionalism to nationalism after Jallianwala Bagh and the first non-cooperation movement, the nascent Assamese Association merging with the Indian National Congress and Gandhi's first visit to that part of the country. (Barpujari, 1993). The Assam Congress Pradesh Committee was formed in 1921 and the first AICC meeting was held in Gauhati in December 1926.

A Congress ministry was elected in Assam after the 1935 constitutional reforms but resigned in 1939 as the Congress objected to the Viceroy's unilaterally declaring India a party to the war on Germany without popular consultation. As the transfer of power drew close, the Muslim League made a bid to incorporate all or as much of the Northeast as possible in Pakistan. The Indian Independence Act passed by the House of Commons provisionally placed the Chittagong Hill Tracts, with its 97 percent non-Muslim population, in West Bengal.

But a surprise was in store. Radcliffe awarded the CHT to Pakistan. The Indian Government of India and the Chittagong Hills Tribes Association protested but to no avail.

The Assam Hills, barring Shillong and Manipur and Tripura, both ancient principalities, had until then virtually remained beyond the ken of the Indian National Congress, though the Naga Club was vaguely known to have petitioned the Simon Commission for a separate status from India in any constitutional settlement, and Jawaharlal Nehru did make passing reference to Rani Gaidinliu's raising the banner of revolt by the Zemi Nagas against the Raj. There had also been the daring Chittagong armoury raid in 1930. For the rest, prevailing attitudes were uninformed, paternalistic or indifferent, with the Northeast being seen by many much in the manner of the *Blind Men of Hindoostan*.

The reasons are not far to seek. The Northeast as we know it today was cocooned between British India and Burma (also administered from Delhi until 1937). The reach of the States People's Congress, when it came into being, was largely limited to the heartland. The 'Seven Sisters' of the Northeast (now eight with Sikkim) were, other than Assam proper, constitutionally designated partially or wholly 'excluded areas', mostly beyond the Inner Line or the settled administrative frontier of India, though certainly included within its outer political frontier. These areas fell outside the scope of dyarchy and provincial rule in the course of the successive constitutional reforms that marked the milestones to Independence.

Addressing a Scheduled Caste-Scheduled Tribe Conference in Delhi in 1952, Nehru admitted that, 'the essence of the struggler for freedom... did not reach these (tribal) areas, chiefly the frontier areas which are the most important tribal areas. The result is that...those frontier areas were not so psychologically prepared (for various changes in India). In fact, they were prepared the other way by British officers or sometimes by missionaries.... The missionaries did very good work there and I am full of praise for them., but politically speaking they did not particularly like changes in India (Singh, 1987).

Tripura, however, had live contact with Bengal. The tribal Maharaja adopted the Bengali language and imported Bengali personnel to administer the state. Bengali peasants were also welcomed to cultivate the narrow plains fringing the Tripura Hills in order to fill the granaries and bring in revenue. Rabindranath Tagore was an honoured guest and wrote some of his works in Agartala. Manipur too, like Assam earlier, forged ties with the heartland through the influence of Vaishnavite missionaries from Nawadwip in Bengal, giving birth to a rich Manipuri-Meitei culture that suffused the Imphal Valley.

For the rest, the Northeast still represents a distinctive part of the country's extraordinarily varied ethnic and racial diversity—Mongoloid India, where southeast Asia begins or ends. It is an equally unique bio-geographic and cultural transition zone. However, even Sardar Patel was uncertain about the loyalty of some of these frontiersmen. Writing to Nehru as Home Minister, the Sardar warned that the Himalaya could no longer be regarded as an impenetrable barrier and that the Tibeto-Mongoloid character of the population on 'our northern and northeastern approaches (consisting of Nepal, Bhutan, Sikkim, the Darjeeling area and the tribal areas of Assam), and the penetration of communist ideologies into some of these areas, posed a new threat'. (Das, 1972).

The Second World War had exposed parts of the Northeast Hills to a wider world from which it had been long secluded. But the Assam and Cachar Valleys were drawn into the cauldron of partition politics with Muslim League claims to include all of Assam and Bengal in East Pakistan. In the background of the abortive 1905-1911 partition of Bengal and the continued planned influx of migrants from Bengal as cheap labour to bring vacant lands under cultivation, Assamese opinion feared that the demographic balance was tilting against it on both linguistic and denominational grounds. It was scarcely reassured when the Congress, albeit reluctantly, agreed—Gandhi dissenting—to Assam's placement with Bengal in Group C in the Cabinet Mission's 1946 plan to avert partition by creating a loose federation with a Hindu majority centred in Group B and two smaller Muslim majority Groups A and C in the northwestern and eastern flanks of the country. The Congress believed the experiment would fail. Assam was in no circumstances prepared to take the risk.

This set the stage for Partition, establishing a new geography and geopolitical reality with the creation of East Pakistan that has coloured the Northeast scene ever since. At one stroke, with its principal arteries of land and inland waterways severed and the loss of its ocean outlet in Chittagong, Assam, formerly one of the country's most globalised states, found itself disconnected, virtually landlocked and a victim of massive market disruption that put its economy back by a quarter century. It was left with no more than a tenuous 20 km link to the Indian heartland through the Siliguri corridor while 98 percent of its external boundary marched with hostile borders closed by civil war and regime change. The trauma and anxiety this caused was not fully understood in Delhi, caught up as it was in the gory aftermath of Partition killings and refugee movements, challenges to its sovereignty in Jammu and Kashmir, Junagadh and Hyderabad, the complex and delicate task of integrating the princely states, and the soon-to-follow

Chinese occupation of Tibet. Pakistan laid claim to Assam, Tripura and Manipur while at least two Khasi durbars, Rambrai and Nongstien, opted for that country and had to be brought back into the fold in short measure. Communist radicalism had swept Southeast Asia and not only Telengana but a swathe of eastern India had been aroused to revolutionary fervour.

This apart, in 1946 some expatriate civil servants had advocated hiving off parts of tribal Northeast and tribal Burma—maybe those with a Christian following—to form a Crown Colony under British tutelage. The Nagas and Mizos rejected this ploy and preferred to cast their lot with a larger and more dynamic Independent India, though on special terms. The Naga 9-point agreement with the Assam Governor, Akbar Hydari, promised local autonomy and a review of the relationship after 10 years. The accord broke down as Phizo, the Naga leader, believed this implied the right to choose independence whereas the Indian view was that the terms of association within India could be renegotiated.

New foreign Christian missionaries were banned from the Northeast after Independence and those remaining were wasted out over time, their place being taken by Indian missionaries, the Catholics entering the scene for the first time. Nevertheless the record of dedicated missionary activity in the educational and cultural development of and social reform in the Northeast is still remembered. The missionaries bestowed on many tribes a written language and script, often English and Roman in the absence of any indigeneous alternative. The Assamese are particularly beholden to the mission-run *Orunodai,* the oldest newspaper in Assam, published from Sibsagar, that kept Assamese alive at a time when it was in danger of being overwhelmed by an officially-patronised Bengali.

NEFA was, however, placed altogether out of bounds for Christian missionaries and encouragement given to the local Donyi Polo faith and Buddhism. The Vivekananada Kendra (not to be confused with the Ramakrishna Mission) became active after 1977 with its emphasis on 'nationalist education' and 'spiritual nationalism'. Yet Christianity has spread in the region, including in Arunachal Pradesh where an anti-conversion law was later adopted.

Two contrary forces were clearly at work in the Northeast after the Second World War, as elsewhere in Asia. Newly independent or decolonised metropolitan powers, China included, raced to secure hitherto outer, political boundaries (as opposed to inner, administrative frontiers) to ensure national consolidation and integration. At the same time, 'excluded' tribes that had been left to their own devices for generations, felt the need to buy time by 'differentiating' themselves by seeking refuge in a new faith, language or script and thereby avoiding the sudden and all too ardent embrace of their metropolitan cousins. These trends were mistakenly read as annexationist or secessionist respectively. Later, 'ethnic nationalism' was manifested among these same people looking for their roots in faith (Seng Khasi and Sanamahi in Meghalaya and the Imphal Valley) and language (Kok Barok in Tripura and adoption of the Roman script elsewhere).

The compromise reached in framing the Constitution was the inclusion of tribal safeguards in the Sixth Schedule, covering the hitherto excluded areas in the Northeast. This provided for autonomy and devolution of administrative and financial powers to district and regional councils and the protection of customary tribal rights with regard to land, forests, laws, and institutions, with the Governor cast in the role of a guardian. For some this appeared a mere sop. Elements among the Nagas and Mizos and some Meitei factions envisioned sovereignty. Others looked for greater autonomy within India and still others, over time, separation from Assam or at least autonomy within it.

Certain other factors completed the backdrop. Both Manipur and Tripura acceded to India in the first half of August 1947, and Dominion Agents were posted in Imphal and Agartala. Merger followed two years later. Some in Tripura believed the merger was hasty. A larger segment of Meitei opinion was resentful in Manipur, which had since conducted elections, written a constitution and established popular rule. It believed the Maharaja had been coerced into extinguishing the separate identity of the state. Meitei opinion was further alienated with the formal waiving by Nehru in 1953 of all claims to Kubaw Valley, long a bone of contention between the kingdoms of Manipur and Burma but virtually ceded to the latter by the British in 1834 for a paltry annual tribute to the former. If these events sowed the seeds of secessionism in certain revolutionary Meitei circles, in Tripura it was the relentless demographic tilt towards Bengali ethnic and linguistic domination that stoked tribal insurrection.

In 1946 Gandhi had told an agitated delegation of Nagas that they had a right to be independent. The Naga National Council (NNC) under Angami Zapu Phizo, declared 'independence' on August 14, 1947 and went on to conduct a somewhat wider though limited 'plebiscite' that ostensibly favoured freedom. The Nagas boycotted the country's first General Elections in 1952 and the district council scheme. Non-cooperation turned to violence and in 1954 a Republican Government of Free Nagaland was announced by Phizo who had turned to Pakistan. This was followed in 1956 by a proclamation establishing a Federal Government of Nagaland from 'Oaking' and an underground army. The Naga insurrection had begun and the Assam

Disturbed Areas Act (1955) was invoked. However, Naga moderates rallied, abandoning independence and seeking fulfillment of their aspirations within the Indian Union.

The economy of the United Khasi and Jaintia Hills and Garo Hills district had been badly hurt by the loss of the East Pakistan market. Things may have settled down but for suggestions in 1952 that Assamese be made the state's official language. This gave rise to fears of Great Assamese chauvinism and encouraged demands for separation of the Hill regions with the birth of the Eastern India Tribal Union (EITU). This, however, yielded to the All Party Hill Leaders Conference (APHLC) which sought statehood for the UKJ and Garo Hills.

The appointment of a States Reorganisation Commission (1953-1956) was greeted with multiple demands. Assam favoured the absorption, if possible, of Cooch Behar, Manipur and Tripura and greater administrative control over NEFA. Though the phrase was not used, this seemed to be a bid for a Greater Assam. The Hill districts had in 1954 pleaded for a Hill State and pressed that case. There were still other demands advocating Kamtapura (Goalpara, Garo Hills, Cooch Behar, Darjeeling and Jalpaiguri) and Purbanchal (for Bengali consolidation through the merger of Cachar and Tripura) but including the Lushai (Mizo) Hills, Manipur and NEFA for good measure). The SRC rejected both Kamtapur and Purbanchal and recommended a new Assam including Tripura but not Manipur in view of its distinctive character. No one was happy. Tripura, already desperate to save its identity, objected to its inclusion in Assam. The Hills were dissatisfied and the introduction of legislation in 1960 to make Assamese the official language of the state intensified their demand for separation. The process of reconfiguring the region's political landscape had begun.

By ending the excluded character of the Northeast hills, Partition set in motion a process of slow but inexorable transition and modernisation. There were multiple transitions, not all with the same trajectory or moving with the same speed—from a subsistence to a market economy, from barter to monetised exchange, from *jhum* to the slow spread of settled cultivation, from isolation to interaction, from a state of being left alone to receiving the attention of a paternalistic government with traditional institutions and the writ of elders giving way to newer administrative structures and procedures despite efforts to preserve customary ways and culture. This was a time of effervescence and change within a new democratic milieu. Silent voices had begun to find tongue.

Nowhere was the transition so challenging as in the various Frontier Tracts that had now been brought together in the North-East Frontier Agency (NEFA) a vast mosaic of tribal peoples that was largely terra incognito. The new Indian Constitution retained it as part of Assam but placed it under the Governor of Assam, acting as Agent of the President. The Daying Ering Committee recommended it be accorded a *panchayati* structure, with village, block and zilla councils and an agency council at the apex. A single line administration was introduced under political officers drawn from a new Indian Frontier Administrative Service reporting to an Adviser to the Governor who headed the NEFA administration in Shillong.

On account of his own deep interest in the matter, NEFA and, later, the Naga area was directly overseen by Nehru. He had appointed a defrocked missionary, Verrier Elwin his Tribal Adviser who, at the Prime Minister's prompting, produced *A Philosophy for NEFA*. Nehru wrote the Foreword to the second edition in which he set out the terms of India's engagement with this sensitive frontier region. 'We cannot allow matters to drift in the tribal areas', Nehru wrote, 'or just not take interest in them. In the world of today that is not possible or desirable. At the same time we should avoid over-administering these areas and in particular, sending too many outsiders into tribal territory'.

Within this broad framework, the Prime Minister set out five principles: permit people to develop along the lines of their own genius; respect tribal rights in lands and forests; train and build up a team of their own administrators and technicians; work through and not in rivalry with their own social and cultural institutions; and judge results not by statistics and outlays 'but by the quality of human character that is evolved'. This was a far sighted and humane charter of development. There were critics who said Nehru wanted to treat NEFA as a cultural museum. They were wrong.

The post-Independence 'awakening' of the Northeast revolved around issues of land and forests, language and ethnicity. The Assam administration had in 1947 designated certain tribal belts and blocks in the Brahmaputra and Barak Valleys as so-called plains tribal homelands. These were steadily eroded by refugee rehabilitation, encroachment, illegal settlers and development. Tribal anger would follow.

Language and ethnicity too were put on a slow boil by the pre- and post-partition influx of Bengali/Muslim settlers who were increasingly seen as illicit immigrants, though East Bengal Hindus were termed refugees. The situation was ambiguous. After the pre-partition riots, the eastern region saw a period of relative quiet even as Western India erupted in violence and a tidal wave of refugees. Then in 1950 and in waves thereafter, the delayed fury of partition engulfed the Eastern region. Refugees streamed across the border both ways. Nehru and his counterpart, Liaqat Ali Khan met and signed a pact under which those who had fled their homes were to be encouraged to return and not remain as refugees. Permanent refugee rehabilitation and evacuee property norms as in the west were eschewed and it was hoped that returning communal harmony would heal the wounds. The Passport Act was accordingly not applied to East Pakistan until 1957 and people travelled on certificates, many of them of dubious validity.

This was to cause enormous problems later in counting numbers and assigning or accepting national status. The 1951 Census was not taken in Assam on account of disturbed conditions and there was subsequent undercounting on one side and over-counting on the other as those who had fled to safety had not returned to their homes. The compilation of a national citizen's register could not be undertaken for the eastern region. The consequences of this omission were painfully to follow.

Assam too was anxious to limit the numbers entering the state, seeing how Tripura had been overrun by Bengalis. On the other hand Nehru was frustrated with Gopinath Bordoloi, Congress chief minister of Assam, for not carrying his share of the national refugee burden and, instead, seeking 'dual citizenship'. Bordoloi had a case. The exchange was acerbic and Nehru did not fully understand the cultural and political implications of the influx.

Matters were not improved by the Centre's later hesitation to locate an oil refinery in Assam to process the crude recently discovered in Upper Assam. Delhi's mandarins preferred to accept the logic of a pipeline to Barauni and Haldia which could more economically refine the limited Assam crude available at these consumption hubs while being able to use imported crude as and when necessary. What was seen as a small 'toy' refinery was finally conceded at Nunmati near Guwahati, then Gauhati. It had been a struggle born of a sense of discrimination and neglect.

From 1956 and more openly by 1959 China had begun to challenge the McMahon Line and lay claim to Arunachal. '*Hindi-Chini bhai bhai*' had turned sour and the flight of the Dalai Lama to Tawang in 1959 marked a turning point. India's defence unpreparedness was soon manifest. Bravado was exposed in 1962. The fall of Se La, the ignominious retreat to the Foothills on November 18-19, and Nehru's 'My heart goes out to the people of Assam...' broadcast to the nation rankled deeply in Assam's wounded psyche, even as the Army and civil administration were ordered to fall back to Guwahati and abandon the North Bank.

The Chinese declared a unilateral ceasefire on the midnight of November 19-20 and pulled back to their (variable) Line of Actual Control. There was, however, a silver lining. The people of Arunachal were steadfast in their allegiance to and support for India. Nor did any

Northeast insurgent group seek to extract any military or political advantage at this time of trouble.

Nehru was shattered. He was a sick man and never regained his authority and composure. He passed away in May 1964, leaving it to Lal Bahadur Shastri and, essentially, Indira Gandhi to pick up the threads.

I

Lal Bahadur Shastri was confronted with a restive Hill population in the Northeast and sought to assuage feelings by appointing a Hill Areas Commission under H.V. Pataskar, a former Union minister. The Commission proposed further devolution and, specifically, a Hill minister in the Assam cabinet with a separate Hill department under a Hill Commissioner, with a distinctive Hill areas budget within the State budget. The Hill MLAs were also to constitute a Hill Areas Committee whose views would ordinarily prevail. A modified package was finally adopted and a Sub-State formed in 1970. But with tensions mounting over Assamese as the official language of the State the experiment was soon doomed and a separate state of Meghalaya came into being in 1972, with the United Mikir (Karbi Anglong) and North Cachar Hills districts opting out to remain autonomous units within Assam.

The 1965 war put the Northeast on alert but there was little or no activity in the eastern theatre. Shastri's tragic death at Tashkent brought Indira Gandhi to office and a fresh mind to bear on the increasingly tangled web of Northeastern affairs.

Even before the new prime minister had settled in, Mizoram went up in flames. The Mizo Union (MU)—the term Mizo being adopted as representing a family of close knit tribes spread over India, Burma and East Pakistan)—was established in 1946 by a rising elite chafing against feudal chiefs. A second conference of the MU submitted a memorandum to the Constituent Assembly seeking self-determination and special safeguards within Assam with a right to secession after 10 years. This front of commoners alarmed the chiefs who joined hands to form the United Mizo Freedom Organisation (UMFO) in 1947 seeking merger with Burma or creation of a British protectorate. These options being found impracticable, all parties accepted the new Sixth Schedule as a sufficient safeguard for Mizo autonomy and identity. District council elections were held and a regional council established for the minority Pawi-Lakher tribes of southern Mizoram which was what the Lushai Hills was renamed in 1954. Hereditary chieftainship was abolished soon thereafter.

Partition had caused grave market disruption in Mizoram with the loss of the East Bengal market and outlet to the sea via Chittagong. Isolated and little developed, the district ranked among the most backward in the region. Assam's inability to offer much assistance and seeming tardiness in dealing with its requirements, situated as it was at the far end of the line, caused growing resentment. The 'mautam', a 40-year cycle of bamboo flowering that causes rodents to multiply manifold and devour the crops, led to famine and distress. The MU became the Mizo National Front (MNF) and under the leadership of Laldenga, established contact with Pakistan for arms and military training. A column of trainees, detected returning from Pakistan, was arrested but released after some months by Chaliha, Assam's chief minister, on a promise of good conduct on which the MNF reneged. Petty grievances mounted and the prospect of inclusion in an autonomous Hill State within Assam offered little satisfaction.

The MNF rose on the night of February 28, 1966. Laldenga proclaimed Mizoram to be an independent sovereign state and launched Operation Jericho to take control of all nodal centres. Aizawl, the civil headquarters, Lunglei and other administrative townships fell to the rebels with little or nothing to oppose them. This was the first challenge to confront Indira Gandhi. She did not flinch. The Air Force was ordered to strafe Aizawl to remove roadblocks and enable the district officials to hold firm while Army relief columns marched in to restore order. The MNF was banned and the Mizo national army and rebel government forced underground, finding sanctuary in the Chittagong Hill Tracts. Lunglei was relieved within a fortnight and the administration restored elsewhere in quick measure.

The crisis had been averted but skirmishes, ambushes and raids continued sporadically over many years. The Mizo Hills were declared a disturbed area and brought under the Armed Forces Special Powers Act. In order to prevent MNF rebels from raiding villages for food, shelter and extorting money, the Army devised a scheme to relocate and group all villages and scattered hamlets in a protected band of territory on either side of the main north-south axis running down the length of Mizo Hills. This had been tried earlier in Nagaland and, prior to that, in Malaya.

Grouping was accomplished in four stages between 1967 and 1970. By the end of the exercise, 466 villages with 236,162 persons accounting for 82 percent of the population of the Mizo Hills had been relocated in 18 protected and progressive villages, 40 new grouping centres, 26 voluntary grouping centres and in 17 hamlets along extended loop areas. All these were placed under civilian administrators and provided with water supply, access to roadheads and other amenities that it was hoped would compensate the people from being torn asunder from their traditional homelands and way of life. The villages were protected. But living was irksome and restricted and 'progressive' development slow in coming in view of logistical and security constraints. There was also some incidental forest loss in the process of clear-felling along roads to preclude ambushes.

The MNF was well ensconced in Pakistan and made forays into Burma and later even sought contact with China. The liberation of Bangladesh in 1971 ended that phase—at least for a while. The Government was sufficiently reassured by these developments to permit a measure of de-grouping, with rehabilitation grants to assist the process, and by 1980 many old villages had been resettled.

With the political reorganisation of Assam in 1972, Meghalaya was granted statehood and Mizoram became a Union Territory with a 30 member territorial assembly and reorganised districts and three new minority district councils. Efforts were made to speed development and, fatigued by an insurgency that seemed to be going nowhere, Laldenga began to think of bringing the MNF back into the fold on honourable terms. As he was to relate later in personal conversations, he had to mask his intentions lest he alienate his radically young supporters and foreign benefactors. He began to feel that he was being used by Pakistan and China, both of whom had their own agenda. He travelled via Pakistan and Europe to Afghanistan where he contacted Indian intelligence which assisted him in coming to Delhi to negotiate a settlement in 1975.

An abortive peace accord was signed in July 1976. This provided for an end to insurgency, a surrender of arms, a political settlement within the framework of the Indian constitution and a corresponding suspension of operations by the security forces. The accord did not last. Some MNF cadres continued on the rampage, forcibly collecting taxes. The security forces struck back leading to further surrenders by MNF cadres, including high ranking officials. Negotiations were resumed by the Janata government. Laldenga formed a council to which he handed over responsibility, clearly to broadbase the negotiations and spread the risk. These talks too stalled and were suspended in 1978.

There was a resumption of hostile activity and matters took a new turn with a call on all non-Mizos or 'outsiders' to quit by July 1, 1979. Laldenga was arrested and pressure brought to bear on the MNF amidst rising violence. Since Laldenga seemed the only person who might be able to deliver the goods, Brigadier T. Sailo, chief minister and head of the People's Conference, a local party in opposition to the Congress but with a national outlook, persuaded Indira Gandhi, now back in office, to reopen fresh peace talks with a suspension of operations on both sides. These talks too proved desultory and Laldenga, who had been released, went off to London.

The 1984 General Elections in Mizoram brought a Congress ministry to power under Lalthanhawla, who once again urged Indira Gandhi to resume talks. Laldenga was recalled from London and an appointment set up for him to meet Mrs Gandhi on October 31, 1984. Alas, she was assassinated that very day. (Prasad and Agarwal, 1991). It was left to her son and successor, Rajiv Gandhi to pick up the threads and reach a final accord in June 30, 1986.

II

Efforts to negotiate a peace had commenced even earlier in Nagaland. Following its formation as a separate entity, a Nagaland Baptist Convention at Wokha sought a dialogue facilitated by a Peace Committee which was ultimately formed with B.P. Chaliha, Jayaprakash Narayan and the Revd. Michael Scott (an unorthodox British missionary who had worked against apartheid and for equality and justice in what was to become Namibia). They gathered in 1964 to establish a peace centre at Chedema near Kohima. Simultaneously, a Peace Observer Mission of Sarvodaya workers was set up under Dr. M. Aram, Nabhakrushna Chowdhury and Marjorie Sykes, a long time acolyte of Gandhi. Its role was to monitor the suspension of operations agreement arrived at that September that bound both sides to stop offensive operations while allowing the security forces to patrol a three-mile strip of territory along the Burma border and 100 yards on either side of all roads.

An official team, accompanied by representatives of the Nagaland administration, was constituted under the Foreign Secretary, Y. Gundevia. Naga Federal Government delegates made out a case for self-determination while Gundevia insisted that with the grant of full autonomy, the Nagas were now self-governing. Having heard both sides, the Peace Mission set out its own proposals. These were that, 'The NFG could of their own volition decide to be a participant in the Union of India and mutually settle the terms and conditions for that purpose. On the other hand, the Government of India could consider to what extent the pattern and structure of the relationship between Nagaland and the Government of India should be adapted and recast so as to satisfy the political aspirations of all sections of Naga opinion and to make it possible for the ideals of peace as expressed in the Naga Peace Declaration to be substantially realised'. (Aram, 1974).

Despite violations of the suspension of operations agreement, five more rounds of talks were held. Scott increasingly began to echo the Naga underground and was ultimately expelled from the country. Phizo sent certain proposals from London but his own position seemed to be somewhat undermined. Extension of underground activity to northern Manipur only aggravated matters. This negative sequence later led to Naga cadres going to China for arms and training.

Indira Gandhi's becoming Prime Minister, had signalled a new beginning. She was not averse to meeting the Naga underground leadership and six further rounds of discussion ensued between February and October 1967 but to no avail. Levels of violence and extortion began to rise with the sabotaging of trains in Assam. Both Jayaprakash Narayan and Chaliha retired and the Peace Mission stood disbanded. The Assam-Nagaland Governor, B.K. Nehru was to say that restraint had been taken for weakness and generosity mistaken for appeasement.

The Nagaland government and Assembly too were getting restive and the Baptist Church increasingly concerned about the underground's consorting with China. An Army encounter with Naga underground cadres in 1968 resulted in the capture of Chinese arms that confirmed an illicit traffic in weapons. The peace talks were suspended. The underground split with one lot under Kughato Sukhai, Kaito and Zuheto deciding to come overground while another faction went on to form a Revolutionary Government of Nagaland under Scato Swu in 'Hongkhin'.

An attempt on the life of the Naga National Organization (NNO) chief minister, Hokishe Sema in August 1972 marked another turning point. The suspension of operations agreement was terminated and the Naga Federal Army (NFA) and Naga National Council (NNC) banned under the Unlawful Activities (Prevention) Act of 1967. Nagaland was taken away from External Affairs and restored to the Union Home Ministry. More seminal was the decision of the Revolutionary Government of Nagaland to surrender and come overground with its armed cadres, some of whom were subsequently absorbed in the Border Security Force (BSF).

With Jasokie becoming chief minister and L.P. Singh Governor of Assam-Nagaland, the Church was again instrumental in promoting peace talks. This was to result in the 1975 Shillong Accord. Under this, the underground agreed of its own volition to accept unconditionally the Indian constitution. The underground was to lay down arms and was thereafter given 'to formulate other issues for discussion for final settlement'. Such issues were, however, never formulated. While many in Nagalnd rejoiced, Thuingaleng Muivah and Isak Swu heard the news while returning home through Burma with an armed band from China. They were outraged by what they considered a sell out by Phizo and others and denounced the Accord in harsh terms.

The following year they joined hands with Khaplang, a Hemi Naga from Burma, to form the National Socialist Council of Nagaland (NSCN). NSCN socialism, under the power of god, was sought to be distinguished from Marxism-Leninism in a tract titled 'Polarisation'. (Ao, 1994). Not long thereafter, the NSCN split, with Khaplang taking on Muivah and Swu in a bloody encounter. The NSCN (IM) and NSCN (K) were born. The Naga movement took a new turn. Muivah, a Thangkul Naga from Ukhrul drew Manipur more directly into the fray. The Angami influence of the NNC waned and internecine and fratricidal killings were to mark and mar the Naga underground movement for quite some time to the great distress of the Baptist Church and Naga Ho Hos or traditional tribal assemblies who saw this strife as the greatest threat to peace and unity.

Through all this period, Nagaland was governed by non-Congress ministries. It was only in 1986 that Hokishe Sema became the first Congress chief minister of the state.

III

The later 1950s had seen the rise of a pan-Mongolian movement. One fall-out of this in Manipur was encouragement to Meitei revivalism, harking back to a pre-Hindu, Sanamahi, Mongoloid past. This was to lay the basis for the establishment of the United Liberation Front (UNLF) in 1964 under Arambam Somorendra dedicated to national self-determination, building a socialist society and forging links with the Naga and Mizo underground. Subsequently, efforts were made to acquire arms from Burma and Pakistan. The UNLF divided on tactics: Somorendra favoured first strengthening the ideological basis whereas the Oinam Sudhir Kumar faction, anxious to launch an armed struggle, established a Revolutionary Government of Manipur. Meitei guerillas made forays into Cachar and Tripura during the 1971 war. (Tarapot, 1993).

The liberation of Bangladesh created a new situation. Disillusioned by the rift within the UNLF, a senior member, Bisheshwar, set out to build a revolutionary rural base to oust the 'mayang (outsider) regime'. Seeking inspiration and support from China he made it to Lhasa via Nepal in 1975, received some training after an initially cautious welcome, and returned home to establish the People's Liberation Army (Eastern Region) in 1978. He hoped to band with other insurgent groups in the region in a revolutionary front to liberate Manipur and oust the 'Delhi bandit government'. (Sanjaoba, 1988). He took early steps to eliminate the 'counter-revolutionary' Revolutionary Government of Manipur.

A familiar pattern of ambushes and extortions followed to raise funds for the purchase of arms. Bisheshwar next turned to Bangladesh and the Kachin Independence Army in Burma. Several other revolutionary formations surfaced, more prominent among them being the People's Revolutionary Party of Kangliepak (PREPAK) under R.K. Tulachandra and the Kangliepak Communist Party (KCP) under K. Binoy. 'Red' and 'socialist' seemed mandatory appellations for most. Divisions were apparent and, probably, personality-oriented. The NSCN remained active in the northern Naga-inhabited Manipur hills and the Mizo National Front in the southern hills. It was a troubled time.

In the face of unabated violence, Imphal Valley was declared a disturbed area and brought under the Armed Forces (Assam and Manipur) Special Powers Act in September 1980. The People's Liberation Army (PLA), PREPAK and KCP were declared unlawful and the induction of military reinforcements soon yielded results. Leading cadres were killed or captured and an ailing Bisheshwar was arrested. He underwent a change of heart in prison and contested the state elections in 1985. He was elected to the Manipur Assembly, only to have his election set aside mid-term. However, he was seen as a renegade and gunned down by his colleagues in 1994.

IV

The influx of refugees in Tripura prior to Independence and certainly thereafter, had kept the state simmering. Forests were felled and additional lands brought under cultivation by the new settlers. A radical tribal organisation, Seng Krak (clenched fist), had sprung up in 1947 in opposition to the Bengali influx. This was outlawed but was resurrected as the Paharia Union in 1954 together with two other bodies to constitute the Adivasi Sansad. The communists too gained ground at the head of a peasant movement, the Rajya Mukti Parishad, under the leadership of Nripen Chakravarty and Dasaratha Deb, both of whom were later to become chief ministers.

Apart from pre-partition in-migrants Tripura absorbed about 610,000 East Pakistan refugees between 1947 and 1971, and the population density rose correspondingly from 49 in 1941 to 196 by 1981, more than a four-fold increase. Tribal numbers had marginally declined from about 53 percent of the total population in 1901 to just under 51 percent in 1941. Thereafter the decline was rapid: the ratio fell to 37 percent in 1951 and to just over 28 percent by 1981. There was a steadily decreasing amount of land available for *jhumia* (swidden farmer) resettlement of tribals in wet rice cultivation. The Tripura Land Revenue and Land Reforms Act, 1960, sought to address the problem by vesting land in the tiller and resuming to the state all other lands in the tribal interest. Nevertheless, restrictions on tribal land alienation proved ineffective and in 1974 the Act was amended to legitimise all lands transferred until 1969. The tribals increasingly felt economically, politically and culturally squeezed, power having passed from the tribal durbar to a majoritarian Bengali/outsider population.

The Communist Party split in 1967 led a disillusioned younger Tripura elite to form the Tripura Upajati Juba Samiti (TUJS) under Samacharan Tripura, a teacher. (Bhattacharjee, 1989). It sought an autonomous district under the Sixth Schedule, restoration of alienated tribal lands and recognition of Kok-Borok in the Roman script as the medium of instruction and official language. The Mizo revolt at this juncture stirred ambitions. The Seng Krak was revived, Bengali settlements raided, and a 100-man army raised to liberate Tripura from base areas in the Northern Tripura Hills and the Chittagong Hill Tracts.

Bijoy Hrangkhawl of the TUJS joined this group, was arrested but released. He subsequently formed an armed wing, the Tribal National Volunteers (TNV), towards the end of 1978, breaking ranks with his previous associates who were themselves soon to form All-Tripura People's Liberation Organisation only finally to surrender in 1983 to the Left Front, now in office under Dasarath Deb. Hrangkhawl had meanwhile secured an autonomous district council in 1979 but ran into opposition from radical 'Amra Bangali' elements who felt this marked the beginning of the partition of Tripura to the disadvantage of the Bengali population. The tribals on the other hand viewed the question as a matter of very survival. (Sarin, 1980). The ensuing confrontation led to a TUJS quit order against all 'foreigners' who had entered Tripura since its merger with India in 1949. Resentments boiled over in a terrible massacre of Bengalis with its epicentre at Mandai in June 1980. An official report placed the number of dead at 550 with over 1800 missing. Elections to the Autonomous State Demand Committee (ASDC) were postponed as attention turned to relief and rehabilitation.

The official Tripura (Inquiry) Committee under Dinesh Singh, a Union minister, advocated more rapid development and 'the psycho-cultural, economic and political integration of the tribal people with development in the rest of the country'. It noted the impact of the non-tribal influx into Tripura but believed the immediate need '(is) to prepare the tribals to face the challenge of the new industrial society and technological age into which the country has entered'.

In 1982, Hrangkhawl formed a government-in-exile in the Chittagong Hill Tracts on the plea that merger with India in 1949 had been a non-consultative process and that tribal interests had been sacrificed. In a letter to Indira Gandhi on March 17, 1983, Hrangkhawl said that, 'armed insurgency was necessary to reach your heart... Either you deport all foreign nationals who entered Tripura after October 15, 1947 or settle them anywhere in India other than in Tripura. Restore tribal majority interest. It may not matter to you much, but delaying implementation of our demands means the TNV will fight for total self-determination. We demand a free Tripura'. (Tarapot, 1993).

The TNV remained active but it did not take too long for it to realise that its struggle was in vain. The Mizo Accord in 1986 paved the way for a return to the fold. A Tripura Accord was finally signed two years later.

V

Even while there was discontent and armed dissension in the Hill regions, Assam remained the major cauldron that kept boiling and bubbling in the Northeast. Partition traumatised Assam, as it did all of the Northeast, and reduced it from one of India's most globalised states to a remote enclave with the severance of its external arteries. It struggled to keep its distinctive ethno-cultural ethnicity alive in the face of demographic and linguistic assaults from outside. This in turn first alienated the hill and then the plains tribals. In the result, Greater Assam yielded to Little Assam, a proud but wounded community which felt neglected, misunderstood and under siege.

Bordoloi, the first post-Independence chief minister and architect of the Sixth Schedule, was solicitous of the tribal interest. Though a staunch Congressman, he failed to win the sympathy of Nehru and Patel in the measure sought with regard to the refugee influx from East Pakistan. This was to shape Assam's subsequent psyche and history. The passing of Bordoloi in 1950 brought the more Assamese rather than Assam-focused Bishu Ram Medhi to office. He confronted the delayed eastern partition riots and the Nehru-Liaqat Pact which left the citizenship status of those affected somewhat fluid and increasingly confused as the demographic lines were not rigorously drawn. There was quibbling and much policy thereafter was informed by equivocation. The situation was admittedly complex and delicate but the Assam Congress somehow did not seem able to get across the urgency of its concerns to the party at the national level.

The stage for Assam's demographic dilemma was set prior to Independence. East Bengal labour had traditionally been imported into Assam to spur its development and bring new and, especially, marginal lands under cultivation. By 1931 this immigration had become a flood. C.F. Mullen, Superintendent of the Assam Census, 1931 wrote: 'Probably the most important event in the province during the last 25 years—an event, moreover, which seems likely to alter permanently the whole future of Assam and to destroy the whole structure of Assamese culture and civililisation—has been the invasion of a vast horde of land-hungry immigrants, mostly Muslims, from the districts of Eastern Bengal, and, in particular, from Mymensingh...Where there is a waste land, thither flock the Mymensinghians'.

Partition aggravated matters. Now political refugees swelled the numbers of what were earlier just economic immigrants. The 1961 Census in India and Pakistan showed a remarkable district-wise fit of East Pakistan population 'deficits' matching a corresponding surge in numbers across the border in Assam. (See Ministry of External Affairs, 1963). Despite all efforts by the Government of India to raise the issue of illegal immigration into Assam during the Indo-Pakistan talks in 1962-63, Pakistan refused to respond and insisted that it would be prepared to discuss infiltration and border issues only if the Kashmir question was settled.

In 1964 the Union Government launched a Prevention of Immigration from Pakistan (PIP) scheme and raised a special Assam police force to man the border. Assam did not, however, follow West Bengal's lead in stipulating official sanction for transfer of any immovable property to a foreigner. Nonetheless some illicit immigrants were apprehended and expelled under the Foreigners (Tribunal) Order. Corruption, vote bank politics and the availability of cheap labour induced laxity in enforcement.

Nepalese immigration was also a matter for concern. But this lacked the linguistic and communal dimension of Bengali Muslim in-migration and was sought to be controlled by enforcement of the protected/restricted areas regulations beyond the Siliguri neck. Census figures indicated a rise in the Nepalese speaking population in Assam from 101,335 in 1951 to 182,925 in 1961 and 353,673 by 1971. According to the All-Assam Students Union (AASU) and the All-Assam Gana Sangram Parishad (AAGSP), the overall figure of foreign nationals in Assam had risen from a million in 1961 to 2.3 million by 1971 and 3.5 million by 1979, with 1.8 million of these enrolled as voters, constituting almost 20 percent of Assam's total electorate. (See Verghese and Ahmed *et al.* (1980). These numbers were to remain a matter of contention with the Government of India projecting a somewhat lesser tally.

The corollary to the territorial shrinkage of Assam through the 1960s and 1970s was shrinking job opportunities for a rising but essentially home-loving Assamese middle class within the region. The winding up of the Joint Steamer Companies plying the Brahmaputra to Calcutta via East Pakistan after the 1965 war added to economic isolation. Followed the agitation to refine new-found Assam oil within Assam rather than pipe it to distant consumption centres in Barauni and Haldia. Resentments were building up.

Matters came to a head in 1978. Addressing a conference of chief electoral officers, the Chief Election Commissioner, S.L. Shakdher referred to 'alarming reports' from the Northeast regarding large scale inclusion of foreign nationals in the electoral rolls. As disturbing was the fact that political parties sought inclusion of the names of migrants without even questioning or properly determining their citizenship status. Shakdher concluded that he intended to communicate to the Union Home Ministry the urgent need for administrative measures to identity foreigners and expeditiously grant citizenship certificates to all eligible persons.

An upcoming by-election to the Mangaldoi parliamentary constituency provided the spark with the demand that the poll be postponed until the electoral rolls had been cleansed of foreign elements. There were cries of popular detection of foreign names by some and counter allegations of victimisation of innocent persons on the other. The dissolution of the Lok Sabha at that juncture and impending General Elections in 1980 magnified the problem. The Chief Election Commissioner took the pragmatic view that the 1977 rolls might be taken as the base and additions and deletions entertained thereafter on the basis of specific objections and applications that might be filed. As a matter of fact, 400,000 objections were filed and 250,000 disposed of by returning officers and special tribunals. But Assamese opinion was incensed by this 'betrayal' and AASU launched what turned out to be a massive though peaceful civil disobedience movement. It is claimed that over three million persons, urban and rural, rich and poor, courted arrest during that satyagraha between November 12 and 17, 1979. The cultural underpinnings to the movement were provided by the Asom Sahitya Sabha and a band of intellectuals.

A shortlived Assam ministry under J.N. Hazarika's Asom Janata Dal, was unable to cope and Assam was brought under President's rule in December 1979. Completely misjudging the situation, the Asom

Janata Dal and other political parties advocated General Elections in January despite the more sober judgment of the Governor, L.P Singh whose view unfortunately did not prevail. The movement intensified. Candidates and campaigners like Dev Kanta Borooah, erstwhile Congress President, and Begum Abida Ahmed, wife of the former President of India, were gheraoed and it was only in Bengali-speaking Cachar that nominations could be filed though polling was limited to just two constituencies. This seeming 'Bengali betrayal' exacerbated tensions and sporadic communal incidents were reported.

The accidental killing of school boy vigilante in Nalbari in Lower Assam gave the Assam movement a new direction. It spread from stopping the polls to preventing the outflow of oil from Assam and picketing government offices. Tempers were rising. Communal killings brought out the CRPF and Army. Military atrocities were alleged. Rumours flew. Picketing at Oil India's installation at Duliajan led to firing and four deaths which sent a wave of anger and emotion throughout Assam. A senior Oil India Limited (OIL) executive, a Bengali, was 'lured' to the hospital to visit the injured and murdered there.

The national elections returned the Congress and Indira Gandhi back to power, ending the short interlude of Janata rule. Sensing an opportunity for talks, AASU put forward an Eight Point Charter of demands:

1. Foreign nationals must be detected and deported.
2. Foreigners must be removed from the electoral rolls before any poll in Assam.
3. A strengthened electoral machinery must prevent future inclusion of foreigners in the electoral rolls.
4. The international border must be adequately protected to prevent further infiltration.
5. Indian voters in Assam must be issued identity cards with photographs.
6. Northeasterners should be provided special safeguards for the next 15/20 years through constitutional provisions for the protection of their indigeneous identity.
7. The Assam Government should be empowered to reject citizenship certificates issued by district authorities in Tripura and West Bengal.
8. The power presently delegated to state governments to issue citizenship certificates should be withdrawn by the Centre so that foreign nationals detected in Assam did not come back

armed with certificates issued by a neighbouring state administration.

An AASU delegation led by its president, Prafulla Mahanta, met Mrs. Gandhi and the Home Minister, Zail Singh, in Delhi on February 4 and 5, 1980. Following the discussions, the Government announced acceptance of the first five demands in principle but remitted the remaining three for fuller consideration, presumably as they involved constitutional amendments and concerned other states as well. Both promised to visit Assam. Returning home, AASU suspended its movement until March 2 except for oil movements outside the state.

The interregnum of President's rule had meanwhile been used to restart quiet talks on the basis of public appeals. The Gandhi Peace Foundation took a lead in the matter and offered its good offices, stationing a representative in Guwahati to act as an intermediary between AASU/AGP and the Governor-cum-Adviser, H.C Sarin.

The critical issues of what should be the base year and cut-off year had been earlier resolved with agreement to tackle the 'foreigners' issue in three segments. Those who entered Assam during 1951-1961 were to be acknowledged as citizens and allowed to remain undisturbed. Those who had come after March 25, 1971 were to be deleted from the electoral list and deported or dispersed to other states. Current discussion now focused on the 1961-1971 segment and modalities for dealing with this number, estimated around 500,000 persons after allowing for earlier expulsions. The Centre was willing to accept the GPF formulation which was that these persons be deleted from the electoral rolls but be granted residence-cum-work permits, though temporarily stateless, until such time as their status was determined or for a period not exceeding five years, whichever was less. The assumption was that some of these persons might by then have proof of eligibility for citizenship by birth or marriage, or have become eligible for naturalisation. Further, if deportation or dispersal was precluded or delayed for whatever reason, Assam should be eligible for special development-cum-rehabilitation grants. After much discussion internally and receipt of official clarifications through the GPF, AASU signified its willingness to accept this as a basis for talks only to go back on this assurance subsequently.

An issue that greatly exercised AASU and to which the Centre had no ready answer was the alienation of lands within the reserved tribal belts and blocks. In reply to a parliamentary Question as far back as 1969, the Union Minister for Rehabilitation had stated that Assam's capacity to absorb more refugees was nearing saturation and that its 'quota' for resettlement of 'new migrants' had accordingly been fixed at 12,000 families (or roughly 60,000 persons). By 1975 some 30,000 'new immigrant' families had been resettled outside the Northeast and Assam, like West Bengal, insisted that even if it were to accept the 1961-1971 migrants, its quota must be limited to the stipulated 12,000 families. The Centre argued that the 'quota' referred only to land resettlement and that many more had been and could be rehabilitated through grants for self-employment, purchase of assets and house construction. Taking these into account, the registered 1961-1971 immigrants numbered 214,000, apart from those who had been self-settled with relatives and could not now be treated as foreigners and uprooted and sent away. Assamese opinion was, however, as concerned with culture as with land and feared that the Assamese language might be swamped if more and more Bengali speakers were accepted. The GPF accordingly proposed that an assurance be given that notwithstanding any demographic changes over the next 20 years, Assamese shall continue to remain the official language of the administration and medium of instruction as at present, without detriment to the legitimate cultural and linguistic interests of other ethnic and linguistic minorities in the state. The alternative of detaching Cachar, a preponderantly Bengali-speaking district from Assam, was not favoured as this would entail further reorganisation of the Northeast region and could have a domino effect.

The process of revising the electoral rolls commenced but an element of disenchantment had set in Assam. AASU split with the formation of an All-Assam Muslim Students Association, and Bengalis, Muslims, Leftists and tribals, including tea tribals, began to distance themselves from the movement. These growing tensions were climaxed when Muslim settlers were massacred at Nellie in Nagaon district by Lalung tribals protesting against usurpation of their supposedly reserved lands and forests by outsiders. Over a thousand were reportedly killed on that black February day in 1983. The Sanskritised 'yellow' plains tribals of Assam—Bodos, Rabhas, Tiwas (Lalungs), Mishings, Sonowals and Deoris among them—had begun to demand territorial and cultural space.

Further talks between AASU and the Centre were unproductive. Triggering the event had been the decision to hold General Elections with unrevised rolls in Assam as President's rule could not be extended beyond a year. The elections were held under heavy security. The overall percentage of polling was no more than 32.66 with some districts like Sibsagar and Lakhimpur reporting considerably lower figures. The wounds took long to heal. Neither side was blameless. The Government lacked clear direction. The AASU leadership was dedicated but immature and carried away by its own rhetoric, ignoring practical considerations.

It was left to Rajiv Gandhi to pick up the threads in 1985 after assuming office as prime minister, aided by a shrewd Congress chief minister, Hiteshwar Saikia who was innovative and ready for bold initiatives.

VI

If the Congress faced many trials and tribulations in the Northeast, the gradual welding of the vast, rugged, remote, unknown and utterly 'excluded' North-East Frontier Agency into Arunachal Pradesh was by any yardstick a remarkable triumph of constructive and democratic nation building that has few parallels anywhere in the world. A motley, disaggregated mosaic of more or less 110 tribes, mostly of Tibeto-Burman stock, along what was soon to be a contested northern border along the McMahon Line, was patiently weaned into the great Indian family of which they are the youngest but very proud members. Nehru established the framework against all criticism. The rest followed.

In 1951, the wheel was unknown in NEFA. Nothing exemplifies its extraordinary transition than the fact that a young Apa Tani boy, Kuru Hasang, who was sent to a Sainik School in Bhubaneswar in 1963 with much trepidation despite an egg sacrifice by his family, was in 1978 commissioned into the Indian Air Force as a jet fighter pilot. Being polyglot and with most tribes, apart from those of Buddhist faith, having no script, Hindi or Nefamese became the *lingua franca.*

Though politically part of Assam, NEFA was administratively brought under the Centre though the Governor acting as the Agent of the Union. It had a single nominated member in Parliament which was authorised to legislate for the territory. Tribal people being essentially communitarian, demands for democratic reform led to the appointment of a committee under the NEFA MP, Daying Ering. This recommended a four-tier structure with elected village councils at the base, with simple customary judicial and development functions; *anchal samitis* under the sub-divisional officer at block level; a *zilla parishad* under the district commissioner or political officer heading a single-line administration under an Indian Frontier Administrative Service established in 1956; and an Agency Council at the apex.

The scheme was adopted in 1969. Five-year plans were launched, with emphasis on connectivity, food security and health, and in 1971, the North Eastern Areas (Reorganisation) Act, severed NEFA from Assam and made it a Union Territory under a Chief Commissioner (Verghese, 1996). NEFA's parliamentary representation was enhanced and the Agency Council was transformed into a Pradesh Council with 26 members enjoying advisory powers. By 1975, the Pradesh Council had become a legislative assembly with an elected council of ministers. The Chief Commissioner was replaced by a Lieutenant-Governor.

A *panchayati raj*-type system had flowered into a fuller representative structure that before long assumed full statehood in 1986. It is no surprise that the first few governments were Congress-led as it is under the tutelage of the Indian National Congress that NEFA, later Arunachal Pradesh, learnt the grammar of politics. Separation from Assam resulted in Arunachal Pradesh, Meghalaya and Mizoram inheriting a legacy of border disputes that remain unresolved to this day.

Arunachal fortunately came together without any 'outsider/ foreigner' complex. But this condition underwent change in 1959 with the flight of the Dalai Lama to India and a consequent influx of Tibetan refugees. This was further aggravated with the relocation of Buddhist Chakma tribals displaced from East Pakistan by the Kaptai Dam in the Chittagong Hill Tracts from Tripura to an Arunachal now imbued with a growing land-territory consciousness. The number of refugees cited varied from 40,000 to 65,000. An anti-Chakma, 'quit Arunachal' movement was to commence later in the 1990s under the All Arunachal Pradesh Students Union (AAPSU).

VII

What is the Northeast? Some in the region are chagrined by what they feel is a demeaning directional characterisation that robs them of identity. Northeast for whom, from where? Yet the Northeast, north and east of the Siliguri neck is a geostrategic entity, accurately and meaningfully described by a nomenclature designating a compact, geo-political, biogeographic and distinctively ethnic part of Northeastern India.

Sikkim became a British protectorate in 1861 and its northern boundary with Tibet was defined and accepted under the Anglo-Chinese Convention of 1890. However, the old Nepalese connection and the need for labour in the region brought more Nepalese immigrants who in course of time began to threaten the political and cultural supremacy of the indigeneous Bhutia-Lepcha community to which the Maharaja belonged. These indigenes sought special preference as 'state subjects'. Gangtok, close by the Nathu La pass, and gateway to trade and exchange with Tibet, became the seat of the British Political Officer for Sikkim, Bhutan and Tibet but remained a Shangri-la within a hermit kingdom best known for its botanical wonders and butterflies.

With the lapse of paramountcy in India, earlier British responsibilities passed to India and a new Indo-Sikkim Treaty was negotiated in 1950 amid rising tensions as the Bhutia-Lepchas were reduced to a 25 percent minority against the dominant Nepalese population which established the Sikkim State Congress and sought accession to India. China's takeover of Tibet added to worries. An Indian Dewan was appointed under the 1950 Treaty which affirmed that Sikkim would remain an Indian protectorate with Delhi responsibile for defence, external affairs, communications and customs. The state's autonomy was limited by the ultimate responsibility of the Indian government 'for the maintenance of good administration and of law and order'.

Years later, the Indian chief executive, B.S. Das was to write that the new structure 'enabled the Maharaja to emerge as the dominant personality on the Sikkimese scene... For the people of Sikkim, the Dewan stood devalued, and with the erosion of power of the Political Officer, the Chogyal became the centre of power for them.' From being the defender of minority ethnic rights in Sikkim, the Government of India slowly found itself protecting the Maharaja against demands for democratisation by an increasingly restive Nepalese population. (Das, 1983).

The weakening of Delhi's power after 1962 was coupled with the more assertive ambitions of the new Chogyal, Palden Thondup Namgyal, which were shared by his American bride, Hope Cooke. Confronting them was Kazi Lhendup Dorji, a leading political figure who had always championed popular rule, and his Belgian wife, Eliza Maria, the no less ambitious Kazini. The third player, Indira Gandhi, wary of China's adamant refusal to accept India's special relationship with Sikkim, finally trumped both.

The Chogyal began to demand Sikkim's admission to the Colombo Plan, ILO and WHO, and pleaded for the stationing of a Sikkim representative in Delhi. The Kazi's Sikkim National Congress on the other hand sought political reforms. Two contending tendencies were clearly discernible. Events moved fast. Elections in 1973 resulted in statewide agitation for reform. The Chogyal was compelled to accept an Indian Administrator or Chief Executive under a tripartite agreement with the Chogyal, the Joint Action Committee (JAC) of agitating parties and Delhi. A 32-member legislature was set up with equal representation for the Bhutia-Lepcha and Nepalese and a seat each for the monks and scheduled castes. The JAC converted itself into the Sikkim Congress under the Kazi while the Palace formed the People's Democratic Party. The Sikkim Congress swept the ensuing polls in 1974, winning 31 seats.

The new ministry immediately sought constitutional clarifications and proposals to forge a closer Sikkim-India relationship 'and for Sikkim's participation in the political and economic institutions of India'. The Chogyal objected, to no avail. With the aid of an Indian constitutional adviser, a new constitution was framed and adopted despite blocking efforts. The new constitution was brought into force on July 15, 1974. Indira Gandhi responded by introducing and passing the 36th Constitution Amending Bill on August 29/30, making Sikkim an 'Associate State' of India and transforming India overnight, and without consultation, into a confederacy.

Not all even in the Sikkim Congress were pleased. *The Statesman* and *Hindustan Times* criticised the gambit, the latter describing the event as 'genteel annexation'. B.S. Das was to say: 'I was never shy of defending the ultimate goal, though I was hesitant on the methods used. International reactions were negative. Shortly thereafter, the Chogyal made some indiscreet remarks in Kathmandu while attending King Birendra's coronation. The Government of India seized upon this as a cause for action. A referendum on merger with India was hastily organised in Sikkim and the result shown as an overwhelming vote in favour. Sikkim formally became an integral part of the Indian Union with special safeguards under Article 371F of the Constitution.

Hope Cooke left Sikkim in 1973 and the Chogyal died a broken man in 1982. He too had overreached himself. The Sikkim Congress merged with the Indian National Congress. The Kazini's protege, a young Nepalese, Narbahadur Khatiwada, formed the Sikkim Youth Congress but switched loyalty to the Janata Party after the Emergency only to break ranks again when Morarji Desai, now Prime Minister, expressed disapproval of Sikkim's merger. The Kazi too had hitched his fortunes to the Janata Party but was in 1979 roundly defeated by the rising star, Narbahadur Bhandari, a former school teacher. Bhandari's Sikkim Janata Party with Bhutia-Lepcha backing took office with a commitment to restore the Sikkimese people their self-respect and sense of dignity. Bhandari called on Bhutia-Lepchas and Nepalese alike to unite so that, 'having merged with India, we will not be submerged'. Indira Gandhi first supported Bhandari but later cooled, as did the Governor, Homi Talyarkhan, who dismissed the chief minister on corruption charges in 1984, replacing him with Gurung, his Finance Minister. The 1985 elections, however, saw Bhandari's Sikkim Sangram Parishad return with an overwhelming majority. (Sikkim Bolcha Prakashan, 1993).

Darjeeling too was soon to have its share of troubles leading the formation of the Darjeeling-Gorkha Hills Council after a movement spearheaded by Subhas Ghising's Gorkha National Liberation Front. But that was to come later, in August 1988.

VIII

Even as politics was playing out in the Northeast, the essential tasks of development remained. After all, the promise of India to the newest members of this enormous joint family was a better and more secure life in a larger commonwealth in which they could aspire to be equal rulers and partners. Partition had delivered a body blow to internal communications and markets while the great post-war convulsions had skewed if not altogether severed critical external cultural and commercial links. There had to be a new beginning.

The imperative was to re-connect physically and emotionally with a now distant heartland separated by what had become a hostile neighbour. The Assam rail and road links were soon established but distances and, with that, costs had multiplied. Agartala was now over three times removed from Calcutta. Access to the sea through Chittagong was lost. The staggered process of national integration, given highly differentiated levels of development and administrative capability and infrastructure on the part of the putative ethno-political units, entailed traversing strange and sometimes difficult territory. Accelerated and possibly involuntary modernisation caused communities to hurtle into modernity from primitivism or early pre-industrialism and to adopt contemporary social mores and economic structures. This was bewildering. So even as India was in transition, the Northeast witnessed multiple transitions with different trajectories and points of departure: from barter to a monetised economy, from *jhum* to more settled cultivation, to a steady opening up as the world entered people's lives.

Planned development came late to the new Northeastern entities as they broke loose from Assam. Much of it was necessarily paternalistic but gradually each state or unit increasingly took its destiny into its own hands. Communications took first priority. Large peripheral mountain tracts were served by civil and military air supply, whether by landings or para-drops, as there was no other quick way of reaching them. This was done by private airline companies using short take-off and landing Dakotas to operate from the dozens of war time airstrips that dotted the fringes of the Brahmaputra and Barak plains. They ran a wonderful air-taxi service that produced an initial connectivity that made strangers neighbours. Alas the Dakotas were phased out in due course and never replaced with comparable aircraft.

The Air Force took on the job. NEFA was better connected by air in the 1950s and 1960s than is Arunachal Pradesh today.

Road building, connecting the 'interior' to certain main axes, was a slow and expensive process in view of heavy, erosive rains and a lack of labour. The looming Sino-Indian conflict brought in the Border Roads Organisation with external labour manning several task forces. This opened up vast areas with a skeletal network of arterial roads, but few laterals. The Railways pushed outwards with new lines and conversion from metre to broad guage. Bridging followed: first a new bridge across the Brahmaputra at Pandu (Gauhati), next at Tezpur and then at Jogighopa near Dhubri in Lower Assam. The Bogibeel bridge near Dibrugarh is currently under construction. The North Bank is no longer quite another country though more flood prone and therefore more backward and less urbanised. Plans for a rail link to each new state and an airport in each capital were mooted in Indira Gandhi's time. Progress has not matched promise.

As a basically agrarian economy at the end of a long line of communications, food security was and remained a most important goal for the Northeast. Population had grown through natural increase and in-migration but food production had not kept pace. The Northeast imported rice, eggs, poultry and fish from distant parts whereas these were products with both considerable potential and markets locally. In the Hills, *jhum* was not favoured by modernising youth and had in many areas become less productive with an increasingly short *jhum* cycle that did not allow for complete natural regeneration. Large *jhum* 'fallows' became agents of erosion. Some areas like the Apa Tani plateau and the beautifully irrigated, terraced slopes hills farmed by the Angamis stood out as exceptions. Nagaland went on to pioneer an excellent environmental promotion and development programme of scientific agro-forestry which is what jhumming was and should be.

The Indian Council of Agricultural Research's (ICAR) experimental station in the region did useful work in three-tiered hill farming practices, with jhumming or terraced paddies on gentler lower slopes, plantation cropping at higher and steeper levels and alpine pasture and forests at the top, on the Himachal pattern. This did not quite take off.

The Assam plains, Imphal Valley and the Tripura plains constitute the region's potential granaries. The latter two did quite well but the failure of basic agrarian reform, irrigation and drainage, credit and input supplies remained an agricultural depressor in the Brahmaputra and Barak Valleys. The lackadaisical approach to flood moderation and management was a major impediment to agricultural development. The

Brahmaputra Board was set up in 1980 and produced a three volume study on harnessing the waters of the main stem of the Brahmaputra, the tributary streams and lesser rivers respectively. (Verghese, 1996). Some of this represented giganticism, as in the proposed twin giant dams on the Dihang and Subansiri. Apart from substantial flood moderation, the proposal envisaged a 100,000 cusec link-canal from Jogighopa through Lower Assam and Bangladesh to fall into the Ganga in West Bengal above Farakka. This was intended to facilitate a Ganga sharing agreement with Bangladesh, then under heated discussion, on the basis of augmentation from the surplus waters of the Brahmaputra. Bangladesh rejected the proposition on technical and political grounds while the then chief minister of Arunachal Pradesh objected to his home in Yingkiong being submerged fathoms deep.

The Dihang-Subansiri projects were each subsequently reworked as three dam cascades to give more or less the same result with less submergence. By then Arunachal Pradesh had moved in favour of run-of-river projects with little or no displacement while Assam gradually turned against large storage dams on vague environmental grounds without any alternative whatsoever for dealing with the floods that cripple it year after year. The absence of any lead from the Centre or the Planning Commission was surprising.

The high potential of the Northeast in horticulture, floriculture, vegetable farming, herbiculture and other plantation crops was largely unexploited. Gone were the days when large tea 'estates' or 'gardens' could flourish. Instead, the wave of the future was to be smallholders organised in cooperatives or in partnership with corporate houses that could provide the necessary technological inputs and management, marketing and processing capability. Smallholders along the Arunachal-Assam border started doing just that in partnership with large, established Assam tea gardens which could not expand acreage but needed more leaf. Tripura too did well with rubber plantations developed by cooperativised smallholders under the aegis of the Rubber Board.

The potential for fruit is vast but simply never took off. The same was the case with fisheries, piggeries and poultry. This was altogether a sad story.

Every household in the Northeast weaves and the region is a treasure house of wonderful crafts. With the invasion of cheap mill made and plastic ware these traditional crafts started languishing and, as elsewhere, became arts for decorative and export purposes. Efforts were made to get the National Institute of Design and others to come and give a new functionality to these traditional wares.

Other than oil, coal and plywood manufactures, other industries were slow in coming and a few small state-owned paper and cement plants setup turned sick. Entrepreneurs were shy of investing from fear of insecurity, long market leads within closed borders, lack of infrastructure and problems in engaging 'outside' manpower. The same gas reserves were oversold to several bidders resulting in uncertainties, delays and loss of economies of scale. Government hand-holding and counter-guarantees, available elsewhere in more favourable situations, were lacking in the Northeast. Resentment and educated unemployment fuelled insurgency.

In the absence of new employment opportunities and expanding economies, government became by far the largest employer. This raised establishment costs and bred parasitism. The underground milked official salaries and project funds as a regular tax, with extortion and illegal levies becoming a way of life. The Northeast 'boasted' more government servants as a ratio of the population, received more development outlays per capita and saw less of the development rupee actually reaching the people than anywhere else in the country. Rent seeking became a way of life and it is the exchequer that financed insurgency. None was free of blame.

In the absence of open borders and regular trade, smuggling flourished and meshed with the narcotics and underground arms mafia. Being near the notorious Golden Triangle, Chinese and Thai crackdowns on drug peddlers caused them to seek new outlets to international markets via the Northeast, which soon found addiction growing. The smuggling of Indian manufactured psychotropic drugs to Burma also showed a marked increase for a while.

The quick suspension of formal border trade by Dhaka, barely a year after an Indo-Bangladesh agreement in 1972, also fostered smuggling. Lack of trade facilitation measures even at licensed trade posts along the border gave an impetus to corrupt practices and smuggling cross the Burma and Bangladesh borders. It took years to address these relatively simple problems in an inward-looking environment.

The inability to reach practical agreements on trade, transit, water sharing, flood moderation, data exchange and border demarcation with Bangladesh aggravated matters. Indian policymakers lacked a broad, forward looking vision while asymmetry and internal politics led East Pakistan and Bangladesh post-1975 to adopt a negative stance. Beggar-my-neighbour policies did no good to anybody and Indian obfuscation and unconscionable delays in implementing the Tin Bigha accord, providing a 100 metre long corridor (flyover or underpass) to

Bangladesh to connect with Dahagram, a tiny enclave within India, exemplified the problem. The same mistrust and lack of vision thwarted sensible agreements on regional cooperation on water resource development. It was only in 1996 that the Gujral Doctrine on non-reciprocity between unequal parties paved the way for the Ganges Accord. Bangladesh too was by no means blameless.

Tourism, which could have opened minds and generated employment all round, was slow to come to the Northeast. A unified view was not taken so that attractive regional packages with related facilities could be offered. One reason for this was that though a North Eastern Council was set up in Shillong, its mandate, structure and staffing left much to be desired. Delhi decided.

More positively, though gradually at first, the Northeast began to manifest a range of talent in music and sport. Northeastern sportspersons now do the nation proud and the music and hospitality industries are doing extremely well.

It would be some time before the external borders opened up with pronouncements on Looking East and infrastructure development picked up some little momentum. But the foundations had been laid and, barring great eye-catching events, not inconsiderable progress had been made, laying the base for Rajiv Gandhi to take the next step forward.

References

Ao, Tajenyuba (1994). "NSCN (Muivah) Massacre", in *The Nagaland Journal,* Kohima, May 4.

Aram, M. (1974). *Peace in Nagaland: Eight Years Story, 1964-72.* Delhi: Arnold Heinemann.

Barpujari, H.K. (1993). *Comprehensive History of Assam.* Vol 5., Assam, Publications Board.

Bhattacharjee, S.R. (1989). "Tribal Insurgency in Tripura: A Study in Exploration of Causes". *Tribal Studies of India Series,* T 136. Delhi: Inter-India Publications.

Das, B.S. (1983). *The Sikkim Saga.* Delhi: Vikas.

Das, Durga (ed.) (1972). *Sardar Patel Correspondence, 1945-50,* Vols. IV, V, VI, VII. Ahmedabad: Navjivan Publishing House.

Ministry of External Affairs (1963). *Infiltration from East Pakistan.* Delhi. August.

Prasad, R.N. and A.K. Agarwal (1991). *Political and Economic Development of Mizoram.* Delhi: Mittal Publications.

Sanjaoba, Naorem (1988). *Manipur Past and Present,* Vol. I. Delhi: Mittal Publications.

Sarin, V.I.K. (1980). *India's Northeast in Flames.* Delhi: Vikas.

Sikkim Bolcha Prakashan (1993). *Now Sikkim Speaks.* Gangtok: Sikkim Sangram Parishad. Singh, B.P. (1987). *The Problem of Change: A Study of North-East India.* Delhi: OUP.

Tarapot, Phanjoubam (1993). *Insurgency Movements in North-Eastern India.* Delhi: Vikas.

Verghese, B.G., Bashiruddin Ahmed *et al.* (1980). *Situation in Assam.* Delhi: Gandhi Peace Foundation. February.

Index

C

N

Q

R